NELSON EDUCATION SERIES
IN HUMAN RESOURCE MANAGEME

SIXTH EDITION

Managing Performance through Training and Development

NELSON EDUCATION SERIES
IN HUMAN RESOURCE MANAGEMENT

SIXTH EDITION

Managing Performance through Training and Development

Alan M. Saks
UNIVERSITY OF TORONTO

Robert R. Haccoun
UNIVERSITÉ DE MONTRÉAL

Series Editor:
Monica Belcourt
YORK UNIVERSITY

NELSON / EDUCATION

Managing Performance through Training and Development, Sixth Edition

by Alan M. Saks and Robert R. Haccoun

Vice President, Editorial Higher Education:
Anne Williams

Acquisitions Editor:
Alwynn Pinard

Marketing Manager:
Dave Stratton

Developmental Editor:
Luciano Nicassio

Permissions Coordinator:
Melody Tolson

Content Production Manager:
Jennifer Hare

Production Service:
MPS Limited

Copy Editor:
Kelli Howey

Proofreader:
Jennifer A. McIntyre

Indexer:
Robie Grant

Manufacturing Manager:
Joanne McNeil

Design Director:
Ken Phipps

Managing Designer:
Franca Amore

Interior Design:
Dianna Little

Cover Design:
Martyn Schmoll

Cover Image:
SCshapecharge/iStockphoto

Compositor:
MPS Limited

Printer:
Edwards Brothers

Library and Archives Canada Cataloguing in Publication Data

Saks, Alan M. (Alan Michael), 1960–
   Managing performance through training and development / Alan M. Saks, Robert R. Haccoun ; series editor, Monica Belcourt. — 6th ed.

(Nelson Education series in human resources management)
Includes bibliographical references and index.
ISBN 978-0-17-650733-6

   1. Employees—Training of—Textbooks. I. Haccoun, Robert R. II. Title. III. Series: Nelson Education series in human resource management

HF5549.5.T7S23 2012
658.3'124   C2012-904406-7

ISBN-13: 978-0-17-650733-6
ISBN-10: 0-17-650733-7

To Kelly, Justin, and Brooke, my best friends
Alan Saks

To Orli and Amit the highlight of Pappy's life
Robert R. Haccoun

BRIEF CONTENTS

CONTENTS

ABOUT THE AUTHORS

Alan M. Saks

Alan M. Saks, PhD, is a Professor of Organizational Behaviour and Human Resource Management at the University of Toronto, where he holds a joint appointment in the Department of Management—UTSC, the Centre for Industrial Relations and Human Resources, and the Joseph L. Rotman School of Management. Prior to joining the University of Toronto, Professor Saks was a member of the Department of Management in the Faculty of Commerce and Administration at Concordia University and in the School of Administrative Studies at York University.

Professor Saks earned his BA in Psychology from the University of Western Ontario, an MASc in Industrial-Organizational Psychology from the University of Waterloo, and a PhD in Organizational Behaviour and Human Resources from the University of Toronto. He conducts research in a number of areas in human resources and organizational behaviour including recruitment, job search, training, employee engagement, and the socialization and on-boarding of new employees. His research has been published in refereed journals such as the *Journal of Applied Psychology, Personnel Psychology, Academy of Management Journal, Journal of Organizational Behavior, Journal of Vocational Behavior, Human Resource Management, Human Resource Management Review, Journal of Business and Psychology,* and the *International Journal of Training and Development* as well as in professional journals such as the *HR Professional Magazine, The Canadian Learning Journal,* and the *Canadian HR Reporter.* In addition to this text, he is also the author of *Research, Measurement and Evaluation of Human Resources,* and co-author of *Organizational Behaviour: Understanding and Managing Life at Work.*

Professor Saks is currently an associate editor of the *Journal of Business and Psychology* and is a member of the editorial boards of the *International Journal of Training and Development, Journal of Vocational Behavior, Human Resource Development Review,* and the *Journal of Leadership and Organizational Studies.*

Robert R. Haccoun

Educated at McGill University (BA 1969) and the Ohio State University (MA 1970, PhD 1973), Robert R. Haccoun is Professor of Psychology at the Université de Montréal. Prior to returning to academia in 1978, Professor Haccoun was a research scientist for Bell Canada in Montreal. He is a founding member and past president of the Industrial-Organizational Psychology section of the Canadian Psychological Association.

He has led a number of research studies, mainly focused on training, absenteeism, and research methodology, and delivered papers at scientific conferences. His research articles are published in Canada in journals that include *Canadian Psychologist, Canadian Journal of Behavioural Sciences,* and the *Canadian Journal of Administrative Studies.* Internationally, his research is published in *Personnel Psychology,* the *Journal of Applied Psychology, Organizational Behaviour and Human Decision Processes,* the *Journal of Organizational Behaviour,* and *Applied*

Psychology: An International Review. He has contributed chapters to several books, and his co-authored research book, *Comprendre l'organisation: Approches de recherches,* has been translated into Spanish. His statistics textbook, published in 2007, is in its second edition (2010). He is a reviewer for many scientific journals and has served on scientific advisory boards for provincial, national, and international research funding agencies.

Active in the transfer of knowledge from academia to applied settings, he has written many non-technical articles and delivered conferences aimed at professional audiences. His consulting services have been called upon by organizations in Canada, the United States, and Europe.

PREFACE

Increasing global competition, an increasingly knowledge-based economy, labour shortages, and demographic changes in the workforce have made learning more important than ever for employees and organizations. These challenges require organizations to provide training and development programs for employees so that they have the knowledge, skills, and abilities that are necessary to be productive and innovative. The ability to compete and survive in today's increasingly competitive and uncertain environment depends in large part on the provision and effectiveness of training and development—the focus of this textbook.

Since the last edition of this text was published, the science and practice of training and development has continued to advance. The increasing use of technology, blended approaches to training delivery, social media, mobile (m) learning, and Learning 2.0 are just some examples of the exciting developments in training and development. The sixth edition of *Managing Performance through Training and Development* reflects the many advances in both the science and practice of training and development.

As with the three previous editions, the sixth edition is co-authored by Alan Saks and Robert Haccoun. The two authors have been involved in training research for over 20 years and have collaborated on numerous research projects. With the sixth edition, they have continued to develop and improve this textbook in many ways.

You will find new content, expanded coverage of existing topics, updated material, new tables and figures, and new *Training Today* and *The Trainer's Notebook* features throughout the sixth edition of *Managing Performance through Training and Development*. Here are some examples to look for:

Chapter 1:   Expanded coverage of performance management
Chapter 2:   Workplace learning
Chapter 3:   Prompting self-regulation
Chapter 4:   Training Today 4.1: Dirty Pools and Poor Training
Chapter 5:   Pre-training interventions
Chapter 6:   Instructional media
Chapter 7:   E-mentoring
Chapter 8:   Virtual classroom
Chapter 9:   Seductive details
Chapter 10: Table 10.1: Transfer of Training in Canadian Organizations
Chapter 11: Expanded coverage of reaction measures
Chapter 12: Training Today 12.1: Investing in People Project
Chapter 13: Effectiveness of safety training
Chapter 14: Leadership development
Chapter 15: Learning 2.0

The sixth edition also includes a new pedagogical feature that complements the other integrative features of the text. In addition to the existing case study questions, we have added an additional set of case questions called *Flashback*

Questions. These questions ask students to use material from a previous chapter in the text that relates to the case study in the current chapter. For example, the case study in Chapter 10 on Transfer of Training includes Flashback Questions that ask about off-the-job instructional methods (Chapter 6), learning and motivation (Chapter 3), and training design (Chapter 5). These questions can be used by an instructor to encourage students to integrate material from previous chapters. In addition, an instructor can now use a case study in any chapter to teach material from other chapters. Thus, it is possible to use more than one case study to teach material in a particular chapter.

The Flashback Questions complement two other integrative pedagogical features in the text—the *Make the Connection* feature and the *Integrative Case Study*. Make the Connection alerts the reader to material in a chapter that has a connection to material that was presented in a previous chapter. For example, when reading about a self-management transfer of training intervention in Chapter 10 (Transfer of Training), the reader is reminded about material on self-regulation and social cognitive theory in Chapter 3 (Learning and Motivation). The purpose of this feature is to help the reader integrate material across the chapters and to understand how material in one chapter is related to material that was presented in an earlier chapter.

Make the
Connection

The Make the Connection feature appears in three ways: an icon in the margin alerts the reader to a Make the Connection feature; the connection is explained to the reader in the text; and at the end of the chapter a Make the Connection section tells the reader the chapter and page number where they can find the relevant material. This feature is meant to help readers understand how the material throughout the text is linked and interconnected.

The Integrative Case Study can be found at the end of Chapter 15. The purpose of this feature is to provide students with an opportunity to work on a case that requires them to use and apply material from many chapters. The relevant chapter for the integrative questions is indicated so that instructors can use the integrative case throughout the course as each particular chapter is covered. Alternatively, the integrative case can be used at the end of a course as a review of all the chapters. This feature is meant to help students integrate and apply their learning throughout the text to one particular training situation.

In addition to these integrative features, the sixth edition continues to provide both students and instructors with a wide range of pedagogical features. Every chapter has a *Case Study* with questions on the main topics, principles, concepts, and theories covered in the chapter. In addition, every chapter has a *Case Incident* that consists of a short description of a training problem followed by several questions. They can be used to begin a discussion at the start of class or later in class when students are ready to apply the chapter material.

As with the previous edition, the sixth edition has two types of exercises in every chapter. *In-Class Exercises* can be completed during class time without any pre-class preparation. *In-the-Field Exercises* require students to gather information in the field by talking to HR and training professionals and by searching the Web to answer chapter-relevant questions (i.e., internet exercises). These exercises can also be used as projects and assignments.

Each chapter also has *Discussion Questions* and *The Great Training Debate*. The Discussion Questions focus on the main issues, principles, and theories described in a chapter. The Great Training Debate presents an issue for students to debate either early in a class to get students thinking about a topic or later in a class so students can begin to apply the chapter material to an important training issue. For example, The Great Training Debate in Chapter 1 asks students to debate whether all provinces should enact training legislation similar to the training law in Quebec.

As in the previous edition of the text, every chapter begins with a chapter-opening vignette. Each vignette tells the story of an actual training program in an organization that is of relevance to the material covered in the chapter. Many of the vignettes feature Canadian organizations, and the sixth edition includes seven new ones that feature a variety of types of organizations (e.g., financial, health, service, energy, consulting, communication) from across the country.

As with previous editions, you will also find in each chapter *The Trainer's Notebook* and *Training Today* features. The Trainer's Notebook presents practical, hands-on information for trainers and practitioners (e.g., Chapter 2, The Trainer's Notebook 2.2: Facilitating Informal Learning in Organizations). The Training Today feature describes the latest in training research and practice (e.g., Chapter 13, Training Today 13.1: Employee Orientation at EllisDon).

Also retained from the previous edition are *Web Links* for students who want to learn more about an organization or association mentioned in the text; they can be found at the end of each chapter. This edition also includes a list of the *Required Professional Capabilities,* or RPCs, at the end of each chapter, to alert students to RPC-relevant content. RPCs represent the learning objectives in the area of Organizational Learning, Development and Training for the national Certified Human Resources Professional (CHRP) designation.

We have also retained other features that appeared in previous editions, including *Chapter Learning Outcomes* at the beginning of every chapter; *Key Terms,* which appear in the text in bold and in the margins and are also listed at the end of each chapter; and a chapter-ending *Summary* that reviews the main content of each chapter.

In sum, the sixth edition of *Managing Performance through Training and Development* offers a wide variety of pedagogical material in every chapter. Our intent is to provide instructors and students with a wide selection of pedagogical material to choose from to best suit their learning needs and preferences.

STRUCTURE OF THE BOOK

Managing Performance through Training and Development is structured in a manner that follows the sequence of the instructional systems design (ISD) model of training and development.

Chapter 1 describes the importance and benefits of training and development for employees, organizations, and society. Training and development is defined and presented within the larger context of the performance management process as well as the organization's external environment, the organizational context, and the human resources management system. Chapter 1 also describes the instructional systems design (ISD) model of the training and development process, which sets the stage for the subsequent chapters in the text.

Chapters 2 and 3 focus on learning, which is first and foremost what training and development is all about. We feel that it is important for students to first understand learning at both the organizational and individual levels before they begin to learn about training and development. Therefore, Chapter 2 describes organizational learning, the learning organization, types of knowledge and intellectual capital, knowledge management practices, informal learning, and communities of practice. The chapter concludes with a multilevel systems model of organizational learning which shows how learning at the organization, group, and individual levels are interrelated.

Chapter 3 focuses on how individuals learn and their motivation to learn. Learning outcomes, stages of learning, learning styles, learning theories, adult learning theory, theories of motivation, and training motivation are described along with their implications for training and development. The chapter concludes with a model of training effectiveness that shows the variables that influence learning and retention, and how learning and retention are related to individual behaviour and performance, and organizational effectiveness. The training effectiveness model is further developed in Chapters 5 and 10.

The training and development process begins with a needs analysis, the focus of Chapter 4. Chapter 4 describes the needs analysis process with particular emphasis on the three levels of needs analysis (organizational, task, and person) and how to determine solutions to performance problems. The chapter also describes the methods and sources of needs analysis and some of the obstacles to conducting a needs analysis.

Chapter 5 describes how to design training and development programs. The chapter begins with an overview of the importance of training objectives and how to write training objectives. The chapter then proceeds to cover the main steps involved in the design of training programs, including whether to purchase or design a training program; requests for proposals; the training content; training methods; active practice and conditions of practice; active learning and adaptive expertise; and error-management training.

One of the most important steps in the design of a training program is the choice of training methods. Given the vast array of training methods and instructional techniques available, Chapters 6, 7, and 8 are devoted to this topic. Chapter 6 describes the most frequently used off-the-job instructional methods, including lectures, discussions, case studies, case incidents, behavioural modelling, role plays, simulations, games, and action learning. Each training method is defined and described, along with tips for trainers. The chapter also describes instructional media and concludes with a discussion of the factors to consider when choosing training methods and the importance of a blended approach.

In Chapter 7, we turn to on-the-job training methods including job instruction training, performance aids, job rotation, apprenticeship programs, coaching, and mentoring. As in Chapter 6, we define and describe each method and provide tips for trainers. The chapter concludes with a discussion of the advantages and disadvantages of off-the-job and on-the-job training methods.

Chapter 8 is devoted to technology-based training methods. The chapter begins with a definition of technology-based training followed by a description of computer-based training and e-learning. Distinctions are made between instructor-led training and self-directed learning and asynchronous and synchronous training. This is followed by a discussion of electronic performance support systems, video and Web conferencing, social media and Web 2.0, and mobile (m) learning. The chapter then describes how to design computer-based training programs, explains advantages and disadvantages, and discusses the effectiveness of computer-based training methods.

The focus of Chapter 9 is training delivery. The chapter begins with a description of a lesson plan and then describes the main components of a lesson plan including the characteristics of good trainers, the selection of trainees, training materials and equipment, the training site, and scheduling training programs. The chapter also describes how to create a climate for learning, Gagné's nine events of instruction, and common training delivery problems and solutions.

One of the biggest problems facing trainers and organizations is the transfer of training, the focus of Chapter 10. The chapter begins with a review of the transfer problem and barriers to transfer, followed by a description of Baldwin and Ford's (1988) model of the transfer process. The chapter then describes strategies that can be undertaken by managers, trainers, and trainees for improving the transfer of training before, during, and after training. The chapter also describes transfer of training interventions, post-training supplements, and the transfer system.

Once a training program has been designed and delivered, it needs to be evaluated. Chapters 11 and 12 are devoted to training evaluation. In Chapter 11, we describe the purpose and barriers of training evaluation and discuss three training evaluation models. The chapter also describes how to measure key variables for training evaluation and the different types of training evaluation designs.

The topic of training evaluation continues in Chapter 12 where the focus shifts to the costs and benefits of training. Chapter 12 describes how to calculate the costs of training programs as well as the benefits (e.g., net benefit, benefit–cost ratio, return on investment, and utility). The importance of the credibility of estimates is also discussed.

Chapters 13 and 14 describe the types of training programs that are provided in organizations. Chapter 13 describes the most common forms of training that employees receive including orientation training, essential skills training, technical skills training, information technology training, health and safety training, total quality management training, team training, sales training, customer-service training, sexual harassment training, ethics training, diversity training, and cross-cultural training.

Chapter 14 is devoted entirely to management development. This reflects both its importance to organizations and the large investments made by organizations in the development of management talent. The chapter begins with a definition of management and management development and then describes the core managerial roles and functions, management skills, and emotional intelligence. Models of management skill development are also described as well as the content and methods of management development programs. The chapter concludes with a discussion of research on the effectiveness of management development.

Finally, Chapter 15 concludes the text with a discussion of the evolution and future of training and development. The chapter begins with a discussion of the role of training professionals, outsourcing training and development, and the ethics of training and development. We then discuss Learning 2.0 and the evolution of learning in organizations. The chapter concludes with a discussion of lifelong learning.

Throughout the text we have tried to maintain a balance between theory and research on the one hand, and practice and application on the other. We have also tried to provide examples of the concepts and principles presented in the text by showcasing organizations, many of them Canadian, that have successfully designed and delivered effective training programs. Overall, we have tried to provide a thorough and comprehensive text on training and development that reflects both the science and practice of the field as well as our excitement and genuine love of the topic. We hope that the combination of text material as well as the pedagogical features will motivate students to learn about the science and practice of training and development.

Instructor Ancillaries

The Nelson Education Teaching Advantage

The **Nelson Education Teaching Advantage (NETA)** program delivers research-based instructor resources that promote student engagement and higher-order thinking to enable the success of Canadian students and educators.

Instructors today face many challenges. Resources are limited, time is scarce, and a new kind of student has emerged: one who is juggling school with work, has gaps in his or her basic knowledge, and is immersed in technology in a way that has led to a completely new style of learning. In response, Nelson Education has gathered a group of dedicated instructors to advise us on the creation of richer and more flexible ancillaries that respond to the needs of today's teaching environments.

In consultation with our editorial advisory board, Nelson Education has completely rethought the structure, approaches, and formats of our key textbook ancillaries. We've also increased our investment in editorial support for our ancillary authors. The result is the Nelson Education Teaching Advantage and its key components: *NETA Assessment, NETA Engagement,* and *NETA Presentation.* Each component includes one or more ancillaries prepared according to our best practices, and a document explaining the theory behind the practices.

NETA Assessment relates to testing materials. Under *NETA Assessment,* Nelson's authors create multiple-choice questions that reflect research-based best practices for constructing effective questions and testing not just recall but also higher-order thinking. Our guidelines were developed by David DiBattista, a 3M National Teaching Fellow whose recent research as a professor of psychology at Brock University has focused on multiple-choice testing. All Test Bank authors receive training at workshops conducted by Prof. DiBattista, as do the copy editors assigned to each Test Bank. A copy of *Multiple Choice Tests: Getting Beyond Remembering,* Prof. DiBattista's guide to writing effective tests, is included with every Nelson Test Bank/Computerized Test Bank package. (Information about the NETA Test Bank prepared for *Managing Performance through Training and Development,* Sixth Edition, is included in the description of the Instructor's Resource CD below.)

NETA Engagement presents materials that help instructors deliver engaging content and activities to their classes. Instead of Instructor's Manuals that regurgitate chapter outlines and key terms from the text, NETA Enriched Instructor's Manuals (EIMs) provide genuine assistance to teachers. The EIMs answer questions like *What should students learn?, Why should students care?,* and *What are some common student misconceptions and stumbling blocks?* EIMs not only identify the topics that cause students the most difficulty, but also describe techniques and resources to help students master these concepts. Dr. Roger Fisher's *Instructor's Guide to Classroom Engagement (IGCE)* accompanies every Enriched Instructor's Manual. (Information about the NETA Enriched Instructor's Manual prepared for *Managing Performance through Training and Development,* Sixth Edition, is included in the description of the IRCD below.)

NETA Presentation has been developed to help instructors make the best use of PowerPoint® in their classrooms. With a clean and uncluttered design developed by Maureen Stone of StoneSoup Consulting, NETA Presentation features slides with improved readability, more multimedia and graphic materials, activities to use in class, and tips for instructors on the Notes page. A copy of *NETA Guidelines for Classroom Presentations* by Maureen Stone is included with each set of PowerPoint slides. (Information about the NETA Presentation PowerPoints prepared for *Managing Performance through Training and Development,* Sixth Edition, is included in the description of the IRCD below.)

Instructor's Resource CD

Key instructor ancillaries are provided on the *Instructor's Resource CD* (ISBN 0176652914), giving instructors the ultimate tool for customizing lectures and presentations. The IRCD includes:

- **NETA Assessment**: The Test Bank was written by Carlos Calao (Kwantlen Polytechnic University). It includes 20 to 30 multiple-choice questions per chapter, all written according to NETA guidelines for effective construction and development of higher-order questions. Each chapter also includes 20 true/false questions and 5 short answer questions with suggested answers. Test Bank files are provided in Word format for easy editing and in PDF format for convenient printing whatever your system. The Computerized Test Bank by ExamView® includes all the questions from the Test Bank. The easy-to-use ExamView software is compatible with Microsoft Windows and Mac OS. Create tests by selecting questions from the question bank, modifying these questions as desired, and adding new questions you write yourself. You can administer quizzes online and export tests to WebCT, Blackboard, and other formats.

- **NETA Engagement:** The Enriched Instructor's Manual to accompany *Managing Performance through Training and Development,* Sixth Edition, was prepared by Stephen G. Robinson, professor at Okanagan College. It is organized according to the textbook chapters and addresses eight key educational concerns, such as typical stumbling blocks student face and how to address them, as well as suggested classroom activities to give you the support you need to engage your students within the classroom.

Other features include chapter summaries, sample lecture outlines, and case incidents with answers.

- **NETA Presentation:** Microsoft® PowerPoint® lecture slides for every chapter have been created by Lori Buchart, professor at Mount Royal University. There is an average of about 30 slides per chapter, many featuring key figures and tables from the text. NETA principles of clear design and engaging content have been incorporated throughout.

We hope that students and instructors find the sixth edition of the text as exciting as we do and that the pedagogical features help to facilitate and maximize learning and retention.

Acknowledgments

Writing a textbook requires the support and assistance of many people who either directly or indirectly make important contributions to the process and outcome. We wish to thank all of those who have played important roles in our lives and in writing this edition as well as previous editions of this text.

First, we thank all the reviewers who provided us with insightful and constructive feedback over the past few editions that led to many changes and improvements:

Lynne Bard of Conestoga College
Gordon Barnard of Durham College
Susan Fitzrandolph of Ryerson University
Morai Forer of the Saskatchewan Institute of Applied Science and
    Technology
Bernadette Gatien of Saint Mary's University
Stefan Groschl of the University of Guelph
Jamie Gruman of the University of Guelph
John Hardisty of Sheridan College
Jill Leedham of Mohawk College
Donna Leibham of the University of Calgary
Barbara Lipton of Seneca College
Jody Merritt of St. Clair College
Grace O'Farrell of the University of Winnipeg
Carol Ann Samhaber of Algonquin College
Wiktor J. Tutlewski of Kwantlen Polytechnic University
Valerie Whyte of the University of New Brunswick
Jeff Young of Saint Mary's University
Tracey Starrett of The Starrett Group

Each one contributed to this text by lending us their expertise and by taking the time to share their teaching experiences. Their comments and feedback have helped us to improve each edition of this text.

Second, we wish to express our gratitude to the team at Nelson Education that helped us develop and produce this text: Acquisitions Editor, Alwynn Pinard; Developmental Editor, Luciano Nicassio; Managing Developmental Editor, Lesley Mann; Content Production Manager, Jennifer Hare; Copy Editor, Kelli Howey; and Amie Plourde, who was our acquisitions editor when we began work on this edition and worked with us on the previous edition. We are grateful for their support and all of their hard work and feel very lucky to be working with a team of professionals who care so much about what they do and their authors.

Finally, we also wish to thank our families, who have had to endure the burden of living with busy, tired, and overworked authors who sometimes don't have time to play or sleep! Alan Saks is grateful to Kelly, Justin, and Brooke for making it all worthwhile. Robert Haccoun is grateful to his family, especially Orli and Amit. Seeing their smiles does not eliminate all difficulties, but it helps.

Alan M. Saks
University of Toronto

Robert R. Haccoun
Université de Montréal

The Training and Development Process

CHAPTER LEARNING OUTCOMES

After reading this chapter, you should be able to:

- understand the meaning of performance management, training, development, and human resource development
- describe the performance management process and the role of training and development
- describe the benefits of training and development for organizations, employees, and society
- discuss training and development in Canada
- understand and explain the role of the environmental and organizational context of training and development and the human resources system
- understand the meaning of strategic human resource management (SHRM), strategic training and development (ST&D), and high-performance work systems (HPWS)
- discuss the instructional systems design (ISD) model of training and development

TD BANK

Several years ago, TD Bank became concerned about the growing number of robberies at its branches. It was clear that something had to be done to protect employees and customers. So in the summer of 2008, a needs analysis was conducted that included focus groups, interviews, and surveys.

The needs analysis revealed the need to design a training program that would focus not just on robbery prevention but also on what happens afterwards. An outline was developed for a training program that centred on three areas: the most common types of robberies, what happens during robbery attempts, and what processes and behaviours are considered best practices in the financial sector.

The objectives of the training program were to reduce the number of robberies, enhance risk-management practices, improve robbery prevention, and reduce financial losses. The instructional designers worked with external subject matter experts and networks to determine learning objectives and partnered with the RCMP and an armed robbery association in the United States to ensure there was a good North America–wide perspective.

That fall, the various components were designed, reviewed, deployed, and tested. By November 2008 the program was piloted with trainers; a train-the-trainer leader's guide was developed, followed by train-the-trainer sessions.

The course content includes strategy tools, tactics for robbery prevention, procedures and actions to follow during a robbery, employee and customer safety standards procedures, documentation and communication strategies, and tips, tactics, and tools for dealing with trauma.

The training program uses a blended learning approach that includes e-learning, in-branch training sessions, and ongoing coaching. The e-learning component focuses on what to do before, during, and after a robbery and includes video clips. It takes about 30 minutes and has to be completed before the in-branch training. Employees also take a test that requires them to achieve a score of 80 percent to receive credit for the course.

The in-branch training program reviews the key learning points from the e-learning training, and includes role plays and debriefing sessions. A second in-branch session is provided six months later. In addition, each year employees are required to review the e-learning course, including a "what's new" section.

The program was rolled out in January 2009 and so far more than 21,000 employees have completed the Robbery Prevention and Awareness training program and are now better prepared to face a robbery situation. Once the training is completed, participants and stakeholders give quantitative and qualitative formal evaluations.

As a result of the program, TD has seen a reduction in the number of robberies, enhanced risk management practices and procedures, improved prevention through ongoing vigilance, and greater safety around customers and employees. In addition, there was a 41 percent reduction in cash losses in 2009 compared to 2008 and an 11 percent decrease in the number of robberies.

In 2010, TD's Robbery Prevention and Awareness training program won a silver award for training excellence from the Canadian Society for Training and Development.[1]

Source: S. Dobson, "Learning to avoid the bad guys," *Canadian HR Reporter*, Nov. 29, 2010, P. 24. Reprinted by permission of Canadian HR Reporter; Employee Performance and Development, Developing our employees, www.td.com (retrieved October 31, 2011).

TD Bank's Robbery Prevention and Awareness training program is a great example of the role and importance of training and development in organizations. It ensures that employees are prepared for robberies and that they and customers will be protected. It is also an excellent example of how to design, deliver, and evaluate training and development programs.

It is not hard to understand how investments in the training and development of employees can improve an organization's success and competitiveness. In fact, later in this chapter you will learn how training and development benefits employees, organizations, and society. But have you ever considered how the training of employees can benefit you and impact *your* life?

Consider the emergency landing of an Air Transat Airbus on an island in the Atlantic Ocean on August 24, 2001. With both engines dead and the lives of 293 passengers and 13 crew members on Flight 236 at stake, the pilots successfully made an emergency landing after gliding for 19 minutes without power.

The loss of power was due to a fuel leak in the right-side engine that caused it to shut down. A chafing fuel line on the right-side engine, which had recently been replaced, leaked during the flight. Although there was a leak in the right-side engine causing a loss of fuel, the left-side engine should have been sufficient to keep the plane in the air. However, fuel from the undamaged left-side engine tanks was pumped to the leaking right side, where it was dumped overboard. This led to a loss of fuel in the left-side engine, which then caused it to lose power as well. The Airbus would have been able to fly safely with just the left-side engine operating had its fuel not been pumped to the leaking right side.

According to Airbus, the maker of the twin-engine A330, Air Transat improperly reconnected the main fuel line to the aircraft's right-side engine when it was changed four days before the near-disaster. The fuel line to the right-side engine chafed against a hydraulic pipe that eventually cracked and created the fuel leak. Air-safety investigators also blamed faulty mechanical work by Air Transat mechanics as the cause of the fuel leak that led to the near-catastrophic emergency landing.

Disaster was averted only by a skilled emergency landing by the pilots, who were hailed as heroes for safely landing the plane. However, one of the pilots, Captain Robert Piché, denied being a hero, stating that landing a plane with no engines is "what you train for."

Transport Canada fined Air Transat $250,000 and ordered the airline to provide pilots and flight crews with special training on fuel management and emergency landings. Senior Transport Canada officials and Air Transat top management agreed that the airline's pilots would take special training sessions. Air Transat also provided Transport Canada with a corrective-action plan to improve the performance of maintenance that included human-factors training for all technical personnel.[2]

In 2004, the official investigation into the incident concluded that the emergency landing could have been avoided if the pilots had followed established fuel-leak procedures. Accident investigators determined that a fuel leak was turned into a near-disaster because the pilots failed to determine the problem and then tried to correct it from memory rather than by following a computer checklist which would have warned them of the possibility of a fuel leak. The pilots believed the problem was a fuel imbalance so they pumped tonnes of fuel overboard. According to the report, the crew did not correctly evaluate the situation before taking action. At the time, there was no adequate training for the pilots in dealing with a catastrophic fuel leak because it was considered a remote possibility.[3]

Although we cannot say that inadequate training was the cause of this near-disaster, we do know that training was required in order to prevent a similar incident from happening again. We also know that experience and training had a lot to do with the pilots' ability to safely land the plane. Air Transat has since reviewed its training programs and enhanced its maintenance and flight operations procedures. Its pilots are now required to attend a new training program on the procedures for overseas flights, which includes a review of fuel management. In 2005, Air Transat agreed to a settlement of $7.65 million to a group of passengers who were aboard Flight 236 and had filed a class-action lawsuit against the airline.[4]

This is just one of many examples that illustrate how the training of employees affects our lives in ways that we are unaware of and seldom, if ever, think about. Another example is the worst subway accident in Canadian history, in which three people were killed and about 140 others injured when two trains collided in Toronto on August 11, 1995. The subway operator, who was only on his second shift, admitted he wasn't ready to operate the train. Although he had successfully completed the 12-day subway training course, he had wanted more instruction behind the controls and was not sure he was ready to operate the train. At an inquest into the accident, he said, "I really didn't understand a lot of this stuff, I really didn't understand the mechanics of the train."

Since then, the Toronto Transit Commission (TTC) has made many changes, including the way it trains its drivers. For example, the 12-day driver training program has been extended to six weeks and operators are now required to take three days of additional training every two years. Emergency training is also required for the recertification of all subway employees every two years. These changes, along with others, have made the TTC one of the safest transit systems in North America.[5]

More recently, an investigation into the 2009 Air France accident in which all 228 people aboard died concluded that the deadliest accident in Air France's history could be blamed on a poorly trained crew. According to the probe into the accident, the crew made a series of fundamental errors that caused the plane to plummet into the ocean off the coast of Brazil. The crew did not realize the plane was stalled and they were insufficiently trained on how to manually handle the aircraft. The investigators recommended an examination of existing pilot training programs and to "make mandatory the creation of regular specific exercises aimed at manual airplane handling." They also recommended mandatory training for learning how to recognize and recover from a high-altitude stall.[6]

As you can see, employees who are poorly trained can make mistakes that result in accidents that threaten the public's safety and well-being as well as the employees' own safety. And while these examples are among the most extreme, it is important to recognize that poorly trained employees produce defective products and provide poor service. Thus, training is of vital concern not just to employees and their organizations, but to all of us who use public transportation and purchase goods and services every day of our lives. Recall from the chapter-opening vignette that TD Bank's Robbery Prevention and Awareness training program was designed in part to protect employees and customers.

For organizations, success and competitiveness are highly dependent on training and development. In fact, continuous learning and education has become a key factor for the success of individuals and organizations. Whether an organization is adopting new technology, improving quality, or simply trying to remain competitive, training and development is a critical and necessary part of the process.

A report by the Conference Board of Canada on learning and development in Canadian organizations concluded that continuous learning and the transfer of knowledge are key factors in fostering creativity and promoting organizational excellence.[7] Not surprisingly, training and education is one of the distinguishing characteristics of the best companies to work for in Canada.[8]

Therefore, it should not surprise you that organizations invest millions of dollars each year on training and development. This textbook will teach you about the training and development process and how to design, deliver, and evaluate training programs.

In this chapter, we introduce you to the topic of training and development and describe the training and development process. We begin with a discussion of performance management, since training and development is first and foremost all about managing performance in organizations.

PERFORMANCE MANAGEMENT

As the title of the textbook indicates, training and development is all about managing performance. **Performance management** is the process of establishing performance goals and designing interventions and programs to develop employees and improve their performance. This process signals to employees what is really important in the organization, ensures accountability for behaviour and results, and helps to improve performance.[9]

Performance management is not a single event, like a performance appraisal or a training program; rather, it is a comprehensive ongoing and continuous process that involves various activities and programs designed to develop employees and improve performance.[10]

As shown in Figure 1.1, the performance management process involves several components that are closely related to each other. The starting point of the performance management process is setting performance goals. Managers meet

Performance management
The process of establishing performance goals and designing interventions and programs to develop employees and improve their performance

FIGURE 1.1

The Performance Management Process

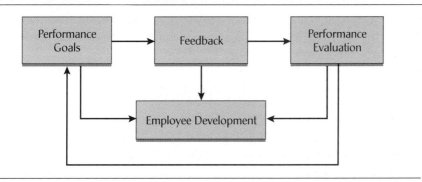

with employees and discuss performance expectations and agree on performance goals. These goals usually stem from organizational or department-level goals and objectives and ensures that employee goals are aligned with department and organizational goals. Once the manager and employee have agreed on goals, it is important for employees to receive ongoing feedback so that they know whether or not they are accomplishing their goals.

In addition to informal feedback, a key part of the performance management process is a formal performance evaluation. This usually involves the use of a standard rating form on which the manager and employee (self-appraisal) evaluate the employees' performance on a number of behavioural/performance dimensions and review the extent to which the employee has accomplished his/her goals. The process then repeats itself with the setting of new or revised goals.

A critical component of the performance management process is employee development and the creation of a development plan for employees. This involves programs and activities that are designed to help employees achieve their goals and improve their performance. This is of course where training and development fits into the performance management process. Employee development can include formal training and development programs in the classroom as well as on-the-job training programs such as coaching and mentoring.

Employee development is shown in the middle of Figure 1.1 because it connects to all of the other components of the performance management process. In other words, each of the components of the performance management process provides information on the developmental needs of employees.[11] For example, when setting goals it might be determined that attending a training program will help an employee achieve his/her goals. Thus, part of the goal-setting process might include a development plan that will enable employees to achieve their goals. Feedback might suggest the need for additional training to address an employee problem or weakness. The formal performance evaluation identifies employee strengths and weaknesses as well as areas that need improvement. This has further implications for employee development and the creation of an employee development plan that will set the stage for the next round of the performance management process.[12] Thus, each component of the performance management process can identify an employee's training needs and lead to action plans for development.

In summary, although the evaluation of performance (i.e., performance appraisal) is a fundamental part of performance management, a critical component of the process is employee development and this requires effective training and development programs.

TRAINING AND DEVELOPMENT

Training and development is one of the most important ways that performance can be improved in organizations. **Training** refers to formal and planned efforts to help employees acquire knowledge, skills, and abilities to improve performance in their current job.[13] Training usually consists of a short-term focus on

Training
Formal and planned efforts to help employees acquire knowledge, skills, and abilities to improve performance in their current job

acquiring skills to perform one's job. You have probably experienced this type of training, such as when your company sends you to a workshop to learn a software package or to learn how to serve customers. The goal is to help you learn to do your current job better.

As indicated at the beginning of the chapter, TD Bank's Robbery Prevention and Awareness training program is designed to provide employees with the knowledge and skills required to effectively respond to robberies.

Development refers to formal and planned efforts to help employees acquire the knowledge, skills, and abilities required to perform future job responsibilities and for the long-term achievement of individual career goals and organizational objectives. The goal is to prepare individuals for promotions and future jobs as well as additional job responsibilities. This process might consist of extensive programs such as leadership development, and might include seminars and workshops, job rotation, coaching, and other assignments. The goal is to prepare employees for future responsibilities and often for managerial careers. You can read more about management development in Chapter 14.

Training and development is part of a larger system and field that is known as human resource development (HRD). **Human resource development** involves systematic and planned activities that are designed by an organization to provide employees with opportunities to learn necessary skills to meet current and future job demands. The main functions of human resource development are training and development, organization development, and career development. The core of all three human resource development functions is learning.[14]

In summary, the creation of an organizational environment conducive to learning and optimum performance is a fundamental first step in the process of a performance management system. All systems are concerned with the goal of improving organizational effectiveness through the improvement of human resources. Key to the achievement of this goal is training and development, which, as described in the next section, has benefits for organizations, employees, and society at large.

> **Development**
> Formal and planned efforts to help employees acquire knowledge, skills, and abilities required to perform future job responsibilities

> **Human resource development**
> Systematic and planned activities that are designed by an organization to provide employees with opportunities to learn necessary skills to meet current and future job demands

BENEFITS OF TRAINING AND DEVELOPMENT

Organizations that invest in the training and development of their employees reap many benefits. But so do employees and the society in which they live. In this section, we describe the benefits of training and development to organizations, employees, and society. As you will see, training and development play a critical role in the success of organizations, individuals, and society.

Benefits to Organizations

Organizations that invest in training and development benefit in many ways that ultimately help them obtain a sustained competitive advantage. Training and development can facilitate an organization's strategy, increase effectiveness, and improve employee recruitment and retention.

Strategy

The goal of all organizations is to survive and prosper. Training and development can help organizations achieve these goals. Organizations can be successful by training employees so they have the knowledge and skills necessary to help organizations achieve their goals and objectives. By linking training to an organization's strategy, training becomes a strategic activity that operates in concert with other programs and activities to achieve an organization's strategic business objectives.

At Providence Health Care, a Vancouver-based health care organization with three hospitals and five long-term care facilities, training is an important component of the organization's people strategy to ensure that the right people, with the right skills, are in the right roles.[15]

Effectiveness

There is a calculable benefit to training employees. Trained employees can do more and better work, make fewer errors, require less supervision, have more positive attitudes, and have lower rates of attrition. Trained employees also produce higher-quality products and services.[16] These benefits have a positive effect on an organization's competitiveness and performance.

The link between training and an organization's performance is strongly supported by research. For example, a survey conducted by American Management Association found that companies that expanded their training programs showed gains in productivity and larger operating profits.[17] In another study, a 10 percent increase in training produced a 3 percent increase in productivity over two years.[18] A review of research on training and organizational effectiveness found that training is positively related to human resource outcomes (e.g., employee attitudes, motivation, behaviours), organizational performance outcomes (e.g., performance and productivity), and to a lesser extent financial outcomes (e.g., profit, financial indicators).[19]

In addition, research has found that companies that invest more in training have higher revenues, profits, and productivity growth than firms that invest less in training.[20] Research by the Conference Board of Canada found that organizations that spend the most on training and development believe they outperform their competitors on a number of performance indicators such as employee satisfaction, customer satisfaction, profitability, and productivity compared with those that spend the least on training and development.[21] A recent study of companies in South Korea found that those that invest more in workplace learning achieve higher levels of learning outcomes (i.e., employee competence, labour productivity, and employee enthusiasm) and financial performance. In other words, investment in workplace training influences organizational performance through learning outcomes.[22]

Training has also been found to be more effective than other interventions. For example, a study that compared the impact of human resource practices to practices that place greater emphasis on operational initiatives, such as advanced manufacturing technology, found that the human resource practices were directly related to the productivity of 308 companies over 22 years while none of the operational manufacturing practices related to productivity. Both empowerment and extensive training were related to productivity and together they accounted for a 9 percent increase in value added per employee.[23]

Training is so important for organizations that it can even make the difference between business success and failure. To find out how, see Training Today 1.1, "Training and Franchise Success."

Employee Recruitment and Retention

Training and development is considered an effective tool for attracting and retaining top talent, especially for employees under the age of 30 who consider their career growth and professional development more important than salary.[24]

Training is often used by organizations to increase their attractiveness to prospective employees and to retain their current employees. For many organizations today, training is the number-one attraction and retention tool. For example, construction company EllisDon offers employees a range of courses and programs through its EllisDon University (EDU), which is part of the company's attraction and retention strategy.[25]

An organization that fails to provide training opportunities to its employees will be at a disadvantage in attracting new employees and retaining current ones. In one study, 99 percent of the respondents said that there are job areas in which training would be useful to them, and in which training decreases their

Training Today 1.1

Training and Franchise Success

What makes a franchise a success? Why do some franchises prosper while others fail? To try to answer these questions, Steven Michael and James Combs examined 88 established restaurant franchisors in the United States.

Although the failure rate of restaurants is very high, the chances of success are greater if the restaurant is a franchise. As a rule, franchises generally do not fail. After all, they benefit from consumer brand recognition, support from the franchisor, buying power, national advertising, and many other factors. But the reality is that some franchisees do fail.

The reasons vary, so the authors considered a number of policy decisions made by franchisors that can influence the success of a franchisee such as franchise industry experience, active owner-managers, the royalty rate, exclusive territories, brand name development, and the length of training (the number of weeks that franchisees underwent initial training).

The results indicated that all of these policy decisions were related to franchisee failure or survival. In particular, a franchisee was more likely to survive if the franchisee had prior industry experience, active ownership, a lower royalty rate, exclusive territory guarantees, a brand name, and a longer length of initial training. The more robust and lengthy the training program for the franchisee, the more likely the franchisee was to succeed. Franchises with the shortest franchisee training programs were the most likely to fail.

According to the authors, the results show that training can reduce the probability of failure and that improving business skills through training might reduce the failure of other businesses as well.

Sources: S.C. Michael & J.G. Combs, "Entrepreneurial failure: The case of franchisees," *Journal of Small Business Management*, Vol. 46 (1), 2008, Pp. 73–90; W. Webb, "Training = franchise success," *Training*, Oct. 2008, Vol. 45 (8), P. 54.

willingness to move to another company.[26] Research conducted by the Conference Board of Canada shows that organizations that spend more per employee on training and development have significantly lower voluntary and involuntary turnover rates.[27]

Not surprisingly, many organizations offer extensive training and development opportunities to retain employees. For example, at Delta Hotels and Resorts, employees are guaranteed ongoing training. If an employee does not receive proper training, he or she can claim an extra week's salary. About 30 employees a year receive an extra week's salary. Delta has an employee retention rate of 89 percent, which is considered one of the best in the hospitality industry. In addition, hotel-school graduates are attracted to Delta because of the training they will receive.[28]

Benefits to Employees

Training and development also has benefits for employees. These can be categorized as internal or intrinsic to an individual, such as knowledge and attitudes, and those that are external to an individual, such as salary.

Intrinsic Benefits

Trained employees benefit by acquiring new knowledge and skills that enable them to perform their jobs better. Research has shown that training has a positive effect on employees' job behaviour and job performance.[29] In addition to improving their knowledge and skills, trained employees also develop greater confidence or self-efficacy (see Chapter 3 for a discussion of self-efficacy) in their ability to perform their job. They describe feelings of increased usefulness and belonging in the organization, and they seek out opportunities to fully exploit their new skills and abilities.[30] Trained employees also have more positive attitudes toward their job and organization.[31]

Extrinsic Benefits

Extrinsic benefits include things such as higher earnings as a result of increased knowledge and skills, improved marketability, greater security of employment, and enhanced opportunities for advancement and promotion. A number of studies have found that company-sponsored training programs increase workers' wages by 4 to 11 percent.[32] According to a recent study, immigrants to Canada who have completed apprenticeship training are more likely to be employed and to earn more money than immigrants who have only a high school diploma.[33] Many workers who have been laid off attend training programs to acquire new skills to obtain employment.[34]

Benefits to Society

Training and development also has benefits for society that extend beyond the workplace. The training and development that organizations provide for their employees helps to create an educated and skilled population that benefits the economy and the standard of living in Canada.

Educated and Skilled Population

The knowledge and skills that employees acquire through workplace training help to create an educated and skilled workforce. For example, some organizations offer literacy and numeracy training for employees who did not obtain it through regular educational channels but who require it to perform their jobs. This training also enables employees to function more effectively in their daily lives and therefore has a number of societal benefits.

Employees who have participated in organization-sponsored training programs report using their new skills to better manage their personal lives. They are more likely to be able to read instructions for assembling products and to be able to calculate bills and expenses. They are also more likely to be able to find employment if they are laid off or their employer closes a plant.

Economy and Standard of Living

Key to a country's standard of living, incomes, and overall prosperity are its productivity and productivity growth. Unfortunately, Canada's economic performance and competitiveness in the global marketplace has been declining. In fact, Canada currently lags behind its major competitors in its productivity growth and innovation. A strong Canadian economy and a high standard of living requires an improvement in the productivity and innovation of Canadian organizations.[35]

There are a number of ways to improve productivity, and one of them is by improving the education and skills of the workforce.[36] An improvement in Canada's productivity will have a positive effect on the economy and the standard of living, and a key factor for improving productivity is education.

The federal government spends billions of dollars annually on education and training because it sees a strong link between an educated workforce and a high-wage economy. Countries with higher education levels have more and better employment opportunities.[37] Training investments also lead to job creation and job opportunities.[38]

Of course, in order for organizations, employees, and society to reap the benefits of training, organizations must invest in training and development. In the next section, we discuss training and development in Canadian organizations.

TRAINING AND DEVELOPMENT IN CANADA

In order to benefit from training and development, organizations must invest in training their workforce and provide employees with training opportunities. In Canada, over 11 million workers receive some type of workplace training each year. In 2008, more than two-thirds (69 percent) of full-time employees in Canadian organizations received training. Part-time and seasonal/contract workers received less training (50 percent and 31 percent, respectively).[39]

Canadian organizations, however, have tended not to be leaders when it comes to investing in training and development. According to the Conference Board of Canada, Canadian organizations under-invest in training and development.[40]

For example, the total average investment in training and development across all industries in Canada was reported to be $4.9 million in 2004.[41] In the United States, organizations spent about $171.5 billion on formal training and development programs in 2010.[42]

Canadian organizations also lag when it comes to the amount spent on training per employee, which has been on a steady decline over the past decade. In 2010, the total average direct investment in training per employee was $688 compared to $787 in 2008, $852 in 2006, $914 in 2004, $824 in 2003, $838 in 2002, $859 in 2000, $798 in 2001, $776 in 1998, and $842 in 1996. This spending decline is evident in both the public and private sector and across all organization sizes.[43] By comparison, organizations in the United States spent on average per employee $1,071 in 2010, $1,176 in 2008, and $1,540 in 2006. Between 2006 and 2010, Canadian organizations spent 64 cents on training and development for every dollar spent by organizations in the United States. Organizations in the United States currently spend about 40 percent more per employee on training and development than do Canadian organizations.[44]

Investments in training, however, vary across sectors, regions, and by organization size. For example, newer knowledge-based sectors (e.g., technology and communications) spend the most (over $1,000 per employee), while more traditional sectors (e.g., wholesale/retail, construction, manufacturing) spend the least. With respect to regional differences, organizations in Quebec spend the most per employee while those in Atlantic Canada spend the least. In terms of organization size, small and medium-sized organizations (SMEs) spend more per employee on training and development than do larger organizations.[45]

In addition, the average number of hours of training received by employees at Canadian organizations dropped from 28 in 2008 to 25 in 2010. As shown in Table 1.1, senior management and executives receive the most hours of training (32) while non-technical employees receive the least (18 hours). Employees in services (32 hours) and not-for-profit organizations (30 hours) receive the most training, while those in wholesale/retail (22 hours) receive the least. By comparison, employees in the United States receive 37 hours of training per employee per year.[46] Canada ranked second last on annual training days per employee in a study that included 12 comparator countries.[47]

The average investment in training as a percentage of payroll in Canada has also dropped to 1.51 in 2008 down from 1.55 percent in 2006 and 1.75 in 2004. By comparison, organizations in the United States spend 2.25 percent of payroll on training and development.[48]

Canadian organizations also spend less on training and development than organizations in other countries, including those in Europe, Asia, and the Pacific Rim. An international comparison of employee training ranked Canada 21st in 2006, down from 12th place in 2002. Ten countries pulled ahead of Canada between 2002 and 2006. According to the Conference Board of Canada, this underinvestment in training and development might lead to a gap in essential knowledge and skills. Further, if Canadian organizations are going to be able to compete effectively, they must increase their investments in training and development.[49]

TABLE 1.1

Training and Development in Canada

- Percentage of Canadian full-time employees who received training in 2008: 69 percent (Part-time employees received 50 hours and seasonal/contract workers received 31 hours)
- Total average training investment per employee in 2010: $688.
- Total average training investment per employee by organization type in 2010: private sector $713; federal/provincial/Crown $498; not-for-profit sector $705.
- Total average training investment per employee by organization size in 2010: fewer than 250 employees $729; 250–499 employees $1,082; 500–1,499 employees $433; 1,500 or more employees $734.
- Total average training investment per employee by level of unionization in 2010: no union $720; low unionized $427; high unionized $770.
- Annual training expenditure per employee by region 2004–2008: Quebec $1,158; Alberta $979; Manitoba/Saskatchewan $829; British Columbia $811; Ontario $802; Atlantic provinces $611.
- Percentage of payroll spent on training in 2008: 1.51.
- Average number of training hours received annually per employee in 2010: 25.
- Average number of training hours received annually by employee category in 2010: senior management and executive, 32; middle management, 27; supervisory, 28; professional, technical, and scientific 29; trades, 25; non-technical, 18.

Sources: P.D. Hughes & A. Campbell, *Learning & development outlook 2009: Learning in tough times*, Ottawa: The Conference Board of Canada, 2009; C. Lavis, *Learning & development outlook 2011: Are organizations ready for learning 2.0?* Ottawa: The Conference Board of Canada, 2011.

Information about training and development in Canada is summarized in Table 1.1. This information will allow you to compare your organization and training experience against that of others. This information also highlights some differences in training across job categories and industries. In the next section, we consider how beliefs that training is an investment or an expense can influence spending on training and development.

IS TRAINING AN INVESTMENT OR AN EXPENSE?

Given the many benefits of training and development it is surprising that Canadian organizations do not invest more, and it begs the question, "Why don't organizations invest more in training and development?"

One reason might be that learning and training is not considered a high priority in Canadian organizations. According to the Conference Board of Canada, the decline in training investment and hours is an indication that learning is not a top priority in many Canadian organizations.[50] In fact, in 2010 Canada was 25th out of 59 countries in the ranking of the importance organizations place on workforce training, which is a drop from the 20th-place ranking Canada earned in 2009. This ranking places Canada just behind China, and behind top-ranking countries such as Japan, Switzerland, and Denmark, but just ahead of the United States, which ranked 31st.[51] In another study, Canadian executives were found to be less likely than those in comparator countries to believe that training is a high priority; Canada ranked 30th out of 55 countries that were surveyed.[52]

Another reason for the underinvestment in training and development is the perception that training, learning, and development expenditures represent a cost rather than an investment. Many organizations view training and development as an expense that can be cut in difficult times. According to the Conference Board of Canada, many organizations in Canada view training and development as a necessary operating expense or cost that should be minimized.[53]

Organizations that view training as a cost tend to limit their training investments to only what is required by law or necessary to survive. As a result, training is often one of the first things to go when times are tough and there are cuts to discretionary spending.[54] Organizations that view training as an investment expect direct benefits and a return on their investment. For these organizations, training is part of the organization's strategy and a key factor for its competitiveness and success.[55]

This is not to say that there are no Canadian organizations that invest heavily in training and development. In fact, there are large differences in the amount spent on training and development across organizations and industries. The Conference Board of Canada found that one in five organizations invests more than 3 percent of payroll in training.[56]

BMO Financial Group invests more than $65 million per year in learning and development programs that include a corporate university, orientation programs, leadership, sales and service programs, and a tuition refund policy or "continuing education assistance plan."[57] TD Bank invested $55.6 million in training in 2009. The average number of days of internal training per employee was 3.88, and TD's investment in training per employee in Canada was $1,241.[58]

However, the overall trend in training investments in Canada is cause for concern. According to the Conference Board of Canada, Canadian organizations are not investing enough resources in training, learning, and development at a time when skilled employees have become increasingly vital to an organization's success, and this threatens Canada's competitiveness. Perhaps not surprisingly, Canada's productivity growth lags behind that of its main competitors.[59]

What can be done to increase training investments in Canadian organizations? What if organizations were required to invest a certain amount of money each year on training and development? That is exactly what the province of Quebec has been doing since 1995, when the government passed the *Act to Foster the Development of Manpower Training* (often referred to by employers as the "1 percent" or "training law"), making it the only payroll training tax in North America. The law requires companies with payrolls of more than $1 million to invest a minimum of 1 percent of their payroll on government-sanctioned training, or pay that amount into a provincial fund. Companies with payrolls of less than $1 million are exempt. The funds acquired from companies that do not invest the 1 percent of payroll on training are placed in a government fund that supports training initiatives in the province.[60]

A 2008 report analyzed the landmark law, concluding that it has had a significant effect on the way Quebec firms organize and deliver training, and has resulted in substantial growth in adult learning and training over the last decade. The main findings of the report are the following:

- the legislation has had a significant impact on the way firms in Quebec structure, organize, and deliver training

- more companies are actively planning and implementing training programs for their employees

- the participation rate in workplace training in Quebec increased from 21 percent to 33 percent between 1997 and 2002 (it increased from 29 percent to 35 percent in Canada), making it the fastest growth rate in Canada and closing the gap between Quebec and other provinces, although Quebec still lags slightly behind the national average in training participation rates

- employers, governments, unions, and community groups are working together to find ways to promote learning and training[61]

As indicated earlier, a study by the Conference Board of Canada found that organizations in Quebec spend on average more per employee on training and development than those in other provinces, providing additional evidence that the Quebec law has had a positive effect on training investments. To find out how the legislation works, see The Trainer's Notebook 1.1, "Quebec's Payroll Training Legislation." To learn about an interesting way that some organizations try to ensure they benefit from their training investments, see Training Today 1.2, "Making Employees Pay for Their Training."

The Trainer's Notebook 1.1

QUEBEC'S PAYROLL TRAINING LEGISLATION

Companies in Quebec with payrolls over $1 million are required by law to spend 1 percent of their payroll on training, or pay a training tax. They must also carefully document their training activities and complete government forms every February. Some have complained that the process is too complicated and choose to pay the tax rather than complete the forms even if they are providing some training. The main aspects of the legislation are as follows:

1. Every February, companies must file paperwork in which they indicate how they spent 1 percent of their total payroll on training.

2. If they have not spent at least 1 percent of their total payroll on training, they must pay the difference to the government, and that money is then used to fund training programs in companies that have invested at least 1 percent in training.

3. Companies must use accredited training bodies, instructors, and services that follow a code of ethics. All types of training are eligible.

4. General information about the participation of employees in training exercises must be provided.

5. Companies that meet the 1 percent training investment can apply for provincial training grants.

Source: K. Harding, "A taxing way to train staff." *The Globe and Mail*, June 4, 2003, P. C1, C6.

Training Today 1.2

Making Employees Pay for Their Training

Organizations that invest in training and development are often concerned that employees will leave the organization soon after they attend a costly training program. When this happens, the organization is unable to reap the benefits of its training investment. In response, some organizations now require employees to sign a training bond.

A **training bond** is a contract between the employer and employee that states that the employer will pay for the employee's training as long as the employee remains with the organization for a minimum period of time following completion of a training program. If the employee fails to remain for the agreed-upon period of time then he/she must reimburse the organization for the cost of the training.

In one such case an employee was hired as a chief pilot with the understanding that he would receive the necessary training and obtain a Transport Canada flight check to fulfill his job duties. The employer agreed to pay for the training and required the employee to sign a training bond. However, the employee resigned after six months of employment and refused to pay for the cost of the training. The employer then successfully sued the employee in small claims court for the prorated portion of the training costs.

Organizations, however, are not always successful in recovering their training investments when employees leave after receiving training. For organizations to successfully recover their investments in employee training, a number of factors need to be demonstrated: the employer's intentions must be made clear to the employee before he/she accepts the investment; the obligations incurred by the employee should be expressed unambiguously and in writing; the employee must be given adequate time to consider the consequences of making the commitment; the employee should be given the opportunity to negotiate the terms; the employee must be made aware the funds are being expended for the benefit of both parties; the employee must not in any way be coerced into the arrangement or be given the impression the commitment is not likely to be enforced; the provisions for recovery must be even-handed and fair to both parties; and the training must be such as to enhance the employee's own marketability in the industry in which he/she works.

Source: Based on T. Mitchell, "When the employer is the victim." *Canadian HR Reporter*, Jan. 17, 2011, Vol. 24 (1), Pp. 13–14.

Training bond

A contract between the employer and employee that states that the employer will pay for the employee's training as long as the employee remains with the organization for a minimum period of time following completion of the training program

THE CONTEXT OF TRAINING AND DEVELOPMENT

Training and development are embedded within a larger context that can influence the extent to which training and development is provided in an organization as well as the type of training provided. As shown in Figure 1.2, training and development is just one part of a system of human resource practices that is influenced by internal and external factors.

The human resources system is influenced by environmental and organizational factors. Environmental factors such as legislation, the economic climate, competition, demographics, and social values have an impact on organizations. For example, if a competitor introduces a lower-priced product, the organization will have to decide whether to match the competitor's actions or compete in other ways, such as providing superior service. This strategic decision can in turn affect costs, the ability to pay employees, and/or the need to train and reward employees for effective performance. Events and concerns inside and outside an organization can lead to the need for new knowledge, skills, abilities, and training programs.

FIGURE (1.2)

The Context of Training and Development

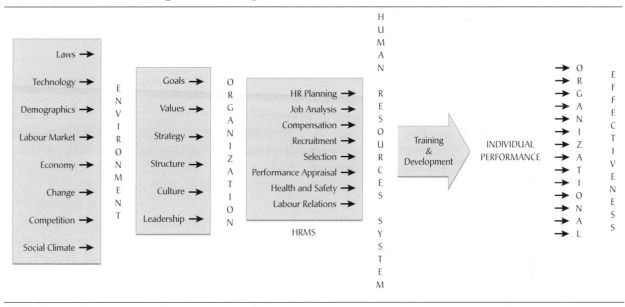

Sometimes sudden and unexpected changes in the environment can lead to changes in organizations themselves and in human resources policies and practices. For example, consider how concerns over terrorism have affected airport and flight security training. The Transportation Security Administration in the United States developed new guidelines for the training of baggage screeners and flight crews and made airport security fully federalized. The training of baggage screeners now includes technical training on metal detectors, X-ray scanners, bag searching, and how to deal with difficult passengers and manage stress. Training was increased to 40 hours of classroom training and 60 hours of on-the-job training. Pilots and flight attendants receive training on how to assess and react to dangerous situations.[62] Other changes in training as a result of the threat of terrorism include a shift to distance technologies and e-learning and an increase in training programs on diversity, security, stress management, and change management.[63]

Let's now consider how changes in specific environmental and organizational factors can impact the human resources system and training and development.

The Environmental Context of Training and Development

Some of the key environmental factors that drive human resources and training and development are global competition, technology, the labour market, and change.

Global Competition

Increasing global competition has forced organizations to improve their productivity and the quality of their goods and services. Improvements in the production process and quality initiatives almost always require employees to learn new skills. And when Canadian organizations send workers on assignments in foreign countries, they need to provide them with cross-cultural training so they will be able to adapt and function in a different culture (see Chapter 13 to learn about cross-cultural training). Thus, global competition can require numerous changes to human resource practices and the need for training and development.

Technology

Technology has had a profound effect on the way organizations operate and compete. New technologies can provide organizations with improvements in productivity and a competitive advantage. However, such improvements depend on the training that employees receive. Technology will lead to productivity gains only when employees receive the necessary training to exploit the technology.[64] Thus, the adoption of new technologies will have a direct impact on the training needs of employees who will be required to use the technology.

The Labour Market

Changes in the labour market can have a major effect on training and development. For example, consider the implications of a shortage of skilled labour in Canada. It has been estimated that a critical shortage of skilled workers in Canada could reach 1 million by the year 2020. To deal with this looming crisis, the country will have to change its approach to education and training.[65] If organizations cannot hire people with the necessary knowledge and skills, they will have to provide more training if they are to compete and survive. Changes in the labour market and the supply of labour require changes in the amount and type of training.

Change

The technological revolution, increasing globalization, and competition have resulted in a highly uncertain and constantly changing environment. In order to survive and remain competitive, organizations must adapt and change. As a result, managing change has become a normal part of organizational life, and training and development is almost always a key part of the process. This often involves training programs on the change process as well as training that is part of the change program. For example, if an organization implements a change program that involves a team-based work system, then employees will require team training (see Chapter 13 for a description of team training).

The Organizational Context of Training and Development

As indicated in Figure 1.2, training and development are also affected by internal events within the organization. Among the most important internal factors are an organization's strategy, structure, and culture.

Strategy

Strategy is one of the most important factors influencing training and development. As indicated earlier, training and development can help an organization achieve its strategic objectives and gain a competitive advantage when it is aligned with an organization's strategy. The alignment of human resources practices with an organization's business strategy is known as **strategic human resource management (SHRM)**. Organizations that have greater alignment between their HR practices and their strategies tend to have superior performance.[66]

HR practices like training and development can also be strategic rather than independent or isolated activities when they are aligned with the organization's business strategy and therefore enable an organization to achieve its strategic goals and objectives. Thus, **strategic training and development (ST&D)** refers to the alignment of an organization's training needs and programs with an organization's strategy and objectives. Whether an organization has a strategy for quality, innovation, or customer service, training as well as other human resources practices must be designed to reinforce and support the strategy.

For example, if an organization decides to improve customer service or product quality, then employees will require training to learn how to provide better service or improve product quality. If an organization's strategy is to grow as rapidly as possible, then employees need to be trained in the management of mergers, acquisitions, joint ventures, and international ventures. All these growth components necessitate the building of new skills, and training is required to do this.

Strategy is often a key factor driving the need for and type of training and development in organizations. For example, several years ago Bayshore Home Health, the largest provider of home and community health care services in Canada, launched a workforce diversity strategy. A key part of the strategy involved employee education about diversity that consisted of workshops on cultural competence and specific diversity workshops to address local needs.[67]

By linking training to business strategy, training becomes strategic rather than an isolated and independent activity, and as a result it is more likely to be effective. In fact, there is some evidence that training can lower an organization's market value when it is not strategically focused.[68]

Figure 1.3 depicts the role that strategy plays in the training and development process. The model shows how an organization's business strategy will have implications for its HRM strategy. The HRM strategy will then influence the organization's strategy for learning and training, which will in turn determine the type of training and development activities and programs required.

Strategic human resource management (SHRM)
The alignment of human resources practices with an organization's business strategy

Strategic training and development (ST&D)
The alignment of an organization's training needs and programs with an organization's strategy and objectives

FIGURE 1.3

A Strategic Model of Training and Development

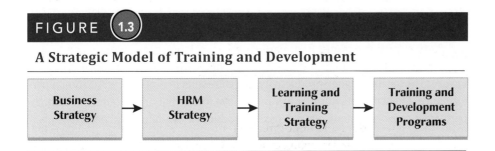

Structure

The structure of an organization also affects training and development activities. Organizations are increasingly becoming flatter, with fewer levels of management. Employees are expected to perform tasks that were once considered managerial tasks and so they must be trained in traditional managerial activities such as problem solving, decision making, teamwork, and so on. Many organizations have experienced dramatic structural changes such as downsizing and reengineering in an effort to survive. These changes to an organization's structure often lead to changes in employees' tasks and responsibilities and necessitate the need for training.

Culture

Organizational culture

The shared beliefs, values, and assumptions that exist in an organization

Organizational culture refers to the shared beliefs, values, and assumptions that exist in an organization. An organization's culture is important because it determines the norms that exist in an organization and the expected behaviours. The culture of an organization and its norms and expected behaviours are often communicated to employees through training programs.

For example, ethical practices are deeply ingrained in the culture of Molson Coors Brewing Company and are communicated to employees through the company's ethics training programs. The company's training programs reflect a culture of integrity and the importance of acting in an honest and trustworthy manner based on business ethics and moral conviction.[69] Thus, the training programs are consistent with the company's core values and are a catalyst for achieving its business goals.

The Human Resources System

The human resources system and other human resource functions also influence training and development. In fact, in addition to being linked to business strategy, human resources practices should also be aligned and linked to each other. Thus, strategic human resource management involves two kinds of linkages. First, human resource practices should be linked to business strategy, as discussed earlier. Second, human resource practices should also be linked to each other so they work together to achieve an organization's strategy. Thus, what is most important is not individual human resource practices but rather the entire system of practices and the extent to which they are aligned with an organization's strategy and with each other. In combination, the practices form an integrated and tightly linked human resources system that is known as a high-performance work system.

High-performance work system (HPWS)

An interrelated system of human resource practices and policies that usually includes rigorous recruitment and selection procedures, performance-contingent incentive compensation, performance management, a commitment to employee involvement, and extensive training and development programs

A **high-performance work system (HPWS)** consists of an interrelated system of human resource practices and policies that usually includes rigorous recruitment and selection procedures, performance-contingent incentive compensation, performance management, a commitment to employee involvement, and extensive training and development programs. High-performance work practices increase employees' knowledge, skills, abilities, and motivation. This leads to more positive attitudes, lower turnover, and higher productivity, which results in higher organizational performance. An increasing number of studies have found that organizations with high-performance work systems have superior productivity and financial performance.[70]

In summary, external factors influence an organization's strategy, structure, and the way human resources are managed, and these factors in turn influence the design and delivery of training and development programs. Training and development should be tightly aligned with an organization's business strategy and the other human resource practices in the human resources system. In other words, there should be a good fit between strategy and training and development, and between training and development and other human resources practices. In this way, training and development is a strategic and important part of a high-performance work system that can improve individual performance and ultimately organizational effectiveness.

THE INSTRUCTIONAL SYSTEMS DESIGN (ISD) MODEL OF TRAINING AND DEVELOPMENT

In this section, we describe a systems approach to training and development that is known as the instructional systems design model. The **instructional systems design (ISD) model** of training and development depicts training and development as a rational and scientific process that consists of three major steps: needs analysis, design and delivery, and evaluation.[71] The ISD model is a streamlined version of an earlier model of instructional design known as ADDIE, in which each letter represents a different action: analysis, design, development, implementation, and evaluation.[72]

> **Instructional systems design (ISD) model**
> A rational and scientific model of the training and development process that consists of a needs analysis, training design and delivery, and training evaluation

According to the ISD model of training and development, the training process begins with a performance gap. A performance gap is something in the organization that is not quite right or is of concern to the organization. Perhaps customer complaints are up, quality is low, market share is being lost, or employees are frustrated by management or technology. Or perhaps there is a performance problem that is making it difficult for employees or departments to achieve goals or meet standards. If some part of the organization has a problem, or if there are concerns about the performance of individual employees or departments, then the problem needs to be analyzed. Recall in the chapter-opening vignette that TD Bank was concerned about the growing number of robberies at its branches.

A critical first step in the ISD model is a needs analysis to determine the nature of the problem and whether training is the best solution. A needs analysis is performed to determine the difference or gap between the way things are and the way things should be. As indicated in the chapter-opening vignette, TD Bank conducted a needs analysis that included focus groups, interviews, and surveys and, based on the needs analysis, it was realized that they had to design a training program that would focus not just on robbery prevention but also on what happens afterwards.

Needs analysis consists of three levels known as an organizational analysis, a task analysis, and a person analysis. Each level of needs analysis is conducted to gather important information about problems and the need for training. An organizational analysis gathers information on where training is needed in an organization; a task analysis indicates what training is required; and a person analysis identifies who in the organization needs to be trained.

Based on the data collected from managers, employees, customers, and/or corporate documents, strategies for closing the gap are considered. Before training is determined to be the best solution to the problem, alternatives must be assessed. The solution to the performance gap might be feedback, incentives, or other human resource interventions. If training is determined to be the best solution, then objectives—or measurable goals—are written to improve the situation and reduce the gap. The needs analysis, the consideration of alternative strategies, and the setting of objectives force trainers to focus on performance improvement, not the delivery of a training program. Training is only one solution and not necessarily the best one to performance problems.

If training is the solution to a performance problem, a number of factors must be considered in the design and delivery of a training program. The needs analysis information and training objectives are used to determine the content of a training program. Then the best training methods for achieving the objectives and for learning the training content must be identified.

After a training program has been designed and delivered, the next stage is training evaluation. The needs analysis and training objectives provide important information regarding what should be evaluated in order to determine whether a training program has been effective. Some of the critical evaluation questions include: Did the training program achieve its objectives? What did employees learn? Did employees' job performance improve? Is the organization more effective? Was it worth the cost? As indicated in the chapter-opening vignette, once training is completed at TD Bank, participants and stakeholders give quantitative and qualitative formal evaluations.

The purpose of all training and development efforts is ultimately to improve employee performance and organizational effectiveness. Thus, it is important to know whether employee job performance has changed and whether the organization has improved following a training program. In this stage, the trainer has to decide what to measure as part of the evaluation of a training program as well as how to design an evaluation study. On the basis of a training evaluation, decisions can be made about what aspects of a training program should be retained, modified, or discarded.

Figure 1.4 shows the instructional systems design model of training and development. As we have described, each stage leads into the subsequent stage, with needs analysis being the first critical step that sets the stage for the design and delivery and evaluation stages. Also notice that there are feedback loops from evaluation to needs analysis and training design and delivery. This indicates the

FIGURE (1.4)

The Instructional Systems Design Model of Training and Development

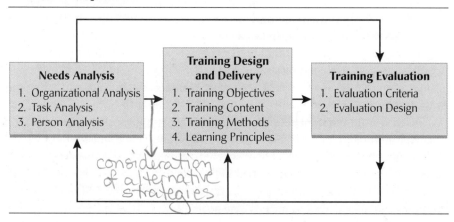

process is a closed-loop system in which evaluation feeds back into needs analysis and training design and delivery. In this way, it is possible to know whether performance gaps identified in the needs analysis stage have been closed, and whether changes are required in the design and delivery of a training program in order to make the training program more effective. Thus, training programs are continuously modified and improved on the basis of training evaluation.

Although the ISD model is considered to be the best approach for managing the training and development process, in reality many organizations do not follow all of the steps of the ISD model. In other words, many organizations do not conduct a needs analysis; rather, they implement training programs that are not well designed, and they do not evaluate their training programs. There has also been some criticism waged against the ISD model in recent years among professionals in the training industry who have seriously challenged its usefulness. However, if used correctly it remains the best approach for managing the training and development process.[73] Training programs often fail because they have ignored an important step in the process such as conducting a thorough needs analysis.

We will have more to say about each of the stages of the training and development process as they are covered in the remainder of the text. For now, you should understand the ISD model and the sequence of activities that are involved in the training and development process. To learn more about how to apply the ISD model, see The Trainer's Notebook 1.2, "The Application of the ISD Model."

The Trainer's Notebook 1.2

THE APPLICATION OF THE ISD MODEL

The instructional systems design model begins when somebody identifies a performance gap in the organization. According to the ISD model, the recognition of a performance gap should lead to the following sequence of activities:

1. Conduct an organizational analysis to investigate the performance gap and determine whether training is a possible solution (when the cause of the problem is a lack of knowledge or skills).

2. If training is a possible solution, conduct a task analysis in order to determine how the job or jobs in question should be performed and the things that a skilled employee must know and be able to do.

3. Conduct a person analysis to determine how employees currently perform the job compared to how they should perform and how best to train them (e.g., training methods).

4. Design a training program using those methods and approaches that will be most effective to train employees who require training. Include specialists in various media and methods to assist in developing training material.

5. Develop and fine-tune the program. Pilot-test it and revise as needed.

6. Deliver the program to its intended audience.

7. Monitor and evaluate the program and its results on an ongoing basis. The program is considered a success if the original performance gap is closed or reduced and if correcting the problem costs less than the cost of not correcting it.

Sources: J. Gordon & R. Zemke, "The attack on ISD." *Training*, April, 2000, Pp. 42–53; R. Zemke & A. Rossett, "A hard look at ISD," *Training*, Feb. 2002, Pp. 26–34.

SUMMARY AND ROAD MAP

This chapter introduced you to the training and development process and emphasized the important role that training and development plays in organizations. The benefits of training and development for organizations, employees, and society were described as well as training investments made by organizations in Canada. We also described how training and development is embedded within the environmental and organizational context and is part of the human resources system. It was also noted that for training to be most effective it should be aligned with the organization's business strategy and with other human resource practices, and part of a high-performance work system (HPWS). Finally, we described the instructional systems design (ISD) model of training and development that sets the stage for the remainder of the textbook.

In the next two chapters, we focus on learning—which is, after all, what training and development is all about. In Chapter 2 you will learn about organizational learning and learning in organizations. In Chapter 3 you will learn about individual learning and motivation. These two chapters are the foundation for the remainder of the text and set the stage for the chapters that follow.

Chapters 4 through 12 focus on the steps of the ISD model. Chapter 4 deals with the needs analysis process. Chapters 5 through 10 focus on the design and delivery of training and development programs. This includes chapters on how to design training programs (Chapter 5), off-the-job training methods (Chapter 6), on-the-job training methods (Chapter 7), and technology-based training methods (Chapter 7). Chapter 9 focuses on how to deliver training programs, and in Chapter 10 you will learn how to design training programs so that employees apply what they learn in training on-the-job or what is known as the transfer of training. Chapters 11 and 12 focus on the final stage of the ISD model, training evaluation. The focus of Chapter 11 is evaluation criteria and evaluation design and the focus of Chapter 12 is how to determine the costs and benefits of training programs.

In Chapter 13 you will learn about different types of training programs, and in Chapter 14 you will learn about management training and development. The text concludes with Chapter 15, which provides an overview of training trends and the evolution of learning, training, and development.

Key Terms

development p. 7
high-performance work system
   (HPWS) p. 20
human resource development p. 7
instructional systems design (ISD)
   model p. 21
organizational culture p. 20

performance management p. 5
strategic human resource management
   (SHRM) p. 19
strategic training and development
   (ST&D) p. 19
training p. 6
training bond p. 16

Web Links

Bayshore Home Health: **www.bayshore.ca**

BMO Financial Group: **www.bmo.com**

Delta Hotels and Resorts: **www.deltahotels.com**

EllisDon: **www.ellisdon.com**

Providence Health Care: **www.providencehealthcare.org**

TD Bank: **www.td.com**

Required Professional Capabilities (RPCs)

The following RPCs are relevant to material covered in this chapter. The RPC number represents the CCHRA number assigned to the RPC as presented on the CCHRA website. All of the RPCs can be found in the Body of Knowledge at **http://www.chrp.ca/rpc/body-of-knowledge/**.

RPC 144: Aligns OLDT with business objectives and needs.

144.01: Strategic HR Management

144.02: The organization's strategic business plan

RPC 155: Ensures performance management information is an integral component of employee development.

155.01: Principles and techniques of effective performance management systems, including assessment, development and performance improvement

Discussion Questions

1. According to the Conference Board of Canada, the investments made by Canadian organizations in training and development have remained relatively constant over the last decade and appear to have reached a plateau in terms of the amount organizations are willing to invest in training and development. Comment on the implications of this for organizations, employees, and the Canadian economy. Should governments get involved and enact laws that require organizations to invest a certain percentage of their payroll in training and development, as they have in Quebec?

2. Studies comparing the competitive performance of Canadian corporations indicate that among the countries in the G8 (Canada, the United States, Japan, Germany, France, Italy, Russia, and the United Kingdom), Canada ranks very low. Do you think that training and development in Canada has anything to do with this? If so, what should governments and businesses do?

3. Discuss some of the reasons why organizations often fail to fully implement the instructional systems design (ISD) model of training and development. Why do you think the ISD model has come under attack in recent years and been seriously challenged and criticized?

4. Refer to the chapter-opening vignette on TD's Robbery Prevention and Awareness training program and discuss the extent to which the instructional systems design (ISD) model was used. In other words, describe the company's approach to the Robbery Prevention and Awareness training program in terms of each stage of the ISD model.

5. Research on training and organizational effectiveness has found that training is positively related to human resource and performance outcomes but to a much lesser extent to financial outcomes. Explain why and how training is related to these outcomes. What are the implications of these findings for organizations? Why is training less strongly related to financial outcomes?

6. Why do some organizations view training, learning, and development as an expense (or an investment)? What are the implications of this? What can be done to change the perception that training is an expense so that organizations view training and development as an investment? What are the implications of changing perceptions for employees, organizations, and society?

7. Discuss some of the reasons why Canadian organizations have not increased their investments in training and development over the last decade. Do you think they should increase their investments in training and development? Explain your answer.

8. Should organizations require employees to sign a training bond in which they agree to pay back the organization the cost of the training they received if they leave the organization? Explain your answer. What would be your response if your organization or an organization that you wanted to work in required you to sign a training bond?

The Great Training Debate

1. Debate the following: Training and development is the single most important factor for the competitiveness and success of an organization.

2. Debate the following: All provinces should enact training legislation similar to the training law in Quebec.

3. Debate the following: Training is an operating cost and should be limited to only what is required by law and absolutely necessary.

4. Debate the following: Employees who receive training from their organization should be required to sign a training bond that requires them to pay the cost of their training if they leave the organization after a specified period of time following training.

Exercises

In-Class

1. Review the training and development facts in Table 1.1. Benchmark your experiences in a current or previous organization against the statistics in the table. Based on the statistics in the table, you might consider things such as: How does your organization compare to the Canadian averages in areas such as the amount of training hours employees receive a year and the amount spent per employee on training? Does your organization fare better or worse than the average Canadian organization? What do the results tell you about your organization? What are the implications of your findings for your learning and job performance and for your organization?

2. Consider how training and development is influenced by, and in turn can influence, other human resource functions. In particular, give an example of how training and development can influence and is influenced by activities within each of the following human resource areas: recruitment; selection; HR planning; performance appraisals; compensation; and health and safety.

3. Using the ISD model of training and development, examine the class your instructor has delivered to you today. In other words, what did your instructor have to do in terms of a needs analysis? How did he or she design and deliver the class? How was the class evaluated or how should it be evaluated?

4. Assume you are a director of training and development in a small organization. In order to reduce expenses, the company president has decided to cut the training budget in half and reduce the amount of training provided to employees. The president has asked to meet with you to discuss these plans. Your job is to prepare a short presentation to persuade the president to change his or her mind. What will you say and what can you do to convince the president of the importance of and need for more, not less, training and development?

5. Recall the last time you attended an organization-sponsored training program. Describe the objectives and content of the training program and whether or not you think the program was strategic. In other words, was it an example of strategic training? Be specific in terms of why you think it was or was not a good example of strategic training. What would have made it more strategic?

6. Recall the last time you attended an organization-sponsored training program. Describe the objectives and content of the training program and whether or not you think the ISD model was used to develop the program. Be specific in terms of each stage of the model and the extent to which it was used in the development of the program. How effective was the training program in terms of your learning and in achieving the program's objectives? Based on your analysis, what could have been done to more fully make use of the ISD model, and what effect might this have had on the effectiveness of the program?

In-the-Field

1. Contact the human resource department of your own or another organization to discuss the organization's training programs. Try to learn about the extent to which the human resource department follows the ISD model of training and development. Find out about each stage of the model and the extent to which it is adhered to in the development of training programs. What aspects of the model are adequately carried out and which ones are not? If some of the stages are not adequately conducted, find out why this is the case and why the human resource department does or does not rigorously adhere to the ISD model. Based on the responses, what advice would you give the human resource department about its training and development programs?

2. A number of associations and government departments provide useful information and services related to learning and training and development. To learn more about some of these associations, visit the following websites:

   www.cstd.ca (Canadian Society for Training and Development)

   www.astd.org (American Society for Training & Development)

   www.ccl-cca.ca/ccl (Canadian Council on Learning)

   www.hrsdc.gc.ca (Human Resources and Skills Development Canada)

   Write a brief report in which you describe the association and the information that can be obtained from each site about learning, education, and training and development.

3. To learn more about the benefits of training for Canadian organizations, go to Industry Canada at **www.collectionscanada.gc.ca/webarchives/20060226114621/http://strategis.ic.gc.ca/epic/internet/incts-scf.nsf/en/h_sl00003e.html**.

   Answer the following questions:
   a. Why is training important?
   b. How is the workforce changing?
   c. What are companies doing to train employees?
   d. What are leading-edge learning organizations doing?

Case Incident

Canadian American Transportation Systems

Canadian American Transportation Systems began running a new high-speed ferry between Toronto and New York State in 2004. The marine industry is highly regulated and most of the workers have no experience so a great deal of training was needed to meet the rigorous standards set by the U.S. Coast Guard and Transport Canada.

There are two mandatory levels of training. One is called SOLAS (safety of life at sea), which involves a very basic familiarization of the vessel, basic life saving procedures, and medical emergencies. There is also a more advanced program of survival training called STCW (seafarers' training certification and watch keeping). Employees were taken to Olympic-sized pools where they had to jump into the water, get people into safety rafts, and learn how to use equipment in cold water conditions.

Questions

1. To what extent has the instructional system design (ISD) model of training and development been used? Discuss how the ISD model is relevant for the training of the new staff and how it can be applied. What are some of the implications of not using the ISD model?
2. Discuss the benefits of the training described in the case for the organization, employees, and society.

Source: Claude Garcia, "CEOs Talk: Training & Development," *Canadian HR Reporter*, May 17, 2004, P. 7. Reprinted by permission of Canadian HR Reporter.

Case Study FLOTATION LTD.

"Great course, Sam!" said the trainees as they walked out the door and headed for the parking lot. Just like all the others. Sam Harris, a veteran trainer with Flotation Ltd., a manufacturer of life jackets and other flotation devices, smiled as he gathered his notes together.

He had just finished two hours of wisecracking and slightly off-colour storytelling as he worked his way through the third session of a human relations course for supervisors. "Keep 'em happy" was Sam's motto. Give the troops what they want, keep your enrolments up, and no one will complain.

Sam was good at it, too! For 20 years, he had earned an easy living, working the politics, producing good numbers (of trainees) for the top brass to brag about ("We give each employee up to 26 hours of training every year!"), and generally promoting his small training group as a beehive of activity.

Everybody knew Sam and everybody liked him. His courses were fun. He had no trouble convincing managers to send their people. He put out a little catalogue with his course list every year in January. He hadn't had a cancellation in more than 10 years. Some managers said that training was the best reward they had. Now, only three years from retirement, Sam intended to coast comfortably into pension-land. All his favourite courses had long been prepared. All he had to do was make adjustments here and there and create some trendy new titles.

But times were changing. The company president was thinking differently. "I need somebody to take a close look at our training function," he said. Sitting in the president's office, Jenny Stoppard, the newly hired Vice President of Human Resources, wondered what he meant. Flotation Ltd. had a reputation as a company with a well-trained workforce.

"We need to increase our productivity per person by 50 percent over the next three years," the president continued. "And you are going to spearhead that effort. We spend a lot on training and we cycle people through a lot of courses. But I'm not satisfied with the bottom line. I know that while Dad was president he swore by Sam and said he was the greatest. I don't know anymore. Maybe a whole new approach is needed. Anyway, I want you to take a close look at Sam's operation."

Later in the day, the president called Sam into his office. "Sam, I want you to meet Jenny Stoppard. I've just hired her as Vice President of Human Resources. She's your new boss. I think the next three years are going to be very exciting around here, and Jenny is going to be a key player in the drive to increase our competitiveness. I want you to do everything in your power to cooperate with her."

Questions

1. Comment on Sam's approach to training. Would you want him working for your company? What are the benefits of his training programs to employees and the organization?
2. To what extent is training and development at Flotation Ltd. strategic? What would make it more strategic?
3. To what extent does Sam use the instructional systems design (ISD) model of training and development? If he were to more fully use the ISD model, what should he do? Comment on each step of the ISD model.
4. How does Sam evaluate his training programs? Compare Sam's evaluation to the president's objectives. If Sam were to evaluate training based on the president's objectives, what would he have to do? What do you think the results might be?
5. The president has asked Jenny to "take a close look at Sam's operation." What should she do, and what should she report back to the president?

REFERENCES

1. Excerpt from Dobson, S. (2010, November 29). Learning to avoid the bad guys. *Canadian HR Reporter, 23(21)*, 24; TD Employee Performance and Development, Developing our employees, www.td.com (retrieved October 31, 2011).
2. Norris, A. (2001, September 1). Transat work faulted. *The Gazette*, A1; Koring, P. (2001, August 31). Transat faces safety crackdown. *The Globe and Mail*, A1; Koring, P. (2002, August 30). Jet crew's handling of fuel leak questioned. *The Globe and Mail*, A1; Brazao, D. (2001, August 29). We had no second chance, pilot in jet emergency says. *The Toronto Star*, A1; Taylor, A., & Verma, S. (2002, August 31). Air Transat told to improve training on fuel handling. *The Toronto Star*, A1.
3. Koring, P. (2004, October 18). Transat report blames pilots; EXCLUSIVE: Emergency landing in Azores could have been avoided if crew followed fuel-management procedures, report says. *The Globe and Mail*, A1; Cernetig, M. (2004, October 19). Pilot's heroic flying tarnished in report; Mishandled fuel leak, probe finds Transat jet glided to safety in Azores. *The Toronto Star*, A7.
4. Koring, P. (2004, October 18); Cernetig, M. (2004, October 19); Koring, P. (2005, March 2). Air Transat agrees to settle lawsuit. *The Globe and Mail*, A6.

5. Campion-Smith, B. (1996, January 24). Rookie driver sorry for crash. *The Toronto Star*, A1, A22; Hall, J. (2005, August 6). Ten years after. *The Toronto Star*, B1, B4–B5.

6. McLean, J. (2011, July 30). Poor training to blame, report claims. *The Toronto Star*, A2.

7. Parker, R. O., & Cooney, J. (2005). *Learning & development outlook 2005*. The Conference Board of Canada: Ottawa.

8. Gordon, A. (2000, February). 35 best companies to work for. *Report on Business Magazine*, 24–33.

9. Gosselin, A., Werner, J., & Hall, N. (1997). Ratee preferences concerning performance management and appraisal. *Human Resource Development Quarterly, 8(4)*, 315–333.

10. Aguinis, H. (2009). *Performance management* (2nd edition). Upper Saddle River, NJ: Pearson Prentice Hall.

11. Aguinis, H. (2009).

12. Smither, J. W., & London, M. (2009). Best practices in performance management. In J. W. Smither & M. London (Eds.), *Performance management: Putting research into action* (pp. 585–625). San Francisco, CA: Jossey-Bass; Squires, P. (2009). The role of on-the-job and informal development in performance management. In J. W. Smither & M. London (Eds.), *Performance management: Putting research into action* (pp. 157–195). San Francisco, CA: Jossey-Bass.

13. Brown, K. G., & Sitzmann, T. (2011). Training and employee development for improved performance. In S. Zedeck (Ed.), *Handbook of industrial and organizational psychology* (Vol. 2, pp. 469–503). Washington, DC: American Psychological Association.

14. Werner, J. M., & DeSimone, R. L. (2009). *Human resource development*. (5th edition). Mason, OH: South-Western.

15. Anonymous. (2008, May 19). CEOs talk: Training & development. *Canadian HR Reporter, 21(10)*, 11–13.

16. Bowsher, J. (1990, May). Making the call on the CEO. *Training and Development Journal*, 65–66.

17. Adams, M. (1999). Training employees as partners. *HR Magazine, 44(2)*, 64–70.

18. Bernstein, A., & Magnusson, P. (1993, February 22). How much good will training do? *BusinessWeek*, 76–77.

19. Tharenou, P., Saks, A. M., & Moore, C. (2007). A review and critique of research on training and organizational-level outcomes. *Human Resource Management Review, 17*, 251–273.

20. Betcherman, G., Leckie, N., & McMullen, K. (1997). *Developing skills in the Canadian workplace*. Ottawa: Canadian Policy Research Networks; Arthur, W. Jr., Bennett, W. Jr., Edens, P. S., & Bell, S. T. (2003). Effectiveness of training in organizations: A meta-analysis of design and evaluation features. *Journal of Applied Psychology, 88*, 234–245.

21. Hughes, P. D., & Campbell, A. (2009). *Learning & development outlook 2009: Learning in tough times*. Ottawa: The Conference Board of Canada.

22. Park, Y., & Jacobs, R. (2011). The influence of investment in workplace learning on learning outcomes and organizational performance. *Human Resource Development Quarterly, 22*, 437–458.

23. Birdi, K., Clegg, C., Patterson, M., Robinson, A., Stride, C. B., Wall, T. D., & Wood, S. J. (2008). The impact of human resource and operational management practices on company productivity: A longitudinal study. *Personnel Psychology, 61*, 467–501.

24. Hirsh, L. (2008, November 3). Non-monetary rewards gaining traction. *Canadian HR Reporter, 21(19)*, 24; Harder, D. (2007, November 5). More than money. *Canadian HR Reporter, 20(19)*, 21.

25. Dobson, S. (2010, February 8). Constructive education. *Canadian HR Reporter, 23(3)*, 14, 15.

26. Schaaf, D. (1998). What workers really think about training. *Training, 35(9)*, 59–66.

27. Hughes, P. D., & Campbell, A. (2009).

28. Roseman, E. (2001, August 29). Delta Hotels knows how to keep workers. *The Toronto Star*, E2.

29. Arthur, W. Jr., Bennett, W. Jr., Edens, P. S., & Bell, S. T. (2003).

30. Garavan, T. N., Costine, P., & Heraty, N. (1995). *Training and development in Ireland: Context policy and practice.* Dublin: Oak Tree Press.

31. Schaaf, D. (1998).

32. Bernstein, A., & Magnusson, P. (1993).

33. Silliker, A. (2011, April 11). Apprenticeships close immigrant wage gap. *Canadian HR Reporter, 24(7),* 8.

34. Howlett, K., & Church, E. (2009, January 13). Training for the new economy. *The Globe and Mail,* A4.

35. Hughes, P. D., & Campbell, A. (2009).

36. Crane, D. (2002, October 27). Innovation means productivity gains. *The Toronto Star,* C2.

37. Klie, S. (2007, December 3). Higher education leads to higher productivity. *Canadian HR Reporter, 20(21),* 7.

38. Bernstein, A., & Magnusson, P. (1993).

39. Hughes, P. D., & Campbell, A. (2009).

40. Harris-Lalonde, S. (2001). *Training and development outlook.* The Conference Board of Canada: Ottawa.

41. Parker, R. O., & Cooney, J. (2005).

42. Green, M., & McGill, E. (2011, November). 2011 state of the industry report. *T+D, 65(11),* 44–50.

43. Lavis, C. (2011). *Learning & development outlook 2011: Are organizations ready for learning 2.0?* Ottawa: The Conference Board of Canada.

44. Lavis, C. (2011)

45. Hughes, P. D., & Campbell, A. (2009).

46. Hughes, P. D., & Campbell, A. (2009); Lavis, C. (2011)

47. Hughes, P. D., & Campbell, A. (2009)

48. Hughes, P. D., & Campbell, A. (2009)

49. Parker, R. O., & Cooney, J. (2005)

50. Lavis, C. (2011)

51. Lavis, C. (2011)

52. Hughes, P. D., & Campbell, A. (2009)

53. Hughes, P. D., & Campbell, A. (2009)

54. Fair, B. (2010, October 18). How to stop C-suite yawn over training. *Canadian HR Reporter, 23(18),* 21, 25.

55. Hughes, P. D., & Grant, M. (2007).

56. Parker, R. O., & Cooney, J. (2005).

57. Dobson, S. (2010, March 22). Reimbursing tuition reinforces development. *Canadian HR Reporter, 23(6),* 14, 18.

58. TD Employee Performance and Development, Developing our employees, www.td.com (retrieved October 31, 2011).

59. Hughes, P. D., & Grant, M. (2007).

60. Bélanger, P., & Robitaille, M. (2008). A portrait of work-related learning in Quebec. Ottawa: Work and Learning Knowledge Centre.

61. Bélanger, P., & Robitaille, M. (2008).

62. (2002, April). Airport training ready to take off. *Training and Development,* 17–18.

63. (2002, February). ASTD survey results: The effect of terrorism on training. *Training and Development,* 28.

64. Crane, D. (1998, March 28). Time to take worker training seriously. *The Toronto Star,* B2.

65. McCarthy, S. (2001, February 27). Skilled-worker shortage could reach one million. *The Globe and Mail,* A1.

66. Becker, B. E., & Huselid, M. A. (1998). High performance work systems and firm performance: A synthesis of research and managerial implications. *Research in Personnel and Human Resources Management, 16,* 53–101.

67. Klie, S. (2009, December 14). Cultural competence affects patient health. *Canadian HR Reporter, 22(22),* 12.

68. Gibb-Clark, M. (2000, February 11). Employee training can backfire on firms: Survey. *The Globe and Mail,* B10.

69. Greengard, S. (2005, March). Golden values. *Workforce Management, 84(3),* 52–53.

70. Becker, B. E., & Huselid, M. A. (1998); Combs, J., Liu, Y., Hall, A., & Ketchen, D. (2006). How much do high-performance work practices matter? A meta-analysis of their effects on organizational performance. *Personnel Psychology, 59,* 501–528.

71. Dipboye, R. L. (1997). Organizational barriers to implementing a rational model of training. In M. A. Quinones and A. Ehrenstein (Eds.), *Training for a Rapidly Changing Workplace,* Washington, DC: American Psychological Association.

72. Gordon, J., & Zemke, R. (2000, April). The attack on ISD. *Training, 37(4),* 42–53; Zemke, R., & Rossett, A. (2002, February). A hard look at ISD. *Training, 39(2),* 26–34; Weinstein, M. G., & Shuck, B. (2011). Social ecology and worksite training and development: Introducing the social in instructional system design. *Human Resource Development Review, 10,* 286–303.

73. Gordon, J., & Zemke, R. (2000, April); Zemke, R., & Rossett, A. (2002, February).

Organizational Learning

CHAPTER LEARNING OUTCOMES

After reading this chapter, you should be able to:

- define organizational learning and describe a learning organization
- explain the five disciplines of a learning organization
- discuss the principles of a learning organization and the four key dimensions that are critical for creating and sustaining a learning organization, and define a learning culture
- define knowledge and give examples of explicit and tacit knowledge
- describe the meaning and types of intellectual capital
- define knowledge management and explain how knowledge is acquired, interpreted, disseminated, and retained in organizations
- define communities of practice and describe what organizations can do to create them
- define workplace learning, informal learning, and formal learning, and describe what organizations can do to facilitate informal learning
- describe the multilevel systems model of organizational learning

VANCITY

Vancity is a member-owned, community-based, full-service financial institution that provides a range of financial products and services to its members across British Columbia. With more than 2,000 employees, 59 branches, and 417,211 member-owners, Vancity is Canada's largest credit union.

In 2009, Vancity made the decision to double its investment in learning and development by 2011. This decision affirmed Vancity's belief in the connection between learning and performance, and was reached following the creation of an organizational accountability framework examining roles, capacity, and capability within the organization. The framework was then tied into a new corporate vision that emphasized clarity about both employee and member expectations. Increased investment in learning directly supports the organization's need to build workforce capacity so that it can execute strategy.

The increased investment in learning and development at Vancity is spread across a number of external programs including tuition subsidies of up to $2,400 to pay for coursework directly related to an employee's position; additional subsidies (covering up to 50 percent of tuition) available for courses not directly related to an employee's current position; subsidies covering the cost of obtaining professional accreditations; a co-operative studies program in Bologna, Italy; and the Saint Mary's University Master of Management, Co-operatives and Credit Unions (MMCCU) program.

Vancity's learning and development expenditures are not limited to external learning opportunities. In-house learning programs cover a variety of topics, including leadership development, financial services, and management training. Additionally, the organization has built an online skills inventory and provides career planning services to employees. Employees and their managers work together on career development. Vancity encourages personal growth through continuous learning and on-the-job development.

In-house learning at Vancity is aligned with its corporate value of "build versus buy," as evidenced by its adoption of the "idevelop" suite for developing e-learning content. There is also a noticeable shift at Vancity toward offering more informal and experiential learning through coaching and internship opportunities.

The final piece of the new learning and development vision at Vancity focuses on accountability. Although the learning and development team is responsible for developing and providing learning opportunities, managers are accountable for ensuring that employees receive the development they need. This new level of responsibility represents a significant change in managers' roles. Vancity has supported this change by providing management development opportunities through programs such as Harvard ManageMentor. The goal of the program is to ensure that these new responsibilities are clarified for management and that it has the right tools in place to provide support to employees.

Vancity has been ranked as one of the most innovative, dynamic, and progressive financial institutions in Canada. Vancity was selected as one of British Columbia's Top Employers for 2010 and 2011 and one of Canada's Top 100 employers for 2012.[1]

Source: C. Lavis, *Learning & development outlook 2011: Are organizations ready for learning 2.0?* Ottawa: The Conference Board of Canada, 2011; www.vancity.com.

Vancity is a good example of how learning can be incorporated into the culture of an organization and how learning is a key component of corporate strategy and performance. It is also an example of how employee learning has a lot to do with the learning systems and infrastructure that exist in an organization.

In organizations like Vancity, learning is considered to be an important investment and receives a great deal of commitment and support from top management. As a result, employees have access to many opportunities for formal and informal learning.

In this chapter, we describe how organizations learn and how learning occurs at all levels of an organization. Training and development is an important part of the learning system in organizations, so you should understand how it fits into the larger picture of organizational learning.

WHAT IS ORGANIZATIONAL LEARNING?

Organizational learning refers to the process of creating, sharing, diffusing, and applying knowledge. However, organizational learning is not simply the sum of individual employee learning, nor is performance management limited to a training system that enables employees to learn and apply that learning. Organizational learning focuses on the systems used to create and distribute new knowledge on an organization-wide basis. Thus, organizational learning is a dynamic process of creating and sharing knowledge.

The traditional perspective of learning has always been strongly associated with training and development. The goals of training have been viewed from a traditional perspective that focuses on developing and improving employees' knowledge, skills, and abilities (KSAs). This is, of course, key for organizational learning because an organization can't learn unless individual employees learn. As noted by Peter Senge, the originator of the concept of the learning organization, "Organizations learn only through individuals who learn. Individual learning does not guarantee organizational learning. But without it, no organizational learning occurs."[2]

The training of employees usually focuses on current needs or deficiencies and is most effective when the future is relatively stable and predictable. However, in today's highly uncertain environment, organizations have realized the need to do more than just train employees for the current state of affairs. In a learning organization, employees learn through a variety of methods and processes, and they also learn how to continuously learn. This is of course the case at Vancity, where employees have a range of opportunities for learning through external and internal programs.

To survive and develop, organizations must learn to manage by managing learning—the capacity to learn and change, consciously, continually, and quickly. A company's knowledge, including that contained in employees' minds, has always been a source of competitive advantage. The ability to learn faster than the competition is a source of sustainable competitive advantage.

For many organizations, creating learning systems and processes requires that they transform themselves into learning organizations. As you will learn in the next section, a learning organization does not represent the latest management fad. It represents a strategic shift and orientation in how organizations learn that can make an organization more competitive and effective.

THE LEARNING ORGANIZATION

In 1990, Peter Senge published a book called *The Fifth Discipline: The Art and Practice of the Learning Organization,* which set in motion a whole new approach to organizations that focuses on learning and, in particular, the "learning organization."

Organizational learning
The process of creating, sharing, diffusing, and applying knowledge in organizations

Learning organization

An organization that creates, acquires, organizes, shares, and retains information and knowledge, and uses new information and knowledge to change and modify its behaviour in order to achieve its objectives and improve its effectiveness

A **learning organization** is an organization that creates, acquires, organizes, shares, and retains information and knowledge, and uses new information and knowledge to change and modify its behaviour in order to achieve its objectives and improve its effectiveness. Learning organizations have established systems and structures to acquire, code, store, and distribute important information and knowledge so that it is available to those who need it, when they need it.

As a result, a learning organization is able to transform itself by acquiring and disseminating new knowledge and skills throughout the organization. Thus, it has an enhanced capacity to learn, adapt, and change its culture.[3]

Embedded in this concept is the ability to make sense of and respond to the surrounding environment. Organizational values, policies, systems, and structures support and accelerate learning for all employees. This learning results in continual improvements in work systems, products, services, teamwork, and management practices—a more successful organization. Organizational learning is learning that actually results in improvements.

In his groundbreaking book, Senge identified the following five "disciplines" to becoming a learning organization:[4]

1. *Personal mastery.* Individuals have to be open to others and willing to learn on a continual basis. People with personal mastery are always in a learning mode. This is fundamental for a learning organization because organizations learn only if the individuals in them learn. If individuals do not learn, then organizational learning will not be possible.
2. *Building a shared vision.* This involves the development of a picture and vision of the future to which everyone can agree and be committed. As indicated in the chapter-opening vignette, Vancity developed a new learning and development vision and learning programs are aligned with the corporate value of "build versus buy."
3. *Mental models.* Mental models refer to the images and assumptions that people have about themselves and the world. People need to be able to examine their mental models and be aware of how they influence their behaviour. Because such models can thwart or inhibit learning, people must understand them and hold them up to scrutiny.
4. *Team learning.* Learning takes place in teams through dialogue, discussion, and "thinking together." People need to be able to learn and act together.
5. *Systems thinking.* This discipline integrates the others and has to do with viewing the organization as a whole and being able to see and understand how its parts are interrelated.

While some people might find the notion of a learning organization to be a fad, there is evidence that learning organizations are highly effective. The Conference Board of Canada found that high learning organizations are almost 50 percent more likely to have higher overall levels of profitability than organizations not rated as learning organizations.[5] High learning organizations also outperform other organizations in terms of employee retention, employee satisfaction, production of quality products and services, and overall organizational performance. High learning organizations believe they are more productive and profitable than their competition, and better able to satisfy their customers than low and medium learning organizations.[6] Research has also found a positive relationship between the practices of learning organizations and financial performance.[7]

PRINCIPLES AND DIMENSIONS OF LEARNING ORGANIZATIONS

Learning organizations have a number of important principles. First, in a learning organization everybody is considered to be a learner. Employees recognize the need for learning and are actively involved in both formal and informal learning programs.

Second, in a learning organization, employees do not learn just by attending formal training programs. They also learn through informal means such as listening to and observing others. People learn from each other in a learning organization.

Third, learning is part of a change process and in fact enables change. When people are open to learning they are able to recognize the need for change, and learning is an important part of any change program. Thus, learning and change are closely related.

Fourth, continuous learning is considered to be a hallmark of learning organizations. Formal and informal learning are considered to be a regular part of every employee's job.

Fifth, learning organizations recognize that learning is an investment in the future of employees and the organization rather than an expense. Just as expenditures on plants and equipment are viewed as long-term capital investments, expenditures on learning are viewed as long-term investments in human capital.[8]

The Conference Board of Canada identified the following four dimensions or pillars of a learning organization, which are described in Table 2.1:

1. Vision,
2. Culture,
3. Learning dynamics and systems, and
4. Knowledge management and infrastructure.

TABLE 2.1

Key Dimensions of Learning Organizations

The Conference Board of Canada has identified the following four dimensions or pillars as critical in creating and sustaining a learning organization.

1. *Vision.* A clear vision of the organization's strategic direction and business goals and learning is part of the vision of the organization.

2. *Culture.* A learning organization has a culture that supports risk taking, experimentation, and learning. Knowledge, information sharing, and continuous learning are considered to be a regular part of organizational life and the responsibility of everybody in the organization. Informal learning is supported and encouraged.

3. *Learning dynamics and systems.* Employees are encouraged and expected to manage their own learning and development and are provided with formal and informal learning opportunities; they are coached and mentored by their managers.

4. *Knowledge management and infrastructure.* Learning organizations learn from their own experience and from competitors, customers, and experts. They have systems and structures to acquire, code, store, and distribute important information and knowledge so that it is available to those who need it and when they need it.

Sources: R.O. Parker, & J. Cooney, *Learning and development outlook 2005.* The Conference Board of Canada: Ottawa, 2005; P.D. Hughes, & M. Grant, *Learning and development outlook 2007.* The Conference Board of Canada: Ottawa, 2007.

In a survey of Canadian organizations, the Conference Board of Canada found that 71 percent of Canadian organizations considered themselves to be a learning organization to at least a moderate extent. To become a learning organization, Canadian organizations can improve on a number of the key dimensions. For example, senior management needs to be more explicit in terms of the type of knowledge that is important in their organization, and serve as learning role models to the rest of the organization (vision). Canadian organizations can also improve by creating a more positive learning culture and by encouraging and rewarding experimentation, risk taking, and challenging the status quo. As well, innovation, knowledge sharing, and productivity improvements should be a more frequent part of organizational life.

Canadian organizations can also improve by providing employees with more opportunities for formal and informal learning, and by supporting and developing managers in their roles as coaches, mentors, and facilitators of learning (learning dynamics and systems). Providing employees with opportunities to improve their learning skills is also necessary. They should be encouraged to participate in learning activities such as communities of practice, mentoring programs, job rotations, and cross training. Finally, Canadian organizations have to develop knowledge management systems and practices so that important information and knowledge that is essential to organizational success can be stored and made available to those who need it, whenever they need it.[9]

Training Today 2.1

Maintaining the Learning Culture at D&D Automation

D&D Automation is a specialty engineering firm based in Stratford, Ontario, that designs and implements industrial automation control systems for industrial machinery, manufacturing lines, process environments, and other automated facilities. The company is a leading provider of discrete and process controls technology.

In the high-tech manufacturing industry, if employees are not up to date on all the latest technologies the company is doomed to fail. That's why training and development is part of the culture at D&D Automation and the firm's 40 employees are all responsible for maintaining this learning culture.

To stay on top, D&D introduced its Tech Leader program about five years ago. The company benchmarks all employees against the technologies they have to use and tracks their progress. The company highlights the technologies that are more important to the business and people can see what they should be learning.

To be at the minimum level in the Tech Leader program, an employee needs in-house or external training on the technology. To move up, the employee needs to log a specific number of hours using the technology in different applications. And to achieve the level of guru, he needs formal, external training, which is paid for by the company.

To keep employees and the company as a whole up to date on new technologies, the company invites technology suppliers to weekly lunch-and-learn sessions. The supplier provides the lunch and 3 to 10 employees attend to learn about the new technology. Suppliers compete to get into the lunch-and-learn sessions, with the best coming back several times a year.

D&D Automation's culture of learning extends into the community as well. The company supports robotics and skills competitions at high schools and co-op education programs at post-secondary institutions.

Sources: Anonymous, "CEOs talk: Training & development," *Canadian HR Reporter*, May 19, 2008, P. 11. Reprinted by permission of Canadian HR Reporter; www.ddauto.com.

The Trainer's Notebook 2.1
THE LEARNING CULTURE INDEX

The Learning Culture Index is composed of the following six items, scored using a 5-point scale ranging from 1 (strongly disagree) to 5 (strongly agree):

1. Learning is a top priority in my organization.

2. Senior management clearly communicates that learning is critical to organizational success.

3. Senior management demonstrates support for learning by serving as role models for the organization.

4. My organization supports knowledge in concrete ways (e.g., funding, policies, resources, systems, technology).

5. Employees are encouraged to continuously upgrade and increase their knowledge and education level.

6. My organization monitors outside trends by looking at what others do (e.g., by benchmarking "best practices," attending conferences, and examining published research).

Source: C. Lavis, *Learning & Development Outlook 2011: Are organizations ready for learning 2.0?* Ottawa: The Conference Board of Canada, 2011; www.vancity.com.

As indicated above, one of the dimensions of a learning organization is a **learning culture**, which refers to the attitudes and practices within the organization associated with organizational learning and people development. Organizations with strong learning cultures have strong support from organizational leaders and they make learning a top priority. Organizations with strong learning cultures spend more on training, provide more hours of training per employee, and report better performance on a number of dimensions (e.g., retention, employee performance, employee engagement, overall productivity) compared to organizations with weak learning cultures.[10]

For an example of a company with a strong learning culture, see Training Today 2.1, "Maintaining the Learning Culture at D&D Automation." To assess the learning culture in an organization, see The Trainer's Notebook 2.1, "The Learning Culture Index."

Learning culture
The attitudes and practices within the organization associated with organizational learning and people development

KNOWLEDGE IN ORGANIZATIONS

Becoming a learning organization involves understanding the importance of knowledge and knowing how to manage it. Knowledge has become a critical resource for organizations in the information economy and is the main resource used to perform work in organizations. Employees require new knowledge to improve the products and services that their organizations provide, and organizations require knowledge to change and remain competitive in today's increasingly competitive and turbulent environment.[11]

Employee knowledge is a synthesis of information: all the facts, theories, and mental representations employees know about the world and, in the context of work, about their jobs and organization. **Knowledge** is the sum of what is known: a body of truths, information, and principles. Knowledge can be found in the minds of employees or transferred and stored in systems in organizations.

Knowledge
The sum of what is known; a body of truths, information, and principles

Knowledge is more than information, which we have in abundance, represented by dusty books filling shelves and facts floating across the Internet. Knowledge, on the other hand, is information that has been edited, put into context, and analyzed in a way that makes it meaningful and therefore valuable to an organization.[12] Knowledge can be grouped in two ways: explicit knowledge and implicit or tacit knowledge.

Explicit Knowledge

Explicit knowledge refers to those things that you can buy or trade, such as patents or copyrights and other forms of intellectual property. The formula for making Coca-Cola and the brand name Coke are examples of intellectual properties that are extremely valuable. These tangible assets can normally be codified or formalized. Explicit knowledge can be written into procedures or coded into databases and is transferred fairly accurately. However, less than 20 percent of corporate knowledge is explicit. The other 80 percent of corporate knowledge is implicit or tacit knowledge and it is difficult to quantify or even describe accurately.[13]

Explicit knowledge
Those things that you can buy or trade, such as patents or copyrights and other forms of intellectual property

Tacit Knowledge

Tacit knowledge
Knowledge that is learned from experience and insight, and has been defined as intuition, know-how, little tricks, and judgment

Implicit or **tacit knowledge** refers to the knowledge learned from experience and insight, and has been defined as intuition, know-how, little tricks, and judgment. Seasoned executives with tacit knowledge of a situation make million-dollar decisions.

Tacit knowledge is used by employees but is almost impossible to transfer. To grasp the concept of explicit knowledge and tacit knowledge, imagine describing the physical characteristics of your best friend; now, try to describe the methods your friend would use to influence a supervisor. The former involves explicit knowledge, while the latter involves your tacit knowledge of your friend.

A well-known example of tacit knowledge is that of the decision-making behaviour of dealers in financial markets. That behaviour appears to be instinctual, but it is based on their past experience, what they read and hear, and the climate of the market. Extracting this knowledge from these dealers and then training others in this winning behaviour is extremely difficult.[14] The transfer of tacit knowledge requires personal contact. The personal contact must be extensive and built on trust and can include partnerships, apprenticeships, and mentoring.

INTELLECTUAL CAPITAL

Intellectual capital is more than knowledge; intellectual capital is more like intelligence. Intelligence is the ability to create knowledge and includes the ability to learn, to reason, to imagine, to find new insights, to generate alternatives, and to make wise decisions.[15] By increasing the general level of intelligence of employees, organizations hope to create new knowledge that will result in new products, services, and processes.

Intellectual capital
An organization's knowledge, experience, relationships, process discoveries, innovations, market presence, and community influence

Intellectual capital refers to an organization's knowledge, experience, relationships, process discoveries, innovations, market presence, and community influence. Intellectual capital is the source of innovation and wealth production—it is knowledge of value.[16] Intellectual capital has to be formalized, captured, and leveraged to produce a more highly valued asset.[17]

Intellectual capital is not like other assets; it grows with use. When an employee learns and uses that learning, he/she usually learns even more, and is motivated to learn again. He/she can share the learning and not deplete it or use it up, like other assets. Sharing learning results in the acquisition of even more knowledge, as you probably learned when you worked on projects with other people.

Intellectual capital is often divided into four types: human capital, renewal capital, structural capital, and relationship capital.

Human Capital

Human capital is the knowledge, skills, and abilities of employees. Included in this type of capital are some basic components of intelligence, such as the ability to learn, to reason, and to analyze. Interpersonal skills, such as the ability to communicate with others and work in teams to generate better work methods, would also be part of an organization's human capital.

Human capital
The knowledge, skills, and abilities of employees

Renewal Capital

Renewal capital refers to what we have labelled intellectual property, which consists of patents, licences, copyrights, and marketable innovations including products, services, and technologies.

Renewal capital
Intellectual property, which consists of patents, licences, copyrights, and marketable innovations including products, services, and technologies

Structural Capital

Organizations are not amoebas; they need a skeleton or structure to function. Although the organizational chart captures some of the concept of **structural capital**, what we really mean are the formal systems and informal relationships that allow employees to communicate, solve problems, and make decisions. Structural capital is the set of structures, routines, and information systems that stay behind when employees go home. Sometimes these structures are represented by policies and procedures. For example, a company might require you to obtain the approval of the vice president of marketing before launching an innovative but costly advertising campaign. Another part of structural capital can be stored in databases and knowledge documents.

Structural capital
Formal systems and informal relationships that allow employees to communicate, solve problems, and make decisions

Relationship Capital

Organizations, like individual employees, do not exist as islands. **Relationship capital** refers to an organization's relationship with suppliers, customers, and even competitors that influence how they do business. These relationships, particularly if they are based on trust and integrity, can be a source of competitive advantage.

Customer capital is a subset of relationship capital. **Customer capital** is the value of an organization's relationships with its customers. For example, many small businesses enjoy high degrees of customer capital. Neighbours will shop at the local milk store even though the milk is more expensive because they know the owner and his/her family. In larger organizations, customer capital refers to all the efforts that a company makes to keep customers returning to buy its products or services.

Relationship capital
An organization's relationships with suppliers, customers, and competitors that influence how they do business

Customer capital
The value of an organization's relationships with its customers

Intellectual Capital Cycle

The four types of intellectual capital work in a cycle to increase intellectual capital. As more investments are made in human capital, employees are more capable of and committed to increasing renewal and structural capital, leading to more productive relationship capital, resulting in better financial performance. The money can then be recycled to increase intellectual capital.

In this chapter, we focus on human capital: the sum and synergy of employee knowledge. Organizations want to develop their intellectual capital, and one way to do it is to create an environment in which learning is valued and actively managed.

The term *learning organization* refers to the programs and culture required to increase an organization's capacity to learn and to create intellectual capital. Creating and leveraging that knowledge has become a goal of many organizations. Training and performance specialists must understand that the creation and transfer of knowledge are strategic imperatives. Learning organizations have to actively manage this knowledge.

In the next section, we discuss the different ways that organizations manage knowledge, or what is known as knowledge management.

KNOWLEDGE MANAGEMENT

Knowledge management
The creation, collection, storage, distribution, and application of compiled "know-what" and "know-how"

Knowledge management involves the creation, collection, storage, distribution, and application of compiled "know-what" and "know-how."[18] The value of knowledge occurs when it is available to those who need it, when they need it, and when it is put into action. Many companies today have realized the importance of knowledge management.

For example, at one automotive supplier, 30 percent of the design engineers' time was wasted solving problems that had already been solved in the company.[19] Companies know that knowledge isn't being shared when work is duplicated, or when expertise is available but hidden in the company and opportunities are lost, or when needless staffing takes place.

Recall from our earlier discussion of a learning organization that knowledge management/infrastructure is one of the four critical dimensions of a learning organization. Knowledge management/infrastructure refers to systems and structures that integrate people, processes, and technology so that important knowledge is coded, stored, and made available to members of an organization when they need it. Thus, in a learning organization, knowledge must be shared and distributed so that the organization can benefit from the cumulative knowledge of all employees.[20]

According to research conducted by the Conference Board of Canada, only 31 percent of respondents indicated that systems and structures exist within their organization to ensure that important knowledge is coded, stored, and made available to those who need it.[21] As noted earlier, Canadian organizations need to develop knowledge management systems and practices to ensure that important information is coded, stored, and made available for use throughout the organization.

In the remainder of this section, we describe four processes through which organizations manage knowledge—acquisition, interpretation, dissemination, and retention.[22] The ability to create and use knowledge is what characterizes a learning organization, and the practices used by organizations to manage knowledge are a critical part of knowledge management.

Knowledge Acquisition

Companies acquire or create new knowledge in many ways. Some focus on well-respected creative processes such as brainstorming. Others may benchmark competitors or the best companies in the world. Some organizations engage in simulations or scenario planning to stimulate new ideas. Most scan the environment looking for new ideas or changing conditions and provide formal training to their employees.

One of the most important ways for organizations to acquire information and knowledge is by scanning the environment. This involves tapping into both internal and external sources of information and establishing internal and external connections.

External sources of information include other organizations, customers, industry watchers, and the marketplace. These sources of information can provide an organization with information on how to improve their practices, services, and products. Internal sources of information include individuals, teams, and departments throughout an organization that might have information and knowledge that would be useful for others in the organization.

Learning organizations establish external connections through partnerships that involve the exchange of information. Internal connections might include the formation of cross-functional teams that meet to discuss changes in the industry and marketplace. Individual members form external connections through participation in professional associations, supplier forums, and through contacts with customers and others in the industry. The cross-functional team is therefore able to keep abreast of industry trends, tactics, and techniques. The key is for the organization to establish both internal and external connections and relationships in order to acquire and share information and knowledge.[23]

Knowledge Interpretation

Learning occurs when employees form their views of the organization and its environment. These views are often called mental models. Peter Senge describes **mental models** as "deeply ingrained assumptions, generalizations, or images that influence how we understand the world and how we take action."[24]

For example, if we have a mental model of managers as manipulators, then we will see all their actions as politically motivated and act accordingly. New knowledge will not be accepted because we cannot recognize and change our mental models. As one researcher noted, the acceptance of new knowledge can be likened to an organ transplant—the possibility of rejection is highly probable.[25] Even when employees are aware of best practices in other companies or units, it might take more than two years for the information to be understood in a way that can be acted upon.

Mental models

Deeply ingrained assumptions, generalizations, or images that influence how we understand the world and how we take action

An effective way to develop shared mental models is to establish teams. The most valuable and innovative work-related learning occurs in work teams, solving real problems.[26] At Chevron Corporation, based in San Francisco, best-practice teams save the company millions of dollars annually by improving processes.[27]

Knowledge cannot be valued unless there is a shared understanding of its importance. Learning is social, and as teams work together they not only learn but also develop a common way of thinking about things, and a common identity emerges. These common perspectives are termed mental maps and are vitally important to the interpretation of the work environment and any lessons it contains. New learning is difficult to accept and apply without this shared perspective.

Knowledge Dissemination

Moving products, services, and money through and between organizations is a standard process for most organizations. Moving ideas requires a different set of skills and even different norms. Companies must design systems or ways of sharing knowledge so that others can improve their work practices. **Knowledge sharing** involves providing task information and know-how to help and collaborate with others to solve problems, develop new ideas, or to implement policies or procedures. Successful knowledge management depends on knowledge sharing.[28]

Research has found that knowledge sharing is positively related to team performance and organizational financial performance.[29] Unfortunately, teams often do not share information even when it is critical for them to do so. Therefore, it is important for organizations to encourage teams to share information and knowledge. This can be done by structuring team discussions, framing team tasks as intellective, which means that a correct answer exists, and promoting a cooperative team climate.[30]

You might say that information has always been shared between employees, and knowledge management is just a new way of describing communication. Although employees have always passed on new ideas by talking with one another, the difference is that these informal systems can be replaced by formal mechanisms grounded in technology.

Information and communication technologies (ICTs) allow for increased codification of knowledge; that is, its transformation into information that can easily be transmitted. Today, most organizations have electronic bulletin boards, libraries, virtual conference rooms, or connected knowledge bases. Through technology, employees can exchange proposals, presentations, spreadsheets, specifications, and so on.

An intranet is a critical component for managing knowledge. An employee who posts a question or seeks advice can receive that information in hours, not weeks. Just as we use the little help wizards in our software, we could use a company expert or subject-matter specialist who would pop up on the monitor while we are working on a new project—an instant coach!

Knowledge Retention

As noted earlier, knowledge resides in the minds of employees or in systems created to store that knowledge. To capitalize on these sources of knowledge, organizations must build tools to quickly compile, store, and retrieve this knowledge, a kind of intellectual inventory. These are called knowledge repositories.

Knowledge sharing
Providing task information and know-how to help and collaborate with others to solve problems, develop new ideas, or to implement policies or procedures

Knowledge repositories should not be seen as sacred libraries in which great books are stored and never read. The system has to be designed to encourage its use, to facilitate interaction. One reason for the growth of interest in this area is that the cost of managing it has been significantly lowered through technology.

There are ways to capture and store knowledge in information systems for later use. Some of these are highly structured databases. Digitalized knowledge can be more easily and cheaply processed, indexed, searched, converted, and transmitted.

Some knowledge repositories are more informal lists of lessons learned, white papers, presentations, and so on. Others are more actively stored in discussion groups. Most have links to the originators of the documents or at least to those who tend to access the repositories, thus signalling who is actively interested in that area. These collaborative filters monitor databases and intranet sites, and can tell you which sites others with interests similar to yours have found useful.

Not all knowledge repositories are based on computer technology. Some knowledge is tacit and not easily codified. Some more traditional means of storing knowledge might include transcripts or audiocassettes from strategic planning sessions, consultants' reports in text or multimedia formats, videotaped presentations, market-trend analyses, and any number of information-rich resources.

Oral histories are another way to capture knowledge, particularly when organizations suffer the memory loss associated with departures and downsizing. For example, in the United Kingdom, Rothschild PLC used an exit interview to capture the vast amount of knowledge that its departing head of public relations held. A professional with HR and PR experience interviewed the executive for an entire afternoon, and the conversation was recorded. Information that would not normally be transmitted to the successor was uncovered, edited, and indexed.[31] Other companies record oral histories from retiring managers.

COMMUNITIES OF PRACTICE

Many organizations today have created communities of practice as a means for people to share, exchange, and acquire information and knowledge. **Communities of practice** refers to groups of employees who share similar concerns and problems and meet regularly to share their experiences and knowledge, learn from each other, and identify new approaches for working and solving problems.[32] The core principles of communities of practice are that learning is social and that people learn from each other while working together on-the-job.[33] Thus, people in communities of practice share information and knowledge and in the process learn with and from each other. Members ask each other for help, exchange best practices, and share information. Very often the information that is exchanged is implicit or tacit knowledge.[34]

According to Etienne Wenger, who along with Jean Lave coined the term communities of practice, three characteristics define a community of practice:[35]

- *Domain.* A community of practice must have a domain of interest that is shared among its members.

- *Community.* In a community of practice, there is interaction, discussion, sharing and exchanging information, and mutual assistance among members.

- *Practice.* Members in a community of practice are practitioners with resources, experiences, stories, and tools that they use to solve problems.

Communities of practice
Groups of employees who share similar concerns and problems and meet regularly to share their experiences and knowledge, learn from each other, and identify new approaches for working and solving problems

Communities of practice can exist within a department in an organization as well as across departments and regions and even include members from different organizations. Some communities of practice meet regularly face-to-face, while others use technology to communicate.[36]

Communities of practice have been found to be an effective method of learning that can improve organizational performance by driving strategy, generating new lines of business, solving problems, promoting the spread of best practices, developing skills, and aiding in the recruitment and retention of talent.[37] A recent study on 250 teams in a global Fortune 100 technology company found that team member participation in face-to-face and technology-mediated communities of practice was positively related to individual tacit and explicit knowledge which were related to team performance.[38] Not surprisingly, communities of practice are now being embraced by organizations all over the world.[39]

Although communities of practice are informal, self-organizing groups that form naturally on their own, they can be created, fostered, and nurtured in organizations. To do so, managers need to focus on three things:[40]

- Identify potential communities of practice that will enhance an organization's strategic capabilities (identify potential members and bring them together).

- Develop an infrastructure to support communities of practice and enable members to share their expertise (they need to be integrated into the organization and supported).

- Assess the value of the organization's communities of practice (listen to stories from members about their experiences of how the community helped them solve a problem, save the company money, etc.).

For an example of an organization that has developed communities of practice, see Training Today 2.2, "Communities of Practice at the Canada School of Public Service (CSPS)."

Training Today (2.2

Communities of Practice at the Canada School of Public Service (CSPS)

The Canada School of Public Service (CSPS) is the learning service provider for the Public Service of Canada. It helps to ensure that public service workers in Canada have the knowledge and skills they need to perform their jobs. The CSPS also plays a vital role in the delivery of the government's Learning, Training and Development Policy.

The CECP breaks the public service into six distinct learning communities. In 2006, the CSPS formed a Centre of Expertise in Communities of Practice (CECP) to provide expert guidance on the design of communities of practice for federal and public service employees. The CECP designs custom structures for each community and offers strategies, techniques, and tools. They also provide multiple methods for interaction such as face-to-face meetings, teleconferences, video conferences, and online functions such as listservs, email distribution lists, and threaded discussions.

So far the CECP has created more than 50 virtual communities of practice with more than 2,000 active participants across the country.

Sources: J. Salopek, "Knowledge in numbers." *T+D*, July, 2008, Vol. 62 (7), Pp. 24–26; www.csps-efpc.gc.ca/index-eng.asp.

INFORMAL LEARNING

Workplace learning refers to the process of acquiring job-related knowledge and skills through both formal training programs and informal social interactions among employees.[41] Although the focus of this book is formal training programs, it is important to recognize that employees also acquire information and learn through informal interactions with each other. In fact, a great deal of what employees learn in organizations is through informal learning.

Informal learning refers to learning that occurs naturally as part of work and is not planned or designed by the organization. Informal learning is spontaneous, immediate, and task-specific. By comparison, **formal learning** has an expressed goal set by the organization and a defined process that is structured and sponsored by the organization.[42] (See Table 2.2 for a more detailed definition of formal and informal learning.) Recall from earlier in the chapter that in a learning organization, employees do not just learn through formal learning; they also learn through informal means such as listening to and observing others. Table 2.3 describes some of the differences between formal and informal learning.

It has been reported that as much as 70 percent of what employees learn and know about their jobs is learned through informal processes rather than through formal programs. This means that only 30 percent of what employees learn is actually acquired through formal training and development programs sponsored by their organization. According to the Conference Board of Canada, informal learning is on the rise in Canadian organizations. One of the main reasons for the increase in informal learning is the increased need for knowledge transfer.[43] As indicated in the chapter-opening vignette, there has been a shift at Vancity toward offering more informal learning.

Employees have always learned through informal means. For example, an employee might show co-workers a way to save time by combining two steps in handling customer complaints. Sometimes learning occurs when an employee returns from a formal training session and teaches others what he or she has learned.

Workplace learning
The process of acquiring job-related knowledge and skills through both formal training programs and informal social interactions among employees

Informal learning
Learning that occurs naturally as part of work and is not planned or designed by the organization

Formal learning
Learning that is structured and planned by the organization

TABLE 2.2

Formal and Informal Learning

Formal Learning
Learning that involves formal, planned, and structured activities or the organized transfer of work-related skills, knowledge, and information. It includes activities such as classroom instruction, structured on-the-job programs, workshops, seminars, e-learning, and courses offered at external institutions.

Informal Learning
Learning that occurs primarily spontaneously and outside of formal, designed activities or the unstructured transfer of work-related skills, knowledge, and information, usually during work. It is initiated by learners and it can involve asking co-workers for help, ad hoc problem solving, incidental conversations, some types of coaching and mentoring, group problem-solving, lunch and learn sessions, and communities of practice.

Sources: P.D. Hughes & M. Grant, *Learning and development outlook 2007*. The Conference Board of Canada, Ottawa, 2007.

TABLE (2.3)

Differences between Formal and Informal Learning

Factor	Formal Learning	Informal Learning
Control	The control of learning rests primarily in the hands of the organization	The control of learning rests primarily in the hands of the learner
Relevance	Variable relevance to participants because it is not tailored to the individual	Highly relevant and need-specific to the individual
Timing	There is usually a delay in that what is learned is not immediately used on the job	What is learned tends to be used immediately on the job
Structure	Highly structured and scheduled	Usually unstructured and occurs spontaneously
Outcomes	Tends to have specific outcomes	May not have specific outcomes

Sources: N. Day, "Informal learning gets results," *Workforce Management*, June, 1998, Vol. 77 (6), Pp. 31–35; R.O. Parker & J. Cooney, *Learning and Development Outlook 2005*. The Conference Board of Canada, Ottawa, 2005.

In fact, when a research team studied informal training at Motorola, they discovered that every hour of formal training yielded four hours of informal training. Thus, there is a strong connection between informal learning and formal training and there is evidence that informal learning has a significant effect on performance.[44]

Organizations are beginning to discover the importance and benefits of informal learning. For example, at Boeing Commercial Airplanes, researchers found that teams, personal documentation, supervisor–employee relationships, and shift changes provided rich examples of informal learning. At Motorola, during shift changes that overlap by half an hour or more assembly-line shift workers and their supervisors update the next shift on any problems that had occurred as well as the probable causes and possible solutions.

McDonald's has begun to focus on informal learning as a result of the large number of new employees who are hired and need to be trained every year. The company is looking for ways to foster episodes of informal learning between crew members. Given the increasing pace of work and the constant changes in technology, organizations are finding that informal learning is more important than ever as there often is not enough time for formal training.[45]

Employees have been found to engage in informal learning to learn about many things such as new general knowledge, teamwork, problem solving, communication skills, new job tasks, computers, health and safety, new equipment, and even politics in the workplace.[46] A recent study found that email was the most-used method for informal learning followed by accessing information from the organization's intranet. Other forms of informal learning include Internet searches, communities of practice, voluntary mentoring, and coaching. Most of the best practices identified by the study involved the use of technology

The Trainer's Notebook 2.2
FACILITATING INFORMAL LEARNING IN ORGANIZATIONS

Here are some strategies for facilitating informal learning in organizations:

- Encourage employees to actively foster informal learning opportunities on their own.
- Form casual discussion groups among employees with similar projects and tasks.
- Create meeting areas and spaces where employees can congregate and communicate with each other (e.g., water cooler, cafeteria).
- Remove physical barriers (e.g., office walls) that prevent employees from interacting and communicating.
- Create overlaps between shifts so shift workers on different shifts or from different departments can get to know each other and discuss work-related issues.
- Create small teams with a specialized focus on a product or problem.
- Allow groups to break from their routines for team discussions.
- Provide work teams with some autonomy to modify work processes when they have found a better way of doing things.
- Eliminate barriers to communication and give employees the authority to take training on themselves.
- Condense office spaces and make room for an open gathering area for coffee breaks and socializing.
- Match new hires with seasoned employees so they can learn from casual interaction and explicit teaching and mentoring.

Sources: C. Lavis, *Learning & Development Outlook 2011: Are organizations ready for learning 2.0?* Ottawa: The Conference Board of Canada, 2011; www.vancity.com.

for information exchange (e.g., a social networking site for the company) and creating time for face-to-face interactions (e.g., team lunches and rearranging office layout to facilitate conversations).[47]

If organizations are to become learning organizations, then they must create a work environment that facilitates informal learning.[48] To learn more about how to facilitate informal learning, see The Trainer's Notebook 2.2, "Facilitating Informal Learning in Organizations."

A MULTILEVEL SYSTEMS MODEL OF ORGANIZATIONAL LEARNING

Before concluding this chapter, it is important to understand that learning in organizations takes place at different levels. This means that to fully understand learning in organizations we have to be aware of the linkages between the different levels of learning.

Figure 2.1 presents a multilevel systems model of organizational learning. The model shows that there are three levels of learning in organizations: the organization level, the group level, and the individual level. Each level is connected to the levels above and below it, which means that learning at each level is influenced by the other levels. The model also shows that there are learning practices associated with each level of learning (e.g., organizational learning practices, group learning practices, and individual learning practices).

FIGURE 2.1

A Multilevel Systems Model of Organizational Learning

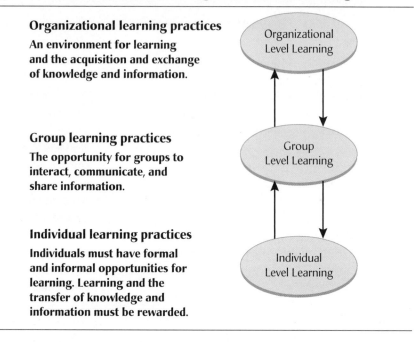

Organizational learning practices

An environment for learning and the acquisition and exchange of knowledge and information.

Organizational Level Learning

Group learning practices

The opportunity for groups to interact, communicate, and share information.

Group Level Learning

Individual learning practices

Individuals must have formal and informal opportunities for learning. Learning and the transfer of knowledge and information must be rewarded.

Individual Level Learning

Organization Level

The organization level consists of the organization's leadership, culture, vision, strategy, and structure. Leadership is extremely important because top management needs to articulate a vision for learning and must support it and devote resources and time to the development of a learning organization. The organization must also develop and implement strategies for knowledge management and learning.

Organizational practices are necessary for the organization and its members to acquire and share information and to distribute it throughout the organization. Thus, an organization must create processes, practices, policies, and structures that enable the acquisition, exchange, and distribution of information and knowledge throughout the organization. As well, the organization's culture for learning will influence the extent to which teams and individuals seek out new information and learning opportunities, and transfer new knowledge and skills on the job. There must be a culture that supports and encourages continuous learning.

Group Level

Important factors at the group level include group climate, culture, norms, dynamics, and processes, as well as the nature of the group task in terms of its complexity and task interdependence. Learning at the group level will be influenced by these factors.

For example, the extent to which informal learning occurs will be influenced by the group's culture and norms for learning, and the extent to which it is rewarded will be influenced by the group's climate. The nature of the group's tasks will also influence learning. Groups that perform more complex tasks are more likely to realize the benefits of training and learning. When the tasks that group members perform are interdependent, there will be a greater need for the group to interact and share information. Thus, these group-level factors will influence the extent to which learning occurs at the group level.

Individual Level

At the individual level, employees must have formal and informal opportunities to learn. This means that the organization needs to provide structured and formal training and development programs in order for employees to acquire new knowledge and skills, as well as opportunities to share and exchange information. In addition, employees must also be rewarded for learning and applying what they learn on the job.

Linkages between the Levels

The multilevel systems model of organizational learning shows that learning is a dynamic process that involves three levels that are interconnected. For example, the systems and processes that exist at the organization level influence the extent to which learning occurs at the group level, and group-level factors influence learning at the individual level. In addition, individual learning will influence group learning, and group learning will influence organization learning.[49]

In summary, the multilevel systems model of organizational learning demonstrates the importance of each level of the organization for learning. In order for organizations to learn, systems and processes must be in place at each level. After all, organizations cannot learn if individuals and groups do not learn, and individuals and groups cannot learn if organizations do not provide opportunities for learning and the sharing and exchange of knowledge and information. Thus, not only does each level act independently to influence learning, but they also interact dynamically to facilitate learning and contribute to organizational performance.[50]

SUMMARY

In this chapter, we described the meaning and importance of learning in organizations and the management of knowledge. The five disciplines and the principles of a learning organization were described as well as four dimensions that are critical for creating and sustaining a learning organization. We also discussed different types of knowledge in organizations as well as four types of intellectual capital. Knowledge management was then defined, followed by a discussion of knowledge management practices that organizations use to acquire, interpret, disseminate, and retain knowledge. We then described how communities of practice and informal learning contribute to individual and organizational learning. The chapter concluded with a description of a multilevel systems model of organizational learning that connects learning at the organizational, group, and individual level. In the next chapter, we will take a closer look at how individuals learn in organizations.

Key Terms

communities of practice p. 47
customer capital p. 43
explicit knowledge p. 42
formal learning p. 49
human capital p. 43
informal learning p. 49
intellectual capital p. 42
knowledge p. 41
knowledge management p. 44
knowledge sharing p. 46

learning culture p. 41
learning organization p. 38
mental models p. 45
organizational learning p. 37
relationship capital p. 43
renewal capital p. 43
structural capital p. 43
tacit knowledge p. 42
workplace learning p. 49

Web Links

Canada School of Public Service (CSPS): **www.csps-efpc.gc.ca**

D&D Automation: **www.ddauto.com**

Vancity: **www.vancity.com**

Discussion Questions

1. Discuss the role of teams and leaders in a learning organization. How do teams and leaders contribute to a learning organization, and what are some of the tasks and activities that they should perform?
2. Discuss the importance and relevance of technology for a learning organization and knowledge management. How important is technology and how should it be used in a learning organization and for knowledge management?
3. Discuss the role of the training function and the role of the trainer in a learning organization. How do these roles change in a learning organization? What knowledge and skills does a trainer require in a learning organization?
4. Discuss the multilevel systems model of organizational learning. How are the three levels related and what should organizations do to facilitate learning at each level?
5. What should Canadian organizations do to become learning organizations?
6. What is the difference between formal and informal learning and what can organizations do to facilitate informal learning? What are the advantages and disadvantages of formal and informal learning?
7. What are communities of practice and how do they contribute to learning and knowledge management in organizations? What can organizations do to create communities of practice?

The Great Training Debate

1. Debate the following: Informal learning is more important than formal learning (e.g., training programs) and organizations should focus more on informal learning and less on formal training programs.
2. Debate the following: The idea of a learning organization is just another management fad that organizations do not really need to be concerned about.

Exercises

In-Class

1. Develop a checklist to determine whether the organization in which you work (or have worked) is a learning organization. How many of the key dimensions and principles of a learning organization are characteristic of your organization? What does your organization have to do to become a learning organization?
2. Think about a previous or current job you have held in terms of what you learned and how you learned it. Make a list of three to five of the most important things you learned on your job. Once you have made your learning list, indicate how each item on your list was learned. Was it through formal or informal means? Be specific in terms of the formal or informal activity that contributed to your learning. What does your list tell you about learning in organizations? What should you do if you want to improve your learning?
3. Imagine that you are a director of training and development in an organization and the company president wants to meet with you to discuss becoming a learning organization. What will you tell him or her about learning organizations and what the organization must do to become a learning organization? Prepare a short presentation in which you present your main ideas and suggestions for becoming a learning organization. When complete, pair up with another member of the class and take turns presenting and evaluating each other's presentation. If time permits, presentations to the class can also be made.
4. Imagine that you are a director of training and development in an organization and the company president wants to meet with you to discuss how the organization can improve the management of knowledge. What will you tell him or her about knowledge management and what the organization must do to improve its management of knowledge? Prepare a short presentation in which you present your main ideas and suggestions for knowledge management. When complete, pair up with another member of the class and take turns presenting and evaluating each other's presentation. If time permits, presentations to the class can also be made.
5. As a student, you spend a great deal of time learning. But how exactly do you learn? Make a list of the formal and informal ways you learn. Do you learn more from formal or informal methods? If you want to improve your learning, what are some of the things you might do? Be specific in terms of both formal and informal ways to improve your learning.

6. If you were asked to help an organization learn about and create communities of practice, what would you tell them and how would you proceed? Prepare an outline for your presentation that describes the following: What is a community of practice? Who should be in a community of practice? What will the community of practice do and how will it do it? What are the potential benefits of a community of practice? When complete, pair up with another member of the class and take turns presenting and evaluating each other's presentation. If time permits, presentations to the class can also be made.

In-the-Field

1. Contact the human resources department of an organization and ask them if you can talk about learning organizations. Ask them if they are a learning organization and what they have done to become a learning organization. How do they rate on the four key dimensions of a learning organization (see Table 2.1)? Do you think they are a learning organization? If so, why? If not, what do they still need to do to become a learning organization?

2. Contact the human resources department of an organization and ask them if you can talk about how they manage knowledge. Ask them about their knowledge management practices and what they do to acquire, interpret, disseminate, and retain knowledge. How can the organization improve its management of knowledge?

3. Conduct an interview with several people you know who are currently employed. Interview them about how they learn in their organization. Ask questions about how and what they have learned through formal and informal learning opportunities. Based on their responses, answer the following questions:
   a. Did they learn more or less from formal or informal learning?
   b. Did they have more or fewer formal or informal opportunities for learning?
   c. Which type of learning was most effective for them: formal or informal learning?
   d. What did they learn from formal and informal learning? Did they learn similar or different things from each?
   e. What kinds of practices were used in their organization for formal and informal learning?

4. Contact the human resources department of an organization and ask if you can talk to them about communities of practice. Once you have found an organization that has communities of practice, ask the following questions:
   a. How many communities of practice does the organization have and why were they implemented?
   b. Who are the members of the communities of practice and how were they chosen?
   c. How were the communities of practice created and how are they structured?
   d. What are the methods used to interact and exchange information?
   e. How effective are the communities of practice and how are they evaluated?

Based on the answers to these questions, prepare a brief report or presentation on how to create and structure communities of practice and how to make them effective.

5. The Conference Board of Canada has developed the Learning Performance Index. To find out about the Learning Performance Index, go to: **www .conferenceboard.ca/topics/humanresource/lpi/default.aspx.**

Answer the following questions:
   a. What is the Learning Performance Index (LPI) and what are its advantages and benefits?
   b. How does the LPI work?
   c. What are the LPI deliverables?
   d. Download the LPI (click Free Assessment Tool) and complete the LPI for an organization you are currently working in or the most recent organization where you were employed. Calculate the total score for each section (vision, infrastructure, culture, learning dynamics, training and investment evaluation) and the overall total score. Refer to Section 4 to interpret your results. Based on your results, what can you say about the organization you evaluated? What does the organization need to improve to become a high-performing learning organization?

6. To find out more about learning organizations in Canada, go to Industry Canada at **www.collectionscanada.gc.ca/webarchives/20060205045403/ http://strategis.ic.gc.ca/epic/internet/incts-scf.nsf/en/sl00019e.html.**

Answer the following questions:
   a. What is a leading-edge learning organization?
   b. What are the performance characteristics of a leading-edge learning organization?

Case Incident

NASA's Knowledge Management Crisis

In the 1990s, NASA's lunar program lost critical knowledge as a result of downsizing when Saturn 5 engineers were encouraged to take early retirement. Commenting on the early retirements, one NASA manager said, "If we want to go to the moon again, we'll be starting from scratch…. All of that knowledge has disappeared. It would take at least as long and cost at least as much to go back." Now NASA wants to ensure that the expertise of other senior engineers isn't lost when they retire.

Questions

1. What kind of knowledge and intellectual capital is NASA losing and what effect does this have on the organization?
2. What should NASA do to prevent the loss of knowledge when senior engineers retire? What do they need to do to ensure that the expertise of other senior engineers isn't lost when they retire?

Sources: J. Foord Kirk, "The cost of disappearing knowledge," *The Toronto Star*, Dec. 3, 2005, P. D10; M. Weinstein, "NASA training program blasts off," *Training*, Dec. 2005, Vol. 42 (12), Pp. 8–9.

Case Study   ALLIEDBARTON SECURITY SERVICES

AlliedBarton Security Services is the largest American-owned security officer services company. The company has over 50,000 employees and 100 offices across the United States and provides high-quality security to more than 3,300 customers including approximately 200 Fortune 500 companies.

AlliedBarton has focused on training for more than 50 years and has long been regarded as a security industry training leader. In 2009, AlliedBarton partnered with Intellum to launch the "AlliedBarton EDGE," an innovative online learning management system designed to provide every AlliedBarton employee with the tools necessary to educate, develop, grow, and engage (EDGE).

Making the transformation from a training company to a learning organization that facilitates the learning of all its employees while continually transforming itself represented the next evolution for the company.

While training employees is absolutely crucial to executing the day-to-day mission at security job sites, preparing their employees and organization for the future means taking their training efforts to the next level.

A learning organization is more future focused and combines basic and ongoing training and employee development and engagement initiatives into a systematic, results-oriented approach that begins even before an employee is hired. The challenge is to create and nurture a culture that reinforces the idea that there are no limits to what can be accomplished if one takes full advantage of available opportunities. Clients and prospects will see a difference in their personnel, and management teams will notice better execution by their staff, a greater sense of ownership of the customer's site, increased morale, and employees moving upward in the organization.

Genuine learning organizations see learning and development opportunities in all facets of their business and strive to constantly look ahead and ensure that everyone is taking full advantage of the learning tools important to their careers. AlliedBarton takes training beyond preparation for entry-level employees or individuals moving to new positions.

The "AlliedBarton EDGE" is AlliedBarton's professionally designed and executed approach to training and development. It starts with the recruiting and screening process (for all levels) and extends throughout the organization to include not only entry-level officers but also managers, executives, and support staff.

As part of the AlliedBarton EDGE, the company's new, online learning management system is an example of the ongoing efforts to continuously improve and enhance the learning offerings. This web-based training solution allows employees to log in and complete modules at their own pace and on their own schedule. Tracking and compliance functionality gives managers the ability to verify course completion and ensure that new and existing security teams are properly trained and prepared for their planned duties, as well as for unexpected occurrences. New modules can be made available instantly to personnel across the country.

It is imperative that security personnel be engaged and guided so that they are best positioned to excel in their current roles and advance as new opportunities arise. To tie all of the critical aspects of employee development together,

AlliedBarton pulled several departments under the umbrella of human capital management. This solidified the company's team approach to employee development and ensured that all efforts aimed at supporting and developing its employees were well coordinated.

AlliedBarton's training extends far beyond security officers in the field to include managers, corporate personnel, and executive leaders. Throughout its history, the company has been committed to developing leaders from within. For example, the leadership platform within the LMS—"The Leaders' EDGE"—includes courses developed in partnership with a major university, which helps ensure that the company's leaders continue to learn and grow. Through a diverse mix of titles such as "budgeting," "time management," and "goal setting," employees from across the organization are able to obtain the skills necessary to advance their careers.

With the understanding that effective development has to take place at all levels on the corporate ladder, AlliedBarton instituted the "Managers' EDGE," consisting of specifically targeted learning modules to support ongoing growth.

In addition to traditional training, the company has also implemented a formal mentoring program. The "Security Academy in Leadership" includes tools for experienced and successful leaders to identify and facilitate the growth and development of future leaders on a one-on-one basis. This structured mentoring process emphasizes the importance of one-on-one development and helps employees at all levels.

AlliedBarton recognizes that in a diverse, multigenerational workforce, employees learn differently. In response, the company began to deliver refresher courses via podcasts (known as "Knowledge Knuggets") for the emerging, technology-savvy employee segment.

The development of a true learning culture has become apparent in every aspect of AlliedBarton's business. Whether it is a natural disaster that requires a coordinated team effort or a single security officer on patrol at a mall who goes out of his way to help a customer burdened with packages, the result of a culture of learning is evident in the performance and attitude of the officers engaged.

Many of AlliedBarton's senior leaders and managers began their careers with the company. Immersion in a culture that promotes constant development encourages employees who may start at any entry-level position to work their way up through the company with the support of the organization. Those who have worked their way up to management or executive positions do not hesitate to reach out and help others do the same.

Learning and development is not a one-size-fits-all process. Developing training modules in a variety of media—such as traditional classroom presentations, self-study guides, and online programs, as well as non-traditional supplemental options such as podcasts and mentoring programs—accommodates a large and diverse employee population. Training is a vital tool that prepares AlliedBarton's employees to perform their jobs with skill and confidence. Learning provides the tools needed to take advantage of opportunities for tomorrow and is critical to developing employees who can grow with the company, respond to unexpected challenges, and serve customers at levels beyond their expectations.

AlliedBarton's development opportunities are not just used by top managers or supervisory personnel. The company's frontline employees and security officers complete voluntary training because they want to increase their knowledge and further their careers. A true learning culture breeds success. Every aspect of a business is stronger because of a company's emphasis on learning and development. Employees prove that through their performance every day.

Sources: C. Rich, "From training company to learning organization," *T+D*, Jan. 2010, Vol. 64 (1), Pp. 60–63; M. Gilley, "Taking training to the EDGE," *T+D*, April, 2010, Vol. 64 (4), Pp. 104–105.

Questions

1. Describe what makes AlliedBarton a learning organization in terms of the following:
   a. the five disciplines to becoming a learning organization
   b. the principles of learning organizations
   c. the key dimensions of learning organizations
   Based on your answers, what can you conclude about AlliedBarton?
2. What is a learning culture and to what extent does AlliedBarton have a learning culture? Refer to The Trainer's Notebook 2.1, "The Learning Culture Index," and use it to assess the learning culture of AlliedBarton. What are your conclusions?
3. Discuss the role that management and technology plays in learning at AlliedBarton. How does management and technology contribute to learning and training and development at AlliedBarton?
4. Use the multilevel systems model of organizational learning (Figure 2.1) to describe learning at AlliedBarton. To what extent does learning occur at each level? Describe some of the individual, group, and organizational learning practices at AlliedBarton.
5. Based on your reading of the case and your answers to the case questions, what can other organizations learn from AlliedBarton about organizational learning, a learning culture, and workplace learning?

Flashback Questions

1. Discuss performance management at AlliedBarton. What role does training and development play in the performance management process at AlliedBarton?
2. Discuss the benefits of training and development at AlliedBarton. What are the benefits to the organization, employees, and society?
3. Provide some examples from the case to support the view that training and development at AlliedBarton is an investment. What can other organizations learn from AlliedBarton about investing in training and development?
4. Refer to the context of training and development (Figure 1.2) to describe training and development at AlliedBarton. Be sure to explain the role of the environment, organization, and the human resources system and how they are connected to training and development at AlliedBarton.

REFERENCES

1. Lavis, C. (2011). *Learning & development outlook 2011: Are organizations ready for learning 2.0?* Ottawa: The Conference Board of Canada; www.vancity.com.

2. Senge, P. M. (1990). *The fifth discipline: The art and practice of the learning organization.* New York: Doubleday, p. 139.

3. Bennet, J. K., & O'Brien, M. J. (1994, June). The building blocks of the learning organization. *Training, 31(6),* 41–49.

4. Senge, P. M. (1990).

5. Harris-Lalonde, S. (2001). *Training and development outlook.* The Conference Board of Canada: Ottawa.

6. Parker, R. O., & Cooney, J. (2005). *Learning & development outlook 2005.* The Conference Board of Canada: Ottawa.

7. Ellinger, A. D., Ellinger, A. E., Baiyin, Y., & Howton, S. W. (2002). The relationship between the learning organization concept and firms' financial performance: An empirical assessment. *Human Resource Development Quarterly, 13,* 5–21.

8. Sigler, J. (1999). Best practices and guiding principles: A training guide to successful development of a learning organization. *Futurics, 23(1&2),* 67–73.

9. Harris-Lalonde, S. (2001); Cooney, J., & Cowan, A. (2003). *Training and development outlook 2003.* The Conference Board of Canada: Ottawa.

10. Lavis, C. (2011).

11. Sigler, J. (1999).

12. Tapscott, D. (1998). Make knowledge an asset for the whole company. *Computerworld, 32(51),* 32.

13. Stamps, D. (1999, March). Is knowledge management a fad? *Training, 36(3),* 36–42.

14. Baets, W. R. J. (1998). *Organizational learning and knowledge technologies in a dynamic environment.* Boston: Kluwer Academic Publishers.

15. Miller, W. (1999, January). Building the ultimate resource. *Management Review,* 42–45.

16. Miller, W. (1999, January).

17. Stewart, T. (1994, October 3). Intellectual capital. *Fortune,* 68–74.

18. Miller, W. (1999, January).

19. Kransdorff, A. (1997, September). Fight organizational memory loss. *Workforce Management,* 34–39.

20. Sigler, J. (1999).

21. Cooney, J., & Cowan, A. (2003).

22. Garvin, D. A. (1998). The processes of organization and management. *Sloan Management Review, 39(4),* 33–50.

23. Jeppesen, J. C. (2002). Creating and maintaining the learning organization. In K. Kraiger (Ed.), *Creating, implementing, and managing effective training and development: State-of-the-art lessons for practice* (pp. 302–330). San Francisco, CA: Jossey-Bass.

24. Senge, P. M. (1990), p. 8.

25. Stamps, D. (1999).

26. Stamps, D. (1997). Communities of practice: Learning is social, training is irrelevant? *Training, 3(2),* 34–42.

27. Neely Martinez, M. (1998, February). The collective power. *HRM Magazine,* 88–94.

28. Wang, S., & Noe, R. A. (2010). Knowledge sharing: A review and directions for future research. *Human Resource Management Review, 20,* 115–131.

29. Mesmer-Magnus, J. R., & DeChurch, L. A. (2009). Information sharing and team performance: A meta-analysis. *Journal of Applied Psychology, 94,* 535–546; Milia, L. D., & Birdi, K. (2010). The relationship between multiple levels of learning practices and objective and subjective organizational financial performance. *Journal of Organizational Behavior, 31,* 481–498.

30. Mesmer-Magnus, J. R., & DeChurch, L. A. (2009).
31. Kransdorff, A. (1997, September).
32. Wenger, E. C., & Snyder, W. M. (2000). Communities of practice: The organizational frontier. *Harvard Business Review, 78(1),* 139–145.
33. Stamps, D. (1997). Communities of practice. *Training, 34(2),* 34–42.
34. Stamps, D. (1997); Salopek, J. (2008, July). Knowledge in numbers. *T+D, 62(7),* 24–26.
35. Salopek, J. (2008, July).
36. Wenger, E. C., & Snyder, W. M. (2000).
37. Wenger, E. C., & Snyder, W. M. (2000).
38. Griffith, T. L., & Sawyer, J. E. (2010). Multilevel knowledge and team performance. *Journal of Organizational Behavior, 31,* 1003–1031.
39. Salopek, J. (2008, July).
40. Wenger, E. C., & Snyder, W. M. (2000).
41. Park, Y., & Jacobs, R. (2011). The influence of investment in workplace learning on learning outcomes and organizational performance. *Human Resource Development Quarterly, 22,* 437–458.
42. Stamps, D. (1998, January). Learning ecologies. *Training, 35(1),* 32–38; Roseman, E. (2001, August 29). Delta Hotels knows how to keep workers. *The Toronto Star,* E2.
43. Day, N. (1998, June). Informal learning gets results. *Workforce Management, 77(6),* 31–35; Dobbs, K. (2000, January). Simple moments of learning. *Training, 37(1),* 52–58; Lavis, C. (2011).
44. Day, N. (1998, June).
45. Stamps, D. (1998); Dobbs, K. (2000, January).
46. Livingstone, D. W., & Scholtz, A. (2006). Work and lifelong learning in Canada: Basic findings of the 2004 WALL survey. Ontario Institute for Studies in Education, University of Toronto.
47. Paradise, A. (2008, July). Informal learning: Overlooked or overhyped? *T+D, 62(7),* 52–53.
48. Squires, P. (2009). The role of on-the-job and informal development in performance management. In J. W. Smither & M. London (Eds.), *Performance management: Putting research into action* (pp. 157–195). San Francisco, CA: Jossey-Bass.
49. Kozlowski, S. W. J., & Salas, E. (1997). A multilevel organizational systems approach for the implementation and transfer of training. In J. K. Ford, S. W. J. Kozlowski, K. Kraiger, E. Salas, and M. S. Teachout (Eds.), *Improving training effectiveness in work organizations.* Mahwah, NJ: Lawrence Erlbaum Associates.
50. Milia, L. D., & Birdi, K. (2010).

Learning and Motivation

CHAPTER LEARNING OUTCOMES

After reading this chapter, you should be able to:

- define learning and describe learning outcomes
- describe the three stages of learning and resource allocation theory
- discuss Kolb's learning styles and describe the learning cycle
- describe conditioning theory and social cognitive theory and their implications for training and development
- describe adult learning theory and its implications for training and development
- define motivation and describe need and process theories of motivation and their implications for training and development
- describe the differences between mastery and performance goals and between distal and proximal goals and their implications for training and development
- define training motivation and discuss its predictors and consequences
- describe the model of training effectiveness and the predictors and consequences of learning and retention

CANADIAN CANCER SOCIETY

Several years ago, the Ontario Division of the Canadian Cancer Society decided to take a more strategic approach to its on-boarding program. The division has hundreds of employees and thousands of volunteers across Ontario.

Senior staff at the society consulted with key groups including the executive team, regional employees, and recent hires so that they could customize an approach that resonates with new hires. One of the objectives of the new program was to reduce voluntary turnover by equipping new hires with a greater understanding of and connection to the work of the society as a whole.

The on-boarding program contains many elements. One part focuses on "foundation knowledge" to provide every new hire, regardless of position or level, with a consistent understanding of the society including things such as key people, portfolios, and programs. Another important element is experience. A new hire needs to engage in certain activities to develop the partnerships and personal insights critical to early visibility, credibility, and success.

Consideration was also given to the timing of different on-boarding activities so the process unfolds in a logical and integrated way throughout the first year of employment. The activities are incorporated into detailed checklists to promote a consistent experience and ensure all elements are covered.

To help guide new employees through the organization's massive intranet, a typical volunteer named Ray was selected as a guide. Through his story as both a volunteer and cancer survivor, Ray helps the new hire absorb information—mission,

cancer research and statistics, organization structure, and fundraising activities—in a more logical, dynamic, and memorable way.

For example, Ray talks about his community work and his family's participation in the Canadian Cancer Society Relay for Life, a national fundraising event. He then invites the new hire to click on appropriate links to drill deeper into fundraising information. Ray's story reinforces the importance of volunteers and provides the perspectives of both a client and volunteer.

Because of the importance of developing quality relationships early in a new employee's tenure, the society also developed a series of discussion guides to help new employees, their managers, and their internal and external clients talk about mutual expectations. In one guide, a new hire and her manager ask each other a set of questions to help define the "soft" side of the working relationship. Another guide helps the new employee interview key clients to understand their priorities and expectations. This helps the employee take action and establish credibility early on.

Another part of the experience is learning how the society's work touches the lives of Canadians. Whether it is a visit to a regional cancer centre, participating in one of many fundraising activities, or sitting in on a call from a cancer patient in the call centre, new employees gain a personal understanding of how the society operates. The end result is that every employee and volunteer feels empowered to be an ambassador in their community by being able to talk from the heart based on their own experiences.[1]

Source: S. Nador, "Canadian Cancer Society launches new onboarding program," *Canadian HR Reporter*, Mar. 10, 2008, Vol. 21 (5), P. 12.

The Canadian Cancer Society's employee on-boarding program focuses on not only *what* new employees must learn but also *how* they learn, two topics that are the focus of this chapter.

In Chapter 2, the focus was organizational learning and learning in organizations. However, in order for organizations to learn and become learning organizations, the people in them must learn. In this chapter, we focus on how people learn and their motivation to learn. First, we define what we mean by learning and describe learning outcomes. Then we discuss the stages of learning followed by a review of learning and motivation theories and their implications for training. We conclude the chapter with a discussion of training motivation and a model that links training and personal and individual factors to learning, behaviour, and organizational effectiveness.

WHAT IS LEARNING?

Although training is the focus of this textbook, it is important to keep in mind that what we are trying to accomplish through training and development is learning. In other words, training is the means for accomplishing the goal, and the goal is learning.

Learning is the process of acquiring knowledge and skills. It involves a change of state that makes possible a corresponding change in one's behaviour. Learning is the result of experiences that enable one to exhibit newly acquired behaviours.[2] Learning occurs "when one experiences a new way of acting, thinking, or feeling, finds the new pattern gratifying or useful, and incorporates it into the repertoire of behaviours."[3] When a behaviour has been learned, it can be thought of as a skill.

New hires and volunteers at the Ontario division of the Canadian Cancer Society acquire knowledge and understanding of the society, fundraising, developing quality relationships, interviewing clients, and how the society operates so that they will be able to perform the behaviours that are important for their job and role. The intent is for them to develop an understanding of and connection to the work of the society as a whole and to be an ambassador in their community, and doing this effectively requires that they exhibit certain actions, thoughts, and feelings.

In the realm of training, the most fundamental issue is whether trainees have learned what was covered in a training program.[4] But what exactly do trainees learn in training? In the next section, we describe two schemes for categorizing learning outcomes.

LEARNING OUTCOMES

Learning can be described in terms of domains or outcomes of learning. Table 3.1 shows the learning outcomes of two categorization schemes. The first one is by Robert Gagné, who developed the best known classification of learning outcomes. According to Gagné, learning outcomes can be classified according to five general categories:[5]

1. *Verbal information.* Facts, knowledge, principles, and packages of information, or what is known as *declarative knowledge.*
2. *Intellectual skills.* Concepts, rules, and procedures that are known as *procedural knowledge.* Procedural rules govern many activities in our daily lives such as driving an automobile or shopping in a supermarket.
3. *Cognitive strategies.* The application of information and techniques, and understanding how and when to use knowledge and information.
4. *Motor skills.* The coordination and execution of physical movements that involve the use of muscles; for instance, learning to swim.

Learning
The process of acquiring knowledge and skills, and a change in individual behaviour as a result of some experience

TABLE 3.1
Learning Outcomes Classification Schemes
Gagné's Classification Scheme
Verbal information (declarative knowledge)
Intellectual skills (procedural knowledge)
Cognitive strategies (how and when to use information and knowledge)
Motor skills (physical movements)
Attitudes (internal states)
Kraiger, Ford, & Salas Classification Scheme
Cognitive (quantity and type of knowledge)
• Verbal knowledge
• Knowledge organization
• Cognitive strategies
Skill-Based (technical and motor skills)
• Compilation (proceduralization and composition)
• Automaticity
Affective (attitudinal and motivational)
• Attitudinal
• Motivational (goal orientation, self-efficacy, goals)

Sources: R.M. Gagné, "Learning outcomes and their effects: Useful categories of human performance," *American Psychologist*, Vol. 39, Pp. 377–385, 1984; K. Kraiger, J.K. Ford, & E. Salas, "Application of cognitive, skill-based, and affective theories of learning outcomes to new methods of training evaluation," *Journal of Applied Psychology*, Vol. 78, Pp. 311–328, 1993.

5. *Attitudes.* Preferences and internal states associated with one's beliefs and feelings. Attitudes are learned and can be changed. However, they are considered to be the most difficult domain to influence through training.[6]

Drawing on Gagné's classification scheme, Kurt Kraiger and colleagues developed a multidimensional classification scheme of learning outcomes that includes some additional indicators of learning. Their classification scheme consists of three broad categories of learning outcomes. Each category has several more specific indicators of learning:[7]

1. *Cognitive outcomes.* The quantity and type of knowledge and the relationships among knowledge elements. This includes *verbal knowledge* (declarative knowledge), *knowledge organization* (procedural knowledge and structures for organizing knowledge or mental models), and *cognitive strategies* (mental activities that facilitate knowledge acquisition and application, or what is known as metacognition).

2. *Skill-based outcomes.* This involves the development of technical or motor skills and includes *compilation* (fast and fluid performance of a task as a result of proceduralization and composition) and *automaticity* (ability to perform a task without conscious monitoring).

3. *Affective outcomes.* These are outcomes that are neither cognitively based nor skills-based and include *attitudinal* (affective internal state that affects behaviour) and *motivational* outcomes (goal orientation, self-efficacy, goals).

A training program can focus on one or more of the learning outcomes and, as you will see in the next section, some of the outcomes are associated with certain stages of the learning process. It is also important to realize that the extent to which a training program has an effect on any of these outcomes depends in large part on the objectives of a training program. In addition, different training methods will be more or less effective depending on the learning outcome a training program was designed to influence. In other words, the best training method for a training program depends in part of the desired learning outcome. According to Gagné, different instructional events and conditions of learning are required for each of the learning outcomes. Furthermore, the learning outcomes are often interrelated, which means that changes in one might result in changes in another.[8]

Regardless of the learning outcome, learning generally occurs over a period of time and progresses through a series of stages as described in the next section.

STAGES OF LEARNING AND RESOURCE ALLOCATION THEORY

In the chapter-opening vignette, you were told that the on-boarding program at the Canadian Cancer Society was designed to unfold in a logical and integrated way throughout the first year of employment. This highlights the fact that learning and the acquisition of new knowledge and skills occur over a period of time and in a meaningful sequence.

A theory developed by John Anderson called the Adaptive Character of Thought theory, or ACT theory, describes the learning process as it unfolds across three stages.[9] According to **ACT theory**, learning takes place in three stages that are known as declarative knowledge, knowledge compilation, and procedural knowledge or proceduralization. A related theory called resource allocation theory explains how people learn during each of the stages as a function of the resources required to learn a new task. According to **resource allocation theory**, individuals possess limited cognitive resources that can be used to learn a new task. Performance of a new task is determined by individual differences in attentional and cognitive resources, the requirements of the task (task complexity), and self-regulatory activities (e.g., self-monitoring and self-evaluation) used to allocate attention across tasks.[10]

As you will see, the amount of cognitive resources an individual can allocate to learning a new task varies across the three stages. Table 3.2 provides a summary of learning and performance at the three stages of learning.

The first stage of learning involves learning knowledge, facts, and information, or what is known as **declarative knowledge**. For example, think of what it was like when you learned how to drive a car. At first, you acquired a great deal

ACT theory
Learning takes place in three stages that are known as declarative knowledge, knowledge compilation, and procedural knowledge or proceduralization

Resource allocation theory
Individuals possess limited cognitive resources that can be used to learn a new task

Declarative knowledge
Learning knowledge, facts, and information

TABLE 3.2
The Stages of Learning
Stage 1
Declarative Knowledge Learning: Knowledge, facts, and information Performance: Resource-dependent
Stage 2
Knowledge Compilation Learning: Integrating tasks into sequences Performance: Fragmented and piecemeal
Stage 3
Procedural Knowledge Learning: Task mastery Performance: Automatic and habitual; resource-insensitive

of information such as what to do when you get into the car, how to start the car and put it in gear, how to change gears if it is a standard shift, and so on. These pieces of information or units are called chunks.

During this first stage of learning one must devote all of one's attention and cognitive resources to the task of learning. In other words, it is not likely that you could make a phone call, listen to the radio, or carry on a conversation during this period of learning to drive a car. This is because all of your attention and cognitive resources are required to learn the task of driving. Furthermore, your driving performance at this stage is slow and prone to errors.

In the declarative stage of learning, performance is resource dependent because all of one's attention and cognitive resources are required to learn the task. Any diversion of attention is likely to affect your learning and lower your performance. Just think of what it is like when you are in class and somebody starts talking to you. Your learning is seriously affected because you need all of your attention and cognitive resources for the task of learning. Listening or talking to somebody during class will require your attention and your learning will suffer.

Knowledge compilation

Integrating tasks into sequences to simplify and streamline the task

The second stage of learning is called **knowledge compilation**. Knowledge compilation involves integrating tasks into sequences to simplify and streamline the task. The learner acquires the ability to translate the declarative knowledge acquired in the first stage into action. During this stage, performance becomes faster and more accurate. For example, when learning how to drive a car, you are able to get into the car and begin to drive without having to think about every single thing you must do. In other words, what was once many single tasks or units and chunks during the declarative stage (e.g., put on your seatbelt, lock the car, adjust the seat, adjust the mirror, start the car, etc.) is now one smooth sequence of tasks. You get into the car and do all of the tasks as part of an integrated sequence.

Although the attention requirements during the knowledge compilation stage are lower than the declarative stage, performance is still somewhat fragmented and piecemeal. So when you are learning to drive a car, this might mean popping the clutch from time to time and occasionally rolling backwards when on an incline, stalling the car, and so on.

The final stage of learning is called **procedural knowledge**, or proceduralization. During this stage, the learner has mastered the task and performance is automatic and habitual. In other words, the task can now be performed without much thought. The transition from knowledge acquisition to application is complete. This is what most of us experience when we drive. We get into a car and drive without giving much thought to what we are doing. The task of driving becomes habitual and automatic.

Because tasks at this stage can be performed with relatively little attention, it is possible to divert one's attention and cognitive resources to other tasks such as conversing with passengers or listening to music. Performance at this stage is fast and accurate and the task can be performed with little impairment even when attention is devoted to another task (as long as we keep our eyes on the road and hands on the wheel!). At this stage, performance is said to be resource insensitive because changes in attention will not have much of an impact on performance.

IMPLICATIONS FOR TRAINING   What are the implications of ACT theory for learning and training? First, ACT theory recognizes the fact that learning is a sequential and stage-like process that involves three important stages. Second, it indicates that different types of learning take place at different stages. And third, motivational interventions might be more or less effective depending on the stage of learning. As you will learn later in the chapter, goal setting is a motivational theory with implications for training and development. However, research has shown that goal setting can be harmful to learning during the early stages of learning when all of one's attention and cognitive resources must be devoted to learning the task. This follows from resource allocation theory, which states that during the early stages of learning, cognitive ability is more important than motivational strategies.

However, when goals are set during the later stages of learning (e.g., procedural knowledge) they can have a positive effect on learning and performance. Cognitive ability becomes less important than it was during the declarative stage of learning. Thus, the effects of both cognitive ability and motivational interventions on learning and performance depend on the stage of learning.[11]

LEARNING STYLES

An important aspect of learning is the way in which people learn. According to David Kolb, individuals differ in terms of how they prefer to learn or what are known as learning styles. A **learning style** is the way in which an individual gathers information and processes and acts on it during the learning process.[12] Table 3.3 shows Kolb's learning styles and the learning modes that they are based on.

Procedural knowledge
The learner has mastered the task and performance is automatic and habitual

Learning style
The way in which an individual gathers information and processes and evaluates it during the learning process

TABLE **3.3**

Learning Styles

Learning Style	Learning Modes	Meaning
Converging	Abstract conceptualization and active experimentation	Thinking and doing
Diverging	Concrete experience and reflective observation	Feeling and watching
Assimilating	Abstract conceptualization and reflective observation	Thinking and watching
Accommodating	Concrete experience and active experimentation	Feeling and doing

Learning modes involve the way people gather information (concrete experience, or CE, and abstract conceptualization, or AC) and the way people process or evaluate information (active experimentation, or AE, and reflective observation, or RO). It is the combination of these "learning modes" (the way a person gathers information and the way a person processes information) that results in a learning style.

People who prefer to gather information through direct experience and involvement are CE types (feeling). Those who prefer to gather information by thinking about issues, ideas, and concepts are AC types (thinking). If you prefer to process information by observing and reflecting on information and different points of view, you are an RO type (watching). If you prefer to process information by acting on it and actually doing something to see its practical value, you are an AE type (doing).[13]

An individual's learning style is a function of how they gather information and how they process information. For example, a *converging* learning style combines abstract conceptualization and active experimentation (thinking and doing). People with this learning style focus on problem solving and the practical application of ideas and theories. A *diverging* learning style combines concrete experience and reflective observation (feeling and watching). People with this orientation view concrete situations from different points of view and generate alternative courses of action. An *assimilating* style combines abstract conceptualization and reflective observation (thinking and watching). These people like to process and integrate information and ideas into logical forms and theoretical models. Finally, an *accommodating* learning style combines concrete experience and active experimentation (feeling and doing). People with this learning style prefer hands-on experience and like to learn by being involved in new and challenging experiences.[14]

Although people might prefer a particular learning style, ideally people can learn best by using all four styles. In fact, Kolb notes the importance of a learning cycle in which people use each of the four modes of learning in a sequence. The learning cycle begins with concrete experience (learning by experience), followed by reflective observation (learning by reflecting), then abstract conceptualization (learning by thinking), and finally active experimentation (learning by doing). This kind of learning cycle has been shown to improve learning and retention as well as the development of behavioural skills. Learning is most effective when all four steps in the learning cycle are part of the learning experience.[15]

IMPLICATIONS FOR TRAINING   Kolb's theory has several implications for training. First, it recognizes that people differ in how they prefer to learn. This means that a person's comfort and success in training will depend on how well the training method matches their learning style. Thus, trainers need to be aware of these differences and design training programs to appeal to people's different learning styles. At AmeriCredit, an auto finance company in Fort Worth, Texas, course facilitators receive a report prior to a training session that allows them to adjust course delivery, content, and design based on the learning styles of the trainees.[16] The use of technology in training makes it much easier to tailor learning and training to a trainee's learning style. To learn more, see Training Today 3.1, "The Personalization of Learning."

Second, training programs should be designed with each learning mode as part of a sequence of learning experiences. At Capital One Financial Corp., after employees are taught a new set of skills they are given work projects to implement the skills and then they must report on the experience. The approach closely mirrors Kolb's learning cycle.[17]

Training Today 3.1

The Personalization of Learning

Personalization makes theory, concepts, and content more relevant for the learner. Learning personalization includes parsing of information that is most relevant to the user based on his or her role, language, culture, learning style, and personal preferences.

Some e-learning requires the learner to take a pre-assessment. With personalization, that pre-assessment can be presented in a specific learning style that is conducive to the individual. If the learner is more comfortable with auditory formats, the online content often will be sound-enabled or have a narrator speaking throughout the lesson.

If the individual is a visual learner, then the bulk of the content may be offered with compelling visuals. Learners who speak English as a second language can take courses that contain captioning in their native language to facilitate learning.

The more personalized the learning content and experiences, the more they will resonate with the learner and the greater chance that the learner will be able to recall the key lessons learned.

Personalization is critical in the information age because a typical worker gets hundreds of emails, dozens of instant messages, multiple phone calls, and several text messages daily, which makes it more difficult to focus on basic tasks. In addition, the amount of time the learner has to focus on learning activities is often compromised by increased expectations, decreased staff, and increased responsibility and accountability.

Thus, spending additional time in the analysis and design phases of training to identify personalization strategies could prove to be an invaluable exercise, especially if the contact time available for the learner and the learning solution is minimized. The key to successful personalization is inclusion of the target audience in the development and delivery of the content.

Source: D. Hartley & K. West, "Taking it personally: Tailoring training for more relevance," *T+D*, Vol. 61 (11), Pp. 21–23, 2007.

LEARNING THEORIES

We know a great deal about how people learn and that the learning process is highly relevant for the design and effectiveness of training programs. The learning process and how people learn is explained in several theories of learning. Learning theories are important because they help us understand how people learn and how to design training programs to maximize learning and retention. In this section, we describe two learning theories that have important implications for training: conditioning theory and social cognitive theory.

Conditioning Theory

The famous psychologist B.F. Skinner defined learning as a relatively permanent change in behaviour in response to a particular stimulus or set of stimuli.[18] Skinner and the behaviourist school of psychology believe that learning is a result of reward and punishment contingencies that follow a response to a stimulus.

The basic idea is that a stimulus or cue is followed by a response, which is then followed by a positive or negative consequence or what is known as positive or negative reinforcement. If the response is positively reinforced, it strengthens the likelihood that the response will occur again and that learning will result.

Behaviourists argue that similar principles are at work when an adult submits an innovative proposal and is praised, and when a pigeon pecks a red dot and is given a pellet of food. When a response is reinforced through food, money, attention, or anything pleasurable, then the response is more likely to be repeated. If there is no reinforcement, then over time the response will cease. If the response is punished, then it will not be repeated. The conditioning process is illustrated in Figure 3.1.

While positive reinforcement involves the application of something positive following a desired response so that the behaviour will continue, negative reinforcement involves the removal of a stimulus after an action. For example, think of your course instructor chewing out the class for not participating in class discussions and threatening to start picking students at random to answer questions. When students participate, the instructor stops chewing them out and threatening to choose students at random. Thus, the response of increased class participation results in the removal of a negative stimulus. Thus, both positive and negative reinforcement are used to increase the likelihood of a desired behaviour.

FIGURE 3.1

The Conditioning Process

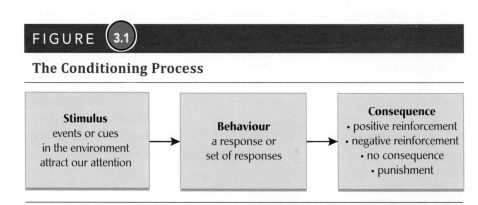

Stimulus events or cues in the environment attract our attention	**Behaviour** a response or set of responses	**Consequence** • positive reinforcement • negative reinforcement • no consequence • punishment

It is important to realize that negative reinforcement is not the same as punishment, which involves the application of a negative consequence in response to an undesirable behaviour in order to decrease or eliminate the occurrence of the behaviour. In the example above, a desirable behaviour is being learned and increased (e.g., class participation) by a negative reinforcer that is removed when the desirable behaviour occurs.

Managers and trainers use conditioning theory principles when they attempt to influence employee behaviour. For example, at Capital One, a financial services company in the United States, new hires attend monthly reinforcement sessions in which they discuss what they did on the job that directly relates to the skills being developed. Once the skills are mastered they are taught new skills, and the reinforcement cycle continues.[19]

The Conditioning Process

The conditioning process involves linking desired behaviour to pleasurable consequences. This is accomplished through three connected concepts: *shaping, chaining,* and *generalization*. **Shaping** refers to the reinforcement of each step in the process until it is mastered, and then withdrawing the reinforcer until the next step is mastered. Shaping is extremely important for learning complex behaviour. Behaviour modelling is a training method (see Chapter 6) that makes extensive use of this concept by rewarding trainees for the acquisition of separate skills performed sequentially.

Chaining is the second concept and involves the reinforcement of entire sequences of a task. During shaping, an individual learns each separate step of a task and is reinforced for each successive step. The goal, however, is to learn to combine each step and perform the entire response. This combination is what chaining involves, and it is accomplished by reinforcing entire sequences of the task and eventually reinforcing only the complete task after each of the steps have been learned.

The third concept is **generalization**, which means that the conditioned response occurs in circumstances different from those during learning.[20] Thus, while a trainee might have learned a task through shaping and chaining, he or she might not be able to perform the task in a different situation or outside of the classroom. To achieve generalization, the trainer must provide trainees with opportunities to perform the task in a variety of situations.

For example, the trainer can change a role-play script from negotiating with one's supervisor on the deadline of a project to negotiating the starting salary with a new employer. As a result, the trainee learns to generalize the skill from a simple, controlled environment to a different, more difficult one. This is a goal of training—that learning acquired during training will be generalized to, and used in, different situations and contexts.

Shaping
The reinforcement of each step in a process until it is mastered

Chaining
The reinforcement of entire sequences of a task

Generalization
The conditioned response occurs in circumstances different from those during learning

IMPLICATIONS FOR TRAINING   When applied to training, conditioning theory suggests that trainees should be encouraged and reinforced throughout the training process. In other words, they should be reinforced for attending training, learning the training material (shaping and chaining), and applying it on the job (generalization). Furthermore, training tasks should be broken into meaningful parts so that they can be reinforced as trainees learn each of them. This will enable the trainer to adequately follow the conditioning process of shaping, chaining, and generalization.

Social Cognitive Theory

If you think about your own learning and how you have learned to do different things, you will realize that learning does not just occur as a result of reward and punishment contingencies as suggested by conditioning theory. Learning also occurs through cognitive processes such as imitation and modelling and this is best explained by social cognitive theory.

Social learning

Learning through interactions with others

The central premise of social cognitive theory is what is known as **social learning**, which involves learning through interactions with others. Social learning can be either formal (e.g., mentoring programs) or informal (e.g., collaborative work).[21] According to social cognitive theory, people learn by observing the behaviour of others, making choices about different courses of action to pursue, and by managing their own behaviour in the process of learning.[22] We observe the actions of others and make note of the reinforcing or punishing outcomes of their behaviour. We then imitate what we have observed and expect certain consequences to follow. Considerable research has shown that people observe and reproduce the actions and attitudes of others.[23]

Social cognitive theory involves three key components: observation, self-efficacy, and self-regulation.

Observation

Observation

Learning by observing the actions of others and their consequences

As you have probably experienced in yourself and others, people learn by **observation**. They observe the actions of others and the consequences of those actions. If the person being observed (the role model) is credible and knowledgeable, their behaviour is more likely to be imitated. The imitation will occur particularly if the role model is reinforced for the behaviour. New recruits watch the intense work hours of the senior staff. They then work the same long hours, in the expectation that they, too, will be rewarded with promotions and pay raises.

Four key elements are critical for observational learning to take place: attention, retention, reproduction, and reinforcement. Learners must first attend to the behaviour (i.e., be aware of the skills that are observable). Second, they must remember what they observed and encode it in their own repertoire so that they can recall the skills. Third, they must then try out the skill (i.e., try to reproduce it) through practice and rehearsal. Fourth, if the reproduction results in positive outcomes (i.e., it is reinforced), then the learner is likely to continue to reproduce the behaviour and retain the new skills.

Many training programs use social cognitive theory concepts in which a model is used to exhibit desired behaviour that is then followed by opportunities for practice and positive reinforcement. Some organizations assign new recruits to mentors or senior co-workers so that they can learn by observing them. The financial services firm Edward Jones has a mentoring program in which new investment representatives are paired with more established ones. New employees shadow their mentor for three weeks to learn about the company and how things are done.[24]

Self-Efficacy

While observation may provide the observer with information necessary to imitate the modelled behaviour, we know that people do not always attempt to do things they observe other people doing. For example, a novice skier might watch his friends make their way down a steep hill but refuse to imitate their behaviour and follow suit. This is because he might not have the confidence or the belief that he will be able to do it. Such beliefs are known as self-efficacy beliefs.

Self-efficacy refers to beliefs that people have about their ability to successfully perform a specific task. Self-efficacy is a cognitive belief that is task specific, as in the example of the skier's confidence that he can ski down a steep hill. The novice skier might have low self-efficacy to ski down the hill but very high self-efficacy that he can get an "A" in a training course!

Self-efficacy is influenced by four sources of information. In order of importance, they are task performance outcomes, observation, verbal persuasion and social influence, and one's physiological or emotional state.[25]

So how would you strengthen the self-efficacy of the novice skier who is afraid to follow his friends down the hill? The self-efficacy of the novice skier can be strengthened not only by having him observe his friends' behaviour, but also by encouraging him and providing assurance that he can do it; making him feel comfortable and relaxed rather than fearsome and anxious; and, most importantly, by ensuring that he first experiences some success—perhaps by trying some less threatening ski hills.

Self-efficacy has been shown to have a strong effect on people's attitudes, emotions, and behaviour in many areas of human behaviour. Self-efficacy influences the activities people choose to perform, the amount of effort and persistence they devote to a task, their affective and stress reactions, and performance outcomes.[26]

Self-efficacy has also been found to be very important for training. Research has shown that the effectiveness of many training programs involves strengthening trainees' self-efficacy to perform the training task. In other words, training increases trainees' self-efficacy to perform a task, and self-efficacy leads to improved task performance.[27]

Self-efficacy
Beliefs that people have about their ability to successfully perform a specific task

Self-Regulation

Conditioning theory takes the position that an individual's behaviour is regulated by external agents who administer rewards and punishments. However, the third component of social cognitive theory suggests that people can regulate their own behaviour and do not always require external rewards and punishment to learn and change their behaviour. This is known as **self-regulation** and it involves managing one's own behaviour.

Self-regulation enables people to structure and motivate their own behaviour through the use of internal processes. These internal processes involve observing and monitoring one's own behaviour (self-monitoring) as well as the behaviour of others, setting performance goals, practising and rehearsing new and desired behaviours, keeping track of one's progress and performance and comparing it with one's goals (self-evaluation), and rewarding oneself for goal achievement.[28]

Self-regulation has been found to be related to cognitive, affective, and behavioural outcomes. It has also been shown to be an effective method of training. For example, one study found that self-regulation training increased the job attendance of employees with above-average absenteeism. Compared to a group that did not receive self-regulation training, employees who received self-regulation training had higher self-efficacy for attending work and increased their job attendance. In a follow-up study, these results were shown to continue for

Self-regulation
Managing one's own behaviour through a series of internal processes

up to nine months following training.[29] An increasing number of studies have also found that self-regulation training leads to improvements in skill acquisition, maintenance, and performance.[30]

IMPLICATIONS FOR TRAINING   Social cognitive theory has important implications for the design of training programs that go far beyond reward and punishment contingencies. In particular, learning can be improved by providing trainees with models who demonstrate how to perform a training task; by strengthening trainee self-efficacy for successfully learning and performing the task; and by teaching trainees how to regulate their behaviour and performance while learning and on the job. These principles have been incorporated into a training method called behaviour modelling, which is described in Chapter 6.

Self-regulation prompts

Asking trainees questions about their learning, goals, and goal progress to encourage self-regulation during training

In addition, there is some evidence that trainees can be encouraged to self-regulate during training by asking them questions about their self-regulatory activities. **Self-regulation prompts** ask trainees questions about their learning, goals, and their goal progress to encourage self-regulation during training. Several studies have shown that trainees who were prompted with questions about their self-regulation during training (e.g., whether they are concentrating on learning the training material, evaluating their knowledge, and monitoring the effectiveness of their learning strategies) showed a significant improvement in their declarative and procedural knowledge over time as well as their performance. Trainees who were prompted to self-regulate also spent more time reviewing the course material and were less likely to withdraw from an online training course before completion.[31]

The Trainer's Notebook 3.1

PROMPTING SELF-REGULATION

The following questions can be used during training to prompt self-regulation. Trainees should be asked these questions periodically throughout a training program. They can respond using a 5-point scale with anchors 1 = not at all to 5 = definitely.

- Am I concentrating on learning the training material?
- Do I understand all of the key points of the training material?
- Are the study strategies I'm using helping me learn the training material?
- Have I spent enough time reviewing to remember the information after I finish the course?
- Am I setting goals to help me remember the material after I finish the course?

- Would I do better on the next quiz if I studied more?
- Am I focusing my mental effort on the training material?
- Do I need to continue to review to ensure I will remember the material after I finish the course?
- Are the study tactics I have been using effective for learning the training material?
- Do I know enough about the training material to remember the material after I finish the course?
- Am I setting goals to ensure I have a thorough understanding of the training material?
- Do I know enough about the training material to answer all of the questions correct on the quiz for this module?

Source: T. Sitzmann & K. Ely, "Sometimes you need a reminder: The effects of prompting self-regulation on regulatory process, learning, and attrition," *Journal of Applied Psychology*, Vol. 95, Pp. 132–144, 2010.

Thus, trainers might incorporate self-regulation prompts into training programs to remind trainees to self-regulate their learning. To be most effective, self-regulation prompts should be provided periodically throughout a training program. To find out how to prompt trainee self-regulation during training, see The Trainer's Notebook 3.1, "Prompting Self-Regulation."

ADULT LEARNING THEORY

In this section, we describe a theory of learning that is based on how adults and children are different and the implications of these differences for learning. First, consider the learning environment most people have experienced throughout their lives. As children, we are told what, when, and how to learn. Learning is supposed to pay off in some unknown way in the distant future. But is this an appropriate way to educate and train adults? To be sure, we first have to consider how adults differ from children.

First, unlike children, adults have acquired a great deal of knowledge and work-related experience that they bring with them to a training program. Adults also like to know why they are learning something, the practical implications of what they are learning, and its relevance to their problems and needs. Adults are problem centred in their approach to learning and prefer to be self directed. They like to learn independently and they are motivated to learn by both extrinsic and intrinsic factors. (See Table 3.4 for some other differences between adults and children.)

TABLE 3.4

Teaching Children versus Adults

Factor	Children	Adults
Personality	Dependent	Independent
Motivation	Extrinsic	Intrinsic
Roles	Student	Employee
	Child	Parent, volunteer, spouse, citizen
Openness to change	Keen	Ingrained habits and attitudes
Barriers to change	Few	Negative self-concept
	Limited opportunities	
	Time	
	Inappropriate teaching methods	
Experience	Limited	Vast
Orientation to learning	Subject-centred	Problem-centred

The Trainer's Notebook 3.2

IMPLICATIONS OF ADULT LEARNING THEORY FOR TRAINING

- Adults need to know why they are learning.
- Adults should have some input into the planning and instruction of training programs.
- Adults should be involved in the needs analysis and have input into things such as training content and methods.
- The designers of training programs should consider the needs and interests of trainees.
- The training content should be meaningful and relevant to trainees' work-related needs and problems.

- Trainers should be aware of trainees' experiences and use them as examples.
- Adults can learn independently, and may prefer to do so.
- Adults are motivated by both intrinsic and extrinsic rewards.
- Adults should be given safe practice opportunities.

Andragogy

An adult-oriented approach to learning that takes into account the differences between adult and child learners

Pedagogy

The traditional approach to learning used to educate children and youth

These differences have led to the development of an adult learning theory known as andragogy. **Andragogy** is a term coined by adult learning theorist Malcolm Knowles and refers to an adult-oriented approach to learning that takes into account the differences between adult and child learners. By contrast, the term **pedagogy** refers to the more traditional approach of learning used to educate children and youth.[32]

Andragogy involves making the learning experience of adults more consistent with their needs and experiences. This means that adult learning should be self directed and problem centred and should take into account the learner's existing knowledge and experience.

IMPLICATIONS FOR TRAINING   Adult learning theory has important implications for training at every stage of the training process as depicted in the instructional systems design model of training and development (see Figure 1.4 in Chapter 1). For example, the design and instruction of training programs should be the joint responsibility of the trainer and trainees based on adult self-assessment of their needs. Adult learners should have some input about the training they will receive (e.g., topics, content) as well as how it will be designed (e.g., training methods) and delivered. You might recall from the chapter-opening vignette that senior staff at the Ontario division of the Canadian Cancer Society consulted with key groups including the executive team, regional employees, and recent hires to customize the on-boarding program so that it resonates with new hires.

The Trainer's Notebook 3.2, "Implications of Adult Learning Theory for Training," describes some of the other implications of adult learning theory for the design of training and development programs.

THEORIES OF MOTIVATION

You might be familiar with theories of motivation as they pertain to employee motivation and job performance. But did you know that learning and the effectiveness of training programs are also a function of people's motivation? As it turns out, motivation is an important predictor of task and job performance and is a key factor for learning and the effectiveness of training programs. Before we discuss motivation in the context of training, however, it is important to understand what motivation is and the major theories of motivation. This sets the stage for learning about the implications of motivation theories for training and development.

Motivation refers to the degree of persistent effort that one directs toward a goal. Motivation has to do with *effort*, or how hard one works; *persistence*, or the extent to which one keeps at a task; and *direction*, or the extent to which one applies effort and persistence toward a meaningful goal. In organizations, motivation has to do the extent to which employees direct their effort and persistence toward organization goals or in a manner that benefits the organization, such as high productivity or excellent customer service.

There are two forms of motivation: extrinsic and intrinsic. **Extrinsic motivation** is associated with factors in the external environment such as pay, fringe benefits, and company policies. These are motivators that are applied by somebody in the work environment such as a supervisor. **Intrinsic motivation** is the result of a direct relationship between a worker and the task. Unlike extrinsic motivation, it is self-applied and includes feelings of achievement, accomplishment, challenge, and competence that are the result of performing a task or one's job.

Theories of motivation can be described as need theories or process theories. Need theories have to do with the things that motivate people and the conditions in which they will be motivated so that they can obtain things that will satisfy their needs. Process theories of motivation address the process of motivation and how motivation occurs. In the remainder of this section, we will describe two need theories of motivation (Maslow's need hierarchy and Alderfer's ERG theory) and two process theories of motivation (expectancy theory and goal-setting theory), and their implications for training and development.

Motivation
The degree of persistent effort that one directs toward a goal

Extrinsic motivation
Motivation that stems from factors in the external environment such as pay, fringe benefits, and company policies

Intrinsic motivation
Motivation that stems from a direct relationship between a worker and the task

Need Theories

Need theories of motivation are concerned with the needs people have and the conditions in which they will be motivated to satisfy them. **Needs** refer to physiological and psychological desires. In organizations, individuals can satisfy their needs by obtaining incentives such as money to satisfy physiological needs, or by challenging work that allows them to fulfill higher-level psychological needs. Therefore, needs are motivational to the extent that people are motivated to obtain things that will satisfy their needs.

Two of the best known need theories of motivation are Maslow's need hierarchy and Alderfer's ERG theory.

Needs
Physiological and psychological desires

Maslow's Need Hierarchy

The best-known theory of motivation is Abraham Maslow's need hierarchy. According to Maslow, humans have five sets of needs that are arranged in a hierarchy, with the most basic needs at the bottom of the hierarchy and higher-order needs at the upper levels of the hierarchy. The five needs from lowest to highest are physiological, safety, belongingness, esteem, and self-actualization needs.[33]

Physiological needs are needs that people must satisfy to survive and include things such as food, water, and shelter. Physiological needs can usually be satisfied with pay. Safety needs refer to needs for security, stability, and freedom from anxiety. Safe working conditions and job security can satisfy safety needs. Belongingness needs have to do with the need for social interaction, companionship, and friendship. The opportunity to interact with others at work and friendly and supportive co-workers and supervision can satisfy belongingness needs. Esteem needs have to do with feelings of competence and appreciation and recognition by others. The opportunity to learn new things and challenging work can satisfy esteem needs.

The highest need in Maslow's hierarchy is self-actualization. Self-actualization involves developing one's true potential as an individual and experiencing personal fulfillment. This can be fulfilled by work experiences that involve opportunities for creativity, growth, and self-development.

According to Maslow, people are motivated to satisfy their lowest-level unsatisfied need. If one's physiological need is unsatisfied, then one will be motivated to satisfy it. The basic premise is that the lowest-level unsatisfied need has the greatest motivating potential, which means that motivation depends on one's position in the need hierarchy. Once a need has been satisfied it will no longer be motivational, and the next highest need in the hierarchy will become motivational. The one exception to this is the self-actualization need, which becomes stronger.[34]

Alderfer's ERG Theory

Alderfer's need theory of motivation is known as ERG theory and it consists of three needs that are represented by the name of the theory (E = existence, R = relatedness, G = growth). Existence needs are similar to Maslow's physiological and safety needs. Relatedness needs are similar to Maslow's belongingness need. And growth needs are similar to Maslow's esteem and self-actualization needs.[35]

Alderfer's ERG theory differs from Maslow's need theory in a number of ways. To begin with, ERG theory is not a rigid hierarchy of needs in which people can only move up the hierarchy in a lock-step fashion. Although both theories argue that once a lower-level need is satisfied the desire for higher-level needs will increase, ERG theory does not state that a lower-level need must be gratified before a higher-level need becomes motivational. Thus, one can be motivated to fulfill relatedness or growth needs even if they have not fulfilled their existence needs. Maslow, however, would argue that a lower need must first be satisfied before a higher-level need will become motivational.

Another difference is that ERG theory states that if individuals are unable to satisfy a higher-level need, the desire to satisfy a lower-level need will increase. Maslow of course would say that this is not possible because once a need has been satisfied it is no longer motivational.

IMPLICATIONS FOR TRAINING   Need theories of motivation highlight the fact that employee needs must be considered in the design of a training program. For example, if trainees' needs are not being fulfilled on the job then their behaviour and performance are not likely to change as a result of a training program unless the training program helps them fulfill their needs. In addition, employees are not likely to be motivated to attend a training program or to learn and apply the training on the job if doing so does not fulfill their needs. Therefore, trainers and managers should be aware of trainees' needs and ensure that training programs are designed in part to fulfill them. This will help to ensure that employees are motivated to attend training programs and to learn and apply the training material on the job.

Expectancy Theory

Expectancy theory is a process theory of motivation. According to expectancy theory, the energy or force that a person directs toward an activity (i.e., motivation) is a direct result of a number of factors. These factors are known as expectancy, instrumentality, and valence:[36]

1. *Expectancy* refers to an individual's subjective probability that they can achieve a particular level of performance on a task. For example, what is the probability that you can get an "A" in this course? What is the probability that you can get a "C" in this course? These outcomes are referred to as first-level outcomes since they are a direct result of one's effort or motivational force.

2. *Instrumentality* refers to the subjective likelihood that attainment of a first-level outcome such as an "A" or "C" in this course will lead to attractive consequences that are known as second-level outcomes. The consequences can be either intrinsic or extrinsic outcomes. For example, what is the probability that an "A" in this course will result in a job offer or a sense of accomplishment? What is the probability that a "C" will result in a job offer or a sense of accomplishment?

3. *Valence* refers to the attractiveness of the first- and second-level outcomes. The attractiveness of a second-level outcome such as a job offer or a sense of accomplishment is simply one's subjective ratings. For example, on a scale of 1 to 10 with 10 being the most attractive, how attractive would you rate receiving a job offer? The valence or attractiveness of a first-level outcome (an "A" or "C" grade in this course) is a result of the instrumentalities multiplied by the valence of each second-level outcome ($I \times V$). For example, the attractiveness of receiving an "A" in this course would be a function of:

$$(I \times V \text{ of receiving a job offer}) + (I \times V \text{ of experiencing a sense of accomplishment})$$

This calculation will determine the valence or attractiveness of the first-level outcome (receiving an "A" in this course). The same calculation would also be done to determine the valence of receiving a grade of "C" in the course.

To determine one's effort or motivation, the expectancy or probability of receiving an "A" or "C" grade must be multiplied by the valence of the first-level outcomes. This would result in a force or motivational value for pursuing an "A" and a "C" grade. In other words, it will indicate what grade you are most motivated to attain. If you feel that you can put in the effort and time required to obtain an "A" (i.e., your expectancy), and you believe that obtaining an "A" will result in a high probability of getting a job offer and experiencing a sense of accomplishment (instrumentality), then chances are you will be motivated to get an "A" in the course.

The expectancy theory linkages can be written as the following equation:

$$\text{Effort} = \text{Expectancy} \times (\text{Instrumentality} \times \text{Valence})$$

In effect, what all this means is that people's effort or motivation is a function of their beliefs that they can achieve a particular level of performance (first-level outcome), and that this will lead to consequences that are attractive to them (the valence of the first-level outcome). The attractiveness of a first-level outcome is simply the probability that it will lead to attractive consequences (e.g., the probability that getting an "A" in the course will result in a job offer and a sense of fulfillment). Thus, you will be motivated to obtain an "A" in this course if you believe that there is a high probability that you can get an "A" and if you believe that getting an "A" will lead to consequences that are attractive to you.

IMPLICATIONS FOR TRAINING   Expectancy theory has a number of implications for training and development. First, trainees must believe that there is a high probability they will be able to learn the training material and fulfill the training objective(s) (high expectancy). Second, learning the training material and using it on the job must result in consequences (high instrumentality) that are attractive to trainees (high valence of second-level outcomes). Simply put, you are more likely to learn something and apply it on the job if you believe that you can in fact learn it (high expectancy) and that you will be rewarded with something that is attractive to you once it has been learned and used on the job (instrumentality). Thus, it is important that employees believe that they can learn the training material and use it on the job and that doing so will result in positive consequences.

Goal-Setting Theory

Goal-setting theory is based on the idea that people's intentions are a good predictor of their behaviour. A **goal** is the object or aim of an action.[37] According to goal-setting theory, goals are motivational because they direct people's efforts and energies and lead to the development of strategies to help them reach their goals. For goals to be motivational, however, they must have a number of characteristics.

First, goals must be *specific* in terms of their level and time frame. General goals that lack specificity tend not to be motivational. Second, goals must be *challenging* to be motivational. Goals should not be so easy that they require little effort to achieve, and they should not be so difficult that they are impossible to reach. Third, goals must be accompanied by *feedback* so that it is possible to know how well one is doing and how close one is to goal accomplishment. Finally, for goals to be motivational, people must accept them and be *committed* to them.[38]

Research on goal-setting theory has provided strong support for the motivational effects of goals. Studies across a wide variety of settings have consistently shown that challenging and specific goals that are accompanied with performance feedback result in higher levels of individual and group performance.[39]

However, although specific and challenging goals have been found to be motivational, the effects on individuals depend on the type of goal that is set. Two important goal distinctions are whether the goal is proximal or distal and whether it is a performance or learning goal.

Goal

The object or aim of an action

Proximal and Distal Goals

An important distinction that needs to be considered is whether a goal is a distal or proximal goal. A **distal goal** is a long-term or end goal, such as achieving a certain level of sales performance. A **proximal goal** is a short-term goal or sub-goal that is instrumental for achieving a distal goal. Proximal goals involve breaking down a distal goal into smaller more attainable sub-goals. Proximal goals provide clear markers of progress toward a distal goal because they result in more frequent feedback. As a result, individuals can evaluate their ongoing performance and identify appropriate strategies for the attainment of a distal goal. Distal goals are too far removed to provide markers of one's progress, making it difficult for individuals to know how they are doing and adjust their strategies.[40]

Proximal goals are especially important for complex tasks. Research has found that distal goals can have a negative effect on the performance of a complex task. However, when distal goals are accompanied with proximal goals they have a significant positive effect on the discovery and use of task-relevant strategies, self-efficacy, and performance.[41]

A study of provincial and federal government managers who attended a self-awareness training program found that trainees who set distal and proximal outcome goals at the end of the training program were more likely to apply what they learned in training on the job six weeks after training than those who set only a distal outcome goal. Thus, distal goals are effective for learning a new task only when they are accompanied by proximal goals.[42]

> **Distal goal**
> A long-term or end goal
>
> **Proximal goal**
> A short-term goal or sub-goals

Goal Orientation

Another important characteristic of goals is goal orientation. There are two general types of goal orientations—a mastery or learning goal and a performance goal orientation.

Mastery goals are process-oriented and focus on the learning process. They enhance understanding of the task and the use of task strategies. **Performance goals** are outcome-oriented goals that focus attention on the achievement of specific performance outcomes.

Goal orientation is important because it can influence task performance as well as cognitive, affective, and motivational processes. The type of goal set (i.e., mastery versus performance) also affects skill acquisition and learning. Trainees who have mastery goals have been found to have higher intrinsic motivation, self-efficacy, and metacognitive activity, and these factors are all related to learning and performance.[43]

Evidence also exists that individuals differ with respect to their goal orientation. Goal orientation has been found to be a stable individual difference such that some individuals have a preference for mastery goals while others have a preference for performance goals. Individuals with a mastery goal orientation are most concerned about developing competence by acquiring new skills and mastering new situations. Individuals with a performance goal orientation are more concerned about demonstrating their competence by seeking favourable judgments and avoiding negative judgments.

> **Mastery goals**
> Process-oriented goals that focus on the learning process
>
> **Performance goals**
> Outcome-oriented goals that focus attention on the achievement of specific performance outcomes

However, high performance goals are not always the most effective. For example, recall from the discussion on the stages of learning and resource allocation theory that goal setting can be harmful for learning during the declarative stage when trainees' attention and cognitive resources are required to learn the task. Setting high performance goals can interfere with learning because they force trainees to focus on the outcomes of their effort rather than learning. This is especially a concern for learning complex tasks where trainees lack the knowledge and skill to perform the task and require all of their cognitive resources for learning. Setting a high performance goal will be more effective for tasks that are less complex and more routine and straightforward.

Mastery goals?   Learning goals, however, are especially important for learning new tasks because individuals must first acquire knowledge and learn strategies required to perform a task. When learning is required rather than motivation, setting a difficult performance outcome goal has been found to be detrimental for performance. This is because performance goals can distract attention from learning. Thus, during the learning process a specific, difficult learning goal should be set as it has been shown to result in higher self-efficacy and performance. Once an individual has acquired the knowledge and skills necessary to perform a new task, he/she can focus on performance goals.[44]

IMPLICATIONS FOR TRAINING   Goal-setting theory has a number of implications for training. For example, prior to a training program trainees should have specific and challenging goals for learning, and they should be provided with feedback during and after the training program so that they know whether they have achieved their goals. Setting specific and challenging goals should improve trainees' motivation to learn as well as their performance on the training task.

However, setting high performance goals during the declarative stage of learning can be detrimental for learning, especially for complex tasks. Therefore, special attention needs to be given to the stage at which goals are set and the complexity of the task. In addition, attention must also be given to the type of goal. For tasks that are novel and complex, a distal goal should be accompanied with proximal goals. Proximal goals should be set for knowledge and skill acquisition during training.

Research on goal orientation suggests that trainers should consider the goal orientation of trainees and the type of goals that are set for training. Learning goals that focus on skill development appear to be particularly important for learning, especially for individuals who have a performance goal orientation and need to be assigned learning goals. Thus, trainers should emphasize the importance of learning and the need to focus on learning goals during training. High learning goals appear to be especially important for challenging tasks and when new skills must be learned. Setting high performance goals for a task that is still being learned can be detrimental for learning and performance. Therefore, learning goals should be set for learning new tasks and performance goals for motivating performance once learning and task mastery have been achieved.[45]

TRAINING MOTIVATION

In the previous section, we described motivation theories and their implications for training and development. In this section, we focus more specifically on the role of motivation in training. In particular, we introduce the concept of *training motivation* and describe the predictors and consequences of trainees' motivation to learn.

Training motivation (also known as motivation to learn) refers to the direction, intensity, and persistence of learning-directed behaviour in training contexts. Research has found that training motivation predicts learning and training outcomes and is influenced by individual and situational factors.[46]

Among the individual factors that predict training motivation, personality variables as well as factors associated with one's job and career are important. Personality variables that predict training motivation include locus of control, achievement motivation, anxiety, and conscientiousness.

Locus of control refers to people's beliefs about whether their behaviour is controlled mainly by internal or external forces. Persons with an internal locus of control believe that the opportunity to control their own behaviour resides within themselves. Persons with an external locus of control believe that external forces determine their behaviour. Thus, internals perceive stronger links between the effort they put into something and the outcome or performance level they achieve. Persons with an internal locus of control tend to have higher levels of training motivation.

In addition, persons who are high in **achievement motivation** or the desire to perform challenging tasks and high on **conscientiousness** (responsible and achievement-oriented) also tend to have high training motivation. Persons with higher anxiety, however, tend to have lower training motivation. Self-efficacy is also positively related to training motivation.

Several job and career variables are also related to training motivation. For example, employees with higher **job involvement** or the degree to which an individual identifies psychologically with work and the importance of work to their self-image have higher training motivation. Organizational commitment and career planning and exploration are also associated with higher training motivation. Organizational factors such as supervisor support, peer support, and a positive climate also predict training motivation.

Training motivation is important because it is related to a number of training outcomes. For example, training motivation is positively related to declarative knowledge and skill acquisition as well as trainees' reactions to training and the likelihood that trainees apply on the job what they learn in training.

In summary, training motivation is an important factor in the training process that is related to training outcomes. Training is more likely to be effective and result in learning, skill acquisition, and improved job performance when trainees have high levels of training motivation.[47]

IMPLICATIONS FOR TRAINING   There are at least two things that trainers and managers can do to ensure that trainees' training motivation is high. First, they can assess trainee motivation prior to a training program and ensure that

Training motivation
The direction, intensity, and persistence of learning-directed behaviour in training contexts

Locus of control
People's beliefs about whether their behaviour is controlled mainly by internal or external forces

Achievement motivation
The desire to perform challenging tasks

Conscientiousness
The degree to which a person is responsible and achievement-oriented

Job involvement
The degree to which an individual identifies psychologically with work and the importance of work to their self-image

trainees are motivated to learn and select only those trainees with high training motivation to attend a training program. In fact, this is what the U.S. auto finance company AmeriCredit does. Employees complete a motivation questionnaire that is used to predict their likelihood of success in learning from a training program.[48]

Second, they can influence the factors that predict training motivation in an effort to increase trainees' training motivation. They might lower trainees' anxiety, increase self-efficacy, improve attitudes, and provide support for learning and training.

A MODEL OF TRAINING EFFECTIVENESS

Make the Connection

In this final section of the chapter, we present a model of training effectiveness that highlights the linkages between training and learning and between learning and individual performance and organizational effectiveness.

Figure 3.2 presents a model of training effectiveness. Recall from Chapter 1 that training involves the acquisition of knowledge, skills, and abilities to improve performance on one's current job, and development involves the acquisition of knowledge, skills, and abilities required to perform future job responsibilities. Thus, the first important link in the model is from training to learning and retention. In other words, training leads to declarative knowledge and the acquisition of skills and abilities and the retention of them over time.

FIGURE 3.2

Model of Training Effectiveness

In addition to training, we also know that there are personal and individual factors that influence learning. Among the most important is **cognitive ability**, which is one of the most often examined individual characteristics in training research. Cognitive or mental ability is similar to intelligence. It reflects an individual's basic information-processing capacities and cognitive resources. It generally refers to the knowledge and skills an individual possesses and may include cognitive skills and psychomotor skills. Examples of cognitive skills include basic numeracy and literacy, the intelligence to learn complex rules and procedures, and so on. Cognitive ability (verbal comprehension, quantitative ability, and reasoning ability) determines how much and how quickly people learn and is related to the ability to learn and to succeed on the job.[49]

Recall the earlier discussion of ACT theory and resource allocation theory in which it was noted that cognitive ability is particularly important during the early stages of learning. In fact, research has consistently shown that general cognitive ability is a strong predictor of learning, training success, and job performance. It is an especially good predictor of job performance on complex jobs. In training research, cognitive ability has been found to predict declarative knowledge, skill acquisition, and the application of trained skills on the job.[50]

Training motivation is also a strong predictor of learning and training outcomes. Like cognitive ability, training motivation predicts declarative knowledge, skill acquisition, and the application of trained skills on the job. Self-efficacy and personality characteristics also have an effect on learning. Trainees with higher self-efficacy are more likely to learn during training. In addition, trainees with an internal locus of control and a high need for achievement also learn more during training.[51]

An additional factor that can influence learning is trainees' attitudes. Three attitudinal variables that are important for learning are job involvement, job satisfaction, and organizational commitment. Employees with higher job attitudes are more likely to learn and apply what they learn in training on the job.[52]

The model also shows a path from learning to individual behaviour and performance. This is called transfer of training (see Chapter 10) and refers to the application of learning on the job. Employees must first learn and retain training content in order to change their behaviour and improve their job performance.

The final path in the model is between individual behaviour and performance and organizational effectiveness. This path indicates that employees' behaviour and job performance have an effect on organizational effectiveness. In other words, more effective employee behaviours and higher job performance result in a more effective organization.

In summary, the training effectiveness model shows how training and individual factors influence learning and retention. We will further develop the model in Chapter 5 when we discuss training design and again in Chapter 10 when we discuss transfer of training.

Cognitive ability
An individual's basic information processing capacities and cognitive resources

SUMMARY

We began this chapter by stating that a major goal of training and development is learning. We also described two classification schemes for learning outcomes. The learning process was described in terms of three stages of learning (declarative, knowledge compilation, and procedural knowledge) and resource allocation theory. Differences in how individuals prefer to learn were then discussed in terms of Kolb's learning styles. Two major theories of learning (conditioning theory and social cognitive theory) as well as adult learning theory were then described along with their implications for training and development. The chapter also described need theories and process theories of motivation and their implications for training. Training motivation was also discussed along with its predictors and consequences. The chapter concluded with a model of training effectiveness that shows the linkages between training, personal factors, and attitudes with learning and retention, individual behaviour and performance, and organizational effectiveness.

Key Terms

achievement motivation p. 85

ACT theory p. 67

andragogy p. 78

chaining p. 73

cognitive ability p. 87

conscientiousness p. 85

declarative knowledge p. 67

distal goal p. 83

extrinsic motivation p. 79

generalization p. 73

goal p. 82

intrinsic motivation p. 79

job involvement p. 85

knowledge compilation p. 68

learning p. 65

learning style p. 69

locus of control p. 85

mastery goals p. 83

motivation p. 79

needs p. 79

observation p. 74

pedagogy p. 78

performance goals p. 83

procedural knowledge p. 69

proximal goal p. 83

resource allocation theory p. 67

self-efficacy p. 75

self-regulation p. 75

self-regulation prompts p. 75

shaping p. 73

social learning, p. 74

training motivation p. 85

Make the Connection

p. 86: the meaning of training and development is discussed in Chapter 1 on pages 6–7

Web Links

Canadian Cancer Society: **www.cancer.ca**

Capital One: **www.capitalone.com**

Edward Jones: **www.edwardjones.com**

Required Professional Capabilities (RPCs)

The following RPCs are relevant to material covered in this chapter. The RPC number represents the CCHRA number assigned to the RPC as presented on the CCHRA website. All of the RPCs can be found in the Body of Knowledge at **http://www.chrp.ca/rpc/body-of-knowledge/**

RPC 150: Applies general principles of adult learning to ensure appropriate development methods and techniques.

150.01: Adult learning principles

150.05: Domains and levels of learning

Discussion Questions

1. Given the importance of motivation for learning and other training outcomes, what should trainers do to ensure that trainees are motivated to learn? What should managers do? Discuss the pros and cons of different approaches.

2. What are the differences between pedagogy and andragogy and what are the implications of adult learning theory for the design of training programs?

3. Discuss Kolb's four learning styles and their implications for the design of training programs. How should training programs be designed if people differ in their learning styles?

4. What are the sources of information that influence self-efficacy? How can trainers improve trainees' self-efficacy? How can supervisors improve trainees' self-efficacy? What can trainees do to improve their own self-efficacy?

5. What are the three stages of learning according to ACT theory? Give an example of how a training program might be designed according to ACT theory.

6. If an instructor of one of your courses wanted to maximize student learning, what should he/she do according to conditioning theory, social cognitive theory, and adult learning theory? If he/she wanted to motivate students to attend class and learn, what should he/she do according to need theories, expectancy theory, and goal-setting theory?

7. Discuss how goal-setting theory can be used to improve trainee learning in a training program. What kind of goal should be set for trainees? Discuss the relevance of task complexity, goal orientation, and type of goal (proximal and distal).

8. Compare and contrast the two learning outcomes classification schemes in Table 3.1. How are they are similar and how do they differ?

9. Based on the description at the beginning of the chapter of the Ontario Division of the Canadian Cancer Society's new employee on-boarding program, what are some of the learning outcomes that the program is designed to achieve? What activities are being used to achieve each learning outcome? Use both classification schemes in Figure 3.1 to answer this question.

10. Describe what self-regulation is and how it can help trainees learn during training? How can self-regulation be encouraged during training and what effect might this have on trainees?

11. Describe resource allocation theory and its implications for learning and training programs.

The Great Training Debate

1. Debate the following: Given that cognitive ability (or training motivation) is a strong predictor of learning, only trainees with high cognitive ability (or high training motivation) should be allowed to attend training programs, since those with low cognitive ability (or low training motivation) are not likely to learn or benefit from costly training programs.

2. Debate the following: When it comes to learning, the only thing that really matters is a person's cognitive ability.

Exercises

In-Class

1. If you had a friend who was about to attend a training program on how to use computers and she had very low self-efficacy about her ability to learn and to use a computer, what would you do to increase her self-efficacy? Describe some of the things you might do prior to the training program to increase your friend's self-efficacy.

2. Consider Kolb's four learning modes and how they might apply to your course on training and development or another course you are taking. How should the course be structured so that students' learning occurs in the following sequence: concrete experience, reflective observation, abstract conceptualization, and active experimentation? Be specific in terms of what the instructor will have students do at each stage of the learning cycle.

3. Using the material on goal-setting theory, set a goal for your training and development course. That is, set a specific and challenging goal that you will be committed to. In addition, determine how and when you will be able to obtain feedback. Be sure to also set a learning goal and a performance goal as well as a proximal and distal goal. Once you have set your goals, meet with another member of the class and review and evaluate each other's goals for the course.

4. Consider a course you are currently taking and examine it in terms of adult learning theory. To what extent does your course incorporate the principles of adult learning theory? What aspects of the course incorporate adult learning theory and what aspects do not? If you were to redesign the course to make it more consistent with adult learning theory, what are some of the things you would change and do?

5. Training motivation is an important predictor of training outcomes, so it is important that trainers ensure trainees' training motivation is high. You might have noticed how your own training motivation influences your

learning and performance in a course or training program. Using each of the theories of motivation (Maslow, Alderfer, expectancy, and goal setting), describe what a course instructor or trainer might do to increase students' or trainees' training motivation. Be specific in describing the techniques that follow from each theory.

6. Review the model of training effectiveness in Figure 3.2. Assess your potential learning and retention of a course you are currently taking by evaluating yourself as best you can on each of the predictors in the model (i.e., cognitive ability, attitudes, self-efficacy, personality characteristics, and training motivation). Based on your assessment, how successful will your learning and retention of the course material be? What predictors can you try to change in order to enhance your learning and retention of the course material?

7. Review the material on self-regulation in the chapter and then design a self-regulation training program to help you learn and improve a skill or behaviour that you want to improve (i.e., making presentations, time management, exercising, quitting smoking, etc.). Once you have chosen a skill or behaviour, prepare a self-regulation program. Be specific in terms of what exactly you are going to do at each step in the process (i.e., how and when you will observe and keep track of your behaviour and observe the behaviour of others; set specific goals; when you will practise and rehearse the desired behaviours; how you will keep track of your progress; and how you will reward yourself for goal achievement). Once you have prepared your program, meet with another member of the class to review and evaluate each other's self-regulation program.

8. Technocell Canada (TCC) is a subsidiary of the German group Felix Schoeller Holding, the world's largest producer of photographic and décor paper (see Chapter 4). After implementing a training program, the benefits listed below were realized. Use Gagné's learning outcomes classification scheme to classify each of the benefits:
   - improved literacy and numeracy skills
   - enhanced understanding by machine operators, managers, and supervisors of the importance of basic skills in the workplace;
   - improved attitudes and behaviour and a stronger sense of community within the workplace;
   - enhanced teamwork
   - improved employee motivation to do better and take pride in their work
   - improved ability of employees to troubleshoot
   - improved workplace safety record
   - increase self-confidence, self-esteem, and activity in the workplace and community

In-the-Field

1. Contact the human resource department of your own or another organization to discuss the organization's training programs. Find out the extent to which aspects of some of the following learning theories are used to improve trainees' learning: conditioning theory, social cognitive theory, and adult learning theory. Then find out the extent to which aspects of

some of the motivation theories (need theory, expectancy theory, and goal-setting theory) are used to motivate trainees to attend training programs and learn. What aspects of these theories are being used for training and what can the HR department do to improve trainee learning and training motivation?

2. How do you like to learn and how do you learn best? Do you have a visual, auditory, or tactile learning style? To find out, go to **http://www.personal.psu.edu/bxb11/LSI/LSI.htm** and take the Learning Style Inventory.

Answer the following questions:
a. What type of learner are you?
b. What do the results tell you about yourself in terms of how you prefer to learn and process information?
c. What are the implications of the results for how you learn? Develop some strategies to enhance your learning potential.
d. How can the information from this quiz be used by trainers and trainees?

Case Incident

Management Training at IKEA

IKEA is a Sweden-based home furnishings chain with stores in Canada and the United States. A single store can have 40 managers, making the task of training enough new managers quickly and well a challenge. To get managers trained for new store openings, IKEA has established certain stores as centres of excellence. These centres of excellence become learning sites for one or more management competencies that managers must master.

Manager trainees have a carefully developed, objectives-based curriculum and access to a 17-module online learning program that covers the basics of each of nine management competencies. Once a trainee has mastered the learning material as well as a series of practicum assignments, he or she is eligible to be certified as successful by the competence centre store manager. Trainees can be at a competence centre for two to six weeks depending on the competency to be mastered and number of competencies to be mastered at each centre. Part of the process involves shadowing successful managers. This is followed by two weeks of classroom training at IKEA Business College where managers are introduced to the philosophies and theories behind IKEA store operations. They get exposed to the "big picture," the theory of how the company operates, and what the IKEA vision is all about. Six months after a location opens, managers begin rotating back to Business College for advanced store operations training.

Questions

1. What are the learning outcomes of the IKEA manager training program? What do managers learn and how do they learn?
2. To what extent does the manager training program follow the learning process and stages of learning according to ACT theory? What changes, if any, would you suggest and why?

3. Discuss Kolb's learning styles, modes, and cycle with respect to the manager training program. To what extent does the program incorporate Kolb's four learning modes and follow the learning cycle? What changes, if any, would you make to the program so that it includes all four learning modes and adheres to Kolb's learning cycle?

Source: R. Zemke, "Training Top 100: Editor's Choice: IKEA U.S.A.," *Training*, Vol. 41 (3), P. 70, 2004.

Case Study THE PERFORMANCE APPRAISAL TRAINING PROGRAM

Supervisors at a large hospital seldom conducted performance appraisal interviews and some refused to do them. They complained that there was no time to meet with every nurse and that it was a difficult and unpleasant process that was a waste of time. Some were uncomfortable with the process and found it to be stressful for everybody involved. They said that it caused a lot of anxiety for them and the nurses.

However, the administration was in the process of introducing a new model of nursing that required the nurses to perform certain critical behaviours when interacting with and counselling patients and their families. It was therefore imperative that performance appraisals be conducted to ensure that nurses were implementing the new model of nursing. The nurse supervisors would be required to evaluate their nurses' performance every six months and then conduct a performance appraisal interview with each nurse in which the previous six months' performance would be discussed. An action plan would then be developed with specific goals for improvement.

The administration decided to hire a performance management consultant to provide a one-day workshop on how to conduct performance appraisals for all nurse supervisors. The training program was mandatory and all nurse supervisors had to attend. Many of them reluctantly did so complaining that it would be a waste of time and that it would not make any difference in how things were done in the hospital.

The training program began with a lecture on performance management and how to conduct performance appraisal interviews. The consultant first explained that the purpose of a performance appraisal interview is to give feedback to employees on how well they are performing their jobs and then plan for future growth and development. He then discussed different types of performance appraisal interviews such as the "tell-and-sell interview," the "tell-and-listen interview," and the "problem-solving interview." This was followed by a list of guidelines on how to conduct effective interviews such as asking the employee to do a self-assessment, focusing on behaviour not the person, minimizing criticism, focusing on problem-solving, and being supportive. The trainees were then instructed on how to set goals and develop an action plan for improvement.

After the lecture, the trainees were asked to participate in a role play in which they take turns playing the part of a supervisor and employee. They were provided with information about a nurse's job performance to discuss in the role play and then develop an action plan. However, some of the trainees left the session, refusing to participate. Others did not take it seriously and made a joke out it. There was a lot of laughing and joking throughout this part of the program.

After the role play there was a group discussion about the role-play experience followed by a review of the key points to remember when conducting performance appraisal interviews.

Although the supervisors were supposed to begin conducting performance reviews and interviews shortly after the training program, very few actually did. Some said they tried to do them but could not find time to interview all of their nurses. Others said that they followed the consultant's guidelines but they did not see any improvement in how they conducted interviews or in how nurses reacted to them. Some said it continued to be a stressful experience that was uncomfortable for them and the nurses and so they decided to stop doing them.

One year later, performance appraisals were still a rare occurrence at the hospital. Furthermore, many of the nurses were not practising the new nursing model and as a result nursing care and performance was inconsistent throughout the hospital and often unsatisfactory.

Questions

1. Consider Gagné's learning outcomes for the performance appraisal interview training program. What were the expected learning outcomes of the training program and what did trainees learn? What learning outcomes were not learned?
2. Explain the success of the training program using conditioning theory and social cognitive theory. How do these theories explain why the training program was not more effective? How could the program be improved by using some of the concepts from each theory?
3. Discuss the extent to which adult learning principles were incorporated into the training program. What principles were included and which ones were absent? What could the consultant have done differently to make better use of adult learning theory?
4. Describe the training program in terms of Kolb's learning styles and the learning cycle. What aspects of the program relate to each of the modes of learning? What learning style or styles are most likely to benefit from the program and which ones are not? How could the program be changed to make better use of Kolb's learning cycle?
5. Comment on the supervisors' training motivation. What effect did their training motivation have on the success of the training program? Consider how the theories of motivation can be applied by the hospital administration and the consultant to increase supervisors' training motivation.

Flashback Questions

1. Explain how the performance appraisal training program can benefit the hospital, employees, and society. What are the potential consequences of an ineffective training program for the hospital, employees, and society?
2. To what extent has the performance appraisal training program followed the instructional systems design (ISD) model of training and development? If you were to redesign the program, what changes would you make based on the ISD model?
3. To what extent would you describe the hospital as a learning organization? Be sure to describe the hospital in terms of the five disciplines of a learning organization, the principles of a learning organization, and the key dimensions of a learning organization. What are the implications of your description of the hospital for the success of the performance appraisal training program? In other words, how does this analysis help us understand why the training program was not more effective and what needs to be done to make it and other training programs in the hospital more effective?
4. Discuss the connection between organizational learning and training and development. How does this connection help us understand why the performance appraisal training program was not more successful?

REFERENCES

1. Nador, S. (2008, March 10). "Canadian Cancer Society launches new onboarding program." *Canadian HR Reporter, 21(5)*, 12. Reprinted by permission of Carswell, a division of Thomson Canada Ltd.
2. Hinrichs, J. R. (1976). Personnel training. In M. D. Dunnette (Ed.), *Handbook of industrial and organizational psychology* (pp. 829–860). Skokie, IL: Rand McNally; Gagné, R. M. (1984). Learning outcomes and their effects: Useful categories of human performance. *American Psychologist, 39*, 377–385.
3. Hinrichs, J. R. (1976), p. 833.
4. Kraiger, K., Ford, J. K., & Salas, E. (1993). Application of cognitive, skill-based, and affective theories of learning outcomes to new methods of training evaluation. *Journal of Applied Psychology, 78*, 311–328.
5. Gagné, R. M. (1984).
6. Zemke, R. (1999). Toward a science of training. *Training, 36(7)*, 32–36.
7. Kraiger, K., Ford, J. K., & Salas, E. (1993).
8. Kraiger, K., Ford, J. K., & Salas, E. (1993).
9. Kanfer, R., & Ackerman, P. L. (1989). Motivation and cognitive abilities: An integrative/aptitude-treatment interaction approach to skill acquisition. *Journal of Applied Psychology, 74*, 657–690.
10. Carter, M., & Beier, M. E. (2010). The effectiveness of error management training with working-aged adults. *Personnel Psychology, 63*, 641–675.
11. Kanfer, R., & Ackerman, P. L. (1989).
12. Kolb, D. A. (1984). *Experiential learning*. Englewood Cliffs, NJ: Prentice-Hall.
13. Kolb, D. A. (1984).

14. Kolb, D. A. (1984).
15. Whetten, D. A., & Cameron, K. S. (2002). *Developing management skills* (5th ed.). Upper Saddle River, NJ: Prentice Hall.
16. Barbian, J. (2002, March). Training top 100: AmeriCredit. *Training, 39(3),* 46–47.
17. Delahoussaye, M. (2001, March). Training top 50: Capital One. *Training, 38(3),* 70–71.
18. Skinner, B. F. (1953). *Science and human behaviour.* New York: McMillan.
19. Delahoussaye, M. (2001, March).
20. Pearce, J. M. (1987). A model of stimulus generalization in Pavlovian conditioning. *Psychological Review, 94,* 61–73.
21. Lavis, C. (2011). *Learning & development outlook 2011: Are organizations ready for learning 2.0?* Ottawa: The Conference Board of Canada.
22. Bandura, A. (1986). *Social foundations of thought and action: A social cognitive theory.* Englewood Cliffs, NJ: Prentice-Hall.
23. Luthans, F., & Davis, T. (1983). Beyond modelling: Managing social learning processes in human resource training and development. In C. Baird, E. Schneier, & D. Laird (Eds.), *The training and development sourcebook.* Amherst, MA: Human Resource Development Press.
24. McLaughlin, K. (2001, March). Training top 50: Edward Jones. *Training, 38(3),* 78–79.
25. Bandura, A. (1997). *Self-efficacy: The exercise of control.* New York: W. H. Freeman & Co.
26. Bandura, A. (1997).
27. Haccoun, R. R., & Saks, A. M. (1998). Training in the twenty-first century: Some lessons from the last one. *Canadian Psychology, 39,* 33–51.
28. Bandura, A. (1986).
29. Frayne, C. A., & Latham, G. P. (1987). Application of social learning theory to employee self-management of attendance. *Journal of Applied Psychology, 72,* 387–392. Latham, G. P., & Frayne, C. A. (1989). Self-management training for increasing job attendance: A follow-up and a replication. *Journal of Applied Psychology, 74,* 411–416.
30. Gist, M. E., Stevens, C. K., & Bavetta, A. G. (1991). Effects of self-efficacy and post-training intervention on the acquisition and maintenance of complex interpersonal skills. *Personnel Psychology, 44,* 837–861.
31. Sitzmann, T., Bell, B. S., Kraiger, K., & Kanar, A. M. (2009). A multilevel analysis of the effect of prompting self-regulation in technology-delivered instruction. *Personnel Psychology, 62,* 697–734; Sitzmann, T., & Ely, K. (2010). Sometimes you need a reminder: The effects of prompting self-regulation on regulatory processes, learning, and attrition. *Journal of Applied Psychology, 95,* 132–144.
32. Knowles, M. (1990). *The adult learner.* Gulf Publishing: Houston, TX.
33. Maslow. A. H. (1970). *Motivation and personality* (2nd ed.). New York: Harper & Row.
34. Maslow. A. H. (1970).
35. Alderfer, C. P. (1969). An empirical test of a new theory of human needs. *Organizational Behavior and Human Performance, 4,* 142–175.
36. Vroom. V. H. (1964). *Work and motivation.* New York: Wiley.
37. Locke, E. A., & Latham, G. P. (2002). Building a practically useful theory of goal setting and task motivation. *American Psychologist, 57,* 705–717.
38. Locke, E. A., & Latham, G. P. (1990). *A theory of goal setting and task performance.* Englewood Cliffs, NJ: Prentice-Hall.
39. Locke, E. A., & Latham, G. P. (1990).
40. Seijts, G. H., & Latham, G. P. (2001). The effect of distal learning, outcome, and proximal goals on a moderately complex task. *Journal of Organizational Behavior, 22,* 291–307; Latham, G. P., & Seijts, G. H. (1999). The effects of proximal and distal goals on performance on a moderately complex task. *Journal of Organizational Behavior, 20,* 421–429.
41. Seijts, G. H., & Latham, G. P. (2001).
42. Brown, T. C. (2005). Effectiveness of distal and proximal goals as transfer-of-training interventions: A field experiment. *Human Resource Development Quarterly, 16,* 369–387.

43. Bell, B. S., & Kozlowski, S. W. J. (2008). Active learning: Effects of core training design elements on self-regulatory processes, learning, and adaptability. *Journal of Applied Psychology, 93,* 296–316; Cannon-Bowers, J. A., Rhodenizer, L., Salas, E., & Bowers, C. A. (1998). A framework for understanding pre-practice conditions and their impact on learning. *Personnel Psychology, 51,* 291–320.

44. Seijts, G. H., & Latham, G. P. (2001); VandeWalle, D., Cron, W. L., & Slocum, J. W. Jr. (2001). The role of goal orientation following performance feedback. *Journal of Applied Psychology, 86,* 629–640; VandeWalle, D., Brown, S. P., Cron, W. L., & Slocum, J. W. Jr. (1999). The influence of goal orientation and self-regulation tactics on sales performance: A longitudinal field test. *Journal of Applied Psychology, 84,* 249–259.

45. Colquitt, J. A., Lepine, A., & Noe, R. A. (2000). Toward an integrative theory of training motivation: A meta-analytic path analysis of 20 years of research. *Journal of Applied Psychology, 85,* 678–707.

46. Colquitt, J. A., Lepine, A., & Noe, R. A. (2000).

47. Colquitt, J. A., Lepine, A., & Noe, R. A. (2000).

48. Barbian, J. (2002, March). Training top 100: AmeriCredit. *Training, 39(3),* 46–47.

49. Brown, K. G., & Sitzmann, T. (2011). Training and employee development for improved performance. In S. Zedeck (Ed.), *Handbook of industrial and organizational psychology* (Vol. 2, pp. 469–503). Washington, DC: American Psychological Association.

50. Colquitt, J. A., Lepine, A., & Noe, R. A. (2000).

51. Colquitt, J. A., Lepine, A., & Noe, R. A. (2000).

52. Burke, L. A. (2001). Training transfer: Ensuring training gets used on the job. In L. A. Burke (Ed.), *High-impact training solutions: Top issues troubling trainers.* Quorum Books: Westport, CT; Colquitt, J. A., Lepine, A., & Noe, R. A. (2000).

The Needs Analysis Process

CHAPTER LEARNING OUTCOMES

After reading this chapter, you should be able to:

- define needs analysis and describe the needs analysis process
- define and explain how to conduct an organizational, task, and person analysis
- define and describe the purpose of a cognitive task analysis and a team task analysis
- describe the process of determining solutions to performance problems
- describe the different methods and sources for conducting a needs analysis
- describe the obstacles to conducting a needs analysis and how to overcome them

TECHNOCELL CANADA (TCC)

Technocell Canada (TCC) is a subsidiary of the German group Felix Schoeller Holding, the world's largest producer of photographic and décor paper. In 2001, Technocell Canada purchased a paper plant in Drummondville, Quebec, as it was the only plant in Canada with the capability of fabricating the specialized paper product needed. The Drummondville plant employs 150 people and exports approximately 80 percent of its production to the United States.

However, most of Technocell's newly acquired workforce was not familiar with the materials or the technology required to produce the quality standard required by Technocell. In addition, the employees had not received any training for the various positions associated with the paper machine production line and they were also lacking in basic skills.

With the introduction of new products, higher quality standards, and significant increases in production volume and speed, staff had difficulty adapting to the new work methods. Furthermore, market requirements demanded a much more in-depth knowledge of the production processes than what was typically required in traditional paper factories.

The reality of an untrained workforce had a direct negative impact on the organization and, in particular, on product quality, efficiency, and productivity. It was clear to both local and German managers that the skill deficiencies were taking their toll on the company and its bottom line. Immediate action was required to stabilize and improve the productivity of the Drummondville plant.

The company's goal of developing a highly skilled workforce was further complicated by difficulties in finding and recruiting specialized and qualified staff. The only solution to overcoming the shortage was to improve the quality of training provided to current employees to ultimately increase both productivity and staff retention.

Before training could take place, a full analysis of the skill set and training needs of each employee was required. To ensure impartiality, an external firm was hired to survey the employees, evaluate and measure their essential skills, analyze the results, and prepare a structured training plan. The audit consisted of preparing, distributing, and analyzing employee surveys and results. The external company then tested the technical and generic competencies of employees at all levels.

In addition to a lack of important skills, the survey results also indicated a need for improvement in employees' attitudes and behaviours as the results indicated that employees were not sensitive to the urgency of completing a task; employees did not take responsibility for product quality; workplace safety was not exercised; management were not necessarily well qualified for their job responsibilities; and employees were not concerned by the consequences of their actions on the company's fragile bottom line.

After analyzing the results, a matrix of training needs was prepared. Training schedules and activities were then put into place. To maintain employee support, the external assessors met with all employees individually to discuss the results of their evaluations, review their training needs, and discuss next steps.

All job descriptions were reviewed and revised and a skill set was identified for each job, including the attitudes and behaviours required to be successful in that position. A proficiency assessment was implemented for each position, identifying a set of competencies which had to be met in order to be proficient in the job. The criteria were based on academic skills, work skills, technical skills, and generic skills. Once all employees had been tested and their skill sets evaluated and identified, the company was in a better position to match jobs to each employee's qualification.

As a result of this process, Technocell Canada was able to tailor the training program to meet the specific needs of individual learners. At the same time, the program ensures that the workforce will acquire the essential job skills specific to the décor paper industry and that workplace safety and pro- ductivity goals are met. The company counts on the training program to improve the quality of its products and services as well as productivity.[1]

Source: Awards for Excellence in Workplace Literacy, Medium Business Winner, 2005. Upgrading Employee Skills to Meet Corporate Standards—Technocell Canada, A Felix Schoeller Group Company. Case Study December 2005 E/F. Ottawa: The Conference Board of Canada, 2005.

The Technocell Canada story highlights an important aspect of the training and development process. It shows how a new business strategy has important implications for training and development, and how a needs analysis is required to determine who needs training and what type of training they need. It also shows how training is often necessary to improve productivity and a company's success. As you can tell from this case, needs analysis is a critical first step in the training and development process.

In Chapter 1 you were introduced to the instructional systems design (ISD) model of training and development, which depicts training and development as a rational and scientific process that consists of three major steps: needs analysis, design and delivery, and evaluation. The process involves an analysis of current performance and ends with improved performance. The critical first step in the ISD model is a needs analysis to determine the nature of the problem and whether training is the best solution. A needs analysis is performed to determine the difference or gap between the way things are and the way things should be. In this chapter, you will learn about the needs analysis process and how to determine whether training is the best solution to performance problems.

Make the Connection

WHAT IS A NEEDS ANALYSIS?

Needs analysis (also known as needs assessment) is the cornerstone and foundation of training and development. In fact, it is often referred to as the most important step in the training and development process.[2] **Needs analysis** is a process designed to identify gaps or deficiencies in employee and organizational performance. Needs analysis is concerned with the gaps between actual performance and desired performance. It is a "formal process of identifying needs as gaps between current and desired results, placing those needs in priority order based on the cost to meet each need versus the cost of ignoring it, and selecting the most important needs (problems or opportunities) for reduction or elimination."[3]

Needs analysis helps to identify gaps or deficiencies in individual, group, or organizational performance. The way to identify performance gaps is to solicit information from those who are affected by the performance problem. A needs analyst gathers information from key people in an organization about the organization, jobs, and employees to determine the nature of performance problems. This information identifies the problem, which is the difference between the way the work is being done and the most cost-effective way of doing it. In the simplest terms, needs = required results − current results.[4]

The goal of needs analysis is to identify the difference between what is and what is desired or required in terms of results, and to compare the magnitude of gaps against the cost of reducing them or ignoring them. Obviously, performance

Needs analysis

A process to identify gaps or deficiencies in employee and organizational performance gaps could be the result of many factors, and the solutions might include training as well as other interventions. A thorough needs analysis can help an organization prioritize its needs and make informed decisions as to what problems need to be resolved. Thus, needs analysis identifies, prioritizes, and selects needs that will have an impact on internal and external stakeholders.[5] Needs analysis helps to identify the causes of and solutions to performance problems.

THE NEEDS ANALYSIS PROCESS

Figure 4.1 shows that needs analysis is a process that consists of a series of interrelated steps. As described in Chapter 1, the process starts with an *itch* or a problem. If the performance problem is important, stakeholders are consulted and a needs

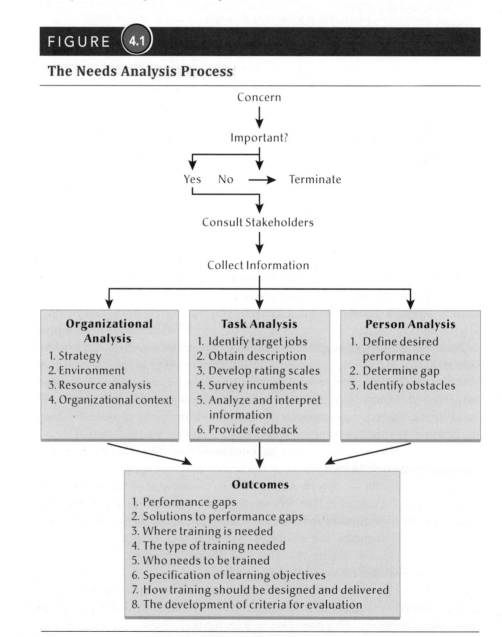

FIGURE 4.1

The Needs Analysis Process

Concern

Important?

Yes   No   →   Terminate

Consult Stakeholders

Collect Information

Organizational Analysis
1. Strategy
2. Environment
3. Resource analysis
4. Organizational context

Task Analysis
1. Identify target jobs
2. Obtain description
3. Develop rating scales
4. Survey incumbents
5. Analyze and interpret information
6. Provide feedback

Person Analysis
1. Define desired performance
2. Determine gap
3. Identify obstacles

Outcomes
1. Performance gaps
2. Solutions to performance gaps
3. Where training is needed
4. The type of training needed
5. Who needs to be trained
6. Specification of learning objectives
7. How training should be designed and delivered
8. The development of criteria for evaluation

analysis is conducted. There are three levels of needs analysis: an organizational analysis, a task analysis, and a person analysis. The collection of information and the needs analysis process concludes with a number of important outcomes.

Step One: A Concern

The process of identifying training needs originates slowly and informally with a concern. This concern is sometimes referred to as an *itch* or a *pressure point,* something that causes managers to notice it. This concern might be as subtle as noticing that employees are treating customers in an abrupt manner, or observing that employees are spending a lot of time asking one another for help with a new system. Other concerns might be recognizing a shift in regular activities, such as an increase in defective parts, accidents, or complaints.[6] At Technocell Canada, there were concerns about product quality, efficiency, and productivity as a result of an unskilled workforce.

At Boston Pizza, the top casual dining chain in Canada, a growing skills gap among the company's store managers was noticed. Although managers are familiar with the Boston Pizza concept and have the necessary hard skills, they were lacking in soft skills because most of them came up through the ranks and have not had any formal management education. In order to remedy the soft-skills concern, the company launched Boston Pizza College, a classroom-based management training program.[7]

Sometimes the pressure comes from the external environment, such as when legislation regarding employee relations is changed, or the competition introduces a highly competitive service feature, or when problems that threaten public health and safety are recognized. For a good example of this, see Training Today 4.1, "Dirty Pools and Poor Training."

Step Two: Importance

After a concern has been raised, the next step is to determine whether the concern is central to the effectiveness of the organization. The training manager must be aware of the strategic orientation of the organization. The goals, plans, introduction of products and services, changes in technology, practices, and regulations should be clear. Human resource policies must be linked with the strategic directions of the company as discussed in Chapter 1, and the training strategy should support the organization's efforts to achieve its goals.[8] As indicated in the chapter-opening vignette, skill deficiencies were having a direct negative effect on Technocell Canada. Immediate action was required to stabilize and improve the productivity of the plant.

Another important concern is the cost implications of a problem. Does current performance cost the company in lost productivity or dissatisfied customers? If the performance problem is important, then there must be some way to demonstrate that correcting the problem will result in increased productivity or client satisfaction. A concern is important (i.e., worthy of further exploration and analysis) if it has an impact on outcomes that are important to the organization and its effectiveness. Clearly, the concern at Technocell Canada was very important as it was affecting the company's bottom line.

Step Three: Consult Stakeholders

The next step in the needs analysis process is to involve the stakeholders who have a vested interest in the process and outcomes. Support from key players in the organization is necessary from the beginning of the needs analysis process. At Technocell

Training Today 4.1

Dirty Pools and Poor Training

In August 2011, the *Toronto Star* conducted an investigation of pools and hot tubs at condominiums, health clubs, and swimming pools across the city of Toronto. What they discovered was that many pools and hot tubs in Toronto have repeatedly violated public health and safety rules. This means that bathers are being potentially exposed to injury and disease.

The data obtained by the *Toronto Star* indicates more than 10,000 violations by pools and spas over the past two years including luxury condominiums, private schools, spas, hotels, and fitness clubs. Health infractions include things such as failure to maintain safe and sanitary conditions and equipment in sanitary and working order, poor water clarity, unsafe storage of chemicals, failing to keep proper records, improper chemical balance such as pH levels, and a hot tub's vacuum release system not working properly (a safety device that prevents the pool's suction mechanism from trapping bathers to the whirlpool floor).

Health inspectors can close a pool for a variety of violations, such as cloudy water, missing emergency equipment such as a spine board or two buoyant safety rings, or loose or missing pool outlet covers. Since 2009, more than 300 pools have been closed for various violations, including faulty mechanics, missing emergency equipment, and dirty water.

Poorly maintained pools can be breeding grounds for bacteria, which can cause serious gastrointestinal illnesses. Recreational water illnesses are caused by germs spread by swallowing or having contact with contaminated water. Illnesses include gastrointestinal, skin, ear, respiratory, eye, and neurologic infections. The most common symptom is diarrhea, which is caused by germs such as cryptosporidium, giardia, shigella, norovirus, and E. coli.

The root of pool problems and infractions is said to be poor training. In Ontario, there are no standardized training requirements. In 2009 and 2010, inspectors reported 114 cases of staff that were not adequately trained to safely run a hot tub or pool. City officials cited 23 facilities multiple times for this infraction suggesting that they failed to get the necessary training despite the inspector's warning.

Following the *Toronto Star* investigation, safety experts have called for the province of Ontario to enforce standardized training for swimming pool operators. Toronto's Board of Health has also asked the province to require standardized training for operators. Ontario's health minister said the province may consider introducing a certification program for pool operators.

Sources: J. McLean & D. Zlomislic, "Toronto pools' dirty secrets," *Toronto Star*, P. A1, A20, Aug. 20, 2011; J. McLean & D. Zlomislic, "Training standards urged to clean up dirty pools," *Toronto Star*, P. A1, A20, Aug. 27, 2011; J. McLean, "Toronto cracks down on bad pools," *Toronto Star*, P. A3, Sept. 14, 2011.

Canada, both local and German managers believed that the skill deficiencies of the workforce were a serious problem and that immediate action was required to achieve the company's goal of developing a highly skilled workforce.

At a minimum, **top management should understand the rationale for the needs analysis**. Training analysts must obtain agreement on why the needs analysis is being done and who will be involved. Managerial expectations must be clarified.[9] Likewise, other stakeholders, such as employees or their collective representatives, should be consulted. At Technocell Canada, the external assessors met with all employees individually to discuss the results of their evaluations, review their training needs, and discuss next steps. All stakeholders must buy into the needs analysis process to ensure that the data collection will result in accurate information and that they have a vested interest in the success of the program.

Step Four: Data Collection

The next stage in the needs analysis process is the most extensive and involves the documentation of the concern through the collection of information from three levels of analysis. Recall from the chapter-opening vignette that before training could take place at Technocell Canada, a full analysis of the skill set and training needs of each employee was required.

The three levels of needs analysis are the *organizational,* the *task,* and the *person* or *employee.* Although overlaps among the three areas of analysis occur, each plays a distinctive role. The analysis of the organization provides information about its strategies and context and answers the question, "*Where is training needed in the organization?*" The task analysis provides information about the tasks and the relevant knowledge, skills, and abilities needed to perform selected jobs and answers the question, "*What knowledge, skills, and abilities are required to perform the job effectively?*" And a person analysis provides information about an employee's level of performance and answers the question, "*Who needs to be trained?*"

Needs Analysis Outcomes

At the beginning of this chapter we referred to needs analysis as the cornerstone of the training and development process and noted that it is one of the most important steps. This is due in large part to the many outcomes of needs analysis as shown in Figure 4.1.

The needs analysis results in a number of outcomes that set the stage for the rest of the training and development process. Besides clarifying the nature of performance gaps, a needs analysis helps to determine whether training and development is a good solution to performance problems or if some other intervention might be more effective. If training and development is part of the solution, needs analysis information is used to determine where training is needed in the organization, what type of training is required, and who in the organization should receive training.

For example, Technocell Canada was able to tailor its training program to meet the specific needs of individuals, to ensure that the workforce acquires the essential job skills specific to the décor paper industry, and to ensure that workplace safety and productivity goals are met as a result of the needs analysis process.

Needs analysis information is also used to write training objectives and to design training programs (e.g., what training content should be included in the training program, what training methods would be most effective, etc.). Finally, the information from a needs analysis is used in the development of measures for training evaluation.

In summary, the needs analysis process helps to determine the best solution to performance problems and how to proceed if training is to be part of the solution. Later in the chapter we discuss a process for determining solutions to performance problems. In the following sections, we describe how to conduct an organizational, task, and person needs analysis.

ORGANIZATIONAL ANALYSIS

Organizational analysis involves the study of the entire organization: its strategy, environment, resources, and context. An understanding of each of these components will provide information not only for the identification of training

Organizational analysis
The study of the entire organization including its strategy, environment, resources, and context

needs, but also on the probability of the success of a training program. Key to an organizational analysis is finding out if a training program is aligned with an organization's strategy, the existence of any constraints, as well as support for the delivery and success of a training program. An organizational analysis can help identify potential constraints and problems that can derail a training program so that they can be dealt with prior to the design and delivery of a costly program. Let's take a closer look at each of the components of an organizational analysis.

Strategy

Most organizations have a strategy that consists of an organization's mission, goals, and objectives such as a dedication to quality or innovation. These broad statements trickle down to specific goals and objectives for each department or unit, and reflect an organization's plan for growth, adaptation, profitability, and survival.

In the past, an organization's strategy was set and implemented independently of the training function and human resources. During the last decade, however, it became increasingly apparent that human resource functions such as training and development are essential for the accomplishment of an organization's strategy and objectives. As a result, vice presidents and directors of human resources are now often involved in the setting of an organization's strategy and the human resource function has become more strategic.

Make the Connection

In Chapter 1, we defined strategic human resource management (SHRM) as the alignment of human resource practices with an organization's business strategy. Although SHRM refers in general to the human resource system, in actuality it involves aligning specific HRM functions and activities with an organization's business strategy. In this regard, we can describe particular HR functions such as training and development as being strategic.

Recall from Chapter 1 that strategic training and development (ST&D) involves the alignment of an organization's training needs and programs with an organization's strategy and objectives. You might recall from Chapter 1 that one of the organizational benefits of training and development is facilitating and supporting an organization's strategy.

An organization's strategy should indicate the type and amount of training required. For example, at construction company EllisDon, the organization's strategic priorities are the basis for determining the competencies that employees will need to move the company forward. They make sure that training is aligned with business needs and the organization's strategic goals.[10]

Training is more likely to be effective and contribute to an organization's success when it is congruent with its business strategy. When training and development programs are designed and implemented in isolation of an organization's strategy, they are not likely to be effective in helping an organization achieve its goals.

As indicated in Chapter 1, there is some evidence that training can actually detract from an organization's bottom line and negatively impact shareholder value if it is not aligned with an organization's strategy. Training that is not linked to an organization's strategy can lower a company's market value by as much as 1.9 percent.[11] In the chapter-opening vignette, the training program was designed to support Technocell's strategy, which included the introduction of new products, higher quality standards, and significant increases in production volume and speed.

Environment

In Chapter 1, we described how training and development is embedded within the external environment and how factors in the environment can impact the organization, human resource practices, and training and development. The environment is dynamic and uncertain. New technologies, competitors, recessions, and trade agreements can profoundly affect not only the need for and content of training, but also employees' receptivity to being trained.

Make the
Connection

Training programs are often a direct result of government regulations (e.g., safety regulations). For example, in the United States a sexual harassment prevention training law in California requires organizations with 50 or more employees to provide at least two hours of sexual harassment training to all supervisory employees.[12] The Sarbanes-Oxley Act of 2002, which was passed in the United States to protect investors from fraudulent accounting activities by corporations in the wake of high-profile scandals such as Enron and WorldCom, requires organizations to provide compliance training which must be documented. The implications for training are especially being felt by accounting firms, where the Act has forced auditors and accountants to do their jobs differently. As a result, some firms have had to double the time their staff spend in training and substantially increase their investment in training.[13] A recent decision by Toronto's Board of Health to disclose inspection reports of pools and spas that violate safety rules along with a request for the province to establish fines for infractions is likely to result in more training for pool operators[14] (see Training Today 4.1).

Besides this regulatory influence, organizations are conscious of the strategies of their competitors. The nature of a training program can be a direct result of an organization's attempt to establish a new market niche. For example, Technocell's need for training is a result of its purchase of the only plant in Canada with the capability of fabricating specialized paper.

Resource Analysis

An important component of an organizational analysis is determining an organization's ability to design and deliver a training program. Does the organization have the resources (money, time, and expertise) to design and deliver a training program if one is needed?

A **resource analysis** involves identifying the resources available in the organization that might be required to design and implement training and development programs. Training programs are costly and require considerable resources. In addition to the financial costs, the design and implementation of a training program requires considerable time and expertise. Not all organizations have the expertise required to design and deliver training programs. In addition, the human resource staff might not have the time required to design new training programs. Training programs also require materials, equipment, and facilities, and these too can be expensive.

A resource analysis enables an organization to determine whether it has the resources required for a training and development solution or whether another less costly solution will be better. Ultimately, one has to answer the question of whether or not the organization has the resources required for

Resource analysis
The identification of the resources available in an organization that might be required to design and implement training and development programs

training if in fact it is needed. Training was of course needed at Technocell Canada and the company invested approximately $2 million in the development of employee skills and expertise, which translated into an average of $30,000 per employee.[15]

Organizational Context

Organizational climate
The collective attitudes of employees toward work, supervision, and company goals, policies, and procedures

Organizations consist of more than buildings, equipment, and paper. They are social entities made up of people. The people within the buildings have feelings, attitudes, and values that make up the climate of an organization. **Organization climate** refers to the collective attitudes of employees toward work, supervision, and company goals, policies, and procedures. One aspect of climate that is particularly important for training is the training transfer climate.

Training transfer climate
Characteristics in the work environment that can either facilitate or inhibit the application of training on the job

Training transfer climate refers to characteristics in the work environment that can either facilitate or inhibit the application of training on the job. A strong training transfer climate is one in which there exist cues that remind employees to apply training material on the job, positive consequences such as feedback and rewards for applying training on the job, and supervisor and peer support for the use of newly acquired skills and abilities. The training transfer climate has been found to be a strong predictor of training effectiveness and whether or not trainees apply newly trained skills on the job.[16]

Make the
Connection

Another important component of an organization's context is its culture. Recall from Chapter 1 that an organization's culture refers to the shared beliefs and assumptions about how things are done in an organization. Organizations can be differentiated from each other on the basis of their culture. For example, some organizations have innovative cultures, while others have risk-taking cultures. One type of culture that is particularly important for training and development is a continuous learning culture.

Continuous learning culture
A culture in which members of an organization believe that knowledge and skill acquisition are part of their job responsibilities and that learning is an important part of work life in the organization

A **continuous learning culture** refers to a culture in which members of an organization believe that knowledge and skill acquisition are part of their job responsibilities and that learning is an important part of work life in the organization.[17]

Information about an organization's training transfer climate and continuous learning culture is important because it can help to determine whether a training program is likely to be effective in an organization as well as whether a pre-training intervention might be required to improve the climate and/or culture prior to the design and delivery of a training program. It might also indicate that an alternative solution to a performance problem would be more effective than a training program. This is an important part of an organizational analysis because training is not likely to be effective in organizations where the climate for training transfer and/or the culture for learning are not strong.

The influence of the training transfer climate and a continuous learning culture on training effectiveness demonstrates the importance of the organizational context for a training program's success and the need to conduct an organizational analysis. Whether or not employees apply what they learn in on-the-job training has a lot to do with an organization's transfer climate and a continuous learning culture, because they can either facilitate or hinder the implementation and success of a training program.

The Trainer's Notebook 4.1

CONTINUOUS LEARNING CULTURE DIAGNOSIS

Here are some ways that you can determine whether an organization has a continuous learning culture. Use the following scale to answer each of the statements below:

1 = Strongly disagree

2 = Disagree

3 = Neither agree nor disagree

4 = Agree

5 = Strongly agree.

- Acquiring knowledge and skills is an essential part of the job.
- Assignments are challenging and are designed to help employees develop new skills.
- Co-workers help each other to learn by sharing their job knowledge and helping to understand how jobs are interconnected.

- Employees are rewarded for learning new things.
- Employees are given opportunities on-the-job to apply what they have learned.
- Employees feel that they work in a place where innovation is encouraged.
- Employees receive excellent on-the-job training.
- Supervisors give employees recognition and credit when they use new knowledge and skills to do their job.
- Supervisors openly express their support of continuous learning.
- Co-workers encourage each other to use new knowledge and skills on the job.

Total your scores for all 10 items. Your total score can range from 10 to 50. Higher scores indicate a stronger learning culture.

Source: Copyright © 1995 by the American Psychological Association. "Applying trained skills on the job: The importance of the work environment," J. Bruce Tracey, Scott I. Tannenbaum, & Michael J. Kavanagh, *Journal of Applied Psychology.* Vol. 80 (2), Apr. 1995, Pp. 239–252. The use of APA information does not imply endorsement by APA.

The Trainer's Notebook 4.1, "Continuous Learning Culture Diagnosis," describes how to determine whether an organization has a continuous learning culture. We discuss the role of the training transfer climate and a continuous learning culture in more detail in Chapter 10.

Once the strategy, environment, resources, and context of an organization have been assessed, the information gathered can be used to determine whether a training program is required to help an organization achieve its goals and objectives and whether it will be successful. However, even if training is needed, it is still not clear what kind of training is needed and who needs to be trained. To answer these questions, additional information is required about the tasks that employees perform and their current level of job performance. This additional information can be obtained by conducting a task analysis and a person analysis.

TASK ANALYSIS

A **task analysis** consists of a description of the activities or work operations performed on a job and the conditions under which these activities are performed. A task analysis reveals the tasks required for a person to perform a job and the knowledge, skills, and abilities that are required to perform the tasks successfully.

Task analysis
The process of obtaining information about a job by determining the duties, tasks, and activities involved and the knowledge, skills, and abilities required to perform the tasks

There are six steps involved in a task analysis:

1. Identify the target jobs.
2. Obtain a job description.
3. Develop rating scales to rate the importance of each task and the frequency with which it is performed.
4. Survey a sample of job incumbents.
5. Analyze and interpret the information.
6. Provide feedback on the results.

IDENTIFY THE TARGET JOBS   After a problem or performance discrepancy has been identified in an organization, the focus shifts to the job level to determine which jobs are contributing to the performance problem and have a performance gap. At Technocell, targeted jobs were from all levels including supervisors, mill operators, laboratory technicians, maintenance and shipping and receiving workers, mill management and support staff, office personnel, and senior management.

OBTAIN A JOB DESCRIPTION   A **job description** lists the specific duties carried out through the completion of several tasks. In large organizations, most positions have a description of the tasks and minimum qualifications required to do the job. If this description has not been updated within the last year, consult with both the manager and several employees in the position (subject-matter experts) to obtain a current listing of tasks and qualifications. The job description should contain a summary of the major duties of the job, a listing of these duties, the knowledge, skills, and abilities required to perform the tasks, and the conditions under which they are performed. All tools and specialized knowledge should be listed.

After preparing a job description, the list of duties should be reviewed with subject-matter experts, managers, job incumbents in interviews, or focus groups. The analyst will then develop a list of tasks to be performed; the knowledge, skills, and abilities needed to perform the tasks; a list of necessary tools, software, or equipment; and an understanding of the conditions under which the tasks are performed. You can see that the result looks very much like a job description with job specifications (a job specification is a statement of the knowledge, skills, and abilities required to perform a job).

Creating job descriptions and making lists of tasks and duties does have its downside. Critics argue that jobs change too rapidly and these lists are quickly out of date. Therefore, some job analysts have begun to develop a list of job competencies. A **competency** is a cluster of related knowledge, skills, and abilities that forms a major part of a job and that enables the job holder to perform effectively.[18] Competencies are behaviours that distinguish effective performers from ineffective performers. Competencies can be knowledge, skills, behaviour, or personality traits. However, most analysts prefer not to use personality traits, such as "charisma," and instead prefer to describe the behaviour underlying the trait.

Examples of competencies for managers include setting goals and standards, coaching, making decisions, and organizing. As you can see, competencies are very similar to skills. Skills, however, can be very specific, such as "negotiate a collective agreement," whereas competencies are generic and universal, such as

Job description
A statement of the tasks, duties, and responsibilities of a job

Competency
A cluster of related knowledge, skills, and abilities that enables the job holder to perform effectively

TABLE 4.1
A Competency Profile for Senior Leaders
Core Competency Ability to obtain buy-in of key stakeholders to new directions
Level 1: Communicates new directions so that everyone affected knows the new directions
Level 2: Leads team through discussions and research to identify key new themes and goals that everyone can accept and use
Level 3: Key stakeholders are consulted and have input into direction-setting
Level 4: All stakeholders are engaged in a process to rewrite the new directions in terms that relate specifically to their roles

Source: D. MacNamara, "Learning contracts, competency profiles the new wave in executive development," *Canadian HR Reporter*, Nov. 16, 1998, P. G8. Reprinted by permission of Canadian HR Reporter.

"win agreement on goals, standards, expectations, and time frames." The Banff Centre for Management has developed competency profiles for senior leaders so that they can assess needs and then train.[19] An example taken from their profile is listed in Table 4.1.

The goal is to develop competencies that are teachable (i.e., we can observe them and describe them). If these competencies are then associated with effective performance, we can use them as a base to increase the effectiveness of an employee's on-the-job behaviour. Competencies can then be used instead of job descriptions.

At Technocell Canada, all job descriptions were reviewed and revised and a skill set was identified for each job that indicated the attitudes and behaviours required to be successful in that position. A set of competencies which had to be met for each position to be proficient was also identified.

DEVELOP RATING SCALES TO RATE THE IMPORTANCE OF EACH TASK AND THE FREQUENCY WITH WHICH IT IS PERFORMED Rating scales must be developed to rate the importance of each task as well as how often a task is performed. Tasks that are more important for the effective performance of a job as well as those that are frequently performed need to be identified. These ratings are important for determining the content of a training program and for identifying what employees must do in order to perform a job effectively.

SURVEY A SAMPLE OF JOB INCUMBENTS Job incumbents as well as supervisors and subject-matter experts who are familiar with the job must then provide task importance and frequency ratings. A questionnaire and a structured interview as well as observation of employees performing their jobs can be used to rate the importance of tasks and the frequency with which they are performed. An example of a survey is shown in Table 4.2.

ANALYZE AND INTERPRET THE INFORMATION Once the tasks have been identified and the importance and frequency ratings have been made, the information must be analyzed and interpreted. This usually involves some elementary

TABLE 4.2

Sample Task Analysis Survey

For each of the following areas of skill, knowledge, and ability, please make two ratings. Looking at your own job, assess the importance of the task by circling a number from 1 (not important) to 5 (very important). Then, consider your own level of competence in that task and rate it from 1 (not at all competent) to 5 (extremely competent).

Task	Importance	Competence
Knowledge: Ability to explain technical information to co-workers	1 2 3 4 5	1 2 3 4 5
Control: Ability to develop procedures to monitor and evaluate activities	1 2 3 4 5	1 2 3 4 5
Planning: Ability to schedule time, tasks, and activities efficiently	1 2 3 4 5	1 2 3 4 5
Coaching: Ability to provide verbal feedback to assist in the development of more effective ways of handling situations	1 2 3 4 5	1 2 3 4 5

statistical analyses to identify those tasks that are the most important and most frequently performed. Statistical software packages can assist in this task and can be used for more complex analyses. Comparisons between groups may reveal additional important information. Job incumbents may rate their own performance highly, while their managers may feel that employees are not working up to standard. New employees may feel that there are no barriers to optimum performance, while those with several years of service might perceive problems.

One study found that experienced police officers spent less time in traffic activities and more in non–crime-related tasks than recent recruits, validating the need to collect background information on respondents.[20] Conducting a training course without understanding the participants and the environment may result in less effective learning and transfer of skills to the workplace.

PROVIDE FEEDBACK ON THE RESULTS   Because employees and managers might not be aware of the need for training, it is important to provide small groups of managers and employees with feedback about the responses to task analysis. This feedback encourages employees to talk about areas of strengths and weaknesses and to propose solutions to problems. By owning the problem and generating the solution, employees may be more willing to change their behaviours and managers will be more likely to support a training program. To maintain employee support at Technocell Canada, the external assessors met with all employees individually to discuss the results of their evaluations, review their training needs, and discuss next steps.

The result of a task analysis should be information on the key task requirements for certain job categories and the associated job specifications (knowledge, skills, and abilities). This sets the stage for the design of training programs because it specifies the tasks that employees must be trained to perform as well as the knowledge and skills that they need to learn. At Technocell Canada, the result was a matrix of training needs along with training schedules and activities.

A limitation of a task analysis, however, is that it emphasizes observable behaviours rather than mental processes, and it assumes that the tasks are performed by individuals rather than groups. Many jobs today, however, involve mental processes and teamwork. In the following sections, we briefly describe two new approaches to task analysis that focus on mental processes and teamwork: cognitive task analysis and team task analysis.

COGNITIVE TASK ANALYSIS

The traditional approach to a task analysis focuses on behaviours rather than mental processes such as decision making. However, many jobs today involve complex mental tasks. How then does one conduct a task analysis for jobs that involve mental tasks that are not easy to observe? The answer is a cognitive task analysis.

A **cognitive task analysis** refers to a set of procedures that focuses on understanding the mental processes and skills required for performing a job.[21] It differs from the more conventional task analysis in that the focus is on the mental and cognitive aspects of a job rather than observable behaviours like typing or driving that are the focus of a traditional task analysis.

Cognitive task analysis describes mental and cognitive activities that are not directly observable, such as decision making, problem solving, pattern recognition, and situational assessment. A traditional task analysis focuses on what gets done, while a cognitive task analysis focuses more on the details of how tasks get done.

Although cognitive task analysis is useful for any job that has cognitive elements, it is especially useful in jobs that require an extensive knowledge base, involve complex judgments in dynamic and uncertain environments, and have high-stakes outcomes.[22] It can identify important elements of job performance such as decisions, cues, judgments, and perceptions that are important for effective job performance and are usually not identified by a traditional task analysis. As a result, important cognitive elements can then be incorporated into training and development programs. The most common approaches used to conduct a cognitive task analysis are interviews and observation.[23]

Cognitive task analysis
A set of procedures that focuses on understanding the mental processes and skills required for performing a job

TEAM TASK ANALYSIS

As indicated earlier, the traditional task analysis is not suited to the analysis of jobs that involve group work. However, many jobs today involve groups. Thus, a task analysis must be able to identify the knowledge and skills required to work in a group. In recent years, there has been an attempt to find ways to conduct a team task analysis.

A **team task analysis** is similar to a task analysis in that the tasks of the job must be identified. However, an assessment of team-based competencies (knowledge, skills, and attitudes) associated with the tasks is also required.

Team task analysis
An analysis of tasks as well as the team-based competencies (knowledge, skills, and attitudes) associated with the tasks

Teamwork competencies include things such as how to communicate, interact, and coordinate tasks effectively with team members. The main objective is to identity the key team competencies required for the tasks of the job, which will be used to write training objectives and to design a training program.[24]

There are a number of important differences between a traditional task analysis and a team task analysis. The main difference is that a team task analysis must identify the interdependencies of the job as well as the skills required for task coordination. Another difference is that a team task analysis must also identify the cognitive skills that are required for interacting in a team.

In general, a team task analysis should focus on the knowledge of task-specific goals; knowledge of task procedures, strategies, and timing; knowledge of team members' roles and responsibilities; interpositional knowledge; and knowledge of teamwork. A team task analysis can be conducted through the use of individual and group interviews, a review of existing documents, observation, questionnaires, and by examining past important events.[25]

PERSON ANALYSIS

Task analysis, cognitive task analysis, and team task analysis identify the tasks an employee must be able to perform and the knowledge, skills, and abilities required. However, they do not indicate how well employees are able to perform the tasks or whether they have the necessary knowledge, skills, and abilities. This information must be obtained from a person analysis, which is the third level of a needs analysis; it focuses on the person performing a job.

Person analysis

The process of studying employee behaviour to determine whether performance meets standards

Person analysis is the process of studying employee behaviour to determine whether performance meets the work standards. A standard is the desired level of performance—ideally the quantifiable output of a specific job. A person analysis examines how well an employee performs the critical tasks and their knowledge, skills, and abilities. The objective is to provide answers to these kinds of questions: How well does the employee perform the tasks? Who, within the organization, needs training? And what kind of training do they need? A three-step process should help answer these questions:

1. Define the desired performance.
2. Determine the gap between desired and actual performance.
3. Identify the obstacles to effective performance.

DEFINE THE DESIRED PERFORMANCE   The first step is to establish standards for performance. These norms will be important in the needs analysis, during training, and in evaluating the effectiveness of training. The idea is to determine the standard or the acceptable level of task performance. This enables a comparison of each employee's performance level against the standard in order to identify discrepancies and the need for training.

As indicated earlier, at Technocell Canada all job descriptions were revised and a skill set was identified for each job, including the attitudes and behaviours required to be successful in that position. In addition, a proficiency assessment was implemented for each position which identified a set of competencies that had to be met in order to be proficient in the job.

DETERMINE THE GAP BETWEEN DESIRED AND ACTUAL PERFORMANCE
In this step, a comparison is made between the standard level of performance and each employee's performance. Employee performance data can be obtained from performance appraisals, work samples, observations, self-assessments of competencies, and formal tests.

At Technocell Canada, the external firm surveyed, evaluated, and measured employees' essential skills as well as their attitudes and behaviours. They also tested the technical and generic competencies of employees at all levels.

IDENTIFY THE OBSTACLES TO EFFECTIVE PERFORMANCE   When a gap exists between the standard and an employee's performance, it is necessary to determine the cause or source of the gap. Performance problems can be the result of deficiencies in execution as well as deficiencies in knowledge, skills, or abilities. Sometimes, the gap is the result of the worker not knowing the standard, not receiving adequate feedback about performance relative to the standard, and not being rewarded for meeting the standard. A lack of goals and feedback is often the reason for substandard performance. At Technocell Canada, the main obstacle to effective performance was the lack of essential job skills specific to the décor paper industry.

Once the obstacles to performance have been identified, the next step in the needs analysis process is to determine solutions to performance problems and whether training is part of the solution to a performance problem. In the next section, we describe a framework for determining solutions to performance problems.

DETERMINING SOLUTIONS TO PERFORMANCE PROBLEMS

Table 4.3 lists a variety of potential barriers to effective performance. If you consider all the barriers to performance listed in Table 4.3, only the first two (lack of knowledge and skills) suggest a training solution. Clearly, the solution

TABLE 4.3

Barriers to Effective Performance

Human	Technical	Information	Structural
Lack of knowledge	Poor job design	Ill-defined goals/objectives	Overlapping roles and responsibilities
Lack of skills	Lack of tools/equipment	Lack of performance measurements	Lack of flexibility
Lack of motivation	Lack of standardized procedures	Raw data, not normative or comparative data	Lack of control systems
Counterproductive reward systems	Rapid change in technology	Resources sub-optimized	Organizational political climate
Group norms	Ineffective feedback	Informal leaders	

Source: Reprinted by permission International Society for Performance Improvement. Copyright 1990. *Performance Improvement*, Vol. 29, No. 10, www.ispi.org. R. Chevalier, "Analyzing performance discrepancies with Line Managers." P. 23.

to performance problems is not always going to be training. Saying "I've got a training problem" is like going to the doctor and saying you have an Aspirin problem.[26] Training, like Aspirin, is a solution, not a problem. How, then, do we determine whether training is the best solution to performance problems?

Figure 4.2 presents a flowchart developed by Mager and Pipe to assist in analyzing performance problems and determining solutions to performance problems. Let's review the steps in the flowchart.

When there is a performance problem, the manager must first describe the problem and decide whether it is worth spending either time or money to correct. Is it worth pursuing? For example, a manager might be irritated by employees who wear their hair shoulder-length, but having short hair will make absolutely no difference to productivity or other measures of performance. The exception might be in a manufacturing environment, where long hair would pose a safety hazard (solved easily by wearing a head covering). When a performance problem is important and worth pursuing the true analysis begins.

First, we consider some basic solutions or quick fixes. For example, are the work expectations, standards, and goals clear? Does the employee have adequate resources? Is the outcome of the employee's performance visible and known to the employee? If the answer to any of these questions is *No*, then the solution might involve clarifying expectations and standards, and setting goals; providing necessary resources; and/or providing performance feedback.

If the problem cannot be solved by these quick fixes, the analyst must then attempt to determine the cause of poor performance by asking a number of additional questions about the environment. For example: Is the person punished for desired performance? While this question seems odd, organizational life is full of examples of punishment for good performance. The assistant who works twice as hard as co-workers is punished by being given more work. The manager who stays within his/her budget is punished by having it slashed the following year. In these and other cases, behaviour that should be rewarded is actually punished. Such penalties and punishments for what is in effect good performance should be eliminated.

Sometimes undesirable performance is rewarded, such as when employees get paid for each unit produced. Under these circumstances you might find that employees are very good at producing lots of defective units. Of course, if they get paid for each unit produced they will continue to produce as many as they can regardless of quality. Thus, it is also important to ensure that undesirable behaviour is not rewarded. High volume should not be rewarded if quality is desired.

The next issue is whether or not rewards are linked to effective performance. Are there positive consequences for performing as desired? Sometimes when an employee does something good, the manager says nothing, on the assumption that the employee is being paid to do the work. Good performance that is not rewarded will eventually disappear. Sometimes, employees assume that their performance does not matter to anyone. When managers sit in their offices and fume over sloppy work but give no feedback to employees, or arrange no consequences for poor performance, the sloppy work will continue.

FIGURE 4.2

Mager and Pipe's Performance Analysis Flowchart for Determining Solutions to Performance Problems

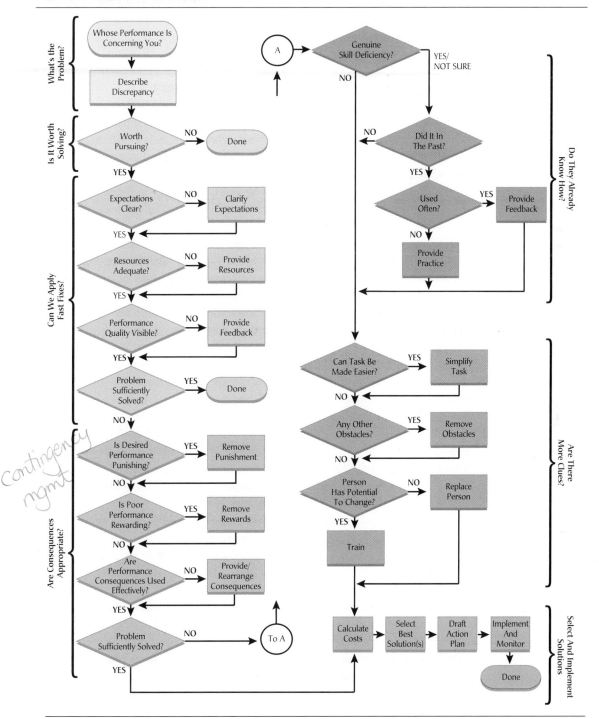

Source: © 1997, The Center for Effective Performance, Inc., Atlanta, Georgia. Adapted from *Analyzing Performance Problems, 3rd Edition* by Robert F. Mager & Peter Pipe. www.cepworldwide.com, 800-558-4237

Contingency management
Practices based on the belief that every act has a consequence and if the consequence is a reward then the act will be repeated

Make the Connection

Working with the human resource staff, managers need to develop contingency management programs that reward employees for good performance. **Contingency management** is grounded in the belief that every act has a consequence and if the consequence is a reward then the act will be repeated. If there is no consequence or the consequence is something negative or punishing, the action will not be repeated. If this sounds familiar to you it is because it has its basis in conditioning theory, which was described in Chapter 3. Recall that according to conditioning theory, learning is the result of reward and punishment contingencies that follow a response to a stimulus. Thus, contingency management represents an application of conditioning theory.

Imagine a classroom where the instructor never acknowledges students whose hands are raised to ask questions. Eventually, the students will learn to keep their hands down. Ensuring that no students ask questions can be done even faster by punishing those who ask questions with sarcastic or humiliating replies. Thus, the behaviour of hand raising or asking questions is eliminated, even when the instructor insists that he/she values classroom participation and discussion.

By analyzing rewards and punishments, managers might realize that they are asking for safe procedures but punishing those who slow down production. Quality might be the all-important word on the sign in the factory, but employees might be praised for quantity. The determination of what constitutes effective performance, and the management of reinforcement for achieving it, is a far more powerful instrument of change than a training program.

If contingency management does not solve the problem, the next step is to consider whether or not there is a genuine skill deficiency. The key to getting at this issue is to ask a critical question: *Could the employee perform the task if his or her life depended on it?* Could your employees produce six units per hour if their lives depended on it? If the answer is *Yes,* then the solution is not to teach them something they already know how to do. Rather, the solution is to provide an environment that allows and encourages them to do it.

Following the right side of Figure 4.2, consider whether the employee has ever performed the task and perhaps does not do it often and just needs some practice. Or perhaps the task is done frequently and the employee needs feedback. Thus, if an employee knows how to perform a task, it is important to consider practice and feedback before training.

To restate the critical question asked earlier: *Could the employee perform the task if his or her life depended on it?* If the answer is *Yes,* they could perform the task if their life depended on it, then say *No* to training. If the employee cannot do the task if his/her life depended on it, then consider a number of other changes before training.

Other solutions might be to lower expectations, simplify the task, or perhaps transfer the employee to a job that better fits his or her knowledge and skills. It is also important to remove any other obstacles in the environment. Training will not be a good solution when the environment is the cause of poor performance.

Environmental obstacles to effective performance might involve a lack of authority, inadequate tools or technology, conflicting responsibilities, work overload, and so on. Removing these obstacles in the work environment and replacing them with a more supportive environment might be the best solution to a performance problem.

The Trainer's Notebook 4.2

THE TRAINING SOLUTION CHECKLIST

Trainers are often asked to provide training to correct a performance problem. However, training is not always the best solution, and trainers should ask the following questions to determine whether training is an appropriate solution:

1. What are the performance (or operating) problems? Don't ask, "What is the training need?"

2. Describe the current performance and desired performance.

3. Could employees perform as desired if they had to? Did they ever perform as expected in the past?

4. If employees have performed as expected in the past, do they need practice, feedback, or specific and challenging goals?

5. If employees perform as you want them to, what are the consequences for them? Are they rewarded for good performance and goal accomplishment?

6. Are there any other reasons why employees might not be performing as desired?

7. If we find a solution to the performance problem, how will we know that the problem has been solved? What behaviours, skills, or results will change?

8. Is training the solution?

Finally, if there exists a genuine skill deficiency and the person does not have the potential to change, then replacing the person might be the only solution. If, however, the person does have the potential to change, then consider training as a potential solution.

In summary, the best way to determine whether training is an appropriate solution to performance problems is to first conduct a thorough needs analysis, identify performance obstacles, and then consider various solutions to a performance problem as shown in Figure 4.2. A checklist of the questions to ask to determine whether training is the best solution to performance problems is provided in The Trainer's Notebook 4.2, "The Training Solution Checklist." Table 4.4 provides a list of the conditions under which training is most likely to be the best solution to performance problems.

TABLE 4.4

Performance Problems and Training

Training is often the best solution to performance problems under the following conditions:

- The task is performed frequently
- The task is difficult
- Correct performance is critical
- The employee does not know how to perform as required (cannot do it)
- Performance expectations and goals are clear, and employees receive feedback on their performance
- There are (or will be) positive consequences for correct work behaviour; there are not negative consequences for performing as required
- Other solutions (such as coaching) are ineffective or too expensive (e.g., terminating employees and rehiring those with required skills)

NEEDS ANALYSIS METHODS

There are many methods and techniques for conducting a needs analysis. The methods tend to differ in terms of the quality and type of information obtained, as well as the time and cost of collecting it. This section describes some of the most common methods of needs analysis.

Table 4.5 describes nine basic needs analysis methods, along with their advantages and disadvantages. The nine methods are: observation, questionnaires, key consultation, print media, interviews, group discussion, tests, records and reports, and work samples.

Some methods of needs analysis are better than others in terms of response rate, quality, usefulness of the data, and cost. One study tested three techniques: closed-ended survey, open-ended survey, and focus groups. A combination of the closed-ended survey and focus-group interviews provided the most practical, useful, and cost-effective information.[27] The best method, however, depends on the time and money available, the experience of the analyst, and the nature of the responses.

TABLE 4.5		
Advantages and Disadvantages of Nine Basic Needs Analysis Methods		
Methods	**Advantages**	**Disadvantages**
Observation • Can be as technical as time–motion studies or as functionally or behaviourally specific as observing a new board or staff member interacting during a meeting. • May be as unstructured as walking through an agency's offices on the lookout for evidence of communication barriers. • Can be used normatively to distinguish between effective and ineffective behaviours, organizational structures, and/or process.	• Minimizes interruption of routine work flow or group activity. • Generates *in situ* data, highly relevant to the situation affected by response to identified training needs/interests. • (When combined with a feedback step) provides for important comparison checks between inferences of the observer and the respondent.	• Requires a highly skilled observer with both process and content knowledge (unlike an interviewer who needs, for the most part, only process skills). • Carries limitations that derive from being able to collect data only within the work setting (the other side of the first advantage listed in the preceding column). • Holds potential for respondents to perceive the observation activity as "spying."
Questionnaires • May be in the form of surveys or polls of a random or stratified sample of respondents, or an enumeration of an entire "population." • Can use a variety of question formats: open-ended, projective, forced-choice, priority-ranking. • Can take alternative forms such as Q-sorts, or slip-sorts, rating scales, either predesigned or self-generated by respondent(s).	• Can reach a large number of people in a short time. • Are relatively inexpensive. • Give opportunity for expression without fear of embarrassment.	• Make little provision for free expression of unanticipated responses. • Require substantial time (and technical skills, especially in survey model) for development of effective instruments. • Are of limited utility in getting at causes of problems or possible solutions.

- May be self-administered (by mail) under controlled or uncontrolled conditions, or may require the presence of an interpreter or assistant.

- Yield data easily summarized and reported.

- Suffer low return rates (mailed), grudging responses, or unintended and/or inappropriate respondents.

Key Consultation

- Secures information from those persons who, by virtue of their formal or informal standing, are in a good position to know what the training needs of a particular group are:
  a. board chairman

- Is relatively simple and inexpensive to conduct.

- Carries a built-in bias, since it is based on views of those who tend to see training needs from their own individual or organizational perspective.

- Permits input and interaction of a number of individuals, each with his or her own perspectives of the needs of the area, discipline, group, etc.

- May result in only a partial picture of training needs due to the typically nonrepresentative nature (in a statistical sense) of a key informant group.

  b. related service providers

- Establishes and strengthens lines of communication between participants in the process.

  c. members of professional associations
  d. individuals from the service population

Print Media

- Can include professional journals, legislative news/notes, industry "rags," trade magazines, in-house publications.

- Is an excellent source of information for uncovering and clarifying normative needs.

- Can be a problem when it comes to the data analysis and synthesis into a useable form (use of clipping service or key consultants can make this type of data more useable).

- Provides information that is current, if not forward-looking.
- Is readily available and is apt to have already been reviewed by the client group.

Interviews

- Can be formal or casual, structured or unstructured, or somewhere in between.
- May be used with a sample of a particular group (board, staff, committee) or conducted with everyone concerned.
- Can be done in person, by phone, at the work site, or away from it.

- Are adept at revealing feelings, causes of, and possible solutions to problems that the client is facing (or anticipates); provide maximum opportunity for the client to represent himself spontaneously on his own terms (especially when conducted in an open-ended, nondirective manner).

- Are usually time-consuming.

- Can be difficult to analyze and quantify results (especially from unstructured formats).

- Unless the interviewer is skilled, the client(s) can easily be made to feel self-conscious.

Group Discussion

- Resembles face-to-face interview technique, e.g., structured or unstructured, formal or informal, or somewhere in between.
- Can be focused on job (role) analysis, group problem analysis, group goal setting, or any number of group tasks or themes, e.g., "leadership training needs of the board."

- Permits on-the-spot synthesis of different viewpoints.

- Relies for success on a skilful interviewer who can generate data without making client(s) feel self-conscious, suspicious, etc.

- Builds support for the particular service response that is ultimately decided on.

- Is time-consuming (therefore initially expensive) both for the consultant and the agency.

TABLE 4.5   (Continued)

Methods	Advantages	Disadvantages
• Uses one or several of the familiar group facilitating techniques: brainstorming, nominal group process, force-fields, consensus rankings, organizational mirroring, simulation, and sculpting.	• Decreases client's "dependence response" toward the service provided since data analysis is (or can be) a shared function. • Helps participants to become better problem analysts, better listeners, etc.	• Can produce data that are difficult to synthesize and quantify (more a problem with the less structured techniques).
Tests • Are a hybridized form of questionnaire.	• Can be especially helpful in determining whether the cause of a recognized problem is a deficiency in knowledge or skill, or by elimination, attitude.	• The availability of a relatively small number of tests that are validated for a specific situation.
• Can be very functionally oriented (like observations) to test a board, staff, or committee member's proficiency. • May be used to sample learned ideas and facts. • Can be administered with or without the presence of an assistant.	• Results are easily quantifiable and comparable.	• Do not indicate whether measured knowledge and skills are actually being used in the on-the-job or "back home group" situation
Records, Reports • Can consist of organizational charts, planning documents, policy manuals, audits, and budget reports. • Employee records (grievance, turnover, accidents, etc.) • Include minutes of meetings, weekly/monthly program reports, memoranda, agency service records, program evaluation studies.	• Provide excellent clues to trouble spots. • Provide objective evidence of the results of problems within the agency or group. • Can be collected with a minimum of effort and interruption of work flow since they already exist at the work site.	• Causes of problems or possible solutions often do not show up. • Carry perspective that generally reflects the past situation rather than the current one (or recent changes). • Need a skilled data analyst if clear patterns and trends are to emerge from such technical and diffuse raw data.
Work Samples • Are similar to observation but in written form. • Can be products generated in the course of the organization's work, e.g., ad layouts, program proposals, market analyses, letters, training designs. • Written responses to a hypothetical but relevant case study provided by the consultant.	• Carry most of the advantage of records and reports data. • Are the organization's data (its own output).	• Case study method will take time away from actual work of the organization. • Need specialized content analysts. • Analyst's assessment of strengths/weaknesses disclosed by samples can be challenged as "too subjective."

Source: Adapted from: Stephen V. Steadham, "Learning to Select a Needs Assessment Strategy," *T+D*, Jan. 1980, Vol. 34 Issue 1, P. 58. American Society for Training and Development. Reprint/Adapted with permission of American Society for Training & Development.

Surveys are one of the most often used methods of needs analysis due to their low cost and the ability to collect information from large numbers of respondents. Some software firms have developed surveys that can be customized to include questions from broad-climate issues to specific job standards. Many firms have designed needs analysis software, some of which can be tailored to clients' needs. This technology allows HR staff to develop customized surveys quickly, and to analyze results by region, unit, and so on.

NEEDS ANALYSIS SOURCES

There are many sources of needs analysis information. Among the most important and often used are employees and managers as well as subject-matter experts who are familiar with a job. Some retail stores assess the competence of their sales staff through the use of professional shoppers who rate sales performance against established standards. A bank tests employee knowledge using a computer-based analysis, and then compares the results with supervisory rankings.[28]

In many cases, data on employees' performance and training needs are obtained from employees who rate their own performance and indicate their training needs. This is usually referred to as self-assessment. Self-assessment has both benefits and limitations. Employees might be more motivated to be trained if they have some input in deciding on their needs. However, expressions of needs include feelings or desires and may have no relation to performance.[29]

Several studies have found weak relationships between employees' self-assessment of performance and managerial assessments.[30] A review of 55 studies failed to find a strong relationship between self-evaluation of ability and other measures of performance.[31] However, a study at IBM demonstrated that employees can be trained in self-assessment by learning to break down a job into its component parts and to analyze skills.[32] This method has the added benefit of the employees accepting ownership of their development plans.

In summary, there are many methods and sources for conducting a needs analysis. Because of the differences in information provided by the various methods and sources, the best approach is usually one that includes multiple methods and sources. Surveying only job incumbents about their perceptions of their own abilities might not result in the most objective information about performance gaps. Employees may have wish lists for training that do not meet the needs of their units or that do not address their own weaknesses. Managers, too, should be asked for their performance evaluations. Those who have frequent interaction with job incumbents, such as customers and employees in other departments, should also be surveyed. These different perspectives will result in more accurate and complete information. It also enables analysts to distinguish between perceived needs (what training employees feel they need), demand needs (what managers request), and normative needs (training needed to meet industry, unit, or job comparative standards).

OBSTACLES TO NEEDS ANALYSIS

Now that you are familiar with the needs analysis process, you might be surprised to learn that many organizations do not conduct a thorough or complete needs analysis, at least not to the extent that they should.[33] Given the importance of needs analysis in the training process, you might wonder why this is the case.

As it turns out, there are a number of obstacles to conducting a formal needs analysis. Understanding these obstacles is important because if you are aware of them then you can also learn how to overcome them.

To begin with, trainers often claim that they are not rewarded for taking the time (and money) to conduct a needs analysis. Managers prefer action over analysis and they want to see training resources used to train employees. They may also feel that they can accurately identify training needs and that more analysis is a waste of time and money. Managers may even have their own agendas, such as rewarding employees by sending them to exotic locations for training, and therefore resist any attempt to identify training needs.

Time can also be a constraint. For example, new equipment might be arriving and it is easier to train all employees on all procedures instead of determining who needs training on which aspects of the new equipment. In fact, time is increasingly a concern and needs analysis can take months to complete, and yet employees need to be trained and back on the job in a matter of weeks or even days.

Ultimately, what everyone is most concerned about is getting people trained as soon as possible. Because needs analysis is costly and time consuming, it is often seen as an unnecessary constraint on resources, staff, and time. The cost, time, and effort necessary to perform a needs analysis means that many organizations will simply not do one.

However, conducting some data collection and analysis, rather than having no information, will almost always result in a better training program. It is therefore important for trainers to persuade management of the importance of conducting a needs analysis, and to ensure that it is included in the training budget. In addition, trainers need to be creative in finding ways to conduct a needs analysis within the constraints that exist in their organizations. To learn about some creative techniques that training experts can use to overcome needs analysis obstacles and to conduct a needs analysis in a timely manner, see The Trainer's Notebook 4.3, "How To Conduct a Just-in-Time Needs Analysis."

SUMMARY

This chapter described the needs analysis process. Three levels of needs analysis were discussed: organizational, task, and person analysis as well as cognitive task analysis and team task analysis. We also described the process of how to determine solutions to performance problems. Needs analysis methods and sources were also described as well as the obstacles to needs analysis. It should now be clear to you that a needs analysis is critical for determining the nature of performance problems and whether or not a training and development program is part of the solution to a performance problem. The importance of a needs analysis, however, does not end here. As you will see in the next chapter, a needs analysis is also necessary for writing training objectives and designing a training program.

The Trainer's Notebook 4.3

HOW TO CONDUCT A JUST-IN-TIME NEEDS ANALYSIS

- *Ask a series of questions.* When a manager demands a training course for employees, the trainer should start by asking questions related to the nature of the problem and its impact on the business. Some trainers even agree to conduct a training course, as per the manager's demand, and then renegotiate the assignment as information emerges from interviews with employees before the course. Managers may be receptive to the emerging data, recognizing the need to design solutions that solve the problem.
- *Use existing information.* Surveys, interviews, and observations are expensive data-collection methods. But most organizations keep customer complaint letters, grievance files, exit interviews, and sales data, which can be re-assessed for needs analysis purposes.
- *Speed up data collection.* Use the company intranet to survey employees. Start discussion groups around issues, concerns, and problems.
- *Link assessment and delivery.* Rather than conduct a lengthy needs analysis and then design a training program, some trainers attempt to join the two together, in small steps. For example, if there are star performers, bring them together in a forum with poorer performers to discuss effective techniques. The poorer performers not only are able to compare performance, but they learn how to improve at the same time.

Source: Adapted from: R. Zemke, "How to do a needs assessment when you think you don't have time," *Training*, Vol. 35 (3), Pp. 38–44, 1998.

Key Terms

cognitive task analysis p. 113
competency p. 110
contingency management p. 118
continuous learning culture p. 108
job description p. 110
needs analysis p. 101
organizational analysis p. 105

organizational climate p. 108
person analysis p. 114
resource analysis p. 107
task analysis p. 109
team task analysis p. 113
training transfer climate p. 108

Make the Connection

p. 101: the instructional systems design model is discussed in Chapter 1 on page 21

p. 106: strategic human resource management is discussed in Chapter 1 on page 19

p. 107: the external environment and training is discussed in Chapter 1 on page 17

p. 108: organizational culture is discussed in Chapter 1 on page 20

p. 118: conditioning theory is discussed in Chapter 3 on page 72

Web Links

The Banff Centre: **www.banffcentre.ca/departments/leadership/**

Boston Pizza: **www.bostonpizza.com**

Technocell Canada: **www.technocell.com**

Required Professional Capabilities (RPCs)

The following RPCs are relevant to material covered in this chapter. The RPC number represents the CCHRA number assigned to the RPC as presented on the CCHRA website. All of the RPCs can be found in the Body of Knowledge at **http://www.chrp.ca/rpc/body-of-knowledge/**

RPC 144: Aligns OLDT with business objectives and needs.

RPC 145: Determines the most effective learning and development initiatives required for organizational success

RPC 160: Conducts training needs assessments

160.02: Training and development needs analysis techniques (i.e., skill assessment strategies and levels of training needs analysis)

RPC 161: Recommends the most appropriate way to meet identified learning needs.

RPC 162: Establishes training priorities based on needs analysis.

Discussion Questions

1. Organizations often have data on file that can be used for the purposes of a needs analysis. Discuss the kinds of information that might exist in an organization and how it might be useful for an organizational, task, and/or person analysis.
2. If needs analysis information has not been used as the basis for the design and delivery of a training program, what are some of the reasons that organizations provide training? Are these good reasons for investing in training and development programs?
3. Discuss the reasons why organizations do not always conduct a needs analysis and what a trainer might do to overcome needs analysis obstacles. What are the implications of designing and implementing a training program without conducting a needs analysis?
4. Discuss the advantages and disadvantages of the different sources of needs analysis information. What sources are best for a person, task, and organizational needs analysis?
5. Discuss the process involved in determining solutions to performance problems. When is training likely to be a good solution? When is training not likely to be a good solution?

6. What is the difference between a training transfer climate and a continuous learning culture? Why should an organization obtain information about the transfer climate and learning culture before designing and implementing a training program?

7. What is the difference between a task analysis, a cognitive task analysis, and a team task analysis? Discuss when and how each type of needs analysis should be conducted.

8. Review the chapter-opening vignette on Technocell Canada and discuss the methods and sources used to conduct the needs analysis. Why do you think they used certain sources and methods, and how useful were they for determining training needs and solutions?

9. In recent years, the Toronto Transit Commission (TTC) has been criticized for its poor customer service and complaints about discourteous employees. Explain how you could use the needs analysis process (Figure 4.1) to address these problems. In other words, discuss the concern, its importance, consulting stakeholders, and collecting information. What can we learn about the TTC and its problems from the needs analysis process?

The Great Training Debate

1. Debate the following: Needs analysis is a waste of time. What is most important is getting people trained as soon as possible rather than wasting precious time to find out who needs training.

2. Debate the following: Training is costly and time consuming for organizations and should only be used after other less costly interventions have failed.

Exercises

In-Class

1. Think of a problem you had or were aware of at an organization that you worked for. Describe the problem and then use Mager and Pipe's flow diagram for determining solutions to performance problems (Figure 4.2) to determine the best solution. Consider each solution in the figure and explain why it would or would not be a good solution to the problem. Finally, if you know what the organization did about the problem, describe what it did and if it was an effective solution.

2. Consider your job and performance as a student and conduct each of the following types of needs analysis: a) task analysis, b) cognitive task analysis, c) team task analysis, and d) person analysis. Based on your results, indicate the critical tasks of a student as well as how well you perform each task, and on which tasks you need to improve your performance. What do you need to do to become a better student?

3. Find a partner in the class and take turns conducting a task analysis interview. Before beginning your interview, prepare a task analysis interview guide with questions that will help you identify tasks; rate their importance and frequency; and determine the task specifications (knowledge, skills,

and abilities). The interviewee can refer to a current or previous job when answering the interviewer's questions. Also consider the relevance of a cognitive task analysis and a team task analysis.

4. Table 4.5 describes nine different methods of needs analysis. Review each method and then explain what methods you think would be most appropriate for each of the following kinds of needs analysis: a) organizational analysis, b) task analysis, c) cognitive task analysis, d) team task analysis, and e) person analysis. Be sure to explain your reasoning as to why a particular method would be best for each type of needs analysis.

5. Recall a training program that you have attended as part of a current or previous job. To what extent do you think the program was based on an organizational, task, and person analysis? Try to relate specific aspects of the training program to each level of needs analysis. What performance problem was the training designed to address, and how effective was the program as a solution to the performance problem?

6. Imagine that you are a trainer in an organization that prides itself on providing employees with frequent opportunities for training. The president of the company has asked you to design and deliver a training program on team skills so that employees will be able to work in groups. He or she wants you to start training employees as soon as possible and does not want you to spend time and money conducting a needs analysis. He or she wants you to develop an action plan for the design and delivery of the program and present it in one week. How will you handle the needs analysis issue and what will you recommend? Prepare your presentation and present it to the class.

In-the-Field

1. To find out about the extent to which organizations conduct needs analyses, contact the human resources staff of an organization and request an interview about needs analysis. In particular, find out whether the staff conduct an organizational, task, and person analysis; the kinds of information they gather when they conduct each level of needs analysis; what methods and sources they use to gather the information; and what they do with the information and how it is used as part of the training and development process. If they do not conduct needs analyses, find out why and how they determine training needs. Students should come to class prepared to present the results of their interviews.

2. Find out how needs analysis was used to identify training needs within the plastics processing industry at: **http://www.cpsc-ccsp.ca/pages/reports_studies_surveys/Training-Needs-Analysis-Report.php**
Download the report, then read the executive summary and answer the following questions:
   a. What was the goal of the study?
   b. What methods of data collection were used in the study?
   c. What are some of the barriers and challenges to providing training? What are some solutions to training barriers?
   d. What are the main conclusions and recommendations of the study?

Case Incident

Beer School

As part of Labatt's training and development strategy, all non-unionized employees attend beer school to learn about the art of brewing and serving. In fact, the company plans to send 4,000 of its employees through the program, either at the employee pub at the company's head office in Toronto or at satellite locations across the country. Labatt employees who have completed beer school can talk knowledgeably about the fine points of beer with clients, friends, and family.

Questions

1. What information from a needs analysis (organizational, task, and person) might have suggested the need for employees to attend beer school?
2. Beer school is part of the company's training and development strategy. Do you think it is an example of strategic training and development? Explain your answer.

Source: T. Humber, "Serving up training." *Canadian HR Reporter*, Nov. 17, 2003, P. G1. Reprinted by permission of Canadian HR Reporter.

Case Study U-HAUL'S PERFORMANCE PROBLEM

In Ontario, the Highway Traffic Act has in place tough sanctions and fines that apply to commercial vehicles. However, there is an exemption in the Act that some refer to as a loophole. The exemption indicates that trucks rented for short-term personal use are not commercial vehicles and are therefore exempt from some of the sanctions and tough penalties. The exemption includes do-it-yourself movers who are the target market for U-Haul. In fact, U-Haul is the market leader among do-it-yourself truck rental companies.

If police feel that the general maintenance on a commercial truck is poor, they can issue a $20,000 fine against the trucking company. However, a company falling under the exemption such as a U-Haul truck is immune from fines and also from having its safety violations recorded against the company's provincial Commercial Vehicle Operating Record (CVOR).

In July 2005, the *Toronto Star* conducted an investigation of the safety of U-Haul vehicles. One of their conclusions was that if you rent a U-Haul, you have a 50–50 chance of getting a truck that will not pass a road safety check. The *Star* based its investigation on three sources: Ontario Provincial Police data that show police failed 109 of 220 U-Haul vehicles during roadside safety checks between 2002 and 2004; an independent test conducted by the Ontario Safety League of four U-Haul vehicles rented at random, in which all four failed a standard North American provincial and state commercial vehicle safety inspection that every truck must pass yearly to continue operating; and U-Haul's driving record, accessed through the Ontario Ministry of Transportation, which showed that 17 of 35 U-Haul vehicles failed safety inspections over a two-year period.

Some of the violations found by the Ontario Safety League included holes on the floor on the driver's side, axle sealant leaking onto brake pads, one flat tire, one bulging tire, one tire with a nail in it, power-steering fluid leaks, coolant leaks, oil leaks, and a loose king pin on the front axle. In all the trucks there were problems with the lights and signals.

Upon hearing of the Ontario Safety League investigation, U-Haul pulled the four vehicles in question out of service and hired independent mechanics to look at them. U-Haul agreed that three of the four trucks had "unacceptable" flaws and should not have been rented. The vice president of U-Haul Ontario said the company was dealing with the four locations that rented the four vehicles and stated that "employees and dealers are responsible for seeing that our equipment is in safe operating condition, scheduling repairs throughout the life of the vehicle."

U-Haul says it runs preventive maintenance inspections at 8,000 kilometres, 24,000 kilometres, and 48,000 kilometres that "meet or exceed the federal specifications." Prior to the rental of a vehicle, the employee or dealer is required to check for fuel leaks, engine-oil leaks and levels, power steering leaks and levels, transmission-oil levels, broken seals, anti-freeze levels, tires for treads and air pressure, and to make sure all lights and signals are working and that the windshield is clean. And after every rental, an employee is required to ask the renter if there are any problems that need to be fixed "before the next customer rents this truck" including braking problems, engine overheating, and electrical problems.

U-Haul operates 1,800 vehicles in Ontario. According to U-Haul's provincial operating record for the past two years, 35 trucks have had safety inspections and 17 failed. If not for the exemption, every OPP citation against U-Haul would be on record. During one weekend safety blitz, U-Haul vehicles failed six of eight inspections and were pulled off the road until they are repaired.

At the time, Harinder Takhar, Ontario's Minister of Transportation, said he would investigate closing the loophole in the Highway Traffic Act. "If we are having some evidence that there are safety concerns out there . . . I will get a full report. I'm asking the Ministry, what kind of problems did we find and if those problems are serious. I want to make sure the consumers are protected and safety is maintained on our highways." Police and the Ontario Safety League are calling for the loophole to be closed.

Following the *Toronto Star* investigation, the Ontario transportation ministry launched a province-wide investigation of the truck rental industry including surprise spot checks of U-Haul vehicles and other major truck rental companies and determined that U-Haul had the poorest safety record. This resulted in high-level meetings among MTO, OPP, and U-Haul executives. U-Haul subsequently promised that it would clean up its act and begin removing older vehicles from service, and more thoroughly check vehicles before they are rented.

However, in December of 2005 a 43-year-old Peterborough man died after being thrown from a U-Haul truck when it flipped over. And in September of 2006, the Ontario government told U-Haul that its licence would be suspended if it did not meet stringent safety benchmarks.

Sources: D. Dale, "U-Haul lags behind in safety," *Toronto Star*, P. A4, Aug. 30, 2007; K. McGran, "Traffic act loophole puts drivers at risk," *Toronto Star*, P. A1, July 4, 2005; K. McGran, "ABCs of do-it-yourself rentals," *Toronto Star*, P. A10, July 5, 2005; K. McGran, "U-Haul rentals to get spot checks," *Toronto Star*, P. A1, July 5, 2005; K. McGran, "U-Haul trails after trucks," *Toronto Star*, P. A10, July 5, 2005; K. McGran, K. "Province to probe truck rental industry," *Toronto Star*, P. A1, July 6, 2005; K. McGran, "Driver faults U-Haul in death," *Toronto Star*, P. A4, Dec. 5, 2005.

Questions

1. Assume that you have been hired by U-Haul to conduct a needs analysis. How can the needs analysis process (refer to Figure 4.1) and each level of needs analysis help you understand the safety problem and whether or not training should be part of the solution to solve it? Describe what you can learn from an organizational, task, and person analysis.
2. If you were to conduct a needs analysis at U-Haul, what methods and sources would you use? Be specific about why you would or would not use a particular method and source.
3. Using the Mager and Pipe flowchart in Figure 4.2, determine some possible solutions to the safety problem at U-Haul. Do you think that training is part of the solution? If so, who should be trained and what kind of training should they receive? What other solutions might be necessary to solve the safety problem?
4. What effect do you think the government's surprise spot checks and threat to suspend U-Haul's licence will have on U-Haul, its employees, and its training? Do you think these actions by the government are a good idea or should it be doing something else?
5. If the Ontario Government closes the loophole in the Highway Traffic Act, what effect do you think this will have on U-Haul? Will it have an effect on training? Explain your answer.

Flashback Questions

1. Refer to Figure 1.2 (The Context of Training and Development) and explain the role of training at U-Haul. What factors might affect the extent to which U-Haul provides training to its employees?
2. Refer to Figure 1.4 (The Instructional Systems Design Model of Training and Development) and describe how it could be used to design and deliver a training program for U-Haul employees. Be specific in terms of training objectives and content as well as how you would evaluate the training program.
3. Do you think U-Haul is a learning organization? Refer to the material in Chapter 2 about learning organizations and perform an audit on U-Haul to determine whether it is a learning organization (refer to the material on the five disciplines, principles of learning organizations, key dimensions, and learning culture). Based on your audit, what can you conclude about learning and training and development at U-Haul?

REFERENCES

1. Based on Scott, L. (2005, December). Awards for Excellence in Workplace Literacy, Medium Business Winner, 2005. *Upgrading employee skills to meet corporate standards—Technocell Canada, A Felix Schoeller Group Company.* Case Study December 2005 E/F. The Conference Board of Canada: Ottawa.

2. Salas, E., & Cannon-Bowers, J. A. (2001). The science of training: A decade of progress. *Annual Review of Psychology, 52,* 471–499.

3. Leigh, D., Watkins, R., Platt, W. A., & Kaufman, R. (2000). Alternate models of needs assessment: Selecting the right one for your organization. *Human Resource Development Quarterly, 11,* 87–93.

4. Kaufman, R. (1991). *Strategic planning plus: An organizational guide.* Glenview, IL: Scott Foreman Professional Books.

5. Leigh, D., Watkins, R., Platt, W. A., & Kaufman, R. (2000).

6. Mills, G. R., Pace, W., & Peterson, B. (1989). *Analysis in human resource training and organization development.* Reading, MA: Addison-Wesley.

7. Hall, B. (2003, February). The top training priorities for 2003. *Training, 40(2),* 38–42.

8. Carr, C. (1992, June). The three Rs of training. *Training, 29(6),* 60–61.

9. Goldstein, I. L. (1993). *Training in organizations* (3rd ed.). Pacific Grove, CA: Brooks/Cole.

10. Dobson, S. (2010, February 8). Constructive education. *Canadian HR Reporter, 23(3),* 14, 15.

11. Gibb-Clark, M. (2000, February 11). Employee training can backfire on firms: Survey. *The Globe and Mail,* B10.

12. Heller, M. (2005, March). State's measure could undercut damage awards. *Workforce Management, 84(3),* 21–22.

13. Johnson, G. (2004, October). The perfect storm. *Training, 41(10),* 38–49.

14. McLean, J. (September 14, 2011). Toronto cracks down on bad pools, *Toronto Star,* A3.

15. Scott, L. (2005, December).

16. Rouiller, J. Z., & Goldstein, I. L. (1993). The relationship between organizational transfer climate and positive transfer of training. *Human Resource Development Quarterly, 4,* 377–390.

17. Tracey, J. B, Tannenbaum, S. I., Kavanagh, M. J. (1995). Applying trained skills on the job: The importance of the work environment. *Journal of Applied Psychology, 80,* 239–252.

18. Parry, S. B. (1998). Just what is a competency? *Training, 35(6),* 58–64.

19. MacNamara, D. (1998, November 16). Learning contracts, competency profiles the new wave in executive development. *Canadian HR Reporter,* G8–G10.

20. Landey, F. J., & Vasey, J. (1991). Job analysis: The composition of SME samples. *Personnel Psychology, 44,* 27–50.

21. Salas, E., & Cannon-Bowers, J. A. (2001).

22. Brown, K. G., & Sitzmann, T. (2011). Training and employee development for improved performance. In S. Zedeck (Ed.), *Handbook of industrial and organizational psychology* (Vol. 2, pp. 469–503). Washington, DC: American Psychological Association.

23. DuBois, D. A. (2002). Leveraging hidden expertise: Why, when, and how to use cognitive task analysis. In K. Kraiger (Ed.), *Creating, implementing, and managing effective training and development: State-of-the-art lessons for practice* (pp. 80–114). San Francisco, CA: Jossey-Bass; Brown and Sitzmann, 2011.

24. Salas, E., Burke, C. S., & Cannon-Bowers, J. A. (2002). What we know about designing and delivering team training: Tips and guidelines. In K. Kraiger (Ed.), *Creating, implementing, and managing effective training and development: State-of-the-art lessons for practice* (pp. 234–259). San Francisco, CA: Jossey-Bass.

25. Salas, E., Burke, C. S., & Cannon-Bowers, J. A. (2002).

26. Mager, R. F., & Pipe, P. (1970). *Analyzing performance problems or you really oughta wanna*. Belmont, CA: Lear Siegler, Inc./Fearon.

27. Preskill, H. (1991). A comparison of data collection methods for assessing training needs. *Human Resource Development Quarterly, 2(2),* 143–156.

28. Tritsch, C. (1991, May). Assessing your training. *Human Resource Executive.*

29. Latham, G. P. (1988). Human resource training and development. *Annual Review of Psychology, 39,* 545–582.

30. McEnery, J., & McEnery, J. M. (1987). Self-rating in management training needs assessment: A neglected opportunity. *Journal of Occupational Psychology, 60,* 49–60. Staley, C. C., & Shockley-Zalaback, P. (1986). Communication proficiency and future training needs of the female professional: Self-assessment versus supervisors' evaluations. *Human Relations, 39,* 891–902.

31. Mabe, P. A., & West, S. G. (1982). Validity of self-evaluation of ability: A review and a meta-analysis. *Journal of Applied Psychology, 67,* 280–296.

32. Bardsely, C. A. (1987, April). Improving employee awareness of opportunity at IBM. *Personnel, 64(4),* 58–63.

33. Saari, L. M., Johnson, T. R., McLaughlin, S. D., & Zimmerle, D. M. (1988). A survey of management training and education practices in U.S. companies. *Personnel Psychology, 41(4),* 731–744.

Training Design

CHAPTER LEARNING OUTCOMES

After reading this chapter, you should be able to:

- define training objectives and describe the four elements and three components of them
- discuss the factors to consider when deciding to purchase or design a training program
- discuss the purpose of a request for proposal (RFP) and how to create an effective one
- describe how to determine the content of a training program
- describe the types of training methods and define blended training
- define practice and active practice and describe the conditions of practice before (pre-training interventions) and during training
- discuss the difference between routine expertise and adaptive expertise and the implications of each for training design
- define active learning and describe how to design training programs for active learning
- define error-management training and describe when it is most likely to be effective

ENBRIDGE

Enbridge transports and distributes energy across North America and employs more than 6,000 people. As part of its leadership development process, Enbridge used to send a few executives each year to take part in a three-week residential executive development program at the Queen's University School of Business in Kingston, Ontario.

In 2007, the Calgary-based oil and gas company began to clamp down on expenditures and Brian Rabinowitz, manager of leadership development with Enbridge, began looking for ways to maximize his training budget.

The training program at Queen's University had three components—leadership, operations, and marketing. In talking with executives who had participated in the program, Rabinowitz found they got most value out of the leadership component. "We decided we would get more value for the dollar if we took that money and did leadership education on a much broader scale," he said.

The company partnered with the school to develop a custom leadership program that could be delivered in-house, which saved on the residential costs. Instead of just five senior executives taking part in the program every year, the new program allowed Enbridge to offer leadership training to about 130 senior leaders just below the executive ranks.

The goal was to offer the two-phase program to four groups of employees over four years. The first phase, offered over three days, focused on general leadership skills, developing the individual as a leader, and how to build and lead teams. The second phase, also three days, focused on strategy execution, decision-making skills, negotiating skills, and building and maintaining collaborative relationships.

In addition to being able to provide training to more senior leaders, Enbridge's custom leadership program is improving employees' engagement and their perception of leadership, said Rabinowitz. Enbridge was recently named one of Canada's Top 100 Employers for 2012 for the eighth year in a row and has also been named one of the Ten Best Companies to Work for in Canada.[1]

Source: S. Klie, "Training important during recession," *Canadian HR Reporter*, June, 2009, P. 1. Reprinted by permission of Canadian HR Reporter; www.enbridge.com.

Enbridge is a good example of a company that invests a great deal of resources in the design of training and development programs. In order to stay competitive and ensure that employees have the knowledge and skills to perform their jobs, companies regularly need to design new training programs. In the case of Enbridge, it designed a customized leadership program to be delivered in-house to senior leaders.

In the previous chapter, we described the process of identifying training needs and determining solutions to performance problems. When it has been determined that training is part of the solution to performance problems, a training program must then be designed. **Training design** involves the process of preparing and planning events to facilitate learning.[2]

As shown in Table 5.1, the design of training and development programs involves many important decisions, such as whether to purchase a training program from a vendor or design it in-house; what content to include; what training methods to use; how to provide trainees with opportunities for practice; and what strategies to include to maximize the potential effects of practice on learning and retention. The starting point is writing training objectives.

Training design

The process of preparing and planning events to facilitate learning

TABLE 5.1
Training Design Activities
1. Write training objectives.
2. Decide to purchase or design a training program.
3. Create a request for proposal (RFP) to purchase training services and programs.
4. Determine the training content.
5. Decide on the training methods.
6. Incorporate active practice and conditions of practice into the training program.
7. Consider design elements for active learning if adaptive expertise is required.

TRAINING OBJECTIVES

A **training objective** is a statement of what trainees are expected to be able to do after a training program, and answers the question, "What should trainees be able to do at the end of a training program?" Put another way, an objective is the expected or intended outcome of training. Training objectives also describe the knowledge and skills to be acquired.

> **Training objective**
> A statement of what trainees are expected to be able to do after a training program

The emphasis of training is usually learning, on-the-job behaviour, and job performance. Learning involves the process of acquiring new knowledge, skills, and attitudes, while performance involves the use of these new skills, knowledge, and attitudes on the job. Training objectives usually refer to the acquisition of knowledge and/or skills as well as behaviour and performance on the job.

Training objectives are an important link between the needs analysis stage and the other stages of the training and development process. In addition to stating what employees will learn and be able to do following a training program, training objectives serve a number of purposes for trainees, trainers, and managers, which are described in Table 5.2. Thus, it is important to write training objectives prior to designing a training program.

Writing Training Objectives

Writing training objectives involves more than making lists of behaviour verbs such as "recognize" and "evaluate." The real skill is the ability to rework needs analysis information into performance outcomes. A training objective should contain four key elements of the desired outcome as follows:

1. *Who is to perform the desired behaviour?* Employees and managers are the easiest to identify. In a training situation more accurate descriptors might be "all first-level supervisors," "anyone conducting selection interviews," or "all employees with more than one month of experience." The trainer is not the "who," although it is tempting for some trainees to write, for example, that the trainer will present five hours of information on communication. The goal of the instructor is to maximize the efficiency with which all trainees achieve the specified objectives, not just present the information.[3]

TABLE 5.2

Purposes of Training Objectives

Training objectives serve a number of purposes for trainers, trainees, and managers.

Trainers

1. Trainees can be assessed prior to training to determine if they have mastered any of the objectives. Depending on the results, trainees can either omit certain sections of a training program or undertake additional training to master the prerequisites.
2. The selection of training content and methods is simplified by objectives. The choice of content and methods will be guided by the need to achieve certain objectives.
3. Learning objectives enable trainers to develop measures for evaluation and to determine how to evaluate a training program and how to calculate the benefits of a program.

Trainees

4. Objectives inform trainees of the goals of a training program and what they will be expected to learn and do at the end of a training program.
5. Objectives allow trainees to focus their energies on achieving specific goals, rather than waste energy on irrelevant tasks or on trying to figure out what is required of them.
6. Objectives communicate to employees that training is important and that they will be accountable for what they learn in training.

Managers

7. Objectives communicate to managers, professional groups, and others what the trainee is expected to have learned by the end of a training program and what the trainee should be able to do.
8. Management and supervisors know exactly what is expected of trainees and can reinforce and support newly trained knowledge and skills on the job.

---

2. *What is the actual behaviour to be employed to demonstrate mastery of the training content or objective?* Actions described by words like "type," "run," and "calculate" can be measured easily. Other mental activities such as comprehension and analysis can also be described in measurable ways.
3. *Where and when is the behaviour to be demonstrated and evaluated (i.e., under what conditions)?* These could include "during a 60-minute typing test," "on a ski hill with icy conditions," "when presented with a diagram," or "when asked to design a training session." The tools, equipment, information, and other source materials for training should be specified. Included in this list may be things the trainee may not use, such as calculators.
4. *What is the standard by which the behaviour will be judged?* Is the trainee expected to type 60 words per minute with fewer than three errors? Can the trainee list five out of six purposes for training objectives?

– How measured
– the criterion

An example of a training objective that includes the four elements is as follows:

> *The sales representative* (who) *will be able to make 10 calls a day to new customers* (what) *in the territory assigned* (where *and* when)*, and will be able to generate three (30 percent) sales worth at least $500 from these calls (*how *or* the criterion).

Training objectives should closely resemble the task analysis. For example, one task of the job of a receptionist could be: *The receptionist* (who) *sorts 100 pieces of incoming mail by categories of complaints, requests for information, and invoices* (what) *within 60 minutes, with less than one percent processing errors* (how). This could easily become a training objective. A training objective that reads like a job behaviour is more likely to be approved, learned, and used on the job.

When the four elements are included in a training objective, the final written objective should contain three key components:

1. *Performance:* What the trainee will be able to do after the training. In other words, what work behaviour the trainee will be able to display.
2. *Condition:* The tools, time, and situation under which the trainee is expected to perform the behaviour. In other words, where and when the behaviour will occur.
3. *Criterion:* The level of acceptable performance or the standard or criteria against which performance will be judged.

Representative workers should be involved in the development of the training objectives. A team consisting of the trainer, trainees, and their supervisors would be ideal.[4] At some point, the objectives should be reviewed with, and approved by, the management and the supervisors of the trainees.

In summary, a training objective contains an observable action with a measurable criterion outlining the conditions of performance. Once training objectives have been developed, the next step is to design a training program. However, at this point the organization has to decide whether a training program should be designed in-house by the HR or training staff or by an external consultant or vendor. This is known as the purchase-or-design decision and is described in the next section.

THE PURCHASE-OR-DESIGN DECISION

Once the training objectives have been developed, the organization faces a make-or-purchase decision. Many private training companies and consultants in Canada offer an extensive array of courses on general topics such as computer training and customer service.

In many cases, it is more economical for an organization to purchase these materials, packaged in a professional format, than to develop the materials themselves, which in many cases will be used only once or twice.

For example, most organizations do not design training courses in basic skills; rather, they form alliances with educational institutions, community colleges, or private organizations that specialize in developing and delivering basic skills training programs.[5] Recall from the chapter-opening vignette that Enbridge partnered with Queen's University School of Business to develop its leadership program.

Organizations are particularly likely to purchase training programs that do not require organization-specific content and are of a more generic nature. For example, organizations prefer to use outside consultants for sexual harassment training.[6]

The advantages of packaged programs are high quality, immediate delivery, ancillary services (tests, videos), the potential to customize the package to the organization, benefits from others' implementation experience, extensive testing, and often a lower price than internally developed programs.[7]

Training programs developed internally by an organization also have some advantages including security and confidentiality, use of the organization's language, incorporation of the organization's values, use of internal content expertise, understanding of the specific target audience and organization, and the pride and credibility of having a customized program.[8]

Let's now consider how an organization decides whether they should design a training program in-house or purchase one from a training vendor or consultant.

Purchase Decision Factors

Given the pros and cons of purchasing and designing a training program, what factors should be considered when making such a decision? One of the most important factors is the cost of each alternative. A cost–benefit analysis would be necessary to determine the best option. Recall that Enbridge decided to partner with the School of Business at Queen's university to develop a leadership program that would be delivered in-house and save on the residential costs. Other organizations such as Shoppers Drug Mart have also brought training programs in-house to save on residential costs.[9]

In addition to the cost of training, other factors should also be considered. For example, the human resource staff must have the time and expertise to design a training program. Designing a training program requires expertise in many areas such as training methods and principles and theories of learning. If the human resource department does not have this expertise in-house then it will need to purchase all or part of a training program. As well, developing a training program is time consuming. Unless a human resource department has a training function and training staff or is otherwise well staffed, it may not have the time to design training programs.

Time is also a factor in terms of how soon the organization wants to begin training. Given the amount of time required to design a new training program, if there is a need or desire to begin training as soon as possible then the organization will need to purchase a training program. In effect, the sooner the organization wants to begin training, the less likely there will be sufficient time to design a new training program.

Another important factor is the number of employees who need to be trained and the extent to which future employees will require training. If a relatively small number of employees require training, then it is probably not worthwhile to design a new training program. However, if a large number of employees need to receive training now and in the future then designing a new training program in-house makes more sense. Thus, to the extent that the training program will be used for many employees in both the short and the long term, a decision to design the program in-house is more likely.

Although we have been referring to the purchase of an entire training program, it is important to realize that an organization can purchase some training materials such as a video package or an entire training program that is specially designed for the organization. Organizations can also purchase off-the-shelf training programs which are already designed and contain all the materials required to deliver a training program. As well, a consultant could be hired to design and deliver a training program or it can be delivered by people within the organization. Recall that Enbridge partnered with Queen's University's School of Business to design a customized program that would then be delivered in-house. For another example, see Training Today 5.1, "Personal Development and Literacy Training at Vecima Networks."

When an organization decides to purchase a training program, it must choose a vendor or consultant who will design and/or deliver the program. This requires a request for proposal and is described in the next section.

Training Today 5.1

Personal Development and Literacy Training at Vecima Networks

Vecima Networks is a manufacturer of computer hardware and software that connects cable, wireless, and telephone networks to the computer for cable and telecom operators to optimize network efficiency. The company is a world-class designer and manufacturer of advanced broadband products.

Based in Victoria, Vecima employs approximately 600 people in western Canada. The industry is small, and there is not a large pool of trained people working in electronics manufacturing. As a result, Vecima has had to design its own training programs to train its 400 manufacturing workers. A few years ago the company partnered with the Saskatchewan Institute of Applied Science and Technology (SIAST) to create a journeyperson curriculum for electronic assembly.

Six full-time trainers provide new hires with 40 hours of training that covers a range of topics, from how to hold a soldering iron to how to inspect a circuit board. Once the base training is complete, new hires go on the line and are trained in a buddy system that brings their training to 60 hours.

However, based on supervisor feedback, the company realized that many issues employees have to deal with are not technical, and a non-technical training program on personal development and literacy was required. Rather than design the program in-house, Vecima went to the community for the expertise. It teamed up with READ Saskatoon and Radium Communication Centre, two not-for-profit agencies that have been offering similar training for years.

Vecima received a $50,000 grant from Saskatchewan-Canada Career and Employment Services. The funding was used to develop a 16.5-hour course that included employability skills such as communication, time management, business etiquette, decision making, and team building. Employees have a personal portfolio to keep a record of their training and their career goals.

The funding also covers the cost of the classroom training to be delivered by the community agencies. When the funding runs out, Vecima training staff will take over and give the course in-house.

Source: Anonymous, "CEOs talk: Training & development," *Canadian HR Reporter*, May 19, 2008, P. 11. Reprinted by permission of Canadian HR Reporter; www.vecima.com/careers.php

REQUEST FOR PROPOSAL (RFP)

Request for proposal (RFP)
A document that outlines to potential vendors and consultants an organization's training and project needs

The process of identifying and hiring a vendor or consultant begins with a **request for proposal (RFP)**, which is a document that outlines to potential vendors and consultants the organization's training and project needs. Vendors and consultants can then review the RFP and determine whether they are able to provide the products and services required by the organization and whether they should prepare a proposal and bid on the job. The organization must then evaluate the proposals it receives and choose a vendor that can provide the best solution and is also a good match for the organization.

A request for proposal should provide detailed information about the organization's training needs and the nature of the project and will often include the following sections:[10]

- Pre-qualification checklist.

- Detailed description of the opportunity.

- Description of the company and its culture.

- Scope of the project.

- Detailed statement of work.

- Detailed instructions on how to respond to the RFP.

- Schedule for the entire RFP and selection process with milestones.

- Basis of the award.

- Definition of the level of service required.

- Request for additional information.

- Confidentiality agreements.

Source: B. Chapman, "Creating the ideal RFP," *Training Magazine*, Vol. 41 (1), P. 40, 2004.

Creating an RFP is an important step in searching for a vendor because it requires the organization to describe its most critical training needs and the nature of the training solution required. This will help to ensure that the organization purchases what it really needs and also communicates the training needs and required project to stakeholders and potential vendors.

Failure to prepare a detailed RFP can result in an organization purchasing a program that it really does not need and at a much higher cost than necessary. There are many stories of companies that failed to create a good RFP and then purchased programs and systems that went well beyond what they really needed.[11] Thus, it is important that an organization determine the extent to which a vendor's products and services match its needs for training services and products. To learn more about how to write an effective RFP, see The Trainer's Notebook 5.1, "An Effective Request for Proposal (RFP)."

TRAINING CONTENT

If a decision has been made to design a training program, the next step is to determine the training content. Recall that in terms of training content, the Enbridge leadership program focused on general leadership skills, developing

The Trainer's Notebook 5.1

AN EFFECTIVE REQUEST FOR PROPOSAL (RFP)

Creating an effective RFP is a difficult and time-consuming task. However, a good RFP will ensure that an organization gets the training program and systems it needs from the right vendor at an appropriate cost. Here are eight things to consider when creating an RFP.

- *Have a clear vision of your overall learning strategy.* There must be a master strategy that is based on the primary needs of the various departments involved.
- *Create proper scope for the project.* Set a budget and align the most critical needs with project requirements.
- *Develop a vendor pre-qualification checklist.* Write a pre-qualification checklist before writing the RFP so that vendors can quickly decide if they can provide the required products and services. The checklist should have between 10 and 20 items and indicate the qualifications for the most critical needs.
- *Create a vendor scorecard.* Create a scorecard to grade vendors before writing the RFP to ensure that you request the necessary information in the RFP. The evaluators should rate each item on the scorecard on a scale of zero to five.
- *Use a template.* Use a template to create the RFP if one exists in the organization. Even one used for non-training purchases can be helpful in creating an RFP.
- *Don't overstate the positive or understate the negative.* Be candid about the project so vendors can adequately determine their suitability for it.
- *Design a request-for-information questionnaire.* The questionnaire should be designed to obtain additional information about a vendor's products, services, experience, and background. Most of the questions should be directly related to the needs of the project and the vendor's ability to provide a solution that meets the organization's needs.
- *Allow sufficient time for responses.* Provide at least two to three weeks for most standard projects so that vendors can carefully analyze the requirements and prepare a detailed response.

Source: B. Chapman, "How to create the ideal RFP," *Training Magazine*, Vol. 41 (1), P. 40, 2004.

the individual as a leader, and how to build and lead teams in the first phase. In the second phase, it focused on strategy execution, decision-making skills, negotiating skills, and building and maintaining collaborative relationships.

This is a crucial stage as the training content must be based on the training needs and objectives. As noted by Campbell, "By far the highest-priority question for designers, users, and investigators of training is, 'What is to be learned?' That is, what (specifically) should a training program try to accomplish, and what should the training content be?"[12]

To understand the importance of this, consider an organization that sells dental equipment and supplies. Although the company regularly offers new products, they do not sell very well. The reason for this is that the sales force concentrates on repeat sales of more common supplies and materials. There are a number of reasons why this might be the case. For example, the sales force might not be sufficiently informed about the new products or they might not have the skills required to sell them. Other reasons could be a lack of motivation or an attitude problem. Obviously, designing a training program to inform the sales force about the new products will not be very effective if what they are actually lacking are sales skills. Getting the content right is one of the most important stages in training design.

A trainer will have a good idea about the required training content from the needs analysis and training objectives. This is another reason why it is important to conduct a thorough needs analysis prior to designing a training program. As well, employees' current levels of knowledge and skills can be compared to the organization's desired levels as indicated by the performance goals or objectives. The gap between the two represents the organization's training needs and the required content of a training program.

According to Donald Kirkpatrick, trainers should ask themselves, "What topics should be presented to meet the needs and accomplish the objectives?"[13] In some cases, the required training is legislated, such as the Workplace Hazardous Materials Information System (WHMIS), which requires that workers in certain occupations receive training on the potential hazards of chemicals in the workplace and emergency procedures for the clean-up and disposal of a spill (see Chapter 13). In such cases, the content of training is specified in the legislation as well as in the requirements for employee certification.

Subject-matter expert (SME)

A person who is familiar with the knowledge, skills, and abilities required to perform a task or job

In other cases, it might be necessary to consult a **subject-matter expert (SME)** who is familiar with the knowledge, skills, and abilities required to perform a task or job and can specify the training content.[14] For example, to determine the content of a training program on sales techniques, one might consult with experienced salespersons, consultants, or managers. At BMO, they survey the highest-ranking commercial account managers in order to identify their best work habits and key drivers of success. Their responses are then incorporated into a guide that is given to all employees within the account management sales force.[15]

TRAINING METHODS

Once the training content has been determined, the next step is to decide what training methods will be used.[16] The topic of training methods is extensive and the next three chapters are devoted to it. For now we will present a brief introduction to this important part of training design.

Training methods can be arranged into a number of different categories such as active versus passive methods, one-way versus two-way communication, or informational versus experiential. For our purposes, we distinguish training methods in terms of where they take place, since this is a fairly tangible distinction. That is, some training methods take place on the job, such as coaching and performance aids, while others take place off the job in a classroom with an instructor. A third category includes methods that use technology to deliver training such as computer-based training and e-learning.

A variety of off-the-job and on-the-job training methods are described in Chapters 6 and 7, and technology-based training methods are described in Chapter 8. These methods differ in terms of their effectiveness for teaching different types of training content and learning outcomes. There are many training methods from which to choose and the choice will be influenced by the training objectives, time, money, and tradition.

Research shows that learning and retention are best achieved through the use of training methods that promote productive responses from trainees and actively engage trainees in learning the training material.[17] **Productive responses** are those in which the trainee actively uses the training content rather than passively watching, listening to, or imitating the trainer. In addition, it is believed that training methods that encourage active participation during training also enhance learning.[18]

Ultimately, the objectives of a training program and the training content should determine the most appropriate training methods. For many organizations, however, the best approach is a **blended training** approach that consists of a combination of classroom training, on-the-job training, and computer technology. According to the Conference Board of Canada, many Canadian organizations use a blend of training methods as opposed to a single training method.[19]

For example, at construction company EllisDon, employees receive classroom training, self-guided e-learning and webinars, lunch and learn programs, as well as on-the-job training.[20] Training for new hires at Best Buy includes role plays as well as on-the-job training and online training.[21]

ACTIVE PRACTICE

One of the most important ways that people learn and acquire new skills is through practice.[22] It is therefore important to incorporate practice into the design of a training program. But what exactly is practice?

Practice refers to physical or mental rehearsal of a task, skill, or knowledge in order to achieve some level of proficiency in performing the task or skill or demonstrating the knowledge.[23] There is a certain degree of truth to the adage "practice makes perfect." A student who practises answering exam questions will learn more than a student who just reads the textbook. A manager will probably learn more about interviewing by actually conducting a mock interview than by listening to a lecture on interviewing. In general, both adults and children learn through practice.

In training, we refer to **active practice**, which means that trainees are provided with opportunities to practise the task or use the knowledge being learned during training. Thus, training programs should include opportunities for active practice. The active engagement in learning training material has been shown to enhance and maximize learning.[24] However, the effectiveness of active practice depends on a number of conditions that occur before and during training.

In the following sections, we describe **conditions of practice** that can be implemented before (pre-training) and during training to enhance the effectiveness of active practice in order to maximize trainee learning, retention, and transfer. Table 5.3 summarizes the conditions of practice before and during training.

Productive responses
The trainee actively uses the training content rather than passively watching, listening to, or imitating the trainer

Blended training
The use of a combination of approaches to training such as classroom training, on-the-job training, and computer technology.

Practice
Physical or mental rehearsal of a task, skill, or knowledge in order to achieve some level of proficiency in performing the task or skill or demonstrating the knowledge

Active practice
Providing trainees with opportunities to practice performing a training task or using knowledge during training

Conditions of practice
Practice conditions that are implemented before and during training to enhance the effectiveness of active practice and maximize learning and retention

TABLE (5.3)

The Conditions of Practice

The following conditions of practice can be implemented before and during training to enhance the effectiveness of practice and maximize trainee learning and retention.

Pre-training interventions

1. *Attentional advice.* Providing trainees with information about the task process and general task strategies that can help them learn and perform a task.
2. *Metacognitive strategies.* Refers to ways in which trainees can be instructed to self-regulate their learning of a task.
3. *Advance organizers.* Activities that provide trainees with a structure or framework to help them assimilate and integrate information acquired during practice.
4. *Goal orientation.* The type of goal that is set during training (mastery or performance).
5. *Preparatory information.* Providing trainees with information about what they can expect to occur during practice sessions.
6. *Pre-practice briefs.* Sessions in which team members establish their roles and responsibilities and establish performance expectations prior to a team practice session.

Conditions of practice during training

1. *Massed or distributed practice.* Refers to how the segments of a training program are divided and whether the training is conducted in a single session or is divided into several sessions with breaks or rest periods between them.
2. *Whole or part learning.* Refers to whether the training material is learned and practised at one time or one part at a time.
3. *Overlearning.* Continued practice even after trainees have mastered a task so that the behaviour becomes automatic.
4. *Task sequencing.* Refers to dividing training material into an organized and logical sequence of sub-tasks.
5. *Feedback and knowledge of results.* Providing trainees with information and knowledge about their performance on a training task.

Pre-training Interventions

Pre-training interventions Activities or material provided before a training program or practice session to improve the potential for learning as well as the efficiency and effectiveness of practice during training.

Conditions of practice that can be implemented prior to a training program to prepare trainees for active practice are known as pre-training interventions. **Pre-training interventions** are activities or material that is provided before a training program or practice session to improve the potential for learning as well as the efficiency and effectiveness of practice during training.[25]

Pre-practice interventions prepare trainees for receiving and utilizing information.[26] In this section, we discuss six pre-training interventions: 1. attentional advice; 2. metacognitive strategies; 3. advance organizers; 4. goal orientation; 5. preparatory information; and 6. pre-practice briefs.

Attentional Advice

Attentional advice involves providing trainees with information about the task process and general task strategies that can help them learn to perform a task. Attentional advice helps to focus or direct trainees' attention on specific aspects of the training or practice session and task strategies and to assimilate the training material with existing knowledge. This can aid in learning and performing a task as well as generalizing what is learned in practice to other situations in which the strategies can be applied. Attentional advice has been found to have positive effects on cognitive learning, skill-based learning, and affective learning.[27]

Attentional advice
Providing trainees with information about the task process and general task strategies that can help them learn and perform a task

Metacognitive Strategies

Trainees can also benefit more from practice if they know how to regulate their learning through a process known as metacognition. **Metacognition** has been described as "thinking about one's thinking" and refers to a self-regulatory process that helps people guide their learning and performance. In this way, people can assess and adjust their progress and strategies while learning to perform a task. You might recall the discussion of learning outcomes in Chapter 3 where metacognition was described as a cognitive learning outcome.

Metacognition
A self-regulatory process that helps people guide their learning and performance

Metacognition consists of two primary functions: monitoring and control. *Monitoring* involves identifying the task, checking and evaluating one's progress, and predicting the outcomes of that progress. *Control* involves decisions about where to allocate one's resources, the specific steps to complete a task, the speed and intensity required to work on a task, and the prioritization of activities.[28]

Make the Connection

Metacognition involves the use of metacognitive activities or strategies to monitor one's progress during training. **Metacognitive strategies** (e.g., thinking out loud, self-diagnosing weaknesses, posing questions to yourself during practice, answering the question, "Why am I doing this?") refer to ways in which trainees can be instructed to self-regulate their learning of a task. Metacognitive strategies can be taught to trainees prior to training so they can self-regulate and guide their own learning and performance during practice sessions. This enables trainees to identify any problems they are having and the need to modify their learning strategies. The use of metacognitive strategies prior to training has been found to enhance cognitive, skill, and affective learning (especially self-efficacy).[29] To find out whether you use metacognitive strategies when learning, answer the questions in Table 5.4.

Metacognitive strategies
Refers to ways in which trainees can be instructed to self-regulate their learning of a task

Advance Organizers

Advance organizers refer to structures or frameworks to help trainees assimilate and integrate training content. In other words, they provide trainees with a structure or framework for organizing the training material and for integrating it with existing knowledge. Advance organizers can include outlines, text, diagrams, and graphic organizers. Research on advance organizers has found that they improve cognitive and skill-based learning and they are particularly useful for learning highly complex and factual material and for low-ability trainees.[30]

Advance organizers
Activities that provide trainees with a structure or framework to help them assimilate and integrate information acquired during practice

TABLE 5.4

Rate Your Metacognitive Activity

Metacognitive activity involves the use of strategies to monitor and control one's learning. More broadly, it has been described as "thinking about your thinking." In a study by Arron Schmidt and J. Kevin Ford, trainees who scored higher on this scale of metacognitive activity acquired more declarative knowledge, had higher levels of self-efficacy, and demonstrated superior training performance. To find out the extent to which you engage in metacognitive activities when learning, answer the following questions the next time you attend a training program or after your next class!

Answer each question using the following scale:

1 = Almost never

2 = Not very often

3 = Sometimes

4 = Often

5 = Almost always

1. During this class or training program, I made up questions to help focus on my learning.

2. During this class or training program, I asked myself questions to make sure I understood the things I had been trying to learn.

3. During this class or training program, I tried to change the way I learned in order to fit the demands of the situation or topic.

4. During this class or training program, I tried to think through each topic and decide what I am supposed to learn from it, rather than just jumping in without thinking.

5. During this class or training program, I tried to determine which things I didn't understand well and adjusted my learning strategies accordingly.

6. During this class or training program, I set goals for myself in order to direct my activities.

7. If I got confused during this class or training program, I made sure I sorted it out as soon as I could before moving on.

8. During this class or training program, I thought about how well my tactics for learning were working.

9. During this class or training program, I thought carefully about how well I had learned material I had previously studied.

10. During this class or training program, I thought about what skills needed the most practice.

11. During this class or training program, I tried to monitor closely the areas where I needed the most improvement.

12. During this class or training program, I thought about what things I needed to do to learn.

13. During this class or training program, I carefully selected what to focus on to improve on weaknesses I identified.

14. During this class or training program, I noticed where I made mistakes and focused on improving those areas.

15. When I practised a new skill in this class or training program, I monitored how well I was learning its requirements.

Source: A.M. Schmidt & J.K. Ford, "Learning within a learner control training environment: The interactive effects of goal orientation and metacognitive instruction on learning outcomes," *Personnel Psychology*, Vol. 56, Issue 2, Pp. 405–429, Blackwell Publishing, 2003.

Goal Orientation

Goal orientation refers to the type of goal that is set during training. You might recall the discussion in Chapter 3 about the two types of goal orientations: a mastery or learning goal orientation and a performance goal orientation. *Mastery goals* focus trainees' attention on the learning process while *performance goals* focus attention on the achievement of specific performance outcomes.

Goal orientation
The type of goal that is set during training (mastery goal or performance goal)

Make the Connection

When used as a pre-training intervention, goal orientation involves having trainees set a goal at the start of the training or prior to a practice session. Since mastery goals focus trainees' attention on the process of learning and skill acquisition, they tend to be more effective for learning. In fact, mastery goals have been found to be related to more metacognitive activity and to result in faster skill acquisition. Thus, mastery goals appear to be most effective for practice because they focus trainees' attention on learning the task rather than on their performance. However, research has found that both mastery and performance pre-training goals result in higher cognitive, skill-based, and affective learning. In other words, any pre-training goal is more effective than no goal at all. Nonetheless, mastery goals have been found to result in higher levels of skill-based and affective learning when compared to performance goals. Thus, it is recommended to encourage mastery goals as a pre-training intervention.[31]

Preparatory Information

Preparatory information involves providing trainees with information about what to expect during training and practice sessions (e.g., events and consequences). This enables trainees to prepare for events that will take place during practice and to develop strategies to overcome performance obstacles. This also helps to minimize the effects of stress. Thus, trainees provided with preparatory information are better prepared to learn and perform a task. They know what to expect and how to deal with performance obstacles.

Preparatory information
Providing trainees with information about what they can expect to occur during practice sessions so that they can develop strategies to overcome performance obstacles

Preparatory information is particularly useful for learning to perform stressful tasks where the ability to cope and overcome obstacles is critical for task performance. Research on the effects of preparatory information has found that it has positive effects on skill-based learning and affective learning (self-efficacy, attitudes toward training, and intention to use training material on the job).[32]

Pre-practice Briefs

The final example of a pre-training intervention is called pre-practice briefs and is specific to team training. **Pre-practice briefs** involve sessions in which team members establish their roles and responsibilities and performance expectations prior to a team practice session. Pre-practice briefs can improve team practice sessions especially for tasks that are fast-paced and stressful. Teams that have engaged in pre-practice briefs have been found to perform better than those that did not. This is partly due to better coordination and communication strategies.[33]

Pre-practice briefs
Sessions in which team members establish their roles and responsibilities and performance expectations prior to a team practice session

Conditions of Practice during Training

Practice conditions can also be implemented during training and include: 1. massed or distributed practice; 2. whole or part learning; 3. overlearning; 4. task sequencing; and 5. feedback and knowledge of results.

Massed versus Distributed Practice

Massed versus distributed practice has to do with how segments of a training program are divided. Massed practice, or cramming, is practice with virtually no rest periods, such as when the training is conducted in one single session instead of being divided into several sessions with breaks or rest periods between them. Distributed or spaced practice conditions include rest intervals during the practice session.

Students might argue that they can succeed on an exam for which they have crammed, but research shows that memory loss after cramming is greater than if a student had studied over several weeks. Furthermore, organizations would prefer that trainees retain material over many months, rather than just knowing it for the course, test, or simulation.

Research has shown that material that was learned under distributed practice is retained longer.[34] Furthermore, a review of research on practice conditions found that distributed practice sessions resulted in higher performance than massed practice conditions.[35] Thus, practice is more effective when practice periods are spread over time, rather than massed together. Trainers teaching a new skill, such as negotiation, could increase learning by spacing the training and practices over a week of two-hour sessions, rather than cramming it into an eight-hour day. Distributed practice is most effective for trainees with little or no experience, when the rest periods are shorter early on but longer later in training, and for learning motor skills.[36]

Whole versus Part Learning

Whole versus part learning has to do with whether all of the training material is learned and practised at one time or one part at a time.[37] For example, piano students often learn complex pieces one hand at a time. Research has found that the best strategy depends on the trainee and the nature of the task. Whole learning is more effective when the trainee has high intelligence, practice is distributed, the task organization of the training material is high, and task complexity is low. Generally speaking, when the task itself is composed of relatively clear and different parts or sub-tasks, it is best for trainees to learn and practise each part at a time and then perform all parts in one whole sequence. However, if the task itself is relatively simple and consists of a number of closely interrelated tasks, then a strategy of whole learning makes more sense.[38]

Overlearning

Overlearning refers to learning something until the behaviour becomes automatic. In other words, trainees are provided with continued opportunities for practice even after they have mastered the task.[39] It is an effective way to train people for emergency responses or for complex skills in which there is little time to think in a job situation. It is also important for skills that employees might not need to use very often on the job.

Overlearning helps ensure that task performance will become habitual or automatic. **Automaticity** refers to the performance of a skill to the point at which little attention from the brain is required to respond correctly.[40] You might recall the discussion of learning outcomes in Chapter 3 where automaticity was described as a skill-based learning outcome.

Massed versus distributed practice
Refers to how the segments of a training program are divided and whether the training is conducted in a single session (massed) or is divided into several sessions with breaks or rest periods between them (distributed)

Whole versus part learning
Refers to whether the training material is learned and practiced at one time or one part at a time

Overlearning
Continued practice even after trainees have mastered a task so that the behaviour becomes automatic

Automaticity
The performance of a skill to the point at which little attention from the brain is required to respond correctly

Make the
Connection

Overlearning has been found to be an effective method for improving retention for both cognitive and physical tasks. The greater the overlearning, the longer the resulting retention of the training material. However, the benefits of overlearning for retention are reduced by half after 19 days and to zero after five to six weeks. Thus, additional training is required after about three weeks to maintain the benefits of overlearning.[41]

Task Sequencing

Task sequencing has to do with the manner in which the learning tasks are organized and arranged. The basic idea is that learning can be improved by dividing the training material into an organized sequence of sub-tasks. The idea behind task sequencing was proposed by Robert Gagné, who argued that practice is not enough for learning to occur.[42] Rather, what is most important is that the distinct sub-tasks are identified and arranged in a logical sequence. In this manner, a trainee will learn each successive sub-task before the total task is performed. The trainee learns to perform each step or task in the proper order or sequence.

According to Gagné, what is most important in the design of a training program is the identification of the component tasks or sub-tasks and their arrangement into a meaningful and suitable sequence.[43]

Task sequencing
Dividing training material into an organized and logical sequence of sub-tasks

Feedback and Knowledge of Results

Feedback and knowledge of results involves providing trainees with feedback and information about their performance on a training task so that they know how they are performing. Research indicates that feedback is critical for learning for at least four reasons.[44] First, feedback lets trainees know whether or not they are effectively performing the training task. This enables them to correct mistakes and improve their performance. Second, positive feedback can help build confidence and strengthen trainees' self-efficacy. Third, positive feedback can be reinforcing and stimulate continued efforts and learning. And fourth, feedback is necessary for trainees to know whether they have attained their goals and whether they need to revise them or set new ones.

During training, feedback can be provided to guide trainees as they attempt new behaviours. This feedback should be designed to correct performance. When incorrect responses are given, the feedback should include the correct response. Negative feedback ("You failed to acknowledge the client's problem") will not be perceived as punishing if the source is knowledgeable, friendly, trustworthy, and powerful enough to affect outcomes like promotions.[45]

To be most effective, feedback should be accurate, specific, credible, timely, and positive.[46] In a study of the effect of feedback on the performance of hourly workers, Miller concluded that the relevance, specificity, timing, and accuracy of the feedback are the critical factors in mastery of learning.[47] Trainees receiving this type of feedback are more likely to adjust their responses toward the correct behaviour, more likely to be motivated to change, and more likely to set goals for improving or maintaining performance.[48] Some training methods such as computer-assisted instruction and behaviour modelling have feedback as an integral component. For guidelines on how to provide feedback, see The Trainer's Notebook 5.2, "How to Give Training Feedback."

Feedback or knowledge of results
Providing trainees with feedback and information about their performance on a training task

The Trainer's Notebook 5.2
HOW TO GIVE TRAINING FEEDBACK

Feedback during training can be very effective for learning and changing behaviour if the feedback is perceived as being constructive rather than critical. Here are some tips on how to give effective training feedback.

- *Timing.* Try to provide the feedback immediately after the behaviour or performance is observed.
- *Be specific.* Feedback works best when it is specific. Don't say, "You moved the arm wrong," but, "You have the arm tilted at 30 degrees."

- *Correct performance.* After discussing what was incorrectly done, provide guidance and demonstrate the correct performance ("You had the arm tilted at a 30-degree angle; you will find it easier or quicker to tilt it 90 degrees.")
- *Reinforce correct performance.* Provide positive feedback and reinforcement following correct performance: "Good, you have the right 90-degree angle."

ACTIVE LEARNING AND ADAPTIVE EXPERTISE

Routine expertise
The ability to reproduce specific behaviours in similar settings and situations

The traditional approach to learning is to train individuals to reproduce specific behaviours in similar settings and situations. This is known as **routine expertise** and many training programs are designed with this in mind. However, routine expertise is not always sufficient or effective for complex jobs that involve novel, unstructured, ill-defined, or changing task demands and work environments.

For complex jobs and tasks employees have to be able to adapt their knowledge and skills to different problems and situations. This requires much more than routine expertise; it requires **adaptive expertise**, which is the ability to use knowledge and skills across a range of tasks, settings, and situations. Adaptive expertise requires a much deeper understanding of a task because the learner has to understand how to use his/her knowledge and skills in new and novel situations. This has important implications for the design of training programs.[49]

Adaptive expertise
The ability to use knowledge and skills across a range of tasks, settings, and situations

Active learning
An approach to training that gives trainees control over their own learning experience

A key factor in training design for adaptive expertise is active learning. **Active learning** is an approach to training that gives trainees control over their learning so that they become active participants in their own learning experience. For example, the learner has responsibility for choosing learning activities and monitoring and judging progress. In contrast, traditional approaches to training give the trainer primary responsibility for learning decisions and limits trainees' control. Active learning promotes an *inductive* learning process in which the learner is provided with unstructured opportunities to discover rules, principles, and strategies for performing a task on their own through exploration and experimentation. Trainees make decisions about what to explore and when to seek guidance and this is what gives them control of and responsibility for their own learning. Traditional approaches to learning are *deductive* because they transmit knowledge to the learner and provide more guidance and structure on how and what to learn.[50]

Exploratory/discovery learning
Trainees are given the opportunity to explore and experiment with the training tasks to infer and learn the rules, principles, and strategies for effective task performance

But how do you design a training program for active learning? Several design elements have been identified including exploratory or discovery learning, error framing, and emotion control. **Exploratory/discovery learning** provides trainees with the opportunity to explore and experiment with training tasks to infer and learn the rules, principles, and strategies for effective task performance. By contrast, **proceduralized instruction** provides trainees with step-by-step instructions on how to perform a task and the rules, principles, and strategies for effective performance.[51]

Error framing involves encouraging trainees to make errors and to view errors as instrumental for learning. In other words, trainees are encouraged to make and learn from errors during practice. We discuss this in more detail in the next section on error-management training.

Emotion control is a strategy to help trainees control their emotions during training, which is important given that active learning can provoke stress and anxiety that can hinder learning and performance. For example, trainees might be instructed to manage negative emotions by increasing positive thoughts and self-statements and avoiding negative ones.[52]

Research on active learning has found that it is effective for developing adaptive expertise. A key reason for the effectiveness of active learning is the development and use of metacognitive strategies. Recall that metacognitive strategies refer to ways in which trainees self-regulate their learning. Research has found that active learning stimulates metacognitive activities to a greater extent than proceduralized instruction and helps to explain the effects of active learning strategies on adaptive learning and performance.[53] Let's now take a closer look at error-management training.

ERROR-MANAGEMENT TRAINING (EMT)

In the previous section, we described training design elements that can be used to promote active learning. One of the design elements encourages trainees to make errors and to view them as instrumental for learning. At first, this might seem like a ridiculous idea. After all, people usually try to avoid errors because they can be frustrating and lead to anxiety, anger, and despair. But think again. Isn't it the case that errors and mistakes happen quite frequently during the learning process? If so, then, why not design training programs so that trainees make errors and learn from them?

First, it is helpful to understand why errors might be important for learning. According to Michael Frese and his colleagues, errors are a source of negative feedback that can actually have a positive and informative function in training. In fact, they argue that negative feedback is a necessary prerequisite for learning. Thus, rather than being avoided, errors should be incorporated into the training process, a method known as error-management training.[54]

Error-management training (EMT) involves explicitly encouraging trainees to make errors during training and to learn from them. This can be done by providing trainees with only basic information or minimal instructions about how to perform a task. As a result, trainees need to try out different approaches when practising a task, which means that they will make a number of errors along the way. In contrast, when the training is **error-avoidant**, it is highly structured and trainees are given detailed step-by-step instructions on how to perform a task so they are less likely to make errors. And if they do make an error, the trainer intervenes and corrects them.[55]

Proceduralized instruction
Trainees are provided with step-by-step instructions on how to perform a task and the rules, principles, and strategies for effective performance.

Emotion control
A strategy to help trainees control their emotions during active learning

Error-management training
Training that explicitly encourages trainees to make errors during training and to learn from them

Error-avoidant training
Training that is highly structured and provides trainees with detailed step-by-step instructions on how to perform a task so they are less likely to make errors

There are two key characteristics of EMT. First, trainees are provided with only basic training-relevant information and introduced to various problems which they are told to explore and solve on their own (active exploration). Thus, trainees are provided with little guidance and active exploration is encouraged. Because they have insufficient information they are very likely to make errors.

Second, because making errors can be frustrating, trainees are told to expect errors and to frame them positively. Thus, making errors is encouraged during training. This is known as **error-management instructions** and involves instructions that errors are a necessary and natural part of learning. Trainees are told that they should make errors and learn from them. Error-management instructions reduce the negative effects of errors and enable trainees to be open to learning from error feedback.[56] For example, when learning a new task, instructors might repeat statements such as "The more errors you make, the more you learn" and "You have made an error? Great! Because now you can learn something new!"[57]

Error training can improve learning and performance for a number of reasons. First, errors inform trainees of knowledge and skills that need improvement and what they should focus on. Second, errors force trainees to develop thoughtful strategies and a deeper processing of information, which leads to mental models of how to perform a task. Third, errors can lead to greater practice because trainees tend to practise those things they have not yet mastered. Fourth, errors force trainees to learn "error-recovery strategies," which means they are better able to respond to and correct errors, which can lead to improved performance. And fifth, errors lead to greater exploration because people often want to find out why an error has occurred. Thus, errors are likely to result in greater learning and therefore better performance of the learned task.[58]

Several studies have found that EMT is more effective than error-avoidant training for learning and performance. However, some studies have found that EMT is not more effective than error-avoidant training and is, in some cases, less effective. To better understand this discrepancy in results, Nina Keith and Michael Frese reviewed all of the studies that have compared EMT to error-avoidant training. They found that overall EMT results in more positive training outcomes than training that does not encourage errors. However, they also found that EMT is especially effective in certain circumstances.[59]

In what circumstances is EMT most effective? First, EMT is effective for post-training performance but not performance during training. This should not be surprising because it is only after training that the benefits of EMT are realized. During training trainees are involved in active exploration and are making errors along the way. Second, EMT was found to be particularly effective on the performance of tasks that require adaptive expertise or what are known as **adaptive tasks** (tasks that differ from those worked on during training and require different solutions) than for tasks that require routine expertise or **analogical tasks** (tasks that are similar to those worked on during training). This follows from the previous discussion of active learning. Recall that EMT is an element of active learning and so it follows that it is more effective for tasks that require adaptive expertise.[60]

Finally, EMT was most effective when it was accompanied by error-management instructions. In other words, it is the combination of active exploration and error-management instructions that results in more positive training outcomes.[61] Interestingly, a recent study found that error-management instructions can

Error-management instructions
Statements that errors are a necessary and natural part of learning and emphasize the positive function of errors

Adaptive tasks
Tasks that differ from those worked on during training and require different solutions

Analogical tasks
Tasks that are similar to those worked on during training

also benefit trainees even when the training is error avoidant. In particular, error-management instructions improved the performance of older trainees as well as younger trainees with lower cognitive ability when the training was highly structured and error avoidant. Thus, error-management instructions can be beneficial with or without error-management training, especially for learning adaptive tasks.[62]

MODEL OF TRAINING EFFECTIVENESS— TRAINING DESIGN

Before concluding this chapter, let's return to the model of training effectiveness that was introduced in Chapter 3. Recall that the model shows that in addition to training, trainees' cognitive ability, training motivation, self-efficacy, personality, and attitudes influence trainee learning and retention; learning and retention lead to individual behaviour and performance; and individual behaviour and performance influences organizational effectiveness.

Based on what you have learned in this chapter, we can add training design to the model. Recall that active practice and practice conditions before training and during training influence learning and retention. As well, design elements that promote active learning (exploratory/discovery learning, emotion control, and EMT) are necessary to develop adaptive expertise.

Figure 5.1 shows a revised model of training effectiveness in which training, trainee characteristics, and training design influence learning and retention. Thus, you know that learning and retention are also influenced by how a training program is designed.

FIGURE 5.1

Model of Training Effectiveness

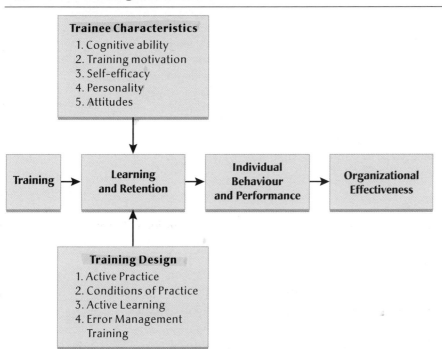

SUMMARY

This chapter described the main activities involved in the design of a training program. First, we described the elements and components of training objectives. Next, we discussed the decision to purchase or design a training program and the factors to consider when making a purchase-or-design decision. The importance of a request for proposal (RFP) was also discussed. We then described the factors involved in the design of a training program including training content, methods, active practice, and the conditions of practice. This was followed by a discussion of active learning and design elements that promote adaptive expertise with particular emphasis on error-management training.

One of the most important design factors discussed in this chapter was training methods. As you will see in the next three chapters, there are many types of off-the-job (Chapter 6) and on-the-job training methods (Chapter 7) as well as many forms of technology-based training (Chapter 8).

Key Terms

active learning p. 152
active practice p. 145
adaptive expertise p. 152
adaptive tasks p. 154
advance organizers p. 147
analogical tasks p. 154
attentional advice p. 147
automaticity p. 150
blended training p. 145
conditions of practice p. 145
emotion control p. 153
error-avoidant training p. 153
error-management instructions p. 154
error-management training (EMT) p. 153
exploratory/discovery learning p. 152
feedback or knowledge of results p. 151
goal orientation p. 149
massed versus distributed
    practice p. 150

metacognition p. 147
metacognitive strategies p. 147
overlearning p. 150
practice p. 145
preparatory information p. 149
pre-practice briefs p. 149
pre-training interventions p. 146
proceduralized instruction p. 153
productive responses p. 145
request for proposal (RFP) p. 142
routine expertise p. 152
subject-matter expert (SME) p. 144
task sequencing p. 151
training design p. 136
training objective p. 137
whole versus part learning p. 150

Make the Connection

p. 147: metacognition is discussed in Chapter 3 on page 66
p. 149: goal orientation is discussed in Chapter 3 on page 83
p. 150: automaticity is discussed in Chapter 3 on page 67

Web Links

BMO Financial: **www.bmo.com**

Enbridge: **www.enbridge.com**

Vecima Networks: **www.vecima.com**

Required Professional Capabilities (RPCs)

The following RPCs are relevant to material covered in this chapter. The RPC number represents the CCHRA number assigned to the RPC as presented on the CCHRA website. All of the RPCs can be found in the Body of Knowledge at **http://www.chrp.ca/rpc/body-of-knowledge/**

RPC 161: Recommends the most appropriate way to meet identified learning needs.

161.02: Principles of effective training, learning and organizational development

161.04: Training and development program design and administration

RPC 166: Develops and reviews requests for proposals (RFP) and reviews submissions by third parties.

166.01: RFP preparation

RPC 168: Participates in course design and selection and delivery of learning materials.

168.02: Instructional design and delivery

168.07: Effective learning objectives

Discussion Questions

1. Discuss the purpose of training objectives for trainees, trainers, and managers. How would trainees, trainers, and managers be affected if a training program did not have training objectives?
2. What factors should an organization consider when deciding to purchase or design a training program?
3. What are the advantages and disadvantages of purchasing a training program and designing a training program in-house?
4. Why is it important to include active practice in a training program? Give an example of how active practice was used in a training program you have attended.
5. Discuss the conditions of practice before (pre-training interventions) and during training and how they can improve learning and retention.
6. Explain how error-management training works and the circumstances in which it is most likely to be effective. When should error-management training be used?

7. Explain what a request for proposal (RFP) is and why an organization should carefully write one before purchasing a training program.
8. What are the main sections of a request for proposal (RFP) and what are the steps involved in creating an effective one?
9. What is the difference between active practice and active learning and what are the implications of each for the design of training programs?
10. Explain how you would design each of the following training programs: a) error avoidant, and b) EMT (error-management training). Describe the training program and how it would proceed if it was designed to be error avoidant and if it was designed in terms of EMT. Be sure to describe the task that trainees are learning to perform.
11. Why do you think error-management instructions have been found to be beneficial even for structured training that is error-avoidant? Why is this especially the case for older trainees as well as younger trainees with lower cognitive ability?

The Great Training Debate

1. Debate the following: Practice makes perfect and enough practice will always lead to learning and retention.
2. Debate the following: Errors are frustrating and upsetting to trainees and should be avoided in training.

Exercises

In-Class

1. Think of the best and worst training experience you have ever had. For each one, indicate the purpose of the training, the objectives, content, and methods. Then, using the material presented in this chapter, make a list of all the reasons why you feel that it was the best or worst training experience you have ever had. Based on your lists, what are some of the things that make a training program effective?
2. If you have a driver's licence then you probably remember what it was like to learn to drive. Chances are you stepped into a car with a friend or family member who told you what to do. And if you have ever taught someone how to drive, you probably did the same thing. Did you remember to tell them everything they needed to know? What did you tell them to do first? Could you have done a better job teaching them to drive? Refer to the section of this chapter on task sequencing. Recall that task sequencing involves dividing a task into its component parts or sub-tasks, and then ordering them into a meaningful or logical sequence. Now try to design a driver training program based on task sequencing. In other words, make a list of all of the sub-tasks involved in driving a car and then organize them into a logical sequence for the purpose of teaching somebody how to drive.

3. Have you ever wondered what your instructor does to prepare for a class? To find out, choose one of your classes and try to describe each of the following:

   - the objectives of the class

   - the content of the class

   - the training methods used

   - opportunities for active practice

   - conditions of practice

   - active learning

   Based on your description, how well was the class designed? How effective was it for your learning? How can it be improved?

4. Recall a training program that you attended in a previous or current job. Describe the objectives and content of the program and any opportunities for active practice. What did you practise and how helpful was it for your learning and retention? Describe the extent to which any of the conditions of practice were used either before or during the training program and how they affected your learning and retention. What changes would you recommend to improve learning and retention?

5. Identify a skill that you would like to acquire. Some examples might be to use a particular software package or perhaps to improve your written or oral presentation skills. Now develop training objectives for a training program on the skill that you have chosen, using the five elements and three components of training objectives described in the chapter. Exchange your objectives with another student and evaluate each other's objectives in terms of the criteria outlined in the chapter for writing training objectives.

6. Read the following training objectives and identify what is wrong with them. Then rewrite them so that they conform to the elements and components of training objectives described in the chapter.

   - The trainer will spend 30 minutes discussing time-management tips.

   - The trainees will be able to manage their time more effectively.

   - The purpose of the seminar is to teach time-management techniques.

   - After attending the course, employees will be able to make lists and put letters beside the items on the list, enabling them to manage time more effectively.

7. Recall a training program that you attended in a previous or current job. Describe the objectives and content of the program and the extent to which errors were part of the program. Did you make any errors while learning and what effect did it have on your learning and the training experience? If you were to redesign this training program, how would you change it so that it included error-management training?

In-the-Field

1. Contact the human resources department of an organization and request a meeting with a department member whom you can interview about the organization's training programs. Prepare some questions so that you can learn about each of the following design factors in terms of a particular training program that the organization has implemented:

   - Was the training program designed by the organization or purchased? What were the reasons for designing or purchasing the program?

   - If the training program was purchased, was a request for proposal (RFP) used and what was included in it?

   - What is the content of the training program and how was it developed?

   - What training methods were used and why?

   - Was active practice designed into the training program and what kind of practice opportunities did trainees have?

   - To what extent were the conditions of practice listed in Table 5.3 incorporated into the training program?

   Based on the information you have acquired, conduct an evaluation with respect to how effectively you think the training program was designed and list some recommendations for improvement.

2. To find out about the kinds of training programs that can be purchased, go to Industry Canada at **www.collectionscanada.gc.ca/ webarchives/20060226034454/http://strategis.ic.gc.ca/epic/ internet/incts-scf.nsf/en/h_sl00010e.html.**

   Answer the following questions:
   a. What can you find out on this site about training suppliers?
   b. What are the different areas of training and types of training providers?
   c. Does your college or university provide training and, if so, what kind of training?

3. To find out about how to choose a training supplier in Canada, go to Industry Canada at **www.collectionscanada.gc.ca/ webarchives/20060201093624/http://strategis.ic.gc.ca/epic/ internet/incts-scf.nsf/en/h_sl00011e.html.**

   Answer the following questions:
   a. When choosing a training supplier, what questions should you ask and what issues should you consider?
   b. What does this site tell you about choosing a training provider? How can you have a successful training experience?

▌ Case Incident

Play to Win at Dofasco

Hamilton-based steel manufacturer Dofasco has a training program that it calls "play to win." Nearly every new hire participates in the program as an initiation to the company which takes place at a resort. Employees go to the resort in groups of between 50 and 70 and there are about four trips a year to the resort.

Over 7,000 employees have taken part in the program since it was launched in 1993. The intent is to get a better understanding of the organization and the things it is trying to accomplish. The program focuses on issues facing the company, what the company does, and who the company's customers are. The program is placed within the context that nobody can do it alone and that they need to look out for each other. Employees also take part in a variety of unique exercises such a rope course and climbing up a pole. In addition, new hires get a chance to sit down with senior management and participate in a question-and-answer session. The context is that when you are back at the company you can help out. The program teaches respect and concern for others, that strength is our people, and what those things mean.

Questions

1. What are the training objectives of Dofasco's play-to-win training program and what purpose do they serve for employees and managers?
2. Discuss the training content and methods used in the training program. What is the nature of the content and what types of methods are used and why?

Source: T. Humber, "Serving up training," *Canadian HR Reporter*, Nov. 17, 2003, P. G1. Reprinted by permission of Canadian HR Reporter.

Case Study ▌ TRAINING THE SALES FORCE

Sales at a large telecommunications company were down for the third quarter. Management reviewed several strategies to improve sales and concluded that one solution would be to improve training for the large, dispersed sales force.

For the sake of expediency, the training department began using a needs analysis it had conducted several years before as a basis to develop enhanced training. Their plan was first to update the original needs analysis, and then to develop new training strategies on the basis of what they found. They also began investigating new training technologies as a possible means to reducing training delivery costs. However, management was so intent on doing something quickly that the training department was ultimately pressured into purchasing a generic, off-the-shelf training package from a local vendor.

One of the features of the package that appealed to management was that the course could be delivered over the Web, saving the time and expense of having the sales force travel to the main office to receive the training. Hence, even though the package was costly to purchase, the company believed that it was a bargain compared to the expense of developing a new package in-house and delivering it in person to the sales force.

Six months after the training had been delivered, sales were still declining. Management turned to the training department for answers. Because no measures of training performance had been collected, the training department had little information upon which to base its diagnosis. For lack of a better idea, members of the training department began questioning the sales force to see if they could determine why the training was not working.

Among other things, the sales people reported that the training was slow and boring, and that it did not teach them any new sales techniques. They also complained that, without an instructor, it was impossible to get clarification on things they did not understand. Moreover, they reported that they believed that sales were off not because they needed training in basic sales techniques, but because so many new products were being introduced that they could not keep up. In fact, several of the sales people requested meetings with design engineers just so they could get updated product information.

The training department took these findings back to management and requested that they be allowed to design a new training package, beginning with an updated needs analysis to determine the real training deficiencies.

Source: E. Salas & J.A. Cannon-Bowers, "Design training systematically," In E.A. Locke (Ed.), *Handbook of principles of organizational behavior*, Oxford, UK. Blackwell Publishers Ltd. 2000, Pp. 56–57. Case questions prepared by Alan Saks.

Questions

1. What were the objectives of the training program? Write a training objective for the program described in the case that contains the three key components of a training objective. How would your training objective have helped in the choice/design of a training program and for trainees and managers?

2. Comment on the company's decision to purchase a generic, off-the-shelf training package by a local vendor. What were the advantages and disadvantages? Do you think that it was a good idea for the company to purchase the training rather than to have it designed in-house? Explain your answer.

3. Explain how the use of a request for proposal (RFP) might have changed the company's decision to purchase the training program. Do you think that the company would have purchased the same training program from the same vendor if they had created a detailed RFP? Explain your answer.

4. What effect did the use of the original needs analysis have on the content of the training program and the decision to have it delivered over the Web? Do you think that a new needs analysis should have been conducted and what effect might it have had on the design of the training program?

5. Comment on the use of the Web as the main method of training. What are the advantages and disadvantages of this method of training? What other methods might have been more effective?

6. If you were to design the training program, describe what you would do differently terms of a) training objectives, b) training content, c) training methods, d) active practice and conditions of practice, and e) active learning. How would your training program be different from the one described in the case and would it be more effective?

Flashback Questions

1. To what extent has the instructional systems design (ISD) model of training and development been used? If it had been used to a greater extent, what would have been done differently? Comment on each step of the ISD model.

2. Comment on how management concluded that one solution to the sales problem was to improve training. Do you think that improving training is the best solution to the sales problem? Explain your answer using Mager and Pipe's performance analysis flowchart for determining solutions to performance problems (see Chapter 4, Figure 4.2). What are some other possible solutions for improving sales?

3. The training department has requested that they be allowed to design a new training program beginning with an updated needs analysis. Explain how they should conduct a new needs analysis. Refer to Figure 4.1 when answering this question.

4. If a new needs analysis is conducted, what will be learned from an organizational, task, and person analysis and how will this information help in the design of a new training program?

REFERENCES

1. Based on Klie, S. (2009, June 1). Training important during recession. *Canadian HR Reporter, 22(11)*, 1, 7; www.enbridge.com.

2. Brown, K. G., & Sitzmann, T. (2011). Training and employee development for improved performance. In S. Zedeck (Ed.), *Handbook of industrial and organizational psychology* (Vol. 2, pp. 469–503). Washington, DC: American Psychological Association.

3. Kibler, R. J., Barker, L. L., & Miles, D. T. (1970). *Behavioral objectives and instruction*. Boston: Allyn and Bacon, Inc.

4. Laird, D. (1985). *Approaches to training and development* (2nd ed.). Reading, MA: Addison-Wesley.

5. Hays, S. (1999, April). Basic skills training 101. *Workforce Management, 78(4)*, 76–78.

6. Ganzel, R. (1998, October). What sexual harassment training really prevents. *Training, 35(10)*, 86–94.

7. Nadler, L., & Nadler, Z. (1990). *The handbook of human resource development* (2nd ed.). New York: John Wiley and Sons.

8. Nadler, L., & Nadler, Z. (1990).

9. Klie, S. (2009, June 1).

10. Chapman, B. (2004, January). How to create the ideal RFP. *Training, 41(1)*, 40–43.

11. Chapman, B. (2004, January).

12. Campbell, J. P. (1988). Training design for performance improvement. In Campbell, J. P. & Campbell, R. J. (Eds.), *Productivity in organizations: Frontiers of industrial and organizational psychology* (pp. 177–216). San Francisco, CA: Jossey-Bass, p. 188.

13. Kirkpatrick, D. L. (1994). *Evaluating training programs: The four levels.* San Francisco, CA: Berrett-Koehler Publishers, p. 11.

14. Campbell, J. P. (1988).

15. Waxer, C. (2005, October 24). Bank of Montreal opens its checkbook in the name of employee development. *Workforce Management, 84(11)*, 46–49.

16. Campbell, J. P. (1988).

17. Campbell, J. P. (1988).

18. Thoms, P., & Klein, H. J. (1994). Participation and evaluative outcomes in management training. *Human Resource Development Quarterly, 5*, 27–39.

19. Hughes, P. D., & Campbell, A. (2009). *Learning & development outlook 2009: Learning in tough times.* Ottawa: The Conference Board of Canada.

20. Dobson, S. (2010, February 8). Constructive education. *Canadian HR Reporter, 23(3)*, 14, 15.

21. Klie, S. (2010, November 1). Social media, training help with holiday hires. *Canadian HR Reporter, 23(19)*, 1, 9.

22. Hinrichs, J. R. (1976). Personnel training. In Dunnette, M. D. (Ed.), *Handbook of industrial and organizational psychology* (pp. 829–860). Skokie, IL: Rand McNally.

23. Cannon-Bowers, J. A., Rhodenizer, L., Salas, E., & Bowers, C. A. (1998). A framework for understanding pre-practice conditions and their impact on learning. *Personnel Psychology, 51*, 291–320.

24. Sitzmann, T. (2011). A meta-analytic examination of the instructional effectiveness of computer-based simulation games. *Personnel Psychology, 64*, 489–528.

25. Mesmer-Magnus, J., & Viswesvaran, C. (2010). The role of pre-training interventions in learning: A meta-analysis and intergrative review. *Human Resource Management Review, 20*, 261–282.

26. Cannon-Bowers, J. A., Rhodenizer, L., Salas, E., & Bowers, C. A. (1998).

27. Mesmer-Magnus, J., & Viswesvaran, C. (2010).

28. Schmidt, A. M., & Ford, J. K. (2003). Learning within a learner control training environment: The interactive effects of goal orientation and metacognitive instruction on learning outcomes. *Personnel Psychology, 56*, 405–429.

29. Mesmer-Magnus, J., & Viswesvaran, C. (2010).

30. Mesmer-Magnus, J., & Viswesvaran, C. (2010).

31. Mesmer-Magnus, J., & Viswesvaran, C. (2010).

32. Mesmer-Magnus, J., & Viswesvaran, C. (2010).

33. Cannon-Bowers, J. A., Rhodenizer, L., Salas, E., & Bowers, C. A. (1998).

34. Baldwin, T. T., & Ford, J. K. (1988). Transfer of training: A review and directions for future research. *Personnel Psychology, 41*, 63–105.

35. Donovan, J. J., & Radosevich, D. J. (1999). A meta-analytic review of the distribution of practice effect: Now you see it, now you don't. *Journal of Applied Psychology, 84*, 795–805.

36. Bass, B. M., & Vaughn, J. A. (1969). *Training in industry: The management of learning.* Belmont, CA: Wadsworth; Donovan, J. J., & Radosevich, D. J. (1999).

37. Baldwin, T. T., & Ford, J. K. (1988).

38. Baldwin, T. T., & Ford, J. K. (1988).

39. Baldwin, T. T., & Ford, J. K. (1988).

40. Yelon, S., & Berge, Z. (1992, September). Practice-centred training. *Performance and instruction*, 8–12.

41. Driskell, J. E., Willis, R. P., & Copper, C. (1992). Effects of overlearning on retention. *Journal of Applied Psychology, 77*, 615–622.

42. Gagné, R. M. (1962). Military training and principles of learning. *American Psychologist, 17,* 83–91.
43. Gagné, R. M. (1962).
44. Baldwin, T. T., & Ford, J. K. (1988).
45. Ilgen, D. R., Fisher, C. D., & Taylor, M. S. (1979). Consequences of individual feedback on behaviour in organizations. *Journal of Applied Psychology, 64,* 349–371.
46. Campbell, J. P. (1988).
47. Miller, L. (1965). *The use of knowledge of results in improving the performance of hourly operators.* General Electric Company, Behavioral Research Service: Detroit.
48. Locke, E. A., & Latham, G. P. (1990). *A theory of goal setting and task performance.* Englewood Cliffs, NJ: Prentice-Hall.
49. Machin, M. A. (2002). Planning, managing, and optimizing transfer of training. In Kurt Kraiger (Ed.), *Creating, implementing, and managing effective training and development* (pp. 263–301). San Francisco, CA: Jossey-Bass; Smith, E. M., Ford, J. K., & Kozlowski, S. W. J. (1997). Building adaptive expertise: Implications for training design strategies. In M. A. Quinones and A. Ehrenstein (Eds.), *Training for a Rapidly Changing Workplace,* Washington, DC: American Psychological Association.
50. Bell, B. S., & Kozlowski, S. W. J. (2008). Active learning: Effects of core training design elements on self-regulatory processes, learning, and adaptability. *Journal of Applied Psychology, 93,* 296–316; Katz-Navon, T., Naveh, E., & Stern, Z. (2009). Active learning: When is more better? The case of resident physicians' medical errors. *Journal of Applied Psychology, 94,* 1200–1209.
51. Bell, B. S., & Kozlowski, S. W. J. (2008).
52. Bell, B. S., & Kozlowski, S. W. J. (2008).
53. Bell, B. S., & Kozlowski, S. W. J. (2008).
54. Heimbeck, D., Frese, M., Sonnentag, S., & Keith, N. (2003). Integrating errors into the training process: The function of error management instructions and the role of goal orientation. *Personnel Psychology, 56,* 333–361.
55. Heimbeck, D., Frese, M., Sonnentag, S., & Keith, N. (2003).
56. Keith, N., & Frese, M. (2008). Effectiveness of error management training: A meta-analysis. *Journal of Applied Psychology, 93,* 59–69.
57. Keith, N., & Frese, M. (2008).
58. Heimbeck, D., Frese, M., Sonnentag, S., & Keith, N. (2003).
59. Keith, N., & Frese, M. (2008).
60. Keith, N., & Frese, M. (2008).
61. Keith, N., & Frese, M. (2008).
62. Carter, M., & Beier, M. E. (2010). The effectiveness of error management training with working-aged adults. *Personnel Psychology, 63,* 641–675.

Off-the-Job Training Methods

CHAPTER LEARNING OUTCOMES

After reading this chapter, you should be able to:

- define instructional methods and instructional media
- describe the following instructional methods: lecture, discussion, case study, case incident, behavioural modelling, role play, games, simulations, and action learning
- list the advantages and disadvantages of each instructional method
- define physical and psychological fidelity
- describe the factors to consider when choosing an instructional method
- define aptitude-treatment interaction and discuss its implications for training
- discuss a blended delivery approach to training

L'ORÉAL CANADA

L'Oréal Canada, headquartered in Montreal, Quebec, is the leader of the cosmetics industry in Canada. Its operations include the manufacture, marketing, sales, and distribution of its colour cosmetics, skin care, sun protection, hair care, and hair colour products.

Training and development is an integral part of L'Oréal Canada. Every year about 100 of its 1,200 employees attend industry-specific and leadership development training and conferences at L'Oréal's management development centres in Tokyo, New York, and Paris.

After three months on the job, product managers at L'Oréal Canada are given their own company and required to market their products to consumers around the world. The company is virtual, the consumers are computer based, and the product managers' success or failure is simply a simulation. But the learning is real, says the company's director of learning and development.

Employees work in pairs and play the "game" for four hours a week over six weeks. Each week, there's an e-learning component where employees have to study a new topic such as market segmentation, brand positioning, and working with media.

This is done online with a trainer and participants from L'Oréal offices around the world.

The next day the pairs go online and use the skills they learned from the e-learning module to make business decisions. Two days later, all participants go back online and, along with the trainer, look at the market share of their companies. This allows them to immediately see the impact of their marketing decisions on the company.

After employees see how they've done, they have a face-to-face meeting with their manager to talk about how they can apply what they learned to their specific job at L'Oréal Canada.

Along with other online simulations and business games, L'Oréal incorporates in-person simulations and role plays to train all employees. L'Oréal uses role plays extensively to train its sales force. Junior sales representatives and key account managers are given information on a product line and the potential clients, such as Shoppers Drug Mart or Walmart. The vice president of sales and sales directors play the role of customers.

L'Oréal Canada recently celebrated its 50th anniversary, and in 2010 the company was named one of Canada's Top 100 Employers for the seventh consecutive year.[1]

Source: S. Klie, "L'Oréal plays games with training," *Canadian HR Reporter*, Oct. 6, 2008, P. 26; S. Klie, "L'Oréal a pretty picture of diversity, training," *Canadian HR Reporter*, Oct. 22, 2007, P. 11; www.loreal.ca.

This chapter is the first of three chapters that focus on training methods. As you learned in Chapter 5, training methods are an important component of the design of training programs. In this chapter, we focus on instructional methods that take place off the job.

Instructional methods

The techniques used to stimulate learning

Instructional methods refer to the techniques used to stimulate learning.[2] Instructional methods usually take place in a classroom or formal setting for the purpose of learning. L'Oréal Canada's, with its use of simulations, games, and role plays, is a good example of a company that uses a number of instructional training methods.

Although the instructional methods presented in this chapter usually take place in a classroom, some methods such as games and simulations can also take place outside of a classroom and can be incorporated into computer-based training like L'Oréal Canada's simulation for product managers.

TABLE (6.1)

Instructional Methods

1. *Lecture*. A training method in which the trainer presents to trainees the training content to be learned.
2. *Discussion*. Two-way communication between the trainer and trainees as well as among trainees.
3. *Case study*. A training method in which trainees discuss, analyze, and solve problems based on a real situation.
4. *Case incident*. A training method in which one problem or issue is presented for analysis.
5. *Behaviour modelling*. A training method in which trainees observe a model performing a task and then attempt to imitate the observed behaviour.
6. *Role play*. A training method in which trainees practise new behaviours in a safe environment.
7. *Simulations*. The use of operating models of physical or social events designed to represent reality.
8. *Games*. Training methods that involve structured competition that allow employees to learn specific skills.
9. *Action learning*. A training method in which trainees study and solve real-world problems and accept responsibility for the solution.

In both Canada and the United States, instructor-led classroom training remains the primary and most popular method of providing training although it has been on the decline in the last decade. In 2000, 80 percent of all training was delivered in the classroom in Canadian organizations, but by 2010 it represented just 58 percent of all training. According to the Conference Board of Canada, instructor-led classroom training is the most widely used training method in Canadian organizations. In the United States, about 70 percent of all training is delivered in the classroom.[3]

This chapter describes the most common instructional training methods. The instructional methods are presented in order of degree of trainee involvement, from passive to active. We start with lectures, because there is relatively little trainee input, and end with action learning, where trainees manage the learning process. Table 6.1 lists the nine instructional methods described in this chapter.

LECTURE METHOD

Most people have experienced a lecture given its widespread use in education and training. A **lecture** is a training method in which the trainer presents to trainees the training content to be learned. It involves a unidirectional flow of information from the trainer to the trainee. Although lectures have a reputation as a boring training method, the research evidence indicates that lectures are effective for training several types of skills and tasks.[4]

The lecture offers a number of advantages. Large amounts of information can be provided to large groups of trainees in a relatively short period of time at a minimal expense, which makes the lecture method very efficient. Key points

Lecture

A training method in which the trainer presents to trainees the training content to be learned can be emphasized and repeated. Trainers can be assured that trainees are all hearing the same message, which is useful when the message is extremely important, such as instructions or changes in procedures. A lecture is also useful as a method to explain to trainees what is to follow in the rest of a training session. For example, a lecture could be used to highlight the key learning points of a video or role play. Many employees are comfortable with the lecture method because they are familiar with it and it requires little participation.

However, as some of us have experienced, a lecture also has some drawbacks as a training method. While useful for the acquisition of declarative knowledge and immediate recall, it is not as effective for the development of skills or for changing attitudes. The lecture does not accommodate differences in trainee ability, and all trainees are forced to absorb information at the same rate. Trainees are also forced to be passive learners with little opportunity to connect the content to their own work environment, or to receive feedback on their understanding of the material. To overcome these disadvantages, trainers often include time for discussion, questions and answers, and other opportunities for trainee involvement.

Tips for Trainers

Trainers can use the lecture method effectively by following a number of guidelines. For example, "Where do I begin?" is a question asked by most first-time trainers. The answer is: "First you have to know what you want to do (the objective) and how much information you need to impart." The trainer should begin a lecture with an introduction to the topic and inform trainees about what they will learn and/or be able to do or accomplish by the end of the lecture.

The trainer must then present the content or body of the lecture. Either through previously gained knowledge or the ability to research a topic, the trainer will gather and arrange information in a logical manner. Logic could dictate a progression from the general to the specific or from the specific to the general, depending upon the subject matter. This information can be transcribed onto cards or sheets of paper. An effective technique is to rule off a wide (5 cm to 8 cm) margin down the right-hand side of each page. Detailed information can then be placed in the body of the page, while headings are written in the margins.

It has been suggested that no more than six major points be presented during each half hour of a lecture.[5] It takes practice to get the timing of a lecture right. Only through experience can one judge the amount of material needed for any given amount of time. It is helpful to break the lecture into 10- to 15-minute segments with a short stretch of time in between and to summarize the material at both the beginning and the end, stopping occasionally to allow trainees to catch up and to write their own summaries.

A trainer who drones on for an entire hour is rarely effective. The delivery should be punctuated with a variety of supplementary material or exercises. Stories, case incidents, graphics, humour, trainee presentations, videos, and question-and-answer sessions are some of the techniques a trainer can use to maintain interest and, perhaps even more important, impart in the trainee the love of—or at the least respect for—the subject matter. The trainer should conclude the lecture with a summary of the key learning points followed by some time for questions and answers.

DISCUSSION METHOD

The **discussion method** is a method of training that allows for two-way communication between the trainer and trainees as well as among trainees. It is one of the primary ways to increase trainee involvement in the learning process. Group discussion serves at least five purposes:

1. It helps trainees recognize what they do not know but should know.
2. It is an opportunity for trainees to get answers to questions.
3. It allows trainees to get advice on matters that are of concern to them.
4. It allows trainees to share ideas and derive a common wisdom.
5. It is a way for trainees to learn about one another as people.[6]

Group discussions facilitate the exchange of ideas and are good ways to develop critical thinking skills. Social and interpersonal skills are also enhanced. However, group discussions are not effective with large numbers of participants because many remain silent or are unable to participate. Some group members will dominate while the contributions of others will not be useful. Still others may become dogmatic in their positions on issues. Group discussions take a lot of training time and must be carefully facilitated to manage the outcomes.

Discussion method
Allows two-way communication between the trainer and trainees as well as among trainees

Tips for Trainers

The discussion method is most effective when the trainer can convince group members that a collective approach has some advantage over individual approaches to a problem.[7] Thus, the trainer should create a participative culture at the beginning of a training program. The trainer's task, then, is to get trainees to buy into the process as an activity that is both interesting and useful.

The major difficulty with the discussion method is that comments tend to be addressed to the trainer. When faced with this situation, it is best to reflect the questions or comments back to the trainees. Positive reinforcement is critical. Reluctant participants are drawn out, while the trainer utilizes the energy of more assertive individuals. When the group strays off topic, the trainer gently refocuses the discussion, supporting the participation while changing the substance.[8]

The key to successful discussions is to ensure that one trainee does not dominate the discussion. The trainer does not have to be obvious (e.g., by putting all the dominant personalities together). More subtle techniques can be used. For example, trainees can be given roles that change with each discussion—scribe, presenter, and discussion leader. If groups are kept small—four to six seems to work best—then most trainees have something to do, increasing participation and decreasing chances for some individuals to dominate the process. It is harder to be aggressive when taking notes or trying to summarize the thoughts of others.

Trainers dealing with groups of mixed educational backgrounds must also be aware of reading speed and literacy problems. Often group discussions require trainees to read a passage, case incident, or problem. Hostility or reluctance to do so might point to illiteracy. Be gentle; work the informal group process by finding a place in a hallway for someone to quietly read the material, or if this process is too obvious, summarize the main points before you assign the work. People who don't read well often have excellent memories; with care, they'll get by.[9]

Groups should be assigned a well-defined, easily understood task, one that is doable within the allotted time frame. Trainees should be given every opportunity to look good in front of their peers, especially if they have to report back to the group. Since many training facilities are less than ideal, seating arrangements will vary. Any configuration that puts trainees in close proximity to one another will do, but a circle arrangement with no obvious leader's position or place is probably best. Size of the group is also important. More than 10 would be hard to handle if everyone is to participate.

CASE STUDY METHOD

Case study

A training method in which trainees discuss, analyze, and solve problems based on a real situation

A **case study** is a training method in which trainees discuss, analyze, and solve problems usually based on a real situation. The primary use of the case study method is to encourage open discussion and analysis of problems and events. Trainees apply business-management concepts to relevant real-life situations. Most cases present situations in which the problems are correctable.

The objectives of a case study are to:

1. Introduce realism into trainees' learning.
2. Deal with a variety of problems, goals, facts, conditions, and conflicts that often occur in the real world.
3. Teach trainees how to make decisions.
4. Teach trainees to be creative and think independently.[10]

The case study method teaches trainees to think for themselves and develop analytical and problem-solving skills while the trainer functions as a catalyst for learning. Case studies develop analytical ability, sharpen problem-solving skills, encourage creativity, and improve the organization of thoughts and ideas.[11]

The case study method is often used in business schools to teach students how to analyze and solve realistic organizational problems. In fact, more than 70 percent of business schools use the case study method. Several studies have found that using cases improves communication skills and problem solving, and enables students to better understand management situations.[12]

Cases vary depending on the intended purpose of the writer and according to the issue being examined. Some case studies disclose what management decisions were made when attempting to solve an organization's problems, while others require one to develop solutions and recommend courses of action.

For the case method to be effective, however, certain requirements must be met. For example, the qualifications of both the trainees and the trainer affect the ability to analyze cases and to draw conclusions. As well, space and time dimensions are important. Trainees need time to analyze cases properly. Finally, case studies and discussions work best in an open and informal atmosphere.[13]

Cases may be written in various styles, presenting either single problems or a number of complex, interdependent situations. They may be concerned with corporate strategy, organizational change, management, or any problem relating to a company's financial situation, marketing, human resources, or a combination of these activities. Some case reports describe the organization's difficulties in vague terms, while others may state the major problems explicitly.

In addition to the various styles of case writing, methods of presentation also differ. Cases do not always have to be in written form. Sometimes it is more effective to present cases using audio-visual techniques. This approach has advantages for both the trainees and the trainers. For example, trainers do not have to do as much research and writing, and trainees are able to identify better with the characters.[14]

A second alternative to a written case presentation is the live case method. Businesses may contact schools to report certain problems. Students then analyze the situation and report back to the company. This approach has been called operational consulting.[15]

Tips for Trainers

Certain requirements should be met when writing a case study. The case should be a product of a real organizational situation. A fictitious case could be regarded with boredom and distrust as the setting might seem too unrealistic.[16] Ideally, cases should be written by more than one person. Collaboration on the presentation of facts ensures a more realistic situation and helps to reduce biases. Although it is difficult, the case writer must not make assumptions and only facts should be included. The author of a case, then, must relate core issues to the reader, not personal bias.

Because a case study is a description of a typical management situation, it is often difficult to know what to include and what to omit. Most cases give an overall description of the company and the industry situation although the length of a case report varies. A typical case, however, will be up to 20 typewritten pages. The key issues and the relevant details should be included to give the reader enough information to make a qualified decision.

A teaching note provides communication between the case writer and those who teach the case. In its strictest sense, a teaching note would include information on approaches to teaching a specific case. Some teaching notes, however, are more detailed, containing samples of analyses and computations. In addition, teaching notes may state the objectives of the case and contain additional company information not available to trainees.[17]

CASE INCIDENT METHOD

Unlike the typical case study, a **case incident** is usually no more than one page in length and is designed to illustrate or to probe one specific problem, concept, or issue. Most management textbooks include a case incident at the end of each chapter. The case incident has become one of the most accessible ways of adding an experiential or real-world component into a lecture.

Case incidents are useful when the trainer wants to focus on one topic or concept. Because they are short, trainees can read them during a training session and valuable time will not be taken up by differences in trainees' reading speeds. When larger, more traditional cases are used, advance preparation is necessary to read and review the case material. The brevity of a case incident reduces the need for preparation and reading skills so all trainees can participate without a lot of advance reading and preparation.

Case incident

A training method in which one problem or issue is presented for analysis

Another advantage of a case incident is that trainees are able to use their own experiences. If the material is written well, the problem presented in each incident will encourage the application of current knowledge, leading to increased confidence and trainee input and participation.

The main disadvantage of case incidents is that some trainees are bothered by the lack of background material. Indeed, at times it is necessary for trainees to make assumptions and trainers may be asked by some trainees to sketch in the background. They can be especially problematic for trainees who have limited knowledge and work experience. A lack of work or life experiences tends to elicit shallow answers based on speculation and ill-informed opinion.

Case incidents have been used successfully in higher education and organizations. Supervisors seem to like the hands-on aspects of solving a specific management problem. Similarly, students have found the case incident method to be a welcome relief from the traditional lecture method.

Tips for Trainers

Case incidents can be used in several ways. Trainees can be divided into groups with one member assigned the task of making notes while another can be designated the group spokesperson. The groups discuss the case incident and answer case questions. The trainer then has each group spokesperson present their answers. This process can then lead into a general group discussion.

Another approach is to have trainees read the case incident, answer the case questions, and then have a class discussion. This method is especially useful when an example is needed to illustrate a specific point. The trainer asks the trainees to read the incident and think about a question, and then leads the group in a short discussion. As soon as the point has been made, the trainer should continue quickly, so as not to lose the trainees' interest. Alternatively, a case incident can be used to illustrate a point at the start of a training program or used as an exercise at the end of a training program.

BEHAVIOUR MODELLING

Behaviour modeling

A training method in which trainees observe a model performing a task and then attempt to imitate the observed behaviour

Make the
Connection

As you know from Chapter 3, people learn by observing the behaviour of others. So it should not surprise you that observational learning is a popular and effective method of training. **Behaviour modelling** is a training method in which trainees observe a model performing a task and then attempt to imitate the observed behaviour. It is based on social cognitive theory and observational learning.

You might recall from Chapter 3 that four key elements are critical for observational learning to take place: attention, retention, reproduction, and reinforcement. These are also important for behavioural modelling training, which is a very effective method for learning skills and behaviours.

Behavioural modelling is one of the most widely used and researched training methods.[18] It has been used to teach interpersonal skills such as supervision, negotiation, communication, and sales as well as motor skills and it is the most popular method for teaching interpersonal and supervisory skills. In recent years it has been extended to other areas such as cross-cultural skills and technical skills.[19]

Behaviour modelling is based on four general principles of learning:[20]

1. Observation (modelling).
2. Rehearsal (practice).
3. Reinforcement (reward).
4. Transfer.

The process is fairly straightforward. Trainees observe a model performing a specific task such as handling a customer complaint or operating a machine and then practise performing the task. The performance of a task can be observed on video or it can be performed live.

The training task should be broken down into key learning points or behaviours to be learned as a series of critical steps that can be modelled independently. After viewing the model, the participants practise the behaviour, one step at a time. When one step is mastered and reinforced, the trainer moves to the next critical skill (recall the discussion of shaping and chaining in Chapter 3). Specific feedback must follow the performance of each step. This step-by-step process results in the development of skills and self-efficacy needed to use them. The final step involves specific actions to maximize the transfer of learning on the job.[21]

A review of research on behaviour modelling training found that it has a particularly strong effect on learning but also has a positive effect on skills development and job behaviour. The effect on skills development was greatest when learning points were used and presented as rules to be followed and when training time was longest. Transfer of learning on the job was greatest when models displaying both positive and negative behaviours were used, when trainees were instructed to set goals, when trainees' superiors were trained, and when rewards and sanctions were provided for using or failing to use newly learned skills on the job.[22]

Tips for Trainers

The model used in behavioural modelling training should be someone with whom the trainee can identify and who is perceived as credible. Under these conditions, the trainee is more likely to want to imitate the model's behaviour. In addition, trainers have to carefully plan behaviour modelling training and ensure that trainees are provided with opportunities to practise the observed behaviour, receive feedback on their performance of the task, and are motivated to use the new behaviour on the job. Trainees will resist behaviour modelling if the behaviours are incongruent with common work practices.

To be effective, trainees must have sufficient trust in the trainer to experiment (i.e., to try new behaviour in front of a group). Sometimes, an ineffective scenario is demonstrated first to increase motivation to try the new positive behaviour (John Cleese of Monty Python fame used this technique very effectively in his humorous video series on interviewing.) In fact, one study found that exposing trainees to a negative and a positive model was more effective for behavioural generalization (using the trained skills on a task that was different from the training task) than exposing trainees to only a positive model. However, exposure to only a positive model was most effective for behavioural reproduction of the training task.[23]

> ### ▶ The Trainer's Notebook 6.1
> #### IMPLEMENTING BEHAVIOURAL MODELLING TRAINING
>
> 1. Describe to trainees a set of well-defined behaviours (skills) to be learned.
>
> 2. Provide a model or models displaying the effective use of those behaviours.
>
> 3. Provide opportunities for trainees to practise using those behaviours.
>
> 4. Provide feedback and social reinforcement to trainees following practice.
>
> 5. Take steps to maximize the transfer of those behaviours to the job.
>
> Source: P.J. Taylor, D.F. Russ-Eft & D.W.L. Chan, "A meta-analytic review of behavior modeling training," *Journal of Applied Psychology*, Vol. 90, Pp. 692–709, 2005.

Make the Connection

Transfer of the new skill and behaviours to the workplace is the weakest link in the process. Old patterns are comfortable and familiar, especially when there is some resistance in the work environment to new ways of doing things. However, by overlearning the skill as discussed in Chapter 5, its use can become automatic. In addition, the reinforcement of newly acquired skills on the job ensures their repetition and continued application. When these reinforcers are in place, behaviour modelling can have long-lasting and positive outcomes.[24]

For guidelines to implement behaviour modelling, see The Trainer's Notebook 6.1, "Implementing Behavioural Modelling Training."

ROLE PLAY

Role play

A training method in which trainees are given the opportunity to practise new behaviours in a safe environment

A **role play** is a method of training in which trainees are given the opportunity to practise new behaviours in a safe environment. In effect, they allow trainees the opportunity to experience a role and what the role entails. Thus, the emphasis is on doing and experiencing. Role plays are most useful for acquiring interpersonal and human relations skills and for changing attitudes. They are often used in training programs that involve interpersonal skills such as communication, sales, performance appraisal, counselling, mentoring, team building, and leadership and in certain settings (e.g., social services) where participants can take on the roles of workers and clients.[25] You might recall that L'Oréal uses role plays to train its sales force.

A role play consists of three phases: 1. development, 2. enactment, and 3. debriefing. First, a role play must be carefully *developed* to achieve its objectives. A role play usually consists of a scenario in which there are two actors. For example, if sales clerks are learning how to interact with customers, a role play might involve a customer returning an item and asking for a refund. The scenario provides information on the time, place, roles, encounter, and instructions on what each role player should do.

During the *enactment* phase, trainees are provided with the role-play information and scenarios and are assigned roles. Usually there are two role players and sometimes a third trainee who is an observer. Trainees are given some time to become familiar with the scenario and their roles, and then act out the role play. Usually the trainees will rotate so that each one spends some time in each role.

By playing a role, trainees can develop empathy for others and learn what it feels like to be in a particular role. For example, when a customer service representative is given instructions to play the part of a disgruntled customer with a major problem, he or she can experience the frustrations of responses like, "That's not my department," and, "Just fill in that form over there, no, not that one."

After the enactment phase is the *debriefing* phase, which is considered to be the most important phase of a role play, and should last two to three times longer than the enactment phase. In this phase, participants discuss their experiences and the outcomes of their role play. Correct behaviours are reinforced and connections with key learning points and trainees' jobs are made. This is done by establishing the facts (what happened, what was experienced), analyzing the causes and effects of behaviours, and planning for skill or attitude changes on the job.

Role playing can take on various forms and does not always have to involve just two actors. A role play can involve groups of trainees acting out various roles in what is known as multiple role playing. They can also vary in terms of how much detail and structure the actors are given. In some role plays the actors are given a great deal of detail about what they are supposed to do and how they should feel, while less structured role plays might just indicate the actors' roles without any detail about them. A role play can also involve one trainee playing him/herself (e.g., manager) while the other trainee acts out a role (e.g., employee who is being coached). Recall that at L'Oréal Canada junior sales representatives participate in role plays in which the vice president of sales and sales directors play the role of customers.

Another variation is to have a single role play performed that is observed by the rest of the trainees. In other cases, it might be preferable to have all of the trainees participate in a role play. The type of role play will depend on the training content and objectives.

Tips for Trainers

While role playing allows trainees to practise and learn new skills, trainees sometimes resist it. As a result, the role of the trainer is crucial. Trust has to be established and an open and participative climate is necessary. Trainees should be warmed up by involving them in minor role situations. The trainer can reinforce risk taking and use mistakes as learning opportunities. Trainers can ask trainees to show all the incorrect ways to handle an angry customer. When a critical mistake is made, the trainer can start again or rewind the case. In one role play, a police officer was testing methods of talking to a potential suicide victim on a bridge. The officer made the fatal mistake of saying, "Go ahead, I dare you," and the role-play partner jumped. The trainer immediately stated, "Well, that approach didn't work, would you like to try another?" He rewound the case and demonstrated the true value of role playing—the opportunity to practise behaviours in a safe environment.

The Trainer's Notebook 6.2
STEPS FOR EFFECTIVE ROLE PLAYS

1. Consider role plays when the training involves communication or interpersonal skills.

2. Define the learning outcomes of the session.

3. Study the relevant organizational roles.

4. Create the role play scripts—one with a general context, and the other that's specific to the role.

5. Prepare the observation sheets with pertinent points to be observed.

6. See that the setting is right for the role play—stage, A/V tools, light, and so on.

7. Call for volunteers.

8. Facilitate and debrief after the role play.

9. Do not leave any issue unresolved.

Source: S. Karve, "Setting the stage for effective role plays," *T+D*, Vol. 65 (11), 2011, Pp. 76–77.

One of the limitations of a role play is that, unlike behaviour modelling, trainees are not shown exactly what to do and how to behave prior to participating in a role play. As a result, some trainees might not be successful in a role play and might even display incorrect behaviours. Furthermore, much of what happens during a role play is left in the hands of the role players. This means that it is extremely important for the trainer to draw out the incorrect and correct behaviours during the debriefing phase. Otherwise, trainees might not learn the appropriate behaviours following a role play. Role plays are most successful when they mirror the reality and setting of the organization and participants relate to it on an emotional level.[26] To learn how to implement roles plays, see The Trainer's Notebook 6.2, "Steps for Effective Role Plays."

SIMULATIONS

Simulations

The use of operating models of physical or social events designed to represent reality

Simulations are a form of training that involves the use of operating models of physical or social events that are designed to represent reality. Thus, a simulation is a working representation of reality.[27] They attempt to recreate situations by simplifying them to a manageable size and structure. They are models or active representations of work situations that are designed to increase trainee motivation, involvement, and learning. They are also used when training in the real world might involve danger or extreme costs. Simulations can involve individuals working alone or groups of individuals working together.

Simulations are a popular method of training and are widely used in business, education, and the military. For example, simulations are typically used in medicine, maintenance, law enforcement, and emergency management settings. The military and the commercial aviation industry are purported to be the biggest users of simulation-based training.[28]

Equipment simulators

Mechanical devices that are similar to those that employees use on the job

Equipment simulators are mechanical devices that are similar to those that employees use on the job. They are designed to simulate the kinds of procedures, movements, and/or decisions required in the work environment. A good example of an equipment simulator is a flight simulator used to train pilots.

Flight simulators mimic flights exactly but pose no risk to humans or equipment. Equipment simulators are also used to train astronauts, air traffic controllers, and maintenance workers. Trucking companies have also begun to use simulations to train new drivers.

Simulations can also be used to develop managerial and interpersonal skills. For example, organizational simulations like the one used for product managers at L'Oréal Canada require participants to solve problems, make decisions, and interact with various stakeholders. Trainees learn how organizations operate and acquire important managerial and business skills.

Simulations are also used to train employees involved in emergency response work, such as firefighters and police officers. For example, in December 2005 a series of truck bombs in Toronto knocked out the city's power, destroyed a terminal at Pearson airport, an office tower on Bay Street, and much of the St. Michael's Hospital. Fortunately, it was just an imaginary scenario that was part of a training simulation for riot police to practise their emergency response strategy. The simulation included army reservists as well as Toronto police, firefighters, and paramedics. The objective of the training was to look for areas that can be improved, to coordinate with other agencies, and to be prepared in case such a scenario ever happens.[29]

A major disadvantage of simulations is that they are expensive to develop and, in the case of emergency response simulations, very expensive to stage. On the positive side, simulations are an excellent method for adding some realism into a training program. They are especially useful in situations where it would be too costly or dangerous to train employees on the actual equipment used on the job.

Tips for Trainers

A successful simulation involves four steps: preparing for the simulation (consider the participants and learning objectives when choosing a simulation), delivering the simulation (let participants know why they are being asked to participate in the simulation and the expected outcomes), debriefing the simulation (discuss the simulation and make connections to the workplace), and following up on the simulation (post-simulation activities to maintain learning). Like role plays, the debriefing is the most important step because it allows the participants to step back and reflect on the experience and understand how it relates to their lives and work.[30]

In order to be most effective, simulations should have physical and psychological fidelity. **Physical fidelity** has to do with the similarity of the physical aspects of a simulation (e.g., equipment, tasks, and surroundings) to the actual job. Simulators should be designed to physically replicate and resemble the work environment. That is, the simulation should have the appearance of the actual work site. For example, a flight simulator should look like the cockpit of an actual airplane with respect to the various controls, lights, and instruments.

Psychological fidelity has to do with the similarity of the psychological conditions of the simulation to the actual work environment. Simulations should be designed so that the experience is as similar as possible to what trainees experience on the job. In other words, the simulation should include on-the-job psychological conditions such as time pressures, problems, conflicts, and so on.

Physical fidelity
The similarity of the physical aspects of a simulation (e.g., equipment, tasks, and surroundings) to the actual job

Psychological fidelity
The similarity of the psychological conditions of the simulation to the actual work environment

Training Today 6.1

Simulations for Sales Success

B. Braun Medical Inc., is a manufacturer of infusion therapy and pain management products. In 2007, the sales of one of B. Braun's flagship products, the Introcan Safety IV catheter, had slowed to 1.5 percent despite a concerted investment of staff and company resources. In addition, customer trial-to-conversions came in at 25 percent, with retention rates measured at only 40 percent six months post-conversion.

The sales representatives didn't feel that they had the clinical expertise necessary to establish credibility with their customers or correctly set expectations for use of the IV catheter. A learning-style survey showed that the sales force collectively held a variety of learning styles, which led B. Braun to create a new blended training program.

B. Braun designed the program to include product training via learning modules, peer coaching, and a teach-back component, followed by hands-on didactic training during live classroom sessions. Then, in September 2010, they launched a two-day simulation training program. The goal was for reps to repetitively practise placing the IV catheter through scenario-based simulation training so they could understand what clinicians experienced when they used the product.

On the first day of the simulation, participants take a pre-test to determine their current knowledge of venipuncture. Part of this assessment includes the reps' immersion within a real-life scenario. They are asked to place an IV catheter using a "demo arm" with blood pressure and fake blood. Participants receive grades based on a 30-point checklist. Following the pre-test, a nurse teaches a venipuncture certification course.

On the second day of the simulation, participants are placed on a computer simulator with a haptics device (which allows them to "feel" the virtual IV catheter insertion) to practise the process of placing the IV catheter. The reps coach one another and engage in clinical discussions while completing the scenarios.

The training concludes with a real-life scenario in which participants work on a patient who is wearing a demo arm. The reps are assigned a scenario and tasked with selecting the correct supplies and placing the IV catheter. An observer uses the 30-point checklist to grade the reps' performance improvement. Participants also complete a written post-training test to measure their knowledge gain.

B. Braun has documented a 22 to 25 percent increase in participants' knowledge and skills. Since the company re-launched the Introcan Safety IV catheter with the new training program, customer trial-to-conversion rates have increased to 95 percent and customer retention rates have increased to better than 85 percent six months post-conversion.

Source: Anonymous, "Simulations for selling success," *T+D*, Jan. 2012, P. 80. Reprint/Adapted with permission of American Society for Training & Development.

Simulations allow a great deal of flexibility as complicating factors or unexpected events can be built into the program. For example, in a pilot-training simulation, a blizzard can be introduced. However, trainers should ensure that simulations have both physical and psychological fidelity. For a good example, see Training Today 6.1, "Simulations for Sales Success."

GAMES

Games
Training methods that involve structured competition that allows trainees to learn specific skills

Games are training methods that involve structured competition that allows trainees to learn specific skills. Games tend to have rules, principles, and a system for scoring. However, unlike simulations, games do not have to represent reality and they are often designed to be entertaining. For example, an employment law game called *Winning through Prevention* teaches human resource managers about lawful termination, discrimination, and workplace safety. Players who answer correctly get promoted and those who answer incorrectly are faced with a lawsuit.[31]

Business games often require teams of players to compete against each other to gain a strategic advantage, to gain market share, or to maximize profits. They can involve all areas of management practice and often require the players to gather and analyze information, and to make business management decisions. As a result, business games tend to focus on the development of problem-solving, interpersonal, and decision-making skills.

Some business games are relatively simple and focus on a particular functional area such as marketing, human resources, or finance. Other games are much more complex and try to model an entire organization. Participants might have to operate a company and make all kinds of decisions and solve business problems. They then receive feedback and have the opportunity to practise particular skills.

Games incorporate many principles of learning such as learning from experience, active practice, and direct application to real problems. They are used to enhance the learning process by injecting fun and competition, generating energy, and providing opportunities for people to work together.

A disadvantage of the use of games is the possibility of learning the wrong things, a weak relation to training objectives, and an emphasis on winning.[32] In addition, trainees sometimes get so caught up in the game that they lose sight of the importance of learning. Although trainees seem to enjoy games and respond enthusiastically to them, there is not very much evidence on how effective they are for improving skills and on-the-job performance.

Tips for Trainers

The design of a game begins with a critical question: "What is the key task to be learned?" At the beginning of the exercise, the trainer should state the learning objective so that trainees don't just focus on winning the game but understand what they will learn. In addition, the roles of the players must be clearly defined.

Games should be as realistic as possible and be a meaningful representation of the kind of work that participants do. If they are not realistic, participants might not take them seriously. This will undermine learning and the application of new skills on the job. To be most effective, games should be well planned and prepared, linked to training objectives, and include a debriefing session so that trainees understand the purpose of the game and the critical skills and behaviours to be learned.[33] As well, because many kinds of games are available, trainers need to be familiar with them and to carefully choose one that best meets an organization's needs and objectives.

ACTION LEARNING

Some training methods that are known as **problem-based learning** require trainees to solve real or simulated open-ended problems.[34] A good example of this is action learning. **Action learning** requires trainees to identify problems; develop possible solutions; test these solutions in a real-world, real-time

Problem-based learning
Training methods that require trainees to solve real or simulated open-ended problems

Action learning
A training method in which trainees solve real-world problems and accept responsibility for the solution

situation; and evaluate the consequences. The aim is to solve an actual business problem and to test theories in the real world. Reginald Revans, the originator of action learning principles, emphasizes that the learner develops skills through responsible involvement in some real, complex, and stressful problem.[35]

Make the Connection

The goals of action learning are to involve and to challenge the trainee and move employees from passive observation to identification with the people and the vision of the organization. This method moves trainees from information receivers to problem solvers. Action learning incorporates more of the adult learning principles than any other method of training. Recall from Chapter 3 that adults are problem-centred in their approach to learning and prefer to be self-directed and to learn independently.

The majority of the time spent in action learning is dedicated to the diagnosis of problems in the field. The problems and the inherent value systems supporting the problems are assessed and challenged. This work is always done in groups, and learning by-products include group and interpersonal skills, risk taking, responsibility, and accountability.[36]

Many professions use action learning to train and socialize their students. For example, students in social work are often sent to work with the homeless or welfare recipients. These students are encouraged to apply their theoretical knowledge in the field. Organizations are using the precepts of action learning when employees take responsibility for quality-improvement projects.

Action learning requires a commitment of energy and time from participants and their managers. Solving real organizational problems can be stressful for trainees. The difficulties of working in teams on real problems can lead to conflict and increased anxiety and stress.

Although action learning is more popular in Europe than in North America, a number of companies in Canada and the United States have developed action learning programs. For example, TD Bank Financial Group has a leadership development program in which action learning plays an integral part. The bank's senior managers attend a three-day course to learn about the competencies that comprise a new leadership profile. Then they must use the learning to solve an action learning opportunity that they identified before attending the courses. TELUS has an action learning program for its director-level managers. The company partnered with several universities to deliver courses in several key areas. After taking the courses, participants are expected to use the learning to solve work-related problems and they are held accountable for applying the learning and making changes.[37] Automatic Data Processing, Inc. (ADP), one of the world's largest providers of business outsourcing solutions, has teams of 10 participants address real business opportunities or challenges and then present recommendations to their executive sponsor(s) and senior leaders.[38]

Tips for Trainers

Action learning projects must be challenging and deal with real organizational concerns. Trainees should buy into the importance of the project and the organizational problem and receive some release time to work on the project. In addition, some training in group skills to enable collaboration might also be necessary. The group working on the project should be small enough (four to seven members) to develop trust but contain a diverse set of skills to enable creative solutions. The learning process should be monitored and the trainees held accountable for their proposed solutions.

INSTRUCTIONAL MEDIA

In addition to instructional methods, the design of training and development programs also involves choosing instructional media that should be distinguished from the training content and instructional methods. **Instructional media** refers to the medium or media used to deliver the training content and methods to trainees. For example, a lecture can be delivered face-to-face in a classroom or through the use of various mediums such as online video or DVD.[39]

Instructional media can also be used with most of the instructional methods. A good example of this is audio-visual methods. **Audio-visual methods** refer to various forms of media that trainers can use in the classroom to illustrate key points or demonstrate certain actions or behaviours. Videos, DVDs, and slides are often used by trainers to supplement lectures and discussions. A video is often used to illustrate how to behave in a certain situation or to demonstrate effective and ineffective behaviours.

For example, at pharmaceutical company Nycomed Canada, a performance management training program for managers uses videos of performance management scenarios to guide managers through the process and to show them how to handle different issues.[40] Many managers have learned correct interviewing techniques through videos. Slides highlight important parts of a lecture or discussion, allowing trainees to remember key points. The use of videos during training has been made easier with the internet as trainers can now find relevant video clips online that can be shown during training.

One advantage of audio-visual methods is the ability to control the pace of training. A slide or a video clip can be used to clarify a concept. Trainees receive consistent information from these methods no matter where or how often the training is given. Most important, a video can show a situation that is difficult for a trainer to describe, such as a hostile customer or a dangerous malfunction in equipment. Video allows a trainer to show complex and dynamic situations in a realistic manner. Not surprisingly, videos remain one of the most popular forms of instructional media.

Tips for Trainers

When using instructional media to supplement an instructional method such as a video, the trainer should discuss the learning objectives and the key points, and instruct trainees to pay particular attention to certain key parts. Trainees should understand how the video fits into the rest of the training program and be given sufficient guidance so that they know what to look for and what they should focus on. Slides should not overwhelm trainees with information and they should be easy to read and follow. Too much information or print that is too small and difficult to read can undermine

Instructional media
The medium or media used to deliver the training content and methods to trainees

Audio-visual methods
Various forms of media that are used to illustrate key points or demonstrate certain actions or behaviours

their usefulness. Finally, it is important to keep in mind that the use of instructional media should be guided by the nature of the training content and the instructional methods being used.

WHAT TRAINING METHOD IS BEST?

In this chapter, we have described some of the most common instructional methods of training. In Chapter 7, you will learn about on-the-job training methods and in Chapter 8 you will find out about technology-based training methods. With so many training methods available, it is natural to ask, "What training method is best?" and "How does a trainer choose a training method?" There is of course no easy or straightforward answer to this question. However, we will try to provide some guidelines for making this important decision. For starters, Table 6.2 summarizes ten on the job and off the job training methods against three criteria (objectives, costs, and on-the-job transfer).

In terms of the effectiveness of the various methods, a survey completed by 150 experienced professional trainers (members of the Canadian Society of Training and Development) revealed a hierarchy of effectiveness. As a general

TABLE 6.2

Choosing a Training Method

Method	Training objectives[1]			Costs[2]		Use on the job[3]
	Knowledge	Skills	Attitudes	Dev$	Admin$	Transfer
Lecture	yes	no	no	low	low	low
Video	yes	no	yes	high	low	med
Discussion	no	no	yes	low	low	low
Behaviour modelling	no	yes	no	high		high
Role play	no	yes	yes	med	med	high
Case study	yes	med	yes	med	low	med
Case incident	med	med	med	med	med	med
Games	no	med	no	med	med	low
Simulations	yes	yes	no	high	high	high
Tech-based training	yes	yes	no	high	low	high

[1] Determine the training objective and match the training methods to that objective
[2] Consider the costs of the method (development and administration) and its potential benefits
[3] Determine suitability for transfer to the job

principle, the more highly involved the trainee in the learning process and the more the training situation resembles the job, the more likely that transfer to the job will occur. These methods include on-the-job and one-on-one training, simulations, role plays, behaviour modelling, self-study, case studies, and multimedia. A combination of these methods results in even greater transfer. Other methods, such as lectures, discussions, video conferencing, and lunch and learn programs, were not as effective for transfer to the job, perhaps because these techniques allow (and indeed require) trainees be passive absorbers of information.[41]

Two large surveys of training directors found that nine different training methods were effective in achieving different types of training goals.[42] For example, the case study method was rated most effective for problem-solving skills and computer-based instruction was rated best for knowledge retention. The role-play method was evaluated best for changing attitudes and developing interpersonal skills. However, these are only individual perceptions and do not provide information on actual trainee achievements.

It is important to realize that the effectiveness of a training method depends on the training objectives and learning outcomes. Thus, the choice of what training method to use for a particular training program should start with the program's objectives. For example, if the objective is declarative knowledge, you might choose the lecture method. However, if the objective is the acquisition of interpersonal skills, you might want to use the role-play method.

In general, the lecture method will be most effective when you want to impart large amounts of information quickly and at low cost to large groups of trainees. To teach interpersonal skills such as interviewing or negotiations, the most effective methods are behaviour modelling and role playing.

In addition to training objectives, other factors that should be considered when choosing a training method include cost and resource availability, on-the-job application, trainer skill and preferences, and trainee preferences and characteristics. We will now briefly discuss each of these factors.

Cost and Resource Availability

A training method might be extremely effective for achieving a program's objectives, but it might be too costly to design and deliver. For example, a simulation might be appropriate for a training objective but very expensive. Thus, trainers must consider the cost and resources available for designing and delivering training methods.

On-the-Job Application

Another important factor to consider is on-the-job applications. Trainers will choose some methods over others if trainees are expected to apply the newly acquired knowledge and skills on the job. For example, a lecture is not a good choice if the objective is on-the-job application. If trainees are expected to apply new knowledge and skills on the job, then a role play or behavioural modelling will be more effective.

Trainer Skill and Preferences

A trainer might be more skilled at using some methods than others and might have a personal preference for using certain methods. For example, if a trainer is not experienced or comfortable conducting role plays or simulations, then these methods might not be considered. Thus, the choice of a training method will also depend on the skills and preferences of trainers.

Trainee Preferences and Characteristics

Make the
Connection

When choosing a training method the trainer should consider what is best for trainees with respect to their preferences and characteristics. For starters, you might recall the discussion of Kolb's learning styles in Chapter 3. Learning style refers to the way individuals gather information and process it during the learning process. Trainees with different learning styles are likely to prefer different training methods (e.g., lecture versus role playing) and will differ in terms of what training methods will maximize their learning.

Also important is a trainee's ability to benefit from a particular method of instruction. There is some evidence that training methods have differential effects on trainees as a result of differences in trainee characteristics and aptitudes (e.g., abilities, skills, knowledge). This is known as an aptitude-treatment interaction.

Aptitude-treatment interaction (ATI)

Situations in which the effect of a training method depends on trainee characteristics

An **aptitude-treatment interaction (ATI)** refers to situations in which the effect of a training method on trainees depends on trainee characteristics (e.g., aptitude, self-efficacy, demographics). For example, some methods of training might be more or less effective depending on a trainee's aptitude. An aptitude is broadly defined as any characteristic of trainees that affects their ability to learn from the training method. For example, there is some evidence that high-ability trainees benefit more from programs with less structure and greater complexity while low-ability trainees benefit more from explicit and structured programs.[43] Thus, it is important that the training methods chosen are suitable for and matched to trainees' aptitudes.

BLENDED TRAINING

Blended training

The use of a combination of approaches to training such as classroom training, on-the-job training, and computer technology.

Although we have been discussing training methods as if only one can be used in a training program, in reality trainers mix and combine them (e.g., case studies with lecturing). In fact, you might recall that in Chapter 5 we defined **blended training** as an approach that combines classroom training, on-the-job training, and computer technology.

Blended training programs are becoming more common and increasingly the norm. A blended delivery approach has a number of benefits. It allows participants to learn in ways that work for them, allows multiple learning outcomes to be achieved, and increases the possibility that the training will be applied on the job. Trainers must therefore be skilled in a variety of training methods.

In conclusion, when it comes to choosing training methods, each method has its place and there are many factors to consider. Ultimately, mixing, adapting, combining, and blending training methods will usually be the best approach for maximizing trainee learning and retention and facilitating the transfer of training.

SUMMARY

This chapter described nine of the most common instructional training methods. The advantages and disadvantages of each method were described as well as suggestions for their use and how to make them most effective for trainee learning and retention. We also discussed instructional media and how they can be used with the instructional methods. The chapter concluded with a discussion of how to choose training methods and the main factors to consider. We also defined aptitude-treatment interactions and how they need to be considered when choosing a training method. The importance of combining instructional methods and using a blended delivery approach was also discussed.

Key Terms

action learning p. 181
aptitude-treatment interaction p. 186
audio-visual methods p. 183
behaviour modelling p. 174
blended training p. 186
case incident p. 173
case study p. 172
discussion method p. 171
equipment simulators p. 178

games p. 180
instructional media p. 183
instructional methods p. 168
lecture p. 169
physical fidelity p. 179
problem-based learning p. 181
psychological fidelity p. 179
role play p. 176
simulations p. 178

Make the Connection

p. 174: social cognitive theory and conditioning theory are discussed in Chapter 3 on page 74 and page 72

p. 176: overlearning is discussed in Chapter 5 on page 150

p. 182: adult learning theory is discussed in Chapter 3 on page 77

p. 186: learning style is discussed in Chapter 3 on page 69

Web Links

Automatic Data Processing, Inc.: **www.adp.com**

L'Oréal Canada: **www.loreal.ca**

Nycomed Canada: **www.nycomed.ca**

TD Bank: **www.td.com**

TELUS: **www.telus.com**

Required Professional Capabilities (RPCs)

The following RPCs are relevant to material covered in this chapter. The RPC number represents the CCHRA number assigned to the RPC as presented on the CCHRA website. All of the RPCs can be found in the Body of Knowledge at **http://www.chrp.ca/rpc/body-of-knowledge/**

RPC 151: Uses a variety of methods to deliver development programs.

151.04: Methods of training and development (Games and simulations, case method, lecturing, on-the-job training, distance learning, role play, videoconferencing, group discussion)

Discussion Questions

1. What is the difference between a role play and behavioural modelling and what are the advantages and disadvantages of each method? What method do you prefer and why?
2. Review the instructional methods listed in Table 6.1 and discuss the advantages and disadvantages of using each method to train airport passenger and baggage screeners. What methods do you think would be most effective and why?
3. What are the advantages and disadvantages of each of the instructional methods listed in Table 6.1, and when would it be best to use each method? What method do you prefer and why?
4. What are the main factors a trainer should consider when choosing a training method? Explain how each factor will suggest some training methods over others.
5. What is the difference between physical fidelity and psychological fidelity and how would you design a training program to have both?
6. What is an aptitude-treatment interaction and how is it relevant when choosing training methods?
7. What is a blended training program and what are the implications of blended programs for trainers and trainees?
8. What is the difference between games and simulations and what are the advantages and disadvantages of each method? When would it be best to use a game versus a simulation?
9. Explain how the four key elements of observational learning (attention, retention, reproduction, and reinforcement) are relevant for behavioural modelling training.

The Great Training Debate

1. Debate the following: Lectures are not a very effective method of training and should not be used as often as they have in the past.
2. Debate the following: No single training method is best and all training programs should use a blended approach to training.
3. Debate the following: Games might make a training program fun for trainees but they are a waste of time and money when it comes to learning and on-the-job changes in behaviour and performance.

Exercises

In-Class

1. Prepare a five-minute lecture on a topic of your choice using the information on lectures described in the text. Find a partner in your class and review each other's lecture. If time permits, give your lecture to the class or a small group and discuss its effectiveness. What would make your lecture more effective?

2. Choose a training program you have taken that you really liked and one that you did not like. For each one, indicate the instructional methods that were used (see Table 6.1) and how they were used. What effect did the methods have on your satisfaction of the program and your learning? What methods might have improved your satisfaction and learning?

3. Think of a work situation you have either experienced or observed that would lend itself to a role play (e.g., a customer complaining to an employee). Design a role play in which you describe a scenario and the role of two role players. Be clear about the purpose of the role play in terms of its objectives and what the role players are expected to learn. Be sure to include instructions to participants about the scenario and the relationship between the characters. The instructor can have you describe your role play to the class and/or have class members enact it. If role plays are enacted, be sure to also include a debriefing session afterwards.

4. Describe the major tasks involved in performing a previous or current job and how employees are trained. Then review each of the instructional methods in Table 6.1 and describe how they might be used to train employees for the job. What training methods do you think would be most effective? What methods would you recommend and why?

5. For this exercise, your task is to design a short game that can be played in class to learn an interpersonal skill such as communication, team skills, leadership, negotiations, etc. In groups of two or three, choose a skill to focus on, and then design a game to learn the skill. Your game must be designed so that other members of the class can play it during class time. Write a brief description of your game indicating the objectives, the players, the rules, and what team members have to do to get points or win. The instructor can either have you describe your game to the class and/or have class members actually play it. After playing the game, be sure to discuss how effective it was for learning the skill and the participants' reaction to it.

6. You have been asked to develop a course to teach senior executives how to use e-mail. What instructional method would you use and why (see Table 6.1)?

7. Consider the potential of action learning as a training method for your course on training and development. Do you think that action learning would be an effective method? Design an action learning project for your training and development course. Be specific in terms of the objectives, the skills to be developed, and the problems to be worked on and solved.

8. For this exercise you are to design a training program for a task you currently perform or have performed on a job. Once you have decided on

a task, prepare an outline of a lecture that you could use to train other employees to perform the task. Be sure to indicate the main content and points you will include in your lecture. When your lecture outline is complete, review the instructional methods in Table 6.1 and consider adding some of them to your training program. What other instructional methods will you include and why? At what point in your lecture will you include them? Be specific when describing how the other instructional methods will be incorporated into your training program and what they will involve.

9. Many organizations today are using structured employment interviews as part of the selection process. However, not all interviewers or managers know how to conduct a structured employment interview. If your task is to design a training program on how to conduct a structured employment interview, what instructional training method(s) would you use and why? For each of the methods in Table 6.1, indicate whether you would use it for your training program. Be sure to explain your reasoning. Once you have decided which method(s) you will use, briefly describe how and why you will use them and for what purpose.

In-the-Field

1. Contact the human resources department of an organization to learn about the instructional methods they use to train employees. In particular, you should inquire about:

   - What instructional methods they use, what they use them for, and why they use them (refer to Table 6.1).

   - Do they use a blended approach to training? Why or why not?

   - Do they use certain methods for particular training programs?

   - Do they prefer to use certain methods more than others?

   - What methods do they believe to be the most effective for training employees in their organization?

   - What factors do they consider when choosing instructional methods?

2. To learn more about action learning, visit the World Institute for Action Learning at **www.wial.org** and answer the following questions:

   a. Provide an overview of action learning and discuss what companies are using it for. Why is action learning effective?
   b. What are the six components of action learning?
   c. What are the benefits of action learning?
   d. Describe some action learning success stories.

Case Incident

In-Flight Crew Training at JetBlue

JetBlue Airways was launched in 2000. In 2005, the company had just over 20,000 applicants for in-flight crew (flight attendant) positions with only 600 selected for training. After a rigorous recruitment and selection process, new hires must attend in-flight crew training in order to learn how to serve customers miles in the air and how to respond to emergencies. JetBlue trainees must also learn how to open cabin doors and shout the appropriate commands to evacuate the aircraft in 90 seconds.

Questions

1. How should JetBlue train new flight attendants? What are the advantages and disadvantages of each of the instructional methods listed in Table 6.1?
2. Which instructional methods do you think are most effective for training new flight attendants and why?

Source: M. Weinstein, "JetBlue: Training in the air," *Training*, April, 2006, Pp. 26–27.

Case Study THE CUSTOMER-SERVICE TRAINING PROGRAM

Intense competition among retailers has made customer service a top priority. At many stores today employees welcome customers into the store with cheery greetings and sales staff must have good communication and interpersonal skills to provide customers with excellent service. They also need to be courteous, polite, friendly, and helpful.

A large retail clothing store decided that it needed to improve customer service to be more competitive. It wanted employees to be more active and involved with customers to provide excellent service and improve customer satisfaction ratings.

The company designed a new customer-service training program to train employees how to greet customers, offer assistance, help them find what they are looking for, solve customer complaints and problems, and provide courteous, helpful, and friendly service. An important objective of the program was to provide employees with better interpersonal and communication skills so that they would be able to spend more time interacting with customers and ensure that every customer leaves the store satisfied with his/her shopping experience.

The training program, which was designed in-house and delivered by the company's training staff, began with a lecture in which the trainer described the importance of customer service and the objectives of the training program. Trainees were instructed on the importance of good customer service and how they should behave when they are interacting with customers.

Following the lecture, a video was shown that consisted of different scenarios in which employees were shown interacting with customers. In one scenario, a customer could not find what he was looking for and asked the employee for assistance. The employee was not friendly and told the customer to try looking in another aisle. In another incident, a customer complained to an employee about something she had purchased that was less expensive at another store. She demanded a price reduction or her money back. The customer began raising her voice and the employee yelled at the customer and told her to leave the store. Similar incidents of poor customer service were also shown in the video.

After the video, the trainer asked trainees what was wrong with each scenario and how the employee should have behaved to provide better customer service. At the end of the discussion, the trainer provided a brief lecture outlining the key points shown in the video. This was followed by a video that showed scenarios of employees providing good customer service. A brief discussion and lecture followed in which the trainees were asked to describe what the employee did in each situation to provide good service. The trainer concluded the session by highlighting the key customer-service behaviours.

Trainees then had to take a test on their knowledge of customer service. The test consisted of multiple choice questions that asked trainees to choose the most appropriate behaviour in different situations with customers. Most of the trainees did very well on the test and received a customer-service qualification certificate upon completing the training program. Trainees reacted positively to the training program, which was considered to be a success.

However, back on the job some employees still had difficulty interacting and communicating with customers. For example, in one incident a customer demanded his money back for a pair of pants that had shrunk after cleaning. He blamed the employee for the store's poor quality and called the employee an idiot. The employee didn't know what to do and just walked away in tears.

In another incident, a customer came into the store to pick up a shirt that he had asked an employee to hold for him. The item had been sold and it was the last one in the store. The employee apologized saying that it had been sold to somebody else by accident. However, the customer insisted that the employee call the customer who bought the shirt and have him return it. The employee said she could not do that and told the customer how sorry she was. The customer refused to leave the store unless the employee called the customer who bought the shirt. The employee threatened to call security if the customer did not leave the store. He finally left but not before causing a big scene in the store in front of many other customers. Later that day the employee quit.

One month after the training program there was no improvement in customer satisfaction ratings and four of the sales staff who had attended the training program had quit. Management began to wonder whether the training program was effective. They were not sure whether more time was needed for the effects of the training program to show up in customer satisfaction scores or whether the training program was a failure.

Questions

1. How effective was the customer-service training program? What are its strengths and weaknesses?
2. Describe the instructional methods that were used in the customer-service training program. Do you think these were appropriate methods to use?
3. What other instructional methods could have been used to make the customer-service training program more effective? Review the methods in Table 6.1 and indicate how effective each one would be using the criteria in the chapter to select training methods.

4. If you were to redesign the customer-service training program, what instructional methods would you use and why?

5. What does this case say about instructional methods and the effectiveness of a training program? What does it say about choosing training methods?

Flashback Questions

1. Refer to the material in Chapter 3 on learning and motivation and consider the following:
   a. What learning outcomes are the focus of the customer-service training program?
   b. What do learning theories tell us about why the customer-service training program was not more effective and how to make it more effective?
   c. What do the motivation theories tell us about why the customer-service training program was not more effective and how to make it more effective?
   d. What role does training motivation play in understanding the customer-service training program?

2. Refer to the material in Chapter 5 on training design and consider the following:
   a. To what extent was active practice used in the customer-service training program and was it used appropriately? How else might active practice have been used?
   b. To what extent were the conditions of practice before (pre-training interventions) and during training used in the customer-service training program? What conditions of practice might have been used and why?
   c. Consider the relevance of adaptive expertise for the customer-service training program. Is adaptive expertise relevant and if so, how might the program been designed to facilitate active learning?

REFERENCES

1. Based on Klie, S. (2008, October 6). L'Oréal plays games with training. *Canadian HR Reporter, 21(17)*, 26; Klie, S. (2007, October 22). L'Oréal a pretty picture of diversity, training. *Canadian HR Reporter, 20(18)*, 11; www.loreal.ca.

2. Brown, K. G., & Sitzmann, T. (2011). Training and employee development for improved performance. In S. Zedeck (Ed.), *Handbook of industrial and organizational psychology* (Vol. 2, pp. 469–503). Washington, DC: American Psychological Association.

3. Lavis, C. (2011). *Learning & development outlook 2011: Are organizations ready for learning 2.0?* Ottawa: The Conference Board of Canada; Green, M., & McGill, E. (2011, November). 2011 state of the industry report. *T+D, 65(11)*, 44–50.

4. Arthur, W. Jr., Bennett, W. Jr., Edens, P. S., & Bell, S. T. (2003). Effectiveness of training in organizations: A meta-analysis of design and evaluation features. *Journal of Applied Psychology, 88*, 234–245.

5. Renner, P. (1988). *The quick instructional planner*. Vancouver: Training Associates Ltd.

6. Zander, A. (1982). *Making groups effective*. San Francisco: Jossey-Bass Publishers.

7. Gabris, G. (1989). Educating elected officials in strategic goal setting. *Public Productivity and Management Review, 13(2)*, 161–175.

8. Conlin, J. (1989). Conflict at meetings: Come out fighting. *Successful Meetings, 38(6)*, 30–36; Renner, P. (1988); Wein, G. (1990). Experts as trainers. *Training and Development Journal, 44(7)*, 29–30.

9. Keller, S., & Chuvala, J. (1992). Training: Tricks of the trade. *Security Management, 36(7)*.

10. Yin, R. K. (1985). *Case study research: Design and methods*. Beverly Hills: Sage Publications.

11. Pearce, J. A., Robinson, R. B., Jr., & Zahra Shaker, A. (1989). *An industry approach to cases in strategic management*. Boston: Irwin Publishing.

12. Wright, P. (1992). The CEO and the business school: Is there potential for increased cooperation? *Association of Management Proceedings: Education, 10(1)*, 41–45.

13. Craig, R. L. (1987). *Training and development handbook: A guide to human resource development* (pp. 414–429). New York: McGraw-Hill Inc.

14. Craig, R. L. (1987).

15. Schnelle, K. (1967). *Case analysis and business problem solving*. New York: McGraw-Hill.

16. Craig, R. L. (1987).

17. Leenders, M. R., & Erskine, J. A. (1973). *Case research: The case writing process*. London: University of Western Ontario Press.

18. Taylor, P. J., Russ-Eft, D. F., & Chan, D. W. L. (2005). A meta-analytic review of behavior modeling training. *Journal of Applied Psychology, 90*, 692–709.

19. Baldwin, T. T. (1992). Effects of alternative modeling strategies on outcomes of interpersonal-skills training. *Journal of Applied Psychology, 77*, 147–154; Taylor, P. J., Russ-Eft, D. F., & Chan, D. W. L. (2005).

20. Robinson, J. C. (1982). *Developing managers through behaviour modelling*. Austin: Texas.

21. Georges, J. C. (1988). Why soft-skills training doesn't take. *Training, 25(4)*, 44–45.

22. Taylor, P. J., Russ-Eft, D. F., & Chan, D. W. L. (2005).

23. Buller, M., & McEvoy, G. (1990). Exploring the long-term effects of behaviour modelling training. *Journal of Organizational Change Management, 3(1)*.

24. Atkins, E. (1999, March) Winning through prevention. *Workplace News*, p. 9.

25. Karve, S. (2011, November). Setting the stage for effective role plays. *T+D, 65(11)*, 76–77.

26. Karve, S. (2011, November).

27. Brown, K. G., & Sitzmann, T. (2011).

28. Salas, E., & Cannon-Bowers, J. A. (2001). The science of training: A decade of progress. *Annual Review of Psychology, 52*, 471–99.

29. Powell, B. (2005, December 5). Troops rehearse for disaster. *Toronto Star*, B1.

30. Musselwhite, C., Kennedy, S., & Probst, N. (2010, August). Best practices for facilitating simulations. *T+D, 64(8)*, 26–28.

31. Greenlaw, B., Herron, M., & Ramdon, L. (1962). *Business simulation in industrial and university education*. Englewood Cliffs, NJ: Prentice-Hall.

32. Baldwin, T. T. (1992).

33. Tannenbaum, S. I., & Yukl, G. (1992). Training and development in work organizations. *Annual Review of Psychology, 43*, 399–441.

34. Brown, K. G., & Sitzmann, T. (2011).

35. Revans, R. W. (1982). *The origins and growth of action learning*. Gock, Sweden: Bratt—Institute for Neues Lernen.

36. Revans, R. W. (1984). Action learning: Are we getting there? *Management Decision Journal, 22(1)*, 45–52.

37. Vu, U. (2005, April 25). Action learning popular in Europe, not yet caught on in Canada. *Canadian HR Reporter, 18(8)*, 1, 17.

38. Anonymous (2011, January/February). Best practices & outstanding initiatives. *Training, 48(1)*, 94–98; www.adp.com.

39. Brown, K. G., & Sitzmann, T. (2011).

40. Anonymous. (2008, May 19). CEOs talk: Training & development. *Canadian HR Reporter, 21(10)*, 11–13.

41. Belcourt, M., & Saks, A. M. (1998, February). Training methods and the transfer of training. *Canadian Learning Journal*, 3.

42. Newstrom, J. W. (1980). Evaluating the effectiveness of training methods. *Personnel Administrator, 25(1)*, 55–60; Carrol, S. J., Paine, F. T., & Ivancevich, J. J. (1972). The relative effectiveness of training methods—expert opinion and research. *Personnel Psychology, 25*, 495–510.

43. Tannenbaum, S. I., & Yukl, G. (1992). Training and development in work organizations. *Annual Review of Psychology, 43*, 399–441.

On-the-Job Training Methods

CHAPTER LEARNING OUTCOMES

After reading this chapter you should be able to:

- describe the following on-the-job training methods: job instruction training, performance aids, job rotation, apprenticeships, coaching, and mentoring
- list the advantages and disadvantages of each training method
- describe how and when to use each training method
- describe the coaching process and how to design a coaching program
- define mentoring and describe how to develop a formal mentoring program
- describe the advantages and disadvantages of on-the-job and off-the-job training methods

WHITE SPOT

White Spot restaurant was founded in Vancouver in 1928 by Nat Bailey. It started as a small log cabin drive-in with a white spot painted on its roof. White Spot now has 64 locations throughout British Columbia and Alberta and employs more than 4,000 people.

As part of its commitment to quality and culinary excellence, White Spot offers its chefs an in-house skills upgrading program. Chefs can learn the skills they need to become a Red Seal certified chef from James Kennedy, the chain's Corporate Training Chef. The Red Seal certification is the standardized certification for Canadian chefs and is a recognized symbol of quality.

In an effort to increase the training and skill of its chefs and the number of nationally certified chefs in its restaurants, White Spot implemented a Red Seal Chef Certification program in 2008. Chefs with the Red Seal certification are in high demand, and finding certified chefs is difficult. The traditional certification process for new chefs takes three years and includes an annual month-long classroom component, which can interfere with an individual's career and leave a restaurant without a chef.

According to White Spot president Warren Erhart, "Unlike the traditional model, where they would have to leave their employer and go to college to get their skill-level training, we can provide that through the White Spot environment. We think it's a more pragmatic way for people to both work in our restaurant and get paid to get their papers. We can customize our learning and training times around the business needs."

White Spot is the first restaurant to offer all the components of a full indentured apprenticeship program in-house, something that has been available only at post-secondary institutions. The program is conducted by White Spot's Corporate Training Chef at its corporate training kitchen and with key industry partners at their facilities. White Spot's Red Seal chefs who complete the skills upgrading program supervise the apprentices while they work in the kitchens. The Corporate Training Chef oversees the classroom component in the chain's corporate kitchen for one day every three weeks.

According to Erhart, the restaurant hopes the program will help the chain retain more of its cooking staff. Before the skills upgrading program was available, White Spot lost several cooks who took jobs at other establishments in order to get their certification. White Spot is now keeping people longer because they can get their chef papers while working.

The Red Seal Certification program is an opportunity for White Spot's chefs to develop their skills and pursue certification on the job without disrupting their regular work schedule and earnings.

Today, White Spot is one of British Columbia's most popular restaurants. In 2010, 87 percent of British Columbians dined at White Spot, which was recognized as one of Canada's 50 Best Managed Companies.[1]

Source: S. Klie, "Restaurant's training a recipe for success," *Canadian HR Reporter*, June 2, 2008, P. 8; www.whitespot.com

White Spot is a great example of an organization that uses on-the-job training to train its employees. In this chapter, we focus on some of the most common methods of on-the-job training. According to the Conference Board of Canada, most Canadian organizations report using on-the-job training to train employees.[2]

Table 7.1 lists the six types of on-the-job training methods described in this chapter. We begin with the most basic form of on-the-job training—when one person trains another person on how to do something—and conclude with some of the more expensive and time-consuming methods such as coaching and mentoring.

TABLE 7.1

On-the-Job Training Methods

1. *Job instruction training.* A formalized, structured, and systematic approach to on-the-job training that consists of four steps: preparation, instruction, performance, and follow-up.
2. *Performance aid.* A device at the job site that helps an employee perform his/her job.
3. *Job rotation.* A training method in which trainees are exposed to many functions and areas within an organization.
4. *Apprenticeship.* Training for skill trades workers that combines on-the-job training with classroom instruction.
5. *Coaching.* A training method in which a more experienced and knowledgeable person is formally called upon to help another person develop the insights and techniques pertinent to the accomplishment of their job.
6. *Mentoring.* A method in which a senior member of an organization takes a personal interest in the career of a junior employee.

ON-THE-JOB TRAINING (OJT) METHODS

The most common method of training is **on-the-job training**, in which a trainee receives instruction at his/her workstation from a supervisor or an experienced co-worker. Most of us can probably remember a time when a co-worker was assigned the job of training us to perform a task such as operating a cash register or learning how to make a request for supplies. Although on-the-job training has been practised since at least the Middle Ages, the United States army formalized the concept during World War II.

There are a number of different approaches for on-the-job training. Table 7.2 provides a description of the various ways in which on-the-job training can be accomplished, such as training a group of employees on the spot, observing performance and providing feedback, and so on.

On-the-job training
A training method in which a trainee receives instruction and training at his or her workstation from a supervisor or an experienced co-worker

TABLE 7.2

Approaches to On-the-Job Training

On-the-spot lecture Gather trainees into groups and tell them how to do the job.

Viewed performance/Feedback Watch the person at work and give constructive feedback, such as when the sales manager makes a call with a new salesperson.

Following Nellie The supervisor trains a senior employee, who in turn trains new employees (showing the ropes).

Job-aid approach A job aid (step-by-step instructions or video) is followed while the trainer monitors performance.

The training step The trainer systematically introduces the task.

Sequence Follows a planned sequence. For example: Provide an on-the-spot lecture, gather trainees into groups, and tell them how to do the job.

On-the-job training (OJT) is an important part of training at McDonald's Canada. As one of Canada's largest employers of youth, the company needs to train thousands of new crew members every year. Although the company once used videos and classroom training, it now uses a buddy system combined with hands-on training and visual aids. A more experienced employee or "buddy" works with a new member individually on the job. In addition, laminated visual aids are used to show the steps in a task at each station and as a form of visual reinforcement. New crew members can refer to it during training and on the job. The combination of hands-on training and visual reinforcement is believed to result in higher levels of trainee self-efficacy and performance.[3]

OJT is especially useful for small businesses because of the limited investment needed to conduct the training. In fact, a survey found that 43 percent of small and medium-sized enterprises use informal training methods such as on-the-job training, tutoring, and mentoring, while just 2 percent use only formal training such as the classroom, seminars, and workshops. Forty-three percent said that they use both on-the-job and formal training methods.[4]

Although on-the-job training is the most common approach to training, it has also been described as the most misused.[5] This is because on-the-job training is often not well planned or structured. Another problem is that most people assigned the task of training others on the job have not received training on how to be a trainer. As a result, managers and employees do not have the knowledge and skills required to be effective trainers and are not familiar with learning principles such as active practice, feedback, and reinforcement.

Another problem is that poor employees teach undesirable work habits and attitudes to new employees and the traditional ways of doing things will be passed on to new employees, which means that existing problems as well as poor attitudes and behaviours will persist.

Other problems occur when those doing the training are worried that newly trained employees will one day take over their jobs. Some trainers might abuse their position by making the trainee do all the dirty work and the trainee might not learn important skills. In addition, OJT can be time consuming and some employees feel penalized when they can't earn as much money or meet their goals because of the time they have to spend training others. Thus, for all these reasons OJT is not always effective and has been referred to as the most used and misused training method.[6]

The main problem with the traditional unstructured approach to on-the-job training is that it results in training that is inconsistent, inefficient, and ineffective. However, when the process is carefully planned and structured, it can be a highly effective and efficient method of training.[7]

In fact, in one of the few studies to test the effectiveness of on-the-job training, structure was shown to be very important. In the study, a group of newly hired workers received training on how to operate a manufacturing process. One group received traditional on-the-job training in which one worker was trained by the supervisor, and then each person trained another one (similar to the Following Nellie approach described in Table 7.2). A second group was trained by a supervisor who used a structured approach to on-the-job training.

The results showed that the structured approach was considerably more effective. Trainees who received structured on-the-job training reached a predetermined level of skill and productivity in one-quarter of the time it took to train the other group. They also produced 76 percent fewer rejects, and their troubleshooting ability increased by 130 percent. This study highlights the importance of building structure into on-the-job training and the positive effect it can have on trainee learning and performance.[8]

In the next section, we describe a structured and effective approach to on-the-job training called job instruction training.

JOB INSTRUCTION TRAINING

While the traditional unstructured approach to on-the-job training has many problems, more structured approaches to on-the-job training can be highly effective. The best known structured approach to on-the-job training is known as job instruction training.

Job instruction training is a formalized, structured, and systematic approach to on-the-job training that consists of four steps: preparation, instruction, performance, and follow-up. To some extent, job instruction training incorporates the principles of behaviour modelling. You might recall from Chapter 6 that behavioural modelling is a training method in which trainees observe a model performing a task and then attempt to imitate the observed behaviour.

With job instruction training, the trainer demonstrates task performance on the job and then provides the trainee with opportunities to practise while the trainer provides feedback and reinforcement. The trainer then monitors the trainees' performance on the job. Thus, like behaviour modelling, job instruction training involves observation, rehearsal, reinforcement, and transfer. Let's now consider each of the steps of job instruction training.

Job instruction training
A formalized, structured, and systematic approach to on-the-job training that consists of four steps: preparation, instruction, performance, and follow-up

Make the
Connection

Step 1: Preparation

During the preparation step, the trainer breaks down the job into small tasks, prepares all the equipment and supplies necessary to do the task, and allocates a time frame to learn each task. A key activity during the preparation step is to develop a communication strategy that fits the trainee and to find out what the trainee already knows. The trainer needs to understand the background, capabilities, and attitudes of trainees as well as the nature of the tasks to be performed before choosing a technique or combination of techniques. If the training is too easy or difficult for a trainee, the trainer can make adjustments to suit his or her needs.

The second part of preparation concerns the trainee. There are three components: putting the trainee at ease, guaranteeing the learning, and building interest and showing personal advantage.[9]

Putting the Trainee at Ease

The trainer must remember that the trainee might be apprehensive. It is unwise to begin too abruptly. Some small talk might be appropriate to relax the trainee and to set the tone for the training session. Most individuals learn more readily when they are relaxed. A short conversation concerning any matter of interest—the weather, sports, a work-related item—should be effective. Obviously, the topic chosen must be suitable for the situation.

Guaranteeing the Learning

When the conversation turns to the training, the trainer needs to guarantee to the trainee that learning is possible. Again, use a simple statement, "Don't worry about this machine, Nadine. In about three hours you will be operating it almost as well as everyone else. I've trained at least 10 people in this procedure." The trainee now knows that it is possible to learn (i.e., learning will take place) and that the trainer has the ability to teach the process, adding to her self-efficacy. Recall from Chapter 3 that self-efficacy refers to judgments people have about their ability to successfully perform a specific task and that it is a key factor in the success of a training program.

Make the
Connection

Building Interest and Showing Personal Advantage

Trainees might be apprehensive or might not understand the effect that training will have on the quality of their work. Developing trainee enthusiasm is sometimes difficult, but pointing out some personal gain helps to create interest. The idea that the training will lead to something positive creates the opportunity to design rewards: more self-esteem, easier work, higher-level work, less routine, more control over work, greater opportunity or security. Once the appropriate reward is found (provided it can be obtained), most employees will respond positively.

Some trainees will resist, as training is change and individuals accept change at different rates. The trainee preparation step will identify those who are not responding. As the trainer is responsible for meeting measurable objectives, it is important to evaluate the likelihood of cooperation among trainees so that individual remedial action can be taken. One way to defuse resistance is to train employees in order of their perceived enthusiasm. When the resisters see others reaping the rewards of training, they usually agree to be trained.

Step 2: Instruction

The instruction step involves telling, showing, explaining, and demonstrating the task to the trainee. If the trainee is to perform a task or an operation, he or she should be positioned slightly behind or beside the trainer so that the job is viewed from a realistic angle. The trainer can then proceed as follows:

Show the Trainee How to Perform the Job

- Break the job into manageable tasks and present only as much as can be absorbed at one time. Remember that individuals learn at different speeds, so while some trainees might be able to learn six or seven sequences at once, others can absorb only four or five.
- Repeat Step 1 as necessary and be patient.
- Explain why as well as how.
- Point out possible difficulties as well as safety procedures.
- Encourage questions.

Repeat and Explain Key Points in More Detail

- Safety is especially important.
- Take the time to show how the job fits into any larger systems.
- Show why the job is important.
- Show why key points are more important than others.
- Repeat Step 2 as necessary and be patient.
- Encourage questions.

Allow the Trainee to See the Whole Job Again

- Ask questions to determine the level of comprehension.
- Repeat Step 3 as necessary and be patient.
- Encourage questions.

Step 3: Performance

During the performance step, the trainee performs the task under the trainer's guidance and the trainer provides feedback and reinforcement. Each task is learned in a similar way until the whole job can be completed without error. This can be done in the following manner:

Ask the Trainee to Perform Less Difficult Parts of the Job

- Try to ensure initial success.
- Don't tell how. If possible, ask questions, but try to keep the trainee's frustration level low.
- Ask the trainee to explain the steps.

Allow the Trainee to Perform the Entire Job

- Gently suggest improvements where necessary.
- Provide feedback on performance.
- Reinforce correct behaviour.

Step 4: Follow-up

Once the performance step is complete, the trainee will be left on his/her own to perform the task. This does, not, however mean that the training is over. In the follow-up step, the trainer monitors the trainee's performance. It is important that the trainer keep track of the trainee's performance and provide support and feedback. The trainer should leave the trainee to work alone, indicate when and where to find help if necessary, supervise closely and check performance periodically, and then gradually taper off instruction as the employee gains confidence and skill.

Tips for Trainers

Sloman developed a set of rules for effective on-the-job training based on a study of three British National Training Award winners.[10] First, job instruction training should not be managed differently from other types of training. Second, it should be integrated with other training methods. Third, ownership must be maintained even when consultants are used. And fourth, trainers must be chosen with care and trained properly. In addition to being experts in the skill area, they must want to be trainers and have good communication skills. Patience and respect for differences in the ability to learn are also important as the trainer sets the initial mood or climate of the learning experience.[11]

Once suitable individuals are found they should be trained (train-the-trainer) and then recognized and rewarded for training others. It is of little use to give training responsibilities to an already busy employee without restructuring his or her job to include a training element. Nor is increased pay always the most sought-after reward (although it doesn't hurt). Recognition, the chance to add variety to the work day, respect from new employees, training certificates, and the prospect of either promotion or cross training help to make the experience worthwhile for the individual.

While the steps of job instruction training might seem elaborate, they must be applied with the complexity and possible safety hazards of the job in mind. Very simple tasks might require only one demonstration. As well, employees bring different skills and backgrounds to the workplace. Competent preparation will eliminate overtraining and the resultant boredom and inattention.

PERFORMANCE AIDS

Performance aid

A device at the job site that helps an employee perform his/her job

A **performance aid**, which is also known as a job aid, is a device at the job site that helps an employee perform his/her job. Performance aids can be signs or prompts ("Have you turned off the computer?"); trouble-shooting aids ("If the red light goes on, the machine needs oil"); instructions in sequence ("To empty the machine, follow the next five steps"); a special tool or gauge (a long stick to measure how much gas is in an inaccessible tank); flash cards to help counsel clients; pictures (of a perfectly set table, for example); or posters and checklists.[12]

For example, employees learning about hazardous-waste management might be provided with a checklist that summarizes the major steps for handling radioactive material. This checklist, if prepared as a colourful poster, will increase the chances of employee application. As indicated earlier, McDonald's uses laminated visual aids to remind trainees of the steps in a task and as a form of visual reinforcement that they can refer to during training and on the job.

The reasoning behind the use of performance aids is that requiring the memorization of sequences and tasks can take too much training time, especially if the task is not repeated daily. They are also useful when performance is difficult, is executed infrequently, can be done slowly, and when the consequences of poor performance are serious.[13] As well, new employees can be on the job more quickly if armed with a series of temporary performance aids. Finally, routine (and not-so-routine) trouble-shooting and repair responses can be performed much more quickly and with less frustration.

Employees who are placed in positions where they must react very quickly might not be able to rely on memory. A panel operator in a nuclear power plant, for example, may have 15 seconds (or less) to perform a series of safety sequences. In the less hectic world of insurance sales, one manager found that a potentially sound sales trainee constantly neglected to complete the entire sales sequence and paperwork. Both these employees, despite their vastly different work environments, were helped by performance aids.

In the first instance, an indexed manual containing various operating sequences was developed and placed on a wheeled trolley within easy reach of all the operators' positions. The sales problem was solved by creating a checklist containing all the steps or tasks to be completed each time the salesperson visited a prospective client. The employee completed and checked off each step and the sheet was signed and dated. The manager then reviewed each call with the trainee. In this case, the checklist was discarded after about three weeks as the sales trainee was performing to the standards set by management.[14]

For an example of a performance aid that can save lives, see Training Today 7.1, "Operating Room Checklist Saves Lives," and Table 7.3.

Tips for Trainers

When designing visual performance aids that help employees remember key information, all the skills of the graphic artist's craft should be utilized. Ease in reading, space between letters, colour, boldness, symbols, and graphic language

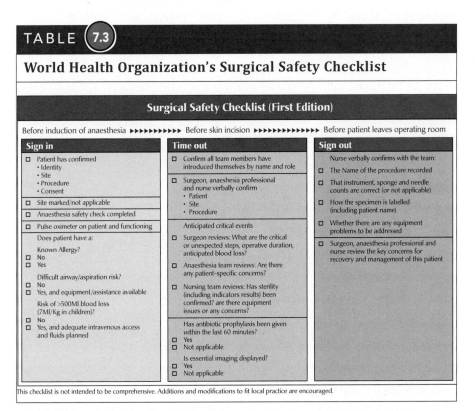

TABLE 7.3

World Health Organization's Surgical Safety Checklist

Surgical Safety Checklist (First Edition)

Before induction of anaesthesia ▶▶▶▶▶▶▶▶▶▶ Before skin incision ▶▶▶▶▶▶▶▶▶▶▶▶ Before patient leaves operating room

Sign in	Time out	Sign out
☐ Patient has confirmed 　• Identity 　• Site 　• Procedure 　• Consent	☐ Confirm all team members have introduced themselves by name and role	Nurse verbally confirms with the team: ☐ The Name of the procedure recorded
☐ Site marked/not applicable	☐ Surgeon, anaesthesia professional and nurse verbally confirm 　• Patient 　• Site 　• Procedure	☐ That instrument, sponge and needle counts are correct (or not applicable)
☐ Anaesthesia safety check completed		☐ How the specimen is labelled (including patient name)
☐ Pulse oximeter on patient and functioning	Anticipated critical events	☐ Whether there are any equipment problems to be addressed
Does patient have a: Known Allergy? ☐ No ☐ Yes	☐ Surgeon reviews: What are the critical or unexpected steps, operative duration, anticipated blood loss?	☐ Surgeon, anaesthesia professional and nurse review the key concerns for recovery and management of this patient
Difficult airway/aspiration risk? ☐ No ☐ Yes, and equipment/assistance available	☐ Anaesthesia team reviews: Are there any patient-specific concerns?	
Risk of >500Ml blood loss (7Ml/Kg in children)? ☐ No ☐ Yes, and adequate intravenous access and fluids planned	☐ Nursing team reviews: Has sterility (including indicators results) been confirmed? are there equipment issues or any concerns?	
	Has antibiotic prophylaxis been given within the last 60 minutes? ☐ Yes ☐ Not applicable	
	Is essential imaging displayed? ☐ Yes ☐ Not applicable	

This checklist is not intended to be comprehensive. Additions and modifications to fit local practice are encouraged.

Source: WHO Surgical Safety Checklist, http://www.who.int/patientsafety/safesurgery/tools_resources/SSSL_Checklist_finalJun08.pdf. © World Health Organization, 2009. All rights reserved.

("Pull Here!") are all used to communicate more effectively.[15] Audio aids also must clearly communicate intent. A taped warning ("Connect your safety harness!") may be useless, but a buzzer alarm is hard to ignore.

When designing a training program, it is important to consider how performance aids might save time and money. With ingenuity, the trainee's work-life not only can be made easier, but significant improvements in performance, downtime, and safety records can result. Performance aids work even better with the use of technology. Performance aids that use technology are called electronic performance-support systems and are described in Chapter 8.

Training Today 7.1

Operating Room Checklist Saves Lives

Surgical complications are a common yet often preventable problem that causes the death and disability of patients all around the world. In an effort to reduce the rate of major surgical complications, the World Health Organization (WHO) has developed a surgical safety checklist to be used during major operations. The Surgical Safety Checklist (see Table 7.3) requires surgeons to perform safety checks at three times during surgical procedures: before induction of anaesthesia (Sign In); before skin incision (Time Out); and before the patient leaves the operating room (Sign Out).

The checklist includes a total of 19 checks and is designed to ensure that the correct surgery site is marked, that prophylactic antibiotics are given, that blood loss is closely monitored, that sponge and needle counts are correct, and that there is effective teamwork by the operating room staff. A check in which members of the surgical team introduce themselves to each other by name is crucial because it increases the chance that a member of the team will speak up when something is going wrong. A checklist coordinator is required to confirm that the team has completed each task on the checklist before proceeding with the operation.

Eight hospitals in eight cities (Toronto, New Delhi, Amman, Auckland, Manila, Ifakara, London, and Seattle) participated in the World Health Organization's Safe Surgery Saves Lives program. Data were collected from 3,733 patients who underwent surgery without the use of the Surgical Safety Checklist and from 3,955 patients who had surgery after the introduction of the checklist.

A comparison of the two groups of patients indicated that the use of the checklist resulted in one-third fewer surgery-related deaths and complications. The rate of major complications following surgery fell from 11 percent to 7 percent after introduction of the checklist. Inpatient deaths following major operations fell by more than 40 percent (from 1.5 percent to 0.8 percent).

The Toronto General Hospital was the only Canadian hospital that took part in the study. The results were so impressive that the checklist has also been adopted by the Toronto Western Hospital and the Princess Margaret Hospital.

The chief executive officer of the Canadian Patient Safety Institute is requesting that health ministers in every province and territory have the checklist implemented in all acute-care hospitals. Countries such as England, Ireland, Jordan, and the Philippines have already established nationwide programs to implement the checklist in operating rooms.

The checklist is considered to be a no-cost innovation and one of the most significant safeguards in the past three decades. The use of the checklist in Canada could prevent an estimated 40,000 complications a year and result in enormous savings to the health-care system.

Source: A. B. Haynes et al., "A surgical safety checklist to reduce morbidity and mortality in a global population," *The New England Journal of Medicine*, 2009, Vol. 360 (5), Pp. 491–499; L. Priest, "Simple checklist saves lives in the operating room, study finds," *The Globe and Mail*, Jan. 15, 2009, P. A4; "Checklist helps reduce surgical complications, deaths," World Health Organization, WHO News Release, www.who.int/en/.

JOB ROTATION

Job rotation is a training method in which trainees are exposed to different jobs, functions, and areas within an organization. It broadens an individual's knowledge and skills by providing him/her with multiple perspectives and areas of expertise.

Job rotation is often used as part of an ongoing career-development program, especially for employees who are destined to management positions. The objective is for an employee to learn a variety of skills both from doing a variety of tasks and by observing the performance of others. Typically the individual will be supervised by a supervisor who is responsible for the individual's training.

More and more companies are using job rotation as part of the training of new graduates and high-potential employees or what they refer to as rotational leadership programs. To learn more, see Training Today 7.2, "Rotational Leadership Programs."

Job rotation is also an effective means of cross training employees. **Cross training** involves training employees to perform each other's jobs so that anyone can step in and perform any member's job if necessary. Cross training is particularly popular with cross-functional teams. By rotating team members to the various positions on a team, each team member learns the skills required to perform all of the team's tasks and jobs. Cross training not only provides greater flexibility for organizations, but also enables employees to learn and use more skills. Toronto Hydro uses cross training for its supervisors so that they can work across specializations.[16]

Job rotation is an effective method of training employees who need to learn a variety of skills. By providing employees with a series of on-the-job experiences in which they work on a variety of tasks, jobs, and assignments, they will acquire the skills required to perform their current job as well as future job responsibilities.

Research on job rotation has generally been supportive. It not only results in an improvement in knowledge and skills but also has a number of career benefits such as higher job satisfaction, more opportunities for career advancement, and a higher salary.[17]

Job rotation
A training method in which trainees are exposed to different jobs, functions, and areas within an organization

Cross training
Training employees to perform each other's jobs

Tips for Trainers

Although job rotation has many benefits, a disadvantage is that if an employee does not spend enough time in a department or working on an assignment, he or she might not have sufficient time to get up to speed and complete an assignment. Thus, a trainee might acquire only a superficial understanding of a job or department and this might result in some frustration. Therefore, it is important that job rotation be carefully planned and structured so that trainees receive sufficient exposure and experience on each assignment to make it a worthwhile learning experience. In addition, the assignments should be tailored to each individual's training.

It is also important that job rotation be part of a larger training program and integrated with other training methods. That is, job rotation should be one component of a training program and learning process and supplemented with classroom instruction and coaching or mentoring. Coaching and mentoring are important because trainees need some guidance and supervision throughout the job rotation process.

Training Today 7.2

Rotational Leadership Programs

Rotational leadership programs provide new graduates, new hires, and high-potential employees an opportunity to try out a variety of roles in different areas of an organization. TELUS has four rotational programs in business transformation, consumer solutions, management, and graduate engineering. While internal employees can come into the program, it is largely directed at new graduates. Those in the first two programs participate in rotations of four to six months while those in the latter two sign on for three one-year rotations. About 70 to 80 new graduates join the program each year, with anywhere from 200 to 300 in the program at one time. Once they have completed their rotations, they move into different positions.

At General Electric, graduates can choose from a variety of two-year leadership development programs: financial management, commercial leadership, engineering, operations management, and human resources. The programs combine rotational work experience with classroom training, mentoring, and performance feedback. About 20 to 30 employees join the programs each year and there are about 8,000 employees at GE in Canada. Participants are given feedback on their performance from their managers at the end of each rotation.

According to Terry Peach, GE manager of organization and staffing, "It accelerates that learning curve by giving you that broader experience. It's really helped (employees) zero in and focus in on what their career interests are because they get a chance to check out the different facets of the business and different types of roles."

RBC launched rotational graduate leadership programs (GLPs) in 2001. Each program is two years long, with four rotations of roughly six to nine months. The enterprise program can include rotations in Canadian banking, operations, IT, wealth management or anywhere there is a need. There is also an annual $3,000 learning budget for participants who are matched with a senior vice-president as a mentor. Four different assignment managers also provide support.

Source: S. Dobson, "Rotating roles put workers on fast track," *Canadian HR Reporter*, Oct. 10, 2009, P. 21. Reprinted by permission of Canadian HR Reporter.

APPRENTICESHIPS

Apprenticeships

Training methods for skilled trades workers that combines on-the-job training and classroom instruction

Apprenticeships are training methods that combine on-the-job training and classroom instruction. It is the primary method of training for skilled trades workers in Canada. The practical on-the-job training component makes up 80 percent of the training and is used to teach the requisite skills of a particular trade or occupation. Classroom instruction, which usually takes place in community colleges, focuses on technical training and comprises a relatively minor portion of apprenticeship programs (20 percent, or 180 hours).[18]

As described at the beginning of the chapter, White Spot apprentices are able to complete their on-the-job training and classroom instruction in-house. Toronto Hydro developed its own trade school and since 2003 it has hired eight overhead power-line apprentices with plans to hire many more of its overhead and underground apprentices.[19]

In Canada, the apprenticeship system covers more than 65 regulated occupations in four occupational sectors: construction (e.g., stone mason, electrician, carpenter, plumber), motive power (motor-vehicle mechanic, machinist), industrial (industrial mechanic, millwright), and service (baker, cook, hairstylist).

The regulation and administration of apprenticeship programs as well as the certification of tradespersons is the responsibility of the provinces and territories. The federal government works with the provinces and territories through the Canadian Council of Directors of Apprenticeship (CCDA) to support the development of a skilled workforce and to facilitate interprovincial mobility of the skilled trades.[20]

In the 1950s the federal, provincial, and territorial governments established the Interprovincial Standards Red Seal Program (also known simply as the Red Seal Program) to facilitate the interprovincial mobility of skilled workers throughout Canada. The CCDA is responsible for the management of the program, which ensures the standardization of training requirements and certification of 49 skilled trades that are covered under the Red Seal program.[21] Recall from the chapter-opening vignette that White Spot's in-house apprenticeship program provides Red Seal certification for its chefs.

Apprentices must be trained and supervised by at least one qualified tradesperson, known as a journeyperson, and pass a provincial government examination to earn a certificate of qualification. Apprentices who pass an interprovincial examination with a minimum grade of 70 percent are awarded a Red Seal certification and achieve the status of journeyperson.

Apprenticeship training differs from other training methods in that it is regulated through a partnership among government, labour, and industry. In Canada, the federal government pays for in-school training and income support. Provincial governments administer the programs and pay for classroom facilities and instructors. Employers absorb the costs of workplace training and apprentices initiate the process by finding employers to sponsor them.

Unlike corporate-sponsored training programs that address the specific needs of an organization, apprenticeships are focused on the collective training needs of specific occupations within broad industrial categories.[22] As a result, the skills learned through apprenticeship training are transferable within an occupation across Canada. This flexibility provides advantages to the worker and the industry when regional fluctuations occur in the supply and demand of skilled labour.

However, the system is highly dependent on employers as they must be willing to sponsor apprentices and provide the on-the-job training component, something that many Canadian organizations are not willing to do.[23]

Many employers are reluctant to provide apprentice training because they do not see the benefits. However, there is evidence that the returns on apprenticeship training investments are realized much sooner than many employers believe. A study by the Canadian Apprenticeship Forum (CAF) found that employers receive a return of $1.47 for every dollar invested in an apprentice and that an apprentice's productive value exceeds the training costs by the end of the second year or earlier. They also found that "homegrown" journeypersons are more productive than externally trained journeypersons.[24]

Tips for Trainers

There has been an increasing demand for skilled tradespersons in Canada and the registration in apprenticeship programs has increased in recent years to record levels. However, the number of people completing apprenticeship programs each year has changed very little over the last several decades.[25]

In addition, Canada's aging population means that many workers in the skilled trades are approaching retirement. As a result, there is a growing skills shortage facing many industrial sectors and it has been predicted that the shortage of skilled workers in Canada could reach one million by the year 2020.[26]

An increased emphasis on apprenticeship training remains the most effective and practical method of teaching skilled trades occupations and dealing with the skills shortage. However, youth interest and entry in apprenticeships has been on the decline and many employers are reluctant to take on apprentices. Recent reports indicate that only 19 percent of Canadian employers sponsor and train apprentices.[27]

Over the years, the federal government has organized a series of round table meetings with government, business, and labour to find ways to address the skills shortage problem and improve apprenticeship training.[28] A number of programs have been implemented to encourage students to enter and remain in the skilled trades and for organizations to sponsor apprentices.

For example, the Apprenticeship Incentive Grant (AIG) is a taxable cash grant of $1,000 that is available to registered apprentices once they have successfully completed their first or second year/level of an apprenticeship program in one of the Red Seal trades. In 2009, the federal government introduced the Apprenticeship Completion Grant (ACG), which is a $2,000 taxable cash grant for apprentices who complete their apprenticeship training in a designated Red Seal trade. Apprenticeship tax credits are also provided by the federal and provincial governments to employers that train apprentices.[29]

The Ontario government is spending $7 million for 700 spaces in pre-apprenticeship training in 38 programs with the aim of increasing the number of people entering full apprenticeships by 7,000 per year. Pre-apprenticeship training provides academic upgrading, technical training, and job placements to prepare potential apprentices in a variety of skilled trades that are facing serious labour shortages.[30]

Another concern is that not all Canadians participate fully in apprenticeship programs. Thus, efforts need to be made to encourage Aboriginal peoples, women, visible minorities, and foreign-trained skilled workers to pursue apprenticeship programs and employment in the skilled trades. Several provinces have implemented programs that introduce women to skilled trades and provide them with hands-on experience.[31]

Finally, human resource and training professionals have a key role to play in promoting and championing apprenticeship training in their organizations and educating their employers on the benefits of apprenticeships. Apprenticeship training can be an effective recruitment and retention strategy that provides organizations with many benefits and can improve their bottom line.[32]

Table 7.4 provides an overview of the benefits of apprenticeship training for organizations. To learn how to increase employer participation in apprenticeship training, see The Trainer's Notebook 7.1, "Increasing Employer Participation in Apprenticeship Training."

TABLE (7.4)

Benefits of Apprenticeship Training

Effective recruitment strategy. Leads to higher retention rates and lower turnover and provides a competitive advantage over non-participating organizations.

Two-way skills development. Mentoring apprentices renews and revitalizes journeypersons' skills, leading to greater productivity.

Higher-quality work. Helps to maintain high standards and quality on the job and develops skills and competencies that meet industry standards and build quality products.

Increased productivity. Productivity is increased because apprentices are trained in the company's systems and work processes.

Improved safety. Makes journeypersons more aware of safe work practices as they teach apprentices; makes employees more familiar with the organization's safety practices leading to fewer accidents which results in reduced compensation costs; and leads to reduced insurance costs for some employers because insurance companies recognize the lower risk of a skilled workforce.

Improve company reputation. Demonstrates an organization's professionalism because it shows it is dedicated to delivering high-quality products through employing highly trained and skilled workers.

Source: *Strategies to increase employer participation in apprenticeship training in Canada.* Ottawa: Canadian Apprenticeship Forum. July, 2008. P. 1.

The Trainer's Notebook 7.1

INCREASING EMPLOYER PARTICIPATION IN APPRENTICESHIP TRAINING

A forum held by the Canadian Apprenticeship Forum made the following recommendations to increase employer participation in apprenticeship training:

- *Educate employers about mentoring.* The process of taking on an apprentice needs to be demystified. Employers may not understand what is involved in mentoring and therefore may be reluctant to take on an apprentice.
- *Inform employers that apprenticeship training is industry driven.* Industry designs the method of delivery in apprenticeship training and a variety of training delivery options are available.
- *Provide incentives to employers.* Incentives are an important way to maintain and enhance participation in apprenticeship training, and some employers might need clarification on the federal/provincial/territorial incentives available.
- *Ensure apprentices understand their value.* Apprentices need to understand their value to

an organization and be informed about wage subsidies and tax credits so they can show what they have to offer to an employer when trying to find a sponsor.

- *Encourage employers to participate in talking to their peers.* Participating employers should inform their colleagues of the benefits of apprenticeship training and encourage non-participating employers to go to schools to discuss with youth a career in the trades; bring non-participating employers to networking events; and give presentations to non-participating employers on the business case for apprenticeship.
- *Build appreciation for skilled labour.* Employers will participate in apprenticeship training if customers and consumers start demanding that they have a skilled labour force and that their employees have trade certification.

Source: *Strategies to increase employer participation in apprenticeship training in Canada.* Ottawa: Canadian Apprenticeship Forum. July, 2008. P. 15.

COACHING

Coaching

An experienced and knowledgeable person is formally called upon to help another person develop the insights and techniques pertinent to the accomplishment of their job

Coaching is a training method in which a more experienced and knowledgeable person is formally called upon to help another person develop the insights and techniques pertinent to the accomplishment of their job. The coach also guides the employee in learning by helping to find experts and resources for learning and development.

Coaching has become popular in many organizations today. For example, SaskEnergy has a coaching program to develop successful leadership behaviours. The program includes assessments, workshops, long-term peer-to-peer coaching triangles involving groups of three people with varying levels of experience, and follow-up evaluations.[33]

Joey Restaurants created a coaching culture that involved training 12 successful senior leaders to be internal coaches so that they can develop the coaching skills of the organization's leaders. The company's new focus on the "leader as coach" has resulted in more than 30 percent revenue growth and a dramatic reduction in turnover. In 2010, Joey Restaurant Group was named one of Canada's Best Workplaces and in 2011 the company was awarded the International Coaching Federation's (ICF) top prize for organizations that have profited through their commitment to coaching as a leadership strategy.[34]

Coaching programs have been effective in enhancing skills and improving performance in a wide range of areas including interpersonal skills, communication skills, leadership skills, cognitive skills, and self-management skills. It is especially effective for helping people apply what they have learned in the classroom on the job.[35]

The coaching process involves the planned use of opportunities in the work environment to improve or to enhance employee strengths and potential. Weaknesses are considered only if they prevent the employee from functioning, or if they are below the manager's tolerance level.[36]

The key elements in the coaching process are "planned," "opportunities in the work environment," and "strengths." First, the process revolves around an agreed-upon plan or set of objectives developed mutually by employee and coach. Development does not occur haphazardly or by chance. The process proceeds in a logical agreed-upon fashion. Second, the work environment is the training laboratory (sometimes expanded to include the community). Transfers, special assignments, vacation replacements, and conference speaking engagements are all potential coaching opportunities. The necessary formal infrastructure, perhaps attached to the firm's appraisal or evaluation system, must be in place for the system to work.[37]

The coaching process begins with a dialogue between coach and employee, during which a set of objectives is defined. Coaching opportunities are then identified by a mutual examination of the environment. A long-term plan is struck, along with an evaluation or measurement procedure. As well, the process is fitted into the employee's career-development goals and made part of the organization's long-term strategies.

The employee performs the agreed-upon task and then reports to the coach both informally and formally during the annual or semi-annual evaluation. They discuss the results of the current program and then plan the next round of activity.[38] With practice, this approach develops into a continual transfer of skills and an ongoing process.[39]

Research has found coaching to be highly effective for both individuals and organizations. In general, the results of a number of studies indicate that individuals who participated in coaching showed dramatic improvements in specific skills and overall performance. Coaching has also been found to improve working relationships and job attitudes, and to increase the rate of advancement and salary increases. Benefits to organizations have been found in productivity, quality, customer service, reduced customer complaints, retention, cost reductions, and bottom-line productivity. Thus, coaching is not only popular, it is also effective.[40]

Tips for Trainers

For coaching to be effective, the employee and the coach must trust each other. Otherwise the employee will see development as extra work. Indeed, perhaps the most important aspect of the coaching process is ongoing dialogue and feedback. It is only under these conditions that employees participate willingly in a two-way process that often requires extra effort and risk taking.[41]

Thus, it is important that the coach build trust and understanding so that employees will want to work with him/her. It is also important that a coach be able to relate to the person he/she is coaching. To be most effective, coaching should be used as part of a broader process of learning rather than a standalone program.[42]

Finally, like any training program, the effectiveness of coaching should be evaluated. Coaching programs are expensive and time consuming so it is important to determine if they are accomplishing what they are supposed to accomplish.

MENTORING

Mentoring is a training method in which a senior member of an organization takes a personal interest in the career of a junior employee. A mentor is an experienced individual, usually a senior manager, who provides coaching and counselling to a junior employee.

Mentors play two major roles: career support and psychosocial support. **Career support** activities include coaching, sponsorship, exposure, visibility, protection, and the provision of challenging assignments. **Psychosocial support** includes being a friend who listens and counsels, who accepts and provides feedback, and who offers a role model for success.[43]

The mentor–protégé relationship was once an informal one with a senior person recognizing the talent of a junior employee and wishing to help. However, organizations now recognize mentoring as a valuable employee development tool and have begun to formalize mentor relationships by implementing formal mentoring programs.

Like coaching, mentoring is popular in organizations today and is also an expensive investment.[44] However, mentoring has a more narrow focus than coaching in that its focus is on the career development of junior employees.

Mentoring
A senior member of an organization takes a personal interest in the career of a junior employee

Career support
Mentoring activities that include coaching, sponsorship, exposure, visibility, protection, and the provision of challenging assignments

Psychosocial support
Mentoring activities that include being a friend who listens and counsels, who accepts and provides feedback, and a role model for success

According to David Peterson, mentoring can serve a number of purposes for organizations. It can help to accelerate the career progress of underrepresented groups; transmit the culture and values to newer managers; and pass on the accumulated wisdom of seasoned leaders.[45] Mentoring involves exposure to senior management activities that are valuable and beneficial for one's growth and development.

Research has found that mentoring is highly effective for those who are mentored and their organizations. Both professional and academic research consistently has indicated that mentored individuals have greater career prospects and higher incomes than those who have not been mentored. A review of mentoring research found that compared to non-mentored individuals, mentored individuals had more promotions and higher compensation, as well as greater career commitment and higher career and job satisfaction. Furthermore, career mentoring was more strongly related to objective indicators of career success such as compensation and promotion while psychosocial mentoring was more strongly related to satisfaction with the mentor.[46]

The use of technology has opened up many new possibilities for mentoring. For example, some organizations have implemented **e-mentoring** programs that allow mentors and protégés to communicate online. The main advantage of e-mentoring is that it allows mentors to connect with protégés anywhere in the world and to reach a larger number of protégés.[47] Another technological innovation is virtual speed mentoring. To learn more, see Training Today 7.3, "Virtual Speed Mentoring at IBM Canada."

E-mentoring

Mentoring programs in which the mentor and protégé communicate online

---

Training Today 7.3

Virtual Speed Mentoring at IBM Canada

IBM Canada has had several kinds of formal mentoring for years, from the short term to the long term, but it was missing the opportunity to have something more ad hoc, where people could easily come together but not demand too much time or effort from executives, managers, or seasoned IBMers, says Chuck Hamilton, virtual learning leader for IBM Canada in Vancouver.

The speed mentoring model, in its second year, is somewhat similar to speed dating, he says. Mentors spend brief 15-minute sessions with a group of protégés sitting in pods and then move on to the next group of avatars seated in the virtual world. With the mentor answering a question from one person, all the protégés in the pod have the advantage of hearing the answer, says Hamilton, and the same is true when it comes to a mentor asking a protégé a question.

The pods are designed for privacy—only avatars sitting down or standing very close can hear the dialogue—and encourage protégés to query the mentors by typing in questions that appear onscreen or by using VOIP (Voice over Internet Protocol).

A coordinator alerts the mentors through an audio channel when it's time to move to a different pod until the allotted time for the overall session is up. About three or four questions are covered at each pod and, if there are two mentors per pod, 30 minutes are allotted.

The speed mentoring area includes a floating boardroom in the Second Life environment that is dedicated to resources for career-building. Larger areas can be used for orientation, to connect people to the overall idea of virtual mentoring or the concept of the avatar world. IBM may also feature a panel of mentors for a larger crowd, with a moderated chat.

Source: S. Dobson, "Virtually speaking—employee avatars," *Canadian HR Reporter*, Nov. 30, 2009, P. 15. Reprinted by permission of Canadian HR Reporter.

Tips for Trainers

Mentoring can be an effective method of training that benefits both the mentor and protégés. However, to be effective it is important that the roles and expectations of the mentor and protégés be clear and well understood. It is also important that they agree on how often they will meet, what types of topics they will discuss, and what career activities will be part of the protégé's development.

Both the mentor and the protégé should have some guidelines on how the process will work. Researchers have highlighted several areas of concern for managers wishing to implement formal mentoring programs:[48]

- *Choice of mentors.* Mentors must be motivated to participate in the program and to make sufficient time available to their protégé. They also need to be knowledgeable about how the organization really works. Participation should be voluntary. Inevitably, some assigned relationships will not work out. A procedure needs to be in place to allow either party to cancel the arrangement without too much loss of face, and employees should feel free to end the relationship without fear of retaliation.

- *Matching mentors and protégé(s).* Matching is an important process that needs to be handled with care. Should males be matched with males and females with females? There may not be enough senior women to mentor all the junior women. Hostility from men when women network with one another makes some women reluctant to take on the mentoring role.[49] Those mentors close to retirement perform better in both the career and psychosocial functions.[50] It is important that the relationship remain confidential and for the protégé to know that it will be confidential. The protégé is unlikely to feel comfortable, for example, if the mentor is his or her boss. Research has also found that having input into the matching process is important. Both mentor and protégé input into the matching process has been found to be related to perceived program effectiveness.[51]

- *Training.* Mentors and protégés both need training. This process should entail more than giving mentors a book to read about mentoring. It should, for example, involve the opportunity to share experiences about mentoring. The training of protégés, usually as part of the induction process, should demonstrate the organization's commitment to mentoring and set appropriate expectations for the mentoring relationship. Mentors could be chosen for this training based on their previous track record in developing employees. Research has found that both the receipt of training and the quality of training is related to perceived program effectiveness for mentors and protégés.[52]

- *Structuring the mentoring relationship.* Some programs set time limits on the relationship and specify minimum levels of contact. Goals, projects, activities, and resources are spelled out. The program is evaluated and those areas in which either mentors or protégés report dissatisfaction are redesigned. While commitment must be made at all levels, it is at the individual level that the process can most easily break down. Signals sent by derailed mentoring schemes include delay between assignment and first meeting with protégé, poor meeting locations (e.g., the cafeteria), and infrequent contacts.

The Trainer's Notebook 7.2

DEVELOPING A FORMAL MENTORING PROGRAM

A well-designed formal mentoring program should consider the following issues:

- *Business objectives*. Determine the business objectives of establishing a mentoring program in order to tie it back to business success.
- *Selection criteria*. Determine key criteria for the recruitment and selection of mentors and mentees (job descriptions, expectations, capabilities).
- *Mentee assessment*. Mentees should be assessed on their appetite for risk, handling mistakes, and their mindset.
- *Training*. Determine the type of training participants should receive.

- *Matching process*. Make sure there is an effective process for optimum matching between participants.
- *Criteria for success*. Determine what the success factors will be. How will you be able to measure success?
- *Rewards*. Decide what the rewards of being involved in the mentoring program should be.
- *Timeline*. Establish a concrete timeline for the mentoring relationship. Most mentoring relationships average one or two years.
- *Feedback*. Build a feedback loop for continuous improvements to ensure a viable and dynamic mentoring program.

Source: S. Butyn, "Mentoring your way to improved retention," *Canadian HR Reporter*, July 27, 2003, P. 13. Reprinted by permission of Canadian HR Reporter.

Finally, to be effective, mentoring programs must receive continued support from management. And because most mentors are volunteers, there should be some benefits and incentives to those who participate as mentors in mentoring programs. To learn more about how to design a formal mentoring program, see The Trainer's Notebook 7.2, "Developing a Formal Mentoring Program."

OFF-THE-JOB VERSUS ON-THE-JOB TRAINING METHODS

In Chapter 6, we discussed some of the factors to consider when choosing a training method. A related issue is whether to use on-the-job or off-the-job training methods. In the final section of this chapter, we review some of the advantages and disadvantages of on-the-job and off-the-job training methods.

Off-the-Job Training Methods

Advantages

A trainer can use a wide variety of instructional training methods when training is off-the-job. For example, a trainer can combine a lecture with discussion, a case study or case incident, or games and simulations, and also use instructional media such as a video and slides. Thus, a trainer has many options when training is off-the-job and can tailor a training program to the needs and preferences of trainees. The trainer can also choose a combination of methods that will be most effective given the objectives and content of a training program.

Another advantage of off-the-job training is that the trainer is able to control the training environment. In other words, the trainer can choose a training site that is comfortable, free of distractions, and conducive to learning. A trainer does not have as much control of the learning environment when training is on-the-job.

A third advantage is that a large number of trainees can be trained at one time. This is especially the case when the lecture method is used. Thus, off-the-job training is generally more efficient given that many more trainees can be trained at one time and in one place. This is of course a huge advantage when many employees need to be trained as soon and fast as possible.

Disadvantages

There are also a number of disadvantages of off-the-job training methods. First, off-the-job training can be much more costly than on-the-job training. This is because of the costs associated with the use of training facilities, travel, accommodation, food, and so on. However, as you will see in the next chapter, such costs can be almost completely eliminated with the use of technology.

A second disadvantage of off-the-job training is that because the training takes place off-the-job in a training environment that is different from the work environment, trainees might have difficulty in the application of the training material on the job. For example, while a trainee might be able to perform a training task in a role play during training, he or she might have difficulty performing the same task on-the-job. Thus, the application of training on the job, or what is known as the transfer of training (see Chapter 10), can be more difficult with off-the-job training.

On-the-Job Training Methods

Advantages

A major advantage of on-the-job training methods is that the cost is much lower given that the need for training facilities, travel, accommodation, and so on is eliminated. Thus, on-the-job training tends to be much less costly than off-the-job training.

A second advantage is the greater likelihood of the application of training on the job. That is, because training takes place in the trainees' actual work area, the application is much more direct and in some cases immediate. Thus, there is less difficulty in the transfer of training since the training environment and work environment are the same.

Disadvantages

There are a number of disadvantages of on-the-job training. First, the work environment is full of distractions that can interfere with learning and interrupt training. Noise might make it difficult for trainees to hear and understand the trainer, and at times the trainer might be interrupted and called away from the training to solve a problem or work on something else.

Second, when trainees are being trained on an actual machine or equipment on the job, there is always the potential for damage to expensive equipment.

This could shut down production for a period of time, adding to the cost of repairing or replacing damaged equipment.

A third problem is the disruption of service or slowdown in production that occurs during training. You have probably had the experience of being served by an employee who is being trained. The result is usually slower service and the potential for errors. Thus, on-the-job training can result in a reduction in productivity, quality, and service.

Finally, when safety issues are associated with the use of equipment or dangerous chemicals, on-the-job training can compromise safety. A trainee learning on the job can make a mistake and harm him or herself, other employees, or customers. Therefore, extra precaution and care need to be taken whenever on-the-job training involves working with equipment or dangerous chemicals.

Combining On-the-Job and Off-the-Job Training Methods

As you can see, there are advantages and disadvantages associated with on-the-job and off-the-job training methods. Being aware of and understanding them can be helpful when choosing a training method. For example, when there is a need to train a large number of employees, off-the-job training would be more practical. When the cost of training is an issue, on-the-job training might be more feasible. Thus, issues of practicality and feasibility are important considerations when choosing training methods.

It should be apparent to you that the choice of a training method is not really a matter of whether training should be on-the-job or off-the-job. In fact, effective training programs often combine on-the-job and off-the-job training methods.

Ultimately, what is most important is mixing and combining training methods to best suit a particular training need and objective. In fact, a government study found that a combination of on-the-job and off-the-job training methods is the best approach for getting employees up to speed. The report found that on average Canadian organizations provide off-the-job or classroom training to 63 percent of their workforce, and on-the-job training to 66 percent of the workforce. However, it also found that larger organizations are more likely to use only off-the-job training while smaller organizations can't afford off-the-job training and therefore tend to rely on on-the-job training.[53]

Thus, once again the best approach appears to be a blended approach that combines different methods of training. This is the case not only with respect to on-the-job and off-the-job training methods, but also for technology-based training methods, which are discussed in Chapter 8.

SUMMARY

This chapter described some of the most common methods of on-the-job training and serves as a complement to the off-the-job instructional training methods described in Chapter 6. We noted that on-the-job training is the most common method of training as well as the most misused. However, job instruction training that is carefully planned and structured can have a positive effect on employee learning and performance. On-the-job training can also involve the use of performance aids and job rotation. Apprenticeship programs combine on-the-job training and classroom instruction and are the primary method of training for skilled-trades workers. Coaching and mentoring are also popular methods of on-the-job training. The chapter concluded with a discussion of the advantages and disadvantages of on-the-job and off-the-job training methods. It was noted that effective training programs mix and combine different methods of on-the-job and off-the-job training as well technology-based training methods, the focus of the next chapter.

Key Terms

apprenticeships p. 208
career support p. 213
coaching p. 212
cross training p. 207
e-mentoring p. 214
job instruction training p. 201

job rotation p. 207
mentoring p. 213
on-the-job training p. 199
performance aid p. 204
psychosocial support p. 213

Make the Connection

p. 201: behaviour modelling is discussed in Chapter 6 on page 174
p. 202: self-efficacy is discussed in Chapter 3 on page 74

Web Links

IBM Canada: **www.ibm.com/ca/en**

Joey Restaurant Group: **joeyrestaurants.com**

McDonald's Canada: **www.mcdonalds.ca**

SaskEnergy: **www.saskenergy.com**

Toronto Hydro: **www.torontohydro.com**

White Spot: **www.whitespot.com**

World Health Organization: **www.who.int**

Required Professional Capabilities (RPCs)

The following RPCs are relevant to material covered in this chapter. The RPC number represents the CCHRA number assigned to the RPC as presented on the CCHRA website. All of the RPCs can be found in the Body of Knowledge at **http://www.chrp.ca/rpc/body-of-knowledge/**

RPC 151: Uses a variety of methods to deliver development programs.

151.04: Methods of training and development (Games and simulations, case method, lecturing, on-the-job training, distance learning, role-play, videoconferencing, group discussion)

Discussion Questions

1. Describe the similarities and differences between coaching and mentoring. When would you use coaching and when would you use mentoring as an on-the-job training method?
2. What are the main issues to consider when developing a mentoring program?
3. How should an organization decide if it should use on-the-job training? What are the advantages and disadvantages?
4. Why do you think on-the-job training is the most common method of training? Why is it also the most misused method of training? What can organizations do to avoid the problems of on-the-job training?
5. Describe the objectives of apprenticeships and how they are different from other on-the-job training methods. What should be done to increase the number of people who pursue apprenticeship training in Canada and why is this important? What should be done to increase the number of employers that are willing to provide apprenticeship training?
6. Describe the four steps of job instruction training and what you would do in each step if you were training someone on the job. Explain how you would train somebody to drive a car or fix a flat tire if you were using job instruction training.
7. Discuss the advantages and disadvantages of on-the-job and off-the-job training methods.

The Great Training Debate

1. Debate the following: On-the-job training can result in employees who are poorly trained and it should be avoided whenever possible.
2. Debate the following: The apprenticeship system in Canada is no longer effective and organizations would be better off if they implemented their own in-house apprenticeship programs.
3. Debate the following: If an employee can perform a job then he/she should be able to train others to do the job.

Exercises

In-Class

1. Recall the most recent job you had and how you were trained. Were you trained on the job? If you were trained on the job, describe your experience. What exactly did the trainer do and how did it influence your learning? Was your on-the-job training experience effective? Why or why not? What could have been done differently to make it more effective? If you were not trained on the job, describe how on the job training might be used to train employees to do your job.

2. As a student, you have probably experienced some problems studying, writing assignments, or perhaps writing exams. If you were to act as a tutor to train another student with some of these problems, what method of training would you use and why? Consider each of the on-the-job training methods in Table 7.1 and indicate how you would use them and how effective they would be for training a student to become a "better" student.

3. Assume that you have just been hired as a trainer in an organization that hires recent college and university graduates every year. The company does not have a formal mentoring program and your job is to try to get one started. Prepare a proposal to convince management of the importance and need for a formal mentoring program. You should also describe how the program will work and what will be required to get it started. You can then either have another member of the class review your proposal and provide feedback or you can present your proposal to the class.

4. Using the job instruction training method, design a training program to perform a task you are familiar with. It could be a task you have had to perform in a current or previous job, or it could be something that is not work related such as how to fix a flat tire, how to drive a car, how to ride a bike, etc. Design your training program following the steps outlined in the chapter. Then have another member of the class review your training program and provide feedback. Alternatively, you can provide a demonstration in front of the class and have the class critique your training program and provide feedback.

5. Very often, experienced employees are called upon to train a new employee on the job. In most cases, the employee has not received any training on how to train others. Chances are that some day you will be asked to train a new employee, or perhaps you have already had to. To prepare yourself for this task, consider how well prepared and qualified you are. What are your strengths and weaknesses? Prepare an action plan to develop areas that need improvement. If you have already had to train somebody on the job, how effective were you and what do you need to work on to improve?

6. On-the-job training can be very effective if the trainer is knowledgeable about learning principles and theories. Make a list of all the principles, concepts, and theories described in the text that can be used to make on-the-job training more effective. Explain the relevance of each principle, concept, or theory on your list for on-the-job training.

In-the-Field

1. Ask your friends if they would accept a paid training experience that consisted of the following benefits:
   - They would be given structured classroom training and on-the-job assignments.
   - They would be coached and supervised throughout the learning experience.
   - They would be paid to learn.
   - They would be certified at the end of learning the job.
   - They would be guaranteed employment at high wages.

If they answer "Yes!" then tell them about becoming an apprentice electrician, carpenter, plumber, or chef. What is their reaction? Do students resist the certification programs in the traditional vocations and embrace certification in human resources or technology? Why? What can be done to increase the likelihood that students will choose a skilled trade and enter an apprenticeship program?

2. Contact the human resource department of an organization to find out about their use of on-the-job training. In particular, you should inquire about the following:

   - Do they use on-the-job training, and if so what do they use it for (what employees, what kinds of job)? Why do they use it? How effective is it?
   - How formal and systematic is their on-the-job training? Is it carefully planned, do trainers receive training and instruction, are the trainers carefully selected, are they rewarded for their efforts? Are they evaluated?
   - Do they follow the steps of the job instruction training method? How well is each of the steps performed?
   - Based on what you have learned in this chapter, is the organization doing a good job in providing on-the-job training? What is it doing right and wrong?
   - What advice would you give the organization to improve its on-the-job training?

3. Do you have what it takes to be a good mentor? To find out, go to **www.mentors.ca** and click on "All about Mentoring" and then click on "Take" to take The Mentor Survey. After you have found out your score, see if you can find a mentor. Click on "Profile" and then "Tips to find and gain a Mentor." What are some of the ways you can find a mentor on your own?

4. To learn more about apprenticeships in Canada, visit the Canadian Apprenticeship Forum (CAF) at **www.caf-fca.org** and answer the following questions:

   a. What is the CAF and what do they do?

   b. What are some of the resources available on the CAF website for employers, educators, and youth?

   c. What are some current activities being undertaken by the CAF? Choose one and write a brief summary of the objectives and project status.

Case Incident

Davco Machine Ltd.

Davco Machine Ltd. is located in Grande Prairie in northern Alberta, where it designs and builds equipment for the forestry, construction, and oil and gas industries. The company has 66 employees, most of whom are machinists, welders, mechanics, or millwrights. Davco formed a partnership with technical schools in Edmonton and was able to generate interest among students to apprentice at the company. However, the facility didn't have enough journeypersons to meet the requirement of one journeyperson for every apprentice.

The company representatives travelled to Germany to take part in a job fair hosted by the provincial government. When a worker in Germany is unemployed the government requires him/her to go back to school. As a result, Germany has a low unemployment rate and a highly educated labour pool. Once in Germany, Davco had no problem recruiting four journeyperson machinists.

Questions

1. What does this case tell you about the importance and need for apprenticeship training in Canada and its future as a method of on-the-job training?
2. What should governments and companies like Davco do to increase the number of apprentices and journeypersons in Canada?

Source: T. Franceschini, "CloseUp: CEOs talk workforce development," *Canadian HR Reporter*, Dec. 2005, P. 7.

Case Study TPK APPLIANCES

When TPK, a manufacturer of small appliances—electric kettles, toasters, and irons—automated its warehouse, the warehouse crew was reduced from 14 to 4. Every one of the displaced employees was assigned to another department, as TPK had a history of providing stable employment.

Jacob Peters, an employee with more than 15 years of service, was transferred to the toaster assembly line to be retrained as a small-parts assembler. When he arrived to begin his new job, the supervisor said, "This may be only temporary, Jacob. I have a full staff right now, so I have nothing for you to do, but come on, I'll find you a locker." As there really was no job for him, Jacob did nothing for the first week but odd jobs such as filling bins. At the beginning of week two, Jacob was informed that a vacancy would be occurring the next day, so he reported for work eager to learn his new job.

The operation was very simple. All Jacob had to do was pick up two pieces of metal, one in each hand, place them into a jig so that they were held together in a cross position, and press a button. The riveting machine then put a rivet through both pieces and an air jet automatically ejected the joined pieces into a bin.

"This job is so simple a monkey could do it," the supervisor told Jacob. "Let me show you how it's done," and he quickly demonstrated the three steps involved. "Now you do it," the supervisor said. Of course, Jacob did it right the first time. After watching him rivet two or three, the supervisor left Jacob to his work.

About three hours later, the riveter started to put the rivets in a little crooked, but Jacob kept on working. Finally, a fellow worker stopped by and said, "You're new here, aren't you?" Jacob nodded. "Listen, I'll give you a word of advice. If the supervisor sees you letting the rivets go in crooked like that, he's going to be really mad at you. So hide these in the scrap over there." The co-worker then showed Jacob how to adjust the machine.

Jacob's next problem began when the air ejection system started jamming. Four times he managed to clear it, but on the fifth try, he slipped and his elbow hit the rivet button. The machine put a rivet through the fleshy part of his hand, just below the thumb.

It was in the first-aid station that the supervisor finally had the opportunity to see Jacob once again.

Questions

1. Comment on the strengths and weaknesses of the on-the-job training that Jacob received. What did the supervisor do that was consistent with job instruction training? What did he fail to do?
2. What does this case tell you about the traditional approach to on-the-job training? What does it tell you about job instruction training?
3. If you were the supervisor, how would you have trained Jacob? What would you do differently and why?
4. If the job instruction training method was used, how would Jacob's training have been conducted? Explain how each step would proceed.
5. Describe any other on-the-job training methods that might be used to train Jacob. Consider each of the methods listed in Table 7.1. What methods do you think would be the most effective? What methods would you use and why?

Flashback Questions

1. Describe any off-the-job training methods that might have been used to train Jacob. Consider each of the methods listed in Table 6.1. What methods do you think would be most effective? What methods would you use and why?
2. Describe how some of the principles, concepts, and theories of learning from Chapter 3 might be relevant for training Jacob. Be sure to consider learning styles, adult learning theory, conditioning theory, and social cognitive theory.
3. Consider the role that active practice played in training Jacob. Did the supervisor provide Jacob with sufficient opportunities for active practice? If you trained Jacob, what would you have done differently in terms of active practice? Consider the conditions of practice before training (pre-training interventions) and during training (see Table 5.3 in Chapter 5). Which ones would you include in the training and why?
4. Consider the use of error-management training (EMT) (Chapter 5) for the training of Jacob. Do you think that EMT might have been effective for training Jacob and would it have prevented his accident? Explain your answer.

REFERENCES

1. Based on Klie, S. (2008, June 2). Restaurant's training a recipe for success. *Canadian HR Reporter, 21(11)*, 8, 9; www.whitespot.com (At 80 years young, White Spot celebrates milestone anniversary; White Spot introduces a ground-breaking Red Seal chef certification program; White Spot Limited named one of Canada's 50 Best Managed Companies).

2. Hughes, P. D., & Grant, M. (2007). *Learning & development outlook 2007*. The Conference Board of Canada: Ottawa.

3. (1999, May/June). McDonald's stresses hands-on training. *The Training Report*, p. 10.

4. Dulipovici, A. (2003, May). Skilled in training: Results of CFIB surveys on training.

5. Sisson, G. R. (2001). *Hands-on training*. Berrett-Koehler Publishers, Inc. San Francisco: CA.

6. Sisson, G. R. (2001).

7. Sisson, G. R. (2001).

8. Sisson, G. R. (2001).

9. Broadwell, M. (1969). *The supervisor and on-the-job training*. Reading, MA: Addison-Wesley.

10. Sloman, M. (1989). On-the-job training: A costly poor relation. *Personnel Management 21(2)*, 38–42.

11. Renner, P. F. (1989). *The instructor's survival kit*. Vancouver: Training Associates Ltd; Tench, A. (1992). Following Joe around: Should this be our approach to on-the-job training? *Plant Engineering, 46(17)*, 88–92.

12. Meyers, D. (1991). Restaurant service: Making memorable presentations. *Cornell Hotel and Restaurant Administration Quarterly, 32(1)*, 69–73; Ukens, C. (1993). Cards help pharmacists counsel patients in a flash. *Drug Topics, 137(1)*, 24–27.

13. Ruyle, K. (1991, February/March). Developing intelligent job aids. *Technical and Skills Training*, 9–14.

14. Arajis, B. (1991). Getting your sales staff in shape. *Graphic Arts Monthly, 63(5)*, 125–127.

15. Arajis, B. (1991); Cowen, W. (1992). Visual control boards are a key management tool. *Office Systems, 9(10)*, 70–72; King, W. (1994). Training by design. *Training and Development, 48(1)*, 52–54.

16. Young, L. (2008, March 24). All in the family at Toronto Hydro. *Canadian HR Reporter, 21(6)*, 16.

17. Campion, M. A., Cheraskin, L., & Stevens, M. J. (1994). Career-related antecedents and outcomes of job rotation. *Academy of Management Journal, 37*, 1518–1542.

18. Ménard, M., Menezes, F., Chan, C. K. Y., & Walker, M. (2007). *National apprenticeship survey: Canada overview report 2007*. Ottawa: Statistics Canada.

19. Young, L. (2008, March 24).

20. Ménard, M., Menezes, F., Chan, C. K. Y., & Walker, M. (2007).

21. Ménard, M., Menezes, F., Chan, C. K. Y., & Walker, M. (2007).

22. Moskal, B. (1991). Apprenticeship: Old cure for new labor shortage? *Industry Week, 240(9)*, 30–35.

23. Galt, V. (2006, March 22). Few employers taking on apprentices: New survey. *The Globe and Mail*, C2.

24. Dobson, S. (2010, June 14). Disconnect between employers, apprentices with hiring: Report. *Canadian HR Reporter, 23(12)*, 6; (2009, June). It pays to hire an apprentice: Calculating the return on training investment for skilled trades employers in Canada. Ottawa: Canadian Apprenticeship Forum; (2008, July). Strategies to increase employer participation in apprenticeship training in Canada. Ottawa: Canadian Apprenticeship Forum; http://www.caf-fca.org/en/.

25. Ménard, M., Menezes, F., Chan, C. K. Y., & Walker, M. (2007).

26. McCarthy, S. (2001, February 27). Skilled-worker shortage could reach one million. *The Globe and Mail*, A1.

27. (2011, June). Employers and apprenticeship in Canada. Ottawa: Canadian Apprenticeship Forum; http://www.caf-fca.org/en/.

28. McCarthy, S. (2001, February 27).

29. Apprenticeship training in Canada. (2006, July 25). www.ccl-cca.ca/CCL/Reports/LessonsInLearning/apprenticeship-LinL.htm

30. Funston, M. (2007, March 29). Free training targets labour shortages. *The Toronto Star*, K2.

31. Apprenticeship training in Canada. (2006, July 25).

32. Starrett, T. (2004, February/March). The eager apprentice: Has HR forgotten about a valuable resource? *HR Professional, 21(2),* 32.

33. Finkelstein, L. (2008, December 1). Coaching SaskEnergy to higher performance. *Canadian HR Reporter, 21(21),* 23.

34. Busse, D., & Hemmingsen, J. (2010, December 13). A pinch of coaching, a dash of training. *Canadian HR Reporter, 23(22),* 25–26; www.joeyrestaurants.com/news (Joey Restaurant Group and BC Housing named 2011 ICF International Prism Award winners).

35. Peterson, D. B. (2002). Management development: Coaching and mentoring programs. In K. Kraiger (Ed.), *Creating, implementing, and managing effective training and development: State-of-the-art lessons for practice* (pp. 160–191). San Francisco, CA: Jossey-Bass.

36. Lovin, B., & Casstevens, E. (1971). *Coaching, learning, and action.* New York: American Management Association; Frankel, L., & Otazo, K. (1992). Employee coaching: The way to gain commitment. *Employment Relations Today, 19(3),* 311–320.

37. Blakesley, S. (1992). Your agency … leave it better than you found it. *Managers Magazine, 67(4),* 20–22.

38. Kroeger, L. (1991). Your team can't win the game without solid coaching. *Corporate Controller, 3(5),* 62–64.

39. Azar, B. (1993). Striking a balance. *Sales and Marketing Management, 145(2),* 34–35; Whittaker, B. (1993). Shaping the competitive organization. *CMA Magazine, 67(3),* 5.

40. Peterson, D. B. (2002).

41. Kruse, A. (1993). Getting top value for your payroll dollar. *Low Practice Management, 19(3),* 52–57.

42. Peterson, D. B. (2002).

43. Noe, R. A. (1999). *Employee training and development.* Boston: Irwin McGraw-Hill.

44. Peterson, D. B. (2002).

45. Peterson, D. B. (2002).

46. Allen, T. D., Eby, L. T., Poteet, M. L., Lentz, E., & Lima, L. (2004). Career benefits associated with mentoring for protégés: A meta-analysis. *Journal of Applied Psychology, 89,* 127–136.

47. Dobson, S. (2011, February 14). Taking mentorship online. *Canadian HR Reporter, 24(3),* 15.

48. Jackson, C. (1993). Mentoring: Choices for individuals and organizations. *The International Journal of Career Management, 5(1),* 10–16; Noe, R. A. (1999).

49. Gallege, L. (1993). Do women make poor mentors? *Across the Board, 30(6),* 23–26.

50. Mullen, E. J. (1998). Vocational and psychosocial mentoring functions: Identifying mentors who serve both. *Human Resource Development Quarterly, 9(4),* 319–331.

51. Allen, T. D., Eby, L. T., & Lentz, E. (2006). The relationship between formal mentoring program characteristics and perceived program effectiveness. *Personnel Psychology, 59,* 125–153.

52. Allen, T. D., Eby, L. T., & Lentz, E. (2006).

53. Harding, K. (2003, May 9). Combined training works best, study says. *The Globe and Mail,* C1.

Technology-Based Training Methods

CHAPTER LEARNING OUTCOMES

After reading this chapter you should be able to:

- define and discuss technology-based training, traditional training, computer-based training, and e-learning
- compare and contrast instructor-led training and self-directed learning
- define and give examples of asynchronous and synchronous training
- define and discuss electronic performance support systems
- define and discuss video conferencing, web conferencing, webinars, webcasts, and the virtual classroom
- define and discuss social constructivism and generative learning
- define and discuss social media, Web 2.0 technologies, and Web 3.0
- define mobile learning and discuss its use for training
- describe how to design computer-based training programs
- discuss the advantages and disadvantages of computer-based training for individuals and organizations
- discuss the effectiveness of computer-based training

THE ECONOMICAL INSURANCE GROUP (TEIG)

The Economical Insurance Group (TEIG) was founded in 1871. Its first insurance policy was written on a barn in Berlin, Ontario. Today, TEIG has more than 2,000 employees and is one of the largest property and casualty insurance companies in Canada. From its head office located in Waterloo, Ontario and an additional 19 branches and member companies across Canada, TEIG offers a wide range of personal, commercial, farm, and surety products.

In 2010, TEIG found that a significant leadership gap existed in the front-line supervisory role (team leader). According to Mary Beth Alexander, director of Learning and Organizational Development, "The struggle lies in the ability to build leadership, coaching, and management skill among this group of leaders. These team leaders are learning how to manage directly from their manager, which further perpetuates the problem."

To respond to this challenge, TEIG launched a new leadership program called Leadership 2010: People and Performance. The three-day workshop was mandatory for all 427 leaders across the company and used a blended learning approach. The program redefined the purpose of performance management in 2010 through a set of guiding principles that were communicated and modelled to managers and employees. Content focused on differentiating among high potentials, high performers, and poor performers; providing effective feedback; coaching for success and coaching for performance; career development; and employee engagement.

The program began with an introductory, interactive, 30-minute webinar using TEIG's virtual classroom technology platform introducing the workshop facilitators and providing the rationale for the program's development. The webinar introduced learning goals and asked polling questions to determine key metrics and measures for the instructor-led portion of the training. Key metrics included self-assessment of ability to manage the performance of direct reports, assessment to determine leadership development support in relation to effectively managing performance, and assessment of the most significant challenge related to people and performance management.

TEIG also used a technical training solution to introduce a new Accident Benefits Claims Regulations program prior to the release of legislative changes. "Delivering the regulations training in our virtual classroom through Dialogue Live technology was the obvious solution," said Alexander. "We incorporated lessons learned from past virtual classroom deliveries and replicated successful components."

The training was delivered to more than 200 participants who included a mix of internal employees and external contractors. To ensure maximum knowledge transfer and interactivity, the training was delivered to approximately 65 participants at a time, and divided into modules of five short deliveries over a period of three days. Participants were encouraged to participate via live chat, submit online poll or quiz answers, and respond to discussion topics over a conference line. Learners received regulations comparisons before the virtual training delivery and had access to materials hosted as e-learning content for their review post-training. As for the results, 85 percent of evaluation respondents said they were confident the training had prepared them for the upcoming legislative changes.

TEIG has wholeheartedly embraced the virtual classroom and blended training. In recognition of its innovative training programs, TEIG was ranked number two on Training Magazine's Training Top 125 for 2011. In the same year, TEIG was also named a top 100 learning-focused organization at Elearning! Media Group's inaugural Learning 100 awards conference. TEIG was recognized for its innovative approach to integrating e-learning technologies into leadership and employee development.[1]

Source: L. Freifeld, "TEIG locks in on leadership," *Training*, Jan/Feb. 2011, Pp. 34–39; "Economical recognized for excellence in workplace learning," March 24, 2011. Found at: www. Econimcalinsurance.com/en/; "Economical Insurance ranks second on 2011 'Training Top 125'," Feb. 11, 2011. Found at: www. Econimcalinsurance.com/en/.

Like many organizations today, the Economical Insurance Group (TEIG) uses technology to deliver training. Besides being able to offer a wide assortment of training programs, technology-based training can be provided to large numbers of employees at any time with many benefits to employees and organizations.

In Chapters 6 and 7, we described off-the-job and on-the-job training methods. In this chapter, we focus on technology-based training methods. You will learn about how technology is being used for training, how to design computer-based training programs, the advantages and disadvantages, and the effectiveness of computer-based training. But first, let's be clear about what technology-based training is and how it differs from traditional training methods.

WHAT IS TECHNOLOGY-BASED TRAINING?

Technology-based training refers to training that involves the use of technology to deliver courses, such as Web-based training; computerized self-study (including CD-ROMs, DVDs, and diskettes); satellite or broadcast TV; and video-, audio-, or teleconferencing. Any technology that delivers education or training, or supports the delivery of these subjects, would be included in the definition.[2]

By contrast, **traditional training** refers to training that does not involve the use of technology to deliver courses, such as classroom training with a live instructor (regardless of the instructor's or learners' use of technology during the class); non-computerized self-study, such as textbooks or workbooks; non-computerized games; seminars; lectures; or outdoor programs.[3]

While most people understand that computers are being used for training, one of the most confusing things about technology-based training is the many different terms used to refer to the various forms of technology-based training. Although there are technical distinctions between some of the methods, the distinctions are generally not apparent to trainees and often have to do with where the programs and data are located and the ease with which they can be updated.[4]

Nonetheless, it is important to understand the terms used to describe the different types of technology-based training. Table 8.1 provides a list and definitions of the major types of technology-based training.

Industry, government, and educational organizations are using technology to deliver training.[5] In Canada, while instructor-led classroom training remains the most widely used training method, three-quarters of organizations offer some sort of self-paced online learning or e-learning which represents 14 percent of overall learning time.[6] In the United States, 21.9 percent of training hours are delivered via online or computer-based technologies and 1.3 percent of training hours are delivered via social networking or mobile devices. Among the learning technologies, the most often used is virtual classroom/webcasting/video broadcasting. However, 54 percent of organizations use virtual training methods for less than 10 percent of their training programs.[7] Thus, although the use of technology for training is becoming more popular, it is doing so at a relatively slow pace and it has not supplanted instructor-led classroom instruction.

That being said, the use of technology for training in Canada has increased over the last decade, and some companies have made major advances.[8] For example, at Cisco Systems Canada Co. most sales training is now done online,

Technology-based training
Training that involves the use of technology to deliver courses

Traditional training
Training that does not involve using technology to deliver courses

TABLE (8.1)

Major Types of Technology-Based Training

Internet: A loose confederation of computer networks around the world that is connected through several primary networks

Intranet: A general term describing any network contained within an organization. It refers primarily to networks that use Internet technology

Extranet: A collaborative network that uses Internet technology to link organizations with their suppliers, customers, or other organizations that share common goals or information

CD-ROM: A format and system for recording, storing, and retrieving electronic information on a compact disc that is read using an optical drive

Electronic performance support system (EPSS): An integrated computer application that uses any combination of expert systems, hypertext, embedded animation, and/or hypermedia to help a user perform a task in real time quickly and with a minimum of support from other people

Electronic simulation: A device or system that replicates or imitates a real device or system

Multimedia: A computer application that uses any combination of text, graphics, audio, animation, and/or full-motion video

Teleconference: The instantaneous exchange of audio, video or text between two or more individuals or groups at two or more locations

Television (cable, satellite): The transmission of television signals via cable or satellite technology

Source: J. Cooney & A. Cowan, *Training and development outlook 2003: Canadian Organizations Continue to Under-Invest.* The Conference Board of Canada. May, 2003.

compared to just a few years ago when 90 percent was done in the classroom. Employees now access the company's website to find out about new Cisco networking products and how to install products. Because the courses are up and running much faster than traditional classroom programs, employees can learn about new products in one week compared to three months.[9]

As part of an initiative to better meet changing customer requirements that involved replacing existing business processes as well as 200 different business systems, Hydro-Québec now delivers training online for close to 3,000 employees.[10]

COMPUTER-BASED TRAINING AND E-LEARNING

Computer-based training
Training that is delivered via the computer for the purpose of teaching job-relevant knowledge and skills

The use of computers to deliver training generally has been referred to as computer-based training or e-learning. Although these terms are often used synonymously, there are differences. **Computer-based training** refers to training that is delivered via the computer for the purpose of teaching job-relevant skills. It can include text, graphics, and/or animation and be delivered via CD-ROMs, intranets, or the internet.[11] Among the various forms of computer-based training, Web-delivered and CD-ROM formats have received the most attention.

A related and increasingly popular term for technology-based training is e-learning. **E-learning** (also known as Web-based instruction or WBI) refers to the use of computer network technology such as the intranet or internet to deliver information or instruction to individuals.[12] Thus, e-learning is a specific type of computer-based learning and refers to the use of computer network technology. It would not include the use of CD-ROMs. In the remainder of this chapter, we will use the broader term, computer-based training, which includes e-learning.

One of the ways that computer-based training methods differ is in terms of whether the training is instructor-led or self-directed, the focus of the next section.

E-learning
The use of computer network technology such as the intranet or Internet to deliver information or instruction to individuals

INSTRUCTOR-LED TRAINING AND SELF-DIRECTED LEARNING

Like traditional training methods, computer-based training can involve an instructor or facilitator who leads, facilitates, or trains online. Computer-based training that is instructor-led is known as **instructor-led training** or **ILT**. Some examples of ILT are online discussions and video conferencing.

In some cases, the instructor is highly involved in the training and leads the process. In other cases, a course or program involves self-study and the instructor is available for answering questions and providing assistance.[13] However, one of the main advantages of computer-based training is that it can be initiated and controlled by the trainee. This is known as self-directed learning.

Self-directed learning (SDL) is a process that occurs when individuals or groups take the initiative and responsibility for learning and manage their own learning experiences. They seek out the necessary resources to engage in learning that will enhance their careers and personal growth. Employees assess their own needs, use a variety of organizational resources to meet those needs, and are helped with evaluating the effectiveness of meeting their needs. SDL can be as simple as a booklet that describes a new procedure or a multimedia program.

Self-directed learning has become increasingly popular because traditional methods of training lack the flexibility to respond quickly to dramatic and constant organizational change and trainees' needs. Self-directed learning allows trainees to access training materials and programs when they want to, at their own pace, and sometimes in the sequence they prefer.

See Table 8.2 for some of the benefits and limitations of self-directed learning.

Instructor-led training (ILT)
Training methods that involve an instructor or facilitator who leads, facilitates, or trains online

Self-directed learning (SDL)
A process in which individuals or groups take the initiative and responsibility for learning and manage their own learning experiences

ASYNCHRONOUS AND SYNCHRONOUS TRAINING

Computer-based training can be asynchronous or synchronous. When training is **asynchronous**, it is available to employees at any time and from any location. For example, an asynchronous program might simply involve the posting of text, information, or instructions on a website. More sophisticated programs can include text, graphics, animation, audio, and video, thereby providing a **multimedia training** program. This, combined with simulations, interactive exercises, tests, and feedback, can result in a much more engaging and active learning experience. While the use of multimedia involves greater

Asynchronous training
Training that is prerecorded and available to employees at any time and from any location

Multimedia training
Computer-based training programs that include text, graphics, animation, audio, and video

facilitator on-site or by allowing for interactive questioning while training takes place.

The use of computer technology is also being used to hold live training programs or what has become known as a virtual classroom. As indicated in the chapter-opening vignette, TEIG uses a virtual classroom for its new leadership program and its Accident Benefits Claims Regulations training program.

Virtual classroom

A web-based platform to deliver live, instructor-led training to geographically dispersed learners

A **virtual classroom** uses a web-based platform to deliver live, instructor-led training to geographically dispersed learners. This allows trainees to participate in live discussions with facilitators and co-workers from any location. It also means that shorter training sessions can be held over a period of weeks rather than having to schedule large blocks of time in which trainees have to be away from their job to attend a training program in a classroom.[20] For example, TEIG's Accident Benefits Claims Regulations training program is divided into modules of five short sessions over a period of three days. The main advantage of a virtual classroom is the cost savings and convenience. Thus, an increasing number of organizations like TEIG are using virtual classrooms to provide training.

Web conferencing

A live meeting or conference that takes place on the internet

Webinar

A seminar that takes place live over the Web

Virtual classrooms are made possible through the use of web conferencing and webinars. Web conferencing is similar to a video conference except that the trainees are connected to the trainer and each other via the internet and participate from their own computer. Thus, **web conferencing** is a live meeting or conference that takes place on the internet. Similar to web conferencing is a **webinar**, which is a seminar or workshop that takes place live over the Web (a web-based seminar). It can be a presentation, lecture, or workshop and can be interactive by allowing participants to ask and answer questions. Many organizations prefer a webinar over a seminar because it reduces the costs associated with renting a room, travel, and catering.[21] TEIG begins its new leadership program with an interactive 30-minute webinar in which they introduce the workshop facilitators and provide the rationale for the program's development.

▶ The Trainer's Notebook 8.1

DESIGNING EFFECTIVE VIRTUAL TRAINING PROGRAMS

To be truly effective, live virtual training has to be designed from the ground up as a unique style of learning experience as follows.

- Design a series of short modules—about 60 to 90 minutes—each followed by a work assignment that immediately applies the learning to the job.
- Move from monologue to dialogue for the delivery.
- Ensure that the delivery is interactive: Ask questions, facilitate conversation, conduct brainstorming sessions, and use breakout rooms.
- Include multimedia content to illustrate complex concepts, such as short pre-recorded audio and video segments.
- Keep the classroom size to a maximum of 20 to 25 learners.
- Attempt to model programs on the structure and style of a phone-in radio show, including guests and compelling narrative.

Source: M. Lewis, "Moving into the live virtual classroom," *T+D*, July, 2011, P. 76.

A **webcast** is a live or recorded video or audio broadcast over the internet. Webcasts are used primarily for presentations, while web conferencing and webinars are used for live meetings and seminars, respectively. Webcasts are usually one-way communications that do not have an interactive component.[22]

To be most effective, virtual classrooms should be designed from scratch and treated as a unique style of learning experience rather than just converting a traditional classroom training program into a virtual training program.[23] To learn more about how to design an effective virtual training program, see The Trainer's Notebook 8.1, "Designing Effective Virtual Training Programs."

SOCIAL MEDIA AND WEB 2.0 TECHNOLOGY

In an article on the future of learning, Kurt Kraiger argued that we are on the cusp of a new model of learning called social constructivism, which places greater emphasis on the learner and learning through social interaction. According to **social constructivism**, "the goal of instruction should be to create interactive learning environments in which training participants learn from instructors, participants learn from each other, and the instructor learns from participants." Kraiger also argues that Web-based instruction is especially well suited for fostering interactive learning environments.[24]

In fact, in the last several years we have seen the emergence of new learning technologies that can facilitate social constructivism. These new technologies are known as Web 2.0 and involve the use of social media and Web-based communities for sharing and exchanging information. **Social media** refers to the use of technology for sharing and exchanging information. **Web 2.0** refers to internet tools that enable the communication and sharing of information and knowledge. With Web 2.0 technology, anybody can create and distribute knowledge and collaborate with others in the process.[25] For a good example of a company that uses social media for training, see Training Today 8.1, "Social Media and Training at Verizon."

One of the benefits of Web 2.0 technologies is that it facilitates generative learning. **Generative learning** is a self-initiated and learner-controlled form of collaborative learning in which individuals in a social network share ideas and information and in the process solve problems and create new knowledge. This involves much more than the traditional approach to learning in which trainees learn the training material provided to them in instructor-led training programs. With generative learning, individuals initiate and control what they learn, when they learn, and how they learn. Web 2.0 technologies make generative learning possible.[26] Table 8.3 describes some other benefits of Web 2.0 technologies.

You are probably familiar with Web 2.0 technologies such as social media networks and interest groups like Facebook and Twitter, wikis, and chat rooms. Some of the most popular Web 2.0 technologies for training are blogs, wikis, and podcasts. A **blog** is a website that contains commentary and information on a subject. It is like a journal in which an individual posts information about a topic or subject. Blogs can include text, video, and audio as well as links to other individuals' blogs. Thus, they provide a network of conversations and the exchange of information on a particular topic, subject, or issue.[27]

Webcast
A live or recorded video or audio broadcast over the internet

Social constructivism
An approach to learning that emphasizes interactive learning environments

Social media
The use of technology for sharing and exchanging information

Web 2.0
Internet tools that enable the communication and sharing of information and knowledge

Generative learning
A self-initiated and learner-controlled form of collaborative learning in which individuals in a social network share ideas and information and in the process solve problems and create new knowledge

Blog
A website that contains commentary and information on a subject

---

TABLE (8.3)

Benefits of Web 2.0 Technologies

Web 2.0 technologies provide learners with the following benefits:

1. Facilitate learner self-initiation and control
2. Combine use of a variety of media
3. Provide a wide range of sources for information search
4. Facilitate data aggregation and analysis
5. Encourage file sharing for joint work
6. Supply interpersonal communication channels for networking and community building
7. Provide access anytime anywhere through web hosts and portable/wireless delivery mechanisms

Source: M. London & M.J. Hall, "Unlocking the value of Web 2.0 technologies for training and development: The shift from instructor-controlled, adaptive learning to learner-driven, generative learning," *Human Resource Management*, 2011, Vol. 50, P. 757.

Training Today (8.1)

Social Media and Training at Verizon

Verizon is a telecommunications company that delivers broadband, video, and other wireless and wireline communication services to mass market, business, government, and wholesale customers. The company is also known for providing consistently high-quality learning and development programs.

In 2010, Verizon made a leap in the use of social media to train employees to support new product and device launches, says Lou Tedrick, vice president, Human Resources, Verizon Wireless. The organization, she says, employs three social media approaches to support these launches: Device Blog, Device Forum, and learning communities. "These approaches help ensure our employees are ready to support customers at launch, as well as increase multigenerational employee engagement, leverage emerging technology, and increase peer-to-peer learning," says Tedrick.

Device Blog was launched in November 2009 to support the company's Droid launch, and has been used ever since to support key wireless device launches. "It is modeled after the external tech blogs our employees visit, and houses general information and updates on our key devices, FAQs, how-to videos, trouble-shooting tips, and 'hot topic' polling," Tedrick explains. "During a typical launch, the site receives thousands of hits per day (even during non-launch periods)."

Device Forum was launched in January 2010 for Verizon's retail employees. These virtual forums enable learning from peers companywide, product experts, and device manufacturers. Reps ask and answer one another's questions, share issues, post tips, submit suggestions, support one another's findings, and serve as a cross-check. A key success factor is the participation of wireless device manufacturers, Tedrick points out. "This gives employees access to subject matter experts," she says. "Plus, our Device Team and manufacturers benefit from early insight into potential customer issues." Tedrick says the forums average thousands of views and user posts per month.

Another key social learning endeavour for Verizon last year was the creation of learning communities to introduce employees to operating systems, says Tedrick. Developed in-house and accessed through the Device Blog, one of Verizon's earliest learning communities included video blogs (vlogs), message boards, links to online training modules, and product demonstrations. Eight reps (representing the target customer) were given pre-launch devices and a flip camera to record and post vlogs every two days. Topics mirrored the customer experience. Employees completed an online device training module and received instructions on how to participate in the learning community, including practice assignments, guidelines (do's and don'ts), and posting directions. More than 20 percent of employees use these learning communities; 90 percent say they'd like to use them more.

Source: M. Weinstein, "Verizon connects to success," *Training*, Jan/Feb. 2011, P. 40.; www22.verizon.com.

A **wiki** is a webpage or collection of webpages in which users share, contribute, and modify information on a topic. Although there are many public wikis (Wikipedia, for example, is the best known), some companies have internal wikis that focus on particular topics such as company products. The content can be created and shared among the users of the website on an ongoing basis. Wikis enable relevant information to be obtained on demand and training material to be constantly revised and updated. Many large organizations now use wikis for team projects.[28]

A **podcast** is a short audio or video recording that can be downloaded and played on a mobile device such as an iPod or cell phone. Employees can access information on-demand from any location at their convenience. For example, a sales team can learn about new products directly from the designers, and truck drivers can learn how to drive in a storm while driving.[29]

Although Web 2.0 technologies are still relatively new and many organizations have not yet adopted them, the next evolution, or Web 3.0, is already on the horizon. **Web 3.0** represents an evolutionary and fundamental shift in how people interact with the Web and consists of three components: the semantic web, the mobile web, and the immersive internet.[30]

The semantic web involves technology that can understand the meaning of data and create customized experiences in which information is tailored to a user's needs, location, and identity. The mobile web allows one to use the Web seamlessly across devices and locations. The immersive internet involves the use of immersive technologies such as virtual worlds, augmented reality, and 3-D environments.[31]

Web 3.0 technologies are expected to improve learning and performance and represent the future of learning. Let's now take a closer look at one of the components of Web 3.0, mobile or m-learning.

MOBILE LEARNING (M-LEARNING)

Technology has made it possible for employees not only to learn whenever they need to but also to learn from any location. This is known as **mobile learning** or **m-learning**, and involves the use of mobile or portable technologies such as iPods, MP3 players, and smartphones. Thus, employees can obtain information and training at any time and from any location with the use of mobile technologies.

Mobile devices can be used to deliver short videos or small amounts of information. For example, if an employee is away from the workplace and needs to

Wiki

A webpage or collection of webpages in which users share, contribute, and modify information on a topic

Podcast

A short audio or video recording that can be downloaded and played on a mobile device such as an iPod or cell phones

Web 3.0

A fundamental shift in how people interact with the web that consists of the semantic web, the mobile web, and the immersive internet

Mobile learning (m-learning)

The use of mobile or portable technologies across locations for obtaining information and training role playing. Trainees interact with animated characters who present different customer-service challenges and learn different approaches for interacting with them. An animated coach provides guidance and feedback.

Rogers noticed improvements in service and employee satisfaction not long after the program was implemented. The role-playing makes the program engaging and the lessons—which are based on real-life scenarios—are having an effect on employees' performance.[42]

STORIES   Stories and narratives have also been used in e-learning in order to engage trainees. Abstract concepts as well as dry material can be livened up with stories that involve dialogue and characters. The characters can be created to be similar to the trainees and learning can occur as the characters solve problems in the story.

Sprint and Volvo have used stories to train employees on how to deliver the company's brand image when interacting with customers. Trainees also practise communicating the brand image in simulated customer interactions.[43]

Customization

Tailoring instructional elements to meet trainee preferences and needs

CUSTOMIZATION   **Customization** involves tailoring instructional elements to meet trainee preferences and needs. This can increase trainee satisfaction with the training and improve learning. Hewlett-Packard is an example of one company that has been very successful at customization. The company has found that preferences for e-learning and other training media differ around the world. For example, it found that employees in Asia prefer instructor-presented or blended learning, while in the United States and Europe employees prefer self-paced and instructor-presented learning approaches, respectively. Differences in e-learning preferences indicate that one type of e-learning program is not likely to meet the needs and preferences of all employees.[44]

Personalization

Structuring the program so that trainees feel that they are engaged in a conversation with the program

PERSONALIZATION   **Personalization** refers to structuring the program so that trainees feel they are engaged in a conversation with the program. This can be achieved by using conversational rather than formal language in the on-screen text and audio recording.[45]

HUMAN INTERACTION   A potential problem of computer-based training for some trainees is the lack of face-to-face interaction with an instructor and other trainees. This can result in trainees feeling isolated and less motivated to learn. One way to overcome this is to include human interaction in the design of computer-based training programs.

Human interaction

The extent to which trainees are able to interact with the instructor and each other during a training program

Human interaction refers to the extent to which trainees are able to interact with the instructor and each other during a training program. This can be built into computer-based programs using a number of formats including email exchanges, chat rooms, discussion boards, and group projects. There is some evidence that more interaction with the instructor and between trainees is associated with higher motivation, more positive attitudes toward learning, and improved learning outcomes.[46]

FEEDBACK   Regardless of the nature of the training experience, it is important that feedback be provided to trainees. In fact, students who received feedback in computer-based training have been found to learn more than students who were not given feedback.[47]

The Trainer's Notebook 8.2

DESIGN PRINCIPLES FOR COMPUTER-BASED TRAINING

The following principles cover many different aspects of computer-based training design and are well grounded in both theory and research.

- *The multimedia principle.* Graphics and text should be used rather than simply text alone. Trainees will engage in a deeper and more active processing of the learning material.

- *The contiguity principle.* When text is used to explain a graphic or vice versa, the text and graphics should be placed near each other on the screen. This permits trainees to focus on the instructional material rather than on trying to match a miscellaneous set of pictures to text.

- *The modality principle.* Audio technology, rather than on-screen text, should be used to present information. Trainees are likely to become overwhelmed with visual information when presented with only text, graphics, illustrations, and figures during learning.

- *The personalization principle.* Text should be written in first and second person and trainees should have access to on-screen virtual coaches that provide guidance and direction. This will help trainees to see the computer as a conversational partner rather than as an information delivery agent.

Source: R.E. DeRouin, B.A. Fritzsche, & E. Salas, "E-Learning in organizations," *Journal of Management*, 2005, Vol. 31, P. 920; R.C. Clark, & R.E. Mayer, *E-learning and the science of instruction: Proven guidelines for consumers and designers of multimedia learning.* San Francisco: Jossey-Bass, 2003.

Feedback can be incorporated into computer-based training in many ways. It can range from a simple prompt indicating that an answer to a question or a quiz is right or wrong to the execution of another program segment in which trainees are routed through a complex maze of reviews and reinforcements based on their responses and answers.

Feedback can also be incorporated into simulations and role plays. For example, in a role play in which trainees must choose from a number of options how to respond to different customers, immediate feedback can be provided following each response chosen by a trainee. In addition, an on-screen virtual coach can be used to provide trainees with feedback about the correctness of their choices, what they did wrong, and hints on how to proceed and improve. Trainees can then take the program again until their performance improves.

To learn about some additional design principles for computer-based training, see The Trainer's Notebook 8.2, "Design Principles for Computer Based Training."

BENEFITS OF COMPUTER-BASED TRAINING

Many see technology as the way to go for all training programs. However, just like on-the-job and off-the-job training methods, computer-based training has both advantages and disadvantages for trainees and organizations.

Advantages

Trainees

A major advantage for trainees is flexibility. For example, trainees do not have to coordinate and arrange their schedule and workload to accommodate training schedules. Trainees do not have to take courses when they are scheduled or wait until a group of trainees are ready to take a course. They can learn when they want to or "just in time." Trainees also do not have to leave work to attend training, and can even learn while they are at home or away from work.

Another advantage for trainees is greater control over their learning, or what is known as learner control. **Learner control** refers to the degree to which the trainee has control over various instructional features during a lesson or training program such as the content, sequence, and/or pace of training.[48] In other words, trainees can choose the content they want to view, the order in which they will view the content, enter and leave training as they choose, and progress at their own pace. **Self-pacing** means that trainees can work on training tasks as quickly or as slowly as they want. In some cases, trainees even have control over various instructional elements of a program such as the sequence of instructional material, the content of instruction, and the amount of instruction during training. There is some evidence to indicate that learner control has a positive effect on trainee satisfaction with training and learning. However, it is important to recognize that too much learner control can detract from the learning experience and have a negative effect on learning.[49]

There is also some evidence that trainees are not as shy online as they are in a classroom. Trainees who encounter difficulties during training are less likely to feel embarrassed about their pace or performance, and they don't have to admit to not knowing something. As a result, they are more likely to be comfortable online than in a classroom and this can improve their satisfaction with the training as well as their learning.[50]

Perhaps most beneficial for trainees is the convenience of being able to learn whenever they want to or need to, and to do so from any location where they have access to a computer. This, of course, is the ultimate example of "just-in-time" training. Employees do not have to sign up and wait for a course to be available; it is available whenever they need it. And during training, employees can pause and continue at a later time without missing a beat. Furthermore, because of the ability to learn at work or at home, employees do not have to spend time travelling to distant training locations. Geographic flexibility is a major advantage.

Organizations

A major advantage for organizations is that they can ensure that all trainees receive the same training regardless of where they are situated. Thus, organizations can deliver standardized and consistent training to large numbers of employees across the organization and even worldwide. This is especially important when employees in many locations require training. Leaving the training to each location could result in differences in content, delivery, and effectiveness.

Another advantage is that large numbers of employees can be trained within a short period of time. There is no limit to the number of employees who can be trained, as one is not constrained by the number of instructors available or the need for classroom space.

Learner control
The degree to which the trainee has control over various instructional features during a lesson or training program such as the content, sequence, and/or pace of training

Self-pacing
Trainees can work on training tasks as quickly or as slowly as they want

Computer-based training also makes it possible to track employees' performance on learning exercises and tests. This kind of tracking is especially important for training programs that are mandatory and completion, certification, or attaining a certain level of performance is legally mandated. The technology can generate tests that can provide legal documentation for proof of competency levels. When an accident or safety incident results in a lawsuit, the employer can prove that a training program was completed and that a desired level of competence was achieved. Such training statistics can reduce corporate liability. Technology also allows trainees to track their own progress and test themselves.

Perhaps the greatest advantage for organizations is the reduction in the cost of training as a result of the elimination of the cost of travel, training facilities, hotel rooms, meals, trainers, and employee time off from work while travelling and attending training.[51] In addition, the high overhead costs of traditional training make computer-based training especially advantageous to companies with national or international employees.

The savings reported by some companies are quite significant. For example, Dow Chemical estimates that the implementation of a Web-based training system saved the company $30 million in one year. It saved $20 million as a result of a reduction in the time employees spend in training, and $10 million due to a reduction in administrative time, classroom facilities, trainers, and the cost of printed material.[52]

Disadvantages

Trainees

A common disadvantage of computer-based training for trainees is that there is less interpersonal contact and interaction with other trainees. Furthermore, individuals have learning preferences and styles, and if a trainee prefers to receive training in a classroom with a trainer and other trainees then computer-based training would disadvantage that employee.

Trainers who are not computer literate might also resist and fear computer-based training. A low-threat opportunity to allow trainees to test the technology is to place the learning stations in the classroom.[53] However, industry analysts perceive these barriers as temporary problems. Computer-based training will become a standard way of providing training, particularly for the current generation which is comfortable with computers and technology.

Organizations

For organizations, a disadvantage is that some employees will be uncomfortable with computers and might refuse training. This is especially likely for older workers who have less experience using computers. There is also the potential for problems to arise if employees do not have access to computers.

However, the major disadvantage for organizations is the cost of development, especially for sophisticated multimedia programs. Estimates are that it takes 200 to 300 hours of design and development time to produce one hour of instruction.[54] Full-motion colour-and-sound courseware would likely cost $200,000 for 30 hours of instruction. This requires a considerable upfront investment in information technology and staff. At Motorola, where about 30 percent of employee training is computer based, it was estimated that $20 million to $27 million will be spent in one year on e-learning.[55]

complete it, they are not likely to do so. Employees have been found to be more likely to complete a computer-based training program when there is an incentive for doing so, some form of accountability, or when the program content is job relevant and useful.

Finally, unless trainees experience technical problems, they tend to respond positively to computer-based training programs. A number of studies have reported that after taking a computer-based training program, trainees report satisfaction with their learning experience, more positive attitudes toward technology-based training, and a willingness to try it again.[60]

SUMMARY

This chapter described technology-based training methods and serves as a complement to Chapters 6 and 7, which described on-the-job and off-the-job training methods. First, we described the meaning of technology-based training, computer-based training, and e-learning. Then we described the differences between instructor-led training and self-directed learning, and between asynchronous and synchronous training. This was followed by a description of different types of technology-based training including electronic performance support systems, video and web conferencing, as well as webinars and webcasts and the use of social media and Web 2.0 technologies. We then described how to design computer-based training programs and their advantages and disadvantages for individuals and organizations. The chapter concluded with a discussion of the effectiveness of computer-based training.

Key Terms

asynchronous training p. 231
blog p. 235
computer-based training p. 230
customization p. 240
e-learning p. 231
electronic performance support system
    (EPSS) p. 232
generative learning p. 235
human interaction p. 240
instructor-led training (ILT) p. 231
learner control p. 242
mobile learning (m-learning) p. 237
multimedia training p. 231
personalization p. 240
podcast p. 237

self-directed learning (SDL) p. 231
self-pacing p. 242
social constructivism p. 235
social media p. 235
synchronous training p. 232
technology-based training p. 229
traditional training p. 229
video conferencing p. 233
virtual classroom p. 234
Web 2.0 p. 235
Web 3.0 p. 237
Web conferencing p. 234
webcast p. 235
webinar p. 234
wiki p. 237

Make the Connection

p. 238: active practice and conditions of practice are discussed in Chapter 5 on page 145 and instructional methods are discussed in Chapter 6 on page 168

Web Links

Cisco Systems Canada Co.: **www.cisco.com**

Dow Chemical: **www.dow.com**

Hydro-Québec: **www.hydroquebec.com**

Motorola Inc.: **www.motorola.com**

Scotiabank: **www.scotiabank.com**

The Economical Insurance Group: **www.economicalinsurance.com**

Verizon: **www22.verizon.com**

Required Professional Capabilities (RPCs)

The following RPCs are relevant to material covered in this chapter. The RPC number represents the CCHRA number assigned to the RPC as presented on the CCHRA website. All of the RPCs can be found in the Body of Knowledge at http://www.chrp.ca/rpc/body-of-knowledge/

RPC 151: Uses a variety of methods to deliver development programs.

151.04: Methods of training and development (Games and simulations, case method, lecturing, on-the-job training, distance learning, role-play, videoconferencing, group discussion)

Discussion Questions

1. In both Canada and the United States, the actual use of training technologies has fallen below projections and, in fact, the adoption of training technologies has been relatively slow. What are some of the reasons for this and what are the potential barriers to the adoption of training technologies?
2. Compare and contrast technology-based training methods to traditional training methods. Why would an organization choose to use technology-based training methods rather than traditional training methods? Are there some types of industries, organizations, or jobs in which technology-based training or traditional training would be more appropriate and effective?
3. What are the advantages and disadvantages of technology-based training for trainees, trainers, and organizations?
4. If you had the choice, would you choose a computer-based training program or a traditional classroom program? Which would you prefer and why? Do you think your satisfaction, learning, and performance would differ in a computer-based program versus a traditional classroom program? Explain your reasoning.
5. Discuss how computer-based training programs can be designed to engage trainees and improve their motivation and learning.

6. Discuss how games, simulations, and role plays can be used in computer-based training programs. If you were designing a computer-based training program, when and why would you use each method?

7. Some have argued that there is nothing uniquely advantageous about technology-based training methods and that any effect they have on learning is not due to the use of any particular technological device. Do you agree or disagree with this position? Explain your reasoning and why you think it might be true or false.

8. Research on the effects of computer-based training has found that it is more effective than classroom instruction when trainees can choose the program (computer-based or classroom) and when the instructional methods used to deliver the programs are different. What are the implications of these two findings for understanding the effects of computer-based training and for the design and delivery of computer-based training programs?

9. What is social constructivism and how can it be facilitated by technology? What is Web 2.0 technology and how can it be used for training? Do you think organizations should use Web 2.0 technologies for training? Explain your answer.

10. What does learner control refer to and what role does it play in computer-based training? How would you design a computer-based training program with and without learner control?

The Great Training Debate

1. Debate the following: Given the many benefits of computer-based training, organizations should convert all of their classroom training programs to computer-based programs and make formal classroom training a thing of the past.

2. Debate the following: There is nothing inherently superior about technology-based training. The effectiveness of a training method depends on how it is designed rather than how it is delivered.

3. Debate the following: The use of technology for training is just the latest fad and it will never be as effective as more traditional methods of training.

Exercises

In-Class

1. Describe the most recent classroom training program you attended in terms of the objectives, content, methods, and conditions of practice. Now think about how the program might be converted to a computer-based training program. Describe what the program would be like and how you would design it. Do you think it would be more or less effective than the classroom training program?

2. Choose a class from a course you are currently taking and describe it in terms of the following design factors from Chapter 5:

   - What are the objectives?
   - What is the content?
   - What training methods are used?
   - What practice conditions are used?

   Now consider how the class might be designed and delivered as a computer-based course. Review your answers to each of the above design factors, and then convert them into a computer-based program. In other words, what would be the objectives, content, methods, and practice conditions?
   How effective do you think the course will be as a computer-based course? Compare and contrast it to the classroom course. What are the advantages and disadvantages for students, instructors, and the university or college? Which course would you prefer and why?

3. One of the concerns about technology-based training is the tendency to focus too much on the technology and not enough on learning and the conditions of practice. Refer back to Chapter 5 and the conditions of practice in Table 5.3. Describe how each of the conditions of practice can be included in the design of a computer-based training program.

4. After learning about computer-based training, you realize that your organization can benefit by converting some of its traditional classroom training programs to computer-based programs. Describe how you would proceed if you were to convert a particular training program (e.g., customer service, sales, negotiations, etc.) to a computer-based program. What would you have to do to convert the program and how would you proceed?

5. You have just been hired by an organization to help convert some of its classroom training programs to computer-based programs. However, the company does not have a tradition of using computers in the workplace and there is likely to be a great deal of resistance from managers and employees. You have to meet with employees and managers to help them understand why computer-based training will be better for them and the organization than classroom training. Prepare a brief presentation of what you will tell the employees and managers and then present it to another student or the class.

In-the-Field

1. Contact the human resource department of an organization and ask them if you can conduct a brief interview with the training staff about their use of computer-based training. Some of the things you might consider include:
   a. Do they use computers for training, and if so, what forms of computer-based training are they using and what are they using them for?
   b. Why did they decide to use computers for training?
   c. How effective has the use of computers been for training? How have they evaluated its effectiveness and what has the impact been on employees and the organization?
   d. Do they plan to use computer-based training in the future, and if so, in what way, for what purposes, and for what reasons?

2. Contact the human resource department of an organization to find out if they have computer-based training programs. Once you have found an organization that has developed a computer-based program, find out how they designed the program and how effective it is. Some of the things to consider include:
   a. What are the training objectives?
   b. What is the training content?
   c. Who are the trainees?
   d. How has the program been designed and does it include interactive elements?
   e. Does the program include active practice and conditions of practice, and if so, how have they been incorporated into the program?
   f. How effective has the program been and how does it compare to traditional classroom training? How have trainees reacted to it?

3. Contact the human resource department of an organization to find out if they are using any Web 2.0 tools for learning. Once you have found an organization that is using Web 2.0 tools, find out what tools they are using and what they are using them for. Some of the things to consider include:
   a. What Web 2.0 tools are being used?
   b. What are the tools being used for and who is using them?
   c. How have employees reacted to the use of Web 2.0?
   d. How effective has Web 2.0 been for learning?
   e. What are some of the benefits and limitations of using Web 2.0 for learning?

4. To learn more about e-learning in Canada, read the report by the Conference Board of Canada, "E-Learning in Canada: Findings from 2003 E-Survey," at **www.conferenceboard.ca/Libraries/EDUC_PUBLIC/ TopLine_report.sflb.** Review the report and summarize the main findings and concerns facing Canadian organizations. Some of the things to consider include:
   a. What are the challenges to implementing e-learning?
   b. What are the benefits of e-learning?
   c. How should e-learning programs be evaluated?
   d. What is the future use of e-learning by Canadian organizations?

5. To find out about technology-based training in Canada, visit Industry Canada at **www.collectionscanada.gc.ca/webarchives/20060201093632/ http://strategis.ic.gc.ca/epic/internet/incts-scf.nsf/en/h_sl00009e.html.** Read the following sections and summarize the main findings:
   a. What is the impact of learning technologies?
   b. Does e-learning help companies save money and improve productivity?
   c. How can you find out which learning technology is right for you?
   d. How can you assess the quality of e-learning products and services?
   e. Read the case studies and briefly summarize how each organization has used technology-based learning and the benefits and outcomes that resulted from it.

Case Incident

SKU at Nike

One of the biggest problems facing retailers is turnover. Retention is very low in certain retail businesses and turnover is 100 percent. This makes training a real challenge. At Nike, for example, every few months an employee leaves and another starts and so does the training process. As a result, training new staff in a classroom setting is not cost effective. So Nike decided to design an online training program that the company could offer to employees in its own stores as well as at other retailers that sell its products. The program would have to convey a lot of information quickly but also be easy to digest.

The solution was a program called Sports Knowledge Underground, or SKU. The layout for the program resembles a subway map with different stations representing different training themes. For example, Apparel Union Station branches off into the apparel technologies line, the running products line, and the Nike Pro products line. The Cleated Footwear Station offers paths to football, whereas the Central Station offers broad lines like customer skills. Each segment is three to seven minutes long and gives the employee the basic knowledge he/she needs about various products.

Questions

1. How effective do you think Nike's SKU e-learning program will be for employee learning? Do you think it will reduce turnover?
2. How should the SKU program be designed to be most effective for learning and retention? Should other retailers design similar e-learning programs?

Source: J. Marquez, "Faced with high turnover, retailers boot up e-learning for quick training," *Workforce Management*, August, 2005, Vol. 84, P. 74.

Case Study E-LEARNING AT FLOTATION LTD.

Jenny Stoppard was excited about her new position as Vice President of Human Resources at Flotation Ltd., a manufacturer of life jackets and other flotation devices. However, she knew she had her work cut out for her.

The president of the company had clearly stated that one of her first tasks was to take a close look at the training function. Although Flotation Ltd. had a reputation as a company with a well-trained workforce, the president now wanted to see some hard evidence to back up the company's training investment. The president wanted to increase productivity per person by 50 percent over the next three years, and Jenny was expected to spearhead the effort.

Sam was the company's veteran trainer and was liked by everybody in the organization. For 20 years he had been training employees at Flotation Ltd. He was only three years away from retirement and was not likely to respond favourably to Jenny and her new mandate.

The president introduced Jenny to Sam as his new boss and the key player in the drive to increase the company's competitiveness. He also asked Sam to do everything in his power to cooperate with her.

Jenny not only had to revamp the training function, but she also had to deal with Sam, who was pretty much set in his ways. How was she going to achieve the president's goals and at the same time get Sam on board?

After thinking about her situation for several days, Jenny came across an article on e-learning and how it has saved some companies millions of dollars a year in training costs. Suddenly, she had an idea.

"Why not convert some of Sam's training courses to e-learning programs on the company's website?" she thought to herself. "This would certainly be a whole new approach and I could save the company money and get Sam involved since he would be responsible for preparing his course material for the program. Surely Sam would be excited to know that his training courses would continue even after he has retired."

Both the president and Sam were very excited about the potential of e-learning at Flotation Ltd. Jenny was given the go-ahead to begin designing the first course. Jenny and Sam decided that the first course would be Sam's sales training program, which was one of his best. It would also be useful for the company's sales staff, who would be able to do the program while they were on the road selling.

The first thing that Jenny did was arrange for Sam to be videotaped delivering the course. Then she had Sam prepare some text material and additional information about some of the key learning points. With the help of the IT people, the video and text were placed on the company's website. The program was designed so that employees would watch the video of Sam and at certain points during the video they could click on an icon for more information. The video would then stop and the additional information would appear on the screen. After reading the material they could then return to the video.

When the program was set up and ready to go, the sales staff received a memo telling them about the company's first e-learning program and how to access it on the company's website. The memo was titled "Learn how to improve your sales skills on the road" and "Attend Sam's best training program any time and anywhere." Everybody was very excited about this new approach to training, and Sam was thrilled to know that he was the main attraction.

However, although the program was launched with much fanfare, the results were less than glowing. In fact, after the first six months very few of the sales staff had taken the course. Many said that they did not have time to take it. And of those who did, fewer than half actually completed it.

When asked about it, some of the sales staff said that it was not very interesting. Some said they would rather attend a live version of the course in the classroom and others said they didn't see the advantage of taking an e-learning course. Some thought it was just a big waste of the company's time and money.

The president asked to see Jenny to find out how things were going and if they were on track for achieving the company's productivity goals. Jenny did not know what she would tell him. Sam tried to console her by telling her that it had only been six months and the sales staff just needed a little more time to get used to e-learning. Jenny wasn't so sure. She began to wonder if the e-learning strategy was a big mistake.

Questions

1. Do you think that e-learning was a good idea for Flotation Ltd.? Could e-learning help the company realize the president's productivity goals?
2. Comment on the e-learning program that Jenny and Sam designed. What are the indicators that suggest it has not been a success? Is it possible there are other indicators that might suggest it is more effective than it appears?
3. If you were Jenny, what would you tell the president and what would you do about e-learning at Flotation Ltd.? Should Jenny give up on e-learning, or wait another six months before making a decision?
4. What do you think are the main reasons for the negative reaction to the e-learning program? What are the most important things that need to be changed to improve the program? How would you change it if you had to redesign it?
5. Consider the use of social media and Web 2.0 technologies for the sales training program. What Web 2.0 technologies would you recommend and how should they be used as part of the sales training program? Explain your answer.

Flashback Questions

1. Comment on how the e-learning program was designed in terms of the material described in Chapter 5, such as active practice and the conditions of practice. Do you think the program could be redesigned and more effective? Refer to Table 5.3 and discuss the potential use of the conditions of practice in the redesign of the e-learning program.
2. Consider the use of active learning and adaptive expertise for the e-learning program. Do you think that the program should be designed for adaptive expertise and active learning? Explain your answer. If you were to redesign the e-learning program for active learning, explain what you would do and why you would do it.
3. Consider the material in Chapter 3 on learning theories and theories of motivation. How can learning theories and motivation theories help us understand why the e-learning program was not more effective? What are the implications of the learning theories and motivation theories for the design of the e-learning program? What would you do to make it more effective?

REFERENCES

1. Based on Freifeld, L. (2011, January/February). TEIG locks in on leadership. *Training, 48(1)*, 34–39; www.economicalinsurance.com/en/ (TEIG Awards: Economical recognized for excellence in workplace learning, March 24, 2011; Economical Insurance ranks second on 2011 "Training Top 125").
2. Dolezalek, H. (2005, December). 2005 industry report. *Training, 42(12)*, 14–28.
3. Dolezalek, H. (2005, December).
4. Brown, K. G., & Ford, J. K. (2002). Using computer technology in training: Building an infrastructure for active learning. In K. Kraiger (Ed.), *Creating, implementing, and managing effective training and development: State-of-the-art lessons for practice* (pp. 160–191). San Francisco, CA: Jossey-Bass.
5. Tomlinson, A. (2002, March 25). T & D spending up in U.S. as Canada lags behind. *Canadian HR Reporter, 15(6)*, 1; Sitzmann, T., Kraiger, K., Stewart, D., & Wisher, R. (2006). The comparative effectiveness of web-based and classroom instruction: A meta-analysis. *Personnel Psychology, 59*, 623–664.
6. Lavis, C. (2011). *Learning & development outlook 2011: Are organizations ready for learning 2.0?* Ottawa: The Conference Board of Canada.
7. Anonymous. (2011, November/December). 2011 training industry report. *Training, 48(6)*, 22–35.
8. Harris-Lalonde, S. (2001). *Training and development outlook*. The Conference Board of Canada: Ottawa.
9. Ray, R. (2001, May 25). Employers, employees embrace e-learning. *The Globe and Mail*, E2.
10. Anonymous. (2007, December 3). Hydro-Quebec takes training online. *Canadian HR Reporter, 20(21)*, 28.
11. Brown, K. G., & Ford, J. K. (2002).
12. Welsh, L. T., Wanberg, C. R., Brown, K. G., & Simmering, M. J. (2003). E-learning: Emerging uses, empirical results and future directions. *International Journal of Training and Development, 7*, 245–258.
13. Welsh, L. T., Wanberg, C. R., Brown, K. G., & Simmering, M. J. (2003).
14. Welsh, L. T., Wanberg, C. R., Brown, K. G., & Simmering, M. J. (2003).
15. Raybould, B. (1990, November–December). Solving human performance problems with computers—A case study: Building an electronic performance support system. *Performance and Instruction*, 4–14.
16. Smith, K. (1996, April). EPSS helps accounting firm reduce training time, improve productivity during transition to new service emphasis. *Lakewood Report on Technology for Learning*, 8.
17. Gebber, B. (1991). Help! The rise of performance support systems. *Training, 28(12)*, 23–29; Ruyle, K. (1991, February/March). Developing intelligent job aids. *Technical and Skills Training*, 9–14.
18. Weinstein, M. (2006, October). On demand is in demand. *Training, 43(10)*, 31–35.
19. Galt, V. (2003, January 22). Bank tunes in to TV training. *The Globe and Mail*, C1, C5.
20. Lewis, M. (2011, July). Moving into the live virtual classroom. *T+D*, 76–77.
21. Shankar, C. (2006, September 25). Rise in webinars among e-learning trends. *Canadian HR Reporter, 19(16)*, 19, 21.
22. Anonymous (2008, September). What does it cost to host web conferences and webcasts? *T+D, 62(9)*, 88.
23. Lewis, M. (2011, July).
24. Kraiger, K. (2008). Transforming our models of learning and development: Web-based instruction as enabler of third-generation instruction. *Industrial and Organizational Psychology, 1*, 454–467; p. 461.
25. Jarche, H. (2008, April). Skills 2.0. *T+D, 62(4)*, 22–24.

26. London, M., & Hall, M. J. (2011). Unlocking the value of Web 2.0 technologies for training and development: The shift from instructor-controlled, adaptive learning to learner-driven, generative learning. *Human Resource Management, 50,* 757–775.

27. Jarche, H. (2008, April).

28. Shankar, C. (2006, September 25).

29. Shankar, C. (2006, September 25); Anonymous (2006, April). Podcast popularity grows. *Training, 43(4),* 14.

30. Green, M. (2011, April). Better, smarter, faster: Web 3.0 and the future of learning. *T+D, 65(4),* 70–72.

31. Green, M. (2011, April).

32. Ally, M. (2008, February 11). Learn anywhere, anytime. *Canadian HR Reporter, 21(3),* 18.

33. Fister Gale, S. (2008, May). Dial M for mobile learning. *Workforce Management Online* (www .workforce.com).

34. Weinstein, M. (2010, January). Be our guest—safely. *Training, 47(1),* 32–33.

35. Garff, M. (2012, January). Implementing M-learning: Make the dream a reality. *T+D, 66(1),* 16.

36. Bowness, A. (2004, September 27). Hands-on learning through computer simulations. *Canadian HR Reporter, 17(16),* 15.

37. Sitzmann, T. (2011). A meta-analytic examination of the instructional effectiveness of computer-based simulation games. *Personnel Psychology, 64,* 489–528.

38. DeRouin, R. E., Fritzsche, B. A., & Salas, E. (2005). E-learning in organizations. *Journal of Management, 31,* 920–940.

39. Sitzmann, T. (2011).

40. Anonymous. (2005, December 12). Simulation games score with trainees. *Workforce Management, 84(15),* 70.

41. Sitzmann, T. (2011).

42. Galt, V. (2004, June 12). Employers jumping on e-learning bandwagon. *The Globe and Mail,* B10.

43. DeRouin, R. E., Fritzsche, B. A., & Salas, E. (2005).

44. DeRouin, R. E., Fritzsche, B. A., & Salas, E. (2005).

45. DeRouin, R. E., Fritzsche, B. A., & Salas, E. (2005).

46. Sitzmann, T., Kraiger, K., Stewart, D., & Wisher, R. (2006).

47. Sitzmann, T., Kraiger, K., Stewart, D., & Wisher, R. (2006).

48. Sitzmann, T., Kraiger, K., Stewart, D., & Wisher, R. (2006); Orvis, K., Fisher, S. L., & Wasserman, M. E. (2009). Power to the people: Using learner control to improve trainee reactions and learning in Web-based instructional environments. *Journal of Applied Psychology, 94,* 960–971.

49. Orvis, K. A., Fisher, S. L., & Wasserman, M. E. (2009). Power to the people: Using learner control to improve trainee reactions and learning in web-based instructional environments. *Journal of Applied Psychology, 94,* 960–971.

50. Galt, V. (2004, June 12).

51. Brown, K. G., & Ford, J. K. (2002).

52. Welsh, L. T., Wanberg, C. R., Brown, K. G., & Simmering, M. J. (2003).

53. O'Keefe, B. (1991, September/October). Adopting multimedia on a global scale. *Instruction Delivery Systems,* 6–11.

54. Miles, K. W., & Griffith, E. R. (1993, April/May). Developing an hour of CBT: The quick and dirty method. *CBT Directions,* 28–33.

55. Eure, R. (2001, March 21). Companies embrace e-training. *The Globe and Mail,* B16.

56. Welsh, L. T., Wanberg, C. R., Brown, K. G., & Simmering, M. J. (2003).

57. Sitzmann, T., Kraiger, K., Stewart, D., & Wisher, R. (2006).

58. Sitzmann, T., Kraiger, K., Stewart, D., & Wisher, R. (2006).

59. Welsh, L. T., Wanberg, C. R., Brown, K. G., & Simmering, M. J. (2003).

60. Welsh, L. T., Wanberg, C. R., Brown, K. G., & Simmering, M. J. (2003).

Training Delivery

CHAPTER LEARNING OUTCOMES

After reading this chapter, you should be able to:

- define a lesson plan and describe how to develop one and the information that should be included in a detailed lesson plan
- describe the characteristics of an effective trainer
- describe how to decide who should attend a training program
- describe what makes an effective training site
- describe the elements of a positive learning climate
- discuss Gagné's nine events of instruction
- discuss some of the problems and solutions of training delivery

SIERRA SYSTEMS GROUP

Sierra Systems Group is a Vancouver-based information technology and management consulting services company in North America with nine Canadian offices and over 900 employees. At Sierra Systems, continuous learning is part of the company's philosophy and culture.

Traditional training methods and online training courses are available to all employees. In addition, Sierra has a career growth program in which each employee is assigned a career adviser who is a manager separate from the employee's project manager. The career adviser assists with matching the employee's goals to his or her career path and is an advocate for obtaining the education required to meet these goals.

The company's employees have access to more than 2,000 online courses and ongoing in-house training. Sierra also covers 100 percent of the tuition cost for some courses unrelated to an employee's position, as well as providing subsidies for professional accreditation and financial bonuses for course completion. According to senior HR manager Stephanie Hollingshead, "Training and development is critical to our business."

All of the company's training is housed under Sierra Systems University, which is a corporate university that was launched in 2000 to meet the career development needs of Sierra employees. The Web-based learning portal provides employees with easy access to in-house courses as well as external courses. It is up to individual managers to approve employee requests for training with input from career advisers. The role of human resources is to make the right courses available at the right time.

The delivery of some of the company's training programs has had to be modified to meet the needs of the company's bottom line. For example, a two-day course on managing people was turned into a series of one-hour webinars. There are still in-person components to the training but most of it is done in the office and incorporates on-the-job training.

HR has also responded to management concerns about lost time by offering a two-day course on a Friday and Saturday rather than scheduling both days mid-week. "That was management pushing to do that," says Hollingshead, as employees didn't want the course to be cancelled and were willing to give up one day on the weekend instead.

In a company with locations across North America, it can be costly to send employees to training. "There was a lot of travel and a lot of push-back on travel costs," says Hollingshead. "Why weren't people going on these courses? Well, because it costs money to send them there and they ended up missing a week of work for a two-day course."

Breaking up training and development into smaller pieces also makes it easier to bring management on board, she says. In one case, HR offered to introduce a larger course in-house in one-hour lunch webinars with one topic per session. "We ended up having to book more sessions because people were talking to other people and everyone wanted to attend," says Hollingshead. "It sort of got a life of its own. Now it's a model we're using and building out."

In 2004, Sierra Systems Group was awarded the University of Alberta/TELUS Partners in Workplace Learning Award of Distinction, which recognizes companies that demonstrate a commitment to providing learning opportunities for their employees. The company has also been recognized as one of Canada's Top 100 Employers several times over the last decade.[1]

Source: D. Harder, "Sierra Systems earns top marks for training," *Canadian HR Reporter,* Feb. 9, 2009, P. 19; Sierra Systems. "News & Events, Sierra Systems Wins Alberta Chamber of Commerce University of Alberta-TELUS Partners in Workplace Learning Award of Distinction," Feb. 19, 2004. Found at: www.sierrasys.com; Sierra Systems. "Online Corporate University Strengthens Sierra Systems' Client Services," July 10, 2000. Found at: www.sierrasys.com; Sierra Systems. "Sierra Systems Awarded Top 100 Employer For 5th Straight Year," October 6, 2004. Found at: www.sierrasys.com.

In the previous four chapters, we described how to design training programs and the different methods of training. However, as you can tell from the description of training and development at Sierra Systems, there are other important

TABLE 9.1
Training Delivery Activities
1. Develop a lesson plan.
2. Choose the trainer.
3. Decide on the trainees who should attend a training program.
4. Determine the training materials and equipment required.
5. Prepare the training site.
6. Schedule the training program.
7. Administer the training.
8. Implement the training program.

aspects of training and development, such as deciding who should attend a training program, scheduling training programs, and choosing the location of the training. These are issues that have to do with the delivery of training programs, the focus of this chapter.

Table 9.1 lists the main activities associated with training delivery that are described in this chapter. The starting point is the preparation of a lesson plan.

THE LESSON PLAN

Once a training program has been designed, the trainer needs to prepare a lesson plan. The **lesson plan** is the blueprint that outlines the training program in terms of the sequence of activities that will take place. As such, it is a guide for the trainer that provides a step-by-step breakdown for conducting a training program. A lesson plan should be prepared for each lesson in a program. A **lesson** is a cohesive unit of instruction with a specific learning objective.[2]

A good lesson plan should be prepared in advance of a training program and be detailed enough that any trainer could use it to guide him/herself through the program. Most of what will be required to deliver a training program will be indicated in the lesson plan. Although there is no one best format for lesson plans, a good rule of thumb is to focus on what the trainee will be doing.[3] A lesson plan should reflect the interaction of content, sequence, trainer, trainee, and the norms of the organization.[4]

Some of the things that should be listed on the first page or cover of a lesson plan are the training objectives, the trainees, the trainer, time allocation, location, classroom requirements and seating, training materials and equipment, and supplies and handouts.[5] The detailed lesson plan for each lesson should indicate the activities that will occur during the lesson as well as what the trainer and trainees will be doing and when they will be doing it.

An important consideration in the development of a lesson plan is the sequencing or ordering of the content for a training program. There is no one best way to order the training content as it will depend on the nature of the content and the trainees. However, there are a number of general approaches for content sequencing that reflect the ease of learning, such as general to specific, easy to difficult, concrete to abstract, old to new, simple to complex, familiar to

Lesson plan
The blueprint that outlines the training program in terms of the sequence of activities that will take place

Lesson
A cohesive unit of instruction with a specific learning objective

TABLE 9.2

Lesson Plan Cover Page

Organization: Vandalais Department Stores
Department: Human Resources
Program Title: Structured Employment Interviews
Instructor(s):   Interview Training Consultant
Time Allocation: 1 day
Trainees: All employees in the Human Resource Department
Where: Vandalais Learning Centre

Training Objectives

Employees will be able to conduct a structured behaviour description interview and correctly perform the seven key behaviours.

Classroom Requirements

Seating for 50 people that allows for high involvement.

Training Materials and Equipment

DVD player and TV monitor; DVD: *How to Conduct a Structured Employment Interview*; computer and projector with screen; flipchart; paper; markers.

Trainee Supplies

Pen and paper.

Trainee Handouts

1. Course objectives and outline.

2. Article on structured employment interviews.

3. Article on behaviour description interviews.

4. List of the seven key behaviours for conducting a structured employment interview.

5. Copy of the behaviour description interview for the sales associate position with interview questions and scoring guide and instructions.

6. Role-play exercise.

unknown, practical to theoretical, and present to future.[6] Beginning with simple and familiar is generally recommended because it builds trainee self-efficacy and allows trainees to see how their current level of knowledge and experience is relevant for the training. This also provides some comfort to trainees and lowers their anxiety about learning.

Table 9.2 presents the cover page of a lesson plan for a one-day training program on structured employment interviews. As shown in Table 9.3, a detailed lesson plan should indicate what will happen and when as well as what the trainees and trainer will be doing. Note that if this training program lasted for more than one day there would be a detailed lesson plan for each day of the program.[7]

TABLE 9.3

Structured Employment Interview Detailed Lesson Plan

Objective

Employees will be able to conduct structured behaviour description employment interview and correctly perform the seven key behaviours.

Trainees:	Members of the Human Resource Department.
Time:	9 a.m.–5 p.m.

Course Outline

9:00–10:00	Introduction lecture on the problem of poor employee performance and high turnover and the use of structured and unstructured employment interviews for selection.
10:00–10:30	Show DVD of an unstructured employment interview followed by a discussion.
10:30–10:45	Break
10:45–11:15	Show DVD of a structured employment interview followed by a discussion.
11:15–12:00	Review the seven key behaviours of conducting a structured employment interview.
12:00–1:00	Lunch
1:00–2:00	Lecture on behaviour description interview questions and review of the interview questions and guide developed for sales associates.
2:00–2:30	Review of the seven key behaviours in conducting a structured employment interview.
2:30–2:45	Break
2:45–3:30	Role-play practice exercise: In groups of three, assign participants the roles of interviewer, interviewee, and observer. Review script for roles and instruct trainees to demonstrate the seven key behaviours of a structured interview using the sales associate behaviour description interview questions. Have observer provide feedback using guidelines contained in the role-play exercise booklet and evaluate the interviewer's performance on the seven key behaviours using the evaluation form provided. Switch roles until each group member has played the role of the interviewer.
3:30–4:30	Regroup for discussion of role-play exercise. Discuss how it felt to be the interviewer and the interviewee, and get the observer's feedback and evaluation.
4:30–4:45	Review the seven key behaviours of the structured employment interview and the importance of using structured interviews and the behaviour description interview for hiring sales associates.
4:45–5:00	Closing. Review objectives and give pep talk about conducting structured employment interviews and using the behaviour description interview. Thank participants and hand out training certificates.

The Trainer's Notebook 9.1

GUIDELINES FOR DEVELOPING A LESSON PLAN

Use the following guidelines to develop a lesson plan.

1. Write the lesson objective (what the trainee will be able to do at the end of the lesson).

2. Determine the knowledge and skills the trainee must learn to accomplish the objective. This enables the developer to determine the subtopics of the lesson.

3. Put the subtopics of the lesson in a preliminary sequence in a way that is most meaningful to the trainee and enables the trainee to master the knowledge and skills.

4. Identify the content of the various subtopics of the lesson. Answer the question: What must the trainee know or be able to do for satisfactory performance of each lesson subtopic?

5. Select the instructional procedures appropriate to the learning of each lesson subtopic. Identify materials and equipment needed.

6. Review the instructional sequence. Adjust as necessary to provide variety and movement for the trainees.

7. Provide a means of monitoring and trainee feedback.

8. Prepare a test to evaluate the degree to which trainees have achieved the learning objective of the lesson.

Source: A.P. Carnevale, L.J. Gainer & A.S. Meltzer, *Workplace basics training manual*. San Francisco, CA: Jossey-Bass Publishers. 1990.

The development of a lesson plan is a critical phase in the design of a training program. It allows for the approval and the smooth operation of training activities. It also enables expenditures to be budgeted for and monitored. The development of a lesson plan sets the stage for the implementation of the training program and it is a signal to other members of the organization that training is to be conducted in a professional manner. In the following pages, we describe the main elements in the lesson plan in more detail. For some guidance on what to include in a lesson plan, see The Trainer's Notebook 9.1, "Guidelines for Developing a Lesson Plan."

THE TRAINER

The lesson plan cover sheet in Table 9.2 indicates that the trainer will be a consultant. But how do you decide who the trainer will be? At first, this might seem like a trivial question. After all, isn't this the job of the human resources department or the training staff? In some cases the answer is yes, but in many training situations the answer to this question depends on a number of factors.

First, it is important to realize the role of a good trainer. Regardless of how well a training program is designed, the success of a program rests in large part on the trainer. In other words, no matter how good the training program, if the trainer is ineffective the program will suffer.

What are the qualities of a good trainer? This question should be easy for students to answer if they consider the courses they have enjoyed and those that they found less memorable. One of the first things that might come to mind is the extent to which the instructor was knowledgeable about the course material, or what is known as a subject-matter expert.

A **subject-matter expert (SME)** is someone who is familiar with the knowledge, skills, and abilities required to perform a task or job and has subject-matter expertise. In Chapter 5 we noted the importance of subject-matter experts in determining the content of a training program. A trainer should also be an expert on the topic or content area being taught. Not only will trainees learn more, but the trainer will be perceived as more credible.

Very often persons who conduct training in an organization do so because they have expertise in a particular area. However, it can be difficult to find subject-matter experts in an organization who are willing to become trainers. To find out how one organization does this, see Training Today 9.1, "Finding Subject-Matter Experts (SMEs)."

An effective trainer must also have the ability to make the material interesting. Students probably have had instructors who knew the material and were able to deliver it, but all the same, they did not make it very interesting. A good trainer should be enthusiastic and excited about the training material and capable of motivating and arousing the interest of trainees.

One way for trainers to generate interest and increase trainee motivation is by being expressive during the delivery of a training program. **Trainer expressiveness** refers to a trainer who uses linguistic devices and is physically animated. Expressive trainers are physically animated (e.g., posture, gesturing, eye contact) and use linguistic devices such as an animated and enthusiastic voice rather than a monotone voice, and vocal fluency rather than speaking with

Subject-matter expert (SME)

A person who is familiar with the knowledge, skills, and abilities required to perform a task or job

Make the Connection

Trainer expressiveness

A trainer who uses linguistic devices and is physically animated

---

Training Today 9.1

Finding Subject-Matter Experts (SMEs)

Export Development Canada (EDC) is a Crown corporation wholly owned by the Government of Canada with headquarters in Ottawa. They specialize in global financing, insurance, and bonding and are a recognized leader in financial reporting and economic analysis. EDC has been named one of Canada's Top 100 Employers for nine consecutive years between 2002 and 2010.

Because the industry in which it operates is heavily regulated, the learning and development team has the good fortune of knowing, at the beginning of each year, which courses it needs to update, develop, and deliver.

Armed with this information, the team meets with the director or vice president of each business unit and provides each leader with a detailed accounting of the company's course development, delivery, and SME needs. Each business unit director, in turn, is responsible for identifying those within his or her group who either are extremely knowledgeable SMEs or who would benefit from delivering or developing training as a professional developmental assignment.

There are many advantages to this approach. The fact that managers themselves handpick SMEs goes a long way toward demonstrating to SMEs that training is important to the organization, has management's buy-in, and deserves their time and attention. In addition, the fact that SMEs' managers enlist SMEs to help with training sends a strong message to SMEs that their managers support and encourage their efforts, and won't penalize them for performing training-related work that isn't directly associated with their regular day job.

Of course, the greatest advantage is that EDC has 120-plus internal SMEs that it utilizes each year to develop and deliver courses.

Sources: S. Boehle, "Subject matter expert trouble?" *Training*, April, 2007, P. 28; www.edc.ca.

hesitancies (e.g., "ums"). Research has found that trainees recall a greater amount of the training content when a trainer is more expressive. There is also evidence that a trainer's expressiveness enhances trainees' training motivation and self-efficacy.[8]

In addition to being expressive, a good trainer is also engaging. In other words, a good trainer is able to draw trainees into the training program and keep them interested, focused, and involved in learning. No doubt you can think of course instructors you have had who either put you to sleep or kept you on the edge of your seat as you were absorbed in what was being taught. When a trainer is engaging, trainees are more likely to be motivated to learn, and they are attentive and absorbed in the learning process. One way a trainer can do this is by using **seductive details**, which refers to the use of entertaining and interesting information during the delivery of a training program (e.g., showing a cartoon, telling a story, or telling a joke) that is only tangentially related to the training material. Although too much seductive detail can be harmful for learning, one study found that when it was combined with an expressive trainer it had a positive effect on problem-solving. The author concluded that trainers should make their instructional material entertaining through the use of seductive details and by being expressive.[9]

But what happens when a subject-matter expert does not know how to train people? This requires a training program known as train-the-trainer.

Seductive details
The use of entertaining and interesting information that is only tangentially related to the training material

Train-the-Trainer

One of the difficulties of finding a good trainer is that individuals who are skilled trainers often do not have the subject-matter expertise to deliver a training program in their organization. On the other hand, individuals who have subject-matter expertise often are not experienced trainers.

Students know, perhaps all too well, that no matter how well informed or knowledgeable an instructor might be, a course can still be poor if the instructor is not effective in delivering the material. In addition to subject-matter expertise, good trainers must also have good verbal and communication skills, interpersonal skills, and organizing and planning skills. The trainer must be able to deliver the training material in a manner that is understandable to trainees. Trainees are more likely to learn and recall training content when the trainer is well organized and easy to follow.[10]

One solution to this problem is to teach subject-matter experts how to be effective trainers. These programs are known as train-the-trainer and focus on the skills that are required to be an effective trainer. **Train-the-trainer** refers to training programs that teach subject-matter experts how to design and deliver training programs. With the increasing use of technology in the workplace, more subject-matter experts are being asked to become trainers and attend train-the-trainer programs. To learn more about train-the-trainer programs, see The Trainer's Notebook 9.2, "Train-the-Trainer Fundamentals."

Train-the-trainer
Training programs that teach subject-matter experts how to design and deliver training programs

THE TRAINEES

The lesson plan cover page indicates that the trainees will be members of the human resources department. This raises another question. Who should attend a training program? This is an important question because money

The Trainer's Notebook 9.2

TRAIN-THE-TRAINER FUNDAMENTALS

Subject-matter experts (SMEs) often are asked to design and/or deliver a training program because of their unique knowledge, the needs of a particular group of training participants, or the requirements of a specific project. However, they may not have experience as a trainer and will require some training on how to be an effective trainer. Here are some things to consider when you need to train-the-trainer:

1. Explain the specific reasons that the SME was selected for the role.

2. Review the training materials with the SME and make sure they are well scripted and marked up with plenty of visual cues for the trainer.

3. Coach the SME on facilitation skills and provide detailed information about the participants.

4. Give the SME permission to delegate tasks during the training (e.g., a volunteer for clicking through the slides).

5. Prepare the SME by providing a checklist of the basics of engaging facilitation, including setting up the room to meet the participants' needs and establishing rapport with the participants by presenting a friendly demeanour and sharing stories. Incorporate tips such as using interactive activities. Review the checklist with the SME and explain the reasons behind each tip.

6. Discuss adult learners' needs and learning styles so that the SME understands how and why to vary the training activities to maximize learning.

Help the SME think about charts, illustrations, and other visuals that would help participants understand the content. Make sure the SME understands the need to design interactive activities that appeal to visual, kinesthetic, and auditory learning styles.

7. Teach the SME how to facilitate a workshop accurately without reading from the leader's guide. Offer tips for remembering content such as creating note cards with key points.

8. Watch the SME conduct a practice session and provide feedback beginning with all the positive behaviours demonstrated and include one or two constructive comments that the SME can work on before the actual training program.

9. Offer assistance during the training with flip-charts or distributing materials.

10. Provide SMEs who must design their programs with PowerPoint templates, sample training materials, and examples they can build on.

11. Provide access to experienced instructional designers who can assist the SME when he/she has questions.

12. Provide the SME with access to a content reviewer to make sure everything is covered clearly and effectively for participants who are not experts.

Source: Trinée Adams, A. Kennedy & M. Marquart, "The reluctant trainer," *T+D*, March 2008, Vol. 62 (3), P. 24.

and time can be wasted, and performance problems are likely to continue, if the wrong people attend training and those who require training do not attend.

According to Donald Kirkpatrick, the following four questions need to be asked when selecting participants for a training program:[11]

1. Who can benefit from the training?
2. What programs are required by law or by government edict?

3. Should the training be voluntary or compulsory?
4. Should the participants be segregated by level in the organization, or should two or more levels be included in the same class?

Some employees stand to benefit from a training program given the tasks they perform and the extent to which the training will provide them with knowledge and skills that will help them improve their performance. Some training programs are required by law, such as health and safety programs for employees who work with hazardous materials. Other training programs are compulsory for all employees in a particular job category or position.

According to Kirkpatrick, some training programs should be compulsory otherwise some employees who will benefit from the training might not attend.[12] However, what if an employee refuses to attend a compulsory training program? To learn more, see Training Today 9.2, "The Right to Train."

As for segregating participants by organizational level or including them in the same training session, this really depends on the culture of the organization and the rapport that exists between different levels in the organization. The main

Training Today 9.2

The Right to Train

If an employer orders an employee to attend a training program and the order is lawful and reasonable, the employer has a right to expect the order to be followed. But what if the employee refuses?

An employee's refusal to obey a reasonable order would constitute insubordination. However, it is important that the directive to train is unambiguous. Condoning the refusal to train, such as allowing an employee to work despite the refusal, could eliminate any consideration of insubordination.

An unreasonable training order would include one that endangers the health and safety of an employee or that is not within the reasonable scope of an employee's work. If an employee argues that he has sufficient work already and training on something new is not needed, it is important that the employer ensure the training is, in fact, necessary.

As well, an employee should be paid for training and not be penalized for the inability to complete existing assignments while undergoing training. To reduce the risk of a constructive dismissal claim, an employer should also avoid saddling an employee with an unreasonable amount of extra work as a result of introducing a new system.

When an employee refuses a lawful and reasonable order to train, discipline may be warranted. Progressive discipline for an employee who continues to refuse training could include warning letters, suspensions, and dismissal.

Although employers generally have a right to order training, unionized and non-unionized employers alike must ensure any order is lawful and reasonable. Employers must act reasonably when employees resist or refuse training. If an employee has a reasonable explanation for refusing training, an employer may be required to accommodate. Moreover, if an employee has a disability that would limit training or his use of a new system, an employer is required to accommodate to the point of undue hardship.

Source: G. Na, "An employer's right to train," *Canadian HR Reporter*, Oct. 6, 2008, P. 25.

issue is whether employees will feel comfortable enough to speak and participate if their supervisors are present. If this is the case then it is often a good idea for different levels to attend a training program together.

One way to know whether an employee is ready to attend a training program is to have them take a trainability test.

Trainability Test

A **trainability test** is a test that measures an individual's ability to learn and perform training tasks in order to predict whether an individual will successfully complete a training program.[13]

This is typically done by having individuals take a mini-course or learn a sample of the training that is representative of the content of a training program. They then take a test that measures their learning and performance of the tasks.

Trainability tests have been shown to be effective in predicting training success and job performance in many jobs such as carpentry, welding, dentistry, and forklift operating. Although they have most often been used for psychomotor skills, they are just as applicable for other types of skills and knowledge tests. Training pre-tests can also be used to determine what kind of remedial training an individual might require to prepare them for a training program or to tailor a training program to one's needs. Thus, managers can maximize trainee learning by assessing employees' readiness to learn and trainability prior to training.[14]

Information on who requires training can be incorporated into a training plan. A **training plan** indicates who in an organization needs training (e.g., human resource staff), the type of training needed (e.g., structured employment interviewing), and how the training will be delivered (e.g., in a formal classroom).[15]

TRAINING MATERIALS AND EQUIPMENT

All training programs require the use of training materials, supplies, and equipment, and this should be indicated on the lesson plan cover page. The content of a training program as well as the methods and exercises determine the materials, supplies, and equipment that will be required.

Training materials refers to expendable items such as note pads, pens, markers, tape, and so on. Common supplies include computer equipment, a projector, and workbooks or manuals. Handouts such as course outlines that indicate the course objectives, the material to be covered, and a schedule of training activities, as well as articles and copies of the trainer's slides, are often required and will have to be prepared in advance. Equipment refers to things that have a life beyond a single use, such as projectors, computers, DVD player, and so on. The trainer must identify the materials and equipment that will be required for a training program.[16]

As shown in Table 9.2, the materials and equipment required for the structured employment interview training program include a TV monitor and DVD player, a DVD on how to conduct a structured employment interview, a computer and projector with screen, a flipchart, pen, paper, and markers. Handouts for trainees include a course outline, readings, a list of the key learning behaviours, and a role-play exercise.

Trainability test
A test that measures an individual's ability to learn and perform training tasks

Training plan
Indicates who in an organization needs training, the type of training that is needed, and how the training will be delivered

Training materials
Expendable items such as note pads, pens, markers, tape, and so on

With the determination of the materials and equipment necessary for training the cost of training and the budget is more easily determined, and the actual training session is more likely to run smoothly.

TRAINING SITE

The **training site** is the facility or room where the training will take place. Off-the-job training can take place at the organization if rooms are available; at an organization's headquarters; or at a rented facility such as a hotel or conference centre. As indicated in Table 9.2, the structured employment interview training program takes place at the company's learning centre.

Some organizations, like the Bank of Montreal, have their own learning centre for training and development. Organizations that do not have a learning centre or training rooms will have to find suitable facilities to conduct the training. In this case, an important concern is the travel time required for trainees to get to the training site and ensuring that trainees have transportation. If trainees have to stay overnight, plans for transportation, accommodation, and meals will have to be made and included in the training budget. This of course can be expensive and can result in employees being away from work for several days. Recall from the chapter opening vignette that Sierra Systems addressed this concern by converting a larger course to one-hour lunch webinars that focus on one topic per session.

Regardless of where a training program takes place, a number of factors need to be considered to ensure the training program runs smoothly. First, the training site should be conducive to learning. This means that the training environment should be comfortable in terms of things like space, lighting, and temperature. This might seem like a trivial point, but have you ever attended a class and the room temperature was on the cold side? Or how about a classroom that was too crowded and you had to stand or sit on the floor because there was not enough seating? Chances are it caused you some discomfort and interfered with your learning.

Second, the training site should be free of noise or distractions that might interfere with or disrupt learning. How often have you been in a class where you had to strain to hear the instructor over the chatter coming from outside the classroom? Obviously, noise can interfere with learning. Distractions can also be a problem. This is one reason why it is sometimes preferable to conduct a training program away from the organization. Otherwise, trainees might be tempted to step out of the training session to check for messages or take care of business. This, of course, is not likely if they are far from their desk and the workplace.

Third, the training site should be set up in a manner that is appropriate for the training program. For example, if trainees will be viewing a DVD, will they be able to see the screen and hear the sound? If trainees will be required to work in groups, will there be sufficient room for them to move around the room and interact with group members? Are break-out rooms necessary for group work? Are the seats arranged in a way that will allow trainees to interact and work with each other, and will the trainer be able to interact with trainees? Are the chairs movable or fixed? These are important considerations that the trainer needs to determine before the training.

Given the importance of the training room for trainee motivation and learning, trainers should inspect and prepare the room in advance of a training program to ensure that it will be conducive to learning. The trainer should arrive early on the day of the training to make sure that the room is properly set up and that the required equipment has arrived and is functioning. As discussed in the next section, one of the most important things that the trainer needs to prepare is the seating arrangement.

SEATING ARRANGEMENT

It is easy to understand how important seating is when you consider how so many students choose a seat in the first class and then continue to sit in the same seat all the time. The seating arrangement is also important because it can facilitate or limit trainee involvement and participation. It can also energize or inhibit trainees and it communicates the trainer's style.[17]

Figure 9.1 shows examples of different seating arrangements for low, moderate, and high levels of trainee involvement. The low-involvement seating represents a traditional classroom arrangement in which the instructor is in control and stands or sits at the front of the room behind a desk or table. With this seating arrangement, communication is one-way and flows from the instructor to trainees. Communication among the trainees is not possible. This arrangement is most common for the lecture method.

When a moderate amount of involvement is desired, the instructor is still at the front of the room. However, trainees are seated around a table, thereby allowing them to interact and exchange ideas with each other. Although the instructor remains in control and one-way communication still dominates, participants can also communicate with and learn from each other.

Finally, with a high-involvement seating arrangement, small groups of trainees are seated together in groups around small tables. As a result, group members can interact and work together on projects. The instructor's role is

---

FIGURE **9.1**

Seating Arrangements

Source: J.E. Eitington, *The Winning Trainer: Winning Ways to Involve People in Learning.* Houston, TX: Gulf Publishing Company. 1989. Reprinted with permission from Elsevier.

more of a resource person or facilitator. This allows the instructor to present material to the class (the work table and flipchart are at the front of the room), engage the class in discussions, move around the room and listen in on groups, provide help and assistance, and spend time with each group while they work on projects and solve problems.[18]

The seating arrangement has important implications for the trainer and trainees and should be arranged in accordance with the objectives of a training program and the desired level of trainee involvement. Thus, the trainer needs to carefully choose a seating arrangement that is appropriate for a particular training program and the methods, activities, and exercises that will be used.

SCHEDULING THE TRAINING PROGRAM

As indicated in Table 9.2, the structured employment interview training program is scheduled as a one-day program. Scheduling a training program must take into consideration a number of factors. In effect, one has to arrange the training schedule to accommodate all of the participants.

For example, when is the best time for employees to attend a training program in terms of the day of the week, the time of day, and the time of year? When will the participants be available to attend training? This will probably depend on the organization and the nature of its business. Most businesses have periods or seasons when they are especially busy and scheduling a training program during these times is likely to result in some resistance and low attendance.

It is also important to be sensitive to the needs and desires of employees and their supervisors. Would it be preferable to hold the training during office hours or after hours, such as in the evenings or on the weekend? Employees and their supervisors should be consulted to determine the best time for them to attend a training program.[19] Recall that in response to management concerns about lost time, a training course at Sierra Systems was offered on Friday and Saturday rather than two days during the week.

Another factor to consider is the availability of the trainer. Whether the trainers are from the human resource department or elsewhere in the organization, they will likely have responsibilities that will restrict their availability. Trainers from within the organization will have to receive release time from their other duties to prepare and deliver the training program. If the trainers are from outside the organization, they will also have some restrictions regarding their availability and will have to be contracted for a particular date.

A third consideration in scheduling a training program is the availability of the training site, equipment, materials, and so on. If the training site and facilities are frequently used a training program will have to be scheduled well in advance. In addition, if materials need to be designed or purchased, they must be prepared and available in time for the training program.

Make the Connection

Finally, when scheduling a training program one must also consider whether it would be best to offer it all at one time, such as one day versus four two-hour sessions in the case of an eight-hour program, or all in one week versus one day each week for five weeks (or once a month for five months) in the case of a five-day program. Recall from Chapter 5 that this distinction refers to massed versus distributed practice. As indicated in Chapter 5, massed practice is practice with no rest periods, while distributed practice includes rest intervals. There are also issues of resources and logistics. Sometimes it is just not feasible to conduct a training program over a longer period of time. For example, a training program at Sierra Systems was broken up into one-hour lunch webinars. Kirkpatrick recommends that it is best to spread the training out as an ongoing program, such as a three-hour session once a month.[20]

TRAINING ADMINISTRATION

Once the lesson plan has been completed, a number of activities must be undertaken to manage and administer a training program. **Training administration** involves the coordination of all the people and materials involved in a training program. The maintenance of trainee records, training histories, customized learning opportunities, schedules, and course and material inventories is a routine, but necessary, activity. In addition to tracking registrations for programs, it is also useful to track individual career development and learning plans. Software is available that can do all these things.

Employees and their supervisors have to be informed of training programs with respect to the objectives and content as well as where and when the training will take place. In addition, employees who are required to attend a training program must be notified and enrolled in the program. Trainers must also be informed as they need to know how many trainees will be attending a training program.

If trainees are to receive training materials prior to a program, then arrangements have to be made for this. In addition, all of the materials and equipment must be ordered and prepared in time for the training program. The training site must be booked and equipment must be made available. In some cases, this might involve renting equipment. As well, supplies such as pens and paper must be ordered.

Finally, the training administrator has to prepare a budget that includes the costs of all of the expenses incurred in the design and delivery of a training program. The calculation of the costs and benefits of training programs is discussed in Chapter 12.

Training administration
The coordination of all the people and materials involved in the training program

IMPLEMENTING THE TRAINING PROGRAM

Once the lesson plan has been prepared and the administrative activities have been completed, the training program is ready to be implemented. For many trainers and especially novices, this is the most difficult part of the training process. There are, however, a number of important steps to follow when implementing a training program. In this section, we describe how to create a climate for learning and Gagné's nine events of instruction.

Learning Climate

When implementing a training program, the trainer has to ensure that the **learning climate** is conducive to learning. This means that trainees should feel relaxed, comfortable, and safe in the training environment. Creating a climate that is conducive to learning involves four elements: pre-arrival factors, greeting participants, the learning facility/environment, and the trainer's style and behaviour.[21]

Learning climate
A climate that is conducive to learning and consists of pre-arrival factors, greeting participants, the learning facility/environment, and the trainer's style and behaviour

Pre-Arrival Factors

Although trainees form perceptions of the learning climate during training, there are some things a trainer can do before their arrival to create a positive learning climate. For example, contacting trainees before the training begins can help set a positive tone. This might just be a welcome message that describes the program and its objectives. However, it can also include information about the location, when the program starts and ends, meals, clothes to wear, what to bring, and so on.

Pre-arrival activities might include pre-work readings or assignments, a pre-session get-together (to hand out materials or perhaps a cocktail party or dinner), or an attempt to find out about trainees' needs, ideas, and input for the program.

Greeting Participants

While the tone can be set before participants arrive, even more important are the perceptions trainees form once they arrive for training. Trainees might be anxious about the training and some will be skeptical about its value. Others will be upset that they are spending time away from work. Therefore, the trainer should meet and greet participants and make them feel welcome when they arrive for training. A nice touch is to have a welcome message posted on the board or a flipchart in the room. Some trainers like to have trainees write their name on a name card to get them doing something simple when they arrive rather than sitting alone and waiting for the program to start. An early-morning welcome session with coffee and refreshments can facilitate interactions among trainees and create a relaxed and comfortable atmosphere.

Learning Facility/Environment

A major factor in trainees' climate perceptions is the training site itself. In this regard, the trainer should ensure that the physical set-up of the training room is attractive, comfortable, bright, relaxing, and clean. Some of the things that the trainer needs to pay attention to include lighting, noise, space, and room temperature, as discussed earlier. Making sure that drinks, refreshments, and lunch arrive on time is also important for creating a positive training climate.

Trainer's Style and Behaviour

Trainees' perceptions of the learning climate will also be based on how the trainer interacts with trainees and conducts the training. If the trainees do not know the trainer, then one of the first things trainers should do is to provide a brief personal introduction about themselves and their involvement in the training program. The trainer should let trainees know how they can address him/her (e.g., first name is fine) and should address trainees by their first name. The trainer should circulate throughout the room during training and at times be seated rather than standing at the front of the room throughout the session. It is also a good idea to take advantage of opportunities to interact with trainees. This can be achieved by mingling with trainees during breaks and joining them at lunch and other meals.

Finally, key to creating a positive learning climate is the style of the trainer. A trainer can create a positive climate by listening with empathy, accepting different ideas, showing sensitivity to the communication process, supporting people who take risks, providing a fun-type atmosphere, stressing opportunities for discovery, making learning gradual, asking for feedback, and making him/herself accessible for questioning.[22]

In summary, creating a positive climate that is conducive to learning is a critical factor in the successful implementation of a training program. Also important is how the trainer actually delivers the training, our next topic.

Gagné's Nine Events of Instruction

Once a positive learning climate has been created, the trainer can deliver the training. According to Robert Gagné, a training program should have nine events of instruction. Following is a brief description of the nine events of instruction. You might notice that some of the design principles discussed in previous chapters are incorporated into them. Table 9.4 lists Gagné's nine events of instruction along with the relevant training design principles.[23]

TABLE 9.4

Gagné's Nine Events of Instruction and Training Design Principles

Gagné's nine events of instruction reflect important principles of training design discussed in previous chapters.

1. *Gain attention.* Reflects adult learners' need to know why they are learning something and their training motivation.

2. *Describe the objectives.* Reflects adult learners' need to know how the learning relates to their job and the importance of goals as indicated in goal-setting theory.

3. *Stimulate recall of prior knowledge.* Reflects adult learners' existing knowledge and experience and how that can be linked to the training material. Providing a framework for learning is similar to an advance organizer.

4. *Present the material to be learned.* Reflects task sequencing as well as incorporating adult learners' job-relevant experiences into the training content.

5. *Provide guidance for learning.* Reflects the use of metacognitive strategies, attentional advice, and advance organizers.

6. *Elicit performance practice.* Reflects the importance of active practice and experiential training methods (e.g., role plays, games, simulations).

7. *Provide informative feedback.* Reflects the importance of feedback and knowledge of results during training.

8. *Assess performance.* Reflects the importance of linking training objectives to trainee learning and ensuring that the objectives are being met as well as the stages of learning.

9. *Enhance retention and transfer.* Reflects generalization from conditioning theory and self-regulation and self-efficacy from social cognitive theory.

1. Gain Attention

The first thing a trainer needs to do is to draw trainees into the learning process. In other words, get the attention of trainees (recall the earlier discussion of trainee engagement). This can be achieved in a number of ways. For example, the trainer might present a thought-provoking problem. For the structured employment interview training program, the trainer might ask trainees, "What should we do to ensure that we hire great employees?" Other questions might focus trainees on the problem at hand and the need for training, such as, "How do you conduct a valid employment interview?" Or the trainer might point out that bad hiring is costing the organization thousands of dollars. Having the CEO make an impassioned plea on the importance of the training program can also get the attention of trainees.

Getting trainees interested and motivated is an important way to begin a training program. Trainees should know why the training program is important for them and the organization.

2. Describe the Objectives

Make the Connection

In Chapter 5, we discussed the purpose of training objectives for trainees, trainers, and managers (refer to Table 5.2). Thus, the trainer must communicate to trainees what they will learn in a training program, what to expect, and what they will be able to accomplish at the end of the program. Trainees should understand what they will learn and how they will be able to use it on the job. The trainer might even provide a demonstration of the desired performance to help trainees form a mental picture of the skill to be performed. This will help trainees begin to focus on what they will need to learn and do after training and think about goals for learning.

3. Stimulate Recall of Prior Knowledge

Make the Connection

It is important to show trainees that they know some things that are related to what they will learn in training. This enables trainees to think about what they know and can do that is related to what they will learn in the training program. You might recall from the discussion of andragogy and adult learning theory in Chapter 3 that adults have a great deal of knowledge and work-related experience that the trainer should ask about and incorporate into the training. One way to stimulate recall of prior knowledge is for the trainer to discuss what trainees already know that is relevant to the training material (facts, rules, procedures, or skills).

The trainer might also provide a framework to help trainees learn and retain the training material. By providing a solid grounding, trainees will feel more confident about their ability to learn. For example, trainees in the structured employment interview training program might begin to think about what they have already learned about hiring and interviewing and how they currently conduct employment interviews.

4. Present the Material to Be Learned

Make the Connection

The organization and presentation of the training material should be done in a logical and consistent manner. As discussed in Chapter 5, this involves teaching the material in a meaningful sequence or one sub-task at a time (i.e., task sequencing). The trainer can ensure learning and understanding by asking questions at various points or junctures during the training and by asking trainees to provide examples from their own work experience.

For the structured employment interview training, the trainer might present each of the seven key behaviours in a logical order and ask trainees how they perform the behaviours when conducting employment interviews (e.g., how have you decided what questions to ask job candidates?).

5. Provide Guidance for Learning

The trainer should provide trainees with guidance and direction on how best to learn the material. This can be done by providing trainees with relevant examples that demonstrate what they need to learn and asking questions to help them generate ideas and solutions. The combination of examples, questions, and discussion should help guide trainees toward the main learning points.

6. Elicit Performance Practice

Trainees should be given the opportunity to practise and apply the training material. You might recall from Chapter 5 that providing trainees with opportunities to practise performing a training task or using knowledge during training is called active practice. Trainers should provide sufficient time for trainees to do something with the information they have received during training.

Make the Connection

In a training program on the employment interview, trainees would have the opportunity to practise conducting an interview. If they have been taught seven key learning points, they would practise them in a mock interview during training.

7. Provide Informative Feedback

Trainees should receive feedback on their performance during training. Recall the discussion of feedback and knowledge of results in Chapter 5, where we described the importance of feedback as a condition of practice during training. It is essential that trainees know and understand what they did correctly, what they did wrong, and how to correct what they did wrong to improve their performance. Trainees should leave training with an understanding of what they can do well and what they need to improve.

Make the Connection

8. Assess Performance

It is important to test trainees on their learning during and after a training program. Ideally, learning should be assessed after each topic is completed. The assessment of learning can be either declarative (recall the discussion of learning outcomes and the stages of learning in Chapter 3), in which case trainees are simply asked to recall information, or it can involve knowledge compilation or procedural knowledge, in which case trainees have to explain how they would do something or to display the learned behaviour in a role play or behavioural demonstration. The assessment of performance can involve a formal test or it might simply involve an informal question-and-answer session. The main issue is to ensure that trainees have learned the material before moving on to new topics.

Make the Connection

9. Enhance Retention and Transfer

Trainees need to know how their learning can be used and applied on the job. Therefore, it is important that trainers discuss how the training material can be applied on the job and in actual work situations. The trainer might show trainees how the material they are learning applies to actual situations that they will encounter at work. Asking trainees to describe situations in which they will be able use the training content in their job can also enhance retention and transfer. More detail about transfer of training and what a trainer can do to facilitate it is described in Chapter 10.

Closing a Training Program

Once a training program has ended, the trainer must close the program. Like the rest of the program, the closing should be well planned and include a closing activity that signals the successful completion of the program. Some kind of event or form of recognition is common, such as a ceremony in which certificates are awarded to trainees who have completed the program. The lasting impression following the closing should be that the next step is a change in behaviour and performance.[24]

TRAINING DELIVERY PROBLEMS

Although Gagné's nine events of instruction might seem straightforward, there are many potential problems that trainers might experience during the delivery of a training program. One of the most common problems is an uncooperative and difficult trainee. While most trainees are cooperative, some can make it difficult for a trainer to deliver a training program by talking too much, putting others down, complaining, displaying negative or hostile behaviour, or just being plain irritating.

Table 9.5 lists different types of problem participants. Dealing with problem participants requires patience and avoiding arguments and put-downs. In most cases, it is best to deal with them in a polite fashion and, if possible, let the group decide how to manage them.[25]

To learn about the types of problems that a trainer might encounter, Richard Swanson and Sandra Falkman conducted a study in which they asked novice trainers about the problems they have had when delivering a training program. After analyzing the responses, the authors identified the following 12 common training delivery problems:[26]

1. *Fear.* Fear that is due to a lack of confidence and a feeling of anxiety while delivering the training program.
2. *Credibility.* The perception that they lack credibility in the eyes of the trainees as subject-matter experts.
3. *Personal experiences.* A lack of stories about personal experiences that can be used to relate to the training content.
4. *Difficult learners.* Don't know how to handle problem trainees who may be angry, passive, or dominating.
5. *Participation.* Difficulty getting trainees to participate.

TABLE 9.5

Types of Problem Participants

Some of the most common types of problem participants in training include the following:

1. *The hesitant one.* Shy, reluctant, and silent most of the time.
2. *The monopolizer.* The "big talker" who will use up all of the available air time if permitted.
3. *The voice of experience.* Has a strong need to be heard and to bring in incidents and anecdotes that are tedious and unnecessary.
4. *The arguer.* Constantly looks for opportunities to disagree, to show up the other participants and the trainer.
5. *The non-listener.* Tends to interrupt, cuts others off, leaps in before others have had their say, and does not listen to others.
6. *The idea zapper.* Puts down other participants' ideas and anything new or different.
7. *The complainer.* A problem magnifier who finds the world unfair and is a specialist in blaming and fault-finding.
8. *The rigid one.* Staunchly takes a position on an issue and will rarely, if at all, move from it.
9. *The hostile one.* Presents highly hostile questions that are designed to embarrass or inflame the trainer.
10. *The angry one.* Will find loopholes in your ideas and present impossible "what-if" scenarios.
11. *The negative one.* Finds the gloomy side of things and will dredge up gripes, past grievances, and cantankerous complaints.
12. *The clown.* Has an abundance of ill-fitting and sometimes irritating and annoying humour.
13. *The show-off.* Likes to parade his/her knowledge before everyone.
14. *The tangent-taker.* Has interesting inputs but they do not relate to the topic.

Source: J.E. Eitington, *The Winning Trainer: Winning Ways to Involve People in Learning*. Houston, TX: Gulf Publishing Company. 1989. Reprinted with permission from Elsevier.

6. *Timing.* Trouble with the timing and pacing of the training material and worries about having too much or too little material.
7. *Adjusting instruction.* Difficulty adjusting the training material to the needs of trainees or being able to redesign the presentation of material during delivery.
8. *Questions.* Difficulty using questions effectively and responding to difficult questions.
9. *Feedback.* Unable to read trainees and to use feedback and evaluations effectively.
10. *Media, materials, facilities.* Concerns about how to use media and training materials.
11. *Opening, closing techniques.* The need for techniques to use as ice-breakers, introductions, and effective summaries and closings.
12. *Dependence on notes.* Feeling too dependent on notes and having trouble presenting the material without them.

The Trainer's Notebook 9.3

SOLUTIONS TO TRAINING DELIVERY PROBLEMS

1. Fear.

A. Be well prepared and have a detailed lesson plan.

B. Use ice-breakers and begin with an activity that relaxes trainees.

C. Acknowledge the fear and use self-talk and relaxation exercises prior to the training.

2. Credibility.

A. Don't apologize. Be honest about your knowledge of the subject.

B. Have the attitude of an expert and be well prepared and organized.

C. Share personal background and talk about your area of expertise and experiences.

3. Personal experiences.

A. Relate personal experiences.

B. Report experiences of others and have trainees share their experiences.

C. Use analogies, refer to movies or famous people who relate to the subject.

4. Difficult learners.

A. Confront the problem learner and talk to them to determine the problem.

B. Circumvent dominating behaviour by using nonverbal behaviour such as breaking eye contact or standing with your back to the person.

C. Use small groups to overcome timid behaviour and structure exercises where a wide range of participation is encouraged.

5. Participation.

A. Ask open-ended questions and provide positive feedback when trainees participate.

B. Plan small-group activities such as dyads, case studies, and role plays to increase participation.

C. Invite participation by structuring activities to allow trainees to share early in the program.

6. Timing.

A. Plan for too much material and prioritize activities so that some can be omitted if necessary.

B. Practise presenting the material many times so that you know where you should be at 15-minute intervals.

7. Adjusting instruction.

A. Determine the needs of the group early in the training and structure activities based on them.

B. Request feedback by asking trainees how they feel about the training during breaks or periodically during the training.

C. Redesign the program during breaks and have a contingency plan in place.

8. Questions.

Answering questions

A. Anticipate questions by writing out key questions that trainees might have.

B. Paraphrase and repeat a question so everyone hears the question and understands it.

These 12 common delivery problems of novice trainers have three basic themes:

1. Problems pertaining to the trainer,
2. Problems pertaining to how the trainer relates to the trainees, and
3. Problems pertaining to presentation techniques.

C. Redirect questions you can't answer back to the trainees and try to find answers during tho break.

Asking questions

A. Ask concise and simple questions and provide enough time for trainees to answer.

9. **Feedback.**

A. Solicit informal feedback during training or breaks on whether the training is meeting their needs and expectations and watch for nonverbal cues.

B. Do summative evaluations at the conclusion of the training to determine if the objectives and needs of trainees have been met.

10. **Media, materials, facilities.**

Media

A. Know how to operate every piece of equipment you will use.

B. Have back-ups such as extra bulbs, extension cords, markers, tape, and so on, as well as bringing the material in another medium in case one has problems.

C. Enlist assistance from trainees if you have a problem and need help.

Materials

A. Be prepared and have all the material placed at trainees' workplace or ready for distribution.

Facilities

A. Visit facility beforehand to see the layout of the room and where things are located and how to set up.

B. Arrive at least one hour early to set up and handle any problems.

11. **Opening, closing techniques.**

Openings

A. Develop a file of ideas based on experimentation and observation.

B. Develop and memorize a great opening.

C. Relax trainees by greeting them when they enter, taking time for introductions, and creating a relaxed atmosphere.

Closings

A. Provide a simple and concise summary of the course contents using objectives or the initial model.

B. Thank participants for their time and contribution to the course.

12. **Dependence on notes.**

A. Notes are necessary.

B. Use cards with an outline or key words as prompts.

C. Use visuals such as notes on the frames of transparencies or your copy of the handouts.

D. Practise and learn the script so you can deliver it from the key words on your note cards.

Source: R.A. Swanson & S.K. Falkman, "Training delivery problems and solutions: Identification of novice trainer problems and expert trainer solutions," *Human Resource Development Quarterly*, Vol. 8, P. 305. © 1997 by Jossey-Bass Inc. Reprinted with permission of John Wiley & Sons, Inc.

The authors also asked expert trainers for strategies and solutions for dealing with the 12 delivery problems. For example, to deal with the problem of fear, a trainer should be well prepared, use ice-breakers, begin with an activity that relaxes the trainees and gets them talking and involved, and acknowledge his/her own fear, understanding that it is normal.[27] See The Trainer's Notebook 9.3, "Solutions to Training Delivery Problems," for solutions to all 12 delivery problems.

SUMMARY

This chapter described the steps involved in training delivery. We began the chapter with a discussion of the lesson plan, which should describe how a training program will proceed and how it will be implemented. This was followed by a description of the characteristics of effective trainers and how to determine who should attend a training program. We also described the training materials and equipment, the training site and seating arrangement, scheduling a program, and training administration. We then described how to create a positive climate for learning and Gagné's nine events of instruction. The chapter concluded with a discussion of common training delivery problems and solutions.

Key Terms

learning climate p. 271
lesson p. 259
lesson plan p. 259
seductive details p. 264
subject-matter expert (SME) p. 263
train-the-trainer p. 264

trainability test p. 267
trainer expressiveness p.263
training administration p. 271
training materials p. 267
training plan p. 267
training site p. 268

Make the Connection

p. 263: subject-matter experts (SME) are discussed in Chapter 5 on page 144

p. 270: massed versus distributed practice is discussed in Chapter 5 on page 150

p. 274: training objectives are discussed in Chapter 5 on page 137

p. 274: andragogy and adult learning theory are discussed in Chapter 3 on pages 77 and 78

p. 274: task sequencing is discussed in Chapter 5 on page 151

p. 275: active practice is discussed in Chapter 5 on page 145

p. 275: feedback and knowledge of results is discussed in Chapter 5 on page 151

p. 275: the stages of learning and learning outcomes are discussed in Chapter 3 on pages 65–69

Web Links

Bank of Montreal: **www4.bmo.com**

Export Development Canada (EDC): **www.edc.ca**

Sierra Systems: **www.sierrasys.com**

Required Professional Capabilities (RPCs)

The following RPCs are relevant to material covered in this chapter. The RPC number represents the CCHRA number assigned to the RPC as presented on the CCHRA website. All of the RPCs can be found in the Body of Knowledge at **http://www.chrp.ca/rpc/body-of-knowledge/**.

RPC 168: Participates in course design and selection and delivery of learning materials.

168.03: Facilitation techniques

168.04: Training and development program design and administration

168.09: Training delivery techniques

RPC 169: Ensures arrangements are made for training schedules, facilities, trainers, participants, and equipment and course materials.

169.02: Instructional design & delivery

169.05: Conditions for successful learning

Discussion Questions

1. Discuss Gagné's nine events of instruction and how they relate to training design principles and adult learning theory.
2. What are some of the common problems and solutions encountered in training delivery?
3. What are the characteristics of a good trainer and what effect do these characteristics have on learning? Do you think that you can learn to be a good trainer, or is it something you are born with?
4. How can you decide whether an employee should attend a training program?
5. Describe the different types of problem trainees and how a trainer might manage them during training.
6. What factors need to be considered when deciding on a training site?
7. Why is it important for subject-matter experts to design and/or deliver training programs? What can organizations do to find and encourage SMEs to get involved in training?
8. What is a train-the-trainer program and how would you proceed if you had to develop and deliver one?
9. What are seductive details and how and why should they be included in the delivery of a training program?

The Great Training Debate

1. Debate the following: Great trainers are born, not made.
2. Debate the following: All training programs should be compulsory.

Exercises

In-Class

1. Think about the last time you attended a course or training program. How effective was the instructor/trainer and what effect did it have on your training motivation and learning? What was it about the instructor/trainer that had a positive or negative effect on your motivation and learning? What could the instructor/trainer have done differently to improve your motivation and learning?

2. How expressive are you as a trainer? To find out and improve your expressiveness, prepare a short lecture (5–10 minutes) on a topic of interest to you or perhaps something on training from the text. Then give your lecture to the class. The class can then evaluate your verbal and nonverbal expressiveness. Make a list of the things you can do to improve your expressiveness. Be sure to refer to your verbal and nonverbal behaviour.

3. Choose a class you are taking and evaluate your instructor's use of Gagné's nine events of instruction. Evaluate the instructor on each of the following events of instruction:

- Gain attention
- Describe the objectives
- Stimulate recall of prior knowledge
- Present the material to be learned
- Provide guidance for learning
- Elicit performance practice
- Provide informative feedback
- Assess performance
- Enhance retention and transfer

Based on our evaluation, how effective was your instructor? How can he/she improve?

4. Recall a training program that you attended in a previous or current job. Describe the extent to which the trainer used Gagné's nine events of instruction. Provide specific examples of how each of the events was applied. How effective was the training program and what might the trainer have done differently to make it more effective?

5. Consider some of the factors that make a training site conducive to learning. Now consider the room of one of your courses. Is the room adequate for learning? What factors, if any, are affecting your ability to learn and what needs to be improved?

6. Think about the last time you attended a training program, or one of the courses you are currently taking. Describe the climate for learning and its effect on your motivation, learning, and satisfaction with the program or course. What can the trainer or instructor do to improve the climate?

7. Think about the last time you attended a training program, or one of the courses you are currently taking. Describe the seating arrangement and its effect on your motivation, learning, and satisfaction with the program or course. Do you think the seating arrangement was/is appropriate? If you could change the seating arrangement, how would you change it and why?

In-the-Field

1. Contact the human resources department of an organization and request a meeting with somebody in the department whom you can interview about the organization's training programs. Develop some questions to learn

about each of the following issues in terms of a particular training program that the organization has implemented:

- Was a detailed lesson plan prepared for the program? If not, why? If so, what things were included in it?
- Who is the trainer of the program and how was he or she chosen?
- Who were the trainees and how and why were they chosen to attend the program?
- What training materials and equipment were used?
- Describe the training site and why it was chosen.
- Describe the seating arrangement and why it was chosen.
- Describe the scheduling of the training program and how it was determined.
- Who administered and coordinated the training program and what did this involve?
- How was the training program implemented (refer to Gagné's nine events of instruction)?
- What are some problems that have occurred in the delivery of the training program and what strategies are used to deal with them?

Based on the information you have acquired, how effectively do you think each of the training delivery activities was performed? List some recommendations for improvement.

2. To find out what it means to be a Certified Training Practitioner (CTP) and a Certified Training and Development Professional (CTDP) in Canada, visit the Canadian Society of Training and Development (CSTD) at **http://www.cstd.ca/?page=Certification.**

Answer the following questions:
a. What does it mean to be a CTP and a CTDP?
b. What are the objectives and requirements of a CTP and CTDP?
c. Describe the CTP and CTDP process.

Case Incident

Training the Trainer at the Running Room

The Running Room is North America's largest specialty retailer of sporting goods, apparel and footwear for runners and walkers. The company operates 111 corporately owned stores in Canada and the United States and has plans for expansion. The Running Room does not have an HR department and relies heavily on a train-the-trainer approach to training. The store managers are in effect the human resource managers and training takes place at the store level.

Each year, all store managers are brought together to talk about training issues, initiatives, and challenges. The focus is usually floor sales training because customer service on the floor is the essence of the business. Training is dynamic and interactive and does not rely on lectures. Role playing is used to teach such things as how to greet customers, how to do merchandising, how to handle security, and how to sell. The goal is to make it fun and enjoyable.

Questions

1. What do you think about the train-the-trainer approach to training used at the Running Room? What are the advantages and disadvantages?
2. As the company grows and expands, do you think it will have to change its approach to training and development? If so, how should it change and why?

Source: R. Rabinovitch, "CloseUp: Training and development," *Canadian HR Reporter,* May 17, 2004, P. 7. Reprinted by permission of Canadian HR Reporter; www.runningroom.com.

Case Study: THE HOUGHTON REFRIGERATION COMPANY

Houghton Refrigeration Company builds refrigerators for large appliance companies. It employs about 300 people, mostly assembly line workers, and is located in a small town in Ohio. The company typically builds, on a contract basis, chest-type freezers and small bar-type refrigerators. On occasion, however, it also builds standard-size refrigerators. The president of the company is a former engineer, as are most of the other executives. These individuals are very knowledgeable about engineering, but have received little training in the basic principles of management.

During the summer months, volume at the factory increases significantly, and the company needs to hire about 40 new employees to handle the heavy workload. Most of these new employees are college students who attend a small private college located about 15 minutes from the plant. Some high school students are hired as well.

When a new employee is hired, the company asks him or her to complete an application blank and then to show up at the plant gate ready for work. Employees receive no orientation. The worker is shown to a work station and, after a minimum amount of on-the-job training, the new employee is expected to start performing a job. Most of the jobs are quite simple and the training is typically completed within 10 minutes. The first-line supervisor usually shows the employee how to do a job once, then watches while the employee does the job once, leaves, and comes back about 20 minutes later to see how the employee is progressing. Typical jobs at the plant include screwing 14 screws into the sides of a freezer, placing a piece of insulation into the freezer lid, and handing out supplies from the tool room.

The company has had excellent experience with college students over the years. Much of the success can be attributed to the older workers coming to the aid of the new employees when difficulties arise. Most new employees are able to perform their jobs reasonably well after their on-the-job training is completed. However, when unexpected difficulties arise, they are usually not prepared for them and therefore need assistance from others.

The older workers have been especially helpful to students working in the "press room." However, Joe Gleason, the first-line supervisor there, finds it amusing to belittle the college students whenever they make any mistakes. He relishes showing a student once how to use a press to bend a small piece of metal, then exclaims, "You're a hot-shot college student; now let's see you do it." He then watches impatiently while the student invariably makes a mistake and then jokingly announces for all to hear, "That's wrong! How did you ever get into college anyway? Try it again, dummy."

One summer, the company experienced a rash of injuries to its employees. Although most of the injuries were minor, the company felt it imperative to conduct a series of short training programs on safe material-handling techniques. The company president was at a loss as to who should conduct the training. The Human Resource Director was a 64-year-old former engineer who was about to retire and was a poor speaker. The only other employee in the Human Resource Department was a new 19-year-old secretary who knew nothing about proper handling techniques. Out of desperation, the president finally decided to ask Bill Young, the first-line supervisor of the "lid-line," to conduct the training.

Bill had recently attended a training program himself on safety and was active in the Red Cross. Bill reluctantly agreed to conduct the training. It was to be done on a departmental basis with small groups of 10 to 15 employees attending each session.

At the first of these training sessions Bill Young nervously stood up in front of 14 employees, many of whom were college students, and read his presentation in a monotone voice. His entire speech lasted about one minute and consisted of the following text:

Statistics show that an average of 30 persons injure their backs on the job each day in this state. None of us wants to become a "statistic."

The first thing that should be done before lifting an object is to look it over and decide whether you can handle it alone or if help is needed. Get help if there's any doubt as to whether the load is safely within your capacity.

Next, look over the area where you're going to be carrying the object. Make sure it's clear of obstacles. You may have to do a little housekeeping before moving your load. After you have checked out the load and route you're going to travel, the following steps should be taken for your safety in lifting:

1.   Get a good footing close to the load.
2.   Place your feet 8 to 12 inches apart.
3.   Bend your knees to grasp the load.
4.   Bend your knees outward, straddling the load.
5.   Get a firm grip.
6.   Keep the load close to your body.
7.   Lift gradually.

Once you've lifted the load, you'll eventually have to set it down. So bend your legs again and follow the lifting procedures in reverse. Make sure that your fingers clear the pinch points. And, finally, it's a good idea to set one corner down first.

After Bill's speech ended, the employees immediately returned to work. By the end of the day, however, everyone in the plant had heard about the training fiasco and all except the president were laughing about it.

Source: From NKOMO/FOTTLER/MCAFEE, *Applications in Human Resource Management, 5E.* © 2005 Cengage Learning.

Questions

1. Comment on the president's choice to have Bill Young conduct the training. Was it a good idea for Bill Young to be the trainer? How else might the president have chosen a trainer?
2. How effective was Bill Young as a trainer? What characteristics of an effective trainer does he display and which ones were lacking? What could have been done to make the training more effective?
3. Discuss how the company determined who should attend the training program. How else might they have decided who should attend the training program?
4. Describe the climate for learning. How positive was the climate? What might Bill Young have done to create a more positive learning climate?
5. Evaluate Bill Young's delivery of the training program in terms of Gagné's nine events of instruction. What events did he use and which ones were absent? Describe what he might have done differently if he had followed Gagné's nine events of instruction.
6. What are the most serious problems in Bill's delivery of the training program and how could they have been avoided?

Flashback Questions

1. Comment on the on-job-training that new employees receive. What is the approach used (see Table 7.2 in Chapter 7), and is it effective?
2. To what extent is the on-the-job training consistent with job instruction training? What changes are necessary to better reflect the steps of job instruction training?
3. Comment on Joe Gleason's approach to on-the-job training. What effect might his approach have on the student workers? If you were the company president, what would you say to him?
4. Comment on Bill Young's training method. What training method is he using (refer to Table 6.1 in Chapter 6), and how effective is it?
5. What other training methods might have made Bill Young's training program more effective? Refer to Table 6.1 in Chapter 6.
6. If you were to design the training program that was delivered by Bill Young, what changes would you make? Refer to the training design activities in Table 5.1 in Chapter 5 to answer this question.

REFERENCES

1. Based on Harder, D. (2009, February 9). Sierra Systems earns top marks for training. *Canadian HR Reporter, 22(3)*, 19; www.sierrasys.com (News & Events, Sierra Systems Wins Alberta Chamber of Commerce University of Alberta–TELUS Partners in Workplace Learning Award of Distinction, February 19, 2004; Online Corporate University Strengthens Sierra Systems' Client Services, July 10, 2000; Sierra Systems Awarded Top 100 Employer For 5th Straight Year, October 6, 2004), retrieved November 10, 2011.
2. Carnevale, A. P., Gainer, L. J., & Meltzer, A. S. (1990). *Workplace basics training manual.* San Francisco, CA: Jossey-Bass Publishers.
3. Carnevale, A. P., Gainer, L. J., & Meltzer, A. S. (1990).
4. Nadler, L. (1982). *Designing training programs: The critical events model.* Reading, MA: Addison-Wesley.
5. Donaldson, L., & Scannell, E. E. (1986). *Human resource development: The new trainer's guide* (2nd ed.). Reading, MA: Addison-Wesley.
6. Nadler, L. (1982).
7. Nadler, L. (1982).
8. Towler, A. J., & Dipboye, R. L. (2001). Effects of trainer expressiveness, organization, and trainee goal orientation on training outcomes. *Journal of Applied Psychology, 86,* 664–673.
9. Towler, A. (2009). Effects of trainer expressiveness, seductive details, and trainee goal orientation on training outcomes. *Human Resource Development Quarterly, 20,* 65–84.
10. Towler, A. J., & Dipboye, R. L. (2001).
11. Kirkpatrick, D. L. (1994). *Evaluating training programs: The four levels.* San Francisco, CA: Berrett-Koehler Publishers.
12. Kirkpatrick, D. L. (1994).
13. Tannenbaum, S. I., & Yukl, G. (1992). Training and development in work organizations. *Annual Review of Psychology, 43,* 399–441.
14. Goldstein, I. L., & Ford, J. K. (2002). *Training in organizations.* Belmont, CA: Wadsworth.
15. Ford, J. K., Major, D. A., Seaton, F. W., & Felber, H. K. (1993). Effects of organizational, training system, and individual characteristics on training director scanning practices. *Human Resource Development Quarterly, 4,* 333–351.
16. Nadler, L., & Nadler, Z. (1994). *Designing training programs.* Houston, TX: Gulf Publishing Company.
17. Eitington, J. E. (1989). *The winning trainer.* Houston, TX: Gulf Publishing Company.
18. Eitington, J. E. (1989).
19. Kirkpatrick, D. L. (1994).
20. Kirkpatrick, D. L. (1994).
21. Eitington, J. E. (1989).
22. Eitington, J. E. (1989).
23. Zemke, R. (1999). Toward a science of training. *Training, 36(7),* 32–36.
24. Nadler, L., & Nadler, Z. (1994).
25. Eitington, J. E. (1989).
26. Swanson, R. A., & Falkman, S. K. (1997). Training delivery problems and solutions: Identification of novice trainer problems and expert trainer solutions. *Human Resource Development Quarterly, 8,* 305–314.
27. Swanson, R. A., & Falkman, S. K. (1997).

Transfer of Training

CHAPTER LEARNING OUTCOMES

After reading this chapter, you should be able to:

- define transfer of training and positive, negative, zero, far, near, horizontal, and vertical transfer
- describe the major barriers to transfer of training
- describe Baldwin and Ford's model of the transfer of training process
- describe the strategies that managers, trainers, and trainees can use before, during, and after training to improve the transfer of training
- define identical elements, general principles, and stimulus variability and explain how they can improve the transfer of training
- explain what a transfer of training intervention is and describe relapse prevention, self-management, and goal-setting interventions
- explain what a post-training supplement is and describe booster sessions, self-coaching, and upward feedback interventions
- define transfer system and describe the transfer system factors

ONTARIO LOTTERY AND GAMING CORPORATION (OLG)

Ontario Lottery and Gaming Corporation (OLG) is the largest gaming organization in Canada and one of the largest in the world. OLG generates more than $6 billion in revenue annually and provides close to $2 billion in profit to the Province of Ontario to support hospitals, education, amateur sport, culture, and charities.

In order to address key leadership competencies demanded by the corporation's strategy, OLG's Corporate Learning Development Department created a Leadership Excellence Model (LEM). LEM is a four-pronged approach to develop the corporation's managers through a combination of an orientation program, a core leadership development program called Launch Pad to Success, follow-up Booster Modules, and In Flight sessions consisting of ongoing application workshops.

OLG partnered with the Rotman School of Management at the University of Toronto to design the Launch Pad to Success program, which includes customized content to support the key competencies and values that OLG leaders are expected to demonstrate. Key content areas include team building, change management, coaching, communications, conflict management, and decision making.

From December 2005 to March 2007, OLG offered 20 Launch Pad sessions for managers and other leaders. A total of 1,896 participants completed the three-day program, which consists of interactive training sessions as well as simulations, self-study, case studies, and team learning activities.

In order to encourage the application of new leadership skills and knowledge provided by the Launch Pad program, several strategies were used. For example, senior leaders demonstrated their support for the program by attending all of the sessions. At the conclusion of each session, participants were asked to write down the key things they learned and one or two skills that they will apply on the job. During the final session of the program, participants prepared action plans for how they will apply three key learning objectives that they will focus on after completing the program to discuss with their manager. Participants were also provided with a Launch Pad follow-up binder that consisted of job aids and behaviour checklists with a suggested uses list. A binder that included posters of the key learning points was also provided so that participants could refresh their knowledge during supervisory team meetings.

Five Booster Modules that cover advanced coaching, problem solving, managing paradoxes, strategic thinking, and negotiation reinforced key learning objectives. In addition, a number of follow-up activities such as pre- and post-tests of learning, individual goal setting, action planning, and a buddy system of coaching, as well as follow-up coaching were provided to support participants' on-the-job application of what they learned in the program. In Flight sessions were also designed to help managers and supervisors in their ongoing application of skills learned through the Launch Pad to Success Program and the Booster Modules.

Surveys completed by participants after attending the Launch Pad to Success program indicated that 95 percent believed their knowledge and skill had increased and 89 percent indicated that they are applying some learning on the job. Many of the comments provided by participants indicated that Launch Pad helped them change their on-the-job behaviour. Furthermore, 80.7 percent of managers observed employees who attended the program applying the knowledge and skills they learned from Launch Pad on the job.[1]

Source: E. Jones & H. Arnold, "Hitting the jackpot in leadership development: A case study," *The Canadian Learning Journal*, 2006, Vol. 10 (1), P. 9.

Transfer of training

The generalization of knowledge and skills learned in training on the job and the maintenance of acquired knowledge and skills over time

Trainees do not always apply what they learn in training on the job. As a result, organizations like the OLG design training programs with strategies to facilitate trainees' application of training on the job. This is known as the transfer of training and it is the focus of this chapter.

WHAT IS TRANSFER OF TRAINING?

Organizations are increasingly concerned about the value-added of human resource programs. When it comes to training, they are concerned about the transfer of training. **Transfer of training** refers to the application of the knowledge and skills acquired in a training program on the job and the maintenance of acquired knowledge and skills over time.[2]

There are two conditions of transfer of training. **Generalization** refers to the use or application of learned material to the job. **Maintenance** refers to the use or application of learned material on the job over a period of time. Transfer of training occurs when learned material is generalized to the job context and maintained over a period of time on the job.

The extent to which a training program transfers to the job can be described as positive, zero, or negative transfer. When transfer is **positive**, trainees effectively apply new knowledge, skills, and attitudes acquired in training on the job. If transfer is **zero**, trainees are not using new knowledge and skills on the job. When transfer is **negative**, training has had a negative effect and trainees are performing worse as a result of a training program. The purpose of this chapter is to find out why transfer is sometimes zero or negative and what can be done to make it positive.

Transfer of training can also be considered in terms of the type of situations in which trainees can apply what was learned in training on the job. For example, **near transfer** refers to the extent to which trainees can apply what was learned in training to situations that are very similar to those in which they were trained. On the other hand, **far transfer** refers to the extent to which trainees can apply what was learned in training to novel or different situations from those in which they were trained.[3]

A final distinction is horizontal and vertical transfer. **Horizontal transfer** involves the transfer of knowledge and skills across different settings or contexts at the same level. This is in fact the focus of this chapter and is consistent with how we have defined transfer of training. That is, we are concerned about the extent to which trainees transfer what they learn in training from the training setting to the job setting.

Vertical transfer refers to transfer from the individual or trainee level upward to the organizational level. In other words, it is concerned with the extent to which changes in trainee behaviour and performance transfer to organizational-level outcomes. For example, will a change in trainees' customer service behaviour and performance result in an improvement in the organization's service and customer satisfaction? Vertical transfer represents the link between employee behaviour and organizational effectiveness.

This is an important distinction because transfer to the job (i.e., horizontal transfer) might not lead to changes in organizational outcomes (i.e., vertical transfer). Furthermore, there are differences in terms of how to improve each type of transfer. The focus of this chapter is on horizontal transfer, which is a necessary condition for vertical transfer.[4]

TRANSFER OF TRAINING PROBLEM

For decades, it has been reported that there exists a transfer of training problem in organizations. Although the estimates of transfer have varied over the years, they have for the most part been quite low, with studies reporting that between 60 and 90 percent of what is learned in training is not applied on the job.[5]

Generalization
The use or application of learned material to the job

Maintenance
The use or application of learned material on the job over a period of time

Positive transfer
Trainees effectively apply new knowledge, skills, and attitudes acquired in training on the job

Zero transfer
Trainees are not using new knowledge, skills, and attitudes acquired in training on the job

Negative transfer
Training has had a negative effect and trainees are performing worse as a result of a training program

Near transfer
The extent to which trainees can apply what was learned in training to situations that are very similar to those in which they were trained

Far transfer
The extent to which trainees can apply what was learned in training to novel or different situations from those in which they were trained

Horizontal transfer
The transfer of knowledge and skills across different settings or contexts at the same level

Vertical transfer
Transfer from the individual or trainee level to the organizational level or the extent to which changes in trainee behaviour or performance transfer to organizational level outcomes

TABLE 10.1

Transfer of Training in Canadian Organizations

Source: C. Lavis, *Learning & development outlook 2011: Are organizations ready for learning 2.0?* Ottawa: The Conference Board of Canada, 2011. P. 37.

According to a recent study by the Conference Board of Canada, only 54 percent of organizations indicated that employees apply learning immediately after a training program to a large extent or completely. This number drops to 15 percent six months after training, and to 11 percent one year after training (see Table 10.1).[6]

Why do you think that training does not always transfer? Table 10.2 provides a list of some of the major barriers to the transfer of training. One of the things you will notice is that many of the barriers have to do with factors in the

TABLE 10.2

Barriers to the Transfer of Training

- Immediate manager does not support the training.
- The culture in the work group does not support the training.
- No opportunity exists to use the skills.
- No time is provided to use the skills.
- Skills could not be applied to the job.
- The systems and processes did not support the skills.
- The resources are not available to use the skills.
- Skills no longer apply because of changed job responsibilities.
- Skills are not appropriate in our work unit.
- Did not see a need to apply what was learned.
- Old habits could not be changed.
- Reward systems don't support new skills.

Source: J.J. Phillips & P.P. Phillips, "11 reasons why training and development fail . . . and what you can do about it," *Training*, 2002, Vol. 39 (9), P. 78.

work environment and can be traced to trainees, managers, and the organization. Furthermore, many of the barriers have to do with a lack of support from supervisors and the organization.

As you can see in Table 10.2, the number one barrier to transfer of training is the immediate manager's lack of support for training. Supervisor support has to do with the extent to which supervisors reinforce and encourage the use of learning on the job.[7] Supervisor support has been found to be one of the most important factors for transfer along with the social support system in an organization.[8]

In the next section we describe the transfer of training process, which sets the stage for understanding how to remove transfer barriers and facilitate the transfer of training.

TRANSFER OF TRAINING PROCESS

One way to understand the transfer of training is to identify the factors that contribute to positive transfer of training. A good place to start is Baldwin and Ford's model of the transfer of training process.[9]

As shown in Figure 10.1, Baldwin and Ford's model of the transfer of training process consists of three main factors: training inputs, training outputs, and the conditions of transfer. The training inputs include trainee characteristics, training design, and the work environment. The training outputs include learning and retention. The conditions of transfer are transfer generalization and maintenance.

According to the model, trainee characteristics, training design, and the work environment have a direct effect on learning and retention. Trainee characteristics, the work environment, and learning and retention have a direct effect on transfer generalization and maintenance.

FIGURE 10.1

Baldwin and Ford's Model of the Transfer of Training Process

Source: T.T. Baldwin & J.K. Ford, "Transfer of Training: A Review and Directions for Future Research," *Personnel Psychology*, Vol. 41, Issue 1, Pp. 63–105, Blackwell Publishing, 1988.

An important implication of the model is that learning and retention are a necessary but not sufficient condition for transfer. This is because trainee characteristics and the work environment also play a critical role in whether or not trainees apply what they learn in training on the job. To better understand the role of training inputs, let's take a closer look at each of them.

Trainee Characteristics

Make the Connection

In Chapter 3, you learned that trainee characteristics are important predictors of trainee learning and retention. Thus, it should not surprise you that trainee characteristics are also important for the transfer of training. In fact, the same trainee characteristics that influence learning and retention are also important for transfer. Trainee differences in these characteristics can help us understand why some trainees are more likely to transfer than others.

In Chapter 3, cognitive ability, training motivation, self-efficacy, job attitudes, and personality traits were discussed in relation to learning and retention. Recall that these factors were included in the training effectiveness model and they have a direct effect on learning and retention. They also have a direct effect on the conditions of transfer. In other words, trainees with higher cognitive ability, training motivation, and self-efficacy are more likely to transfer. In addition, trainees with an internal locus of control and a high need for achievement are more likely to apply what they learn in training on the job, and employees with higher job involvement, job satisfaction, and organizational commitment are more likely to learn and transfer. Among the trainee characteristics, cognitive ability has been found to be the most strongly related to transfer.[10]

Make the Connection

Motivation to transfer
A trainee's intended effort to utilize skills and knowledge learned in training on the job

Another trainee characteristic that is particularly relevant to transfer is motivation to transfer. Recall from Chapter 3 that training motivation refers to the direction, intensity, and persistence of learning-directed behaviour in training contexts. **Motivation to transfer** is a trainee's intended efforts to utilize skills and knowledge learned in training on the job. Motivation to transfer has been found to be a significant predictor of positive transfer.[11]

Training Design

A number of design elements that are known as learning principles can be incorporated into a training program to improve the transfer of training. These learning principles include identical elements, general principles, and stimulus variability.

Identical Elements

Identical elements
Providing trainees with training experiences and conditions that closely resemble those in the actual work environment

Identical elements involve providing trainees with training experiences and conditions that closely resemble those in the actual work environment. Identical elements theory states that transfer will occur only if identical elements are present in both the old (training course) and new situations.[12] Identical elements are especially important for near transfer and have been shown to increase trainees' retention of motor and verbal behaviours.[13]

Make the Connection

But what exactly is identical? In Chapter 6 it was noted that to be most effective, simulations should have physical and psychological fidelity. Physical fidelity involves making the conditions of a training program such as the surroundings, tasks, and equipment similar to the work environment. Psychological fidelity has to do with the extent that trainees attach similar meanings to the training experience and the job context.

General Principles

General principles involve teaching trainees the general rules and theoretical principles that underlie the use and application of trained knowledge and skills. In other words, the training program provides trainees with an explanation of the theory and principles behind a skill or task that they are learning to perform. On-the-job application is more likely when trainees are taught the general rules and theoretical principles that underlie training content.[14]

General principles
Teaching trainees the general rules and theoretical principles that underlie the use and application of particular skills

Stimulus Variability

Stimulus variability involves providing trainees with a variety of training stimuli and experiences such as multiple examples of a concept or practice experience in a variety of situations. The idea is that trainees' understanding of training material can be strengthened by providing numerous examples of a concept because they will see how the concept can be applied in a variety of situations. This will enable greater generalization of the new skills and prevents the potential problem that learning will be limited to a narrow range of situations.[15]

Stimulus variability
Providing trainees with a variety of training stimuli and experiences, such as multiple examples of a concept, or practice experiences in a variety of situations

Stimulus variability can be incorporated into a training program by using different models that vary in terms of their characteristics (e.g., gender or age), by modelling different situations (e.g., different types of negotiation scenarios for a training program on negotiation skills), and by using models with different levels of competence in performing the training task (successful and unsuccessful). Trainers can also increase stimulus variability by describing a variety of examples and experiences related to the training content, and by asking trainees to discuss their own work experiences in relation to the training material. Using several examples has been found to be more effective than simply repeating the same example.[16]

Work Environment

Characteristics of the work environment before training (the pre-training environment) as well as after training (the post-training environment) also influence transfer.

Pre-training Environment

Management actions prior to a training program send signals and messages to employees about the importance of training and the extent to which the organization supports training. These messages can influence employees' training motivation. For example, if management actions convey messages that training is not important, employees will not be motivated to attend training and less likely to learn. In addition, if employees face constraints in their job such as a lack of time, equipment, and/or resources, they will not be highly motivated to learn given that the work environment would prevent them from using new skills.[17]

Post-training Environment

Events that occur after a training program in the post-training environment can also influence transfer of training. Factors in the post-training environment can encourage, discourage, or prevent employees from applying new knowledge and skills on the job. As indicated earlier, one of the most important characteristics of the post-training environment is the amount of support provided by trainees' supervisors. In fact, both supervisor support and peer support have been found to be strong predictors of transfer. Trainees who have supervisors and colleagues who are more supportive of training are more likely to be motivated to attend training, to learn and retain training content, and to transfer what they learn in training on the job.[18]

Training Transfer Climate

Make the Connection

Training transfer climate
Characteristics in the work environment that can either facilitate or inhibit the application of training on the job

In Chapter 4 we described the importance of the organizational context as part of an organizational analysis. At that time, two important aspects of the work environment were described: the training transfer climate and a continuous learning culture. As described in Chapter 4, a **training transfer climate** refers to characteristics in the work environment that can either facilitate or inhibit the application of training on the job. A positive transfer climate is one in which there exist cues that remind employees to apply training material on the job, positive consequences such as feedback and rewards for applying training on the job, and supervisor and peer support for the use of newly acquired skills and abilities. A positive and supportive transfer climate has been shown to result in greater learning, retention, and transfer of training. Further, a recent review of transfer research found that among the work environment factors, a positive transfer climate was the strongest predictor of transfer.[19]

Continuous Learning Culture

Continuous learning culture
A culture in which members of an organization believe that knowledge and skill acquisition are part of their job responsibilities and that learning is an important part of work life in the organization

A **continuous learning culture** refers to a culture in which members of an organization believe that knowledge and skill acquisition are part of their job responsibilities and that learning is an important part of work life in the organization. Research has shown that the transfer of training is greater in organizations that have a continuous learning culture.[20]

Now that you are familiar with the transfer of training process, see Training Today 10.1, "What Do Training Professionals Know about Transfer of Training?" to find out what training professionals know about transfer.

TRANSFER OF TRAINING STRATEGIES

In this section, we describe strategies that can be implemented before, during, and after training to improve the transfer of training. We will also show that positive transfer of training requires the involvement of three key role players (management, trainers, and trainees) and describe transfer strategies for each role player at each of the three time periods. Table 10.3 presents a summary of the transfer of training strategies discussed in this section of the chapter.

Training Today 10.1

What Do Training Professionals Know about Transfer of Training?

Research on the transfer of training has provided some important information about the factors that can hinder or facilitate transfer. However, given the low rates of transfer reported in several studies, one has to wonder if training professionals are aware of the research findings from transfer of training research.

To find out, Holly Hutchins and Lisa Burke conducted a study to assess the extent to which there is a gap in transfer knowledge among training professionals. They sent a survey to training professionals who had on average 15 years of professional experience in training or workplace learning. The survey included items about the training inputs in Baldwin and Ford's model of the transfer of training process as shown in Figure 10.1.

The results indicated that the average participant correctly answered 78 percent of the survey items. However, the participants differed on the extent to which they agreed on specific items and specific categories, which suggests that there are some areas where knowledge gaps exist.

In terms of the three main input factors, knowledge differences were greatest for trainee characteristics (i.e., cognitive ability, personality, and motivation). In other words, training professionals' knowledge of how trainee characteristics influence transfer varies widely and/or is limited. Most of the participants were in agreement on the importance of training design factors for the transfer of training, especially the use of specific design elements (i.e., identical elements, stimulus generalization, modelling, practice, and feedback). Training professionals were also in agreement on the importance of the work environment for transfer of training, especially manager support and peer support.

Some training professionals were more knowledgeable about transfer research than others. In particular, those with more education, training certification, and higher job levels were more knowledgeable of transfer of training research findings. The results of this study suggest that there exists a research-to-practice gap among training professionals in some areas of transfer of training knowledge.

Source: H.M. Hutchins & L.A. Burke, "Identifying trainers' knowledge of training transfer research findings—closing the gap between research and practice," *International Journal of Training and Development*, Vol. 11, Pp. 236–264, 2007.

TABLE 10.3

Transfer of Training Strategies

Transfer of Training Strategies before Training

Management
- Decide who should attend training.
- Meet with employees prior to training to discuss training programs (e.g., WIIFM).
- Get employee input and involvement in the training process.
- Provide employees with support for learning and training (e.g., release time to prepare for training).

Trainer
- Ensure application of the ISD model.
- Make sure that trainees and supervisors meet and discuss the training.
- Find out supervisor and trainee needs and expectations.
- Make sure that trainees are prepared for the training.

Trainees
- Find out about training programs prior to attendance.
- Meet with supervisor to discuss the training program and develop an action plan.
- Prepare for the training program.

Transfer of Training Strategies during Training

Management
- Participate in training programs.
- Attend training programs before trainees.
- Reassign employees' work while they are attending training.

Trainer
- Incorporate conditions of practice, adult learning principles, and other learning principles (e.g., identical elements) in the design of training programs.
- Include content and examples that are relevant and meaningful to trainees.
- Provide transfer of training interventions at the end of the content portion of a training program (e.g., relapse prevention, self-management, goal setting).
- Have trainees prepare and commit to a performance contract for the transfer of trained skills on the job.

Trainees
- Enter a training program with a positive attitude and the motivation to learn.
- Engage yourself in the training program by getting involved and actively participating.
- Develop an action plan for the application of training on the job.

Transfer of Training Strategies after Training

Management
- Ensure that trainees have immediate and frequent opportunities to practise and apply what they learn in training on the job.
- Encourage and reinforce trainees' application of new skills on the job.
- Provide positive feedback for the use of new skills on the job.
- Develop an action plan with trainees for transfer and show support by reducing job pressures and workload, arrange practice sessions, publicize transfer successes, give promotional preference to employees who have received training and transfer, and evaluate employees' use of trained skills on the job.

Trainer
- Stay involved in the training and transfer process by conducting field visits to observe trainees' use of trained skills, provide and solicit feedback, and continue to provide support and assistance to trainees.

Trainees
- Begin using new knowledge and skills on the job as soon and as often as possible.
- Meet with supervisor to discuss opportunities for transfer.
- Form a "buddy system" or a network of peers who also attended the training program.
- Consider high-risk situations that might cause a relapse and develop strategies for overcoming them and avoiding a relapse.
- Set goals for transfer and use self-management.

TRANSFER OF TRAINING STRATEGIES BEFORE TRAINING

Strategies for positive transfer of training should begin before a training program. A number of factors in the pre-training work environment have a direct effect on trainees' motivation, learning, and transfer. The work environment sends messages to employees about the importance of training and should therefore be carefully constructed and managed. This means that management has an especially important role to play.

Management

One of the first things that a manager should do before a training program is to decide who should attend training. This involves more than just the identification of employees' needs for training. Recall from our earlier discussion that trainee characteristics are an important determinant of learning and retention as well as transfer. Therefore, it is important that trainees who are selected to attend training programs will learn the training material and apply what they learn on the job.

The extent to which a trainee is likely to learn and benefit from a training program is known as readiness to learn or trainability. **Readiness to learn/ trainability** refers to the extent to which an individual has the knowledge, skills, and abilities and the motivation to learn the training content. An equation for readiness to learn and trainability combines ability, motivation, as well as perceptions of the work environment as follows:[21]

Readiness to Learn and Trainability = (Ability × Motivation × Perceptions of the Work Environment)

According to this equation, trainees are more likely to learn and are more trainable when they have the ability to learn the training content, when they are motivated to learn, and when they perceive the work environment as supportive of their learning and use of new knowledge and skills on the job. All three of these components are important and they are not additive. In other words, being high on one factor will not make up for a low rating on another factor. For example, a trainee might have the ability to learn and be motivated to learn, but if he/she does not believe that the work environment will support learning, then he/she will score low on readiness to learn and trainability. Therefore, it is important that all three components are high before trainees are sent to a training program.

One way to determine whether an employee has the ability to learn the training content is to have him/her take a trainability test as described in Chapter 9. Recall that a trainability test measures an individual's ability to learn and perform training tasks.

If employees lack the motivation to attend training, there are several ways for managers to increase training motivation. First, they can meet with employees to discuss their training needs and decide on a training plan to meet those needs. Prior to actually attending a training program, managers can discuss the content and the benefits of a training program with employees and set goals for learning and how they will apply what they learn on the job. They should also discuss the objectives of a training program so that employees know what is expected

Readiness to learn/ trainability

The extent to which an individual has the knowledge, skills, and abilities and the motivation to learn the training content

Make the Connection

and what they will be accountable for in terms of learning and the use of new knowledge and skills on the job. Trainees who know that they will be required to participate in follow-up activities or will be evaluated have stronger intentions to transfer.[22]

Employees also need to know why they are attending a training program and the potential benefits. It is up to management to inform trainees about the importance and relevance of a training program and the benefits of learning and transfer. Trainees need to know what's in it for them, or what is sometimes referred to as **WIIFM** (what's in it for me?).

Some evidence exists that trainees will be more motivated and will achieve greater learning when they are given the choice of attending a training program than when attendance is mandatory. In one study, managers who could choose whether to attend a performance-appraisal workshop achieved more from attending the workshop than those who were forced to attend. Providing detailed information about the workshop, which was designed to facilitate the managers' attendance decision, rather than just providing the typical positive overview, also resulted in greater achievement.[23]

Some, however, argue that it is better to make attendance mandatory. The idea behind this argument is that by making attendance mandatory, managers communicate the importance of training and ensure that all employees are using the same skills.[24] One study found that a mandatory training course resulted in higher intentions to transfer.[25] However, this appears to be the case when training is highly valued in an organization, which is the case with OLG's Launch Pad to Success program. When training is not so highly valued, however, providing employees with some choice is beneficial. The main point is that trainee involvement and input in the training process, whether discussing training needs, allowing trainees to decide what training programs to attend, and/or providing input regarding training content and methods, can enhance training motivation, learning, and transfer.

Finally, managers also need to show their support for training before an employee is sent to a training program. One way to do this is to have them complete a questionnaire and respond to questions about the need for and potential application of training material. For example, managers who have requested training might be required to answer questions such as: What is the training need? What are the employees doing now and what should they be doing? Why do you feel that training will solve the problem? What would you want employees to be able to do after the training? Having managers complete a contract can also commit them to a training program and ensure their support for it (an example of a contract is shown in Table 10.4). Supervisors can also demonstrate their support for training by providing employees release time to prepare for training and by providing encouragement.[26]

Trainer

One of the first things a trainer should do is ensure that the training system is operating according to the instructional systems design (ISD) model presented in Chapter 1. That is, a trainer should ensure that a needs analysis has been conducted, that appropriate training objectives have been developed, and that important learning and design principles have been incorporated into the design

WIIFM
What's in it for me?

to attend or not—voluntary is mandatory

Make the
Connection

TABLE 10.4
Training Support Contract—Supervisor

I, _____, agree to

- provide time for the employee to complete pre-course assignments.
- provide release time for attendance, and ensure that the employee's workload is undertaken by others to eliminate interruptions.
- review the course outline with the employee, and discuss situations in which the newly acquired knowledge and skills can be used.
- provide timely opportunities to implement the skills, and reinforce new behaviours upon the return of the trainee.

Signature _____

Title   _____

of the training program. As described at the beginning of this chapter, the Launch Pad to Success program was customized to meet the needs of the OLG Leadership Excellence Model and the program was designed based on behavioural and measurable learning objectives.

Second, the trainer should ensure that supervisors and trainees are prepared for the training program. For example, the trainer should see that supervisors have taken appropriate actions with respect to trainees' readiness to learn/trainability. The trainer should also make sure that supervisors and trainees have met to discuss the training objectives, content, and benefits of the training program, and that trainees know what they are expected to learn and do after training.

Third, the trainer should know what supervisors and trainees expect from the trainer and the training program. Thus, to some extent a trainer might have to tailor a training program to the particular needs and expectations of supervisors and trainees. The trainer should also be aware of the needs of trainees in terms of relevant content, examples, and methods. In other words, the trainer must ensure that the training program is relevant and meaningful for trainees.

Finally, the trainer should ensure that trainees have taken any required prerequisite courses and have the necessary readings, assignments, and/or pre-training exercises. Preparation might also include asking trainees to think about work-related problems and issues that they are currently dealing with and how the training program might help solve them. Thus, when trainees show up for a training program they should be ready and motivated to learn.

Trainees

Trainees often show up for training with little knowledge of what they are going to learn or what is expected of them. This is obviously not going to lead to a high level of motivation, learning, or transfer. Trainees must be involved in their training and the training process. But what can trainees do before a training program to increase their involvement and the likelihood that they will learn and transfer?

First, trainees should find out why they are being asked to attend a training program, what the training objectives are, and what is expected of them in terms of learning and on-the-job behaviour and performance. Second, trainees should meet with their supervisor to discuss the training program and develop a plan of action for learning and transfer. Trainees should also ask their supervisor about the support they can expect while they are away from work and attending a training program, and the support they will receive when they return to work.

Finally, trainees should prepare for the training program to ensure that they are ready to learn and that they will benefit from the training. This might involve preparatory reading, pre-training exercises or assignments, or simply thinking about work-related problems that they can bring with them to discuss during the training program. These activities will help ensure that trainees are knowledgeable about the training program and its objectives and they are prepared and motivated to learn.

TRANSFER OF TRAINING STRATEGIES DURING TRAINING

Although it is the responsibility of the trainer to implement and deliver a training program, there are also strategies that trainees and managers can perform during training to improve learning and transfer.

Management

Managers can facilitate the transfer of training during training by showing their support for training. One way of doing this is to attend a training program. If managers cannot attend a training program, then they should consider speaking about the importance and relevance of the training at the start of a program or participating as a trainer if possible. At the very least, they should visit the training session at some time to show their support.[27] In the case of the OLG's Launch Pad to Success program, senior executives were actively involved in the design of the program and demonstrated their support for the program by attending all of the sessions and as speakers during the program.[28]

It also helps if managers have already taken a training program. Managers are more likely to support training if they have been trained or have participated as trainers in a training program. In this way, managers can model the behaviour and observe its occurrence. Senior executives at Vancouver-based Finning Ltd., the world's largest Caterpillar dealer, are the first to attend training and help deliver the training.[29] This cascading effect tells employees that management is serious about learning and the application of new skills on the job. In addition, when managers are required to teach the new skills, they learn them very well. They are also aware that their employees are watching them to see if they practise what they preach.

Management can also do a number of things to assist employees while they are away from work and attending a training program. For example, they can reassign some of their workload so that they don't worry about falling behind while they are being trained. They can also ensure that trainees will not be interrupted during training. This not only puts trainees at ease while they are being trained, but also signals to employees that management supports training and considers it a high priority.

Trainer

There are several things a trainer can do during training to facilitate the transfer of training. For starters, as described in Chapter 5, training programs should include active practice and the conditions of practice (e.g., task sequencing, feedback, and knowledge of results) to maximize learning and transfer. In addition, as discussed earlier in this chapter, the principles of learning (i.e., identical elements, general principles, and stimulus variability) are especially important design factors for transfer of training. Adult learning theory should also be considered (Chapter 2). In fact, the OLG's Launch Pad to Success program was built on adult learning principles.[30]

Make the Connection

Trainers can also increase trainees' training motivation during training. This can be achieved by explaining the value of a skill and by using training content and examples that are familiar and meaningful to trainees.[31] Trainees learn and remember meaningful material more easily than material unrelated to their work.[32] Trainers can use information, problems, and anecdotes collected from the needs analysis to demonstrate the link between the training material and work situations. New material should be introduced using terms and examples familiar to trainees. The customization of the Launch Pad to Success program resulted in the use of tools and examples that the trainees could relate to.[33]

Trainers can also have trainees prepare a performance contract. A **performance contract** is a statement, mutually drafted by the trainee and the trainer near the end of a training program, that outlines which of the newly acquired skills are beneficial and how they will be applied to the job. A copy can then be given to the trainer, a peer, or the supervisor, who will monitor progress toward these goals. Trainees submit progress reports to human resources and their supervisor. A variation on the timing (i.e., signing the contract jointly before a training program) alerts the trainee to the critical elements of the program and commits the supervisor to monitoring progress.[34] Recall that the participants of the Launch Pad to Success program were asked to write down the key things they learned and one or two skills that they would apply on the job at the conclusion of each session.

Performance contract
An agreement outlining how the newly learned skills will be applied to the job

Trainees

Trainees should begin a training program with a positive attitude and be motivated to learn. During the training, trainees should engage themselves by taking notes, participating in discussions and exercises, asking and answering questions, and interacting with the trainer and the other trainees.

Before leaving a training program, trainees should develop an action plan for the application of training on the job and be prepared to discuss their learning and action plan with their supervisor and co-workers. You might recall from the chapter-opening vignette that the Launch Pad to Success participants prepared action plans during the final session of the program for how they will apply three key learning objectives that they will focus on and will discuss with their manager. These activities help maximize trainee learning and facilitate the transfer of training.

TRANSFER OF TRAINING STRATEGIES AFTER TRAINING

After a training program has ended and trainees return to work, they may be motivated to use their new skills on the job. However, only some trainees are able to do so successfully. Some will stop trying after a few attempts because they receive no support or reinforcement for the use of their new knowledge and skills on the job. Others will give up because they encounter barriers and obstacles that make it difficult if not impossible for them to apply their new knowledge and skills. Still others will give up just because the old ways of doing things are easier and faster. Therefore, it is important that managers, trainers, and trainees implement strategies after training that facilitate the transfer of training.

Management

One of the most important things that managers can do following a training program is ensure that employees have immediate and frequent opportunities to practise what they learned in training on the job. Training programs that include opportunities to practise newly learned skills have been shown to have higher rates of transfer.[35] Thus, assignments and opportunities to try new skills should be given as soon as trainees return from a training program. Managers can also help by allowing trainees time to experiment using new behaviours without adverse consequences.

Managers should also encourage and reinforce the application of new skills on the job. In fact, one of the major reasons for a lack of transfer is that reinforcement is usually infrequent or nonexistent. Behaviour that is not reinforced is not repeated. If the sales representative dutifully submits the reports as learned in training but no one even notices they are filed, then the representative will waste no further energy doing this task. Thus, trainees who use new skills on the job should be provided with praise, recognition, more challenging assignments, additional opportunities for training, and other extrinsic rewards. It is also important that managers provide trainees with positive feedback about their use of new knowledge and skills on the job. Feedback has been found to be a significant predictor of transfer of training.[36]

Recognition and positive feedback not only directly reinforces employees for their transfer behaviour, but also sends a signal to other employees that training is important and learning and transfer will be rewarded. In effect, it helps to demonstrate management support and to create a positive transfer climate.

Managers can do many other things to facilitate transfer, such as developing an action plan for transfer, reducing job pressures and workload, arranging for co-workers to be briefed by trainees about a training program, arranging practice sessions, publicizing successes, giving promotional preference to employees who have received training, and evaluating employees' use of trained skills on the job.[37] Calgary-based Western Gas Marketing Ltd., a subsidiary of TransCanada PipeLines Ltd., rates its managers on the application of new skills on their performance-appraisal forms.[38] At the Bank of Montreal, managers conduct performance assessments to gauge the transfer of learning to the job.[39]

Trainer

Some trainers might believe that their job is finished after a training program has been delivered. However, it is important for trainers to remain involved in trainees' learning and transfer after a training program has been delivered. Trainers should maintain their involvement in the training and transfer process by conducting field visits to observe trainees' use of trained skills, provide and solicit feedback, and provide continued support and assistance to trainees.[40] Sometimes a trainer might meet with trainees for a follow-up session to review the training program and discuss transfer problems and solutions (see the section on booster sessions later in the chapter).

Trainees

After attending a training program, trainees should begin to use their new knowledge and skills on the job as soon as possible. Failure to use the training material when a trainee returns to work is likely to result in a low likelihood of transfer. To ensure adequate opportunities for skill application and support, trainees should meet with their supervisor and discuss opportunities for transfer. Trainees might also benefit by establishing a "buddy system," or a network of peers who have attended a training program and can provide assistance and support, and reinforce each other for using their trained skills on the job.[41] One of the follow-up activities used for OLG's Launch Pad to Success program was a buddy system of coaching.

The Trainer's Notebook 10.1

BEST PRACTICE STRATEGIES FOR TRANSFER OF TRAINING

According to a sample of training professionals, the best practice strategies for transfer of training are the following:

1. *Supervisory support and reinforcement.* Recognize and reinforce the use of new knowledge and skills on the job.

2. *Coaching and opportunities to practise.* Provide time to practise skills immediately when returning from training.

3. *Use of interactive activities to encourage participation.* Collaborative activities, role plays, small group exercises.

4. *Post-training evaluation of skills.* Tracking and measuring transfer of training.

5. *Making the content relevant to actual job duties.* Activities that resemble work behaviours, challenges, and scenarios.

Source: L.A. Burke & H.M. Hutchins, "A study of best practices in training transfer and proposed model of transfer," *Human Resource Development Quarterly*, 19, Pp. 107–128, 2008.

Now that we have described transfer of training strategies, you might be wondering which ones are most effective. To find out, see The Trainer's Notebook 10.1, "Best Practice Strategies for Transfer of Training."

TRANSFER OF TRAINING INTERVENTIONS

In addition to transfer strategies, many studies have found that **transfer of training interventions** provided at the end of a training program can be effective for improving the transfer of training. In this section, we discuss three types of transfer of training interventions: relapse prevention, self-management, and goal-setting.

Relapse Prevention

Relapse prevention (RP) is an intervention that instructs trainees to anticipate transfer obstacles and high-risk situations in the work environment and to develop coping skills and strategies to overcome them. A relapse occurs when trainees revert back to using the old skills or their pre-training behaviour. Relapse prevention sensitizes trainees to the possibilities of a relapse and "immunizes" them against obstacles in the environment that might cause one.[42] RP sensitizes trainees to barriers in the workplace that might inhibit or prevent successful transfer.

Relapse prevention interventions make trainees aware that relapses can occur and that temporary slips are normal. Trainees are asked to identify obstacles and barriers to transfer and high-risk situations in which a relapse is likely to occur. Some high-risk situations that might lead to a relapse are time pressure and deadlines, work overload, lack of necessary tools, equipment, and resources, and the lack of opportunities to apply trained skills on the job.[43]

For each barrier or high-risk situation, trainees develop a coping strategy. For example, if workers think they will abandon their new skills when there is too much work, time-management techniques could be discussed and used to prevent a relapse. Thus, RP prepares trainees to anticipate, prevent, and recover from temporary lapses. Table 10.5 provides an outline of a relapse prevention intervention.

Relapse prevention programs have been found to be effective. Trainees who receive RP interventions have higher levels of course knowledge and use the knowledge on the job more than trainees who do not receive it. Relapse prevention has also been found to improve trainees' ability and desire to transfer. There is also evidence that relapse prevention interventions are especially effective when the transfer climate is not very supportive of training.[44]

Self-Management

In Chapter 3, we discussed self-regulation as one of the components of social cognitive theory. We also noted that employees can be trained to learn how to regulate their behaviour and the use of self-regulation prompts. **Self-management** interventions focus on behavioural change and have their basis in self-regulation and social cognitive theory. Self-management interventions involve teaching trainees to perform a series of steps to manage their transfer behaviour.

Transfer of training interventions
Interventions provided at the end of a training program to facilitate the transfer of training

Relapse prevention
An intervention that instructs trainees to anticipate transfer obstacles and high-risk situations in the work environment and to develop coping skills and strategies to overcome them

Make the Connection

Self-management
A post-training transfer intervention that teaches trainees to manage their transfer behaviour

TABLE (10.5)

Relapse Prevention Intervention

Step 1. State the trained skill you wish to apply and maintain from this training.

Step 2. Set your skill maintenance goal, based upon this training. Set a specific, measurable, short-range goal. Then, specifically define a slip and a relapse.

Skill Maintenance Goal: ___

Slip: ___

Relapse: ___

Step 3. Understand positive and negative consequences of using the skill at work.

Positive consequences of using your new skills: ___

Negative consequences of not using your new skills: ___

Positive consequences of not using your new skills: ___

Negative consequences of using your new skills: ___

Step 4. Apply the relapse prevention strategies to maintain trained skills.

RP Strategy: Trainee Notes/Comments

1. Understand the relapse process (i.e., slip, then relapse).
2. Understand the difference between the training environment and job contexts.
3. Create a support network.
4. Be aware of subordinate skepticism of new skills.
5. Identify high-risk situations.
6. Apply skills in the appropriate setting.
7. Understand seemingly unimportant behaviours that may lead to a relapse.
8. Reduce interfering and unproductive emotions.
9. Retain your self-confidence, despite slips.
10. Diagnose support skills needed to maintain training.
11. Review disruptive lifestyle patterns.
12. Mix enjoyable and tedious work tasks.
13. Diagnose support back at work for skill application.
14. Create meaningful self-rewards for skill retention.

Step 5. Describe the nature of circumstances that will likely surround a first slip.

Step 6. Generate ideas for how you will deal with such difficult situations.

Step 7. Monitor your behaviour at work using a self-monitoring record.

Sources: L.A. Burke "Training transfer: Ensuring training gets used on the job," in L.A. Burke (Ed.), *High-impact training solutions: Top issues troubling trainers.* 2001. Wesport, CT: Quorum Books; H.M. Hutchins & L. Burke, "Has relapse prevention received a fair shake? A review and implications for future transfer research," *Human Resource Development Review,* Vol. 5 (1), Pp. 8–24, 2006.

The steps of self-management interventions include anticipating performance obstacles, planning to overcome obstacles, setting goals to overcome obstacles, monitoring one's progress, and rewarding oneself for goal attainment. Research has found self-management interventions to result in greater skill generalization and higher performance on a transfer task.[45]

Make the Connection

Goal-Setting

In Chapter 3, we described goal-setting theory and its implications for training and in Chapter 5 we described how mastery goals can be set as a pre-training intervention to improve learning during practice sessions. Many studies have shown that individuals who set specific, difficult, and challenging goals achieve higher levels of performance.[46]

The importance of goal-setting for training has been the focus of many studies in recent years. From these studies, we know that learning and transfer is more likely when trainees set specific and challenging goals. Therefore, it makes sense to use goal-setting as a transfer intervention.

Goal-setting interventions teach trainees about the goal-setting process and how to set specific goals for the use of trained skills on the job. This usually involves a discussion of why goal-setting is important and a definition of goals; a description of the goal-setting process; characteristics of effective goals (specific and challenging); an explanation for the effectiveness of goals; examples of how goal-setting has been used in organizations; and a discussion of how goal-setting can be effective in one's own organization.

Following a discussion of how to set specific and challenging goals, trainees develop their own goal-setting plan that indicates the steps they will take to achieve their goals and the date that each step will be achieved.[47] In the chapter-opening vignette it was noted that individual goal setting and action planning were used to support participants' application of what they learned in the Launch Pad to Success program on the job.

Goal-setting interventions have been shown to improve learning and the extent to which trainees apply their newly learned skills on the job. In addition, one study found that goal-setting was particularly effective for enhancing transfer for trainees who work in a supportive work environment.[48]

Goal-setting intervention

An intervention that instructs trainees about the goal-setting process and how to set specific goals for the use of trained skills on the job

POST-TRAINING SUPPLEMENTS

Post-training supplements are transfer interventions that take place on the job following a training program and include booster sessions, self-coaching, and upward feedback.

Post-training supplements

Transfer interventions that take place on the job following a training program

Booster Sessions

A common post-training supplement is a booster session or a refresher course following a training program. **Booster sessions** are extensions of training programs that involve a review of the training material. A booster session can also involve a discussion of problems that trainees are having using their trained skills on the job as well as success stories. Recall that the Launch Pad to Success program includes five booster modules, and the In Flight sessions are designed to help managers apply the skills learned in the program. In addition, a number of follow-up activities such as coaching were also used to support participants' application of learning on the job.

Booster sessions

Extensions of training programs that involve a review of the training material

Self-Coaching and Upward Feedback

Self-coaching involves reflecting on one's performance and setting transfer goals for several weeks following completion of a training program. Trainees complete an assessment in which they examine the extent to which they have

Self-coaching

Trainees examine the extent to which they have engaged in trained behaviours and establish performance maintenance and improvement goals engaged in trained behaviours and then establish performance maintenance and improvement goals. An **upward feedback** supplement involves providing trainees with data on the frequency with which they engaged in the trained behaviours along with written comments from subordinates on their performance. Trainees then establish performance maintenance and improvement goals.[49]

A study of newly hired managers of a large restaurant chain found that both self-coaching and the upward feedback supplements resulted in greater post-training performance following a training program on interpersonal skills development. Thus, both supplements proved to be effective extensions of formal classroom training for improving transfer of training.[50]

Upward feedback
Trainees receive data on the frequency with which they engaged in trained behaviours and written comments from subordinates on their performance

TRANSFER SYSTEM

In this chapter, we have described strategies and interventions that can facilitate and improve the transfer of training. These strategies can occur throughout the training process and have to do with the training program itself as well as trainees, trainers, management, and the organization. One way of thinking about all of the variables that can influence the transfer of training is in terms of a transfer system. According to Elwood Holton and colleagues, the **transfer system** refers to all factors in the person, training, and organization that influence transfer of learning to job performance.[51]

Sixteen factors make up the transfer system. The 16 factors represent important predictors of transfer of training that we have already discussed in the chapter, including trainee ability, motivation, and the work environment. Learning as well as the transfer system factors influence transfer performance, which in turn influence organizational performance.[52]

Holton and his colleagues have developed a diagnostic instrument called the Learning Transfer System Inventory (LTSI) to assess the transfer system in organizations. The instrument consists of 16 factors that have been found to be the most important in transfer research. Some of the factors are used to assess a specific training program while others are general factors that are important for all training programs. Table 10.6 lists the 16 factors and their definitions.

The LTSI can be used by organizations to diagnose their transfer system. It is usually administered to trainees after a training program to identify potential barriers in an organization's transfer system and to determine the type of intervention to overcome barriers and facilitate transfer. Factors with particularly low scores can be identified and made the focus of interventions.[53]

One of the benefits of this approach to transfer is that it recognizes the importance of a systematic approach to the transfer of training. Organizations are able to diagnose their transfer system, identify barriers, and implement programs to eliminate the barriers. This is important because transfer systems differ across organizations, which means that the barriers and the most effective interventions to eliminate them will also differ across organizations.[54] It should also be evident that there is no one best strategy for improving transfer of training and that multiple transfer strategies should be used in combination.[55]

To learn more about how to diagnose and change a transfer system, see The Trainer's Notebook 10.2, "Learning Transfer System Change Process."

Transfer system
All factors in the person, training, and organization that influence transfer of learning to job performance

TABLE (10.6)

Transfer System Factors

The Learning Transfer System Inventory (LTSI) consists of sixteen factors that assess the transfer system in organizations. Eleven factors are for specific training programs (Factors 1 to 11) and the remaining five (Factors 12 to 16) are more general and apply to all training programs.

Specific Factors

1. **Learner readiness.** The extent to which individuals are prepared to enter and participate in training.

2. **Motivation to transfer.** The direction, intensity, and persistence of effort toward utilizing in a work setting skills and knowledge learned.

3. **Positive personal outcomes.** The degree to which applying training on the job leads to outcomes that are positive for the individual.

4. **Negative personal outcomes.** The extent to which individuals believe that not applying skills and knowledge learned in training will lead to outcomes that are negative.

5. **Personal capacity for transfer.** The extent to which individuals have the time, energy, and mental space in their work lives to make changes required to transfer learning to the job.

6. **Peer support.** The extent to which peers reinforce and support use of learning on the job.

7. **Supervisor support.** The extent to which supervisors and managers support and reinforce use of training on the job.

8. **Supervisor sanctions.** The extent to which individuals perceive negative responses from supervisors and managers when applying skills learned in training.

9. **Perceived content validity.** The extent to which trainees judge training content to reflect job requirements accurately.

10. **Transfer design.** The degree to which (1) training has been designed and delivered to give trainees the ability to transfer learning to the job, and (2) training instructions match job requirements.

11. **Opportunities to use.** The extent to which trainees are provided with or obtain resources and tasks on the job enabling them to use training on the job.

General Factors

1. **Transfer effort–performance expectations.** The expectation that effort devoted to transferring learning will lead to changes in job performance.

2. **Performance–outcomes expectations.** The expectation that changes in job performance will lead to valued outcomes.

3. **Resistance or openness to change.** The extent to which prevailing group norms are perceived by individuals to resist or discourage the use of skills and knowledge acquired in training.

4. **Performance self-efficacy.** An individual's general belief in the ability to change performance at will.

5. **Performance coaching.** Formal and informal indicators from an organization about an individual's job performance.

Source: E.F. Holton III, R.A. Bates, & W.E.A. Ruona, "Development of a generalized learning transfer system inventory," *Human Resource Development Quarterly*, 11, Pp. 333–360, 2000.

The Trainer's Notebook 10.2

LEARNING TRANSFER SYSTEM CHANGE PROCESS

Assessing and improving the transfer system is a change process that involves the following steps:

1. **Plan system assessment.** An effective diagnosis begins with good planning and involves logistical issues and political issues with managers. Sub-steps include:

   - Determine employee groups to be assessed.
   - Build partnerships with managers.
   - Address confidentiality issues.
   - Obtain management support.
   - Decide logistical issues.

2. **Diagnose system.** Use the Learning Transfer System Inventory (LTSI) to collect diagnostic data as a pulse-check to identify areas for further inquiry. Sub-steps include:

   - Collect initial diagnostic data.
   - Conduct focus groups to understand meaning behind data.
   - Identify key transfer system gaps.

3. **Provide feedback to system members.** It is recommended that the diagnostic findings be reported to system members who should be involved if diagnosis is to become action and solution oriented. Sub-steps include:

   - Arrange feedback meeting (or meetings, if needed).
   - Report diagnostic data.
   - Avoid blame and criticism.
   - Overcome objections to identified gaps.

4. **Plan system changes.** Attempts should be made to involve system members in joint change planning as they are frequently best equipped to recommend specific improvements. Sub-steps include:

   - Build support from management and transfer agents for change.
   - Engage transfer agents in collaborative decision making.
   - Make realistic decisions.

5. **Implement system improvements.** System improvements are most likely to endure if ownership is shared with system members. Sub-steps include:

   - Share ownership of system improvements.
   - Overcome resistance of system members.
   - Monitor change progress.
   - Plan for reassessment.

Source: E.F. Holton III ,"What's really wrong: Diagnosis for learning transfer system change," In E.F. Holton III & T.T. Baldwin (Eds.), *Improving learning transfer in organizations*. San Francisco, CA: John Wiley & Sons, Inc., 2003.

MODEL OF TRAINING EFFECTIVENESS— TRANSFER OF TRAINING

Let's now return to the **model of training effectiveness** that was presented in Chapters 3 and 5. Recall that the model shows that: 1. trainee characteristics (i.e., cognitive ability, training motivation, personality, self-efficacy, and attitudes) and training design (i.e., active practice, conditions of practice, active learning, error-management training) have a direct effect on trainee learning and retention; 2. learning and retention have a direct effect on individual behaviour and performance; and 3. individual behaviour and performance has a direct effect on organizational effectiveness.

As shown in Figure 10.2, we can now add a number of other factors to the model based on the material presented in this chapter. First, we can add the work environment which includes the training transfer climate, a continuous learning

FIGURE 10.2

Model of Training Effectiveness

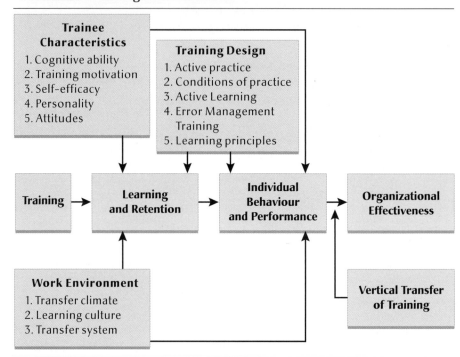

culture, and the transfer system. Second, we can add the learning principles (i.e., identical elements, stimulus variability, and general principles) to the training design factors.

In terms of the linkages, we can add a direct link from trainee characteristics and the work environment to individual behaviour and performance. This follows from Baldwin and Ford's model of the transfer process. We can also add a direct link from training design to individual behaviour and performance given that the learning principles are important for transfer. The model now shows that individual behaviour and performance (i.e., transfer) is influenced by trainee characteristics, training design, the work environment, and learning and retention.

The final linkage in the model is from transfer behaviour and performance to organizational effectiveness. Recall that this linkage is known as vertical transfer. Vertical transfer refers to the link between individual-level training outcomes and organizational outcomes. While a change and improvement in employees' behaviour and performance (i.e., horizontal transfer) is necessary for vertical transfer, it is important to realize that the relationship is not one-to-one. In other words, positive horizontal transfer does not guarantee vertical transfer because many other factors also contribute to organizational effectiveness.

SUMMARY

This chapter described the importance of transfer of training and the transfer problem in organizations. Baldwin and Ford's model was presented as a framework for understanding the transfer of training process. Strategies for facilitating the transfer of training were described in terms of when they can be used (before, during, and after training) by managers, trainers, and trainees. The use of transfer of training interventions and post-training supplements for improving transfer were also described. The chapter concluded with a discussion of the transfer system and the importance of a systematic approach to transfer of training that involves all of the key stakeholders throughout the training process and the need to use multiple transfer strategies to improve the transfer of training in organizations.

Key Terms

booster sessions p. 308
continuous learning culture p. 296
far transfer p. 291
general principles p. 295
generalization p. 291
goal-setting intervention p. 308
horizontal transfer p. 291
identical elements p. 294
maintenance p. 291
motivation to transfer p. 294
near transfer p. 291
negative transfer, p. 291
performance contract p. 303
positive transfer p. 291

post-training supplements p. 308
readiness to learn/trainability p. 299
relapse prevention p. 306
self-coaching p. 308
self-management p. 306
stimulus variability p. 295
training transfer climate p. 296
transfer of training p. 290
transfer of training interventions p. 306
transfer system p. 309
upward feedback p. 309
vertical transfer p. 291
WIIFM p. 300
zero transfer p. 291

Make the Connection

p. 294: trainee characteristics that predict trainee learning and retention are discussed in Chapter 3 on pages 86–87

p. 294: training motivation is discussed in Chapter 3 on page 85

p. 294: physical and psychological fidelity are discussed in Chapter 6 on page 179

p. 296: training transfer climate and learning culture are discussed in Chapter 4 on page 108

p. 299: a trainability test is discussed in Chapter 9 on page 267

p. 300: the instructional systems design (ISD) model is discussed in Chapter 1 on pages 21–23

p. 303: active practice and the conditions of practice are discussed in Chapter 5 on pages 11–12 and adult learning theory is discussed in Chapter 3 on page 77

p. 306: self-regulation is discussed in Chapter 3 on page 75

p. 308: goal setting theory is discussed in Chapter 3 on page 82 and goal orientation as a pre-training intervention is discussed in Chapter 5 on page 149

Web Links

Finning Ltd.: **www.finning.com**

Ontario Lottery and Gaming Corporation: **www.olg.ca**

Western Gas Marketing Ltd.: **www.transcanada.com**

Required Professional Capabilities (RPCs)

The following RPCs are relevant to material covered in this chapter. The RPC number represents the CCHRA number assigned to the RPC as presented on the CCHRA website. All of the RPCs can be found in the Body of Knowledge at **http://www.chrp.ca/rpc/body-of-knowledge/**.

RPC 163: Facilitates post training support activities to ensure transfer of learning to the workplace.

  163.05: Issues regarding the transfer of training to the job

  163.06: Conditions necessary for training success

Discussion Questions

1. Refer to Table 10.2, "Barriers to the Transfer of Training." For each of the barriers, indicate who is responsible for the barrier (trainer, trainee, management) and when the barrier is most likely to occur (before, during, and/ or after).
2. Refer to Table 10.2, "Barriers to the Transfer of Training." For each of the barriers, describe what can be done to remove the barrier and facilitate the transfer of training. Be sure to indicate at what stage in the training process you would do something to remove the barrier (i.e., before, during, and/or after), and who would be involved (i.e., manager, trainer, and/or trainee).
3. Refer to the OLG vignette at the beginning of the chapter and describe the strategies that were used to facilitate the transfer of training. At what point during the training process were these strategies implemented and how effective were they?
4. What is the difference between horizontal and vertical transfer and how are they related? What is the difference between near transfer and far transfer and what should a trainer do to maximize each of them?
5. Describe the main factors in Baldwin and Ford's model of the transfer of training process and how they are related. What are the practical implications of the model for improving transfer of training?
6. What is the transfer system and what are the specific and general factors associated with it? Review each of the factors in Table 10.6 and discuss who is responsible for each factor (i.e., trainee, trainer, supervisor) and what can be done to improve them.

7. Discuss how technology can be used to facilitate the transfer of training in organizations. Be specific in describing the technology and how it can be used.
8. Who is responsible for the transfer of training? Explain your answer and indicate why you believe that someone is or is not responsible. If you believe that someone is responsible, explain what you think they should do as part of their responsibility for transfer of training.

The Great Training Debate

1. Debate the following: Low rates of transfer of training are inevitable and will always be a problem for trainers and organizations.
2. Debate the following: Trainers should be responsible only for trainee learning and retention because what happens when trainees return to the work environment and the transfer of training is beyond their control.
3. Debate the following: Trainees and trainees alone are responsible for the transfer of training and they should be held accountable for applying what they learn in training on the job.

Exercises

In-Class

1. After the final exam, many students claim to forget most of what they learn in their courses. How could you design a course for students so that they will remember and use most of what they learned in the classroom after the course has ended?
2. Think about the most recent training experience you had in a current or previous job. What did you learn and to what extent did you apply what you learned on the job? Did you transfer immediately after training? Six months after training? One year after training? What factors explain why you did or did not transfer what you learned in training on the job? Is there anything that the trainer or your supervisor could have done to increase your transfer? Is there anything you could have done yourself to improve your transfer? (*Note:* This exercise can also be done by interviewing somebody about their training experiences, e.g., another member of the class, a friend, or family member.)
3. Students acquire a great deal of knowledge and information from their courses, but does it transfer to their work experiences? Describe any courses you have taken that resulted in transfer to a job. What factors do you think contributed to your transfer and could they be used in the design of other courses?
4. Describe how you would use identical elements, general principles, and stimulus variability to improve the learning and transfer of your courses. In other words, how can an instructor incorporate these learning principles into his/her classes?

5. Assume the role of a training consultant who has been hired by an organization with a transfer of training problem. Your task is to conduct a diagnosis of the transfer system to find out why there is a transfer problem. Therefore, you need to develop a diagnostic tool to find out what barriers exist. Using the material in this chapter, develop some questions that take into account the different time periods of the training process (i.e., before, during, and after) and the main role players (management, trainer, and trainees) to assess the transfer problem in the organization. What questions will you ask and who will you interview and/or survey?

6. Review the transfer of training interventions (relapse prevention, self-management, and goal-setting) described in the chapter and think about how they might be used to help students learn their course material and apply it on the job. You could consider your course on training and development or perhaps a course on managerial skills. Your task is to design one of the following interventions: relapse prevention, self-management, or goal-setting. You can then have another member of the class review your intervention and provide feedback, or if time permits present your intervention to the class.

In-the-Field

1. To find out about transfer of training in an organization, contact the human resource department of an organization and ask the following questions:

   - To what extent do trainees apply what they learn in training on the job immediately after training, six months after training, and one year after training?

   - What are the main barriers or obstacles to transfer of training in your organization and who is responsible for them?

   - What strategies do you use to improve the transfer of training?

   - Are there things you do before, during, and after training to facilitate the transfer of training?

   - What are the responsibilities of managers, trainers, and trainees for the transfer of training?

   - What have you found to be most effective for ensuring that trainees apply what they learn in training on the job?

     Based on your interview, how well do you think the organization is managing the transfer of training process? What recommendations do you suggest for the organization to improve its transfer system and the transfer of training?

2. To find out how to conduct a learning transfer system audit, visit Learning Transfer Solutions at **http://ltsglobal.com/free-resources.html.**
     Download the Learning Transfer System Audit Checklist and then perform an audit on the transfer system in an organization you currently work in or have worked in; or, if possible, interview a person or persons currently

employed in an organization. Based on your audit, answer the following questions:

a. What general conclusions can you make about the organization's transfer system?

b. What are the main barriers in the transfer system?

c. Based on your audit, do you think transfer of training is a problem in the organization? Explain your answer.

d. What recommendations would you make to the organization to improve the transfer system?

Case Incident

BC Assessment

BC Assessment is a provincial Crown organization whose 350 to 400 professional appraisers determine the market value of land and improvements for taxation purposes. Each year, about 2 percent of property owners file a formal complaint or appeal with the agency. Complex appeals that are not resolved might proceed to an appeal board, which could lead to a formal hearing. The appeal process represents a significant cost, mainly in staff time. To help cut back, the agency decided to train appraisers to develop the skills needed to resolve appeals earlier.

Thirty-six appraisers took part in a two-day, face-to-face workshop that included group discussions, team summaries, case studies, and mock role-playing exercises. Before training, 20 percent of the trainees rated their knowledge and skill levels as high. After training, that number rose to 56 percent. In addition, 69 percent of the trainees said they had a high level of confidence in effectively applying the learning to their jobs.

However, six months after the training the value of the course was significantly diminished at the transfer of learning stage. More than one-half of respondents saw little or no improvement in tasks associated with appeals management.

Questions

1. What effect did the training have on trainees? What should the trainees be able to do on the job after attending the training program?

2. Use Baldwin and Ford's model of the transfer of training process (Figure 10.1) to explain why so many of the trainees reported little or no improvement in tasks associated with appeals management.

3. Discuss some of the strategies you would recommend before, during, and after training to improve trainees' performance of tasks associated with appeals management. Be sure to indicate strategies for the trainer, trainees, and managers.

Source: S. Dobson, "Logitech, BC Assessment fine-tuning training," *Canadian HR Reporter,* Mar. 22, 2010, P. 8. Reprinted by permission of Canadian HR Reporter.

Case Study THE SCHOOL BOARD

For years, parents, students, and teachers complained that nobody listened, that decisions were made without participation, and that good ideas went unacknowledged. A needs analysis that involved a survey of teachers and students confirmed that these problems were widespread.

Carlos DaSilva, who was recently appointed trainer at the School Board and had a strong background in teaching, had to address the communications problem as his first assignment. He designed what he considered to be an excellent three-day communications program. He spent months on the design: finding videos, exercises, and games that taught active listening, upward communication, brainstorming, and other areas identified in the survey.

Carlos was excited to deliver his new training program and was sure that the participants would like it. On the first day, Carlos began with a brief introduction on the importance of communication, followed by a lecture on communication channels. Afterwards, he showed a video about manager–employee communication problems and how to improve communication. This was followed by a discussion of the key points in the video and what the trainees might do to improve their communication skills.

On day two of the training program, Carlos began with a lecture on brainstorming. He then had trainees participate in a group brainstorming exercise. Each group had to brainstorm as many ideas as possible for improving communication in the school board. Afterwards, the groups presented their ideas followed by a discussion of the most creative ways to improve communication with teachers, students, and parents.

On the third day of the training program, Carlos began with a lecture on active listening. Trainees then participated in an exercise in which they had to develop a message and then communicate it to the other trainees. At the end of the exercise, each trainee had to recall the message sent by the other trainees. This was then followed by a discussion of how to be a more effective listener and with tips on active listening.

Carlos ended the training program by having trainees participate in a communication game. First, he had trainees complete a self-assessment of how they send messages and the channels they use for communication. Then groups of trainees had to develop a message that they would communicate to the other groups. Each group had to determine the best way for their message to reach the other groups as accurately and quickly as possible. At the end of the game, each group read out the message they received from the other groups. Carlos then scored each group in terms of the accuracy of the message received by the other groups as well as how long it took for each group to receive the message.

The game was a lot of fun for the participants, who left the training program on a high. Carlos thanked them for attending the training program and encouraged them to apply what they learned in training when they returned to work. The trainees applauded Carlos and thanked him for providing such an enjoyable training experience.

Two months after the training program, Carlos was sitting at his desk, thinking about his meeting scheduled for 2 p.m. with the school board superintendent. He was looking forward to the meeting, knowing that he would be praised for the successful interactive communications program he had designed and delivered.

However, the meeting with the superintendent went poorly. Although some participants had loved the exercises and games in the communications course, most had not changed their work behaviour. Furthermore, a review of the situation showed that the old problems persisted and communication remained a serious problem at the school board. Carlos did not know what to say or what he should do.

Several days later, Carlos approached some of the participants who had attended the training program and asked them how things were going. One participant laughed at him and said, "Well that was a lot of fun, but training is training and work is work. Besides, nothing ever changes around here." Carlos asked her what she meant and she explained to him that supervisors don't get it and continued to call the shots. "The only thing they know about communication is downward," she said. "Maybe they should have attended your training program!"

Questions

1. What are some reasons that Carlos's training program did not transfer?
2. Discuss some of the barriers to transfer that might be operating at the School Board. Who is responsible for these barriers and when do they occur during the training process?
3. Describe some of the things that Carlos might have done before, during, and after the training program to improve the transfer of training. What could have the trainees and supervisors been asked to do before, during, and after training to improve transfer?
4. Discuss the training transfer climate and the transfer system at the School Board. How might they have contributed to the transfer problem?
5. What should Carlos do about the transfer problem at the School Board? What changes should he make next time he delivers a training program?

Flashback Questions

1. Describe the training methods that were used in the communications training program. Do you agree with the use of these methods, and do you think they are appropriate given the content and objectives of the training program?
2. What other training methods would you recommend for the communications training program? Refer to Table 6.1 and consider each of the off-the-job instructional methods. Explain why you would recommend some methods, and why they might be more effective than the methods that were used.

3. Describe how some of the principles, concepts, and theories of learning and motivation from Chapter 3 might be relevant for understanding why the communications training program was not more effective. What can Carlos learn from the material in Chapter 3 that would make the communications training program more effective if he were to redesign it?

4. If you were to redesign the communications training program, what changes would you make? Refer to the training design activities in Table 5.1 in Chapter 5 to answer this question.

REFERENCES

1. Jones, E., & Arnold, H. (2006, Spring). Hitting the jackpot in leadership development: A case study. *The Canadian Learning Journal, 10(1),* 9–11; (2007, May). *Launch pad to success program evaluation report.* Ontario Lottery and Gaming Corporation; Personal communication with Priscilla Fraser, Senior Manager Training & Development—Gaming, Ontario Lottery and Gaming Corporation.

2. Baldwin, T. T., & Ford, J. K. (1988). Transfer of training: A review and directions for future research. *Personnel Psychology, 41,* 63–105.

3. Broad, M. L., & Newstrom, J. W. (1992). *Transfer of training.* Reading, MA: Addison-Wesley.

4. Kozlowski, S. W. J., Brown, K. G., Weissbein, D. A., Cannon-Bowers, J. A., & Salas, E. (2000). A multilevel approach to training effectiveness: Enhancing horizontal and vertical transfer. In K. J. Klein & S. W. J. Kozlowski (Eds.), *Multilevel theory, research, and methods in organizations* (pp. 157–210). San Francisco: Jossey-Bass.

5. Phillips. J. J., & Phillips, P. P. (2002, September). 11 reasons why training and development fails . . . and what you can do about it. *Training, 39(9),* 78–85.

6. Lavis, C. (2011). *Learning & development outlook 2011: Are organizations ready for Learning 2.0?* Ottawa: The Conference Board of Canada.

7. Cromwell, S. E., & Kolb, J. A. (2004). An examination of work-environment support factors affecting transfer of supervisory skills training to the workplace. *Human Resource Development Quarterly, 15,* 449–471.

8. Tracey, J. B., Tannenbaum, S. I., Kavanagh, M. J. (1995). Applying trained skills on the job: The importance of the work environment. *Journal of Applied Psychology, 80,* 239–252.

9. Baldwin, T. T., & Ford, J. K. (1988).

10. Colquitt, J. A., Lepine, A., & Noe, R. A. (2000). Toward an integrative theory of training motivation: A meta-analytic path analysis of 20 years of research. *Journal of Applied Psychology, 85,* 678–707; Blum, B. D., Ford, J. K., Baldwin, T. T., & Huang, J. L. (2010). Transfer of training: A meta-analytic review. *Journal of Management, 36,* 1065–1105.

11. Burke, L. A., & Hutchins, H. M. (2007). Training transfer: An integrative literature review. *Human Resource Development Review, 6,* 263–296.

12. Bass, B. M., & Vaughn, J. A. (1969). *Training in industry: The management of learning.* Belmont, CA: Wadsworth.

13. Baldwin, T. T., & Ford, J. K. (1988).

14. Baldwin, T. T., & Ford, J. K. (1988).

15. Baldwin, T. T., & Ford, J. K. (1988).

16. Baldwin, T. T., & Ford, J. K. (1988).

17. Tannenbaum, S. I., & Yukl, G. (1992). Training and development in work organizations. *Annual Review of Psychology, 43,* 399–441.

18. Baldwin, T. T., & Ford, J. K. (1988); Tannenbaum, S. I., & Yukl, G. (1992); Blum, B. D., Ford, J. K., Baldwin, T. T., & Huang, J. L. (2010); Martin, H. J. (2010). Workplace climate and peer support as determinants of training transfer. *Human Resource Development Quarterly, 21,* 87–104.

19. Rouiller, J. Z., & Goldstein, I. L. (1993). The relationship between organizational transfer climate and positive transfer of training. *Human Resource Development Quarterly, 4,* 377–390; Blum, B. D., Ford, J. K., Baldwin, T. T., & Huang, J. L. (2010).

20. Tracey, J.B., Tannenbaum, S. I., & Kavanagh, M. J. (1995)

21. DeSimone, R. L., Werner, J. M., & Harris, D. M. (2002). *Human resource development.* Orlando, FL: Harcourt.

22. Baldwin, T. T., & Magjuka, R. J. (1991). Organizational training and signals of importance: Linking pretraining perceptions to intentions to transfer. *Human Resource Development Quarterly, 2,* 25–36.

23. Hicks, W. D., & Klimoski, R. J. (1987). Entry into training programs and its effects on training outcomes: A field experiment. *Academy of Management Journal, 30,* 542–552.

24. Broad, M. L., & Newstrom, J. W. (1992).

25. Baldwin, T. T., & Magjuka, R. J. (1991).

26. Tannenbaum, S. I., & Yukl, G. (1992).

27. Burke, L. A. (2001). Training transfer: Ensuring training gets used on the job. In L. A. Burke (Ed.), *High-impact training solutions: Top issues troubling trainers.* Westport, CT: Quorum Books.

28. Jones, E., & Arnold, H. (2006, Spring).

29. Clemmer, J. (1992, September 15). Why most training fails. *The Globe and Mail,* B26.

30. Jones, E., & Arnold, H. (2006, Spring).

31. Bass, B. M., & Vaughn, J. A. (1969).

32. McGehee, W., & Thayer, P. W. (1961). *Training in business and industry.* New York: Wiley.

33. Jones, E., & Arnold, H. (2006, Spring).

34. Leifer, M. S., & Newstrom, J. W. (1980, August). Solving the transfer of training problems. *Training and Development Journal,* 34–46.

35. Taylor, P. J., Russ-Eft, D. F., & Taylor, H. (2009). Transfer of management training from alternative perspectives. *Journal of Applied Psychology, 94,* 104–121.

36. Velada, R., Caetano, A., Michel, J. W., Lyons, B. D., & Kavanagh, M. J. (2007). The effects of training design, individual characteristics and work environment on transfer of training. *International Journal of Training and Development Journal, 11,* 282–294.

37. Broad, M. L., & Newstrom, J. W. (1992).

38. Clemmer, J. (1992, September 15).

39. Waxer, C. (2005, October 24). Bank of Montreal opens its checkbook in the name of employee development. *Workforce Management, 84(11),* 46–48;

40. Burke, L. A. (2001).

41. Baldwin, T. T., & Ford, J. K. (1988); Burke, L. A. (2001).

42. Tziner, A., Haccoun, R. R., & Kadish, A. (1991). Personal and situational characteristics influencing the effectiveness of transfer of training improvement strategies. *Journal of Occupational Psychology, 64(2),* 167–177.

43. Burke, L. A. (2001).

44. Burke, L. A. (2001).

45. Gist, M., Bavetta, A., & Stevens, C. (1990). Transfer training method: Its influence on skill generalization, skill repetition, and performance level. *Personnel Psychology, 43,* 501–523; Gist, M., Stevens, C., & Bavetta, A. (1991). Effects of self-efficacy and post-training intervention on the acquisition and maintenance of complex interpersonal skills. *Personnel Psychology, 44,* 837–861.

46. Locke, E. A., & Latham, G. P. (1990). *A theory of goal setting and task performance.* Englewood Cliffs, NJ: Prentice-Hall.

47. Richman-Hirsch, W. L. (2001). Posttraining interventions to enhance transfer: The moderating effects of work environments. *Human Resource Development Quarterly, 12,* 105–120; Wexley, K. N., & Nemeroff, W. F. (1975). Effectiveness of positive reinforcement and goal setting as methods of management development. *Journal of Applied Psychology, 60,* 446–450.

48. Richman-Hirsch, W. L. (2001).

49. Tews, M. J., & Tracey, J. B. (2008). An empirical examination of posttraining on-the-job supplements for enhancing the effectiveness of interpersonal skills training. *Personnel Psychology, 61,* 375–401.

50. Tews, M. J., & Tracey, J. B. (2008).

51. Holton, E. F. III. (2003). What's really wrong: Diagnosis for learning transfer system change. In E. F. Holton III & T. T. Baldwin (Eds.), *Improving learning transfer in organizations.* San Francisco, CA: John Wiley & Sons, Inc.

52. Holton, E. F. III. (2003).

53. Holton, E. F. III. (2003).

54. Holton, E. F. III., Chen, H., & Naquin, S. S. (2003). An examination of learning transfer system characteristics across organizational settings. *Human Resource Development Quarterly, 14,* 459–482.

55. Blum, B. D., Ford, J. K., Baldwin, T. T., & Huang, J. L. (2010).

Training Evaluation

CHAPTER LEARNING OUTCOMES

After reading this chapter, you should be able to:

- define training evaluation and the main reasons for conducting evaluations
- discuss the barriers to evaluation and the factors that affect whether or not an evaluation is conducted
- describe the different types of evaluations
- describe the models of training evaluation and the relationships among them
- describe the main variables to measure in a training evaluation and how they are measured
- discuss the different types of designs for training evaluation as well as their requirements, limits, and when they should be used

BELL CANADA

Years ago, when Bell Canada installed a new telephone system for its business clients, it also sent out service advisers whose task it was to train the employees to use the new system. These training sessions consisted of "show-and-tell" activities in which the instructors demonstrated the use of the telephone. Simple as the training was, it was expensive, costing millions of dollars annually. With the introduction of electronic equipment, the functionality of the telephone systems—and complexity for the users—increased exponentially.

Initially, the company attempted to use its traditional training approach with purchasers of the electronic systems. However, a training evaluation was conducted and it showed that following the training experience, customer knowledge of the operation of the electronic telephones was quite low. Training was not effective.

A number of attempts were then made to improve the situation. Different types of training, presented by either Bell Canada or user personnel, were tried and evaluated. None made any significant difference in terms of training effectiveness.

However, these training evaluation studies did detect an important fact. No matter how training was conducted, the users' knowledge of a limited number of functions—those they used a lot—increased after training, indicating that practice seemed to have a significant effect on learning.

This suggested that providing end users with an instructional aid might help them gain greater benefit from the electronic system. To that end, a special instruction booklet was carefully prepared and trainees were provided with a brief instructional session teaching the users how to use the instruction booklet. The evaluation of this approach showed, empirically, that the use of the instruction booklet resulted in greater user mastery than the formal training course.

Thus, the training evaluations conducted throughout this process demonstrated a) that the traditional training method was ineffective, b) that changing the instructors had no effect, but c) that the use of a well-developed instruction booklet had greater effect.

This demonstrates the two main objectives of training evaluation: to assess the effectiveness of training and, equally important, to identify ways of enhancing that effectiveness. At Bell, the traditional program was discontinued and replaced with an inexpensive booklet that was both more effective and considerably cheaper.

Training programs are designed to have an effect on learning and behaviour. However, as the Bell Canada story demonstrates, this is not always the case. Fortunately, in that case, the organization launched an evaluation program that involved several studies, the results of which served not only to assess the effectiveness of the existing training but also to identify and test different strategies for improving the situation.

In this chapter, you will learn several training evaluation models, the many types of evaluations, the variables to measure and how to do so, as well as the strengths and weaknesses of different data collection designs used in the conduct of evaluations.

WHAT IS TRAINING EVALUATION?

Organizational training and development is intended to improve technical competencies (e.g., learning new software), to modify attitudes (e.g., preparing a manager for an international assignment), and/or to modify behaviours (e.g., better communication skills). Organizations invest in this organizational function because it is expected that training makes a positive contribution to them and to their employees.

Training evaluation is concerned with whether or not these expected outcomes materialize as a result of training. They are designed to assist decision making: Should the organization cancel or continue a training program? Should it be modified? How?

Training evaluation is a process designed to assess the value—the worthiness—of training programs to employees and to organizations. Training evaluation assesses this value by analyzing data collected from trainees, supervisors, or others familiar with the trainees and with the job context. Using a variety of techniques, objective and subjective information is gathered before, during, and after training to provide the data required to estimate the value of a training program.

Training evaluation
A process to assess the value—the worthiness—of training programs to employees and to organizations

Training evaluation is not a single procedure. Rather, it is a continuum of techniques, methods, and measures. At one end of the continuum are simple evaluations that focus on trainee satisfaction: Trainees indicate on a brief questionnaire if they liked the course. Certainly simple and easy to implement, they regrettably yield minimal information.

At the other end of the training evaluation continuum lie more elaborate procedures and more complete questionnaires and interviews that provide managers with more information of a richer quality about the value of a training program. These evaluations may assess job performance improvements and even isolate the unique role that training played in it. Others assess the psychological states of trainees immediately after training: Have they learned the skills? Are they motivated to apply them? Are they confident they can? Will the work environment help or hinder them? The more sophisticated the evaluations, the better the information they provide, the surer the conclusions and the greater the confidence with which they can be stated.

However, more sophisticated evaluation procedures are more costly and more complex and difficult to implement. Conducting elaborate evaluations may entail disruptions to the training program and/or to the job. Specialized consultants may be required in some cases.

But these factors are not required in every case. At times a simple and cheap evaluation procedure will do while a more complex and sophisticated approach might be overkill.[1] In other cases the reverse is true. In the end, training evaluation choices are a trade-off, balancing between quality and complexity/costs, between the informational needs of decision makers and the difficulty and resources required to obtain that information.

WHY CONDUCT TRAINING EVALUATIONS?

Organizations invest in the training of employees and managers as it is a necessity for competitiveness in the current global environment. With chronic understaffing (one result of cost-cutting layoffs), the amount of time available for training has become smaller and must be used more wisely. In this context, management has a stake in ensuring that the resources invested in training bear fruit. Training evaluation is therefore of value to:

- Help fulfill the managerial responsibility to improve training.

- Assist managers in identifying the training programs most useful to employees and to assist management in the determination of who should be trained.

- Determine the cost benefits of a program and to help ascertain which program or training technique is most cost-effective (see Chapter 12).

- Determine whether the training program has achieved the expected results or solved the problem for which training was the anticipated solution.

- Diagnose the strengths and weaknesses of a program and pinpoint needed improvements.

- Use the evaluation information to justify and reinforce, if merited, the value and credibility of the training function to the organization.

Do Organizations Conduct Training Evaluations?

By the year 2000 most organizations in North America were conducting some evaluation of most of the training programs offered to their employees.[2] However, there has been a gradual decline in the evaluation activities of organizations. The survey of the American Society for Training and Development (ASTD) and the latest Conference Board of Canada survey of organizations confirm this result.[3] In 2002, 89 percent of Canadian organizations assessed training in some manner, but by 2010 fewer than 50 percent still did. This significant decline occurred even though the actual proportion of staff time invested in evaluation remained steady (hovering between 4 percent and 10 percent). Notwithstanding the fact that the same evaluation time is spent on fewer courses, the level of sophistication of the evaluations has not shown demonstrable growth. Most evaluations are reaction based.

As depicted in Figure 11.1, although many organizations have abandoned evaluation, almost half have not. Most (92 percent) of these organizations gauge training success by soliciting the trainees' opinions (their "reactions"), and they do this for most (80 percent) of the courses held. Figure 11.1 also shows the rarity of organizations that measure learning, behaviour, or job performance improvements to evaluate training success. Such evaluations are more useful, but they are more complex. Longitudinal data collected by the Conference Board indicates little change to these percentages since the survey began a decade ago: the percentage of organizations that evaluate reactions has remained the same.

The new finding, however, is the confirmation that organizations are not simply abandoning reaction measures: they are abandoning evaluation altogether! Perhaps dissatisfied with reaction-based evaluations, and unable or willing to consider the use of better approaches, many organizations have chosen to forgo training evaluation.

FIGURE 11.1

The Percentage of Organisations that Evaluate Training and the Percentage of Courses Evaluated at various Evaluation Levels

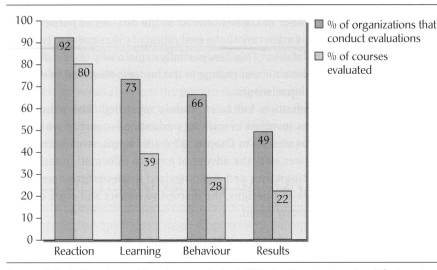

Source: C. Lavis, *Learning and Development Outlook 2011: Are Organizations Ready for Learning 2.0?* The Conference Board of Canada, 2011.

BARRIERS TO TRAINING EVALUATION

Studies of training professionals showed that some employers do not conduct training evaluations because they are perceived to be too complicated to implement, too time consuming, and/or too expensive.[4] Indeed, this may explain why companies that conduct evaluation choose the simplest of procedures (reaction-based evaluations). In some cases, training managers resist evaluation because of the difficulty of isolating from other variables the unique impact that training has on employee effectiveness. In yet other cases, training managers do not conduct evaluations because top management does not demand them, while others do not because they may not wish to know. Thus, barriers to training evaluation fall into two categories: pragmatic and political.

Pragmatic Barriers to Training Evaluation

Increasingly, training departments, as with all other departments, are expected to demonstrate their usefulness, their contribution to job performance improvements, and ultimately to the company's bottom line. Based on the ASTD and The Conference Board of Canada reports, the training departments in most companies are finding it a challenge to fulfill this obligation. Collecting training success data that addresses management's needs requires more complex evaluation procedures.

Fundamentally, evaluation requires that perceptual and/or objective information furnished by trainees, their supervisors, and even others—such as peers, subordinates, and/or clients—be gathered before, during, and/or after the training session. These data gathering and analytical efforts require extensive collaboration from the trainees, their supervisors, and so on, which is disruptive and understandably difficult to obtain.

2. **The purpose of the evaluation:** Evaluations also differ with respect to their purposes. Worthen and Sanders distinguished between *formative evaluation* and *summative evaluation*.[12]

Formative evaluations

Provide data about various aspects of a training program

a. **Formative evaluations** are designed to help evaluators assess the value of the training materials and processes with the key goal of identifying improvements to the instructional experience (the clarity, complexity, and relevance of the training contents, how they are presented, and the training context). Hence, formative evaluation provides data that are of special interest to training designers and instructors.

Summative evaluations

Provide data about the worthiness or effectiveness of a training program

b. **Summative evaluations** are designed to provide data about a training program's worthiness or effectiveness: Has the training program resulted in payoffs for the organization? Cost–benefit analyses (see Chapter 12) are usually summative. Economic indices are often an integral and important part of these types of evaluations; consequently, organizational managers show great interest in these results.

Descriptive evaluations

Provide information that describes the trainee once he or she has completed a training program

Causal evaluations

Provide information to determine whether training caused the post-training behaviours

A further distinction can be made between *descriptive* and *causal evaluations*. **Descriptive evaluations** provide information describing trainees once they have completed the program. What has the trainee learned in training? Is the trainee more confident about using the skill? Is it used on the job? Most evaluation designs have descriptive components. **Causal evaluations** are used to determine whether the training caused the post-training behaviours. Was the performance improvement caused by the training program? Causal evaluations require more sophisticated experimental and statistical procedures.

MODELS OF TRAINING EVALUATION

Models of training evaluation specify the information (the variables) that is to be measured in training evaluations and their interrelationships. The dominant training evaluation model is Donald Kirkpatrick's hierarchical model.[13] However, research and practical experience has indicated that Kirkpatrick's model can be improved. The COMA model and the Decision-Based Evaluation model are two recent efforts in that direction; both are discussed below.[14]

Kirkpatrick's Hierarchical Model: The Four Levels of Training Evaluation

Kirkpatrick's hierarchical model is the oldest, best known, and most frequently used training evaluation model. For example the Conference Board of Canada data summarized in Table 11.1 are organized using that model. The model identifies four levels of training evaluation criteria. According to this model, a training program is "effective" when:

L1. Trainees report positive reactions to a training program (Level 1 = reactions).
L2. Trainees learn the training material (Level 2 = learning).
L3. Trainees apply what they learn in training on the job (Level 3 = behaviours).
L4. Training has a positive effect on organizational outcomes (Level 4 = results).

TABLE 11.1

The Main Variables Measured in Training Evaluation

Variable	Definition	How Measured
Reactions	Trainee perceptions of the program and/or specific aspects of the course.	Questionnaires, focus groups, interviews.
Learning	Trainee acquisition of the program material. Declarative learning is knowing the information. Procedural knowledge is being able to translate that knowledge into a behavioural sequence.	Multiple choice or True-False tests (declarative); situational and mastery tests (procedural).
Behaviour	On-the-job behaviour display, objective performance measures.	Self-reports, supervisory reports, direct and indirect observations, production records.
Motivation	Trainee desire to learn and/or transfer skills.	Questionnaires.
Self-efficacy	Trainee confidence in learning and/or behaviour display on the job.	Questionnaires.
Perceived and/or anticipated support	The assistance trainees obtain and/or the assistance trainees expect.	Questionnaires.
Organizational perceptions	How trainees perceive the organization's culture and climate for learning and transfer.	Standardized questionnaires.
Organizational results	The impact of training on organizational outcomes.	Organizational records.

In a more recent articulation, an additional level has been added to the Kirkpatrick model. Level 5 refers to return on investment (ROI), which is designed to assess the financial benefit of training to the organization. However, for simplicity's sake we continue this description using the original four-level version of the model proposed by Kirkpatrick (ROI and the financial benefit of training programs is discussed in Chapter 12).

The model states that the four levels are arranged in a hierarchy, such that each succeeding level provides more important (though more difficult to obtain) information than the previous one. The model also assumes that all levels are positively related to one another, each level having a causal effect on the next level. Hence, positive trainee reactions (L1) cause trainees to learn more (L2), which in turn leads to the behavioural display of the new skill at work (L3), which in turn impacts on organizational effectiveness (L4)—the ultimate reason for conducting training in organizations. Thus, a complete training evaluation, according to Kirkpatrick, would assess all four levels.

Critique of Kirkpatrick's Model

Kirkpatrick's model makes good sense to managers and trainers alike as it is a clear and simple systematic framework for assessing training. The contribution the model has made to training evaluation cannot be underestimated. It has greatly demystified training evaluation and popularized its routine use. It is the main model used by the many organizations that evaluate training. The extensive application of the model has permitted much research. As a result, we now know considerably more about the model than was the case when it was introduced more than 50 years ago. Whereas there is general agreement that the four levels are indeed important outcomes to be assessed, several aspects of the model including its completeness have been questioned.

Research studies, especially those conducted by Elwood Holton (who concludes that Kirkpatrick's is *not* a model!) and by George Alliger and his colleagues have thrown doubt on the validity of the hierarchical aspect of the model.[15] The model would be valid if a positive correlation exists among the four levels. Hence, enjoyment (L1) would be correlated with learning (L2), and learning correlated with transfer (L3), and so on. In fact, that is not the case. The correlations among the levels are small or non-existent. Most students can easily explain this result: you may have learned little from an otherwise pleasant course or learned a great deal from a hated one (as exemplified by biochemistry for one of the authors!). As a further example, most people know that smoking is not healthy, yet many still do—knowledge and behaviours are not synonymous. In short, the hierarchical aspect of the Kirkpatrick model lacks empirical support.

Relying on the Kirkpatrick model can prove a handicap in formative evaluations where the goal is to use the results to improve training effectiveness. When "something goes wrong" with a training program (e.g., low transfer), this model cannot diagnose the specific nature of the problem or what to do about it. For example, as the relationship between learning and behaviour is small, improving L1 (reactions) or L2 (learning) is unlikely to improve transfer levels. As the model collects no other information (such as trainee motivation, self-efficacy, or conditions of the organization) the causes for that ineffectiveness cannot be identified. Yet that is the very information required. The Kirkpatrick model is not well suited to formative evaluation.

This limit to the model does not affect the effectiveness of the Kirkpatrick model for conducting summative evaluations, where global payoff is the main interest. The model remains helpful because no matter the relationships among the levels, there is intrinsic value in assessing whether the training program leads to learning (L2), results in a payoff to the organization (L4), or is boring (L1).

The model has also been criticized for its lack of precision in the outcomes. For example, it fails to specify what is meant by "L2-learning" (declarative? procedural? see Chapter 3), or by "behaviours": Are we to measure the specific rote reproduction of a specific learned task, or do we measure the degree of application of the new skill to several job aspects? Moreover, does that behaviour level refer to the actual demonstration of the learned skill or does it refer to noticeable job performance improvements?

But perhaps the most important critique has been that Kirkpatrick requires *all* training evaluations to rely on the same variables and outcome measures. The current view is that the type of evaluation, as well as the measures and procedures, should be selected as a function of the organizational situation and the purposes of the evaluation. One model does not fit all in training evaluation situations.

Overall, then, the Kirkpatrick model suffers from a number of weaknesses. To that end, two alternative models have been introduced: COMA and DBE.

COMA Model

The **COMA** model has been proposed as a mechanism for enhancing the usefulness of training evaluation questionnaires by identifying and measuring those variables that research has shown to be important for the transfer of training.[16] Instead of relying exclusively on reaction and declarative learning measures, COMA suggests the measurement of variables that fall into four categories: cognitive, organizational environment, motivational, and attitudinal variables (spelling the acronym COMA). These can all be measured by questionnaires administered before and immediately after the training session.

COMA

A training evaluation model that involves the measurement of Cognitive, Organizational, Motivational, and Attitudinal variables

- *Cognitive* variables refer to the level of learning that the trainee has gained from a training program. Both declarative and procedural learning might be measured, but the latter is more important because it is more strongly related to transfer than the former.

- *Organizational* environment refers to a cluster of variables that are generated by the work environment and that impact transfer of training. This includes the learning culture, the opportunity to practise, and the degree of support that is expected as well as the level actually provided to trainees once they return to the job.

- *Motivation* refers to the desire to learn and transfer on the job what was presented in training. As indicated in Chapter 10, motivation has been shown to be a powerful and persistent influence on the transfer of training. COMA suggests that training motivation (measured at the onset of the program) and motivation to transfer (measured immediately after) both be measured.

- *Attitudes* refer to individuals' feelings and thinking processes. Chief among these beliefs are self-efficacy, perceptions of control, and expectations about self and the environment.

According to the COMA model, training evaluation should assess the degree to which trainees have mastered the skills ("**C**"); accurately perceive the degree to which the organizational environment (including peers and supervisors) will support and help them apply the skills ("**O**"); are motivated to learn and to apply the skills on the job ("**M**"); and have developed attitudes and beliefs that allow them to feel capable of applying their newly acquired skills on the job ("**A**").

At the conclusion of training, the trainees answer questionnaires that assess the COMA components. The specific questions are custom-fitted as they list the trained skills. The participants indicate whether they know (C), are motivated to (M), and are confident (A) that they can display the learned skills while being in a work environment that is supportive of their efforts to do so (O). When scores on the COMA variables are positive, the chances of transfer are greater. But the reverse is also true: when scores are lower on one or more COMA dimensions, transfer is likely to be weaker. An analysis of each of the COMA dimensions might well identify the specific element (C, O, M, or A) that is problematic, pinpointing where to improve the training experience.

COMA improves upon the Kirkpatrick model in four ways:

- It transforms the typical reaction questionnaires by incorporating a greater number of measures (the COMA variables).

- It is especially useful for formative evaluations.

- The measures chosen for inclusion in the evaluation *are* those known to be causally related to training success (see Chapter 10, Transfer of Training).

- It defines these new variables with greater precision.

As the COMA model is still relatively new, it is too early to draw conclusions as to its value. Further, COMA's focus is only limited to an analysis of the factors that impact on transfer. Moreover, COMA is not well suited for summative evaluation purposes.

Kirkpatrick may be more suited to summative evaluations, while COMA is better for formative ones. Decision-Based Evaluation, the third evaluation model to be discussed, is an attempt for more versatility. It provides a template to guide the evaluator through a number of choices.

Decision-Based Evaluation Model

Decision-Based Evaluation (DBE) is a model developed by Kurt Kraiger. As with the COMA model, Decision-Based Evaluation specifies the categories of variables to be measured. However, it goes further. DBE invites evaluators to custom fit their evaluations to the requirements of the situation. Hence, assessors need to identify the *target* of the evaluation (what do we wish to find out from the evaluation?); identifies its *focus* (what are the variables we will measure?); and suggests the *methods* that may be appropriate for conducting the evaluation.

The model specifies three potential "targets" for the evaluation: 1. trainee change, 2. organizational payoff, and 3. program improvement. Once that is decided, the evaluator specifies the "focus" of the change, as there are many changes that can be measured. Are we interested in assessing the level of trainee changes with respect to learning behaviours, or to the psychological states (such as motivation and self-efficacy)? Each evaluation study may include one or more foci. Once the focus or foci are selected, the model suggests the appropriate data collection method (e.g., surveys, job sample information, objective data, questionnaires, interviews, etc.).

Decision-Based Evaluation may well be a marked improvement, for different reasons, over both Kirkpatrick's model and the COMA model. Unlike Kirkpatrick's model or COMA, it allows for different variables (focus) to be measured depending on the goals (target) of the evaluation. In contrast to COMA and Kirkpatrick, DBE is more flexible, being useful for both formative and summative evaluations.

Most importantly, DBE does not advocate a *single best way* for training evaluation, nor does it compel the measurement of a single set of variables for all evaluations. DBE is the only training evaluation model that clearly specifies that evaluations must always be guided by key questions, chief amongst which are What do we choose to evaluate, and How can we do so? However, as with COMA, this model is recent and still needs to be tested more fully.

The Kirkpatrick, COMA, and DBE models of training evaluation all require that for each training course people with somewhat specialized skills develop the evaluation measures and questionnaires, and analyze and interpret the data.

Decision-Based Evaluation (DBE)

A training evaluation model that specifies the target, focus, and methods of evaluation

Training Today 11.2

The Learning Transfer System Inventory (LTSI)

The Holton-Bates approach is the Learning Transfer System Inventory (LTSI), which was described in Chapter 10. It is a questionnaire containing 89 questions that assess the 16 variables described in Chapter 10. These variables include all of the COMA dimensions plus additional ones such as learner readiness (e.g., "I knew what to expect from the training before it began"), resistance/openness to change (e.g., "People in my group are open to changing the way they do things"), and opportunity to use learning (e.g., "The resources I need to use what I learned will be available to me after training"). Trainees answer the 89 questions using a five-point scale (strongly agree to strongly disagree). The LTSI is available in both English and French (advantageous for use in organizations that operate in different cultural milieu). Importantly, the LTSI is also a research instrument that is being constantly refined with questions added or withdrawn depending on research results.

There are, however, some limitations with LTSI. It is a proprietary instrument, and organizations that wish to use it must obtain the authors' permission, must administer all 89 questions, and are required to provide the data collected to the authors. Organizations that do not wish to release their training evaluation data (e.g., for confidentiality or legal reasons), that believe the questionnaire taps dimensions of no relevance to their assessment, and/or that are unable to administer a lengthy questionnaire may judge this approach less applicable.

Source: C. Devos, X. Dumay, M. Bonami, R. Bates, & E. Holton III, "The Learning Transfer System Inventory (LTSI) translated into French: internal structure and predictive validity," *International Journal of Training and Development*, Vol. 11, Pp. 181–199, 2007.

In some organizations such resources are not always available. To help alleviate this constraint on training evaluation, Elwood Holton and his colleagues have proposed a more generic approach, described in Training Today 11.2, "The Learning Transfer System Inventory (LTSI)."[17]

TRAINING EVALUATION VARIABLES

Training evaluation requires the measurement of variables, many of which are specified in the training evaluation models. Table 11.1 provides a more complete list of the main variables that can be measured in training evaluation, while Table 11.2 shows sample questions and formats for measuring each type of variable.

TABLE 11.2

Examples of Questions and Formats Used in Training Evaluations

Variable	Example of Question	Example of Answer Format
Reactions	"How much of the course content can be applied in your job?" (utility reaction measure)	1 = None, 2 = Little, 3 = Some, 4 = Much, 5 = All
	"How satisfied were you with the content of the program?" (affective reaction measure)	1 = Not at all satisfied, 2 = Not satisfied, 3 = Somewhat satisfied, 4 = Satisfied, 5 = Very satisfied

Declarative learning	Declarative: True or False: The earth is square.	Declarative True ___ False ___
	Multiple choice: What statement best describes Earth?	Multiple choice: round, square, triangular, flat
Procedural learning	Procedural Mastery: You need to write a letter using a computer. From the list below pick the four steps required to do so and list them in the order with which they should be performed.	Procedural Step Required Order Turn computer on Yes 1 Set the margins Yes 4 Select "new document" Yes 3 Open the word processor Yes 2 Test the hard drive No —
Behaviour	Self-report: How many "cold calls" have you made in the last week? Observation: By others including the supervisor and the analyst. May also include subordinates or customers.	Open-ended frequency scale (number of times) or rating scale: 1 = Many, 2 = Some, 3 = A Few, 4 = None
Motivation	How important is it to reduce accidents at work?	1 = Very important, 2 = Important, 3 = Neither important nor unimportant, 4 = Somewhat unimportant, 5 = Very unimportant
	The consequences to you of applying the behaviour at work?	Will make my job: 1 = much harder, 2 = somewhat harder, 3 = no effect, 4 = somewhat easier, 5 = much easier

	How likely is it that if you do apply the trained behaviours there will be fewer accidents?	1 = Extremely likely, 2 = Somewhat likely, 3 = Neither likely nor unlikely, 4 = Unlikely, 5 = Extremely unlikely
	The product of the three sets of questions produces the motivator scores.	
Self-efficacy	How confident are you that you can explain the new policy to your subordinates?	1 = Not at all confident, 2, 3, 4, to 5 = Very confident
Perceived and/ or anticipated support	I expect that my supervisor will help and support me in my attempts to apply my new skills on the job.	1 = Completely disagree, 2, 3, 4, to 5 = Completely agree
Organizational perceptions	Supervisors give recognition and credit to those who apply new knowledge and skills to their work.	Standardized questionnaires
Organizational results	How much has quality improved as a result of the training program?	Number of units rejected per day; number of items returned per month; number of customer complaints per week

Reactions

Trainee opinions and attitudes about a training program—so-called *reaction measures*—are the most common variables measured in evaluation studies. Typically measured by questionnaires, trainees answer questions using rating scales immediately following training. Reaction measures are easy to administer, collect, and analyze, and the questions may focus on the trainees' overall reactions to a training program (e.g., Overall, how satisfied were you with the training program?) and/or on specific elements of a program (e.g., To what extent were you satisfied with the instructor?).

In a major study involving thousands of responses to reaction questionnaires, Morgan and Casper identified six dimensions that underlie reaction measures: satisfaction with the instructor, the training process, the materials, the course structure, the assessment process, and the perceived usefulness (utility) of the training.[18]

Reaction measures can be quite different, but two types have received the most attention: affective and utility reaction measures. **Affective reactions** assess trainees' *likes and dislikes* of a training program. **Utility reactions** refer to the perceived *usefulness* of a training program.

Whereas trainers are interested in the likes and dislikes of trainees, research has shown that such affective reaction measures bear little relationship to other important training outcomes including learning and behaviour. On the other hand, *utility* reaction measures demonstrate some relationship to learning and behaviour.[19] Hence, collecting utility reactions is important because they indicate to some degree whether transfer is likely or unlikely. Affective reaction measures do not.

Affective reactions

Reaction measures that assess trainees' *likes and dislikes* of a training program

Utility reactions

Reaction measures that assess the perceived *usefulness* of a training program

A recent study provides data that contest, to some degree, the previously thought advantage of utility measures over reaction ones: in this case there does not seem to be much proof that utility measures are superior to affective reactions in predicting learning outcomes.[20] Most interestingly, that same study found a significant correlation between reactions and outcomes for courses that utilize a high level of technology as opposed to those that rely on less technology. That result may serve as a warning for internet-delivered courses. It may be especially important that they stimulate trainee interest: trainees can easily lose their concentration and/or withdraw from a boring course.

There are many ways to gather reaction measures. Open-ended discussions with trainees using focus groups or interviews gather data that are expressed more freely. This technique can provide more nuanced and rich data. However, the success of this technique depends in part on the openness and verbal abilities of participants, but it also depends to a large degree on the skills and objectivity of the interviewer. If interviewer biases slant or taint the discussion, the results may be quite worthless. For this reason, it is a usual practice that such focus groups are not led by the course designer or instructor.

The most common method for collecting reaction measures is a post-training questionnaire. It is efficient, time/cost-effective, and can be used repeatedly. Because they can be quite generic, the same reaction measures can be used for most or even all of the courses given by the company. This can allow organizations to compare the reactions of people across different courses.

As illustrated in Table 11.3, reaction questions may be formatted in any number of different ways: 1. in the form of a statement (e.g., "The course materials captured my interest"), for which the trainee indicates his/her degree of agreement (from strongly agree to strongly disagree); or 2. in the form of direct questions (e.g., "How effective was the instructor?"), to which the trainee chooses a response from a linear rating scale (from very effective to

---

TABLE 11.3

Reactions Rating Form

Course or Session: ___
Instructor: ___

Content:
_____

Please answer the following questions using the scale below:
1. strongly disagree 2. disagree 3. neither disagree nor agree 4. agree 5. strongly agree
___ The material presented will be useful to me on the job.
___ The level of information was too advanced for my work.
___ The level of information presented was too elementary for me.
___ The information was presented in manageable chunks.
___ Theories and concepts were linked to work activities.
___ The course material was up-to-date and reliable.

Instructor:

Please rate the instructor's performance along the following dimensions:

___ Needs improvement.

___ Just right, or competent, effective.

___ Superior or very effective performance.

The instructor:

___ Described the objectives of the session.

___ Had a plan for the session.

___ Followed the plan.

___ Determined trainees' current knowledge.

___ Explained new terms.

___ Used work and applied examples.

___ Provided opportunities for questions.

___ Was enthusiastic about the topic.

___ Presented material clearly.

___ Effectively summarized the material.

___ Varied the learning activities.

___ Showed a personal interest in class progress.

___ Demonstrated a desire for trainees to learn.

Perceived Impact:

___ I gained significant new knowledge.

___ I developed skills in the area.

___ I was given tools for attacking problems.

___ My on-the-job performance will improve.

Please indicate what you will do differently on the job as a result of this course.

Overall Rating:

Taking into account all aspects of the course, how would you rate it?

___ Excellent ___ Very Good ___ Good ___ Fair ___ Poor

Would you take another course from this instructor? ___ Yes ___ No

Would you recommend this course to your colleagues? ___ Yes ___ No

very ineffective). Typically, the questions are listed on one side of the page and a rating scale is placed next to each question. Most rating scales have between four and seven response choices, though more or fewer points can be used.

No matter their relationship to other training outcomes, immediate post-training questionnaire measures remain popular because: 1. they are easy to collect and analyze and are easily understood by managers and employees alike; 2. they provide trainers with immediate feedback on their course; 3. trainees who have had a chance to comment on a program and make suggestions for improvements might be more motivated to transfer their learning than others who leave a program without providing input; and 4. they are an easy and convenient mechanism for measuring levels 1 and 2 of the Kirkpatrick model, as well as the dimensions of the LTSI and COMA models.

Learning

Make the Connection

Although there are many types of learning outcomes that can be measured (Jonassen and Tessmer identify more than 10), most training evaluations measure "declarative" learning, which was described as a learning outcome in Chapter 3.[21] In rare cases, some evaluators also assess "procedural" learning. The contents of both the declarative and procedural learning measures are selected from the training content.

Declarative learning is by far the most frequently assessed learning measure. As described in Chapter 3, it refers to the acquisition of facts and information. **Procedural learning** involves the organization of facts and information into a smooth behavioural sequence. Research has shown that declarative learning has only a minor effect on behaviours. Procedural learning, however, is more strongly related to a number of training outcomes including transfer of training.

Declarative learning is usually assessed with multiple choice or true-false type questions. Students familiar with college or university exams know about these tests of learning. Table 11.4 presents an array of these options. The test items listed in Part A are termed "objectively scored" tests because there is only one correct answer possible. Part B gives some examples of "subjectively scored" test items. Test items that are considered subjective are essay questions, oral

Declarative learning

Refers to the acquisition of facts and information and is by far the most frequently assessed learning measure

Procedural learning

Refers to the organization of facts and information into a smooth behavioural sequence

---

TABLE 11.4

Declarative Learning Test Formats

Part A: Objectively Scored Tests

True or False

1. A test is valid if a person receives approximately the same result or score at two different testing times. True ___ False ___

Multiple Choice

2. The affective domain of learning refers to
   ___ skills
   ___ attitudes
   ___ knowledge
   ___ all of the above
   ___ 2 and 3

Matching

3. For each of the governments listed on the left, select the appropriate responsibility for training and place its letter next to the term.

___ 1. federal	a. displaced workers
___ 2. provincial	b. language training
___ 3. municipal	c. student summer work

Short Answer

4. Kirkpatrick identified four levels of measurement. These are:

    ____

    ____

    ____

    ____

Part B: Subjectively Scored Tests

Essay

5. Describe the similarities among Kirkpatrick, COMA, and DBE.

Oral

6. The measurement of training has many potential benefits. Identify these benefits. Discuss the reasons why, given these advantages of measurement, most trainers do not evaluate training.

Observation Checklist

7. The customer-service representative:

    ____ greeted the customer

    ____ approached the customer

    ____ offered to help

Rating Scale

8. Indicate the degree to which you agree or disagree with the statements below:

    Scale: 1 = strongly disagree, 2 = disagree, 3 = agree, 4 = strongly agree

    During a selection interview, the interviewer:

    used behavioural-based questions 1 2 3 4

    looked for contrary evidence 1 2 3 4

    used probing questions 1 2 3 4

Diaries, Anecdotal Records, Journals

9. In your journal, write about your experiences working with someone from a different culture. Record the date, time, and reason for the interaction. Describe how you felt and what you learned.

interviews, journals, and diaries. Here, several answers might be acceptable, and markers have some latitude in their interpretation of the correctness of the answer, which potentially exposes that judgment to "subjective" biases.

Procedural learning, however, is rarely measured because the development of such measures is much more complex. Desjardins developed a procedural learning measure for a course training police officers into the do's and don'ts when tasked to "protect a crime scene."[22] She interviewed task experts who demonstrated the proper actions and proper sequence of behaviours required and then summarized these steps, added some unnecessary and incorrect steps, and shuffled the order of the steps. Trainees had to distinguish between the required and erroneous steps and reposition them into the correct order. Completing this task successfully requires procedural understanding of the training content.

Cheri Ostroff used another approach to develop a measure of procedural learning.[23] Education managers were instructed on how to interact with parents more effectively in tense situations. Different anecdotes drawn from real experience were presented to trainees along with four different ways of handling each situation. The four options were carefully constructed. Trainees who had acquired a limited comprehension of the principles of conflict management would tend to select one option, while those with sophisticated comprehension levels would select another. The intermediate choices reflected comprehension levels between these extremes.

Procedural learning measures can also involve simulations conducted in realistic situations. For example, a pilot could be tested in a virtual-reality airplane. The skills of a drug counsellor could be tested using actors as drug addicts. A test could be conducted as a role play (for negotiation skills) or a practice session (for tennis certification). These tests are usually called performance tests or work sample tests.

Learning measures also vary in terms of when they are administered. For example, some researchers have divided learning measures into three subcategories: 1. immediate post-training knowledge, which measures trainee learning immediately after a training program; 2. knowledge retention, which measures trainee learning sometime after a training program; and 3. behaviour or skill demonstration, which also are indicators of procedural knowledge acquisition.

Learning measures are useful for a number of reasons besides determining whether trainees have learned the training material. Research has shown that participants anticipating a post-training test were more motivated to learn the material.[24] For trainees at General Dynamics, this was important because they were not allowed access to the manufacturing resource planning software until they had passed a competency test. What's more, trainers became extremely motivated because the trainees had to learn and could not be brushed off by hinting that they could "always learn misunderstood material back on the job."

The information that learning tests provide to trainers is invaluable. In cases of accidents and litigation, the employer can prove that the employee was trained to the necessary levels. Furthermore, if trainees consistently score low on some aspect of the course, the trainer is alerted to the fact that this component needs to be revised. More information may be required or exercises might have to be added to ensure that learning does occur. However, the trainer cannot assume that scoring well on tests necessarily means changed and improved job performance. It is on the job that the real measurement of the payoff of training begins.

Behaviour

Make the
Connection

Behaviour refers to the display of the newly learned skills or competencies on the job. This is also what we have referred to in Chapter 10 as "transfer of training" and is arguably the most important of all training effectiveness criteria.[25] The behaviours assessed should be those identified by the training objectives (see Chapter 5). Behaviours can be measured using three basic approaches:

a. *Self-reports*: The trainee indicates if and/or how often he/she has used the newly trained behaviours on the job. Use of self-reports is dominant in the field because they are the easiest and most practical measure to collect.

b. *Observations*: Others observe and record whether and/or how often the trainee has used the newly trained behaviours on the job. Typically it is supervisors who provide these observations, but depending on the opportunity to observe, the trained person, trainers, subordinates, or even clients can provide it.

c. *Production indicators*: The trainee's objective output is assessed through productivity records, such as sales or absenteeism.

Self-reports remain the most frequently used measures of behaviour.[26] However, the accuracy of self-report measures can be problematic. How do we know that people are accurately remembering and reporting their own behaviours? It is generally agreed that self-reports tend to be *inaccurate,* although they might yet be *valid*. The distinction between accuracy and validity is important. Studies comparing self-reports of absenteeism with company records of absence show that, in general, people tend to report fewer absences than were actually taken (low accuracy). However, people who are more absent tend to self-report more absences than those who have fewer absences (validity). Hence, although self-reports are unable to measure transfer in absolute terms, they are able to reveal trends.

Observations by others (mainly supervisors) are sometimes used to measure behaviour. Typically, the observer rates whether or not the person has used the behaviour and/or how often that has occurred. As with self-reports, the issue of accuracy is of significance here. Observation data are more reliable and useful when the observer has extensive contact with the trainee. These conditions are easily met in call centres where interactions with customers are routinely recorded or monitored "live." These recordings and direct observations can be very precise and useful, provided that the observer has a clear understanding of the behaviours the employee is expected to display and those he/she needs to avoid. And, of course, the manner with which the observer provides feedback to the employee is an important determinant of how that feedback will be taken by the employee.

For both self-report and observational data, it is important that the measure focus on specific behaviours (how many times in the last month has the trainee used the new machine?) as opposed to general ones (has the trainee applied the skill on the job?). Measures of specific behaviours are more likely to be valid and accurate.

Productivity indicators (sometimes called "objective" measures) are a third type of behaviour data that might be gathered in an evaluation of behaviour. Performance indicators, such as sales performance, can often be obtained directly from company records. They are more frequently used when the evaluator is interested in measuring the impact of training on job performance, in the context of summative evaluations (see Chapter 12) and when the data collection plan is a time series (see "Data Collection Designs in Training Evaluation," below).

In some cases, performance records can provide highly precise data on specific behaviours. For example, "number of times a trainee has accessed a database" can be automatically recorded by the computer, providing highly accurate behaviour data for evaluating a training program designed to train people in the use and application of a database. In the Bell Canada chapter-opening vignette, computerized records were used to accurately measure, for each trainee, his/her extent of use of each feature of the electronic telephone.

However, performance indices are *not always* the best measure as they sometimes contaminate individual performance with other events that impact performance. For example, one "objective" measure of a telephone operator might be the number of calls he/she has taken in an hour. However, those data might lead to inaccurate conclusions as the number of calls an operator takes is also affected by the number of calls that are received. Similarly, the performance of a salesperson is influenced by external factors such as sales territory and competition in addition to the salesperson's behaviour.

Xerox uses many methods to ascertain behaviour, including post-course observations of trainees performing their jobs, interviews with their managers, and a review of performance-appraisal forms.[27] TD Bank uses a very simple approach. Participants in training programs are asked to describe three or four examples of when they used the new knowledge or skill on the job.[28]

Whatever the approach used, behaviour data collection should take place only after the trainee has become comfortable with the newly acquired skills and has had opportunities to demonstrate them on the job. The time lag for the assessment of behaviour can range from a few weeks to two years or more in the case of managerial skills. It is recommended that the measurement of behaviour take place at several points following a training program in order to determine the long-term effects of a training program.

Motivation

Make the
Connection

Training evaluators consider the measurement of two types of motivation in the training context: training motivation, which we described in Chapter 3, and the motivation to transfer the skill on the job, which we discussed in Chapter 10. As described in Chapter 3, training motivation is a very important factor that influences training success. A number of scales have been designed to measure training motivation and motivation to transfer.[29]

One important technique for measuring transfer motivation relies on expectancy theory (described in Chapter 3). Three sets of items are used to respectively measure the valence (the attractiveness of transfer outcomes), instrumentalities (the positive or negative consequences of transfer), and expectancies (the probability that transfer will result in successful performance). The principle is that trainees will be motivated to apply the training when they attach importance to the end result of training (valence), that the attainment of that end result leads to positive consequences or avoids negative ones (instrumentalities), and that applying the training is likely to lead to the desired end result (expectancies).

A study by Haccoun and Savard exemplifies the measurement of motivation to transfer.[30] Trainees (supervisors) were trained to apply a new organizational policy designed to reduce employee absenteeism (among other things). Motivation was measured through three sets of questions. 1. *valence:* How important is it that absence be reduced in your work group? 2. *instrumentality:* If you reduce absence, what would be the consequences (positive or negative) for you? and 3. *expectancy:* If you did apply the behaviours taught in training, how likely is it that absence levels would drop? Each question was rated on a five-point rating scale. The product of the three sets of answers (Valence $\times$ Instrumentality $\times$ Expectancy) produces the transfer motivation score.

Expectancy theory eg:

Self-Efficacy

As described in Chapter 3, self-efficacy refers to the beliefs that trainees hold about their ability to perform the behaviours that were taught in a training program. That is, self-efficacy assesses a person's *confidence* in engaging in *specific* behaviours or achieving specific goals. Changing one's work behaviour is often a difficult process, as many obstacles and ambient forces within the work environment may not be supportive of it. Thus, self-efficacy is important because people who do not feel capable of applying a new skill at work are unlikely to exert much effort to do so, especially when they are faced with obstacles.

Self-efficacy is measured relative to a specific behavioural target. Measures of self-efficacy vary, but most tend to focus on assessing trainees' level of confidence for performing specific tasks and behaviours. In one option people rate the likelihood of obtaining a certain result followed by ratings of the confidence they have in obtaining that result. For example, a measure of self-efficacy for an exam on this chapter might read as follows: "Are you likely to obtain 50%; 60%; 70%; 80%; 90%; 100% on an exam on training evaluation?" (Yes/No response to each option). Next, the person rates how confident they are about obtaining the grade for each "Yes" response. The question might read: "How confident are you that you can obtain that grade?" (0 = Not confident at all, 10 = Totally confident). Another simple method lists the key behaviours demonstrating transfer and asks trainees to rate each on a confidence scale, such as: "How confident are you that you will obtain at least 70% on the training evaluation exam?" The response scales would range from totally confident to not at all confident. Although 10-point rating scales are common, scales employing a smaller number of points are also frequently used. Of course, self-efficacy scales can assess confidence in behaviours as well.

Perceived and/or Anticipated Support

As indicated in Chapter 10, the support provided to trainees as they return to work is a very important component of transfer and training effectiveness. Two important measures of support are perceived support and anticipated support. **Perceived support** refers to the degree to which the trainee reports receiving support in his or her attempts to transfer the learned skills. **Anticipated support** refers to the degree to which the trainee *expects* to be supported in his/her attempts to transfer the learned skills.

Perceived support

The degree to which the trainee reports receiving support in his or her attempts to transfer the learned skills

Anticipated support

The degree to which the trainee expects to be supported in his or her attempts to transfer the learned skills

The measurement of perceived and/or anticipated support can be easily constructed for any training program. Specific questions can be designed to include the source of the support (e.g., supervisor, co-workers, or the organization) and the support (perceived or anticipated) in applying the training content in general and/or in transferring specific aspects of the training program.

For example, in a study on the effects of a training program that trained nurses on a model of nursing, questions about anticipated support included: "If I am having difficulty writing a nursing care plan, I know I can obtain (very little— very much) help from my supervisor." An alternative phrasing could be, "Based on my previous experiences, I think I can count on (very little—very much) support from my co-workers in applying the training content to my job."

Notice that in the nursing study, the first formulation of the question refers to a specific component of the training program (i.e., nursing care plan), while the latter refers to the training program content in general. These two items also differ in terms of the source of support, with the former being one's supervisor and the latter being co-workers. The respondents use a rating scale to fill in the blank spaces (1 = Very little, 5 = Very much). Similar items can be constructed to refer to key parts of a training program. Anticipated support is measured before and/or immediately after training while perceived support is measured once trainees have returned to work. In their study, Haccoun and Savard measured anticipated support (immediately after training) and both (perceived) actual support and transfer as assessed two years later. They show that trainees who expect more support than they actually receive tend to engage in lower levels of transfer. Unrealistic expectations of support, this study shows, have a strong negative impact on transfer.

Organizational Perceptions

Make the Connection

Several researchers have designed scales to measure perceptions of the transfer climate and a learning culture, which were discussed in Chapter 4 on needs analysis and Chapter 10 on transfer of training. Transfer climate can be measured via a questionnaire developed by Janice Rouiller and Irwin Goldstein.[31] The measure consists of a number of questions that identify eight sets of "cues" that can trigger trainee reactions that encourage or discourage the trainee to transfer the skill. The eight scales include goal cues, social cues, task and structural cues, positive feedback, negative feedback, punishment, no feedback, and self-control. Trainees are asked questions about training-specific characteristics of the work environment, such as "In your organization, supervisors set goals for trainees to encourage them to apply their training on the job" (1 = Strongly disagree, 5 = Strongly agree). Rouiller and Goldstein have shown that transfer is stronger when the organizational transfer climate is more favourable.

In addition, J. Bruce Tracey, Scott Tannenbaum, and Michael Kavanagh proposed a scale to measure if an organization has a continuous-learning culture. The questions measure trainees' perceptions, beliefs, expectations, and values with regard to individual, task, and organizational factors that support the acquisition and application of knowledge, skill, and behaviour. The Trainer's Notebook 4.1 in Chapter 4 presents some of the items from this scale. Once again, research indicates that transfer levels are higher with organizations that have a stronger learning culture.

p. 109

Make the Connection

Finally, the LTSI approach (described in Training Today 11.2 and in Chapter 10) is an example of yet another approach to assessing the role of the organization in fostering training transfer.

Organizational Results

An evaluation may also focus on "results criteria." These criteria focus on the effects of training on the organization rather than on the trainee: How has the organization benefited from the training program? Have profits increased? Results criteria are considered to be the "ultimate" criteria for training evaluation and may include such measures as turnover, productivity, quality, profitability, customer satisfaction, accidents, and so on. However, some of these may be difficult to measure and, in any case, it is very difficult to clearly attribute changes in these variables specifically to the training program. Testing causality requires experimental designs that are generally difficult to implement in organizations (see the section titled "Data Collection Designs in Training Evaluation"). In some instances, the objective is to cost the program and determine the net benefit. Chapter 12 is devoted to procedures for doing cost–benefit analysis.

Hard and soft data can be useful in assessing the results of training. **Hard data** are measured objectively. They are of particular and direct relevance to upper management partly because of their "objectivity" but mainly because they assess the bottom line. **Soft data** are not objective and usually involve a judgment, observation, or perception of an outcome.

Phillips has produced a taxonomy of hard data and soft data that may be measured in training evaluations.[32] Hard data may include quantities (number of items sold or produced), quality (scrap rates and product returns), time (downtime or time to complete assignments), and costs (sales expenses, benchmarks). Soft data may include beliefs, attitudes, and perceptions.

ACCO Brands Corporation, a manufacturer of school supplies ranging from paper clips to binders, uses hard data (quantity) to track the effect of training on new production hires. After training, new hires were able to produce vinyl binders at a 5 to 10 percent higher rate than tenured operators, a clear payoff to the organization.[33]

Hard data are not always available nor are they always essential to the purpose of the evaluation. For formative evaluations, where the goal is to improve training, the use of "soft data" is prevalent. These include measures such as the LTSI (see Training Today 11.2) and/or questionnaires assessing self-efficacy, motivation, post-training support, and so on (see the section titled "Models of Training Evaluation"). They can also be self-reports of difficult-to-measure skills like decision making. Unlike hard data, soft data are not direct indicators of organizational outcomes (providing dollar values). Rather, soft data are important because the feelings, beliefs, and attitudes they measure are reasoned to be linked to concrete results. For example, communication skills are not bottom-line measures, but they may ultimately have an impact on the organization's bottom line. And self-efficacy, another soft data, may indirectly affect the bottom line because of its influence on the display of communication skills.

In some cases it is difficult or impossible to adequately assess the impact of training directly. An alternative is to calculate **return on expectations**. Those who are involved in training decide exactly what they expect from the training. These expectations form the goals for training, and some time after the course managers decide whether the performance results are in line with their expectations.

For example, an organization that was restructured into product-performance teams was unable to place a dollar value on the cross-functional training employees had received, but managers were able to articulate improvements they noticed after the training. The numbers are not absolute, but managers imply that time is managed better in that 95 percent of deadlines are being met. They feel that this anecdotal evidence does have an impact on the bottom line, and that profit improvements are noticeable.

According to a recent Conference Board of Canada survey (see Figure 11.1), few Canadian organizations measure training impact using hard data (similar findings have been reported for the United States by the ASTD). There are good

Hard data
Results that are assessed objectively

Soft data
Results that are assessed through perceptions and judgments

Return on expectations
The measurement of a training program's ability to meet managerial expectations

reasons for this. Not only is it more costly in terms of time (it may take months or years for a training program's effects to manifest themselves on the bottom-line results) and resources, it is very difficult to link training to organizational results. The fact that productivity increases after training may not be automatically attributed to training. Many other things unrelated to training may have caused the effect and improved productivity. To illustrate, consider the ACCO Brands study described earlier, where the new hires at ACCO Brands Corporation, trained with a new program, were more effective. But was that improvement because of training or because the participants were more motivated, as new hires tend to be? It is not enough to demonstrate change. Attributing that change to training is the next and final step of the evaluator's task. This speaks to the issue of data collection designs for training evaluation, a topic to which we now turn.

DATA COLLECTION DESIGNS IN TRAINING EVALUATION

Data collection designs, of which many exist, are a very important component of training evaluation as they determine the conclusions that can be validly drawn. The more sophisticated training evaluation data collection designs can detect the effect of training in precise ways. Other designs, though useful in some situations, produce more limited conclusions about the value of training.

Data collection designs in training evaluation refers to the manner in which the data collection is organized and how the data will be analyzed. All data collection designs compare the trained person to something. They may compare 1. trained people with untrained ones, 2. the same people before and after training, or 3. each trained person to an absolute standard. When the comparison does not involve another group of (untrained) people, the designs are labelled **non-experimental**. When that comparison is to another group of people similar to those trained but that do not receive the training, the designs are called **experimental** or **quasi-experimental**. The main difference between an experimental design and a quasi-experimental design has to do with whether assignment-to-conditions is random or not random.

In experimental designs, the assignment of people to the trained group (labelled the "experimental" or "trained" group) and to the untrained group (labelled the "control" group) is done randomly. In quasi-experimental designs, we also compare trained to untrained employees but the assignment to the groups is not done randomly. In that case, instead of speaking about a "control" group we refer to it as a "comparison" group.

Figure 11.2 graphically represents several data collection designs. The uses and limitations of each data collection design are explained below, and Table 11.5 summarizes the main differences between the various methodologies. In general, non-experimental designs do not establish if trainee learning and behaviours were *caused* by the training program (with the partial exception of the IRS, design G below). On the other hand, they are easy to organize and practical for use in organizations. Quasi-experimental and experimental designs do provide evidence of causality but are more complex to plan and implement. Compared with quasi-experimental designs, experimental designs provide even stronger evidence of causality. However, they are difficult to use in practice.

Data collection designs in training evaluation

The manner in which the data collection is organized and how the data will be analyzed

Non-experimental designs

When the comparison is not made to another group of (untrained) people

Experimental designs

When the trained group is compared to another group that does not receive the training and when the assignment of people to the training group and the untrained group is random

Quasi-experimental designs

When the trained group is compared to another group that does not receive the training but when the assignment of people to the training group and the untrained group is not random

Training Evaluation Data Collection Designs

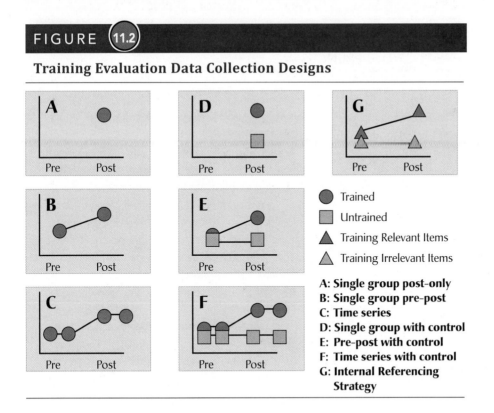

A: **Single group post-only**
B: **Single group pre-post**
C: **Time series**
D: **Single group with control**
E: **Pre-post with control**
F: **Time series with control**
G: **Internal Referencing Strategy**

Experimental (and to a lesser extent quasi-experimental) designs provide stronger evidence of causality, demonstrating that changes in trainees' learning and behaviour are due to the training and not to something else. To learn more about some of the other factors that might explain a change in trainees' learning and behaviour, see The Trainer's Notebook 11.1, "Understanding Pre-Post Differences."

Uses and Limitations of Non-Experimental, Quasi-Experimental, and Experimental Training Evaluation Designs

Non-experimental designs cannot provide causal information (except for the Internal Referencing Strategy). Hence, such designs can't be used to infer the quality of the training program. However, they are most practical and can provide useful information when the evaluator has an external standard against which post-training performance can be compared and/or when demonstrating that training is the cause of that proficiency does not matter.

Experimental designs estimate the degree to which a training program has caused trainee proficiency. They are used to establish whether the training program should be eliminated or expanded to other parts of the organization. The downside is that experimental designs are more difficult to use in organizational settings.

Quasi-experimental designs provide indications of cause but the proof is not definitive. However, because they do not require random assignment they are generally more accessible to organizations. Hence, quasi-experimental designs may be appropriate when experimental designs cannot be used and when the training manager is willing to live with some risk.

The Trainer's Notebook 11.1

UNDERSTANDING PRE-POST DIFFERENCES

Suppose we wish to evaluate this chapter's effectiveness in teaching training evaluation. We select a pre-post design in which knowledge is measured with a multiple choice test administered on the first day of class (pre-test) and again on the last day (post-test). The results show the average score of the students on the post-test is significantly higher than the pre-test scores. Can it be concluded that reading this chapter *caused* this gain in knowledge? Before jumping to conclusions, you should consider four alternative explanations:

History or Time. Events in the environment that coincide with this course and that have nothing to do with it may, in fact, have caused pre-to-post changes. For example, the class may have done better because many students saw a PBS program on training evaluation that was aired the week before the final exam.

Maturation. People mature and change over time. As the students are taking this course they are also taking other courses. Even if none of the other courses deals explicitly with training evaluation, they may have helped the students develop higher levels of reasoning and critical thinking skills. This growing general competence may translate into better performance on the post-test.

Testing. Taking the pre-test may have made it easier for students to perform better on the post-test. Some students may have remembered some of the questions asked on the pre-test, while others may have gained a better "feel" for the kinds of questions that are asked. Hence, the post-test performance may be due, at least in part, to the mere experience of being pre-tested.

Mortality. Whereas most students who enrol in a course stay until the end, it is almost always the case that some students drop the course. Those who remain in the course and from whom post-test information will be available may be systematically different from those who dropped the course—they may be more interested in the subject matter, more motivated, more able than those who leave, and/or have more time to meet the course demands. These students may very well show large improvements in learning, shifting the average class performance on the post-test upward.

Source: Adapted from T.D. Cook & D.T. Campbell, *Quasi-experimentation: Design and analysis issues for field settings.* Skokie, IL: Rand McNally, 1979.

NON-EXPERIMENTAL, EXPERIMENTAL, AND QUASI-EXPERIMENTAL TRAINING DATA COLLECTION DESIGNS FOR TRAINING EVALUATION

Training evaluation designs
The process by which evaluation information is gathered

Training evaluation designs were developed from the principles of experimental scientific research, and there are many research designs within each of the three general types described in the previous section. Each data collection scheme is graphically described in Figure 11.2.

Designs A, B, and C are non-experimental designs because the employees who are trained are not compared to untrained employees. Designs D, E, and F are causal models that compare trained and untrained people and, depending on trainee assignment, they may be experimental or quasi-experimental. Finally, design G—the Internal Referencing Strategy—is a hybrid design that permits some of the conclusions made by the causal designs (D, E, F) without the need for a control or comparison group (design B).

In general, all training outcome measures may be used irrespective of the training evaluation design chosen: affective, cognitive, or skill-based as well as reactions and behaviours. *Hence, the choice of an evaluation design has less to do with the measures collected but much more to do with the inferences or decisions required about the effectiveness of the training program.*

In the remainder of this section we describe each of the seven designs represented in Figure 11.2. Design A is the most simple, while design F is the most complex, with the others falling in between these extremes. Designs A, B, and C are non-experimental because the trained group is not compared to another group. Designs D, E, and F are experimental when subjects are randomly assigned and quasi-experimental when subject assignment to trained and comparison groups is not random. Design G is a hybrid model.

Non-Experimental Designs

DESIGN A: THE POST-ONLY DESIGN is the simplest training evaluation data collection design. Data are gathered once after training and only from those who have completed training. Each trainee is compared to a pre-determined criterion of success and training is considered "effective" when trainees meet that standard of proficiency. Three common examples of such programs include university exams, a course for new drivers, and the basic training program administered to new call centre employees. The basic strength (and popularity) of this design is its practicality. However, this design is plagued with two main drawbacks: 1. it cannot indicate whether the trainees have changed (e.g., trainees may have been proficient before training), and 2. it cannot indicate that the achieved outcome is a result of training (their observed proficiency may have been "caused" by some other experience coincidental to training). In general, these types of evaluations do not require statistical analyses.

DESIGN B: THE SINGLE GROUP PRE-POST DESIGN is a non-experimental design because the comparison is not made to another group. Instead, the comparison is made to the trainees themselves prior to training. This is the second most frequently used evaluation design. Training outcome data are gathered from trainees both before and after training. Used to assess *changes* in trainees, this design infers training effectiveness when the post-training data show statistically significant improvement from pre-training. Typically, the analysis required to test the difference is a repeated measures analysis of variance or a t-test for non-independent samples. Although superior to the post-only design, the pre-post remains problematic as it cannot prove that the noted difference results from training (see The Trainer's Notebook 11.1).

DESIGN C: THE TIME-SERIES DESIGN is, in principle, an extension of the pre-post-only data collection technique. It requires several data collection points before and after training (the pre-post design requires only one pre- and one post-measure). For example, in a time-series design to assess a course on "selling earthquake insurance," the analyst would retrieve for each trainee the number of earthquake policies sold during each of the four quarters prior to training and each of the four quarters after training. Training is considered effective when the number of policies sold jumps after training and remains consistently higher.

The use of several pre- and post-measures, essential to this design, yields the decided advantage of this technique over the simple pre-post design. However, the quality of the conclusions depends on the number of times data are collected: The greater the number of data points the more valid the conclusion. Moreover, because it requires several measurements, the data are rarely collected by questionnaire. Instead, the design principally relies on hard measures of job performance that can be collected without disturbing the employee.

Objective performance measures tend to fluctuate (up or down) due to many circumstances that may have little to do with the employee's competencies. The time-series data collection design is a marked improvement over the pre-post because multiplying the measurement moments will tend to cancel out these fluctuations. Further, the time-series design allows the evaluator to test whether post-training improvements are persistent and stable over time. The drawback to this design is that the statistical analyses required to assess the results are more complex than the ones needed with the simpler designs. They are typically statistically analyzed with trend analyses or forecasting techniques.

Experimental and Quasi-Experimental Designs

Data collection designs D, E, and F compare the trainees to another group of "equivalent" people who have not been trained. These designs can be either experimental or quasi-experimental depending on whether or not trainees are assigned to the comparison and trained group randomly.

DESIGN D: THE SINGLE-GROUP DESIGN WITH CONTROL/COMPARISON GROUP is the simplest experimental or quasi-experimental design. Post-training data are collected from both trainees as well as a group of people who were not trained. Effectiveness is inferred when those trained obtain higher scores on the outcome measures than those who were not trained. With this design, it is possible to state with considerable confidence that the training program caused the higher outcomes obtained by the trained group. We have greater confidence in this conclusion when the design is experimental (because random assignment ensures that both groups are initially equal). However, the statistical properties of randomness will equate the groups only when the number of people involved is large. This latter restriction is important because many training programs in organizations are administered to a limited number of people. When assignment to groups cannot be randomized (as is typical in organizational settings), the design becomes quasi-experimental and it cannot be categorically stated that the groups were initially equal. In that case the attribution of causality is more risky. The statistical procedure used for this design is the independent sample t-test or analysis of variance.

DESIGN E: THE PRE-POST DESIGN WITH CONTROL/COMPARISON GROUP With this design, data are gathered from trainees both before and after training. Simultaneously, data are also gathered from an untrained group. This is a more complete training evaluation design because it allows one to examine the two most important questions about training programs: "Did the trainees change?" and "To what degree was the training program responsible for that change?" Training effectiveness is inferred when pre-post changes are greater for the trained than the untrained group. In Chapter 14, Training Today 14.4, "Are Corporate Universities Useful?" illustrates this design.

The main drawback of this model is its practicality: rare are the cases where comparison groups are available and random assignment to condition is even more difficult to arrange. Analytically, factorial analysis of variance with repeated measures is the proper statistical tool used to evaluate effectiveness.

DESIGN F: THE TIME-SERIES DESIGN WITH CONTROL/COMPARISON GROUP is identical to the time-series design C except that data are simultaneously gathered from a comparison group. This additional group allows for stronger conclusions about changes as well as about the role that the training intervention played in creating that change. Take for example the course on "selling earthquake insurance" described above (see design C). Suppose that shortly after the course is offered, an earthquake does occur. Selling earthquake insurance is likely to become a lot easier and all salespeople, whether or not they had taken the training, would show a marked increase. Had we not had a comparison group, we would have falsely concluded that the training program was responsible for the pre-post changes. Once again, trend analyses are used to statistically evaluate the results.

A Hybrid Model

DESIGN G: THE INTERNAL REFERENCING STRATEGY Design G is a hybrid model developed by Haccoun and Hamtiaux for use in those frequent cases where the pre-post design is used but where no comparison group can be assessed (design B).[34]

The heart of this technique is the careful construction of the pre-test and the post-test measures that are administered to participants before and after training. Two types of test items—"relevant" and "irrelevant but germane"—are constructed. *Relevant* items are those that test the mastery of the knowledge and behaviours that are taught in the training program. *Irrelevant but germane* items test knowledge of contents that could have been included in a training program but were not. For example, in testing the effectiveness of this chapter for teaching evaluation designs, one could ask questions about the time-series design. One could also ask questions about the interrupted time-series design. Questions testing knowledge of a time-series design would be "relevant" because the topic is covered in this chapter. Questions testing knowledge of the interrupted time-series would be "irrelevant" because the chapter does not cover this design but "germane" because the interrupted time-series is a legitimate evaluation design that could have been included in the training content.

The analysis of the data is straightforward: The evaluator calculates the pre-post differences separately for the relevant and irrelevant items. These two differences are then compared statistically. With effective programs the pre-post performance change on the relevant items is greater than the pre-post differences on the irrelevant ones. Hence, the statistical procedure is a repeated measures analysis of variance or an analysis of co-variance.

The IRS is a useful addition to the evaluator's tool box: It is as practical to implement as design B yet provides conclusions that are similar to those than can be reached through the much superior and complex design D, the pre-post with control. Research conducted to date has shown that the IRS is scientifically robust and it has been recommended that evaluators consider relying on it instead of the pre-post design without control.[35]

Summary of Data Collection Designs

As stated at the onset of this chapter, the choice of evaluation strategies always involves trade-offs (between the quality and the scope of the information gathered and their costs and practicality). The same is true of data collection approaches. To obtain better information more complex designs are required, even as they are difficult to implement in organizations. The evaluator will choose the design that meets the information that management needs. If that is impractical, alternative designs of lower quality are available but management needs to be advised of the limits of the selected design.

SUMMARY

This chapter reviewed the main purposes for evaluating training programs as well as the barriers that prevent training evaluation. Models of training evaluation were presented, contrasted, and critiqued. Although Kirkpatrick's evaluation model is the most common and frequently used model, for formative evaluations at least, the COMA model may be more appropriate. Also described are the variables required for an evaluation as well as some of the methods and techniques required to measure them. Whereas many of these are measured through questionnaires administered to trainees, their supervisors, or others, objective data can also be used. Advantages and disadvantages of each were discussed. The main types of data collection designs were also described along with the limits to the interpretation they permit. The choice of data collection design, as with most aspects of training, was seen as a trade-off among costs, practicalities, and the information needs of management.

Key Terms

affective reactions p. 337
anticipated support p. 345
causal evaluations p. 330
COMA p. 333
data collection designs in training
  evaluation p. 348
Decision-Based Evaluation (DBE) p. 334
declarative learning p. 340
descriptive evaluations p. 330
experimental designs p. 348
formative evaluations p. 330

hard data p. 347
non-experimental designs p. 348
perceived support p. 345
procedural learning p. 340
quasi-experimental designs p. 348
return on expectations p. 347
soft data p. 347
summative evaluations p. 330
training evaluation p. 325
training evaluation designs p. 350
utility reactions p. 337

Make the Connection

p. 340: declarative and procedural knowledge are discussed in Chapter 3 on page 69

p. 342: transfer of training is discussed in Chapter 10 on page 291; training objectives are discussed in Chapter 5 on page 137

p. 344: training motivation is discussed in Chapter 3 on page 83; motivation to transfer is discussed in Chapter 10 on page 294; expectancy theory is discussed in Chapter 3 on pages 81–82

p. 345: self-efficacy is discussed in Chapter 3 on page 75

p. 345: manager support for transfer of training is discussed in Chapter 10 on page 300

p. 346: training transfer climate and a continuous learning culture are discussed in Chapters 4 and 10 on pages 108 and 296, respectively.

p. 346: the learning transfer system inventory (LTSI) is discussed in Chapter 10 on page 310

Web Links

ACCO Brands Corporation: **www.acco.com**

American Society for Training and Development (ASTD): **www.astd.org**

Bell Canada: **www.bell.ca**

Conference Board of Canada: **www.conferenceboard.ca**

General Dynamics: **www.generaldynamics.com**

TD Bank: **www.td.com**

Xerox: **www.xerox.com**

Required Professional Capabilities (RPCs)

The following RPCs are relevant to material covered in this chapter. The RPC number represents the CCHRA number assigned to the RPC as presented on the CCHRA website. All of the RPCs can be found in the Body of Knowledge at **http:// www.chrp.ca/rpc/body-of-knowledge/**.

RPC 147: Monitors and reports on the impact of development activities on organizational performance.

  147.01: Data gathering techniques

  147.02: Stakeholders in training & development

  147.05: Research methods and designs (including measurement of HR)

  147.06: Measurement and assessment tools and techniques (and their limitations)

RPC 154: Statistical analyses and evaluation

Discussion Questions

1. Discuss the similarities and the differences between the evaluation models discussed in the chapter. In your discussion be sure to include the practical implications of preferring one model over another.
2. You have two training programs: a) a course designed to teach the use of a PC, and b) a course to improve supervisory feedback to employees. Which evaluation design would you use in each case? What if you wanted to determine whether training caused the outcome? Which design would you use?

3. Many organizations do not evaluate their training programs. If you had to convince a manager to evaluate a training program, what would you tell him or her? Why should organizations evaluate their training programs and what should they evaluate?

4. What are the barriers to training evaluation? Discuss the main types of barriers and what a trainer might do to overcome them and evaluate a training program.

5. Discuss the different types of training evaluation and how they can be distinguished from one another.

6. What is the difference between formative and summative evaluation and between descriptive and causal evaluation?

7. Discuss the assumptions of Donald Kirkpatrick's hierarchical model of training evaluation. What are the implications for training evaluation if the assumptions are valid? What are the implications if the assumptions are not valid?

8. Explain each of the following and give an example: hard data, soft data, and return on expectations. What are the advantages and disadvantages of each type of measure?

9. Explain each of the following and give an example: non-experimental designs, experimental designs, and quasi-experimental designs. What are the advantages and disadvantages of each type of evaluation design?

The Great Training Debate

Conducting evaluation studies using full experimental designs and sophisticated data collection is almost impossible in real organizations. Some managers argue that training evaluations can provide meaningful conclusions only when conducted using these techniques. They therefore conclude that in most cases training evaluations are a waste of time and money.

Debate this conclusion: Is it the case that training evaluations should be conducted only when it is possible to use the more sophisticated procedures?

In preparation for this debate you should review the chapter's sections on barriers to training evaluation and models of training evaluation as well as data collection designs.

Exercises

In-Class

1. Training evaluation principles and variables can also be used to make important individual decisions.

   Following her graduation, your best friend Sally felt she lacked "work-life skills." To remedy her perceived problem, she enrolled in a private school that specializes in "enhancing the skills needed for a successful work life." You are graduating at the end of the year and, for the same reasons, are considering enrolment in that program. However, the school fees are very high. But you'll accept that burden, provided you believe that graduates of this program are indeed better prepared for the world of work.

Six months into her program you meet Sally for lunch. Assume that Sally is your only source of information about the school and remember that she has yet to enter the world of work.

What are the changes in Sally that you will be looking for to help you decide whether the school is worthwhile or not? Are there specific questions you would ask Sally? Refer to the models and variables of training evaluations to guide your thinking. Remember that Sally has not yet completed her course, so we cannot know at this point whether or not she is indeed "better prepared" for work.

2. In most universities and colleges, students fill out an end-of-course questionnaire in which they evaluate the course. Describe how these evaluations are typically conducted in your university or college. What variables are measured, how is that done, and what type of data collection design is used? Keeping in mind each model and the variables in Table 11.1, what other variables do you think should be included as part of the evaluation process? Design an evaluation form that you would like to see used to evaluate your university/college's courses. For each variable you include, develop one sample question and/or a procedure for measuring it.

3. Suppose your university or college has decided to switch all computers from PC to Mac (or, if your university's current system uses Mac, to PC). Although some staff members already know both systems, the majority will need to learn and master the new system (Mac or PC). The university administration has therefore authorized Human Resources and the IT group to work together to develop and deliver a compulsory training program to all staff members. The top university administration has hired you to conduct an evaluation of the effectiveness of this program as it needs to know if the training program was worthwhile.

   a. Decide whether your client's request calls for a summative or formative evaluation, and
   b. Depending on that decision, develop the training evaluation plan. Keeping in mind the data collection designs (Figure 11.1) and the models and the variables of training evaluation, describe what will be measured, how, and when that will be done to meet the client's needs.

4. Suppose that in the same circumstances described in question 3, it is Human Resources and the IT group who are your clients. They are interested in identifying possible improvements to the course. Would the design you established in #3 be applicable? Would you change anything? If so, what would you change and how? What would the plan look like if your clients were simultaneously both the administration and the HR/IT departments?

5. Consider a situation in which you are the director of training and development in an organization that is going to deliver a very expensive training program. It is very important to find out how effective the training program is, given the expense and the large number of employees who will be trained over the next several years. Your job is to develop a plan for the evaluation. Discuss what you will do in terms of the type of evaluation: What data

should be gathered and analyzed? What is the purpose of the evaluation and should it be formative or summative? Should it be a descriptive or causal evaluation? Now consider the different types of evaluation designs in Figure 11.1. What type of evaluation design do you think would be most appropriate? Consider the pros and cons of the various alternatives. Present your training evaluation strategy to the class.

In-the-Field

1. Identify the training manager of a local company, set up an appointment, and meet with him or her. During that interview, identify
   - The types of training programs that are given in that company and the types of training evaluations (if any) that are conducted.
   - Is the same type of evaluation used across different programs or are different evaluations designs adopted for different ones?
   - How are the evaluation data used and by whom?
   - Finally, based on all of the information gathered, assess the quality of that company's evaluation efforts: What can the company conclude about training effectiveness given the types of evaluations it conducts, and what can it not conclude?
2. Identify a member of your family or a friend who is currently working and who has recently taken a training course and interview him or her. The purpose of the interview is for you to estimate the likelihood that the training program was "effective." Establish the interview guide (the questions you will ask) in advance of the interview. Your questions should focus on the dimensions to be measured using both the Kirkpatrick and the COMA models.

Case Incident

The Social Agency

A large governmental social agency, employing thousands of social workers and other specialized workers, trained all of its front-line professionals on a new service-delivery system. Simultaneously, it taught managers how to actively support and encourage their employees to implement the new system: that is, transfer their new skills. A consultant was asked to evaluate the effectiveness of the program directed to the managers and to offer suggestions for improvements.

Questions

1. What information should be collected and from whom should it be collected?
2. Discuss when and how the information should be collected.
3. What should the criteria for "effectiveness" be?

Case Study | THE ALCOHOL/DRUG ABUSE PREVENTION PROGRAM (ADAPP)

The North American Transportation Company (NATC) is a very large organization that provides continent-wide facilities for the shipping of goods, from tonnes of wheat and iron ore to individual parcels. Headquartered in Canada, the company uses all forms of heavy equipment to load, transport, and deliver goods and materials for its clients.

In recent years, a number of accidents and near-accidents had occurred. In some cases the accidents caused injuries to people (mainly employees, though some injuries were sustained by bystanders). They also caused substantial material damage to property and/or the environment. In three cases in the last five years, people were killed.

Investigation of these accidents indicated that drug and/or alcohol abuse by company personnel was relatively common and that these may have been contributing factors to the accidents. This analysis also uncovered that absenteeism and job performance problems were also the result of drug/alcohol use by employees.

The CEO of the company asked the Human Resource department to solve the problem. In response, the department formulated a zero-tolerance policy toward workplace alcohol and drug abuse. The policy outlawed alcohol/drug use on the job and made the implementation and enforcement of the policy the direct responsibility of all supervisory personnel in the company. They further developed and implemented a training program to instruct all supervisors of the policy, the means to implement it, and the specific behaviours expected of them. This training program became known as the Alcohol/Drug Abuse Prevention Program (ADAPP).

The day-long training program explained that it was the responsibility of supervisors to be vigilant with respect to drug/alcohol use on the job and to act immediately when there was a problem.

There were three main aspects to the ADAPP policy that supervisors were to learn and to transfer to the job: 1. Explain the policy to their employees as a group; 2. Watch for employees who show signs of being "under the influence" and 3. To correctly choose the specific supervisory action required.

Were problematic employees detected, supervisors were instructed to a) assess the situation with the employee, b) immediately relieve the employee from his post should the impairment prevent safe and effective job performance, and c) direct the person to the Employee Aid Program for further investigation and treatment. Supervisors who failed to implement the procedure would face disciplinary actions including, in some cases, immediate dismissal.

The training program consisted of lectures and video presentations, followed by various role-playing exercises and discussions designed to help them learn the policy, to motivate supervisors into implementing it, and to enhance their confidence in their ability to do so.

Questions

1. Design a training evaluation for the ADAPP. The training evaluation must be both *summative* (has ADAPP led to an increase in the desired supervisory behaviours and has it led to a decrease in employee absence and workplace accidents and injuries?) and *formative* (what aspects of the training program, if any, should be improved?).
2. What model or models of training evaluation would seem appropriate in this case? Explain your answer.
3. What variables should be measured and how should this be done?
   a. Determine the main variables to measure.
   b. Determine the information to be collected to address program improvements.
4. What data collection design or designs would you consider most appropriate for the evaluation? Explain your reasoning.

Flashback Questions

1. Suppose that in the ADAPP case the evaluation results showed little transfer. Refer back to the sections on trainee characteristics and the other conditions of transfer described in Chapter 10. What would you suggest be done to improve the situation? Should the company change the training? How?
2. The ADAPP mobilized the entire company, costing it thousands of work hours. One of the main advantages of e-learning (Chapter 8) is that it can considerably reduce those costs. Do you think this a viable alternative in this case? What e-learning approach would you think appropriate in the situation? In thinking about your answer, consider, amongst other things, the issue of active practice discussed in Chapter 5.
3. Trainee motivation to learn and transfer are important elements that should be assessed in a training evaluation because of their known impact on the adoption of new job behaviours. Chapter 3 deals extensively with motivation. What kinds of interventions during training would enhance the ADAPP managers' motivation? What can be done on the job to maintain and enhance motivation?

REFERENCES

1. Sackett, P. R., & Mullen, E. J. (1993). Beyond formal experimental design: Towards an expanded view of the training evaluation process. *Personnel Psychology, 46,* 613–627.
2. Twitchell, S., Holton, E. F. III, & Trott, J. R. Jr. (2001). Technical training evaluation practices in the United States. *Performance Improvement Quarterly, 13(3),* 84–109.
3. Sugrue, B., & Kim, K-H. (2004). *ASTD's annual review of trends in workplace learning and performance.* The American Society for Training and Development; Lavis, C. (2011). *Learning and development outlook 2011: Are organizations ready for Learning 2.0?* The Conference Board of Canada
4. Grider, D. T. (1990). Training evaluation. *Business Magazine, 17 (1),* 20–24.

5. Laroche, R., & Haccoun, R. R. (2003). Buts complémentaires and contradictoires de la formation du personnel: Une typologie intégratrice. (Complementary and contradictory goals of employee training: An integrative typology) *Psychologie du travail et des organisations, 9*, 3–4, 147–166.

6. Kraiger, K., Ford, J. K., & Salas, E. (1993). Application of cognitive, skill based and affective theories of learning outcomes to new methods of training evaluation. *Journal of Applied Psychology, 78(2),* 311–328; Colquitt, J. A., Lepine, J. A., & Noe, R. A. (2000). Toward an integrative theory of training motivation: A meta-analytic path analysis of 20 years of research. *Journal of Applied Psychology, 85(5),* 678–707.

7. Pace, R. W., Smith, C. P., & Mills, G. E. (1991). *Human resource development: The field.* Englewood Cliffs, NJ: Prentice-Hall.

8. Roullier, J. Z., & Goldstein, I. L. (1993). The relationship between organizational transfer climate and positive transfer of training. *Human Resource Development Quarterly, 4(4),* 377–390; Tracey, J. B., Tannenbaum, S. I., & Kavanagh, M. J. (1995). Applying trained skills on the job: The importance of the work environment. *Journal of Applied Psychology, 80(2),* 239–252.

9. Tracey, J. B., Hinkin, T. R., Tannenbaum, S., & Mathieu, J. E. (2001). The influence of individual characteristics and the work environment on varying levels of training outcomes. *Human Resource Development Quarterly, 12,* 1, 5–23.

10. Quinones, M. A. (1995). Pretraining context effects: Training assignment as feedback. *Journal of Applied Psychology, 80,* 226–238.

11. Montesino, M. U. (2002). Strategic alignment of training, transfer-enhancing behaviors and training usage: A posttraining study. *Human Resource Development Quarterly, 13(1),* 89–108; Saks, A. M., Tagger, S., & Haccoun, R. R. (2002). Is training related to firm performance? *The HRM Research Quarterly, 6(2).*

12. Worthen, B. R., & Sanders, J. R. (1987). *Educational evaluations: Alternative approaches and practical guidelines.* White Plains, NY: Longman.

13. Kirkpatrick, D. L. (1976). Evaluation of training. In R. L. Craig (Ed.), *Training and development handbook: A guide to human resource development* (2nd ed). New York: McGraw-Hill.

14. Kraiger, K. (2002). Decision-based evaluation. In K. Kraiger (Ed.), *Creating, implementing, and managing effective training and development: State-of-the-art lessons for practice* (pp. 331–375). San Francisco: Jossey-Bass

15. Holton, E. F. III. (1996). The flawed four-level evaluation model. *Human Resource Development Quarterly, 7,* 5–21; Alliger, G. M., Tannenbaum, S. L., Bennett, W., Traver, H., & Shortland, A. (1997). A meta-analysis on the relations among training criteria. *Personnel Psychology, 50,* 341–342.

16. Haccoun, R. R., Jeanrie, C., & Saks, A. M. (1999). Concepts et pratiques contemporaines en évaluation de la formation: Vers un modèle diagnostic des impacts. In D. Bouthilier (Ed.) *Gérer pour la performance.* Montreal: Presses de HEC.

17. Holton, E. F., Bates, R. A., & Ruona, W. E. A. (2000). Development of a generalized learning transfer system inventory. *Human Resource Development Quarterly, 11(4),* 333–360.

18. Morgan, R. B., & Casper, W. (2000). Examining the factor structure of participant reactions to training: A multidimensional approach. *Human Resource Development Quarterly, 11,* 301–317.

19. Alliger, G. M., Tannenbaum, S. L., Bennett, W., Traver, H., & Shortland, A. (1997). Meta analysis of the relationship among training criteria. *Personnel Psychology, 50,* 341–357.

20. Sitman, T., Brown, K. G., Casper, W. J., Ely, K., & Zimmerman, R. D. (2008). A review and meta-analysis of the nomological network or trainee reactions. *Journal of Applied Psychology, 93(2),* 280–295.

21. Jonassen, D., & Tessmer, M. (1996–97). An outcomes-based taxonomy for instructional systems design, evaluation and research. *Training Research Journal, 2,* 11–46.

22. Desjardins, D. (1995). Impact de la présentation d'un organisateur avancé sur l'apprentissage et le transfert en formation du personnel. Unpublished Master's Thesis, Université de Montréal, Département de Psychologie.

23. Ostroff, C. (1991). Training effectiveness measures and scoring schemes: A comparison. *Personnel Psychology, 44,* 353–374.

24. Smith, J. E., & Merchant, S. (1990). Using competency exams for evaluating training. *Training and Development Journal, 44(8),* 65–71.

25. Flynn, G. (1998). The nuts and bolts of valuing training. *Workforce Management, 17(11),* 80–85; Kozlowski, S. W. J., & Salas, E. (1997). A multilevel organizational systems approach for the implementation and transfer of training. In J. K. Ford (Ed.) *Improving training effectiveness in work organizations* (pp. 247–287). Hillsdale, NJ: Erlbaum.

26. Salas, E., & Cannon-Bowers, J. A. (2001). The science of training: A decade of progress. *Annual Review of Psychology, 52,* 471–499.

27. Olian, J. D., & Durham, C. C. (1998). Designing management training and development for competitive advantage: Lessons from the best. *Human Resource Planning, 21(1),* 20–31.

28. Larin, N. (April, 1998). Who understands return on investment better than a bank? *Canadian HR Reporter,* 2–8.

29. Noe, R. A., & Schmitt, N. (1986). The influence of trainee attitudes on training effectiveness: Test of a model. *Personnel Psychology, 39,* 497–523.

30. Haccoun, R. R., & Savard, P. (2003). Prédire le transfert des apprentissages à long terme role du soutien anticipé et perçu, de la motivation et de l'efficacité personnelle. (Predicting long term transfer of learning: The role of anticipated and actual support, motivation, and self efficacy). In G. Delobbe, C. Karnas, & C. Vandenberghe (Eds.), *Evaluation et développement des compétences au travail.* UCLs: Presses Universitaire de Louvain, pp. 507–516.

31. Roullier, J. Z., & Goldstein, I. L. (1993). The relationship between organizational transfer climate and positive transfer of training. *Human Resource Development Quarterly, 4(4),* 377–390; Tracey, J. B., Tannenbaum, S. I., & Kavanagh, M. J. (1995). Applying trained skills on the job: The importance of the work environment. *Journal of Applied Psychology, 80(2),* 239–252.

32. Phillips, J. (1996). How much is the training worth? *Training & Development,* 20–24.

33. Flynn, G. (1998). The nuts and bolts of valuing training. *Workforce, 17(11),* 80–85.

34. Haccoun, R. R., & Hamtiaux, T. (1994). Optimizing knowledge tests for inferring learning acquisition levels in single group training evaluation designs: The internal referencing strategy. *Personnel Psychology, 47,* 593–604.

35. Frese, M., Beimel, S., & Schoenborn, S. (2003). Action training for charismatic leadership: Two evaluation studies of a commercial training module on inspirational communication of vision. *Personnel Psychology, 56,* 671–697; Neuhengen, M. J., Cigularov, K., & Scott, S. B. (2010). Effectiveness of the internal referencing strategy design for training evaluation. SIOP conference; Taylor, P. J., Russ-Eft, D. F., & Taylor, H. (2009). Transfer of management training from alternative perspectives. *Journal of Applied Psychology, 94(1),* 104–121.

The Costs and Benefits of Training Programs

CHAPTER LEARNING OUTCOMES

After reading this chapter, you should be able to:

- explain why trainers should calculate the costs and benefits of training programs
- describe how to calculate the cost of training programs
- explain the difference between cost-effectiveness and cost–benefit evaluation
- describe how to calculate the benefits of training programs
- describe how to conduct a net benefit analysis, benefit–cost ratio, and return on investment
- define utility analysis and describe how to calculate the utility of training programs
- discuss the importance of credibility when estimating the benefits of training programs

ACCENTURE

Accenture is a global management consulting, technology services, and outsourcing company with more than 244,000 employees in more than 120 countries. A core value of the company is attracting and developing the best people and providing them with opportunities for personal and professional growth.

Accenture invests heavily in training and development. Entry-level employees receive more than 750 hours of training during their first five years and during the next eight years they receive an additional 550 hours of training. More than 70 percent of Accenture's new hires say that training was an important factor in joining the firm.

Several years ago, in the midst of changes in the global economy, the company experienced a dramatic transformation. Among the many challenges facing the firm was a realization of the need to reinvent its learning programs in order to deal with the many changes facing the company.

A critical part of the reinvention was that it would no longer be acceptable to treat training as a cost centre. Rather, it would be necessary to demonstrate and prove the added value of learning programs to the company. With this in mind, the company conducted a major return on investment (ROI) study to determine the ROI of its training programs.

The study involved analyzing the ROI of training for all of the company's employees over the history of the company. They did this using a technique that begins with a comprehensive analysis of employee records and measures the impact of learning on recruiting, retention, chargeability, and performance. To isolate the training effect on a per-person margin, the analysis factors out the effects of inflation, market cycle, experience, and employee level.

The study indicated that the net benefit of training was $1.27 billion. To calculate the return on investment (ROI), they divided the net benefit by the total cost of training ($358 million). The result was that for every dollar invested in training, there was a return of $3.53 or an ROI of 353 percent. In other words, for every dollar invested in learning, the firm receives the dollar back plus an additional $3.53 to its bottom line.

The study also showed that employees who take more training (the top 50th percentile) are more productive. They have 20 percent higher bill rates to clients, they are more "chargeable" to clients, and they stay with the company 14 percent longer compared to the bottom 50 percent.

The ROI study got the attention and respect of the company's most senior executives. It secured their ongoing support for the learning transformation and made it clear how important learning is for achieving business objectives and driving high performance.

Accenture's learning strategy is now aligned with its business strategy, and learning has had a positive impact on financial performance. Accenture has an evaluation system that collects data on all of its training programs, allowing the company to measure the ROI of each course. The company has won numerous awards for its ROI evaluation process, which is featured in a book called *Return on Learning*.[1]

Source: D. Vanthournout, K. Olson, J. Ceisel, A. White, T. Waddington, T. Barfield, S. Desai & C. Mindrum, *Return on learning: Training for high performance at Accenture.* Evanston, IL, 2008: Agate; T. Galvin, G. Johnson, & J. Barbian, "The 2003 training top 100," *Training*, March, 2003, Pp. 18–38; Galvin, T., "The 2002 Training Top 100," *Training*, March, 2002, Pp. 42–60; www.accenture.com.

Organizations have become increasingly concerned about the costs and benefits of their training and development programs and the value added to the bottom line. As you can see from the Accenture story, it is possible to calculate the benefits of training programs in monetary terms and the return on training investments. Accenture's learning transformation shows that learning programs can be run like a business and that learning can have a financial impact on an organization's bottom line by maximizing the return on learning.

Information on the costs and benefits of training programs is an important part of the training evaluation process. In fact, some experts consider the calculation of return on investment (ROI) to be Level 5 in Kirkpatrick's evaluation model (see Chapter 11).[2]

This chapter describes different approaches for calculating the costs and benefits of training programs. In this chapter, you will learn how to calculate the costs, benefits, net benefit, benefit–cost ratio, return on investment (ROI), and utility of training programs. But first, let's discuss training and the bottom line.

TRAINING AND THE BOTTOM LINE

In Chapter 11, we described the process of training evaluation. This usually involves measuring trainees' reactions, learning, behaviour, and organization results. The intent is to show some improvement in employees' knowledge, on-the-job behaviour, and organizational outcomes. Typically, one hopes to see an improvement in employees' learning and on-the-job behaviour and a positive effect on organizational effectiveness.

Make the
Connection

But what about the cost of a training program? What if a training program is very expensive? That is, what if the cost is greater than the benefit? Would improvements in employee behaviour and organizational outcomes be worthwhile? Would the training program be worth the cost?

Without information on the cost of training and the monetary value of training benefits, one cannot adequately answer these questions. Clearly, the effectiveness of a training program also depends on its costs and benefits. Managers might be pleased to know that a training program has improved customer satisfaction, but they will be even more impressed by the financial value of an improvement in customer satisfaction. Recall how the ROI study at Accenture got the attention and ongoing support of senior executives.

Costing is a complex and time-consuming process that many training specialists prefer to avoid. Some managers are skeptical about the theoretical underpinnings of costing, while others suggest, rightly, that in business not everything is quantifiable. Indeed, many managers suggest that some quality and processes—job satisfaction, communication techniques—make people feel good about themselves and the company they work for, and you just cannot put a dollar value on them.

However, there is increasing pressure for human resource and training professionals to demonstrate the financial value of their programs. Organizations increasingly want to know the return on their training investments and in a time of declining budgets, the training function faces increased pressure to justify the costs of training programs.[3] A recent survey of CEOs found that 96 percent of them want to see learning and development connected to business impact data, and 74 percent want to see return on investment (ROI) data.[4] Therefore, trainers and human resource professionals must be able to calculate and demonstrate the results of training and development investments. This not only shows the value of training programs to management and the organization, but it also justifies the training function's share of the budget and improves its status and influence within the organization.[5]

Make the
Connection

Furthermore, other members of an organization are more likely to see training and development as an investment rather than a cost and training budgets are less likely to be slashed during economic downturns. You might recall from Chapter 1 that many organizations in Canada view training and development as an operating expense or cost that should be minimized rather than as an investment. Calculating the costs and benefits of training programs is necessary for viewing training as an investment. Financial information about the benefits of training programs also places human resource and training professionals on an equal footing with other functions in an organization.

TRAINING AND THE BOTTOM LINE IN CANADIAN ORGANIZATIONS

According to the Conference Board of Canada, although most training programs in Canada are evaluated at Level 1 (trainee reactions), only 24 percent are evaluated at Level 5 (cost–benefit analysis) and only 21 percent of organizations perform Level 5 evaluations.[6] However, more organizations are beginning to conduct financial evaluations of their training programs.

For example, 15 supervisors at Firestone Canada attended a problem-solving workshop after a lack of skills was identified as the source of an internal problem. After the training the supervisors used their new skills to solve the problem. An assessment of the program's impact on the supervisors indicated that supervisors acquired new problem-solving skills, strengthened their analytical thinking, participated in more dynamic teamwork, and had better quality control. As for the bottom line, the company realized a cost savings of $10,000 per month.[7]

In order to calculate the effect of training on the bottom line, you must first calculate the costs and benefits of training. In the next section, we describe how to calculate training costs and in subsequent sections we describe how to calculate the benefits of training.

COSTING TRAINING PROGRAMS

Costing
The process of identifying all the expenditures used in training

Costing is the process used to identify all the expenditures used in training. This is an important procedure in both the design and evaluation of a training program. In Chapter 9, we noted that the trainer must prepare a budget that includes the costs of all of the expenses incurred in the delivery of a training program.

The calculation of the cost of a training program usually involves the assignment of various costs to a number of meaningful cost categories. Over the years, a number of approaches have been developed. One approach categorizes the costs of training according to the stages of the training process. For example, one might calculate the cost of needs analysis, training design, delivery, and evaluation. These costs are usually listed on a costing worksheet. One can then calculate and compare the cost of each stage as well as the total cost of a training program.

Another approach to costing training programs is to categorize the costs according to the nature or kind of cost. An example of this approach uses the following five cost categories: direct costs, indirect costs, development costs, overhead costs, and trainee compensation costs.[8]

Direct Costs

Direct costs are costs that are directly linked to a particular training program. This would include the trainers' salary and benefits, equipment rental, course materials, instructional aids, food and refreshments, and the cost of travel to and from the training site. These costs are so directly linked to a particular training program that they would not be incurred if a training program were cancelled.

Direct costs

Costs that are directly linked to a particular training program

Indirect Costs

Indirect costs are costs that are not part of a particular training program per se but they are expenses required to support training activities. Indirect costs include clerical and administrative support, trainer preparation and planning, training materials that have already been sent to trainees, and the cost of marketing training programs. These costs would still be incurred even if a training program were cancelled. In other words, unlike the direct costs, these costs cannot be recovered.

Indirect costs

Costs that support training activities and are not directly linked to a particular training program

Developmental Costs

Developmental costs are costs that are incurred in the development of a training program. This would include the cost of doing a needs analysis, the cost of developing instructional media such as videotapes, the design of training materials, and the cost of evaluating a training program.

Developmental costs

Costs that are incurred in the development of a training program

Overhead Costs

Overhead costs refer to costs incurred by the training department but not associated with any particular training program. Such costs are required for the general operation of the training function such as the cost of maintaining training facilities (e.g., heat and lighting) and equipment and the salaries of clerical and administrative support staff. A portion of these costs must be allocated to each training program.

Overhead costs

Costs incurred by the training department but not associated with any particular training program

Trainee Compensation Costs

Trainee compensation refers to the cost of the salaries and benefits paid to trainees while they are attending a training program. This might also include the cost of replacing employees while they are in training. The logic behind this cost is simply that employees must be paid while they are not working and this is a cost of the training program.

Trainee compensation

The cost of the salaries and benefits paid to trainees while they are attending a training program

TRAINING COSTS AT THE WOOD PANEL PLANT

Table 12.1 presents a training cost analysis using the five cost categories described above. The example is from a company that produces wood panels. The company had three problems that it wanted solved. First, it wanted to improve the quality of wood panels because they were experiencing a 2-percent rejection rate each day due to poor quality. Second, they wanted to lower the number of preventable accidents, which was higher than the industry average. Third, they wanted to improve the housekeeping of the production area, which was considered poor and a cause of some of the preventable accidents. Visual inspections that used a 20-item checklist indicated an average of 10 problems in housekeeping each week.[9]

TABLE 12.1

Training Cost Analysis for Wood Panel Plant

Direct costs. The travel and per diem cost was zero, because training took place adjacent to the plant. Classroom space and audiovisual equipment were rented from a local hotel; refreshments were purchased at the same hotel. Because different supervisors attended the morning and afternoon sessions, lunch was not provided.

Direct Costs	
Outside instructor	0
In-house instructor—12 days × $125 a day	$1,500
Fringe benefits—25 percent of salary	375
Travel and per-diem expenses	0
Materials—$60 × 56 participants	3,360
Classroom space and audiovisual equipment—12 days × $50 a day	600
Refreshments—$4 a day × 3 days × 56 participants	672
Total direct costs	**$6,507**

Indirect costs. Clerical and administrative costs reflect the amount of clerical time spent on making arrangements for the workshop facilities, sending out notices to all participants, and preparing class rosters and other miscellaneous materials.

Indirect Costs	
Training management	0
Clerical and administrative salaries	750
Fringe benefits—25 percent of clerical and administrative salaries	187
Postage, shipping, and telephone	0
Pre-and post-learning materials—$4 × 56 participants	224
Total indirect costs	**$1,161**

Development costs. These costs represent the purchase of the training program from a vendor. Included are instructional aids, an instructor manual, videotapes, and a licensing fee. The instructor-training costs are for a one-week workshop the instructor attended to prepare for facilitating the training. Front-end assessment costs were covered by the corporate training budget.

Development Costs	
Fee to purchase program	3,600
Instructor training	
Registration fee	1,400
Travel and lodging	975
Salary	625
Benefits (25 percent of salary)	156
Total development costs	**$6,756**

Overhead costs. These represent the services that the general organization provides to the training unit. Because figures were not available, we used 10 percent of the direct, indirect, and program-development costs.

Overhead Costs	
General organization support, 10 percent of direct, indirect, top management's time and development costs	. . . .
Total overhead costs	**$1,444**

Compensation for participants. This figure represents the salaries and benefits paid to all participants while they attended the workshop.

Compensation for Participants	
Participants' salaries and benefits (time away from the job)	
Total compensation	**$16,696**
Total training costs	**$32,564**
Cost per participant	**$ 582**

Source: D.G. Robinson & J. Robinson, "Training for impact," T+D, Aug. 1989, Pp. 34–42, American Society for Training & Development. Reprint/Adapted with permission of American Society for Training & Development.

The solution was to train supervisors in performance-management and interpersonal skills. Forty-eight supervisors as well as seven shift superintendents and a plant manager attended a three-day behavioural-modelling skill-building training program. The objectives of the program were to teach the supervisors how to discuss quality problems and poor work habits with employees; to recognize improvements in employee performance; to teach employees on the job; and to recognize employees for above-average performance.

The cost of the training program was calculated for each of the five cost categories. As shown in Table 12.1, the total cost of the training program was $32,564, or $582 per trainee. This was based on total direct costs of $6,507; indirect costs of $1,161; development costs of $6,756; overhead costs of $1,444; and compensation costs of $16,696.

It is important to recognize that the costing process presented in Table 12.1 is only an example. It represents one approach for categorizing training costs and might need to be modified to suit an organization's unique circumstances. The idea is to identify the main costs of a training program and not to worry too much about the labels assigned to them. The trainer should be most concerned about how to design a costing approach that has credibility within an organization and that will be accepted by management.

Once the costs of a training program have been calculated, they can be used for at least two purposes. First, they can be used to prepare a budget for a training program and to compare and contrast the costs of different programs. This is important when making decisions about whether to adopt a particular training program. Second, they can be used along with benefit information to calculate a training program's net benefit, benefit–cost ratio (BCR), and return on investment (ROI).

In the next section, we describe how to determine the benefits of training programs.

THE BENEFITS OF TRAINING PROGRAMS

The benefits of a training program can be calculated in monetary or non-monetary terms. When the benefit is calculated in monetary terms, it is referred to as cost-effectiveness evaluation. **Cost-effectiveness evaluation** involves comparing the monetary cost of training to the benefit of training in monetary terms.

Sometimes, however, it is not possible to determine the monetary value of training benefits or to express them in financial terms. Further, in some cases there might be important benefits of a training program that are not monetary benefits. This kind of evaluation is called cost–benefit evaluation.

Cost–benefit evaluation compares the cost of training in monetary terms to the benefits of training in non-monetary terms. Non-monetary benefits are similar to what was described as results or Level 4 evaluation criteria in Chapter 11 and include organization outcomes such as the rate of turnover, absenteeism, customer satisfaction, and so on. It is worth noting that such benefits might have a financial effect on the performance of an organization even though they might not be described in monetary terms.

Cost-effectiveness evaluation

A comparison of the monetary cost of training to the benefit of training in monetary terms

Cost–benefit evaluation

A comparison of the cost of training in monetary terms to the benefits of training in non-monetary terms

Net benefit

The estimated value of the benefit minus the cost of the training program

Benefit–cost ratio (BCR)

The benefit divided by the cost of the training program

For example, if a training program is expected to reduce the amount of scrap in the production of a product, then a cost–benefit evaluation would indicate how much the training program cost and the amount or percentage reduction in scrap. On the other hand, a cost-effectiveness evaluation would calculate the monetary value of the reduction in scrap.

Once we know the cost of a training program as well as the benefit in monetary terms, it is possible to determine the net benefit of the program. The **net benefit** of a training program refers to the benefit minus the cost of the training program. Thus, to conduct a net benefit analysis one simply subtracts the cost of a training program from its financial benefit. A related calculation is the **benefit–cost ratio (BCR)**, which is derived by dividing the benefit by the cost.

Another way to determine the financial return of a training program is the calculation of the return on investment or ROI, which is described in the next section.

RETURN ON INVESTMENT (ROI)

Return on investment (ROI)

A comparison of the cost of a training program relative to its benefits that involves dividing the net benefit by the cost of the training program

The most popular approach for determining the benefits or return of a training program is the return on investment. This is what Accenture did to demonstrate the value of its training programs to the company. You might recall that Accenture found that for every dollar invested in training, there was a return of $3.53—or an ROI of 353 percent.

Return on investment (ROI) involves comparing the cost of a training program relative to its benefits by dividing the net benefit by the cost of the training program. For example, Cisco Systems calculates the ROI of e-learning by having employees complete a Web-based survey shortly after they have attended a training program. Employees are asked to select a percentage range that indicates the time savings or quality improvement in their performance since taking the course. The results are used to calculate the ROI of e-learning, which has been found to be 900 percent per course. In other words, every dollar the company spends on training results in a gain of $9 in productivity.[10]

However, many companies in Canada still do not calculate the ROI of their training programs. As indicated earlier, the Conference Board of Canada found that only 21 percent of organizations conduct a Level 5 evaluation. This is partly due to the difficulty and complexity involved in the process. To help companies learn how to calculate the ROI of their training programs, a program called Investing in People was launched several years ago to provide Canadian organizations with methods and tools to assess the impact of their training investments. To learn more about this program, see Training Today 12.1, "The Investing in People Project."

The calculation of ROI involves dividing the net benefit (benefits − cost of the program) by the cost of a training program:

$$\text{Return on Investment} = \frac{\text{Benefits} - \text{Cost of the program}}{\text{Cost of the program}}$$

As an example, if a training program cost $100,000 and the financial benefit is $300,000, then the calculation of ROI is simply $300,000 − $100,000/ $100,000 = 2. In other words, there is a return of $2 for every $1 spent on training (1:2). When the ROI is above 1 it indicates that the return of a training program is greater than the investment. A higher ratio of results to costs

Training Today (12.1

The Investing in People Project

A project called Investing in People was launched in 2007 to help Canadian organizations evaluate the return on investment (ROI) of training programs and to provide evidence that training results in positive business outcomes. The main objective of the project was to provide evidence that training results in a positive return on investment (ROI) and is crucial to business success and economic growth. The program also aims to encourage Canadian organizations to invest more in training and to identify best training practices based on the most successful training programs.

Investing in People was a three-year project sponsored by Human Resources and Social Development Canada (HRSDC) as part of the Workplace Skills Initiative (WSI). The $1.3-million project was awarded to the Canadian Society of Training and Development (CSTD) and was implemented by Learning Designs Online. Return-on-investment case studies were carried out in 12 organizations where a chosen training program was evaluated. The project involved organizations from all geographic regions and includes a wide variety of training programs across the country.

The aim of the program was to develop practical and innovative methods, tools, and instruments for Canadian organizations to use for assessing the impact of their training investments. The program focused on small and medium-sized companies in the manufacturing, services, and retail sectors. The results of the project along with the best practices and evaluation tools have been made available to other Canadian organizations.

To calculate ROI, Learning Designs uses a methodology called the Learning Value Chain, which evaluates a training program at each of four "links" (capability, transfer, business results, and ROI). At each link, data is gathered to assess the extent to which the training has achieved key outcomes, added value, and enabled the next critical event in the chain to occur.

Business Development Bank of Canada (BDC) is one of the 12 workplaces that participated in the program. The Crown corporation has 1,700 employees and invests on average about 4.5 percent of its payroll in training. BDC evaluated a coaching program for banking branch managers that achieved an ROI of 74 percent. A training program at WestJet on running efficient meetings achieved an ROI of 558 percent.

Sources: S. Dobson, "Rallying for ROI around training," *Canadian HR Reporter,* Oct. 19, 2009, P. 15; S. Dobson, "Project connects dots between T&D, profit," *Canadian HR Reporter,* April 21, 2008, P. 3; A. Bailey, "Meeting Canada's productivity challenge," *The Canadian Learning Journal,* Fall, 2008, P. 25; L. Gillis & A. Bailey, *Meta study of evaluation findings.* Toronto: Canadian Society for Training and Development, 2010.

indicates a greater financial benefit to the organization. When the ROI ratio is less than 1 it indicates that the investment or cost is greater than the return. And when the ROI is 1, the return is equal to the investment and the training program breaks even.

The percentage return can also be calculated by simply multiplying the ratio by 100; so, in this case, the return is 200 percent. This can also be described as a 200-percent return on investment (the gain of $200,000 is 200 percent of the $100,000 investment).

For another example of the calculation of ROI, let's return to the wood panel plant. Recall that a supervisor training program that cost $32,564 was designed to improve the quality of wood panels by lowering the daily rejection rate; to improve the housekeeping of the production area; and to reduce the number of preventable accidents.[11]

Table 12.2 shows how the benefits were measured in each of the three areas. The results in each area before and one year after training as well as the differences are shown. Before training, the rejection rate of wood panels was 2 percent per day or 1,440 panels. After training, this was reduced to 1.5 percent or 1,080 panels. The difference of .5 percent per day or 360 wood panels was calculated to be a saving of $720 per day or $172,800 per year. Housekeeping was measured in terms of a visual inspection using a 20-item checklist. Before the training there was an average of 10 defects per week while after training it was reduced to two defects. Thus, the training program resulted in a reduction of eight defects per week (this could not be calculated in monetary terms). The number of preventable accidents before training was 24 per year at a cost of $144,000. After training this was reduced to 16 per year or eight fewer accidents at a cost of $96,000 and a savings of $48,000.

By comparing this information to the cost information in Table 12.1, we can calculate the net benefit, BCR, and the ROI of the training program. Recall that the total cost of the training program was $32,564. The net benefit of the training program in monetary terms can be determined by adding the savings from the reduction in rejected wood panels ($172,800) with the savings from the reduction in preventable accidents ($48,000) and then subtracting the cost of the training program ($32,564). Thus, the net benefit of the training program is: $220,800 − $32,564 = $188,236. The BCR is $220,800/$32,564 = 6.78.

TABLE 12.2

Benefits Calculation Worksheet for Wood Panel Plant

Operational Results area	How Measured	Results before Training	Results after Training	Differences (+ or −)	Expressed in $
Quality of panels	percent rejected	2 percent rejected–1440 panels per day	1.5 percent rejected–1080 panels per day	5 percent 360 panels	$720 per day $172,800 per year
Housekeeping	Visual inspection using 20-item checklist	10 defects (average)	2 defects (average)	8 defects	Not measurable in $
Preventable accidents	Number of accidents	24 per year	16 per year	8 per year	$48,000 per year
	Direct cost of each accident	$144,000 per year	$96,000 per year	$48,000	

Total savings: $220,800

Net Benefit = $220,800 − $32,564 = $188,236

Cost–benefit ratio = $220,800/$32,564 = 6.8

$$\text{ROI} = \frac{\text{Benefits} - \text{Training Costs}}{\text{Training Costs}} = \frac{\$220,800 - \$32,564}{\$32,564} = 5.78 \times 100\% = 578\%$$

Source: D.G. Robinson & J. Robinson, "Training for impact," T+D, Aug. 1989, Pp. 34–42, American Society for Training & Development. Reprint/Adapted with permission of American Society for Training & Development.

The Trainer's Notebook 12.1
CONVERTING BENEFITS TO MONETARY VALUES

One of the most difficult aspects of calculating ROI is determining the monetary value of the benefits of training. Jack Phillips, one of the leading experts on the calculation of ROI, suggests the following five steps for converting benefits to monetary values.

Step 1: Focus on a single unit. Identify a particular unit of improvement in output (e.g., products, sales), quality (e.g., errors, product defects), time (to respond to a customer order or complete a project), or employee behaviour (e.g., one case of employee turnover).

Step 2: Determine a value for each unit. Place a value identified on the single unit identified in step 1. This will be easier for hard measures such as production, quality, and time because most organizations record the value of one unit of production or the cost of

a product defect. It will be more difficult to do for softer measures such as the cost of one employee absence.

Step 3: Calculate the change in performance. Determine the change in performance following training after factoring out other potential influences. This change in units of performance should be directly attributable to the training.

Step 4: Obtain an annual amount. The industry standard for an annual performance change is equal to the total change in the performance data during one year.

Step 5: Determine the annual value. The annual value of improvement equals the annual performance change, multiplied by the unit value.

Source: J.J. Phillips, "How much is the training worth?" *T+D*, April, 1996, Pg. 20–24. Reprinted with permission of American Society for Training & Development.

To calculate the ROI, we simply divide the net benefit of the program ($188,236) by the cost of the training program ($32,564): $188,236/$32,564 = 5.78. Therefore, the ROI for one year after training is equal to 5.78 or 578 percent. It is worth noting that while this analysis is an example of cost-effectiveness evaluation, the results for housekeeping (i.e., a reduction of eight defects per week) is an example of cost–benefit evaluation.

In summary, this example provides a good illustration of how the benefits of training programs can be measured in a manner that is consistent with the objectives of a training program (e.g., reduction in preventable accidents), and can then be translated into monetary terms and used to calculate a training program's net benefit, BCR, and ROI.

To learn more about how to convert benefits into monetary values, see The Trainer's Notebook 12.1, "Converting Benefits to Monetary Values."

UTILITY ANALYSIS

As described in Chapter 11, in a typical training evaluation study a training group is compared to an untrained or control group that did not receive training in order to determine how effective a training program is for learning, a change in behaviour, and/or job performance. While the results of this comparison might indicate a significant difference between the two groups, it does not indicate the dollar value associated with the change or improvement in

Make the Connection

learning, behaviour, or job performance. Utility analysis, however, can do this and it is another approach for determining the costs and benefits of training programs.

Utility analysis is a method for forecasting the financial benefits that result from human resource programs such as training and development. Utility analysis involves procedures in which the effectiveness of a training program can be translated into dollars and cents.[12]

To calculate the utility of a training program, several factors must be considered. One of the most important is the effectiveness of the training program. In other words, what is the difference in job performance between employees who are trained and those who do not receive training? This is referred to as the *effect size*. The larger the effect size, the more effective a training program will be and the greater the utility.

A second factor is the *standard deviation of job performance* in dollars of untrained employees. This has to do with how much of a difference there is in the job performance of untrained employees and the monetary value of this difference. The standard deviation of job performance in dollar terms is an important factor because in jobs in which the performance of individual employees is widely different, an effective training program will improve the performance of a greater number of employees and will, therefore, result in larger dollar gains. When the job performance of employees is relatively similar, an effective training program is less likely to result in large dollar gains. Therefore, it is necessary to estimate the standard deviation of job performance of untrained employees to make estimates of utility. There are several approaches for doing this, such as asking supervisors to provide an estimate of the dollar value of performance. The larger the standard deviation of job performance of the untrained group the greater the utility of a training program.

A third factor is the *number of employees trained*. The more employees who are trained the greater the utility. A fourth factor is the expected length of *time that the training benefits will last*. The longer the effects of training will last, the higher the utility of a training program.

Utility is equal to the multiplication of all of these factors minus the *cost of the training program* (cost per employee × number of employees trained). The following formula is used to estimate the utility of a training program:[13]

$$\Delta U = (T)(N)(d_t)(SDy) - (N)(C)$$

where

ΔU = utility, or the dollar value of the program
T = the number of years the training has a continued effect on performance
N = the number of people trained
d_t = the true difference in job performance between the average trained and untrained employee in standard deviation units (effect size)
SDy = the standard deviation of job performance in dollars of the untrained group
C = the cost of training each employee

Consider the following example. To increase the number of toys produced in a toy factory, a training program is implemented and 50 of the plant employees attend. Compared to a group of workers who do not attend the training program,

Utility analysis
A method to forecast the financial benefits that result from human resource programs such as training and development

the performance of the 50 trained employees is found to be twice as high (e.g., they produce 100 toys per day compared to 50 produced by untrained workers). We will assume that this equals an effect size of 2. We also assume that the standard deviation of job performance of the untrained employees is $100. The expected length of time that the training will last is estimated to be five years. The cost of the training program is $300 per employee. Using the utility equation above, we can calculate the utility of the training program as follows:

$$\Delta U = 5(50)(2)(\$100) - 50(\$300)$$
$$\Delta U = \$50,000 - \$15,000$$
$$\Delta U = \$35,000$$

Thus, the expected utility of the training program for the 50 employees trained is $35,000. This amount might be even greater if the training program lasts longer than five years or if the untrained employees learn how to improve their performance by working with and observing the trained employees. The BCR can also be calculated by dividing the utility by the total cost of the program ($35,000/$15,000 = 2.33) and the ROI can be calculated by dividing the net benefit of the program by the total cost of the program ($35,000 − $15,000/$15,000 = 1.33).

Break-Even Analysis

An extension of the use of the utility formula is to conduct a **break-even analysis** or to find the value at which benefits equal costs and utility is equal to zero.[14] This can be calculated for any of the terms in the utility equation. However, it is most meaningful to conduct a break-even analysis for the effect size or the standard deviation. For example, what is the break-even effect size for the example presented above? This can be calculated by dividing the cost of the training program ($15,000) by the multiplicative function of the other factors: (N)(T)(SDy) or (50)(5)(100). The calculations are as follows:

Break-even analysis	Finding the value at which benefits equal costs and utility is equal to zero

$$d_t = 15,000/25,000$$
$$d_t = .6$$

Thus, a training program with an effect size of .6 will result in a utility of zero, and an effect size greater than .6 will result in a utility that is greater than zero. Therefore, a training program that is considerably less effective than the one in the example would still be likely to result in a financial gain as long as the effect size is greater than .6.

Break-even analysis can be very useful because it helps reduce the uncertainty associated with the estimates of the various parameters used to calculate utility. For example, to the extent that the break-even effect size is far below the actual effect size used to calculate utility, the greater the confidence one can have in the results.[15]

THE CREDIBILITY OF BENEFIT ESTIMATES

We have been discussing the costs and benefits of training programs and how to calculate the ROI and utility of training programs. However, it is important to realize that this is not an exact science. Assumptions and judgments are made when estimating the monetary benefits of a training program. As a result, the process works only if managers and clients accept the assumptions. The estimation of benefits is an inexact procedure and trainers should be concerned about professional credibility.

Credibility is a major issue in cost-effectiveness evaluation and the data must be accurate and the process believable.[16] Consider the example of a large bank that was experiencing a high rate of turnover. A training program was designed to counter the turnover problem. The cost of employee turnover needed to be estimated to calculate the ROI. However, the actual cost calculation was difficult because of the many interacting variables—administrative costs, interviewing, testing, relocation, orientation, increase in supervisory time, initial less-than-optimal performance, on-the-job training—that make up the cost of replacing one person. As the bank did not want to devote the considerable resources necessary to developing a precise calculation, turnover was classified as a soft cost and a combination of approaches was used to derive an acceptable figure.

Initially, a literature search was used to determine that another institution in the same industry had calculated a cost of $25,000 per turnover. This figure, derived by an internal-audit unit and verified by a consulting specialist in turnover reduction, was used as a starting point. The application of this statistic to another (even though quite similar) organization, however, was in question. The training staff then met with senior executives "to agree on a turnover cost value to use in gauging the success of the program. Management agreed on an estimate that was half the amount from the study, $12,500. This was considered very conservative because other turnover studies typically yield statistics of greater value. Management felt comfortable with the estimate, however, and it was used on the benefits side of program evaluation. Although not precise, this exercise yielded a figure that was never challenged."[17]

The term "never challenged" is significant. Trainers must perform cost-effectiveness evaluations from a position of strength. In this example, senior managers were brought on-side when they were used as experts. It mattered little that the turnover cost was set at $12,500 rather than $25,000, because the benefit estimation produced from these data was credible and accepted by those with the power to make investment decisions.

Thus, despite the appearance of quantitative rigour, virtually all but the simplest cost-effectiveness evaluations are dependent to a greater or lesser extent on some assumptions and expert opinion.[18] Trainers must ensure that their clients and management agree on the cost factors and the measurement and estimation of benefits. Management and clients must perceive benefit estimates as credible, believable, and acceptable. It is therefore critical that trainers find out what management deems to be most important in terms of the benefits and expected results, and whenever possible, obtain cost estimates (e.g., the cost of turnover) from management.

It also helps to use internal and external experts to assist in making benefit estimates. Because they are experts who are familiar with the situation, they are likely to be seen as credible by management. For example, if one wanted to estimate the cost of employee grievances, a good expert would be a manager of labour relations. Estimates might also be obtained from other sources who are close to the situation, such as trainees and their supervisors.[19]

The Trainer's Notebook 12.2

INCREASING THE CREDIBILITY OF BENEFIT ESTIMATES

Following these guidelines can increase the credibility of estimates of the benefits of a training program.

1. Take a conservative approach when making estimates and assumptions.

2. Use the most credible and reliable sources for estimates.

3. Explain the approaches and assumptions used in the conversion.

4. When results appear overstated, consider adjusting the numbers to achieve more realistic values.

5. Use hard data whenever possible.

Source: J.J. Phillips, "How much is the training worth?" *T+D*, April, 1996, P. 20.

For some guidelines on how to increase the credibility of the estimates of training benefits, see The Trainer's Notebook 12.2, "Increasing the Credibility of Benefit Estimates."

SUMMARY

This chapter described the methods and approaches for calculating the costs and benefits of training programs. Cost and benefit information is important not only for budgeting purposes and for comparing the costs of training programs, but also for training evaluation. Five cost categories for costing training programs were described as well as the differences between cost-effectiveness evaluation and cost–benefit evaluation. Descriptions and examples were then provided for the calculation of the net benefit, benefit–cost ratio (BCR), and return on investment (ROI) of training programs. Utility analysis was also described as an alternative approach for calculating the financial benefits of training programs. The chapter concluded with a discussion of the importance of credibility when estimating the financial benefits of training and development programs.

Key Terms

benefit–cost ratio (BCR) p. 370
break-even analysis p. 375
cost–benefit evaluation p. 369
cost-effectiveness evaluation p. 369
costing p. 366
developmental costs p. 367
direct costs p. 367

indirect costs p. 367
net benefit p. 370
overhead costs p. 367
return on investment (ROI) p. 370
trainee compensation p. 367
utility analysis p. 374

Make the Connection

p. 365: types of training evaluation are discussed in Chapter 11 on page 329
p. 366: training as an expense versus an investment is discussed in Chapter 1 on page 13
p. 373: training evaluation designs are discussed in Chapter 11 on pages 350–353

Web Links

Accenture: **www.accenture.com**

Cisco Systems: **www.cisco.com**

Firestone Canada: **www.bridgestone-firestone.ca**

Required Professional Capabilities (RPCs)

The following RPCs are relevant to material covered in this chapter. The RPC number represents the CCHRA number assigned to the RPC as presented on the CCHRA website. All of the RPCs can be found in the Body of Knowledge at **http://www.chrp.ca/rpc/body-of-knowledge/**.

RPC 152: Develops and implements measurement tools and processes to evaluate program effectiveness.

152.03: Training cost–benefit analysis and training evaluation techniques

Discussion Questions

1. Discuss the pros and cons of calculating the ROI of training programs. Should trainers always do this as part of a training evaluation?
2. What can trainers do to increase the credibility of monetary estimates of the benefits of a training program?
3. What is the difference between cost–benefit evaluation and cost-effectiveness evaluation? What are some situations in which a trainer might want to calculate a cost–benefit evaluation and a cost-effectiveness evaluation?
4. What is a utility analysis and how is it used to determine the cost and benefits of a training program? What is a break-even analysis and how can it help to understand the value of a training program?
5. Why should trainers be concerned about calculating the costs and benefits of training programs? What are the advantages and disadvantages of doing so?
6. What are the different costs associated with training programs and what information is required to calculate each type of cost?
7. Why do so few Canadian organizations evaluate the financial benefits of training programs? Do you think that more organizations should do so? What needs to be done to increase the number of organizations that evaluate the financial benefits of training programs?

8. Explain how to calculate each of the following: net benefit, benefit–cost ratio (BCR), return on investment (ROI), and utility. What are the differences among each of these calculations?

The Great Training Debate

1. Debate the following: Calculating the monetary benefits and ROI of training and development is the most important way to evaluate training programs.
2. Debate the following: The calculation of a training program's ROI is more art than science and should not be part of the training evaluation process.

Exercises

In-Class

1. In order to calculate the benefits of training programs, measures have to be developed that are consistent with a training program and its objectives. As well, some of these measures will need to be converted into monetary terms. For each of the following training programs, identify some of the benefits and how they can be measured for the purpose of cost–benefit evaluation and cost-effectiveness evaluation:
   a. Sales training
   b. Ethics training
   c. Customer-service training
   d. Health and safety training
   e. Total quality management training
   f. Sexual harassment training
   g. Diversity training

   To learn more about these training programs, refer to Chapter 13.

2. Consider a situation in which you, a trainer for an organization that manufactures sportswear, must present information on the costs and benefits of a training program to management, which is about to decide whether the program will be implemented organization-wide. You have already designed the training program and delivered it to one group of employees and you want to begin offering it to the rest of the organization. How will you present the information to management? Will you present information on the net benefit, BCR, ROI, and/or utility analysis? Will you present cost–benefit information or cost-effectiveness information? What are the advantages and disadvantages of presenting information on each of these? Do you think that trainers should present financial information about the benefits of training to management? What are the advantages and disadvantages of doing so?

3. Consider the costs and benefits of a university or college course such as the training and development course you are now taking. Using the five cost categories discussed in the chapter, identify the major costs of the course and try to estimate the costs of each category. Now consider the benefits. What benefits would you include if you were to conduct a cost-effectiveness analysis and a cost–benefit analysis? How would you determine the ROI and utility of your course? Consider the costs and benefits from the institution's perspective and the student's perspective.

4. Think about the last time you attended a training program. Based on what you know about the program, make a list of the costs in each of the following cost categories: direct costs, indirect costs, development costs, overhead costs, and compensation for participants. In addition, make a list of the potential benefits of the program. What information would you need to determine the monetary value of these benefits? What additional information do you require to calculate the utility of the program?

In-the-Field

1. To find out about the costs and benefits of training in an organization, contact the human resource department of an organization and ask the following questions:

   • To what extent do you determine the cost of training programs, how do you do it, and who does it? What cost categories are used?

   • Do you determine the benefits of training programs and if so, how do you do it? Who is involved in calculating the monetary value of training?

   • Do you conduct a cost-effectiveness evaluation and a cost–benefit evaluation? If so, who does it?

   • Do you determine the net benefit, benefit–cost ratio (BCR), and return on investment (ROI) of training programs? If so, who is responsible for it?

2. To find out about some of the organizations that participated in the Investing in People project, visit the Canadian Society of Training and Development at **www.cstd.ca** and click on Professional Development and then Investing in People. Then in the box at the top of the page, choose "Investing in People: Case Studies." Choose one of the companies listed and prepare a brief report (written or class presentation) of the company in which you discuss the following:
   a. Overview of the company
   b. Training rationale and training program
   c. The learning value chain
   d. The costs and benefits of the training program
   e. The evaluation results and main findings

Case Incident 1

The Harmony Remote

The Harmony remote is a universal remote control that can replace up to 15 remote controls. While it sounds simple, many consumers have questions and they keep Harmony's call centre very busy. Maintaining this centre can be expensive and poorly trained support agents can affect customer satisfaction, and subsequently, the success of the product.

So Logitech, makers of the remote, decided to redesign the training program used to educate new support agents about the Harmony technology. Harmony's redesigned training program blended e-learning technology with a traditional classroom setting while reducing the training from 12 to eight days. The goal for Logitech was to improve the support experience for customers in terms of quality and call-handle time, along with reducing the overall cost of the training. For the purpose of evaluation, they looked at the average handle time of a call, customer satisfaction ratings, and first call resolution (dealing with the customer's concerns during the first call without any other follow-up required).

Immediately after the training, the 162 participants completed a survey about the training program. The results revealed considerable success in enhancing capability—78 percent said they had acquired a high level of knowledge and skills and 74 percent had a high level of confidence in their ability to apply their learning in their new jobs. When it came to the transfer of learning to the job, 73 percent of respondents reported a high level of learning application and proficiency one month after training.

Sources: Based on: S. Dobson, "Logitech, BC Assessment fine-tuning training," *Canadian HR Reporter,* March 22, 2010, P. 8; L. Weisser, "Is training the answer? Project partners discover what's really important in measuring training initiatives," *The Canadian Learning Journal,* Spring, 2009, P. 14.

Questions

1. Describe how you would do a cost-effectiveness evaluation and a cost-benefit evaluation of the Harmony remote training program. What additional information do you require?
2. Describe how you would calculate the net benefit, benefit–cost ratio (BCR), and return on investment (ROI) of the Harmony remote training program. What additional information is required?
3. How would you conduct a utility analysis of the Harmony remote training program? What information do you have and what additional information do you require to conduct a utility analysis?

Case Incident 2

Renswartz Realty Company

As the housing market began to heat up, the Renswartz Realty Company set high goals for increasing the number of listings and sales. In order to accomplish these goals, the company president believed they would have to do two things. First, they would have to better market the company's superior customer service. Second, they would have to train their agents to improve their sales and customer-service skills. Choosing an advertising company turned out to be much easier than choosing a training program. Two consulting firms were contacted to provide a proposal to design and implement a training program that would be attended by all 200 of the company's sales agents.

The first consulting firm proposed a five-day program that would consist of lectures on "how to get more listings," "how to improve your service," and "making the sale," and would involve videos and behavioural modelling. According to the consulting firm, research has shown that the sales performance of those who have attended the training is significantly better than those who have not; the effect size of the program is .35. The training is expected to last for two years and will cost $1,500 per employee.

Flashback Questions

1. Do you think that training is the best solution to DATAIN's problems? Explain your answer using Mager and Pipe's performance analysis flow-chart for determining solutions to performance problems (see Chapter 4, Figure 4.2). What are some other possible solutions to the problems described in the case?

2. What do you think the objectives should be for the proposed training programs? Refer to Chapter 5 and write several training objectives for the training programs that DATAIN is considering. Be sure to include the five key elements of training objectives. For each objective, be sure to include the three key components of training objectives (i.e., performance, condition, criterion).

3. DATAIN has not prepared a request for proposals (RFP). What are some possible consequences of this? If they were to create an RFP, what should it include and what should they consider when creating it? (Refer to the section in Chapter 5 on Request for Proposal and The Trainer's Notebook 5.1.)

4. Describe how the proposed training programs should be evaluated according to: a) Kirkpatrick's model, b) the COMA model, and c) the decision-based evaluation (DBE) model. Be specific in terms of what should be measured.

5. If you were to evaluate the proposed training programs, how would you design your evaluation study? Refer to Figure 11.2 in Chapter 11 and describe how you would evaluate the proposed training programs using each of the designs. What design would you recommend and why?

REFERENCES

1. Vanthournout, D., Olson, K., Ceisel, J., White, A., Waddington, T., Barfield, T., Desai, S., & Mindrum, C. (2008). *Return on learning: Training for high performance at Accenture.* Evanston, IL: Agate; Galvin, T., Johnson, G., & Barbian, J. (2003, March). The 2003 training top 100. *Training, 40(3)*, 18–38; Galvin, T. (2002, March). The 2002 training top 100. *Training, 39(3)*, 42–60; www.accenture.com.

2. Phillips. J. J. (1996, February). ROI: The search for best practices. *Training and Development,* 42–47.

3. Salas, E., & Cannon-Bowers, J. A. (2001). The science of training: A decade of progress. *Annual Review of Psychology, 52,* 471–499; Lavis, C. (2011). *Learning & development outlook 2011: Are organizations ready for learning 2.0?* Ottawa: The Conference Board of Canada.

4. Phillips, J. J., & Phillips, P. P. (2010, January). Confronting CEO expectations about the value of learning. *T+D, 64(1),* 52–57.

5. Phillips, J. J., & Phillips, P. P. (2009, August). Measuring what matters: How CEOs view learning success. *T+D, 63(8),* 44–49.

6. Lavis, C. (2011). *Learning & development outlook 2011: Are organizations ready for learning 2.0?* Ottawa: The Conference Board of Canada.

7. Everson, B. (2007, November 5). Canadian companies lag foreign firms in training. *Canadian HR Reporter, 20(19)*, 23.

8. Robinson, D. G., & Robinson, J. (1989, August). Training for impact. *Training & Development Journal, 43(8)*, 34–42.

9. Robinson, D. G., & Robinson, J. (1989, August).

10. Gale, S. F. (2002, August). Measuring the ROI of e-learning. *Workforce Management,* 74–77.

11. Robinson, D. G., & Robinson, J. (1989, August).

12. Cascio, W. F. (1991). *Costing human resources: The financial impact of behavior in organizations.* Boston, MA: Kent.

13. Schmidt, F. L., Hunter, J. E., & Pearlman, K. (1982). Assessing the economic impact of personnel programs on workforce productivity. *Personnel Psychology, 35,* 333–347.

14. Cascio, W. F. (1991).

15. Mathieu, J. E., & Leonard, R. L. Jr. (1987). Applying utility concepts to a training program in supervisory skills: A time-based approach. *Academy of Management Journal, 30,* 316–335.

16. Bedinham, K. (1998). Proving the effectiveness of training. *Education & Training 40(4),* 166–167; Phillips. J. J. (1996, April). How much is the training worth? *Training & Development,* 20–24.

17. Phillips, J. J. (1991, Autumn). Measuring the return on HRD. *Employment Relations Today, 18(3),* 329–342, p. 337.

18. Geroy, G. D., & Wright, P. C. (1988). Evaluation research: A pragmatic program-focused research strategy for decision makers. *Performance Improvement Quarterly, 1(3),* 17–26; Wright, P. C. (1990). Validating hospitality curricula within associated-sponsored certification programs: A qualitative methodology and a case study. *Hospitality Research Journal, 14(1),* 117–132.

19. Phillips. J. J. (1996, April).

Training Programs

CHAPTER LEARNING OUTCOMES

After reading this chapter, you should be able to:

- describe orientation training and essential skills training
- describe technical skills training and information technology training
- discuss WHMIS legislation and health and safety training programs
- describe total quality management (TQM) training
- describe team training and the skills required of team members
- describe sales training and the skills required to be effective in sales
- discuss customer-service training and the skills that employees require to interact effectively with customers
- define sexual harassment and describe sexual harassment training
- describe ethics training, diversity training, and cross-cultural training

BAYSHORE HOME HEALTH

Bayshore Home Health is a Canadian-owned and -operated home and community health-care provider with more than 50 home care offices, 20 community care clinics, and 8,000 employees. Bayshore is the largest provider of home and community health care services in Canada offering a wide range of home care services that it delivers to more than 70,000 clients each year.

Bayshore is committed to being a great place to work and an employer of choice. So to ensure that employees are more culturally competent and able to provide high-quality care, the company introduced a diversity strategy to help attract, recruit, and retain a more diverse workforce that reflects the Canadian population and the company's clientele.

The diversity strategy includes a three-year goal to hire more visible minorities, Aboriginals, and people with disabilities and create a culture that respects and includes diversity. The strategy also includes employee education about diversity and the impact that different cultural traditions, gender, age, sexual orientation, and physical or cognitive abilities have on attitudes towards health, illness, and treatment.

"Our goal is not only to increase representation of these groups in middle management and other positions, but also to shift the mindset of our leadership and employees to ensure we continually create a culture that respects and includes diversity today and in the future," says Bayshore employee relations innovation leader Soraiya Walji.

To create that culture and launch the strategy, Bayshore held workshops across the country on cultural competence. The workshop "Embracing Cultural Diversity & Developing Cultural Competence" was held in Moncton, Vancouver, and Oakville. The goal of the workshops was to raise awareness about how different cultural traditions, as well as age, gender, sexual orientation, and physical or cognitive abilities, can affect health outcomes.

Listening to patients and asking the right questions is key to providing quality health care, says Walji. "If we don't know how to ask the questions that are in tune with that culture, then that might affect the diagnosis and the treatment there onwards," she said.

Bayshore will also be implementing specific diversity workshops in branches to address local needs. "We really want to make sure that we improve client care and outcomes. Culture plays a big part in patient safety—diagnosis, treatment, and outcome. We want to make sure we're doing everything we can to be in tune with our patients' needs," says Walji.

According to Holly Quinn, chief nursing officer for Bayshore, the company is committed to making Bayshore a great place to work. "Our new strategy will help ensure that workforce diversity exists at all levels of our organization by educating and training staff throughout the company and encouraging them to embrace diversity as a source of strength and innovation," says Quinn.

It seems that they have succeeded in making Bayshore a great place to work: the company was recognized as one of Canada's 50 Best Managed Companies in 2011 for the fifth consecutive year.[1]

Source: Based on: S. Klie, "Cultural competence affects patient health," *Canadian HR Reporter*, Dec. 14, 2009, P. 12; www.bayshore.ca, Press Release: "Bayshore Home Health Launches Workforce Diversity Strategy", Sept., 16, 2009; www.bayshore.ca, Press Release: "Bayshore Home Health named one of Canada's 50 Best Managed Companies for fifth consecutive year," Feb. 23, 2011.

By now you should be familiar with the training and development process. We have covered the major steps of the instructional systems design (ISD) model of training and development: needs analysis, training objectives, training design, training methods, delivery, transfer of training, and the evaluation and costing of training programs. At this point, you might be asking yourself, "What types of training programs do organizations provide for their employees?"

Organizations offer many different types of training like the diversity training at Bayshore Home Health. The purpose of this chapter is to describe

TABLE 13.1

Training Content in Canadian Organizations

Training content	% of overall content	% of organizations offering
Management and supervisory skills	15	91
Professional and technical training	13	67
Occupational health and safety/compliance	11	80
New employee orientation	10	85
Interpersonal skills	9	77
Product knowledge	8	51
Executive development	7	69
Information technology skills training	7	68
Customer relations and/or service	7	65
Sales (excluding product knowledge)	5	41
Quality, competition, and business practices	5	59
Other	2	6
Basic skills (e.g., literacy, numeracy)	1	20

Source: C. Lavis, *Learning & development outlook 2011: Are organizations ready for learning 2.0?* Ottawa: The Conference Board of Canada, 2011.

the major types of training programs that are designed and delivered by organizations today. Table 13.1 shows the percentage of overall content for different types of training and the percentage of organizations in Canada that offer each type. Notice that most organizations offer all of the training content listed except for basic skills training, which is offered by only 20 percent of the organizations.

Table 13.2 lists 14 common types of training programs that will be described in this chapter. As you read about each type of training, you might think about how

TABLE 13.2

Types of Training Programs

1. *Orientation training.* Programs that introduce new employees to their job, the people they will be working with, and the organization.
2. *Essential skills training.* Training programs that are designed to provide employees with the essential skills required to perform their job and adapt to workplace change.
3. *Technical skills training.* Training in specific job-related skills that all employees need to perform their jobs.
4. *Information technology training.* Training programs that focus on the use of computers and computer systems.
5. *Computer software training.* Training programs that focus on how to use a specific computer software application.

6. *Health and safety training.* Training programs that educate employees in safe work methods and practices and how to recognize the chemical and physical hazards in the workplace so that they are prepared and capable of taking corrective action in the event of an accident.

7. *Total quality management (TQM) training.* Training programs that involve team training as well as training in the use of statistical tools that are used for problem-solving and decision-making processes.

8. *Team training.* Training programs that are designed to improve the functioning and effectiveness of teams in areas such as communication and coordination.

9. *Sales training.* Training programs that are designed to upgrade sales professionals' skills and help them deal with new competitive challenges.

10. *Customer-service training.* Training programs that are designed to provide employees with interpersonal and service skills that are required for interacting with customers and for providing quality service.

11. *Sexual harassment training.* Training programs that are designed to educate employees about sexual harassment and the organization's policies and procedures regarding sexual harassment.

12. *Ethics training.* Training programs that educate employees about the organization's values and ethical policies and on making ethical decisions.

13. *Diversity training.* Training programs that focus on differences in values, attitudes, and behaviours of individuals with different backgrounds.

14. *Cross-cultural training.* Training programs that prepare employees for working and living in different cultures and for interactions with persons from different backgrounds.

some of the material described in earlier chapters (e.g., needs analysis, training methods, transfer of training, training evaluation) is important for making each type of training program effective. Let's now take a closer look at the different types of training.

ORIENTATION TRAINING

Orientation training

Programs that introduce new employees to their job, the people they will be working with, and the organization

Orientation training refers to training programs that introduce new employees to their job, the people they will be working with, and the organization.[2] Formal orientation and training programs are one of the main methods used by organizations to socialize new employees.[3]

Most organizations provide some type of orientation for new employees. For example, a study of 100 major British organizations found that an overwhelming majority provided new hires with formalized, off-the-job induction training within four weeks of entry. Most of the organizations provided standardized programs that were designed and conducted by in-house human resource practitioners. The content of induction training was general in nature and pertained mostly to health and safety, terms and conditions of employment, organizational history and structure, specific training provisions, and human resource management policies and procedures.[4]

Employees who attend orientation training programs have been found to be more socialized in terms of their knowledge and understanding of the organization's goals and values, history, and involvement with people and to have higher organizational commitment.[5] Effective orientation programs can also shape corporate culture, increase new employees' speed-to-proficiency, and lower turnover.[6] Furthermore, a recent study on the training of new hires in a large fast-food organization found that those units that used the new hire training program to a greater extent had higher customer service performance, greater retention, and higher financial performance.[7]

For a good example of orientation training, see Training Today 13.1, "Employee Orientation at EllisDon."

Training Today 13.1

Employee Orientation at EllisDon

At construction company EllisDon, new employee orientation involves face-to-face programs as well as an online orientation system. When newcomers first arrive, HR sits down with them for an hour. This gives them a level of comfort and establishes a relationship so employees know whom to contact if they have questions. HR also goes through the online portal with them, outlining where to find information.

About two months later, HR sends an email to the managers to ask how the new employees have been doing. The managers are encouraged to sit down with each employee for an informal conversation to open up some dialogue.

The online orientation system begins with an automatic but customized welcome message sent to the new employee's email address. The employee is then told how to access the system and encouraged to complete several modules, at various stages: from day one, week one, month one, leading up to year one.

The first module includes a president's welcome in a 20-minute video that explains the company and its values. A 10-minute welcome video from HR follows talking about mentoring, EllisDon University, learning and development opportunities, and role expectations. There is also a link to a web page on the company's core values. New employees are also shown a high-level organizational chart from the top down in the director level. This gives them a sense of how the organization is structured and includes photos, titles, and responsibilities. Sections about the payroll process and health and safety, featuring another video clip, are also included.

An hour-long video that describes the history of EllisDon and what makes it unique and successful is also delivered in the first week. There is also a copy of the employee handbook and a benefits summary. New employees are also introduced to "Edge Builder," a project financial management system. This gives them a high-level overview of the tool and explains that more structured training will happen later.

At the end of each section, an interactive "Do you recall?" section features a series of questions about the modules to make sure employees are taking away the information provided. If they answer correctly, they are told, "Congratulations." If not, they are told the correct answer.

At the 90-day mark, the system delivers a voluntary new-hire employee satisfaction survey. It asks for honest feedback about their first 90 days, such as meetings with senior leaders, clarity around performance evaluations, the orientation process, and their biggest challenges. Those who complete the survey are sent a leather portfolio branded with the EllisDon name; if people provide really positive feedback, their managers are sent an approving email.

At the end of the first year, the online orientation tells employees about the performance management program—what to expect from your leader, how it's a collaborative process, and how it's also about actively helping yourself in your own development.

Source: S. Dobson, "Mix of online, face-to-face programs ensure success in orientation," *Canadian HR Reporter,* Mar. 28, 2011, P. 13. Reprinted by permission of Canadian HR Reporter.

ESSENTIAL SKILLS TRAINING

Essential skills
Skills required for work, learning, and life

Many working adults today have difficulty reading, writing, and understanding mathematics. They lack what are known as essential skills. **Essential skills** are the skills required for work, learning, and life. They are necessary and a foundation for learning other skills and being able to adapt to workplace change. The Government of Canada and other agencies have identified nine types of essential skills: reading text, document use, numeracy, writing, oral communication, working with others, continuous learning, thinking skills, and computer use. Essential skills are required for most occupations and in one's daily life.[8]

Literacy
The ability to understand and employ printed information in daily activities, at home, at work, and in the community—to achieve one's goals, and to develop one's knowledge and potential

Many of the essential skills (e.g., reading text, document use, numeracy) are known as literacy skills. **Literacy** refers to the ability to understand and employ printed information in daily activities, at home, at work, and in the community—to achieve one's goals, and to develop one's knowledge and potential.[9] A report by the Conference Board of Canada found that 42 percent of all Canadians aged 16 to 65 score at the lowest literacy levels and are only semi-literate. About 4.7 million Canadians score in the upper Level 2 and low Level 3 range and their limited literacy skills pose a significant challenge to their workplace performance and success. Further, only 58 percent of Canadian adults can read well enough to meet most day-to-day requirements. It has been reported that low literacy levels cost Canadian businesses $2.5 billion each year in lost productivity.[10]

It is becoming increasingly clear that organizations must provide their workforces with essential skills training if they are to compete and survive in a global and high-tech workplace. Evidence suggests that without first providing trainees with essential skills training, other programs and initiatives will not succeed.[11]

Essential skills training
Training programs that are designed to provide employees with the essential skills required to perform their job and adapt to workplace change

Essential skills training provides employees with the essential skills that are required to perform their job and adapt to workplace change. Organizations that have implemented essential skills training have not only experienced improvements in productivity, efficiency, and quality, but some also report a decrease in absenteeism and the number of workers' compensation claims made, and an improvement in cross-cultural communication and morale.

Essential skills training also has advantages for employees. Not only does the training improve their skills, self-esteem, and confidence, but it also improves their chances of remaining employed. The percentages of employees who receive essential skills training and remain employed or are promoted are higher than employees who do not receive training.[12]

Unfortunately, Canadian organizations spend very little on essential skills training. As shown in Table 13.1, only one percent of overall training content is devoted to basic skills and only 20 percent of organizations indicated that they provide basic skills training. The Conference Board of Canada has described this underinvestment as "troubling" given that employees who improve their essential skills are more likely to learn new job-related skills more quickly and accurately, make fewer mistakes, work more efficiently, and be less resistant to change. Literacy is critical to productivity, which in turn is essential to Canadian competitiveness and prosperity.[13]

TECHNICAL SKILLS TRAINING

Technical skills training is training in specific job-related skills that all employees need to perform their jobs. Among manufacturing firms, training for specific job skills is the most frequent type of training provided. This is not surprising given the changes in the workplace that have occurred over the past two decades. With increasing global competition, organizations have had to find new ways to stay competitive and to survive, often by adopting new technologies and the redesign of work arrangements and systems. As a result, employees have had to undergo a considerable amount of technical skills upgrading and training. Nowhere is this more apparent than in the manufacturing sector, where low-skilled employees have had to become highly skilled to keep their jobs and for their organizations to survive.[14]

Technical skills training
Training in specific job-related skills that all employees need to perform their jobs

INFORMATION TECHNOLOGY TRAINING

Information technology training refers to computers and computer systems training. Information systems training is a key factor in the successful implementation of information systems technology.[15] Research has shown that technological failures in the workplace are most often the result of training issues rather than the technology.[16]

Information technology training usually involves either introductory computer training programs in which trainees learn about computer hardware and software, or applications training in which trainees are instructed on specific software applications to be used within the organization.[17] Applications training is required whenever an organization upgrades its computer systems.

One of the most common types of information technology training is computer software training. **Computer software training** refers to the planned, structured, and formal means of delivering information about how to use a specific computer software application.[18] Computer software training has been shown to increase trainees' ability to use the system and their motivation to use software.

Information technology training
Training programs that focus on the use of computers and computer systems

Computer software training
Training programs that focus on how to use a specific computer software application

HEALTH AND SAFETY TRAINING

Workplace health and safety has become an increasing concern in Canadian organizations. The costs of work-related injuries and illnesses are on the rise and present a serious threat to employees and their organizations. Approximately 1,000 workers die each year in Canada as a result of workplace accidents, and some 340,000 workers suffer an injury serious enough to warrant missing time from work or what is known as a lost-time injury. The cost of workplace injuries is estimated to exceed $12 billion a year.[19]

One of the most important ways to deal with accidents before they occur is education. **Health and safety training** programs educate employees in safe work methods and practices and how to recognize the chemical and physical hazards in the workplace so that they are prepared and capable of taking corrective action in the event of an accident. Unfortunately, many workers in Canada do not receive adequate safety training.[20] However, safety training is so important that one of the recommendations of a recent report by the Ministry of Labour in

Health and safety training
Training programs that educate employees in safe work methods and practices and how to recognize the chemical and physical hazards in the workplace so that they are prepared and capable of taking corrective action in the event of an accident

Ontario is to provide mandatory safety training for all construction workers. The report is the result of a construction accident in Toronto in 2009 in which four construction workers fell to their death.[21]

An important component of health and safety training involves the handling of hazardous materials and chemicals. The **Workplace Hazardous Materials Information System (WHMIS)** legislation is designed to ensure that workers across Canada are aware of the potential hazards of chemicals in the workplace and are familiar with emergency procedures for the clean-up and disposal of a spill.

An important component of WHMIS legislation is employee training. Training in WHMIS is designed so that employees can identify WHMIS hazard symbols, read WHMIS supplier and workplace labels, and read and apply the information on material safety data sheets (MSDS), which outline the hazardous ingredient(s) in a product and the procedures for the safe handling of that product.[22]

Research on safety training has found that it can have a significant positive effect on employee learning (i.e., safety knowledge) and safety performance. However, the effectiveness of safety training depends on the training method and the severity of exposure to workplace hazards. Safety training that involves the use of highly engaging instructional methods (e.g., behavioural modelling, simulations, hands-on training) is more effective for both learning and safety performance than less engaging instructional methods (e.g., lectures, films, reading materials, and video-based training). This is especially the case when the training is for work situations that involve high exposure to hazardous conditions that could result in severe illness, injury, or death.[23]

TOTAL QUALITY MANAGEMENT TRAINING

To remain competitive, many organizations have implemented quality programs. One of the most popular examples is total quality management (TQM). **Total quality management** is a systematic process of continual improvement of the quality of products and services. In addition to an emphasis on quality and continual improvement, TQM also involves teamwork and a customer focus.[24]

TQM places the training function in a pivotal position, as the process often requires significant changes in employees' skills and the way employees work. **TQM training** involves team training as well as training in the use of statistical tools that are used for problem-solving and decision-making processes. Most TQM advocates emphasize the importance of training and development.[25] Training and development is the primary method of reinforcing employee commitment to the consistent delivery of high-quality products and services.[26]

TEAM TRAINING

Team training is designed to improve the functioning and effectiveness of teams in areas such as communication, coordination, compensatory behaviour, mutual performance monitoring, exchange of feedback, and adaptation to varying situational demands.[27]

According to Bottom and Baloff, team training is an "attempt to improve a group's process through the use of interventions targeted at specific aspects of the process such as effective communication."[28] Group processes are usually the focus of team training; however, because team members are often expected

Workplace Hazardous Materials Information System (WHMIS)

Legislation to ensure that workers across Canada are aware of the potential hazards of chemicals in the workplace and are familiar with emergency procedures for the clean-up and disposal of a spill

Total quality management (TQM)

A systematic process of continual improvement of the quality of an organization's products and services

Total quality management (TQM) training

Training programs that involve team training as well as training in the use of statistical tools that are used for problem-solving and decision-making processes

Team training

Training programs that are designed to improve the functioning and effectiveness of teams in areas such as communication and coordination to perform a variety of the group's tasks, they often must also receive technical training to become multi-skilled.

Thus, team training focuses on two general types of skills: *task-work skills* refers to skills that are required to perform the team's tasks, and *teamwork skills* are skills that team members require in order to interact, communicate, and coordinate tasks effectively with other team members. Both types of skills need to be included in team training programs, and it is recommended that team members first master task-work and technical skills before they are trained on teamwork skills.[29]

SALES TRAINING

Sales professionals must develop a different set of skills to be successful in today's competitive sales environment. They need to be more knowledgeable about their products and their business, as well as their customers' businesses. As a result, sales training has become more than simply sending the sales troops off to a motivational pep rally.[30]

Today, **sales training** programs are being designed to upgrade sales professionals' skills and help them deal with new competitive challenges. At the centre of these new training initiatives is an emphasis on "relationship-based" sales training. Sales professionals are being trained to develop more strategic and complex relationships with clients, and to create relationships across client functions. They are also being trained to become knowledgeable about their customers' business needs, and to develop customized sales strategies. Rather than just selling a commodity, integrated teams of people from sales, support, and service are learning to sell solutions that combine support and service agreements.

Sales training
Training programs that are designed to upgrade sales professionals' skills and help them deal with new competitive challenges

CUSTOMER-SERVICE TRAINING

Organizations with a strong commitment to customer service invest heavily in training their employees. **Customer-service training** programs are designed to provide employees with interpersonal and customer service skills that are required for interacting with customers and for providing quality service. The training can be either informal or formal. Informal training might involve pairing new hires with the organization's best employees in terms of customer-service behaviour and philosophy. The kind of formal training required will depend on the type of service business that an organization is in and its service strategy. In other words, the training program must be tailored to an organization's strategy and characteristics as well as its customers.[31]

Service employees must have both the *ability* and *motivation* to perform effectively. Because you cannot always hire people with the required abilities or motivation, you must be able to train them. Many organizations that have reputations for superb customer service are successful because of their commitment to training. Organizations that provide the best service also provide the most training.

At Delta Hotels and Resorts, employees are trained and empowered to provide customers with excellent service such as settling a disputed mini-bar charge or offering a complimentary room if a guest has a reasonable complaint. As part of its training program, Delta has produced an award-winning training video and promises employees a certain amount of training every year.[32]

Customer-service training
Training programs that are designed to provide employees with interpersonal and service skills that are required for interacting with customers and for providing quality service

SEXUAL HARASSMENT TRAINING

Sexual harassment
Unwelcome sexual advances, requests for sexual favours, and verbal or physical conduct of a sexual nature that is a condition of employment, interferes with work performance, or creates a hostile work environment

Sexual harassment is defined as "unwelcome sexual advances, requests for sexual favours, and other verbal or physical conduct of a sexual nature . . . when submission to requests for sexual favours is made explicitly or implicitly a term or condition of employment; submission to or rejection of such requests is used as a basis for employment decisions; or such conduct unreasonably interferes with work performance or creates an intimidating, hostile, or offensive work environment."[33]

The most effective way for organizations to prevent sexual harassment is to develop sexual harassment policies and procedures for filing complaints and to provide **sexual harassment training** to educate employees about sexual harassment and the organization's policies and procedures regarding sexual harassment.[34]

Sexual harassment training
Training programs that are designed to educate employees about sexual harassment and the organization's policies and procedures regarding sexual harassment

Training is especially important because the definition of what constitutes sexual harassment is not always clear or understood, and problems have occurred in situations in which employees and managers were unaware of an organization's sexual harassment policy or did not know how to report it and proceed with a complaint.

ETHICS TRAINING

Ethics training
Training programs that educate employees about the organization's values and ethical policies and on making ethical decisions

While many companies provide ethics training to comply with legal mandates and to gain liability protection, ethics training is also important for creating an ethical culture and workplace, and for attracting and retaining the right type of employee. **Ethics training** programs educate employees about the organization's values and ethical policies and on making ethical decisions. This usually involves opportunities for employees to practise applying company values and its code of ethics to hypothetical situations. It is important that ethics training programs go beyond ethical guidelines and focus on how to effectively recognize and respond to common ethical problems in the workplace. As a result, employees learn to recognize ethical dilemmas and how to respond to them.[35]

To be most effective, ethical training programs must be mandatory for all employees and include a copy of the organization's code of ethics, a discussion of relevant compliance laws, an ethical decision-making model, resources for help, and role-playing scenarios. Organizations should first set standards for ethical behaviour and determine what the training should accomplish. Key elements of strong ethical programs are responsibility, respect, fairness, honesty, and compassion. Employees should be trained on the laws that apply to their jobs as well as decision-making models with questions they can ask themselves to help them make ethical decisions. Employees should also be taught how to report ethics violations and where they can go for assistance. Practical scenarios should be included in the training so employees can test their ethical knowledge. Ethical topics can include workplace romance, email appropriateness, internet use, confidentiality, security, and harassment (physical, verbal, and emotional).[36]

Molson Coors Brewing Company has one of the most comprehensive ethics programs in North America. Its training program includes interactive online courses, ethics leadership training, a decision map, a detailed set of policies, and a help line that complements and supports a user-friendly and accessible code of conduct.[37]

DIVERSITY TRAINING

Diversity training programs are one of the most common and effective ways for organizations to manage diversity. **Diversity training** programs are designed to address the differences in values, attitudes, and behaviours of individuals with different backgrounds. The objectives are to increase awareness and understanding of cultural diversity, and to improve interaction and communication among employees with different backgrounds and between employees and the organization's customers and clients. As indicated in the chapter-opening vignette, Bayshore Home Health implemented diversity training to ensure that employees are more culturally competent and able to provide high-quality care to patients with diverse backgrounds.

Diversity training is reported to be one of the most widely used strategies for managing diversity in the workplace and there has been a dramatic rise in diversity training programs in the last decade.[38] According to a study by the Conference Board of Canada, in 2008 thirty-seven percent of organizations provided diversity learning and development programs to help employees understand and work with non-traditional groups.[39]

Diversity training has three main objectives: 1. increase awareness about diversity issues, 2. reduce biases and stereotypes, and 3. change behaviours to those required to work effectively in a diverse workforce.[40] Some diversity training programs are designed to change people's attitudes by creating an awareness of diversity and an understanding of differences in values and behaviours. The expectation is that, by creating awareness and understanding of these differences, people will change their behaviour and overcome any stereotypes they might hold. Another approach to diversity training is to change behaviour. This approach emphasizes learning new behaviours that might then lead to changes in attitudes.[41]

Diversity training, however, has been controversial. Some organizations believe that it is well worth the investment while others feel that it is a waste of time and that it does not work.[42] However, a study on diversity in the workplace found that diversity experts rated training and education programs as one of the best strategies for managing diversity. The study also suggested that diversity training should focus on increasing *awareness* of what diversity is and why it is important; providing *skills* required to work effectively in a diverse workforce; and providing *application* strategies to facilitate the use of diversity awareness and skills to improve work performance, interactions, and communication.[43]

In Canada, many organizations like Bayshore Home Health have implemented diversity programs. For example, L'Oréal Canada has an intergenerational training program that was designed to help different age groups communicate with each other. The program has become one of the company's most popular training programs.[44] The Winnipeg Division of Boeing Canada Technology provides diversity training that includes formal educational classes on respecting and honouring co-workers' origins, leanings, and affiliations in four target groups of people (women, Aboriginals, visible minorities, and people with disabilities).[45]

Diversity training
Training programs that focus on differences in values, attitudes, and behaviours of individuals with different backgrounds

CROSS-CULTURAL TRAINING

Many companies send their employees on assignments in foreign countries. While these foreign assignments can be good for one's career, they can also be difficult if an individual is not familiar with the foreign culture. The purpose of **cross-cultural training** is to prepare employees for overseas assignments by developing the skills and attitudes necessary for successful interactions with persons from different backgrounds.[46]

A critical factor in the success of cross-cultural training is training rigour. **Training rigour** refers to "the degree of mental involvement and effort that must be expended by the trainer and the trainee in order for the trainee to learn the required concepts."[47] Training rigour also refers to the length of time spent on training.

Table 13.3 lists some of the most common methods of cross-cultural training. Cross-cultural training programs that are considered to have a high degree of rigour include interactive language training, cross-cultural simulations, and field trips. Programs with a moderate degree of training rigour include role plays, cases, and survival-level language. Cross-cultural training programs that are considered to be the lowest in terms of training rigour include lectures, films, books, and area briefings. More rigorous cross-cultural training programs require trainees to be much more active and involved in practising cross-cultural skills.[48]

The degree of cross-cultural training rigour required by an expatriate for a particular foreign assignment depends on three dimensions: cultural toughness, communication toughness, and job toughness. *Cultural toughness* refers to how difficult it is to adjust to a new culture. Generally speaking, cultural toughness will increase the greater the difference or distance between one's own culture and the foreign culture.

Communication toughness is a function of the extent to which the expatriate will have to interact with the locals of the host country. When an expatriate will

Cross-cultural training
Training programs that prepare employees for working and living in different cultures and for interactions with persons from different backgrounds

Training rigour
The degree of mental involvement and effort that must be expended by the trainer and the trainee in order for the trainee to learn the required concepts

---

TABLE 13.3

Cross-Cultural Training Methods

- Environmental briefings about a country's geography, climate, housing, and schools.
- Cultural orientation to familiarize expatriates with cultural institutions and the value systems of the host country.
- Cultural assimilators that use programmed learning approaches to expose persons of one culture to the concepts, attitudes, role perceptions, and customs of another culture.
- Language training.
- Sensitivity training to develop attitudinal flexibility.
- Field experience such as visiting the country where one will be assigned to see what it is like to work and live with people in a different culture.

Source: R.L. Tung, "Selection and training procedures of U.S., European, and Japanese multinationals," *California Management Review*, Vol. 25 (1), P. 57. 1982.

be required to have frequent interactions with host nationals that will involve face-to-face, two-way, and informal communication, the level of communication toughness will be high, and more rigorous communication training will be required.

Job toughness refers to how difficult the tasks will be for the expatriate compared to what he/she is used to doing. If the expatriate will be working in a new area and the demands of the job will be different and require new responsibilities and challenges, then the degree of job toughness will be greater. As a result, the expatriate will require more rigorous job-specific training.[49]

As the levels of these three dimensions increase, the type of cross-cultural training required will need to be more rigorous. In addition to pre-departure training, it is also important that the expatriates and their families also receive follow-up or in-country cross-cultural training in the host country.[50]

Research on the effectiveness of cross-cultural training has found that it is effective for enhancing one's success on overseas assignments and is related to expatriate adjustment and performance. However, the effectiveness of cross-cultural training depends on a number of factors such as the timing of the training and the cultural differences between one's own country and the assignment country.[51]

For guidelines on how to design a cross-cultural training program, see The Trainer's Notebook 13.1, "How to Design an Effective Cross-Cultural Training Program."

▶ The Trainer's Notebook 13.1

HOW TO DESIGN AN EFFECTIVE CROSS-CULTURAL TRAINING PROGRAM

Here are some recommendations for the successful design and implementation of a cross-cultural training program:

1. Cross-cultural training should be considered a mandatory process.

2. The location of training should be established in accordance with the needs of the family as part of the preparation process and corporations need to accept that training can be done at home or in the host country.

3. The depth of training is of utmost importance. If corporations are going to provide cross-cultural training, it needs to be done properly with depth and with care.

4. Families must be incorporated into the training process. Training for expatriates alone is only sufficient if the expatriate is on an individualized assignment.

5. Language training should be incorporated into cross-cultural training wherever possible and should be encouraged as an ongoing aspect of the assignment.

6. Education and expectations of training must be laid out by training companies for international human resource professionals and in turn be easily translated for the preparation of each individual expatriate. This can be through appropriate written information being prepared for the expatriate and reinforced by the service provider reiterating the goals and expectations prior to the training.

Source: A. Bross, A. Churchill, & J. Zifkin, "Cross-cultural training: Issues to consider during implementation," *Canadian HR Reporter*, June 5, 2000, P. 10.

SUMMARY

This chapter has provided an overview of the different types of training programs provided by organizations. You should now be familiar with orientation training, essential skills training, technical skills training, information technology training, health and safety training, total quality management training, team training, sales training, customer-service training, sexual harassment training, ethics training, diversity training, and cross-cultural training. Many of these training programs have become key components of an organization's corporate strategy and are major factors in their efforts to remain competitive.

Key Terms

computer software training p. 393
cross-cultural training p. 398
customer-service training p. 395
diversity training p. 397
essential skills p. 392
essential skills training p. 392
ethics training p. 396
health and safety training p. 393
information technology training p. 393
literacy p. 392
orientation training p. 390

sales training p. 395
sexual harassment p. 396
sexual harassment training p. 396
team training p. 394
technical skills training p. 393
total quality management (TQM) p. 394
total quality management (TQM)
    training p. 394
training rigour p. 398
Workplace Hazardous Materials
    Information System (WHMIS) p. 394

Web Links

Bayshore Home Health: **www.bayshore.ca**

Boeing Canada: **www.boeing.ca**

L'Oréal Canada: **www.en.loreal.ca**

WHMIS: **www.hc-sc.gc.ca/hecs-sesc/whmis/**

Discussion Questions

1. Diversity training programs have been criticized for doing more harm than good. In fact, there is some evidence that they may be ineffective at best and harmful at worst. Why do you think this is the case? Do you think this is true, and should organizations abandon diversity training or embrace it?
2. Why do you think Canadian organizations invest so little in essential skills training (see Table 13.1, basic-skills training)? What are the implications of this for employees, organizations, and society? Should Canadian organizations spend more on essential skills training? What are the advantages and disadvantages?

3. What would be your reaction if your employer wanted to send you on an overseas assignment? What would be your reaction if the assignment were in: 1. England, 2. France, 3. China, or 4. Egypt? Would you accept the assignment, and if so, what training would you require? Describe the training you would need in terms of the content and methods.

4. What aspects of a cross-cultural training program affect its degree of training rigour? Discuss the factors that need to be considered to determine the degree of cross-cultural training rigour required by an expatriate for a particular foreign assignment. If you were sent on a foreign assignment to France to manage a restaurant chain, what degree of cross-cultural training rigour would you require?

5. What is the Workplace Hazardous Materials Information System (WHMIS) and what are its implications for safety training? What should be covered in a health and safety training program?

6. Why is team training important for organizations that want to implement teams? What skills should be the focus of team training programs?

7. Why should an organization provide orientation training? If you were going to design an orientation program, what material would you include and how would your program be delivered?

8. Who is responsible for literacy in the workplace and what is the effect of low literacy levels on individuals, organizations, and the economy?

9. Research has found that the effectiveness of safety training depends on the instructional method and the severity of workplace hazards. Explain the nature of this relationship and its implications for organizations and employees.

The Great Training Debate

1. Debate the following: Diversity training programs result in more harm than good and organizations should abandon them.

2. Debate the following: Essential skills and literacy training are the responsibility of government, not organizations.

Exercises

In-Class

1. The extent to which organizations provide certain types of training programs is often driven by external and internal factors. In other words, social, political, and economic changes in the external environment, as well as internal changes to organizational systems and work arrangements, have a substantial influence on training activities (see the section on the context of training and development in Chapter 1 and Figure 1.2). Choose one of the following training programs and discuss the role of external and internal factors and how these factors might influence the need for and importance of each type of training:
   a. Orientation training
   b. Essential skills training

c. Technical skills training
d. Information technology training
e. Health and safety training
f. TQM training
g. Team training
h. Sales training
i. Customer-service training
j. Sexual harassment training
k. Ethics training
l. Diversity training
m. Cross-cultural training

2. Assume you are a training director for a large retail organization. To increase your training budget for next year, you have to make a persuasive argument to convince other members of the organization of your need for an increase in resources. An important part of your argument will involve proving the need for and importance of several training programs. For one of the training programs listed in Table 13.2, describe how you will argue that it is important, the impact it will have on employee attitudes and behaviour, the benefits it will have for employees and the organization, and how it can help the organization gain a competitive advantage.

3. Design a training program for one of the types of training discussed in this chapter. In designing your program, specify each of the following:
a. The training objectives
b. The training content
c. The trainer
d. The trainees who should attend the program
e. The training methods to be used
f. The required training materials and equipment
g. The training site
h. The schedule for the training program
i. The lesson plan
j. The criteria you will use to evaluate the program

4. Describe the orientation training you received in the most recent job that you held. Some of the things to consider are:
a. How long was the orientation training?
b. What content was included?
c. What methods were used?
d. What did you learn from it?
e. Were you satisfied with the program and did it help you perform your job?
f. What did you like about it and what did you not like?
g. How would you change the orientation training you received to make it more effective?

5. Choose one of the types of training programs described in this chapter that you have attended in a current or previous job. Describe the content and methods used and how effective the training was for your learning, on-the-job behaviour, and performance. Based on the material in the chapter, how effective was the training program? How would you change it, improve it, and make it more effective?

6. Imagine your employer has just informed you that you are going on a foreign assignment for three years to a country that you have never been to and know nothing about. Furthermore, the culture is very different from your own. Your employer has informed you that you will be receiving some written information about the country and its culture as well as a videotape to help you prepare for your assignment. Prepare a memo to your employer in which you evaluate the training they are offering you and describe the type of cross-cultural training that you require if you are going to accept the assignment.

7. Students often have to work in groups on course projects without any knowledge of how groups function and what it takes for them to be effective. Some students experience difficulties when working in groups and some groups fall apart and the work is not completed. Therefore, it might be helpful if students receive team training. Your task is to design a training program for students to prepare them for group work. Describe the nature of your training program including the objectives, content, and methods.

8. Prepare a brief presentation in which you have to convince management to invest in essential skills and literacy training. Be sure to explain why investing in essential skills and literacy training is important and the consequences of investing and not investing in it.

In-the-Field

1. To learn more about the training programs discussed in this chapter, contact a training professional or a human resource professional to arrange an interview about the types of training programs provided in their organization. Choose several of the types of training programs described in this chapter and ask them the following questions:
   - Does your organization provide this type of training?
   - What are some of the reasons you do or do not provide this type of training?
   - What are the objectives of this type of training program?
   - What is the content of this type of training?
   - How is this training program designed (e.g., what methods, techniques, etc.) and who is the trainer?
   - What effect does this type of training have on employees' attitudes and behaviours?
   - What effect does this type of training have on the organization?

   Based on your interview, what is your evaluation of the training programs provided by the organization? Do you think they could be improved, and if so what would you recommend and why?

2. Contact several employees you know who work in different organizations, and ask them the following questions about some of the types of training programs discussed in the chapter:
   - Have you ever received this type of training?
   - If yes, what was the reason you attended the training program?
   - What were the objectives of the training program?

- What was the content of the training program?
- How was the training program designed (e.g., methods, techniques, etc.) and who was the trainer?
- What was your reaction to the training program and what did you learn?
- What effect did the training have on your behaviour and job performance?
- What effect did the training have on the organization?

Based on your interview, do you think the training program was effective? What changes do you recommend to make it more effective?

3. To learn more about workplace literacy and essential skills in Canada, visit ABC Life Literacy Canada at: **http://abclifeliteracy.ca/workplace_literacy/home**. Answer the following questions:
    a. What are the five signs that employees may be struggling with literacy and essential skills?
    b. Click on Case Studies and Testimonials and then choose one of the case study articles at the bottom of the page. Prepare a brief report or presentation about the organization in which you discuss the company's training program and the effect it has had on employees and/or the organization. What can other organizations learn from this organization?

4. To learn more about the types of safety training programs available, visit the Canadian Centre for Occupational Health and Safety at **www.ccohs.ca/education/**.
    Answer the following questions:
    a. What kinds of training programs are available?
    b. Choose one of the programs and find out what the program is about, the topics covered, the program objectives, target audience, and delivery options.

5. To find out about WHMIS education and training go to **www.ccohs.ca/oshanswers/legisl/whmis_education.html**.
    Answer the following questions:
    a. What is WHMIS education and training?
    b. Who should be educated and trained in WHMIS?
    c. What is the purpose of WHMIS training?
    d. What, in general, is the content of a WHMIS training program?
    e. Can people in the same plant receive different training?
    f. What are the criteria of a successful program?

Case Incident

Saving Theatre Calgary

Theatre Calgary is one of the largest professional theatres in Western Canada, with a 40-year history. However, lagging ticket sales and competing claims on the philanthropy dollar brought Theatre Calgary to near bankruptcy in 1996. A decision was made to overhaul the company's marketing approach that would raise the standard of performance expected from employees, especially those in the areas of sales and customer service.

To support the new approach, the company invested in training for aggressive marketing and up-selling. Employees attended seminars on a range of techniques from how to cross-sell to how to analyze demographics for marketing opportunities and how to create a customer profile from the client database. Employees also had to improve their customer contact skills, from telephone manner to up-selling to meet-and-greet. They spent time developing scripts and rehearsing how to deal with people and how to deal with people with problems.

Questions

1. How important is training for saving Theatre Calgary from bankruptcy and what type of training is required?
2. What do you think about the training programs provided to employees at Theatre Calgary? What would you recommend for improving them?

Source: R. Rabinovitch, "Close Up: Training and development," *Canadian HR Reporter,* May 17, 2004, P. 7. Reprinted by permission of Canadian HR Reporter.

Case Study (THE POLICE SENSITIVITY TRAINING PROGRAM

On September 14, 2000, several police officers raided a special event known as the Pussy Palace, a lesbian bathhouse in Toronto in which 355 scantily clad women were gathered. Two undercover female officers entered the bathhouse to check for possible liquor violations. They then called in five male officers, who raided the palace and spent 90 minutes walking around on what was described as a routine liquor licence inspection.

The officers allegedly opened doors, entered private rooms, questioned the women, and lingered in areas where the patrons' nudity was most evident in rooms such as "the sling room" and "the photo room." Complainants alleged that their feelings of violation and intimidation were akin to being strip-searched. Police charged two organizers with six liquor violations and three counts of permitting disorderly conduct. The raid outraged the gay community.

Justice Peter Hryn of the Ontario Court threw out the liquor licence infractions and ruled that the defendants' privacy rights had been seriously violated in a situation that did not require urgent police action. He compared the officers' entry into the club to a strip-search, calling it outrageous, flagrant, deliberate, unjustified, and a violation of the women's Charter rights.

During the defamation trial that followed, Justice Janet McFarland of the Ontario Superior Court described the raid as a violation of the Charter of Rights of the women present and declared, "It is no part of a police officer's job to breach the Charter of Rights of any citizen. To do so is misconduct of the most serious kind."

The Toronto Women's Bathhouse Committee launched a human rights complaint, and several of its members also initiated a $1.5-million class-action lawsuit alleging harassment and discrimination. In December 2004, a settlement between the Toronto Police Services Board and seven complainants was announced and approved by the Ontario Human Rights Commission.

The settlement required all current and future Toronto police officers to attend gay and lesbian sensitivity training. The Toronto Police Service also had to pay $350,000 to the complainants, which went toward charities and to cover legal fees. In addition, the five male officers who raided the bathhouse provided a signed apology to the women who were attending the event stating that they did not intend to breach their rights or privacy. As a result of the settlement, the $1.5-million class-action suit and the complaint to the Ontario Human Rights Commission were dropped.

According to the settlement, everyone on the 7,260-member force—from rookie constables to the chief of police—will be required to take training on gay and lesbian sensitivity. The training will pay particular attention to searches involving the gay, lesbian, and transgendered communities as well as inspections of gay and lesbian venues, businesses, and bathhouses. The program will be designed in consultation with the Ontario Human Rights Commission and members of the gay community.

Then-Police Chief Julian Fantino responded to the settlement by stating that the Toronto Police are already bogged down in training programs and scarcely need the added burden of enforced gay and lesbian sensitivity training, which he called an unnecessary overreaction. He told a local newspaper that, "it's being forced on us," and "we are conscientious about diversity and sensitivity issues and all those kinds of things. Is it necessary? I think that in many respects this is a duplication of much of the work we already do." He went on to say that the force shouldn't have to "bow to all kinds of pressures," and "we have made extraordinary efforts to reach out and work with all entities in the community." Then Toronto Mayor David Miller called the sensitivity training "a very positive step" and "a very good part" of the settlement.

Sources: K. Makin, "Toronto police to face gay-sensitivity training," *The Globe and Mail,* Dec. 17, 2004, P. A1; C. Porter, "Fantino attacks deal; Sensitivity training "being forced" on police force, chief says: Agreement ends lawsuit over 2000 raid on lesbian bathhouse," *Toronto Star,* Dec. 18, 2004, P. A1; K. Makin & J. Gray, " . . . but calls sensitivity training a burden," *The Globe and Mail,* Dec. 18, 2004, P. A17; A. Reinhart, "Fantino has proved he can exemplify tolerance . . . ," *The Globe and Mail,* Dec. 18, 2004, P. A17; D. Brown, "Toronto cops grudgingly accept sensitivity training," *Canadian HR Reporter,* Jan. 31, 2005, P. 1.

Questions

1. Do you agree with the settlement that requires all current and future Toronto police officers to attend gay and lesbian sensitivity training? What effect do you think this will have on the police and the gay and lesbian community?

2. What aspects of diversity training are relevant and might be used in the design of the sensitivity training program? Are there are other types of training programs that are relevant and might be part of the sensitivity training program? Explain your answer.

3. Do you think the sensitivity training program will be effective? What else might be required in order for it to result in a significant change in police attitudes and behaviour?

4. Refer to the chapter-opening vignette on Bayshore Home Health. What aspects of their diversity strategy might be useful in the design and delivery of the police sensitivity training program?

Flashback Questions

1. What do you think the training objectives should be for the police sensitivity training program? Refer to Chapter 5 and write several training objectives for the sensitivity training program. Be sure to include the five key elements of training objectives. For each objective, clearly indicate the three key components of training objectives (i.e., performance, condition, and criterion).

2. If you were to design the police sensitivity training program, how would you design it in terms of the training content and methods? Develop a lesson plan for your training program.

3. Describe how the sensitivity training program should be evaluated according to: a) Kirkpatrick's model, b) the COMA model, and c) the decision-based evaluation (DBE) model. Be specific in terms of what variables you will need to measure according to each model.

REFERENCES

1. Based on Klie, S. (2009, December 14). Cultural competence affects patient health. *Canadian HR Reporter, 22(22)*, 12; www.bayshore.ca Press Releases (Bayshore Home Health launches workforce diversity strategy, September, 16, 2009; Bayshore Home Health named one of Canada's 50 Best Managed Companies for fifth consecutive year, February 23, 2011), retrieved on November 25, 2011.

2. Klein, H. J., & Weaver, N. A. (2000). The effectiveness of an organizational-level orientation training program in the socialization of new hires. *Personnel Psychology, 53*, 47–66.

3. Feldman, D. C. (1989). Socialization, resocialization, and training: Reframing the research agenda. In I. L. Goldstein (Ed.), *Training and development in organizations* (pp. 376–416). San Francisco: Jossey-Bass.

4. Anderson, N. R., Cunningham-Snell, N. A., & Haigh, J. (1996). Induction training as socialization: Current practice and attitudes to evaluation in British organizations. *International Journal of Selection and Assessment, 4*, 169–183.

5. Klein & Weaver (2000).

6. Ostroff, C., & Kozlowski, S. W. J. (1992). Organizational socialization as a learning process: The role of information acquisition. *Personnel Psychology, 45*, 849–874; Schettler, J. (2002, August). Welcome to ACME Inc. *Training, 39(8)*, 36–43.

7. Van Iddekinge, C. H., Ferris, G. R., Perrewé, P. L., Perryman, A. A., Blass, F. R., & Heetderks, T. D. (2009). Effects of selection and training on unit-level performance over time: A latent growth modeling approach. *Journal of Applied Psychology, 94*, 829–843.

8. Understanding essential skills. Human Resources and Skills Development Canada. www.hrsdc.gc.ca/eng/workplaceskills/essential_skills/general/understanding_es.shtml

9. Campbell, A. (2005, December). *Profiting from literacy: Creating a sustainable workplace literacy program*. The Conference Board of Canada: Ottawa.

10. Campbell, A. (2005).

11. Kuri, F. (1996, September). Basic-skills training boosts productivity. *HRMagazine 41(9)*, 73–79; www.abclifeliteracy.ca/workplace-literacy-facts.

12. Kuri, F. (1996, September).

13. Harris-Lalonde, S. (2001). *Training and development outlook*. The Conference Board of Canada: Ottawa; Campbell, A. (2005).

14. Baker, S., & Armstrong, L. (1996, September 30). The new factory worker, *BusinessWeek*, 59–68.

15. Harp, C. G., Taylor, S. C., & Satzinger, J. W. (1998). Computer training and individual differences: When method matters. *Human Resource Development Quarterly, 9*, 271–283.

16. Martocchio, J. J. (1992). Microcomputer usage as an opportunity: The influence of context in employee training. *Personnel Psychology, 45*, 529–552.

17. DeSimone, R. L., & Harris, D. M. (1998). *Human resource development* (2nd ed.). Fort Worth, TX: Dryden Press.

18. Harp, C. G., Taylor, S. C., & Satzinger, J. W. (1998).

19. Kelloway, E. K., & Francis, L. (2008). *Management of occupational health and safety* (4th ed.). Toronto: Nelson Canada.

20. Kelloway, E. K., & Francis, L. (2008).

21. Silliker, A. (2011, January 17). Ontario report calls for overhaul of OHS. *Canadian HR Reporter, 24(1)*, 1, 23.

22. Kelloway, E. K., & Francis, L. (2008).

23. Burke, M. J., Salvador, R. O., Smith-Crowe, K., Chan-Serafin, S., Smith, A., & Sonesh, S. (2011). The dread factor: How hazards and safety training influence learning and performance. *Journal of Applied Psychology, 96*, 46–70.

24. Dean, J. W. Jr., & Bowen, D. E. (1994). Management theory and total quality: Improving research and practice through theory development. *Academy of Management Review, 19*, 392–418.

25. Oakland, J. S. (1989). *Total quality management.* Oxford: Butterworth-Heinemann Ltd; Schonberger, R. J. (1992). Total quality management cuts a broad swath—through manufacturing and beyond. *Organizational Dynamics, 20(4)*, 16–28; Tenner, A. R., & DeToro, I. J. (1992). *Total quality management, three steps to continuous improvement.* Reading, MA: Addison-Wesley.

26. Harper, L. F., & Rifkind, L. J. (1994). A training program for TQM in the diverse workplace. *Human Resource Development Quarterly, 5*, 277–279.

27. Tannenbaum, S. I., & Yukl, G. (1992). Training and development in work organizations. *Annual Review of Psychology, 43*, 399–441.

28. Bottom, W. P., & Baloff, N. (1994). A diagnostic model for team building with an illustrative application. *Human Resource Development Quarterly, 5*, 317–336, p. 318.

29. Salas, E., Burke, C. S., & Cannon-Bowers, J. A. (2002). What we know about designing and delivering team training: Tips and guidelines. In K. Kraiger (Ed.), *Creating, implementing, and managing effective training and development: State-of-the-art lessons for practice* (pp. 234–259). San Francisco, CA: Jossey-Bass.

30. Stamps, D. (1997). Training for a new sales game. *Training, 34(7)*, 46–52.

31. Schneider, B., & Bowen, D. E. (1995). *Winning the service game.* Boston, MA: Harvard Business School Press.

32. Anonymous. (1999, May 31). Delta promotes empowerment. *The Globe and Mail*, C5.

33. Schneider, K. T., Swan, S., & Fitzgerald, L. F. (1997). Job-related and psychological effects of sexual harassment in the workplace: Empirical evidence from two organizations. *Journal of Applied Psychology, 82*, 401–415, p. 401.

34. Ganzel, R. (1998); Peirce, E., Smolinski, C. A., & Rosen, B. (1998).

35. Tyler, K. (2005, February). Do the right thing: Ethics training programs help employees deal with ethical dilemmas. *HR Magazine, 50(2)*, 99–102; Sekerka, L. E. (2009). Organizational ethics education and training: A review of best practices and their application. *International Journal of Training and Development, 13*, 77–95.

36. Tyler, K. (2005, February).

37. Greengard, S. (2005, March). Golden values. *Workforce Management, 84(3)*, 52–53.

38. Chrobot-Mason, & Quinones, M. A. (2002). Training for a diverse workplace. In K. Kraiger (Ed.), *Creating, implementing, and managing effective training and development: State-of-the-art*

lessons for practice (pp. 117–159). San Francisco, CA: Jossey-Bass; Wentling, R. M., & Palma-Rivas, N. (1998).

39. Hughes, P. D., & Campbell, A. (2009). *Learning & development outlook 2009: Learning in tough times.* Ottawa: The Conference Board of Canada.

40. Hanover, J. M. B., & Cellar, D. F. (1998). Environmental factors and the effectiveness of workforce diversity training. *Human Resource Development Quarterly, 9,* 105–124.

41. Noe, R. A., & Ford, J. K. (1992). Emerging issues and new directions for training research. *Research in Personnel and Human Resources Management, 10,* 345–384.

42. Cocchiara, F. K., Connerley, M. L., & Bell, M. P. (2010). "A GEM" for increasing the effectiveness of diversity training. *Human Resource Management, 49,* 1089–1106.

43. Wentling, R. M., & Palma-Rivas, N. (1998). Current status and future trends of diversity initiatives in the workplace: Diversity experts' perspective. *Human Resource Development Quarterly, 9,* 235–253.

44. Klie, S. (2007, October 22). L'Oréal a pretty picture of diversity, training. *Canadian HR Reporter, 20(18),* 11.

45. Shaw, A. (2008, May 5). Boeing puts diversity to work—silently. *Canadian HR Reporter, 21(9),* 18.

46. Noe, R. A., & Ford, J. K. (1992).

47. Black, J. S., Gregersen, H. B., & Mendenhall, M. E. (1992). *Global assignments.* San Francisco, CA: Jossey-Bass, p. 97.

48. Black, J. S., Gregersen, H. B., & Mendenhall, M. E. (1992).

49. Black, J. S., Gregersen, H. B., & Mendenhall, M. E. (1992).

50. Black, J. S., Gregersen, H. B., & Mendenhall, M. E. (1992).

51. Aguinis, H., & Kraiger, K. (2009). Benefits of training and development for individuals and teams, organizations, and society. *Annual Review of Psychology, 60,* 451–474.

Management Development

CHAPTER LEARNING OUTCOMES

After reading this chapter you should be able to:

- define management and management development and explain how it is different from employee training
- describe the main roles, functions, and critical skills of managers
- discuss emotional intelligence and its relevance for management
- describe the models of management skill development
- describe the use of error-management training for management development
- describe the content of management skills development programs
- discuss the different types of management development programs
- describe outdoor wilderness training programs and their effectiveness for management development
- define job rotation and coaching and discuss the characteristics of great coaches, the five conditions that are necessary to ensure the development of managers, and the challenges of coaching
- discuss the research on the effectiveness of management development programs

IBM

As an industry leader in training and development, IBM is a world leader when it comes to the development of sophisticated training programs. It invests more than $1 billion a year on training. Perhaps, then, it is no surprise that the company has been able to launch a new two-year companywide program to transform the role of the manager.

The program is called Role of the Manager@IBM and is the largest management development initiative in the company's history. It involves 32,000 IBM executives and managers and is designed to transform the role of the manager and to create a new model of 21st-century leadership.

Manager@IBM uses cutting-edge technology to provide managers with a new kind of learning experience that includes a blended program for leadership teams, performance support, and an online "e-coach" to guide managers in creating personal management development plans.

The program allows employees to manage their training using three "tracks," thanks to a sophisticated system called Edvisor. In track one, employees can access more than 150 online best practice management-support modules. In track two, managers' learning activities are assessed as they prepare for a two-day, face-to-face workshop focused on improving organizational climate and coaching skills. Edvisor helps managers to master specific Web-based program modules that prepare them for the face-to-face learning.

In the third track, an "intelligent agent" analyzes a manager's 360-degree leadership survey feedback and online responses. Edvisor then provides leadership advice and assists managers in building a personalized management development plan that includes access to a customized list of management development programs.

More than 22,000 managers have participated in the program and the financial impact of manager action plans has been substantial. More than $280 million in new revenue has been generated resulting in a net gain of $200 million over the $80-million cost of the program. Managers credit the program with enabling them to achieve these results. In addition, survey results indicate that business units with greater participation in Role of the Manager@IBM show greater improvements in employee satisfaction, clarity, and leadership ratings than units with less or no participation. In 2002, *Training* magazine ranked IBM fourth on its list of the *Training* Top 100, thanks to its Manager@IBM program.

Another successful program at IBM is called Basic Blue for Managers, which is a blended learning program for new first-line supervisors. The program combines four tiers of training. Three technology-delivered labs and one week-long classroom learning lab teach first-line managers to become better people managers. This year-long program immerses managers in a combination of online self-study, simulations, competency assessments, management coaching, and classroom experiences. In 2003, Basic Blue for Managers was highlighted by *Training* magazine as a best practice.[1]

Sources: J. Schettler, "Training Top 100: IBM," *Training,* March, 2002, P. 48; J. Schettler, "Training top 100: Best practices," *Training,* March, 2003, P. 58; G. Johnson, H. Johnson, H. Dolezalek, T. Galvin & R. Zemke, "Top five profile and ranking," *Training,* March, 2004, P. 42.

The management of our global economy is no simple matter, challenging companies, even smaller ones, to excellence. Evidence indicates that the single characteristic that best distinguishes a successful organization, large or small, from others is the calibre of the management team.[2] As exemplified in the chapter-opening vignette, the development of the skills required of successful managers is a very serious business. This is because, like many companies, IBM understands the impact that managers have on the company's performance. It will be no surprise to learn that *Training* magazine has consistently ranked IBM's training program among the very best in North America.

This chapter is placed near the end of the book, but this is not because the training of managers is unimportant. On the contrary, developing managers is among the most important, complex, and difficult of the challenges that trainers face today. It is also one of the major issues now facing organizations, as the Baby Boomer generation has reached retirement age. Organizations must recruit and develop those high-potential men and women—referred to as "bench strength"— who will soon take over the leadership of organizations. It is increasingly recognized that a major shift in the leadership of organizations is upon us (for more, see Training Today 14.1, "Bench Strength").[3] To meet this challenge, management development experts make use of the full slate of principles and techniques described in the earlier chapters.

As you have learned in previous chapters, successful training and development involves three key aspects: 1. the identification of training needs, which

Training Today (14.1

Bench Strength

Every two years or so, Executive Development Associates (EDA) conducts a major survey of managerial and leadership development practices and priorities by sampling 100 of the largest companies in the USA. Although the survey is concerned with many aspects of managerial development, the most striking result is the importance currently attached to the development of future managers (known as the development of "bench strength"). Clearly, as the Baby Boomer generation retires the replenishment of the leadership pipeline is an increasingly urgent priority. Interestingly, although companies still make use of the full gamut of development activities including formal courses and informal learning, they are increasingly turning to three mechanisms for creating that bench strength: leader-led development, action learning, and executive coaching.

Leader-led development refers to having top executives share their experiences and insights with future leaders. Action learning refers to job rotations and special assignments specifically designed to enhance certain specific competencies. Executive coaching remains a very important development activity, the use of which is increasing.

The Conference Board of Canada's 2007 survey shows similar results for Canada, where mentoring and coaching are increasingly favoured. This trend is also evident in Quebec. Daoud and Gosselin, researchers from the École des Hautes Études Commerciales in Montreal, report a qualitative study conducted with Quebec-based pharmaceutical and insurance companies. In-depth interviews held with managers from these companies reveal that whereas both are assigning increasing importance to managerial development, insurance companies are motivated to do so, as with the USA study, because of the demographic concerns (i.e., retirement of the Baby Boomers). Pharmaceutical companies in Quebec are smaller and more recently created than are insurance companies, and as such are likely to have a younger work force. Yet both emphasize the same techniques for growing their future managers.

The broader USA and Canadian studies, as well as the narrower Quebec study, report the same fundamental issue: All see the development of managers as a critical priority and, within this, the development of soft skills—such as human interaction skills—as much more important than the development of hard skills— such as technical ones. Clearly, these results are telling us that new managers should be better at handling people.

Sources: J.F. Bolt, "Mapping the future of leadership development," *The 2007 Pfeiffer Annual: Leadership development.* John Wiley & Sons, 2007; M. Daoud & A. Gosselin, *Évolutionrécente du développement des gestionnaires dans les secteurs pharmaceutique et de l'assurance au Québec.* Paper presented at the Annual meeting of Administrative Sciences Association of Canada, 2007.

requires an understanding of the jobs and an identification of the skills required of people who do them (see Chapter 4); 2. the choice of training design and delivery techniques (see Chapters 5–9); and 3. an integration, within the training experience, of elements that contribute not only to learning, but also to other psychological forces like motivation and self-efficacy (see Chapter 3). These, as shown in the training evaluation context (Chapter 11), enhance the odds for successful transfer (see Chapter 10).

To grasp management training, it is important to explore, as this chapter does, what managers do (their roles and functions) and the critical skills they need. We describe the techniques and guiding principles that create the training experience (management training design and delivery). The chapter also describes several types of management development programs and their content. Finally, the chapter closes with a research-based analysis of the effectiveness of management training. We begin by explaining what management is.

WHAT IS MANAGEMENT?

Management

The process of getting things done, efficiently and effectively, through and with other people

The work of managers is to orchestrate the work of others: "**Management** refers to the process of getting things done, efficiently and effectively, through and with other people."[4] Figure 14.1 describes what managers do: their roles (interpersonal, informational, decisional) and the functions these roles serve (controlling, organizing, planning). They also perform the important role of "leadership." Whereas all managers assume these roles and perform these functions, their relative saliency differs as a function of the specific environment in which they work. As an example, controlling budgets or organizing a task may have very different meanings for the National Ballet of Canada or Petro-Canada managers, yet accomplishing these tasks requires of them both to have conceptual, technical, and interpersonal skills as grouped in Figure 14.1.

It is axiomatic to management development that managerial skills and competencies are learnable and that they can and should be nurtured and developed through training and related experiences. These development experiences (indicated in Figure 14.1) occur on and/or off the job with instructional systems that are informational and experiential.

MANAGEMENT DEVELOPMENT VERSUS EMPLOYEE TRAINING

The topic of management development is separated from employee training for a number of reasons. First, managers work mainly through other people: They are effective when those they manage are effective. Whereas some management development programs are strictly technical (project planning or budget preparation, for example), since managers mostly deal with people most management training programs are focused on the development of interpersonal and other "people skills." This is a training task of considerable difficulty. Second, and as a result of this different focus and its inherent difficulties, the training design techniques tend to be different (training for managers tends to be experiential and informational). Third, and related to the previous point, the work of management is more influenced by individual managerial preferences or personalities.

FIGURE (14.1)

Managerial Roles, Functions, Skills, and Development Approaches

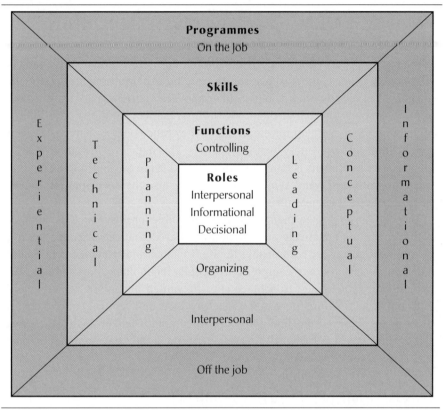

Successful training programs need to take into account these important individual differences. Fourth, management development is a longitudinal and gradual *process* by which the complex skills and competencies required of managers are built—that is, developed—over time, with training and with experience. Fifth and most important, incompetent managers can have a catastrophic effect on an entire organization's ability to survive: Management development is different from employee training because it has unique strategic significance.

WHAT IS MANAGEMENT DEVELOPMENT?

Management development refers to the "complex processes by which individuals learn to perform effectively in managerial roles."[5] Management jobs are not easy. Managers are responsible for delivering tangible results while tending to unforeseen problems and obstacles of all types such as supply problems, machinery breakdowns, and, most importantly, personnel issues, all within the current organizational context characterized by change. A diverse and sometimes international work force, frequent technological changes, increased competition, shorter time frames, and a focus on efficiency are all serving to make the

Management development

The complex process by which individuals learn to perform effectively in managerial roles job of managing ever more complex. Successful adaptation to this difficult reality requires extensive managerial skills that need strengthening and updating to retain their currency and effectiveness. That is the mission of management development.

IS MANAGEMENT DEVELOPMENT IMPORTANT?

Management development, a multi-billion-dollar business, is without doubt one of the most important applications of training in organizations.[6] In Canada as well as many other countries, per capita training expenditures are greater for managers than for any other category of employees: more managers are trained and more is spent on each of them. North American corporations pour billions of dollars into management development as they fund courses, seminars, executive education, and university business schools. This high level of commitment to managerial development is true in countries as diverse as the United Kingdom, Lithuania, Spain, and Iran.[7] Why is that? It is because the development of managers is a prudent business investment.

To a very large degree, managers are responsible for ensuring that the organization functions effectively and efficiently. They define the organization and it is they who are most responsible for its financial and psychological health. Organizations are systems composed of people, technologies, procedures, and communications designed to achieve specific valued objectives. It is management's purpose to define these objectives (products and services) and to ensure that they are achieved on time and with acceptable levels of quality. In effect, organizations invest more heavily in managers and in their development because theirs is *the* pivotal role in organizations.

MANAGEMENT DEVELOPMENT

As you will see, the fundamental roles that managers play in organizations are interpersonal, informational, and decisional ones. These three roles are core for the main functions of managers: controlling, organizing, and planning (which makes the convenient acronym COP). However, the last 20 years have seen a growing recognition of the exercise of leadership as a fundamental function of managers. **Leadership** refers to the individual qualities and behaviours that define and shape the direction of the organization and that inspire others to pursue that direction in the face of obstacles and constraints.

Leadership
The qualities and behaviours that shape the direction of the organization and that inspire others to pursue that direction in the face of obstacles and constraints

Although most managers will have to accomplish these roles and functions, the relative emphasis placed on them will vary as a function of the hierarchical position, the organizational and social-cultural context, the organizational strategies, and the technologies and structures in which they operate. For example, the interpersonal roles may be particularly significant for the manager of a classical ballet company, while the decisional role may be even more critical for the management of a production department. Clearly, managers play a complex role requiring sophisticated skills.

The starting point for a discussion of management development is the identification of training needs. To define these needs, as discussed in Chapter 4, a thorough understanding of the managerial job is required. We therefore begin by reviewing research results that describe what managers do in order to identify the skills they require. This step is especially crucial for managers, as recent research has shown that the effectiveness of the training programs will be highly influenced by the quality and accuracy of job information.

CORE MANAGERIAL ROLES

Henry Mintzberg analyzed management from the perspective of the manager's day-to-day activities.[8] Derived from the formal authority and status that a manager has, Mintzberg broke these activities into three roles: interpersonal, informational, and decisional. This research is important because it helps define, with greater precision, the skills required of managers and hence the focus of training and development efforts.

Interpersonal Roles

Interpersonal roles refer to the relationships that managers develop with other people because these can provide significant help (or obstacles) to the attainment of group goals. As such, the manager is the organizational person who provides *leadership* (motivates others), and who *liaises* with others both within and outside the unit with the goal of securing information that is of use to the attainment of goals. The manager also plays a *figurehead* or representational role wherein he or she stands in for the managed group in routine (e.g., administrative meetings), social (e.g., local school board), and legal contexts (e.g., municipal zoning officials).

Informational Role

Managers must *monitor* the environment (both internal and external) to accumulate information pertinent to the attainment of organizational goals. He or she reciprocates by assuming the role of *disseminator* of information by informing others about the unit and informing the unit about relevant developments occurring outside the unit. The manager also acts as a *spokesperson*, informing others and "selling" them on the plans, values, or goals of the unit (such as explaining to others the environmental impact of a new plant). Hence, managers require communication skills.

Decisional Role

Managers must make decisions about people and about goals and the means to attain them. As an initiator of change, the manager is an *entrepreneur* moving the unit in directions that take advantage of opportunities or shifting the activities of the group to reduce threats. The manager *allocates resources,* choosing from competing proposals and projects those that will receive additional funding and personnel and those to be curtailed or discontinued. Downsizing or staff expansions are such resource-allocation decisions.

The manager is also called upon to act as a *negotiator,* interacting and bargaining with others in both the external (e.g., regulatory agencies, suppliers), or internal (e.g. budget allocation, policy choices) environments. Mintzberg's data also note that the manager is also a *troubleshooter* reacting to unanticipated and unplanned environmental events that can severely disrupt the unit (e.g., a sudden job action or a delivery problem).

MANAGERIAL FUNCTIONS

Functions of management

Controlling, organizing, planning, and leading

Traditionally, the **functions of management** have been summarized to be controlling, organizing, and planning (COP). That is, managers are responsible for ensuring that things get done. They monitor the work processes and progress toward goal attainment (controlling); they allocate resources and tasks (organizing); they establish what should be done and how (planning). Moreover, as is discussed below (see "Leadership: A Critical Function of Management"), they are further tasked to maintain the motivation and zeal of those who do the work. That is, they are to lead. In completing these functions, they play one or more of the interpersonal, informational, or decisional roles and rely on the skills that each implies.

Controlling

Controlling, as its name suggests, refers to the process by which the activities of the organization and its members are monitored to ensure that they contribute positively to the attainment of organization goals and objectives. It involves establishing mechanisms to monitor and resolve performance gaps and address any constraints and problems that hinder the attainment of performance goals.

Organizing

The accomplishment of most contemporary organizational goals requires the efforts of a diversity of units, each composed of many individuals. Major activities are identified and components of these major tasks assigned to units and individuals. The manager's job is to establish systems that ensure these efforts are efficiently and effectively coordinated and organized.

Planning

Planning, in the context of management, means defining the direction toward which the efforts of individuals are to be directed. It involves defining objectives and developing goals to be met by the organization and the departments or the units for which the manager is responsible. The scope of the goals and objectives depends on the level of management, and the specifics of the planning tasks depend on the nature of managerial responsibility. As one moves from the lowest to the highest levels of the organization, the objectives and goals become broader and more strategic.

Leading

Leading is a critical people-oriented function of management. It means influencing the actions of others such that these actions are coordinated to produce the desired outcomes. Managers mainly operate through others. Hence, managers require people skills.

Leadership: A Critical Function of Management

In the past, the "leadership" function was thought to belong more exclusively to the apex of the organizational pyramid: the senior managers.[9] However, in line with current thinking (e.g., Kotter, or Whetten and Cameron), we subscribe to the view that the exercise of leadership is a function of *all* management.[10] Hence, the functions of managers are now thought to be controlling, organizing, planning, and leading (which makes COPL, though some prefer the less literal but more colourful acronym CLOP).

Managers are responsible for obtaining and keeping employees committed to their goals. This is facilitated when employees believe that the attainment of the goal is important, when they believe that attaining the goal will result in positive outcomes, and when they also believe that their individual efforts make a difference in goal attainment. A leader, according to Kouzes and Posner, is successful by being a role model (i.e., preaching by example), by inspiring a shared vision, by challenging the status quo and encouraging others to do the same (asking why), and by recognizing the contributions of others (through verbal feedback and tangible outcomes).[11]

Adapting to the global economy and its competitive pressures requires ever-increasing levels of resiliency and flexibility in organizations. This flexibility requires that people at all levels of the organization, from the top to the bottom, adapt their job behaviours in response to the changing requirements of their jobs and the contexts in which they are to be performed. As Kotter explains, managers are the motors that propel this process of adaptation to change. From first-line supervisors to CEOs, from production to R&D, managers need to possess the knowledge, skills, attitudes, and behaviours that enable them to foster in the people they manage the attitudes and behaviours that are conducive to the attainment of the individual and organizational goals. The current economic realities compel managers to assume this challenge. They need to lead.

Although managers are still viewed as those responsible for "getting things done" through the functions of controlling, organizing, planning, and leading, increasingly managers must provide support to their employees, assist them in the development of new skills, and act as coaches and facilitators for employee task accomplishment.[12] Some leading organizations have formalized these functions by integrating them into the performance appraisal system for managers. To learn more about this, see Training Today 14.2, "Taking Management Development Seriously: The PricewaterhouseCoopers Story."

Training Today 14.2

Taking Management Development Seriously: The PricewaterhouseCoopers Story

PricewaterhouseCoopers (PwC) is one of the largest professional services organizations in the world. PwC takes the development of its people seriously. It has instituted widespread coaching and mentoring programs for managers, but it has gone one step further.

As part of the performance management program, all managers must indicate the steps they have taken to develop their own subordinates. The performance assessment—and the rewards and bonuses paid out to managers based on it—is determined, in part, by the degree to which they have helped their employees achieve higher levels of competencies, both managerial and technical.

Moreover, all partners in the firm are offered a series of workshops delivered by leading professionals to help them gain a deeper understanding of the help that they can provide to their employees and the importance of that function for the organization.

Why would a prestigious organization like PwC attach importance to this policy? Because it is good for their employees and good for business! Such policies help the company retain its valued employees and help them service their clients even better. Developing and growing the competencies of employees also increases their employability, both on client projects with PwC and even if they should leave the organization.

In the end, the value of these practices is that they seamlessly and simultaneously provide benefits both to the organization and to employees. It's a win-win scenario.

MANAGEMENT SKILLS

Skills

Sets of actions that individuals perform and that lead to valued outcomes

Skills may be defined as sets of actions that individuals perform and that lead to valued outcomes.[13] The literature is replete with descriptions of the types of skills that are needed to accomplish the managerial roles and functions. Two types of approaches have been used to identify the skills required of managers. Some authors rely on their extensive experience with management to infer the skills needed for effective management (or leadership). They then propose mechanisms by which these can be developed.

Others have used empirical surveys of managers, sometimes within a single firm and sometimes across several, to guide their prescriptions. Managers rate the importance of many potential skills and statistical analyses are conducted to identify those skills and competencies that distinguish successful managers from their less successful counterparts.

One such comparative study involved observations of 52 successful managers and less successful ones in three organizations. Successful managers were better equipped with technical skills (such as paperwork, planning, and goal setting) as well as in working with people (building power and influence, communicating, managing conflict, decision making, and developing others).[14]

A rather unusual other study conducted group interviews (focus groups) with 830 U.S. managers who were identified as *less* successful, the results of which closely mirror those found in other studies.[15] Unsuccessful managers tended to be poorer in both technical and people skills. They were poorer at planning, monitoring performance, and providing feedback and they tended to be less effective in identifying and removing obstacles to effective performance. They tended to display ineffective communication and interpersonal skills, failed to clarify expectations, were poorer in delegating and empowering subordinates, tended to be more distrustful of others, and were less able to organize and encourage teamwork. As a result, they had more trouble motivating others.

Some further research has helped identify the relative importance of the various managerial skills. Cameron and Tschirhart asked a large sample of managers working in 150 organizations to identify the most important skills and competencies required of managers.[16] The results showed that the managerial skills fall into four basic clusters. One cluster focuses on human relations skills and includes skills such as providing support, communication, and team building. Another focused on competitiveness and control. A third cluster focused on behaviours that foster individual entrepreneurship and innovativeness, and the fourth focused on order and rationality. Hence, effective managers support and encourage the work of their employees (cluster 1) while focused on achievement and results (cluster 2). They encourage employees to display innovation and creativity (cluster 3), while maintaining control and rationality (cluster 4).

Re-read the previous paragraph. You might note, as Cameron and Tschirhart do, that the skills required of successful managers are "paradoxical," seemingly contradictory. For example, it may appear that cluster 3 (fostering individual entrepreneurship) is the opposite of cluster 4 (maintaining control). Yet Whetten and Cameron showed that successful managers do indeed resolve this paradox: Even as they were controlled, stable, and rational, they were still able to help employee creativity and flexibility!

TABLE (14.1)
The Most Frequently Cited Skills of Effective Managers
Verbal communication (including listening)
Managing time and stress
Managing individual decisions
Recognizing, defining, and solving problems
Motivating and influencing others
Delegating
Setting goals and articulating a vision
Self-awareness
Team building
Managing conflict

Source: D.A. Whetten & K.S. Cameron, *Developing Management Skills (5th ed.)* Upper Saddle River, NJ: Prentice Hall, 2002.

Based on these research studies, a number of critical managerial skills have been identified. Table 14.1 presents a summary of the most frequently mentioned skills of effective managers. As you will see, many of these involve "people skills" (communicating, motivating others, delegating, self-awareness, team building, and conflict management). From this it is generally recognized now that the "people" side of management and its subsequent salience for management development cannot be underestimated. As an example, the Stanford Graduate School of Business produces a large number of briefings videos delivered by corporate and academic stars and intended for the development of managers. Whereas these DVDs cover a wide range of topics (such as mergers and acquisitions, preparing financial statements, supply chain strategies, etc.), the single most frequent topic, about a third of all videos, focuses on dealing with people (such as coaching and providing feedback).

A manager controls, organizes, plans, and leads people. In practice, this means that one of the most important aspects of management involves interacting, communicating, and dealing with other people: their peers, subordinates, and superiors, as well as customers and, in many cases, suppliers and members of the general public. You will not be surprised to learn that some managers are better at it than others. Research has shown that managers who are more effective tend to display superior people skills. They are thought to hold higher levels of a specific type of intelligence called "emotional intelligence," a topic to which we now turn.

EMOTIONAL INTELLIGENCE

Most human interactions have an emotional component and the success of these interactions often depends on how well emotions are managed. Moreover, because of the heavy responsibilities of the management role and the sheer number of tasks that managers perform, they must often deal with their own emotional issues and pressures. Thus, they have to cope with conflict, performance pressures, and uncertainty. Because much of this involves emotions, managers must develop skills in managing their own emotions and in understanding those of others. The skills that people have in managing emotions—their own and those of others—have been labelled *emotional intelligence* (EI).[17] Search the internet using the key words "emotional intelligence" or "emotional quotient (EQ)" to obtain an appreciation for the prominence of this concept. You will find thousands of entries!

Emotional intelligence has to do with the ability to manage and cope with emotions—one's own emotions as well as those of others. This involves five sets of skills.

Emotional intelligence
The ability to manage your own and others' emotions and your relationships with others

1. *Self-awareness:* Being aware of, and understanding, oneself and one's emotions when interacting with others.
2. *Self-control:* Managing and regulating one's emotions (both positive and negative) that arise from encounters and events.
3. *Motivation or drive:* Channelling emotions and energies in support of one's goals.
4. *Empathy:* "Reading" and recognizing the emotions of others and responding to them appropriately.
5. *Interpersonal skills:* The ability to manage interactions with others in an appropriate and effective manner, through an understanding, integration, and management of emotions—their own and those of the people with whom they interact.

Notice that the components of EI (self-awareness, interpersonal skills, etc.) are listed as skills. That is, they are believed to be controllable and learnable behaviours rather than "fixed" character-like traits. Unlike intellectual intelligence (IQ), which is a relatively stable and enduring characteristic of people's cognitive abilities, EI is believed to be a learnable and changeable factor (see the section "Project Management and Emotional Intelligence").

Through appropriate management development and training, emotional intelligence can be modified and improved. However, unlike project planning or the other technical skills associated with management, emotional intelligence involves people-oriented skills that often are labelled as "soft skills." As you read in Training Today 14.1, the development of soft skills is considered to be even more important for managers.

EI, as with other "soft skills," tends to be developed indirectly, through enhanced skills in dealing with others. As people learn to receive and deliver feedback, to manage stress, or to defuse conflicts, for example, they also simultaneously enhance their own levels of emotional intelligence.[18] Training in emotional intelligence involves group and individual activities that include role plays, assessments, and practical exercises all intended to enhance self-management and empathy.

It is believed that emotional intelligence can be developed. This is extremely important because empirical research has shown that managers with higher levels of emotional intelligence are more effective and successful than managers with lower levels of EI. They are more likely to be promoted and to rise to the highest levels of management in their organizations. Furthermore, while cognitive intelligence levels (IQ) is important, emotional intelligence has been found in some cases to be even more important than IQ in predicting a manager's success. Not surprisingly, research indicates that organizations prefer to hire for management positions people with higher levels of the skills associated with emotional intelligence.[19]

In summary, emotional intelligence involves the ability to manage one's own and others' emotions and relationships with others. Given that managers spend most of their time interacting and communicating with others and that the main functions and roles of management involve people, emotional intelligence is a critical factor in management development and effectiveness. Therefore, in addition to training experiences that are directly focused on its development, those programs that include activities and experiences that encourage self-awareness and self-control, motivation, empathy, and interpersonal skills serve to enhance emotional intelligence.

Project Management and Emotional Intelligence

Whereas only some managers are involved with project *planning,* most if not all will be tasked with the *management* of projects. Planning involves determining the resources (human, technical, and financial) required to achieve an objective and to organize these such that they will converge to achieve the final product within the projected time frames and budgets. Managing a project, on the other hand, requires of managers that they control, lead, organize and plan (CLOP) the workforce to achieve the desired end result. Project management, therefore, refers to the day-to-day functioning of the manager in the accomplishment of the plan.

While poorly planned projects are unlikely to be successful, research has shown that well planned projects can and sometimes do fail. That unfortunate result often stems from weak project management. Planning is one thing—getting it done is another.

All plans, once initiated, are subject to unexpected and disruptive events: poor weather, wildcat strikes, supply problems, and influenza outbreaks are but four examples. Even under the best of circumstances changes to the plan are often required: for example, the plan for the construction of the Freedom Tower, built over the old World Trade Center site in New York City, called for the building facade to be encased in special glass. However, it was discovered that the type of glass earmarked for use was unable to meet safety standards. As a result, the architectural and engineering plans had to be modified and work previously accomplished had to be demolished and redone to accommodate the new specifications.

Whatever the circumstances, managing a project also means managing feelings. These may range from the frustrations of workers who must sometimes redo work; the concerns of clients who fear delays and cost overruns; the anxieties that accompany the heavy responsibility for achieving specific results within tight time frames; and the anger and conflicts that occur when people are under pressure.

This raises two interrelated questions: 1) is it the case that managers with higher levels of emotional intelligence—that is, those who cope better with emotions—manage projects better, and 2) can EI be developed through structured training? The answer to both questions appears to be yes.

Research conducted by Muller and Turner[20] analyzed leader cognitive and emotional intelligence across different types of projects run in different countries. Their results show that emotional intelligence dimensions and success in question. This is essential because people must recognize a need for development before development can take hold. That is, skill assessment affects and contributes to training motivation.

Initial skill assessment also serves to identify the learning and the behavioural styles of managers such that these can be taken into account when developing and implementing training programs. Remember that the purpose of management development is *not* to change individual personalities, but rather to help managers translate these personal preferences into practices and behaviours that are appropriate to their work context and that are effective in meeting the goals of the organization. No wonder that skill assessment is a key component of IBM's Managing@IBM program and is developed in close symmetry with the learning objectives set for the training program (see Chapter 5).

Initial skill assessment is usually established through self-administered (and often self-scored) standardized validated questionnaires given to training participants at the onset of training. For this reason these questionnaires are relatively short, easily administered, and scored under themes that directly reflect the training content. For example, the initial (PRE TRAINING) questionnaire for a stress-coping program would ask trainees to describe the degree to which they engage in behaviours that are known to be associated with stress reactions. Typically, trainees retain their answers and following training participants answer the same questionnaire (POST TRAINING) again. Comparing the pre- and post-answers allows managers to see progress, if any.

Although initial skill assessment is of importance to all training programs, it is especially critical for management development because "development" is a gradual process where *improvement* in skills is the main objective. Managers will need to practise and rehearse the skill before mastery can be achieved. People are more likely to rehearse a skill when they are motivated and have confidence in their ability to develop it. Reinforcement is one very important mechanism that helps enhance motivation. Skill assessment before and after the development experience can be reinforcing as it helps managers perceive the degree of growth in their level of skills mastery. Helping managers perceive improvements helps to build motivation, thus encouraging managers to continue to exert the efforts (practice and rehearsal) that lead to mastery. Hence, skill assessment and growth is immediately useful to the trainer (to know how things are going), but it also makes an indirect contribution to the motivation of the learner.

b. *Skill learning.* Learning is the core focus of training programs. However, in contrast to most technical training where the trainee is taught specific procedures and steps required to accomplish a task, the managerial role is more diffuse, requiring that managers recognize the need for the skill in a diverse number of circumstances and the importance of using the skill in different ways for different cases. Hence, management development programs will almost invariably include group discussions and role plays where managers help each other discover the opportunities for application that may exist on the job, the obstacles that may inhibit skill use, and the strategies and tactics that may be used to circumvent these obstacles.

In management development, the purpose is to help managers learn managerial principles and processes that can be integrated with their personal styles and applied to the conditions they are likely to meet on the job. Hence, most management development programs will include substantial lectures or presentations that outline the reasons for the training and the principles that will guide their future actions. For example, performance planning and reviews (PP&R) tend to be more constructive when subordinate and managerial anxiety and defensiveness are minimized. To achieve this, most PP&R training programs emphasize the importance for the manager of clearly explaining the evaluation process to the subordinate ahead of time. There are many ways of explaining the same thing, and no specific manner, or set of words, will be appropriate for all managers and/or with all subordinates. Therefore, the effectively trained manager will have understood the principle (reducing subordinate defensiveness) but will "choose" his or her own specific words and approaches depending on the specifics of the person under review and the specifics of the situation. The ultimate objective of these development programs is to help managers attain procedural learning (see Chapter 3). Attaining that goal generally requires *practice,* the third major component of management development programs.

c. *Skill practice.* As described in Chapter 5, practice is the key to learning how to do most things well. The practice of learned skills serves three fundamental purposes. First and most obvious, practice reinforces learning and, more formally, helps shift the learning from the declarative to the procedural learning stage (see Chapter 3). This is essential if the manager is to integrate the learned skill with his or her own style. A second purpose of practice is to enhance the manager's belief in his or her ability to perform the skill. That is, practice contributes to the development of self-efficacy and, as you have read in both Chapters 3 and 11, the development of self-efficacy is one of the keys to successful training. Managers who feel more confident of their capacity to learn and display the skill on the job are more likely to learn and transfer that skill. Third, skill practice can take a variety of forms including role plays, simulations, and videotaped behaviour with feedback. These activities are inherently more active, maintaining trainee interest, attention, and motivation on the learning task. However, as training time is invariably limited in the North American context, it is not realistic to expect that the amount of time devoted to practice during training will be sufficient to automatically produce high levels of transfer on the job. As rehearsal and practice on the job is essential, all development models include as a final component "skill application on the job."

d. *Skill application on the job (transfer).* This final step in management development has to do with the transfer process (see Chapter 10). Managers establish, during the training session, specific plans for the application of the learning on the job. Once on the job, however, organizational

Make the
Connection

Make the
Connection

support in the form of follow-ups, additional coaching, and reinforcement is frequently required to ensure that managers transfer their newly learned skills. The reason for this is that in light of the very numerous tasks that managers perform, usually under pressure, it is very easy and tempting for them to relapse into their traditional, well-honed pre-training behaviours. Specific immediate post-training interventions such as relapse prevention (see Chapter 10) can also be integrated at this point to augment the odds of successful transfer.

In summary, models of management skill development focus on a number of important steps or stages in the development process. This usually begins with self-assessment and then proceeds to skill learning, practice, and application. These steps favour the development of the motivational, self-efficacy, learning, and/or transfer outcomes that define successful training.

ERROR TRAINING FOR MANAGEMENT DEVELOPMENT

Traditional models such as TIMS regard errors as undesirable and detrimental to learning. Trainee skills are assessed, then skills are taught, then they are practised and applied. This sequential approach is designed to focus the training content and processes to reduce errors until, at the application stage, they are mostly eliminated. However, errors are inevitable when mastering new content or a new task, and that can be very discouraging. As most students know, it is very difficult to exercise continued effort in the face of failure.

Make the Connection

In Chapter 5 we discussed error-management training (EMT), which involves allowing and encouraging trainees to make errors. Let's consider how EMT can be used for management development. Recall that EMT has been found to be more effective when the trainee has to generalize learning to new tasks. Thus, if the training transfer task is to reproduce—more or less mechanically—a learned skill, EMT programs do not offer much advantage over traditional ones, designed using TIMS approaches. However, for jobs that require problem-solving skills, where reproduction of learned behaviours is not sufficient, EMT may prove superior.

This latter result is of special relevance for management jobs, where constant adaptation to an ever-changing environment is the norm. Trained managers must be able to use new skills flexibly in a variety of contexts. In Chapter 5 this was called adaptive expertise. As EMT appears pointedly more effective in producing adaptive expertise, and since that type of transfer is required for management jobs, organizations might consider EMT when developing managers.

THE CONTENT OF MANAGEMENT DEVELOPMENT PROGRAMS

Based on our earlier discussion, management skills can be clustered around three general categories: conceptual, technical, and interpersonal skills. These three clusters of skills are not completely independent. For example, the mastery of conceptual skills (planning a project) often requires technical skills (such as linear programming). Similarly, interpersonal skills (e.g., convincing

R&D scientists of the importance of respecting deadlines) often require specific technical skills (understanding the complexities of research). Nevertheless, this categorization provides a useful way to organize management development programs.

We now describe the content of programs used to develop some of these managerial skills. More complete descriptions of management development programs may be found in texts specialized in management development (e.g., Whetten and Cameron or Hunsaker) and by consulting the weblinks identified at the end of the chapter.

Conceptual Skills

To accomplish the control, organizing, and planning functions of management, managers require various conceptual skills. We will limit the discussion to three especially important conceptual skills—problem solving and decision making, planning, and performance management.

a. *Problem-solving and decision-making skills.* Because managers are required to make myriad decisions—small and large—it is essential that they have the skills to do so. Many years ago, James March and Herbert Simon, in one of the most influential studies of managerial decision making, showed that most people are uncomfortable making decisions, and that they tend to adopt solutions to problems that are not optimal but "adequate."[23] Moreover, as Mintzberg showed, managers are invariably under time pressure. They need to make very quick decisions. As a typical consequence of these pressures, the first solution that minimally solves the problem is selected. That is not always a good idea.

   Contemporary decision-making programs are designed to train managers into specifically avoiding this tendency. As a result, most programs are organized around four basic steps:

   1. Definition of the problem.
   2. Generation of alternative solutions.
   3. Evaluation and selection of a solution.
   4. Implementation of the solution and follow-up.

   The actual training programs include introductory lectures where the basic steps required for effective decision making are explained and defended. Videotapes, role plays, and structured individual exercises are used to reinforce each learning point, and to provide some of the all-important skills practice.

b. *Planning skills.* Planning is an essential requirement of management. Planning involves first the clarification and specification of the goals the manager wishes to achieve. Next, the manager is taught to scan the environment to ensure that the plans are relevant and have a high probability of being successfully implemented. This second step is referred to as a "SWOT" analysis. That is, the manager is taught how to identify the strengths (S) and weaknesses (W) of the unit managed (i.e., its capabilities and weaknesses) relative to the opportunities (O) and threats (T) that exist in the environment. Based on this analysis, the manager is taught to translate these strengths and weaknesses, opportunities, and possible threats into specific actions in order to establish the strategies and tactics required for implementation. Finally, managers learn the processes by which the success (or lack thereof) of the plan is evaluated.

c. *Performance management and goal-setting skills.* Almost all organizations in North America require managers to review, assess, and manage the performance of their units and the people in them. Performance appraisal involves two distinct steps: assessing the performance of people (to provide feedback on past performance and to ensure that rewards and sanctions are applied fairly), and establishing goals and directions to encourage improved future performance. Whereas these two steps are usually associated with a yearly formal review session, it is now widely acknowledged that managers need to review the performance of others on an ongoing basis. Motivating employees to improve performance is one of the key skills that successful managers possess.

Make the Connection

Goal setting is an integral part of this process. As discussed in Chapter 3, goals have strong motivational effects and are one of the most important mechanisms for managing one's own performance as well as the performance of others.[24] Goals focus and direct one's efforts and can be self-reinforcing by providing specific feedback information that allows people to evaluate their progress.

However, in order for goals to be motivational, they must be SMART goals. That is, they must be Specific, Measurable, Achievable, Relevant, and specified in Time. Managers need to know how to structure such SMART goals. Moreover, goals are motivating and effective only when they are perceived to be challenging yet achievable, and when there is commitment to goal attainment. Most goal-setting training programs are structured to teach managers how to obtain the employees' commitment to the set goals and to provide feedback relevant to goal attainment.

Goal setting is now an integral part of performance management, and many managers are trained in this area in order to enable them to conduct performance appraisals and to help their employees improve their performance. Many Canadian organizations including PricewaterhouseCoopers, the National Research Council of Canada, and Bell Canada have provided their managers with performance management and assessment training courses that include goal setting as one of the key dimensions of the program.

Performance management training programs emphasize, through lectures and discussions, the key advantages of performance reviews and the fundamental difficulties of the process. Such programs include many experiential components such as role plays and simulations. These interventions are designed to provide skill practice and to enhance both procedural learning as well as self-efficacy. As discussed in Chapters 10 and 11, these are important elements for successful transfer from the training situation to the job.

Technical Skills

Managers of marketing departments know something about marketing, and research directors know something about research. Such knowledge and skills are generally acquired through university programs that may be general (such as a general MBA) or more specialized (such as a university program in human resource management, marketing, statistics, or accounting). Additionally, technical skills can be further developed through targeted training courses and workshops and/or readings. For example, controlling budgets requires expertise in computer spreadsheet programs such as Excel, and the informational role requires presentation skills, which in turn often requires knowledge of how to use presentation programs such as PowerPoint.

As additional examples, university professors tend to build technical skills by reading scientific journals and by attending conferences, and medical doctors and pharmacists in Canada are required to attend a certain number of conferences and workshops that instruct them on new research, treatments, or diagnostic procedures in their areas of practice. Accountants and lawyers are also required to attend periodic specialized information sessions, such as when there are changes to auditing standards or tax regulations or when new laws are enacted. These are essentially informational interventions.

Interpersonal Skills

Interpersonal skills refer to the manager's ability to interact with others in a constructive manner. This includes skills in communication, in coaching (see "Coaching" later in the chapter), and in managing conflict and stress. Although we limit our discussion in this chapter to these skills, it is important to note that other skills are also important. For example, there is a growing recognition of the importance for managers to develop "political" skills designed to help them gain power and influence. Moreover, as organizations move toward knowledge-based systems, they require that their members increasingly self-manage their behaviour and show initiative in their own development, including innovative ways of integrating Web-based learning, as with Kraiger's "third-generation" models of learning.[25] Although that particular approach is somewhat controversial, it remains that managers need to learn how to function in this new environment by learning how to empower and motivate their employees and to build effective teams.[26]

a. *Communication.* Communication skills are central to most management positions because much of a manager's time involves gathering and disseminating information from the environment to the people in the unit and from the unit to higher management and/or to the external environment. Often managers must communicate expectations to employees and provide feedback—not all of which is positive—to employees. In communicating effectively, managers are taught to recognize their own *biases and styles* in "hearing" and in "speaking" with others. Hence, managers need to understand their *frame of reference* (knowing "where they are coming from"), how their interpretations of what they hear and communicate are affected by their *values,* and their *trusts* or distrusts of others. These in turn affect *selective listening* (hearing what we want to hear) and *filtering* (telling only that which others want to hear). In addition to alerting managers to these tendencies that obscure communication, most communication training programs teach managers the principles and the practice of effective communication. This involves *congruency* (ensuring that the message sent is in line with their own actions), *clarity* (using language that is appropriate for the listener), and most importantly to ensure *comprehension* by actively soliciting feedback from the listener. These complex skills are developed through training programs that place a large emphasis on practice. Hence, these programs devote much of their time to analyzing cases and engaging in role plays with other training participants and the instructor's main role is to provide constructive feedback.

b. *Managing conflict.* Managing conflict is an essential skill for managers because they are invariably competing for resources with other managers and because they may be involved in managing the competition and conflict between employees.

Conflict can be described as being of one of two types—conflict that is *interpersonal* (co-workers who may dislike one another) or *issue-based* (people who may have conflicting views on a problem or its solution).[27] Conflict is not an inherently "bad" thing, because issue-based disagreements often enhance the quality of the final decision.[28] However, when conflict is not properly managed it can quickly create organizational problems.

There are five ways of managing conflict: *avoidance* (ignoring it), *accommodation* (giving in), *forcing* (getting your way), *compromise* (providing each party with some of the things they want), and *collaboration* (finding a solution together that gives the parties what they both want).

Collaboration is the ultimate conflict resolution outcome but it is not always possible or appropriate. Which style is appropriate depends on the situation faced by the manager. Forcing, for example, may be appropriate when the resolution requires an unpopular decision and when gaining the commitment of people to that decision is not important. Hence managers are taught to recognize and choose the conflict management response that is appropriate to the circumstances they face. This, above all, requires of managers that they pay attention to the emotional aspects of the conflict. To do so requires that the manager

- Treats the parties with respect.
- Listens to the other party and ensures that they know they have been heard and understood.
- Shares his/her needs and feelings.

c. *Managing stress.* Considering the scope, time pressures (managers spend about nine minutes on each problem!), difficulties, responsibilities, and ambiguities of managerial life, it is no surprise that managerial jobs tend to be very stressful. A stress reaction is a person's emotional and physical response to a perceived threat. Stress reactions, like pain, are useful warning mechanisms that inform people that "something is wrong" and that they should do something about it. However, how a person deals with stress may or may not be particularly functional. Reacting to someone cutting you off on the highway by tearing after them with vengeance on your mind is unlikely to lead to an enjoyable or safe driving experience!

Stress reactions are responses to events that emanate from the work itself and/or from the organization. For example, two well-known work-related stressors are role conflict and role ambiguity. *Role conflict* is associated with having contradictory task demands (e.g., jobs that require experimentation and innovation in organizations that do not tolerate errors); *role ambiguity* refers to not knowing what is expected. Stressors that affect work behaviours might also find their source in non-work events (a family or health problem, for example). Managers need to recognize stress reactions both in themselves and in those they manage, because some stress reactions can be quite dysfunctional, damaging one's health and/or work performance.

The *Canadian HR Reporter* published several articles that describe what it calls "problem managers"; that is, managers who "abuse" or make inappropriate comments to employees.[29] Often these dysfunctional behaviours are a result of the stresses experienced by the manager.

There are two basic ways to deal with stress. First, one can change the environment by removing the stressors. Second, one can learn to cope with and manage stressors more effectively. Learning how to react to stressful situations is more likely to be successful, as changing organisations requires forces, strategies and actions that are not under the control of the individual.

Most people experience stress and are unaware of it. In learning how to cope with stress, the first and most important step, then, is to recognize the signs of stress: to know when one is in fact experiencing it. As a result, the initial "skills assessment" phase of such training is critical and these programs spend considerable time helping managers become aware of their own reactions to stress. The manager can then learn proactive behavioural and cognitive tactics and strategies (learning how to perceive these situations differently) that will reduce the harmful effects of a stress reaction.

Stress-related training programs rely on the typical informational (reviewing basic principles related to stress and its management) and experiential (principally simulations and role plays) techniques. Usually, these programs offer concrete stress-reduction techniques that can be beneficial to managers not only in the context of work but also in their non-work lives.

In summary, management development programs are often designed to focus on the development of conceptual, technical, and interpersonal skills. There are of course many different approaches and methods for developing these skills, some on-the-job and others off-the-job, a topic to which we now turn.

METHODS OF MANAGEMENT DEVELOPMENT

Whereas virtually all of the on-the-job and off-the-job training methods described in Chapters 6 and 7 can and have been used by some management development programs, management training methods tend to rely on highly informational and highly experiential procedures.

At the informational level, management training programs focus on the principles and the applications of the skill or technique being taught. That is, they teach principles relevant to specifics in the core roles and functions of management. You may have noticed that in the sections describing management training programs (conflict management, decision making, etc.), emotional intelligence, or coaching (see below), we emphasized their principles. Lectures, readings, informative videos, and group discussions structured around these principles and their concrete applications constitute major elements in management training programs. This informational, principles-based approach is of great importance in management development because managers operate in fluid and varied environments and each manager needs to develop his/her own idiosyncratic ways of comfortably applying the principles learned in training. Management development cannot consist of memorizing and applying a set of prescriptions. If, for example, all computer operators can be drilled in exactly the same behaviours for loading a hard drive, all managers cannot be equivalently drilled into using the same words to communicate with all employees effectively. It is only by understanding and integrating the principles taught that different managers can correctly apply them in a manner that is appropriate to them and to the work group situation.

Helping managers adapt principles and techniques in conformity with their personal styles, given the context in which they work, requires effort on the part of the learner and that effort requires motivation. Managers who do not believe in the usefulness of a training program are unlikely to exert the efforts required to learn and apply its content. Focusing on the principles (and their application) contributes motivationally to successful management training: It sells it!

Experiential learning

Learning experiences that include skill practice exercises that actively engage and involve the learner

To further enhance the all-important trainee motivation, management training programs tend to be experiential. **Experiential learning** refers to learning experiences that include skill practice exercises that actively engage and involve the learner. Hence role plays with feedback, active exercises, and simulations are important components of the programs. Experiential approaches provide, in addition to motivational benefits, two other important ones. First, extensive hands-on practice builds procedural knowledge (see Chapters 3 and 11). That is, direct experience helps managers integrate the newly learned skills. Second, experiential learning is favoured because it contributes to managerial self-efficacy, which is an important precursor for transfer of training (see Chapter 10). As you will recall from the COMA model (see Chapter 11), motivation, self-efficacy, and procedural knowledge all have important effects on training success and transfer.

Make the
Connection

Although informational and experiential components are present in most management development programs, their relative emphasis vary across different programs. Many short-term programs (such as the Stanford Graduate School of Business DVDs) are essentially informational.

At the other extreme, some development programs are more fully experiential, providing few if any formal informational components. One such example is outdoor wilderness training. The interesting origins of this popular technique are described in Training Today 14.3, "The Origins of Outdoor Wilderness Training," and its effectiveness as a training strategy is discussed later in this chapter.

There are three general approaches to and techniques for management development: management education programs, management training programs, and on-the-job management development.

Training Today 14.3

The Origins of Outdoor Wilderness Training

During World War II, the allied navies played a major role, conveying and protecting ships supplying England. German U-boats opposed these convoys, taking a heavy toll on men and ships. Hundreds of ships were torpedoed, forcing thousands to confront the rigours of survival in rafts and lifeboats. Many successfully escaped their burning ships only to perish awaiting a rescue that did not come.

Paradoxically, casualty reports revealed that older, less physically able shipwrecked men had better survival rates than younger, fit sailors. Discussions held with survivors indicated that younger sailors adopted unsuccessful life strategies such as panic, while the older sailors, those with greater life experience, remained calmer and hence

were better able to meet the demands of their extreme situation.

Years after the war ended, this experience spawned "outdoor wilderness training," an experiential team and management development technique. For several days trainees are tasked with arduous and/or hazardous duties that are intentionally stressful, such as winter wilderness camping or rock climbing.

These stressful situations bring out the best and the worst in ourselves and others, allowing us to gain direct experience with what we and others are capable of doing. With its exposure to extreme conditions, outdoor wilderness training is intended to build "life experience" which, in turn, is supposed to contribute to the development of coping skills.

Management Education Programs

The development of managers has typically involved management education. **Management education** refers to the types of activities that are typically conducted by colleges and universities and that develop a broad range of knowledge, principles, and general conceptual abilities relevant to the managerial role.[30] These education programs target the development of the principles and techniques required to effectively control, organize, plan, and lead. Examples and case studies drawn from specific organizations are often used to exemplify the general principles and techniques of management that are presented through lectures and discussions. Three examples of such content areas are accounting, organizational behaviour, and business statistics.

The ever-popular MBA that most business schools offer provides the classic example of a management education program. Executive MBA programs are especially desirable for individuals who are already in managerial roles and want to advance in their organization. These programs provide individuals with a general education in management. Although they tend to be highly informational they typically include experiential learning as well. Students not only learn about management concepts and theory, but also are expected to develop managerial skills. In fact, many MBA programs offer managerial skills courses such as those listed in Table 14.1.

Management education programs make use of the full gamut of instructional methods described in Chapter 6. That includes lectures, group discussions, role plays, games, simulations, and behaviour modelling. The case study method, however, is the method most often used to teach management skills in MBA programs.

Management education
The acquisition of a broad range of managerial knowledge and general conceptual abilities

Make the Connection

The training materials are sometimes developed by the training department, even by the trainer in some cases. These highly customized training products can be very effective or not, depending on the degree to which they a) are constructed around solid need analyses, b) strongly respect adult learning principles, and c) integrate practice and other active learning experiences.

Some training programs, on the other hand, are supplied by specialized firms (such as Xerox). Commercially available programs are generally well developed as they incorporate adult learning principles (see Chapter 2) as well as some practices and/or role plays. They are generally affordable and the training packages include all required materials including those needed by the trainer (acetates, lecture notes, etc.). However, as they are designed for use in many organizations, their content may sometimes be inappropriate. For example, a role play simulating a sales context may be less meaningful to trainees in construction jobs. Concerns about "identical elements" (see Chapter 10) are pertinent here.

An increasing number of management development programs are now being made available through electronic media (see Chapter 8). IPM, for example, offers an integrated package of 12 CD-based training modules that covers key management skills including staffing, performance management, team building, and employee relations (more details are available from www.workplace.ca).

On-the-Job Management Development

On-the-job management development
Programs designed to provide individuals with managerial learning experiences on the job

On-the-job management development programs are designed to provide individuals with managerial learning experiences on the job. Two of the most common examples are job rotation and coaching.

Make the
Connection

Job Rotation

Job rotation
Exposing an individual to different areas and experiences throughout the organization

Recall from Chapter 7 that **job rotation** is a planned process that involves posting the manager to different jobs, areas, or functions of the organization. In effect, once a manager has mastered one job, he or she is moved to a different one. As briefly described in Training Today 14.1, this technique continues to enjoy high levels of popularity. With job rotation, the individual not only acquires new skills from working on different projects and interacting with a diversity of people and functions, but also learns about the organization itself. Job rotation as a development technique is particularly useful for the development of managers when the match between the skills the managers possess and those required in the new job is well thought out: rotating managers to jobs that require the manager's skills and provide opportunity for building others are best. As indicated in the TIMS model, accurate initial skills assessment is especially important when job rotation is contemplated as a development technique for managers.

Make the
Connection

Coaching and Mentoring

In Chapter 7 it was noted that coaching and mentoring are common methods of on-the-job training. Both are very popular tactics for the development of managerial competencies and particularly useful because they focus on the organization to which the manager belongs. That is, they are highly congruent with and relevant to the specific organizational culture. In most cases they involve one-on-one sessions held between the manager and another person: mentors and coaches. Both mentoring and coaching share the same distal goal of helping managers be more effective.

Coaching and mentoring have grown into major management development approaches for many companies. The 2007 Conference Board of Canada *Learning and Development Outlook* reports that more than one-third of Canadian organizations maintain coaching and/or mentoring programs, and 55 percent of these consider them effective tools for the development of their people.[32]

MENTORING   **Mentors** contribute to the strategic development of managers by helping less experienced managers to understand and to gain perspective on the general managerial problems and difficulties with which they are confronted. They are usually continuous interventions in which trainees and mentors might work together for years and are most useful as career development strategies. Although the mentor and the manager may discuss specific problems, the goal of mentoring is broader and more diffuse. The mentor's task is to nurture the manager's growth as a manager.

COACHING   On the other hand, **coaching** is more specifically goal-oriented than is mentoring. It is a one-on-one individualized learning experience in which a more experienced and knowledgeable person is formally called upon to help the manager develop the insights and techniques pertinent to the accomplishment of specific aspects of their job.

The coach interacts with and provides feedback to the manager with the intent of developing his or her insight, skills, attitudes, and motivation for dealing with more specific challenges. For example, a coach might help a manager develop a presentation explaining how a particular problem can be solved.

Coaches may be external or internal to the company depending on budgets, coaching goals, and the organizational contexts. For example, the CEO who is struggling with a downsizing decision may well prefer to be coached by an external person. However, the manager who needs to hone her selling skills might benefit more from a trusted internal coach.

Many coaches are specialized in specific sectors such as pharmaceuticals or manufacturing, or in specialized contents as the following example illustrates. A marketing manager was promoted to head a different group: the organizational learning group in the Canadian operations of a multinational pharmaceutical organization. Her boss, the vice president of human resources, asked her to develop and present to upper management six weeks hence a training plan for the marketing division. Although experienced in marketing, the new manager lacked direct experience and knowledge of "organizational learning." She therefore signed a six-week contract with an external coach who was an expert in training and development with extensive experience in the pharmaceutical industry. The coach's role was *not* to produce the training plan, but rather to help the manager develop hers. During the weekly two-hour coaching sessions they discussed best practices, what other companies did, the advantages and disadvantages of various options, the obstacles likely to be encountered and how best to prepare for them, and how to present the plan, including setting up the actual slides for the presentation to her bosses. This coaching episode ended when the manager presented (successfully, as it turns out) her training plan.

Mentors
Help less experienced managers gain insight and perspective on the general managerial problems and difficulties with which they are confronted

Coaching
One-on-one individualized learning experience in which a more experienced and knowledgeable person is formally called upon to help another person develop the insights and techniques pertinent to the accomplishment of specific job tasks

In this very typical case, the coach was an external consultant hired to help a manager complete one major task within an established six-week deadline. However, many organizations require that managers serve as coaches to subordinate employees and managers on an ongoing basis. In that case the mandate may be much broader (the issues to be coached are not specified in advance) and/or more open-ended (without a specific end date). The coaching system in place in the Canadian branch of PricewaterhouseCoopers (see Training Today 14.2) provides one such example.

When coaching is to be provided to all employees on an ongoing basis, managers are expected to serve as coaches to some subordinates. However, to be competent in that role supervisors need to be trained in the science of coaching. David Peterson has uncovered some of the key ingredient of a "great coach," of which three stand out: Great coaches are goal-oriented, challengers, and person-focused.[33]

1. *Goal orientation.* Great coaches are great listeners who empathize with the learner and who are honestly interested in helping people achieve their goals. Hence, great coaches work diligently to help the manager clarify the goals pursued.
2. *Challengers.* Great coaches are able to "feel" the mood state of the learner and know when to listen and when to challenge the beliefs and thinking of the learner. They know when to be supportive and when to be critical.
3. *Person-focused.* Great coaches focus their efforts and attention on the learner. They do not try to impose their views on the learner by insisting that there is "one best way" to do things. Rather, they focus on helping the learner use his/her own previous knowledge and experience to develop his/her own perspective, understanding, and styles in dealing with the problems to be solved.

The coach who is goal oriented, challenging, and person focused is more likely to develop the manager. This is because these are the skills that will help the person coached to develop insight, motivation, capabilities, real-work practice, and accountability, the five conditions of successfully accomplished coaching. These five form what Peterson labels the "development pipeline." Coaches are maximally helpful when they structure their efforts to help managers develop:

- *Insight.* Recognizing and understanding their own strengths and weaknesses.

- *Motivation.* Understanding and caring about changing the ways in which they operate.

- *Capabilities.* Identifying resources and best practices for dealing with complex decisions/situations and exploring alternative ways of dealing with them.

- *Real-world practices.* Identifying opportunities to implement, on a day-to-day basis, the little changes that should be made and developing the critical perspective needed to assess what works, what does not, and why.

- *Accountability.* Encouraging the manager to demonstrate the new skills and knowledge through commitment to specific actions.

To achieve these objectives, coaches face a number of important challenges. First and foremost, coaches must act to gain the trust of the "coachee." Confidentiality, discretion, and honesty are three of the key behaviours coaches must demonstrate. With this developing trust it becomes easier for the coach to provide constructive feedback. For example, advice from a trusted coach is likely to be well received.

Applying new skills is difficult and attempts to do so are often subject to obstacles and hurdles that can discourage their deployment. Coaches have a special responsibility to be attentive to these situations and to help managerial persistence. Building self-efficacy, helping managers construe obstacles as "problems" rather than "failures," and providing emotional support are three techniques successful coaches use. Finally, coaches who are in a position to do so sometimes intervene elsewhere in the organization to remove obstacles. That is, successful coaches are sometimes proactive as opposed to strictly passive in their interventions. Compared to external ones, internal coaches are often in a better position to help in this way.

A number of research studies have shown that coaching does help managers become more successful and more effective in accomplishing their tasks. Coached executives showed progress in a number of dimensions including the management of people, relationships with others, communication skills, goal setting, engagement, and productivity.[34] This study also showed that the effects are greater when the coaches are committed to change and when the organizational environment actively supports them in their attempts to change. Yet another study—this one relying on a very large sample of executives using a quasi-experimental research design—showed similar results, although here the changes were significant but somewhat modest.[35] Finally, other research has shown that managers who received coaching experiences as part of their executive education program in a university also reported higher levels of self-efficacy and improved skills in developing others.

While this evidence speaks highly of coaching, it is important to note that most of the research has relied on self-report measures and/or on the perception of others (mainly supervisors and/or subordinates) to assess the effectiveness of coaching as a management development technique. Perceptions of effectiveness may not always be accurate substitutes for objective criteria.

We now conclude this chapter by turning to the key question: How effective is management development?

IS MANAGEMENT DEVELOPMENT EFFECTIVE?

The Conference Board of Canada estimates that only one-quarter (26 percent) of organizations are pleased with the results of their leadership development practices.[36] This result is highly consistent with those shown by multiple studies demonstrating that the effectiveness of these development efforts is highly dependent on careful planning and on environmental support.

The Conference Board results are derived from perceptions rather than from hard facts, and they represent the results of one specific survey conducted at one specific moment. More general results have been obtained from meta-analyses. A meta-analysis is a powerful statistical technique that allows researchers to summarize, in quantitative terms, the results obtained from many evaluation studies that have focused, in this case, on the effectiveness of management training.

In 1986, Burke and Day analyzed all studies conducted prior to the early 1980s and concluded that management training was, at best, "modestly" effective.[37] However, because few studies actually collected objective data and even fewer measured level 3 or 4 outcomes (see the discussion of the Kirkpatrick model in Chapter 11), the results of that meta-analysis have been considered tentative by all—including its authors.

Twenty years later, Collins and Holton returned to the literature and reported a meta-analysis of all pertinent studies published since Burke and Day's.[38] Here, the focus was on investigating the degree to which managerial leadership development efforts produced positive results with regard to learning, expertise, and organizational outcomes. Both perceptual and objective data were considered in this study, as were many different types of training evaluation studies both with and without control or comparison groups (see Chapter 11).

The results indicate that training programs are highly effective in increasing learning levels. However, they are only moderately effective in building expertise, though that result varies depending on the specific training evaluation design used. As for system outcomes—such as impact on firm effectiveness or profits—the results are less complete, as few studies actually assessed such outcomes. Fewer still were able to isolate the effect of management training from all other potential impacts on these outcomes. Nevertheless, the data indicate that, on average, leadership development programs do seem to contribute to the organization's effectiveness: Management training has a major impact on learning and a more modest one on expertise and organizational outcomes. Perhaps more important is the finding that there remains much variation in results across development efforts: while many training programs are effective, others remain ineffective.

Unfortunately, the data available from the Collins and Holton study do not permit us to clearly identify the characteristics of training programs that are effective versus those that fail. For example, we do not clearly understand the conditions under which coaching or mentoring programs are effective.

More recently Taylor, Russ-Eft, and Taylor have provided data that begin to explain the difference between successful and less successful training programs.[39] They performed a meta-analysis of 107 management training evaluation studies that focused on transfer of training. In those studies managerial effectiveness—the degree of training transfer—was assessed in some studies by self-reports, and/or by the trainee's boss, peers (other managers), or own subordinates. They also related certain characteristics of the training program to the transfer outcome for different types of training programs. In particular, they researched evaluation studies that focused on training programs centred on the development of the manager's interpersonal skills. The data analysis uncovered some significant trends.

Although different studies reported somewhat different results in general, trainees and their supervisors tended to report reasonably high levels of transfer. This result was not obtained when transfer levels were rated by the manager's employees and/or peers. They rated transfer levels as negligible! In other words, managers and their bosses tended to view managerial training as being more effective than did the manager's subordinates and his/her colleagues.

A decade earlier Collins and Holton cautioned against the use of self-reports for training evaluations and they too noted the variations in results: some programs are more effective than others. But where do the differences lie?

Taylor et al.'s data suggest an answer: effective training programs were built on thorough needs analysis and they provided, during training, significantly more practice of learned skills. Ineffective programs did not. The conclusion seems inescapable: organizations that experience weak transfer levels should consider reviewing both their needs analysis (Chapter 3) process and the training contents to ensure additional practice time. As with all training, these two components remain essential ingredients for success.

SUMMARY

This chapter described the roles, functions, and critical skills of managers and how they are developed. Managers engage in a number of interpersonal, informational, and decisional activities in order to accomplish their organizational goals of controlling, organizing, planning, and leading the work of others. This requires them to master and display conceptual, technical, and interpersonal skills, and to have emotional intelligence. Management development programs are designed to develop these skills. Models of management development involve skill assessment, skill acquisition, skill practice, and skill application. The content of management development programs was described in terms of conceptual, technical, and interpersonal skills. Management development programs involve both informational and experiential learning and include management education, management training, and on-the-job management development. Management education programs such as an MBA provide individuals with a general management education. A popular example of a highly experiential management training program is outdoor wilderness training. Examples of on-the-job development include job rotation, mentoring, and coaching. The chapter concluded with an assessment of the effectiveness of managerial development programs for improving organizational performance and a discussion of the research findings as to the effectiveness of management development efforts.

Key Terms

coaching p. 439
emotional intelligence p. 422
experiential learning p. 434
functions of management p. 418
job rotation p. 438
leadership p. 416
management p. 414
management development p. 415

management education p. 435
management training p. 437
mentors p. 439
on-the-job management development
　p. 438
outdoor wilderness training p. 437
skills p. 420

Make the Connection

p. 427: practice and active practice are discussed in Chapter 5 on page 145; the stages of learning are discussed in Chapter 3 on page 68; self-efficacy is discussed in Chapter 3 on page 75

p. 427: the transfer process and transfer interventions are discussed in Chapter 10 on page 289 and pages 308–309

p. 427: error-management training is discussed in Chapter 5 on page 153

p. 430: goal setting is discussed in Chapter 3 on page 82

p. 434: procedural knowledge is discussed in Chapter 3 on page 69; the COMA model is discussed in Chapter 11 on page 333

p. 435: off-the-job instructional training methods are discussed in Chapter 6 on page 168

p. 438: job rotation is discussed in Chapter 7 on pages 207–208

p. 438: coaching and mentoring are discussed in Chapter 7 on pages 212–216

Web Links

Bell Canada: **www.bell.ca**

IBM Canada: **www.ibm.com/ca**

Links to Managerial and Professional Training Programs: **www.trainingreference.co.uk/directory**

Microsoft: **www.microsoft.com**

National Research Council of Canada: **www.nrc-cnrc.gc.ca**

PricewaterhouseCoopers: **www.pwc.com**

Required Professional Capabilities (RPCs)

The following RPCs are relevant to material covered in this chapter. The RPC number represents the CCHRA number assigned to the RPC as presented on the CCHRA website. All of the RPCs can be found in the Body of Knowledge at **http://www.chrp.ca/rpc/body-of-knowledge/**.

RPC 154.05: Positions and their requirements.

RPC 156.03: Core competencies required for organizational success

RPC 163.03: Methods to establish interpersonal effectiveness

RPC 161.06: Domains and levels of learning

RPC 167.07: Training and development program design and administration

RPC 156.06: Methods of training and development (games and simulations, case method, lecturing, on-the-job training, distance learning, role-play, videoconferencing, group discussion)

RPC 163.02: Coaching

Discussion Questions

1. What are some of the differences between management development and employee training?
2. Why is management development important?

3. Imagine the CEO of a company who has read this chapter and the section on coaching. She decides that coaching is a good idea and sends a memo to all managers telling them to formally take on the role of coach for each of their subordinates. Is this a good idea? How likely is it to improve performance? Had the CEO consulted you prior to announcing her decision, what would you have suggested she do?

4. Compare and contrast management education, management training, and on-the-job development. What are the advantages and disadvantages of each of these approaches for management development? How effective do you think each approach is for teaching the skills listed in Table 14.1?

5. What is emotional intelligence and what does it have to do with management and managerial skills? Can managers be trained to improve their emotional intelligence? If yes, how can this be done?

6. What is outdoor wilderness training and how effective is it for developing managers? What would be your advice to an organization that was considering sending its managers to an outdoor wilderness program?

7. What is the difference between informational learning and experiential learning and when should each be used for management development?

8. Describe the four basic commonalities of models of management skill development.

9. What is the difference between the traditional models of skill development and error-management training?

The Great Training Debate

1. Debate the following: Some people have argued that management development is a waste of time and money because great managers are born, not made. Is it the case that managers cannot be developed?

Exercises

In-Class

1. In an article called "The smart-talk trap," Jeffrey Pfeffer and Robert Sutton (1999) described a phenomenon in organizations that they call the "knowing–doing gap." According to the authors, many managers are knowledgeable and very good at talking but not very good at doing or acting. In other words, talk substitutes for action. An especially dangerous form of talk is "smart talk," where the speaker is particularly good at sounding confident, articulate, and eloquent. Unfortunately, smart talk tends to focus on the negative and is often unnecessarily complicated. It tends to result in inaction or what the authors call the "smart-talk trap." Problems are discussed and plans for action might be formulated, but in the end nothing is done. This can have serious negative consequences for organizations. The authors suggest that one of the main reasons for the knowing–doing gap and the smart-talk trap is that managers have been trained to talk.

a. What do you think about the knowing–doing gap and the smart-talk trap? Do you think that this is a serious problem in organizations?

b. The authors argue that one of the reasons for the existence of the knowing–doing gap and the smart-talk trap is the training that managers receive. Do you agree with this assertion? How can management training result in so much knowing and talking and so little doing?

c. Discuss the knowing–doing gap and the smart-talk trap with somebody you know in a managerial position. Find out what they have to say about the prevalence of it in their organization, why it might or might not be a problem, and what can be done to avoid it.

d. What advice would you give organizations about how to develop managers in order to avoid the knowing–doing gap and the smart-talk trap?

2. This task will help you integrate much of the material in this book. Starting with the TIMS model, construct a table, similar to Table 14.2, in which you indicate for each of the 10 steps of the model the probable impact on trainees for each step.

3. Think of your manager from a current or previous job. Keeping in mind his/her behaviour and performance, how effective do you think he/she was in his/her performance of the core functions and roles of management? What skills do you think he/she needs to improve? What would you recommend your manager do to improve his/her performance and managerial skills?

4. If you were hired in a managerial position and you were told to design your own plan for development, what would you do? Refer to the section on models of management skill development, and for each step in the process develop a plan for your own management development. Be sure to indicate what you will do in each step.

In-the-Field

1. To find out more about management development, contact a human resource professional and ask about management development in his/her organization. To guide your discussion, consider the following issues:

- Describe the main skills that are the focus of management development programs. What are these skills and why are they the focus of management development?

- Describe the process of management development. What are the main steps involved in the process?

- How is a typical management development day spent?

- What types of management development programs are used and why? Does the organization use experiential learning approaches, and if so, what are they? Does the organization use management education programs, management training programs, job rotation, and/or coaching and how effective are they?

- How effective is management development for improving managerial and organizational effectiveness?

2. Contact several people who work full-time for an organization. In each case, focus the interview on their perceptions of their own immediate supervisor/manager/boss. Focus on the skills of managers as described in the chapter. Do they perceive the manager as competent or not and what are the skills they think the manager should most urgently improve? Summarize your results in a report in which you discuss the extent and nature of management skills that subordinates feel should be improved.

Case Incident

Middle Manager Burnout

In a recent article in *Harvard Business Review*, Morison, Erikson, and Dychtwald surveyed more than 7,000 mid-career employees between the ages of 35 and 55. The authors report that many middle managers are burned out, dissatisfied, or feel that they are in dead-end jobs, and most are no longer energized by their work. Feeling neglected, many are actively searching for new jobs. As a result, many organizations face a stark choice: risk losing some of their best people or continue to work with a host of unhappy managers.

Your consulting advice is requested by the company president. She is asking you to provide suggestions for combating this growing managerial apathy in her organization.

Questions

1. What do you think are some of the causes of this growing problem?
2. In order to improve the situation, what, if anything, should be done with the middle managers, the bosses of the middle managers, and the subordinates of the middle managers, by top management?

Case Study MARKET RESEARCH INC.

Market Research Inc. is a Vancouver-based firm that specializes in conducting surveys and interviews with members of the general public. The company has a number of different teams that work on many different projects for its many corporate clients. It is usually the case that several projects are conducted at the same time.

The company is composed of three departments: production, technical, and marketing. The marketing group is responsible for selling the company's services to corporate clients. The technical department is mainly composed of research personnel who are responsible for developing and analyzing the results of the surveys, focus groups, and interviewing studies for the clients. The production department is composed of several teams of interviewers. It is that department's job to conduct the data collection. They are responsible for identifying the customers who will be interviewed or surveyed, for enlisting their cooperation, and for interviewing them either personally, by phone or mail, depending on the project.

Thomas Waterfall (Tom) is the manager of the production department. The department is responsible for ensuring that all of the data-collection projects are conducted in a professional and timely manner. More specifically, Tom is responsible for ensuring that there is always enough staff on hand to conduct each study (never too many or too few), for hiring (or dismissing) the interviewers, for training them on the specific project requirements, and for ensuring and controlling the quality of the work done by the production department. He must keep himself informed of the activities of the marketing and technical departments to ensure that his department meets the demands of these other groups. Finally, the production department is a high-pressure environment where tensions among interviewers and between interviewers and the technical staff can sometimes flare up, threatening the efficient and effective production of the studies. The production manager must often act as an arbiter of disputes and soothe people when they get upset, a skill for which Tom is famous.

Mary Milend has been working for the last five years in the production department of Market Research Inc., where she is an interviewer. She has been doing a remarkable job, conducting her interviews with professionalism and competence. She always meets her deadlines and has never been the object of a complaint, either by consumers or by her co-workers. She has always shown great cooperation, often volunteering to help other interviewers with their tasks when they were submerged. Finally, in the tense atmosphere of conducting the data collection under tight deadlines, she has always maintained extremely good relationships with the technical staff with whom the production department interacts routinely.

Tom, the manager of the production department, has announced that he will be retiring next year. Because of her superb record as an employee and her extensive hands-on knowledge of the production department, the vice president has offered to promote Mary to the job of production manager when Tom retires.

Mary is quite interested in the job, as this would mean a much higher salary, better benefits, vacations, and greater influence in the company. However, as Mary is a very honest person, she told the VP, when he offered her the promotion, that although she was keenly interested in the job, she was not sure that she was the best choice. She explained that she had never acted in a managerial role before and that she felt uncertain that she had the skills to do the job well. Impressed by Mary's honesty, the VP indicated to her that he would be willing to provide her with all of the training she requires to acquire the managerial skills that she will need to perform her new job.

Questions

1. What are the main skills that Mary will need to develop if she accepts the promotion?
2. What are some of the training experiences that might benefit Mary?
3. Should Tom be invited to play a role in Mary's development? If so, what could that role be?

4. How effective do you think each of the following programs would be for Mary's development: management education programs, management training programs (i.e., outdoor wilderness training), and on-the-job development (i.e., job rotation and coaching). What are the advantages and disadvantages of each, and which one(s) do you recommend and why?

Flashback Questions

1. Clearly, Mary's managerial skills need development. However, this may take quite a long time. Can you identify training methods that could be delivered more quickly? In answering this question, think back to Chapter 8, which discusses technology-based training.
2. Thinking back to Chapter 7 (about on-the-job training programs), can you suggest some of the things that can be done, on the job, to sharpen Mary's skills?
3. Chapter 11 discusses training evaluation and Chapter 12 describes the costs and benefits of training programs. How would you evaluate the effectiveness of the training and development provided to Mary?

REFERENCES

1. Schettler, J. (2002, March). Training top 100: IBM. *Training, 39(3)*, 48–49; Schettler, J. (2003, March). Training top 100: Best practices. *Training, 40(3)*, 58–59; Johnson, G., Johnson, H., Dolezalek, H., Galvin, T., & Zemke, R. (2004, March). Top five profile and ranking. *Training, 41(3)*, 42–58.
2. McCallum, J. (1993). The manager's job is still to manage. *Business Quarterly, 57(4)*, 61–67; Brown, T. L. (1995). Leadership is everyone's business. *Apparel Industry Magazine 56(9)*, 14; Tannenbaum, S. I., & Yukl, G. (1992). Training and development in work organizations. *Annual Review of Psychology, 43*, 399–441.
3. Bolt, J. F. (2007). Mapping the future of leadership development. *The 2007 Pfeiffer Annual: Leadership development*. John Wiley & Sons.
4. Robbins, S. P., De Cenzo, D. A., Condie, J. L., & Kondo, L. (2001). *Supervision in Canada today* (3rd ed.). Toronto: Prentice-Hall, p. 7.
5. Whetten, D. A., & Cameron, K. S. (2002). *Developing management skills* (5th ed.). Upper Saddle River, NJ: Prentice Hall, p. 270.
6. Baldwin T. T., & Patgett, M. Y. (1994). Management development: A review and commentary. In C. L. Cooper & I. T. Robertson (Eds.), *Key reviews in managerial psychology*. New York: Wiley.
7. Marquardt, M. J., Nissley, N., Ozag, R., & Taylor, T. L. (2000). International briefing 6. Training and development in the United States. *International Journal of Training and Development, 4(2)*, 138–149; Mabey, C., & Thomson, A. (2000). Management development in the UK: A provider and participant perspective. *International Journal of Training and Development, 4(4)*, 272–286; Cornuel, E., & Kletz, P. (2001). An empirical analysis of priority sectors for managers' training. *Journal of Management Development, 20(5)*, 402–413; Agut, S., & Grau, R. (2002). Managerial competency needs and training requests: The case of the Spanish tourist industry. *Human Resource Development Quarterly, 13(1)*, 31–51; Analoui, F., & Hosseini, M. H. (2001). Management education and increased

managerial effectiveness. The case of business managers in Iran. *Journal of Management Development, 20(9)*, 785–794.

8. Mintzberg, H. (1973). *The nature of managerial work.* New York: Harper & Row; Mintzberg, H. (1975). The manager's job: Folklore and fact. *Harvard Business Review, 53(4)*, 49–61.

9. London, M. (2002). *Leadership development*: Mahwah, NJ: Lawrence Erlbaum Associates; Tichy, N. M., & Cardwell, N. (2002). *The cycle of leadership: How great leaders teach their companies to win* (3rd ed.). New York: HarperCollins Publishers; Ketz de Vries, M. (2001). *The leadership mystique.* London: Prentice-Hall.

10. Kotter, J. P. (1996). *Leading change.* Boston, MA: Harvard Business School Press; Whetten, D. A., & Cameron, K. S. (2002).

11. Kouzes, J. M., & Posner, B. Z. (2002). *Leadership challenge* (3rd ed.). San Francisco, CA: Jossey-Bass.

12. Orth, C. D., Wilkinson, H. E., & Benfari, R. C. (1987, Spring). The manager's role as coach and mentor. *Organizational Dynamics,* 67–74.

13. Whetten, D. A., & Cameron, K. S. (2002).

14. Luthans, F., Rosenkrantz, S. A., & Hennesy, H. W. (1985). What do successful managers really do? An observation study of managerial activities. *Journal of Applied Behavioral Science, 21*, 255–270.

15. Camp, R., Vielhaber, M., & Simonetti, J. L. (2001). *Strategic interviewing: How to hire good people.* San Francisco, CA: Jossey-Bass.

16. Cameron, K., & Tschirhart, M. (1988). Managerial competencies and organizational effectiveness. Working Paper, School of Business Administration, University of Michigan.

17. Goleman, D. (1998). *Working with emotional intelligence.* New York: Bantam.

18. Ryan, A. M., Brutus, S., Greguras, G. J., & Hakel, M. D. (2000). Receptivity to assessment-based feedback for management development. *Journal of Management Development, 19(4)*, 252–276.

19. Pfeffer, J. (1998). *The human equation: Building profits by putting people first.* Boston, MA: Harvard Business School Press.

20. Muller, R., and Turner, R. (2010). Leadership competency profiles of successful project managers *International Journal of Project Management, 28*, 437–448.

21. Clark, N. (2010). The impact of a training programme designed to target the emotional intelligence abilities of project managers. *International Journal of Project Management, 28*, 461–468.

22. Hunsaker, P. L. (2001). *Training in management skills.* Upper Saddle River, NJ: Prentice Hall.

23. March, J. G., & Simon, H. A. (1958). *Organizations.* New York: Blackwell.

24. Locke, E. A., & Latham, G. P. (1990). *A theory of goal setting and task performance.* Englewood Cliffs, NJ: Prentice-Hall.

25. Kraiger, K. (2008). Transforming our models of learning and development: Web-based instruction as enabler of third-generation instruction. *Industrial and Organizational Perspectives: Perspectives on Science and Practice, 1*, 454–467.

26. Saks, A. M., & Haccoun, R. R. (2008). Is the "third-generation model" new and is it the holy grail of adaptive learning? *Industrial and Organizational Perspectives: Perspectives on Science and Practice, 1*, 480–483.

27. Eisenhardt, K. M., Kahwajy, J. L., & Bourgeois, L. J. III (1997, July-August). How management teams can have a good fight. *Harvard Business Review*, 77–85.

28. Haccoun, R. R., & Klimoski, R. J. (1975). Negotiator status and accountability source: A study of negotiator behavior. *Organizational Behavior and Human Performance, 14*, 342–359.

29. Klie, S. (2011, Jan. 17). "Problem" managers a big problem: survey. *Canadian HR Reporter, 24*, 1.

30. Wexley, K. N., & Baldwin, T. T. (1986). Management development. *Journal of Management, 12*, 277–294.

31. Hattie, J., Marsh, H. W., Neill, J. T., & Richards, G. E. (1997). Adventure education and Outward Bound: Out-of-class experiences that have a lasting effect. *Review of Educational Research, 67*, 43–87.

32. Hughes, P. D., & Grant, M. (2007). *Learning and development outlook 2007*. The Conference Board of Canada.

33. Peterson, D. B. (2002). Management development: Coaching and mentoring programs. In K. Kraiger (Ed.), *Creating, implementing, and managing effective training and development: State-of-the-art lessons for practice* (pp. 160–191). San Francisco, CA: Jossey-Bass.

34. Kombarakaran, F., Yang, J., Baker, M., & Fernandes, P. (2008). Executive coaching: It works! *Consulting Psychology Journal: Practice and Research, 60(1)*, 78–90.

35. Smither, J. W., London, M., Flautt, R., Vargas, Y., & Kucine, I. (2003). Can working with an executive coach improve multisource feedback ratings over time? A quasi-experimental field study, *Personnel Psychology, 56*, 23–44.

36. Grant, M. P., & Hughes, D. (2007). *Learning and development outlook 2007: Are we learning enough?* The Conference Board of Canada.

37. Burke, M. J., & Day, R. R. (1986). A cumulative study of the effectiveness of managerial training. *Journal of Applied Psychology, 71*, 232–246.

38. Collins, D. B., & Holton, F. E. III. (2004). The effectiveness of managerial leadership development programs: A meta analysis of studies from 1982 to 2001. *Human Resource Development Quarterly, 15(2)*, 217–248.

39. Taylor, P. J., Russ-Eft, D. F., & Taylor, H. (2009). Transfer of management training from alternative perspectives. *Journal of Applied Psychology, 94(1)*,104–121.

The Evolution and Future of Training and Development

CHAPTER LEARNING OUTCOMES

After reading this chapter, you should be able to:

- describe the changing role of training professionals
- discuss the outsourcing of training and development
- explain the role of ethics in training and development
- define Learning 2.0 and describe the evolution of training and development in organizations
- define lifelong learning and describe the four pillars of lifelong learning

TELUS

TELUS is a national telecommunications company in Canada with more than 35,000 team members globally and $10.1 billion of annual revenue. TELUS provides a wide range of communications products and services including data, Internet protocol (IP), voice, entertainment, and video.

In 2008, TELUS completely restructured all aspects of its existing corporate learning by creating an organization-wide vision called "Learning 2.0." At TELUS, Learning 2.0 represented a fundamental shift from the traditional model of "training as an event" to "learning as a continuous, collaborative, connected, and communicative process." This ideological shift required an approach to learning that encompassed three interconnected facets of learning: formal, informal, and social.

The impetus for the shift at TELUS was a recognition that learning does not occur solely in a classroom and dissatisfaction with the existing delivery methods and distribution of learning expenditures. Prior to the restructuring, TELUS dealt with more than 250 external learning providers, as 95 percent of its learning offerings were provided through outsourced instructor-led training. External providers were typically self-selected by team members in search of learning opportunities. This largely individualized outsourced approach led to frequent inconsistencies in the ways that vendors interpreted TELUS's specific training needs. As a result, the two main goals of the restructuring were to reduce the number of external providers used and to ensure that all learning providers delivered material consistent with the Learning 2.0 vision and philosophy.

After conducting a thorough assessment of external providers and team member learning needs, the move to Learning 2.0 allowed TELUS to reduce the number of external providers from 250 to roughly 70; shift expenditures from 95 percent outsourced formal learning to 60 percent formal and 40 percent informal within only two years; include more opportunities for social, team-member-driven, and developed learning; and maintain spending at previous levels through a "value-for-money" mindset.

Accomplishing such a radical shift in such a short time frame required a two-pronged approach. First, TELUS mobilized its 25-person Learning and Collaboration team to manage the change process. Those new to social learning educated themselves quickly through consultations with the Learning 2.0 experts who were brought on board. Additionally, a grassroots 2.0 Adoption Council was formed within the organization. This group met biweekly to share their collective intelligence and discuss the ways in which social media could be used to benefit the organization and drive some of their social learning goals.

When the time came to pilot the new approach, TELUS relied on ambassadors and on early adopters to use as case studies for promoting Learning 2.0 within the organization. Once the seeds were sown by these early cases, Learning 2.0 was launched enterprise-wide and has been met with enthusiasm throughout the organization.[1]

Source: C. Lavis, *Learning & development outlook 2011: Are organizations ready for learning 2.0?* Ottawa: The Conference Board of Canada, 2011; www.about.telus.com

The restructuring of learning at TELUS and its new Learning 2.0 vision is an excellent example of how training and development is changing in organizations. In this chapter, we discuss the role of training professionals, the outsourcing of training and development, ethical issues associated with training and development, Learning 2.0 and the evolution of training and development, and lifelong learning.

ROLE OF TRAINING PROFESSIONALS

During the last decade, the trainer's traditional status as a staff employee of HR has been changing. Trainers have begun to move out of the training department to work with management to solve organizational problems and create learning opportunities that support the organization's strategy. This reflects a movement and evolution of the trainer from staff employee to strategic business partner.

While many training professionals spend most of their time designing and delivering training programs, they are increasingly becoming more involved in strategic functions such as facilitating organizational change, managing organizational knowledge, career planning, and talent management.[2] According to the Conference Board of Canada, the role of learning and development professionals is shifting from knowledge-keeper to that of learning facilitator. This involves creating environments and activities that enable and facilitate knowledge sharing and transfer between employees.[3]

A study conducted by the American Society for Training and Development (ASTD) on the areas of expertise and competencies expected of training and development professionals identified four key roles for training professionals: learning strategist, business partner, project manager, and professional specialist.[4] These four roles are part of the ASTD competency model for learning and performance and the foundation for its professional certification program. Figure 15.1 shows the ASTD competency model. The certification program covers the nine areas of expertise found in the middle tier of the model.

The Canadian Society for Training and Development (CSTD) has also developed a set of competencies for training and development professionals. As shown in Figure 15.2, the competencies are organized into five categories: assessing performance needs, designing training, facilitating training, supporting transfer of learning, and evaluating training. Within each competency category there are first-, second-, and third-level competencies. These competencies form the basis of the CSTD certification process which includes two designations (Certified Training Practitioner, or CTP, and Certified Training and Development Professional, or CTDP).[5]

The training and development function is transforming into a learning and performance strategic function. It will focus more on results rather than activities and it will be integrated into the business of the organization at a strategic level; learning will be embedded into the jobs that individuals perform.[6] In addition, training functions will become performance consulting centres and training professionals will become performance consultants. As a **performance consultant**, the role of the trainer is not just to provide training and development, but also to provide solutions to performance problems.

Performance consultant
Responsible for providing solutions to performance problems

Finally, given the increasing importance of lifelong learning and the learning organization, the role of the trainer is increasingly shifting from training to learning. Thus, the role of the trainer is to facilitate and create learning opportunities throughout the organization, and to help organizations manage the transition to a learning organization.

OUTSOURCING TRAINING AND DEVELOPMENT

In the chapter-opening vignette, it was noted that one of the main goals of the restructuring at TELUS was to reduce the number of external learning providers being used as 95 percent of its learning offerings were provided through outsourced instructor-led training. The restructuring allowed TELUS to reduce the number of external providers from 250 to about 70 and to shift expenditures

FIGURE (15.1)

ASTD Competency Model

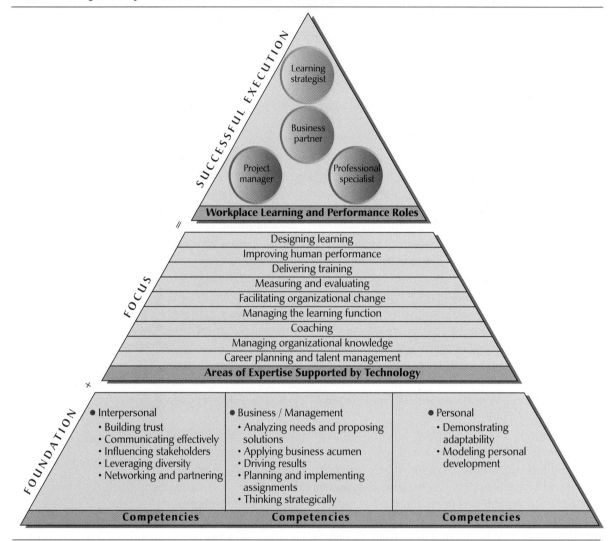

Outsourcing
The use of an external supplier to provide training and development programs and services

Make the
Connection

from 95 percent outsourced formal learning to 60 percent formal and 40 percent informal within two years.

The use of external sources to provide training and development is known as outsourcing. **Outsourcing** involves the use of an external supplier to provide training and development programs and services. This is related to the discussion in Chapter 5 on purchasing training programs and services. Outsourcing involves the purchase of training services and products from external suppliers rather than using in-house services.

According to one survey, 57 percent of HR and training professionals outsource all or part of their training and development programs.[7] In Canada,

FIGURE (15.2)

Canadian Society for Training and Development Competencies for Training and Development Professionals

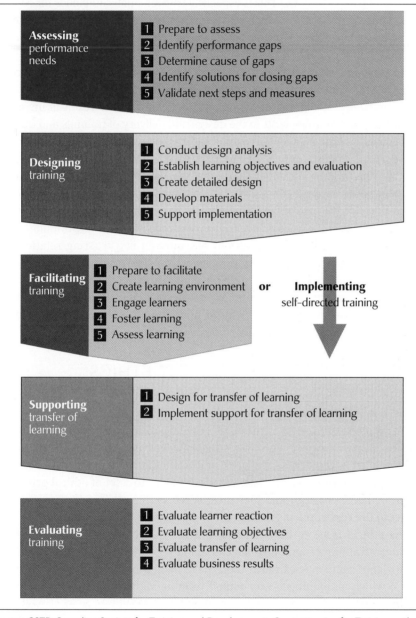

Assessing performance needs
1 Prepare to assess
2 Identify performance gaps
3 Determine cause of gaps
4 Identify solutions for closing gaps
5 Validate next steps and measures

Designing training
1 Conduct design analysis
2 Establish learning objectives and evaluation
3 Create detailed design
4 Develop materials
5 Support implementation

Facilitating training
1 Prepare to facilitate
2 Create learning environment
3 Engage learners
4 Foster learning
5 Assess learning

or **Implementing** self-directed training

Supporting transfer of learning
1 Design for transfer of learning
2 Implement support for transfer of learning

Evaluating training
1 Evaluate learner reaction
2 Evaluate learning objectives
3 Evaluate transfer of learning
4 Evaluate business results

Source: CSTD Canadian Society for Training and Development. *Competencies for Training and Development Professionals 2010.*

it has been reported that organizations allocate more than half of their direct training expenditures to external sources including external learning providers and employee tuition. The research reported by the Conference Board of Canada indicates a drop in spending on internal learning and a slight increase in expenditures to external providers which represents the largest proportion of training and development budgets.[8]

There are a number of reasons for outsourcing training and development. For example, outsourcing provides organizations with access to specialists who have expertise in a particular training area. In addition, external vendors can provide a greater variety of training programs more efficiently and less expensively than in-house training departments.[9] This is especially true for small companies that do not have in-house expertise or enough staff to train to justify the expense of in-house training design and delivery. In addition, the use of external vendors can often result in trainees being trained and back on the job much faster than designing a new training program in-house. One study found that the top reasons for outsourcing included cost savings, time savings, and improvements in compliance and accuracy.[10]

Outsourcing training and development has been found to result in increased performance and improvements in the design and delivery of training, and training professionals report a high level of overall satisfaction with their training suppliers. However, outsourcing does have certain risks such as a loss of control, situations in which the vendor does not understand the organization's culture, loss of in-house expertise, and increased vulnerability that can result in harmful consequences for an organization.[11] In the case of TELUS, outsourcing training and development resulted in inconsistencies in the ways that vendors interpreted their specific training needs.

An important factor for successful outsourcing is a trusting relationship between the organization and its external vendor. Furthermore, the positive outcomes associated with outsourcing have been found to be higher when there is frequent vendor–client interaction, when contractual agreements are explicit, when there is greater trust in the vendor, and when the organization's primary motivation for outsourcing is quality improvement.[12]

TRAINING AND DEVELOPMENT ETHICS

Ethics

Systematic thinking about the moral consequences of one's actions and decisions on various stakeholders

Ethics involves systematic thinking about the moral consequences of one's actions and decisions on various stakeholders. Stakeholders refer to people inside or outside of the organization who might be affected by one's actions and decisions. For training professionals, ethics involves following a set of standards and principles in the design, delivery, and evaluation of training and development programs. Training professionals must adhere to a set of ethical principles that guide their behaviour and they must serve as role models of proper ethical conduct to the rest of the organization.

One ethical issue of particular concern is the refusal of employees from attending a training program, which can result in workplace discrimination and human rights complaints. In fact, there have been a number of cases in recent years in which an employee was denied training and then filed a complaint of discrimination. The Canadian Human Rights Act at the federal level, as well each of the provincial human rights codes, governs human rights issues that can be invoked when an employee is denied training.[13]

Ethical codes and standards are often set by organizations and associations. For example, the Canadian Society for Training and Development (CSTD) has a member code of ethics that sets standards of practice and professionalism for its members (see Table 15.1). To learn more about the kinds of ethical issues that are important for training and development professionals, see The Trainer's Notebook 15.1, "Ethical Guidelines for Training and Development Professionals."

TABLE (15.1)

Canadian Society for Training and Development (CSTD) Member Code of Ethics

In its ongoing quest to promote the profession and set standards of practice, CSTD has approved a code of ethics for members. To ensure that the highest levels of professionalism, competence, and discretion are maintained within the Training & Development community, CSTD members must practise and promote the following ethical standards:

- Incorporate the principles of adult learning in human resource development
- Respect individual differences and human rights
- Honour client confidentiality
- Advance the field of knowledge in human resource development and management
- Provide high quality consulting and development services
- Offer only services that you are qualified and experienced to deliver
- Empower people to realize their potential
- Support the growth and integrity of CSTD throughout Canada
- Refrain from personal gain through improper use of the organization's platform and resources
- Ensure that your conduct is professional, legal, and honest
- Observe all laws and restrictions of copyright
- Acknowledge the authors of original material and concepts

Source: CSTD Canadian Society for Training and Development. CSTD Member Code of Ethics. Found at: http://www.cstd.ca/?page=CodeofEthics.

The Trainer's Notebook 15.1

ETHICAL GUIDELINES FOR TRAINING AND DEVELOPMENT PROFESSIONALS

Trainers must conduct themselves according to a set of ethical guidelines and standards as follows:

1. Voluntary consent: Trainers should not implicitly coerce unwilling or skeptical participants into self-revealing or physical activities.

2. Discrimination: Age, sex, race, or handicaps should not be used as barriers to determine who receives training.

3. Cost-effectiveness: Training activities should be based on demonstrated utility, should show a demonstrated benefit vis-à-vis costs, and should not be undertaken simply to spend a training budget.

4. Accurate portrayal: Claims for the benefits of training need to be accurate; training should be consistent across time and trainers; training materials should be appropriately depicted.

5. Competency in training: Teaching methods that do not work, such as talking down to audiences, should be avoided.

6. Values: Trainers should believe in the value of what they teach.

Source: R.L. Lowman, "Ethical human resource practice in organizational settings," In D.W. Bray (Ed.), *Working with organizations*. New York: Guilford, 1991.

LEARNING 2.0

At the beginning of this chapter, you read about how TELUS has completely restructured all aspects of its learning system and created a new organization-wide vision that represents a fundamental shift in and new approach to learning that includes formal, informal, and social learning. These changes represent how learning in organizations has evolved and is changing.

Throughout this textbook you have learned about a variety of ways in which employees in organizations learn, such as informal and formal learning, on-the-job and off-the-job training methods, and the use of technology and e-learning. When you consider these various approaches, one can begin to see how training, development, and learning in organizations has evolved. As shown in Figure 15.3, learning has evolved from classroom-instructor–led training, to e-learning, then blended learning, and most recently to a more employee-driven and collaborative process. This evolution represents a shift from formal learning to social learning and from an individual focus to a group focus. This paradigm shift is known as Learning 2.0 and it involves the increasing use of technology.[14]

Learning 2.0 represents a shift from learning as a product that is created for learners by organizations to a learner-initiated collaborative process. Learning 2.0 can involve informal learning (e.g., during meetings) as well as formal learning (e.g., mentoring programs, apprenticeships), and can happen either face-to-face or through the use of social media.[15] As described in the chapter-opening vignette, TELUS restructured its corporate learning based on a Learning 2.0 vision and philosophy that involved a fundamental shift in how it provides training and development.

The evolution of learning toward Learning 2.0 is a result of changes in the workplace and the changing nature of work (e.g., knowledge- and team-based), shifting demographics, an increase in employee-initiated learning, and social media.[16]

As a result of these changes, learning can no longer be treated as a static and organization-driven event or product. Rather, learning is becoming a more continuous, fluid, and employee-driven collaborative process. Thus, Learning 2.0 represents an important trend in training and development. An increasing number of organizations like TELUS are likely to embrace Learning 2.0 in the coming years.[17]

Learning 2.0

A shift from learning as a product that is created for learners by organizations to a learner-initiated collaborative process

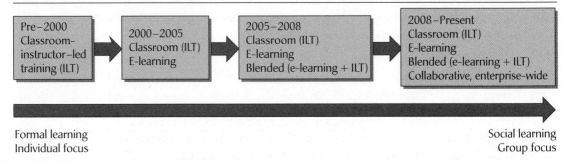

FIGURE (15.3)

The Evolution of Learning

Pre–2000
Classroom-instructor–led training (ILT)

→ 2000–2005
Classroom (ILT)
E-learning

→ 2005–2008
Classroom (ILT)
E-learning
Blended (e-learning + ILT)

→ 2008–Present
Classroom (ILT)
E-learning
Blended (e-learning + ILT)
Collaborative, enterprise-wide

Formal learning
Individual focus

Social learning
Group focus

Source: The Conference Board of Canada, "The Evolution of Learning," *Conference Board of Canada Learning and Development Outlook 2011*, Exhibit 1, P. 4, 2011.

LIFELONG LEARNING

Although the focus of this text has been on learning at work and in organizations, it is important to understand that training and development is part of a larger approach to learning that is known as lifelong learning.

Lifelong learning is an approach to learning that recognizes that learning takes place throughout a person's life and involves all aspects of one's life including the workplace, personal development, the community, and physical well-being. The Canadian Council on Learning (CCL) has developed a measure called the Composite Learning Index (CLI) to measure Canada's progress in lifelong learning. The CLI measures the following four pillars of lifelong learning:[18]

- *Learning to know* refers to the development of skills and knowledge needed to function in the world (e.g., literacy, numeracy, critical thinking, and general knowledge).

- *Learning to do* refers to applied skills that are often required for occupational success (e.g., computer training).

- *Learning to live together* refers to developing values of respect and concern for others, social and interpersonal skills, and an appreciation of the diversity of Canadians.

- *Learning to be* refers to learning that contributes to the development of a person's body, mind, and spirit (e.g., personal discovery and creativity).

The CLI recognizes that lifelong learning is critical to the success of an individual, the community, and the country. Individuals benefit from better jobs and higher wages and Canada benefits from higher productivity and a stronger economy.[19] Training and development is an important contributor to lifelong learning.

Unfortunately, a recent report by the Canadian Council on Learning (CCL) concluded that Canada is falling behind the international competition in many stages of education and learning and is not making progress in adult and workplace learning. As a result, productivity in Canada remains low, adult literacy levels are poor, and opportunities for lifelong learning are limited. The report concludes that "Canadian productivity will struggle until Canadian industry responds to the need for enhanced training of all kinds which it itself routinely acknowledges is present and pressing."[20]

Thus, there is much work to be done and those who have training and development competencies will have an especially important role to play in helping organizations design and deliver effective training and development programs and in providing employees with opportunities for lifelong learning.

Lifelong learning
An approach to learning that recognizes that learning takes place throughout a person's life and involves all aspects of one's life.

SUMMARY

This chapter began with a discussion of the changing role of the trainer and the outsourcing of training and development. We then discussed ethical issues in training and development, the evolution of learning in organizations, and the trend toward Learning 2.0. The chapter concluded with a discussion of lifelong learning.

CONCLUSION

It should now be clear to you that training and development is an important part of the management of performance in organizations. Training and development plays a critical role in helping organizations meet the challenges of an increasingly complex and competitive environment. Unfortunately, training programs often fail to achieve their objectives and, as a result, hinder an organization's ability to remain competitive. The good news is that the science of training, as described in this textbook, contains practical information on how to design, deliver, and evaluate effective training and development programs. By applying the theories, concepts, and principles described in this text, it is possible to design and deliver effective training programs that will benefit individuals, organizations, and society.

You now know the science of training; it is up to you to translate training science into training practice!

Key Terms

ethics p. 458
Learning 2.0 p. 460
lifelong learning p. 461

outsourcing p. 456
performance consultant p. 455

Make the Connection

p. 456 the decision to purchase or design a training program is discussed in Chapter 5 on page 139

Web Links

American Society for Training and Development: **www.astd.org**

Canadian Society for Training and Development: **www.cstd.ca**

TELUS: **www.telus.com**

Discussion Questions

1. What are some of the ethical issues for training professionals?
2. How has the role of the trainer changed and what are the new and emerging competencies and roles of trainers?
3. Why do organizations outsource training and development and what are the advantages and disadvantages of outsourcing? Do you think that organizations should outsource training and development?

4. Describe the evolution of training and development in organizations and the implications for the design and delivery of training programs. What are the main changes taking place and what are the implications of these changes for trainers and employees?
5. Define Learning 2.0 and discuss how it is different from more traditional approaches to learning. What are the implications of Learning 2.0 for employees, trainers, and organizations?
6. What is lifelong learning and how is it related to training and development? What is the role of organizations in lifelong learning?

The Great Training Debate

1. Debate the following: Organizations should outsource all of their training and development programs.

Exercises

In-Class

1. If an organization wanted to hire a training professional today, what should it look for? Find several job advertisements for a training manager or director in your local newspaper. Bring the advertisements to class and summarize the main competencies and responsibilities of the position. Describe how the job matches the traditional role of a trainer as well as more current roles and expectations described in the chapter.
2. Consider the ethics of the most recent training experience you have had either in a current job or in a previous job. Review the six ethical guidelines listed in The Trainer's Notebook 15.1, "Ethical Guidelines for Training Professionals," and determine how well they stand up against your most recent training experience. Based on your analysis, were the trainer and the training program ethical? Be prepared to explain and defend your answer.
3. If you were responsible for training in your organization and management decided that it wanted to outsource most of the company's training and development programs, what would you do? Prepare a brief presentation in which you must present your case to management. What will be your position and what will you present to management in order to defend it?
4. Think about your knowledge and skills and the extent to which you are prepared for the new competencies and roles expected of training professionals today. Conduct a self-assessment using the material presented in this chapter, with particular attention to the ASTD competency model and the CSTD competencies for training and development professionals. What competencies do you have and which ones do you still need to develop? Prepare an action plan that describes some of the things you can do to develop your competencies.

In-the-Field

1. Contact the training manager in an organization to find out how his/her role has changed and how it will change in the future. What was his/her role five years ago? What is his/her role today? What will be his/her role in five years? What skills and experiences do trainers need in order to perform their current and future roles, and how has this changed over the last five to 10 years?

2. To find out about lifelong learning and the Composite Learning Index (CLI), visit the Canadian Council on Learning at **http://www.cli-ica.ca/en/about/about-cli/what.aspx.** Answer the following questions:
   a. What is the Composite Learning Index (CLI) and how does it work?
   b. What is lifelong learning?
   c. What are the effects of lifelong learning?
   d. What are the most recent CLI scores for your city or town and how do they compare to the average CLI score in Canada?

Case Incident

Outsourcing at Nestlé Canada and Hudson's Bay Company

Nestlé Canada has been outsourcing parts of HR services to external providers for years in areas such as payroll, pension administration, and benefits administration. Although the company is using external providers more often for training and development, there are no plans to outsource all of it. If they are planning to develop a course in a particular area, they look for a provider who has experience in that area and then partner with them to develop something specific for the company. For example, the company partnered with an external organizational psychologist to develop a new leadership development program.

Hudson's Bay Company keeps most of its human resources in-house. The company believes it is best served when HR support is delivered by those who most understand the organization—its own employees. In the case of training and development, it is important to have employees who started out working in stores deliver customer-service training. They have an understanding of the customer and the way the stores operate.

Questions

1. Comment on the two companies' approaches to outsourcing training and development. What are the advantages and disadvantages of each approach?
2. What advice would you give each company about its current and future outsourcing of training and development?

Source: T. Cook, J. Household, B. Cormier & B. Kolida, "HR leaders talk-The constant pressure to add value and control costs combined with the growing desire to play a strategic business role has caused many HR leaders to at least consider outsourcing some part of their operations—if they haven't done so already," *Canadian HR Reporter*, Sept. 8, 2003, P. 13.

Integrative Case Study — TRAINING SECURITY GUARDS

In 1999, Patrick Shand was wrestled to the ground by security guards at a grocery store in Toronto. He was handcuffed and kept face-down on the ground where he died of asphyxiation after being accused of shoplifting baby formula.

In February of 2004, a coroner's inquest into Shand's death ruled that his death was accidental and that he died of restraint asphyxia with complications from chronic and acute cocaine use. One of the findings of the inquest was that Shand might not have died if the guards who apprehended him had been trained in the use of force and life-saving.

The inquiry made 22 recommendations to reform Ontario's security industry. For example, it recommended that all in-house security guards and bouncers in Ontario be licensed and receive mandatory training in areas such as first aid, CPR, and use of force training that identifies the hazards of restraint asphyxia and excited delirium as well as appropriate training in the use of handcuffs and expandable batons. The inquest concluded that "It is important that the government act quickly, responsibly and diligently."

The Ontario government responded to the inquest's 22 recommendations with the Private Security and Investigative Services Act in 2005. This was the first time the act had been updated since it was passed in 1966. The act went into effect in August 2007, with a deadline of August 2008 for 22,000 previously unlicensed security guards and bouncers to get licensed.

In addition to mandatory licensing for all security personnel and standards for uniforms, equipment, and vehicles used by security personnel, the act also includes mandatory training standards. The basic training standard would be developed to include knowledge of relevant legislation (the new Private Security and Investigative Services Act, Trespass to Property Act); power of arrest; use of force; communications and public relations skills; first aid and cardiopulmonary resuscitation; on-the-job skills (report writing, note taking, and diversity sensitivity); and the use of equipment (batons, handcuffs).

Security guards and bouncers in Ontario now must pay $80 to meet the new requirements. However, the Ministry of Community Safety and Correctional Services did not implement the training program that is part of the licensing. Those in the industry were left questioning the law.

Thus, despite a proposed curriculum and government plans for a 40-hour mandatory training program, the licence requirements only required in-house security guards and bouncers to submit an application to the ministry, pay a fee, and pass a criminal record check. There was no use-of-force training and no first-aid training was required. As a result, security guards continued to work at local stores and nightclubs without the basic training needed to safeguard lives.

In May of 2008, the ministry announced that it was pushing back plans to implement the training program from November 2008 to an undetermined later date because the curriculum for training had only recently been finalized. However, according to the director and registrar of the ministry's private security and investigative services branch that is responsible for the new licensing procedures, "The onus of responsibility is at this state on the employer to make sure that their staff are adequately trained." As for the province's slow pace in implementing the training, he said that it takes time to implement such a wide range of changes in an industry that has never had to be licensed or trained.

However, other provinces already have similar training programs in place. British Columbia has a 40-hour course for security guards that is taught by the same people who train the police.

Unfortunately, the problem did not go away. In 2008, a 20-year-old man died in Hamilton after being pinned to the ground by a security guard and store employees who suspected him of stealing a $15 radiator hose from a Canadian Tire store. In June of 2008, bouncers found a woman unconscious and frothing from the mouth in the back of an after-hours club. The bouncers did not have first-aid training and did not know how to help the woman, who later died.

In February of 2009, two security guards at St. Michael's Hospital in Toronto were dismissed following the alleged beating of a man who had broken ribs and a punctured lung. The hospital said that it will assess and review its use-of-force policy and procedures and intends to provide additional diversity training to its security officers.

Finally, on April 15, 2010, the new basic Training and Testing Regulation came into effect. The regulation requires that individuals must take a mandatory training and testing program before they are eligible to apply for a security guard or private investigator licence. The security guard training program must consist of at least 40 in-class hours and it must include certification in Emergency Level First Aid and CPR. Basic security guard training obtained through web-based, instructor-led distance learning (e.g., virtual classroom) meets the ministry's requirement for in-class training.

Sources: B. Popplewell, "Training lag angers guards," *Toronto Star,* July 14, 2008, P. A1, A9; "Security industry cleanup overdue," *Toronto Star,* Aug. 23, 2007, P. AA6; D. Black, "Tough rules on security demanded: 'This is Patrick's legacy,' Shand's mother says of coroner's jury findings," *Toronto Star,* April 24, 2004, P. B1; "McGuinty government introduces new legislation to make Ontarians safer," Ministry of Community Safety and Correctional Services. Government of Ontario. www.ogov.newswire.ca/ontario. Dec. 9, 2004, Retrieved on March 16, 2009; M. Henry, "Man says ribs broken by hospital guards," *Toronto Star,* Feb. 19, 2009, P. A2; M. Henry, "Hospital CEO apologizes to beaten man," *Toronto Star,* Feb. 27, 2009, P. GT4.

Questions

Chapter 1

1. Explain how a mandatory training program for security guards is an example of performance management. What effect will it have on security guards and their organizations?
2. Describe the role of the environmental context for mandatory security guard training. How will the organizational context and the human resources system in organizations influence the training and the effect it has on organizations and society?
3. Explain how the instructional systems design (ISD) model can be used in the development, delivery, and evaluation of a security guard training program.

Chapter 2

4. Explain the use and potential effects of formal and informal training for security guards. Are both necessary, or is formal training sufficient?

Chapter 3

5. What are the learning outcomes of security guard training?
6. Explain the relevance of learning styles for a security guard training program. How can Kolb's four learning modes be used to train security guards?
7. What are the implications of conditioning theory and social cognitive theory for the security guard training program? How can principles from each theory be used in the training of security guards?
8. What are the implications of adult learning theory for the security guard training program? Explain how adult learning theory principles might be included in the training.
9. How important is training motivation for the training of security guards? Explain how motivation theories can be used to ensure that security guards are high in training motivation.

Chapter 4

10. Refer to the needs analysis process in Figure 4.1 and explain its use and relevance for the mandatory security guard training program.
11. Explain the relevance and use of an organizational, task, and person analysis for the security guard training program. What information can be obtained from each level of needs analysis and how can it be useful in the design of the training program?
12. Is training the best solution to the security guard problem? Run the situation through Mager and Pipe's Performance Analysis Flowchart (Figure 4.2) to determine solutions to the problem indicated in the case. Is training the best solution and are there other possible solutions? Explain your answer.

Chapter 5

13. Write some training objectives for the security guard training program.
14. Describe the content of the program and some potential training methods that should be considered.
15. Explain how active practice can be used for the security guard training program. How can the conditions of practice before (pre-training interventions) and during training be used? Explain the use and relevance of each condition of practice.
16. Is active learning and adaptive expertise relevant for the security guard training program? Explain how active learning elements might be included in the training.
17. Is error-management training (EMT) relevant for the security guard training program? Explain how you might use EMT in the training and its potential effects.

Chapter 6

18. What off-the-job training methods should be used for the security guard training program? Consider each of the instructional methods described in Chapter 6 (Table 6.1). Which methods would you recommend and which ones would you not use? Explain your answer.

Chapter 7

19. Consider each of the on-the-job training methods described in Chapter 7 (Table 7.1) for the security guard training program. Which methods would you recommend and which ones would you not use? Explain your answer.

Chapter 8

20. Can technology-based training methods be used for the security guard training program? How might technology-based methods be used and do you think they would be effective? What are the advantages and disadvantages? Explain your answer.

21. Review the material on the design of computer-based training programs in Chapter 8. If you were to design a computer-based training program for security guard training, what instructional methods and design factors would you use? Be sure to explain your reasoning for using or not using the methods and design factors described in Chapter 8.

Chapter 9

22. Develop a lesson plan for the security guard training program. Be sure to indicate the training objective, classroom requirements, training materials and equipment, supplies, and handouts. You should also indicate the sequence of activities and events that will occur during the training program as well the timing of them.

23. Who should be the trainer for the security guard training program? Explain your answer.

24. Explain how you would use Gagné's nine events of instruction for the security guard training program. Be sure to give specific examples.

25. What are some training delivery problems that might occur in the security guard training program? What can a trainer do to avoid them or manage them during training?

Chapter 10

26. What are some barriers that might inhibit the transfer of the security guard training program? Who is responsible for these barriers?

27. How can the security guard training program be designed to facilitate the transfer of training?

28. What are some strategies that can be used before, during, and after training to facilitate the transfer of training? Be sure also to indicate strategies for the trainer, trainees, and management.

Chapter 11

29. How should the security guard training program be evaluated? Be sure to indicate the type of data to be collected, the purpose of the evaluation, and whether it should be a descriptive and/or causal evaluation.

30. Explain the application of Kirkpatrick's model, the COMA model, and the decision-based evaluation model for evaluating the security guard training program. What model would you recommend and why?
31. What variables would you include in the evaluation of the security guard training program and how would you measure them?
32. What data collection design would you use to evaluate the security guard training program? Explain the advantages and disadvantages of non-experimental, experimental, and quasi-experimental designs. What design would you use and why?

Chapter 12

33. What are the main costs of the security guard training program? Be sure to indicate the main cost categories.
34. What are the main benefits of the security guard training program? Explain how you would conduct a cost-effectiveness evaluation and a cost–benefit evaluation.
35. How would you estimate the net benefit, benefit–cost ratio, return on investment, and utility of the security guard training program? Be sure to indicate what you would include in the estimation of each (e.g., what costs and what benefits).

Chapter 15

36. Security guard basic training can be provided by training providers (e.g., an agency licensed under the Private Security and Investigative Services Act to sell security guard services) as well as a business entity that employs its own in-house security personnel. Should businesses train their own security personnel or outsource the training to a licensed agency? What are the advantages and disadvantages of each option? Explain your answers.

REFERENCES

1. Based on Lavis, C. (2011). *Learning & development outlook 2011: Are organizations ready for Learning 2.0?* Ottawa: The Conference Board of Canada; www.about.telus.com.
2. Vu, U. (2004, July 12). Trainers mature into business partners. *Canadian HR Reporter, 17(13)*, 1, 2.
3. Lavis, C. (2011).
4. Vu, U. (2004, July 12).
5. (2011). *Competencies for training and development professionals.* Toronto, ON: Canadian Society for Training and Development.
6. Robinson, D. G., & Robinson, J. C. (2005, Anniversary issue). A heightened focus on learning and performance. *HR Magazine, 50(13)*, 65–67.
7. Johnson, G. (2004, August). To outsource or not to outsource . . . that is the question. *Training, 41(8)*, 26–29.
8. Lavis, C. (2011).
9. Kraiger, K. (2003). Perspectives on training and development. In W. C. Borman, D. R. Ilgen, & R. J. Klimoski (Eds.), *Handbook of psychology: Industrial and organizational psychology* (pp. 171–192). Hoboken, NJ: John Wiley & Sons, Inc.

10. Johnson, G. (2004, August).
11. Gainey, T. W., & Klaas, B. S. (2002). Outsourcing the training function: Results from the field. *Human Resource Planning, 25,* 16–22.
12. Gainey, T. W., & Klaas, B. S. (2002).
13. Macdonald, N. C. (2004, November 22). Workplace discrimination prohibited—and that includes training. *Canadian HR Reporter, 17(2),* G3, G11.
14. Lavis, C. (2011).
15. Lavis, C. (2011).
16. Lavis, C. (2011).
17. Lavis, C. (2011).
18. Canadian Council on Learning. About the CLI. www.ccl-cca.ca/CCL.
19. Canadian Council on Learning. About the CLI. www.ccl-cca.ca/CCL.
20. (2011, October). *What is the future of Learning in Canada?* Ottawa, ON: Canadian Council on Learning. http://www.ccl-cca.ca/CCL/AboutCCL/PresidentCEO/20111011FutureLearning.html